PRAISE FOR
What Is a Man?

"*What Is a Man?*, Waller R. Newell's new book, is an asteroid hurtling toward our planet—and, if I am not mistaken, it is headed straight for the Tower of Babel, the construction that produced the babble about sexual matters that we all now speak. Brilliantly timed, conceived, edited, and introduced by Professor Newell, *What Is a Man?* is an anthology of buried treasures. It is unlike any recent book for the general reader I know of on the relations between the sexes. Newell's inspiring book is about how to build manly virtue—which sounds antiquated because manly virtue is all but forgotten or remembered only in parody. But manly virtue, he argues, is our best hope of bringing men and women together with respect and dignity."

—Norman Doidge, department of psychiatry, Columbia University

"Newell's anthology covers an astonishing range and is a constant source of ideas about a neglected, almost a suppressed, virtue."

—Kenneth Minogue, London School of Economics

"*What Is a Man?* is that rare sort of book that rewards serious study while delighting and inspiring the casual reader. The meanings and the perplexities of manhood are illuminated by an assemblage of literary gems culled from the greatest writers at their most incandescent."

—Thomas Pangle, University of Toronto

"This book—3,000 years of reasoned arguments and wisdom about manly virtue by the greatest minds in history—is an outstanding achievement and a great gift for any boy or man, or girl or woman, frightened or confounded by manliness; it's an ideal bar mitzvah gift, since for Jews becoming a man is a religious rite. . . . It is the perfect Father's Day gift for the man who has everything, except manliness. Or who has it, but might wish to remind himself why."

—*National Post*

"Waller R. Newell is breaking the taboo, daring to speak the unspoken, to discuss answers to the whispered question: What is a man? But Newell is no Iron John. He's skeptical about men's consciousness and his answer to feminism is not to dress in wolfskins, bang drums and howl in the forest. What he has tried to do was to find cultural traditions of manliness from the time before feminism, when masculinity was supposedly so self-evident that it didn't need to be defined. He found enough to fill the pages of this book and then some."

—The Canadian Press

WHAT IS
A MAN?

WHAT IS

3,000 YEARS OF WISDOM
ON THE ART OF MANLY VIRTUE

A MAN?

EDITED WITH COMMENTARY BY
WALLER R. NEWELL

ReganBooks
An Imprint of HarperCollins*Publishers*

Frontispiece: *Tristan und Isolde (1865) by Richard Wagner.* From *Fantastic Opera: The Great Operas Illuminated* by John Martinez, text by F. Paul Driscoll. Copyright © 1997 by Harry N. Abrams, Inc., New York, NY. Used by permission of the artist.

Permissions appear on pages 529–532, which constitute an extension of this copyright page.

A hardcover edition of this book was published by ReganBooks, an imprint of HarperCollins Publishers, in 2000. It has been revised and abridged for this paperback.

HarperCollins books may be purchased for educational, business, or sales promotional use. For information please write: Special Markets Department, HarperCollins Publishers Inc., 10 East 53rd Street, New York, NY 10022.

First paperback edition published 2001.

Library of Congress Cataloging-in-Publication Data

What is a man? : 3,000 years of wisdom on the art of manly virtue / [edited by] Waller R. Newell.—1st ed.
    p.   cm.
  ISBN 0-06-039296-7
  1. Men—Conduct of life Literary collections. 2. Nobility of character Literary collections. 3. Virtues Literary collections.
I. Newell, Waller Randy.
PN6071.M387B66   1999
808.8'0353—dc21   99-36304

ISBN 0-06-098758-8 (pbk.)

01 02 03 04 05 ❖/RRD 10 9 8 7 6 5 4 3 2 1

Contents

ACKNOWLEDGMENTS   XV

IINTRODUCTION   XVII

1. THE CHIVALROUS MAN   1

The Manly Lover   4
Orpheus and Eurydice *Thomas Bulfinch*   4
The Art of Courtly Love *Andreas Capellanus*   6
Love and Self-Perfection *Baldesar Castiglione*   8
The Rules of Love *Andreas Capellanus*   10
Love and Valor *Thomas Bulfinch*   11
Older Men Make Better Lovers *Baldesar Castiglione*   12
Love or Wisdom? *Francis Bacon*   14
Love or Duty? *Xenophon*   15
Lancelot and Guenever *Thomas Bulfinch*   19
Dido and Aeneas *Thomas Bulfinch*   21
Breaking Up Is Hard to Do *Aristophanes (from Plato)*   22
Diana and Actaeon *Thomas Bulfinch*   25
On Adultery *Ovid*   27
Apollo and Daphne *Thomas Bulfinch*   28
The Narcissist *Thomas Bulfinch*   30

Manliness Toward Women   33
Never Use Force Against a Woman *Sir Thomas Malory*   33
Every Man Thinketh His Own Lady Fairest
    Sir Thomas Malory   34
Stalkers Beware! *Sir Thomas Malory*   35
The Death of Robin Hood *Thomas Bulfinch*   37
Revenge Against Women Is Shameful
    Sir Thomas Malory   38
What Women *Really* Want in a Man *Thomas Bulfinch*   39

Stick Your Neck Out and Close Your Eyes
   Geoffrey Chaucer   42
Can a Businessman Make a Good Lover?
   Andreas Capellanus   44
Sigh No More, Ladies *William Shakespeare*   45
Pyramus and Thisbe *Thomas Bulfinch*   46
Emile and Sophy *Jean-Jacques Rousseau*   48
The Sorrows of Youth *Johann Wolfgang von Goethe*   53
The Age of Innocence *Edith Wharton*   57

2. THE GENTLEMAN   67
A Well-Bred Man   71
Austen on Gentlemanliness *Jane Austen*   71
A Gentleman Avoids Vulgarity *Lord Chesterfield*   80
The Sun King *The Duke of Saint-Simon*   82
The Importance of Good Grooming and Good
   Company *Lord Chesterfield*   83
The Boor *Theophrastus*   84
The Art of Good Manners *Jonathan Swift*   85
A Club Man *Sir Richard Steele*   87
Gentlemanly Reserve *William Shenstone*   88
The Ugly Club *Sir Richard Steele*   90

Manly Character and Conduct   91
The Rules of Harvard College (1643)   91
Pride and Prejudice *Jane Austen*   92
Do Not Be a Rake *Lord Chesterfield*   102
John Grey, the Worthy Man *Anthony Trollope*   103
The Knight *Geoffrey Chaucer*   114
Honor and Reputation *Francis Bacon*   115
Temperance *Baldesar Castiglione*   116
The Man Without Moral Feeling *Theophrastus*   118
Practice Makes Perfect *John Locke*   119
On Friendship *Aristotle*   120
The Lover of Bad Company *Theophrastus*   122

3. THE WISE MAN   125
The Wise Man of Affairs   128
Where Do You Shop for Wisdom? *Diogenes Laertius*   128
My Son, Be Admonished! *Ecclesiastes*   129
How Should a Young Man Live? *Plato*   130
Daedalus and Icarus *Thomas Bulfinch*   134

The Man of Discipline *The Bhagavad-Gita*   135
The Value of Study *Francis Bacon*   139
Why a Man Must Be Liberally Educated If He Is
    to Gain Eternal Fame *Baldesar Castiglione*   140
Men's Happiness or Misery Is Mostly of Their
    Own Making *John Locke*   141
The Contemplative Man and the Active Man
    Aristotle   142
The Dream of Scipio *Cicero*   145
A Man of Principles *John Locke*   150
How a Grown Man Should Live *Plato*   151

A Wise Man Within   154
The Child Is Father of the Man
    William Wordsworth   154
The Painful Path to Manhood *St. Augustine*   154
Youth *John Woolman*   158
The Four Ages of Man *W. B. Yeats*   161
Reflections on a Man's Success *William James*   162
A Man Must Stand Erect *Marcus Aurelius*   164
Intimations of Immortality from Recollections
    of Childhood *William Wordsworth*   166
Death Is Not to Be Feared *Desiderius Erasmus*   173
The True Spirit of Man *The Bhagavad-Gita*   174
The Two Paths *St. Augustine*   177
The Myth of the Cave *Plato*   180
Levin Wonders About the Meaning of Life
    Leo Tolstoy   182

4. THE FAMILY MAN   195
Boys into Men   198
Telemachus's Search for a Father *Homer*   198
Educating Boys *Michel de Montaigne*   202
The Value of a Fair Fight *Thomas Hughes*   203
Telemachus Finds His Father *Homer*   205
The New Kid in Town *Mark Twain*   207
The Education of Cyrus *Xenophon*   210
An Early Critic of Rock Music? *Jacopo Sadoleto*   211
Bringing Up a Prince *Desiderius Erasmus*   212
The Lion and the Mouse *Aesop*   214
It Is Held That Schools Corrupt the Morals
    Quintillian   215

Shame Is Good in a Boy *Jacopo Sadoleto*   217
The Hare and the Tortoise *Aesop*   218
The Duties and Education of Children
    Leon Battista Alberti   219
The Shepherd's Boy and Wolf *Aesop*   220
The Right Kind of Boy: Brave and Tender
    Theodore Roosevelt   220
The Value of a Boy's Friendships *Thomas Hughes*   222

The Manly Father   225
I Have a Boy of Five Years Old *William Wordsworth*   225
Apply Yourself, My Boy *Lord Chesterfield*   227
A Father Pays Attention All the Time
    Leon Battista Alberti   229
A Father's Parting Advice *Thomas Hughes*   230
This Fair Child of Mine *William Shakespeare*   232
A Father Sets the Example *Leon Battista Alberti*   232
Son, What Have I Done to Deserve This?
    William Shakespeare   234
On the Affection of Fathers for Their Children
    Michel de Montaigne   238
A Roman Father *Plutarch*   239
Fathers Must Earn Their Authority *Jacopo Sadoleto*   241

A Man's Journey   243
The Seven Ages of Man *William Shakespeare*   243
Odysseus Comes Home *Homer*   244
Married or Single? *Francis Bacon*   246
A Son's Mixed Feelings *John Stuart Mill*   247
Hektor and Andromache on the Walls of Troy
    Homer   251
The Joys of Parents Are Secret *Francis Bacon*   252
Advice to a Young Man on Marrying Early
    Benjamin Franklin   253
My Wife Is My Best Friend *John Stuart Mill*   255
At His Brother's Grave *Robert G. Ingersoll*   258
Mother o' Mine *Rudyard Kipling*   260
Youth Versus Age *Francis Bacon*   260
Why Should Not Old Men Be Mad?
    William Butler Yeats   261

5. THE STATESMAN 263

The Kingly Man 268

Two Kings Clashing: Achilles and Agamemnon
  Homer 268
David and Goliath *1 Samuel* 270
The Kingdom of the Lion *Aesop* 274
The Good Prince and the Evil Prince
  Desiderius Erasmus 274
Theseus, the Minotaur and Other Adventures
  Thomas Bulfinch 275
Henry the Fifth Rallies His Troops Before the Walls
  of Harfleur *William Shakespeare* 278
Napoleon, Man of the World *Ralph Waldo Emerson* 279
Alfred the Great, a Model King and Man
  John Richard Green 280
Tyrants Will Always Be with Us *Aesop* 283
The Outstandingly Virtuous Prince
  Niccolo Machiavelli 283
The Patriot King *Henry St. John, Viscount Bolingbroke* 286
To Be a King *Queen Elizabeth I* 289
Who Should Pilot the Ship of State? *Plato* 291
The Midas Touch *Thomas Bulfinch* 293
The Career of Charlemagne *Francois P. G. Guizot* 294
We Few, We Happy Few, We Band of Brothers
  William Shakespeare 295

Manly Leaders and Citizens 297

The Man of Character *Charles de Gaulle* 297
The Model Citizen *Plutarch* 301
The Mice in Council *Aesop* 304
Everything That Entitles a Man to Praise *Cicero* 304
The Need for Good Laws *Aristotle* 305
Liberty Is Order, Liberty Is Strength
  Charles James Fox 306
Comparing the Statesman and the Soldier
  Charles de Gaulle 307
Always Be Prepared for War *Niccolo Machiavelli* 309
The Wolves to the Sheep: Give Peace a Chance
  Aesop 310
What Is the Duty of a Statesman to the Voters?
  Edmund Burke 311

At Last I Had the Authority. I Slept Soundly.
    Winston S. Churchill   313
Pericles's Funeral Oration and Thucydides's Assessment
    of His Statesmanship *Thucydides*   318
The Wolves to the Sheep Dogs: Give Peace a Chance
    Aesop   326

6. THE NOBLE MAN   327

The Man of Valor   331

The Virtues of the Soldier *Charles de Gaulle*   331
Not One Step Back Unless Ordered! The Battle
    of Stalingrad *M. S. Shumilov*   335
The Meaning of Courage *John Fitzgerald Kennedy*   336
A Young Man's First Battle *Leo Tolstoy*   339
He Had Dreamed of Battles All His Life
    Stephen Crane   341
On Courage *Aristotle*   350
The Coward *Theophrastus*   351
"Oh, to Die, to Die for Him!" *Leo Tolstoy*   352
The Good War *Studs Terkel*   355
In Flanders Fields *Lieutenant-Colonel John McRae, M.D.*   359

The Man of Integrity and Honor   360

The Great-Souled Man *Aristotle*   361
A Counterfeit Man *William Shakespeare*   362
Moral Courage *Charles Dickens*   363
Conquer Fortune with Patience
    Leon Battista Alberti   364
The Generous Majesty of His Nature:
    Lawrence of Arabia *Winston S. Churchill*   365
Toussaint L'Ouverture: Soldier, Statesman, Martyr
    Wendell Phillips   369
If *Rudyard Kipling*   370
The Happy Warrior *William Wordsworth*   371
The Value of Adversity to a Great Man *Seneca*   374
Triumphing over Adversity *Frederick Douglass*   375
What Is a Man? *William Shakespeare*   379
There Was a Time When Our Forefathers Owned
    This Great Island *Red Jacket*   380
My Forefathers Were Warriors *Tecumseh*   382
The Hero Deepened *Homer*   383
The Ascent *Aleksandr Solzhenitsyn*   386

7. THE AMERICAN MAN   395

The American Hero   399

Freedom in All Just Pursuits *Thomas Jefferson*   399
The Call to Arms *Patrick Henry*   401
It Is Natural to Believe in Great Men
   Ralph Waldo Emerson   403
The Glory of Our Fathers *Josiah Quincy*   404
Democracy and the Great Man *Alexis de Tocqueville*   405
The Sword of Washington! The Staff of Franklin!
   John Quincy Adams   407
Illustrious Man! *Charles James Fox*   408
Such Men Cannot Die *Edward Everett*   409
Manly Honor in Democracy and Aristocracy
   Alexis de Tocqueville   410
"Towering Genius Disdains a Beaten Path."
   Abraham Lincoln   412
Why There Are So Many Men of Ambition in
   the United States but So Few Lofty Ambitions
   Alexis de Tocqueville   417
His Life Now Is Grafted Upon the Infinite
   Henry Ward Beecher   421
I Have a Dream *Martin Luther King Jr.*   423
A Man Among Men *Theodore Roosevelt*   427
Were We Truly Men? *John Fitzgerald Kennedy*   429

Manhood in America   430

The Democratic Dad *Alexis de Tocqueville*   430
An American Father: Robert E. Lee
   Captain Robert E. Lee   433
"A Natural Made Gentleman" *William H. Herndon*   438
Men and Women in America *Alexis de Tocqueville*   442
Men Who Greatly Dared *Theodore Roosevelt*   443
Young Husbands *Albert J. Beveridge*   445
Moral Force Gives a Man Both Fearlessness and
   Tranquillity *Ralph Waldo Emerson*   447
Family Life and the Average Man's Duty
   Theodore Roosevelt   449
The Whistle *Benjamin Franklin*   451
The College Man *Albert J. Beveridge*   452
A Man Must Be a Nonconformist *Ralph Waldo Emerson* 455
No Man Is Happy If He Does Not Work
   Theodore Roosevelt   458

8. THE INVISIBLE MAN   461

Rebellion and Despair   464

The End of Something *Ernest Hemingway*   464
Oh Damn Them All, Thought the Adolescent
   John Cheever   468
"Most Young Men Do Not Stand Like Ramrods
   or Talk Like Demosthenes." *James Dean*   469
What Then Shall We Choose? Weight or Lightness?
   Milan Kundera   470
Video Games Get Very Very Ugly: Masochism,
   Mutilation, Prostitution *Charles Mandel*   471
Television's Virus of Violence and
   the Jonesboro Schoolyard Shootings
   Lieutenant-Colonel Dave Grossman   474
Why the U.S. Won't Go to War *Michael Kelly*   478
Gender Traits Tie T.V. Execs in Knots *Brian Lowry*   481
Marginal Men *Barbara Ehrenreich*   484

The Confusions of Love   488

The Dangerous Game of Dating *Jonathan Foreman*   488
Collecting Broken Glass *Nino Ricci*   491
The Sinking of Mature Romance *Michael Medved*   495
Enchanting and Repulsive: What Is Gothic?
   Michelle Wauchope   498
Dad? I Wish I'd Known You When You Were Little
   Raymond Carver   502
Born to Lose in 1962 *Social Distortion*   505
Sex and That Postmodernist Girl
   David Foster Wallace   506
Each Other *Patrick Buckley*   513
"I Don't Want to Sacrifice Myself or My Family."
   Interview with Kurt Cobain by Robert Hilburn   516

CONCLUSION: A RETURN TO MANLINESS?   519

ACKNOWLEDGMENTS

I am grateful to Judith Regan for her early and unflagging enthusiasm for this project, and to my editor, Cal Morgan, for an enjoyable and fruitful partnership. I am also indebted to the friends and colleagues who offered me encouragement and advice about this anthology and its theme. They include Peter Ahrensdorf, David Blankenhorn, Amitai Etzioni, Norman Doidge, Charles Fairbanks, Joan Fairbanks, Bryan-Paul Frost, Francis Fukuyama, Barbara Garner, Barbara Laine Kagedan, William Kristol, Harvey C. Mansfield Jr., Kenneth Minogue, D. Gregory MacIsaac, Patrick Malcolmson, Arthur M. Meltzer, Rick Meyers, Linda Rabieh, Michael Rabieh, Farhang Rajaee, Robert Sibley, Nathan Tarcov, Micheline White, and Claudia Winkler.

I owe a special word of thanks to my principal researcher, Timothy Voronoff, my erstwhile student. Tim's energy and imagination sustained me at every stage of a sometimes grueling creative marathon. I am grateful as well to my other researchers, Geoffrey Kellow, David Tabachnick, Jarrett Carty, and John Colman, for their hard work and sound instincts.

I cannot end without mentioning Allan Bloom, beloved teacher and friend of my wife's and mine during many years and the greatest man I have known. This book is dedicated to his memory.

Finally and above all, I am profoundly grateful to my wife, Jacqueline Etherington Newell. Without her wealth of insight, learning, discriminating judgment, and prodigious labor on every aspect of this anthology, this book would not exist. She is my true partner in this as in everything.

INTRODUCTION

As America heads into the twenty-first century, there is an increasingly widespread feeling that we have forgotten the meaning of manliness. On first reflection, this might seem like an absurd proposition. Across the nation, millions of men do their daily best to meet their responsibilities as husbands, fathers, partners, friends, and citizens. We expect men to behave decently and honorably in those capacities and to pull their weight in families and relationships. But at the same time, we are curiously adrift as a society when it comes to knowing precisely what we mean by manliness—how to describe it, encourage it, and discourage its opposite. Especially in our public discourse, in the worlds of academia, government, the social welfare bureaucracy, the educational establishment, and the learned professions, an open discussion of manliness as a positive form of behavior is almost taboo. In many of these circles, to suggest without a sneer of irony that one should "be a man" would produce ripples of cringing embarrassment over the after-dinner decaf. There is a huge vacuum in our moral vocabulary about the whole subject of the manly virtues, a feeling that even to raise such a matter is retrograde or at least a faux pas, like ordering Chardonnay with beef. We feel manly passions and impulses, but we don't know how to articulate them. This is especially noticeable among young men in their teens and twenties, or even older. They have the same strong passions, the same need for love, that youths their age have always experienced. But, much more so than with previous generations, their passions are sometimes baffled and stifling because they lack the means to express them in a refined yet heartfelt way.

The aim of this anthology is to help fill this vacuum, and to restore a sense of the positive meaning of manliness that we have somewhat mysteriously forgotten. I say mysteriously because, as the reader will see, there is an extraordinary continuity in the understanding of the manly virtues from their earliest origins in the ancient world until, so to speak, just yesterday. Despite considerable differences in content, style, and intrinsic quality among ancient and modern artists, thinkers, historians, poets, and statesmen from the classical era to the twentieth century, there is also an unbroken pedigree in the Western conception of what it means to be a man. Honor tempered by prudence, ambition tempered by compassion for the suffering and the oppressed, love restrained by delicacy and honor toward the beloved—from Plato to the twentieth century, there is a common store of richly textured observations, maxims, illustrations, and confirmations of this enduringly noble standard of conduct. Thus, although that tradition can be easily parodied and ridiculed today as something hopelessly outmoded and far away, in fact it is very close. Depending on our ages, many of us have parents and grandparents still living who embody the aspiration to those manly virtues; the rest of us, as adults, still carry their letters, their diaries, and their childhood influence on us. We don't need to reinvent manliness. We only need to will ourselves to wake up from the bad dream of the last few generations and reclaim it, in order to extend and enrich that tradition under the formidable demands of the present.

What are the tenets of manly pride and honor that we need to impart to young men? How might we recover an understanding of what it means to be a man in the positive sense—brave, self-restrained, dignified, zealous on behalf of a good cause, imbued with sentiments of delicacy and respect for one's loved ones? These are the questions explored by *What Is a Man?* In its pages, the reader will find a panoply of examples of manhood at its best. And among the cases made consistently throughout its pages is that the surest way of convincing men to treat women with respect is to expose them to those traditional virtues of manly character that make it a disgrace to treat anyone basely. Reclaiming the positive tradition of manly refinement and civility is the surest antidote to the much-decried balkanization of the sexes that has characterized the last thirty years. As *What Is a Man?* illustrates through a wide variety of sources, reverting to the blond beast of either sex is no answer to our present romantic ills. With all due respect to the proponents of "men's rights," such adversarial visions of our culture simply mirror the distortions of the most extreme, exclusionary versions of academic feminism. The answer is not to return to the worship of a primordial Mother Goddess, or to primeval fantasies of male shamanism and campfire dances, in order to breathe some life back into contemporary eros. Real and responsible friendships between men and women can only be lost in the pursuit of a sectarian and rejectionist "gender identity." Instead, we need a return to the highest fulfillment of which all people are capable—moral and intellectual virtues that are the same for men and women at their peaks—while recognizing the diverse qualities that men and women contribute to this common endeavor for excellence. We need a sympathetic reengagement with traditional teachings that stress that men and women share what is highest, while accepting that their passions, temperaments, and sentiments can differ, resulting in different paths to those high standards shared in common. This anthology is meant to be a contribution to genuine friendship between men and women, through a recognition that each makes a distinct contribution to this common feast of excellence.

The original idea for this book grew out of my eighteen years' experience as an educator. During this period, and especially in the last decade, the young men in my university classes have seemed especially lost—shy, confused, lonely, afraid to assert themselves, their trepidation broken only by occasional bursts of pointless cockiness and attitudinizing. At the same time, I was always struck (although officially forbidden by my university to say or even think as much) that my male and female students were very different, although they did equally well or poorly in my courses. Young men are still openly competitive, attention-grabbing, and eager to impress, looking for someone with whom to lock horns but also someone to praise them for doing well, like a brave soldier getting a battlefield promotion. They view a class as both a comradely collective enterprise and a contest in which they need to outshine the other young men. By contrast, female students still seem more self-sufficient, less prone to grab the spotlight, more quietly competent, less in need of hand-holding. They don't need to lock horns or to be constantly assured that they're doing fine. These observations are limited to my experiences as a professor, but similar observations could doubtless be made in many occupations and vocations. Maleness still exists, but in a baffled, confused kind of way. This is especially noticeable when students open up about their erotic relationships. Young men and women today face all the traditional quandaries of love that you will sample in these pages—jealousy, possessiveness, wounded pride, shame, competition for female attention and affection. But they lack the vocabulary even to express these feelings, let alone grapple with them constructively. This culture of romantic bafflement is compounded by the dramatic rise in kids from broken homes, almost the norm now among my students rather than the exception. It is both appalling and deeply touching to see how many young men, even into their thirties, are still so badly hurt by the childhood horror of watching their families disintegrate. It doesn't incline them to trust that love can last. They fear that by saying "I love you," they're making themselves vulnerable to another betrayal like the one inflicted upon them by their parents.

It was musing on these observations that made me wonder what past ages had to say about manliness. What might we learn from history? Would it offer any consistent lessons? What I found can only be described as buried treasure. As I burrowed into the annals of our Western literary heritage, I found hundreds of readings from every period on the theme of manliness—ancient, medieval, Renaissance, early modern and Romantic, down almost to today. Throughout this treasure hunt, I selected the readings for inclusion here by relying on a few fundamental questions: What is a real man like? How does he act and feel? On this basis, the readings sorted out into the eight main sections that comprise this book.

The book is arranged thematically rather than chronologically, allowing readers, if they so choose, to explore the eight chapters out of sequence and browse within each chapter in any order they find appealing. Whenever an author appears for the first time, I provide some essential biographical information for the reader. There is a degree of overlap among some of the eight themes and certain historical periods—chivalry, for instance, is closely associated with medieval knighthood, while gentlemanliness is a favorite theme of both Renaissance- and Enlightenment-era writers. But the primary aim isn't chronological, and the reader will find a wide range of historical eras covered in each of the eight sections. My purpose is to present a conjunction of timeless virtues that can still inspire us today with a series of vividly contrasting portraits of manliness and an appreciation for the enticing variety of manly types. The one exception to this approach is the final section, "The Invisible Man," which appropriately brings us full circle by looking at the confused but in some ways promising signals being sent about manliness in the late 1990s. My aim has been to explore the manly virtues as the key to understanding the male psychology and character, and to refresh our acquaintance with the vibrant, fully rounded knights, lovers, gentlemen, thinkers, artists, statesmen, spouses, and warriors who people our history.

Before letting that chorus of suppressed voices take over, however, let's think a little more about the crisis of manliness in the
present, beginning with fatherhood.

• • •

Fatherhood and manliness have always been closely connected, not only because fathering a child is a palpable proof of
manhood, but because fathers are supposed to provide their sons
with a model of how to live. And yet, as a culture, we have never
been more unsure or conflicted about what we mean by manhood.

In a recent novel by Chuck Palahniuk, *Fight Club,* a group of
young men in their twenties, stuck in typical Gen-X jobs as office
temps and couriers, relieve their boredom by meeting after hours
in the basement of a bar and beating each other senseless. Sometimes they show up for work with black eyes and stitches as a warrior's badge of honor. Aside from their jobs—white collar, but holding out no clear career prospects—what these young men have in
common is that they are underfathered, the product of divorce
and of fathers who had no time for them. "I'm a thirty-year-old
boy," says the novel's protagonist. "I knew my dad for about six
years, but I don't remember anything. . . What you see at fight club
is a generation of men raised by women."

In the absence of a clear idea from their distant, distracted
fathers of what it means to be a man, these bored and frustrated
youths react against their antiseptic jobs by reverting to the crudest
stereotype of "macho" violence. The club's founder, Tyler, pro-
gresses from consenting violence among buddies to random murder—a slacker Raskolnikov. The novel is chillingly insightful about
the unmapped psyche of young males in the nineties.

Given these signals from the culture, confirmed every day by
real acts of mayhem, some hold that we should try to abolish ideals of
manliness altogether and make more rigorous efforts to create a genderless personality free of male violence. The recent horrific shootings in American schools from Arkansas to Colorado, with little-boy
killers waiting in army fatigues to ambush their classmates and teachers, might suggest that this view is right. Add to this the fact that the
majority of violent crimes are committed by young men between the
ages of fifteen and twenty-five, and there seems further good reason
for discouraging male children from embracing any notion of manly
pride.

But it is not so simple. The last thirty years have in fact witnessed a prolonged effort at social engineering throughout our

public and educational institutions. Its purpose is to eradicate any psychological and emotional differences between men and women, on the grounds that any concept of manliness inevitably leads to arrogance and violence toward women, and to rigid hierarchies that exclude the marginalized and powerless. This experiment was meant to reduce violence and tensions between the sexes. And yet, during this same period, "macho" violence and stress between men and women may well have increased. Recent crime statistics suggest as much in the United States, Canada, and the United Kingdom—the countries where the feminist social experiment stigmatizing manliness has had the greatest latitude to prove itself.

As a recent book by Barbara Dafoe Whitehead confirmed, the absence of a father is one of the strongest predictors of violence among young men in the United States, at least as important as poverty, lack of education, or minority status. The ease with which men of my baby boomer generation have abdicated their roles as fathers is undoubtedly connected with feminism and with the sexual revolution of the 1960s. Boomers were told not to be hung up about providing masculine role models for children, reassured that we should do whatever made us happiest, including escaping an unsatisfying marriage. After all, to hold things together for the sake of the children would restrict both men and women to old-fashioned "patriarchal" responsibilities. The casualties of this hard, bright credo of selfishness are today's underfathered young men, many of them from broken homes, prone to identify their maleness with aggression because they have no better model to imitate.

This generation's experience is summed up in a brilliant, pathetic scene from a film by Atom Egoyan called *Family Viewing*. The central character, a teenage boy, drifts in and out of his divorced father's house. The father is totally preoccupied with his relationship with a younger woman. The boy's only solid human contact is with his dying grandmother, shunted to a nursing home lest she spoil the father's swinging lifestyle. One day the boy digs out some family videos. At first, he sees a backyard barbecue with happy children and his parents when they were still together. Suddenly, the film jumps to the father and his new girlfriend having sex. The father simply taped over the family movies, literally erasing his son's connection with the only secure part of his childhood.

It seems plain enough that we are missing the boat about manliness. A strong case can be made that manly honor, and shame at failing to live up to it, are the surest means of promoting respect for women. Moreover, manly anger and combativeness can provide energy for a just cause. Horrified as we are by the cult of warrior violence in the Balkans or Rwanda, we may have gone too far toward the opposite extreme in the Western democracies. As Michael Kelly recently observed, "There are fewer and fewer people, and they are older and older people, who accept what every twelve-year-old in Bihac knows: that there are some things worth dying for and killing for." Abolitionism in the antebellum United States, the Allies' defeat of Nazi Germany, or the civil rights movement of the sixties, would never have succeeded without the legitimate expression of anger against injustice. The point is not to eradicate honor and pride from the male character, but to rechannel those energies from the nihilistic violence of *Fight Club* or the Arkansas schoolyard to some constructive moral purpose.

To do this, we must recover a positive sense of manhood. For, if young men are cut off from this positive tradition of manly pride, their manliness will reemerge in crude and retrograde forms. Some thirty years ago, the Rolling Stones recorded a misogynist rant called "Under My Thumb." Today, it is one of the songs that fans most request of these aging shamans of adolescent attitudinizing. In three decades, tension between men and women not only has not disappeared but may actually have intensified, and we must wonder whether the experiment in social engineering itself is one reason why.

For hostility toward women is an aberration of male behavior. If, as the prevailing orthodoxy contends, the male gender were intrinsically aggressive, hegemonic, and intolerant, then by definition male behavior could never improve. The message young males receive from feminist reasoning is not *You should be ashamed of liking "Under My Thumb,"* but *That's the way your gender thinks about women.*

So the first step toward a sensible debate about manly pride is to rescue the positive tradition of manliness from three decades of stereotyping that conflates masculinity with violence, hegemony, and aggression. We have to recognize that men and women are moral and intellectual equals, that decent and worthy men have always known this, and that, while men and women share the most important human virtues, vices, and aptitudes, they also have different psychological traits that incline them toward different activities.

According to the reigning orthodoxy, men and women should have exactly the same kinds of capacities and ambitions. They should be equally interested in becoming tycoons, winning battles, driving tractors, and nurturing children. But this is not the reality.

In general, men don't want to work in day-care centers or teach kindergarten, and women don't want to be truck drivers or join the military. Moreover, women are far more likely than men to leave successful jobs to devote time to families; in fact, women under thirty are more eager for lasting marriages and numerous children than women of their parents' generation (in what may be a yearning for what their parents denied them). We should recognize at last that, as long as women are guaranteed an equal opportunity to pursue whatever occupation they want, it does not matter that men and women on the whole still choose different vocations. We must stop trying to reengineer the human soul to prevent boys from being boyish, while encouraging all forms of self-expression in girls.

All that thirty years of behavioral conditioning has done is drive manliness underground and distort it by severing it from traditional sources of masculine restraint and civility. The gurus of sensitivity have tried to convince men to become open, fluid, genderless beings who are unafraid to cry. But little boys still want to play war and shoot up the living room with plastic howitzers, and we can't give them all Ritalin. Psychologists have begun to express concern about our educational institutions' readiness to pathologize what once would have been regarded as boyish high spirits—roughhousing, "hating" girls, locker-room language—and the use of powerful drugs to extirpate their perfectly ordinary immaturity.

Again, the point is to channel these energies into the development of character. Boys and young men still want to be heroes, and the way to teach them to treat girls and women with respect is to appeal to their heroism, not try to blot it out. Look at those kids performing daring flips on their skateboards, or sailing on their Rollerblades into downtown traffic like warriors contemptuous of fear or danger. Look at that squeegee kid with his shaved head and horsehair plume, decked out like some road-warrior Achilles. Walk into one of those high-voltage computer emporiums, selling our century's most potent icon for the extension of human mastery over the cosmos. Who are the salespeople? Almost always cocky young men, celebrities-in-waiting in dark suits and moussed hair, hooked on the sheer power of it all.

Channel surf on your television late at night and sample the rock videos. Nearly all the bands in rock videos are male, snarling or plaintive over the world's confusions and their erotic frustrations, oozing male belligerence alternating with Byronic alienation and a puppyish longing for attention. Their names (Goo Goo

Dolls) and attitudes (the lead singer of Radiohead is wheeled around a supermarket in a giant shopping cart curled up like an overgrown five-year-old) combine an infantile longing to return to childhood with an in-your-face attitude of distrust and suspicion.

And what else would one expect, since so many of the families into which they were born ended in divorce? By denying and repressing their natural inclination to manliness, we run the risk of abandoning them to such infantile posturing. When they pierce their bodies, it is because they want to experience moral and erotic constraint. Having failed to find an authority they can respect, someone to guide them from boyish impetuosity to a mature and manly vigor of judgment, they confuse authority with oppression. Still, cast adrift in a world without any limitations, they long to pay a price for their hedonism. Since no one is leading them back to the great ethical and religious traditions that set these limits on the highest intellectual and spiritual level, they pierce their bodies in a crude simulacrum of traditional restraint. In that very gesture, they reveal not only the wondrous capacity of spirited young people to see through the aridity of the establishment, but also the potential for an ennobling transformation.

It is precisely in traditional understandings of manly pride and honor that we will find the only sure basis for respect between men and women. The best way of convincing young men to treat women with respect is to educate them in those traditional virtues of character that make it a disgrace to treat anyone basely, dishonestly, or exploitively. Moreover, the surest way of raising young men to treat young women as friends rather than as objects for sexual exploitation is to appeal to their natural longing to be honored and esteemed by the young women to whom they are attracted. When our erotic attraction to another is properly directed, it leads us to cultivate the virtues of moderation, honesty, gratitude, and compassion, all of which make us worthy of love in the eyes of the beloved. We try to be virtuous because we want to be worthy of being loved.

One thing is sure: Given our current confusion over the value and meaning of manliness, we have nothing to lose by reopening the issue. If academic feminism is correct that violence toward women stems from traditional patriarchal attitudes, our grandparents' lives must have been a hell of aggression and fear. Yet, if anything impresses us about our forebears, judging from their lives, letters, and diaries, it is the refinement of their affections for one another, and of men's esteem for women in particular. Perhaps we cannot return to that world. But boys and young men today need to be reintroduced to the tradition of manly civility, to supplement our contemporary insistence that all romantic stress between men and women can be solved by the adjudication of rights and the stigmatization of exclusively male traits of character

Despite recent caricatures of the Western tradition as one long justification for the oppression of women, poets and thinkers from Homer to Rousseau have explored the delicate interplay of love and self-perfection. In Homer's *Odyssey*, Telemachus, son of the great war hero Odysseus, embarks on a search to find his missing father and thereby save his mother from the oppressive noblemen who want her to give up her husband for dead and marry one of them. As he searches for his father, in an adventure parallel to Odysseus's own search for a way home to his long-lost wife and child, Telemachus is educated by his adventures and grows from a boy into a man, guided by the wise goddess Athena who is also his father's best friend among the gods. Telemachus's search for his missing father, guided by the goddess, in effect provides him with the upbringing Odysseus was unable to give him. Even so, Odysseus still inspires his son from afar, because Telemachus learns during his travels of his father's exploits and wants to prove himself the hero's worthy son.

Whenever I describe Telemachus, this boy from a broken home, forced at a too-early age to be his mother's protector from oppressive men, compelled to bring himself up in a way that he hopes his absent father will be proud of, the young men in my undergraduate classes tend to become very quiet and reflective. They are Telemachus.

1

THE
CHIVALROUS
MAN

We OFTEN HEAR THAT CHIVALRY IS DEAD. BUT THE VERY FACT that we can lament its passing suggests we still have some recollection of it. What does it mean for a man to be chivalrous? Refined manners, courtesy toward others, respect for women, and a character bred to the virtues of honor, courage, and self-restraint—these would all be part of what we have in mind when the concept of chivalry is invoked. Chivalry is often associated with the ideals of medieval knighthood, as portrayed in the legends of King Arthur and his knights. The perfect knight was thought to embody a distinct array of ideals: piety, valor, gentleness, compassion for the suffering; knights were expected, moreover, to lead a sublime and spiritual inner life. In matters of love, the perfect knight always acted with moderation, composure, and patience in wooing his fair damsel. The chivalrous man wanted his lady to love him for his worthy character and his courage in defending justice, faith, and duty.

Chivalry, then, means much more than simply good manners—opening doors for ladies, for instance, or spreading one's trench coat over a puddle. These are the outward signs of a deeper experience—the process by which a man's love for a woman helps to perfect his own character. A common theme throughout the readings in this section is that love gives a man the strongest motive to overcome and avoid bad behavior, so as to make himself admirable and worthy of affection in the eyes of his beloved. They demonstrate, again and again, one of the paradoxes of the chivalric ideal: that an overwhelming romantic passion can furnish the surest inducement to moral decency. Readers will find in this section guidance from all ages on how a man can make himself worthy of a woman's love, how to avoid the temptations of lust and other excesses of erotic passion, and how to conduct himself toward his beloved in a gracious and admirable fashion.

THE MANLY LOVER

Orpheus and Eurydice

From Thomas Bulfinch,
Bulfinch's Mythology

A man's love for a woman can conquer even death. From the influential Victorian-era collection of ancient and medieval myths.

Orpheus was the son of Apollo and the Muse Calliope. He was presented by his father with a lyre and taught to play upon it, which he did to such perfection that nothing could withstand the charm of his music. Not only his fellow-mortals, but wild beasts were softened by his strains, and gathering round him laid by their fierceness, and stood entranced with his lay. Nay, the very trees and rocks were sensible to the charm. The former crowded round him and the latter relaxed somewhat of their hardness, softened by his notes.

Hymen had been called to bless with his presence the nuptials of Orpheus with Eurydice; but though he attended, he brought no happy omens with him. His very torch smoked and brought tears into their eyes. In coincidence with such prognostics, Eurydice, shortly after her marriage, while wandering with the nymphs, her companions, was seen by the shepherd Aristaeus, who was struck by her beauty and made advances to her. She fled, and in flying trod upon a snake in the grass, was bitten in the foot, and died. Orpheus sang his grief to all who breathed the upper air, both gods and men, and finding it all unavailing resolved to seek his wife in the regions of the dead. He descended by a cave situated on the side of the promontory of Taenarus and arrived at the Stygian realm. He passed through crowds of ghosts and presented himself before the throne of Pluto and Proserpine. Accompanying the words with the lyre, he sung, "O deities of the underworld, to whom all we who live must come, hear my words, for they are true. I come not to spy out the secrets of Tartarus, nor to try my strength against the three-headed dog with snaky hair who guards the entrance. I come to seek my wife, whose opening years the poisonous viper's fang has brought to an untimely end. Love has led me here, Love, a god all powerful with us who dwell on the earth, and, if old traditions say true, not less so here. I implore you by these abodes full of terror, these realms of silence and uncreated things, unite again the thread of Eurydice's life. We all are destined to you, and sooner or later must pass to your domain. She too, when she shall have filled her term of life, will rightly be yours. But till then grant her to me, I beseech you. If you deny me, I cannot return alone; you shall triumph in the death of us both."

As he sang these tender strains, the very ghosts shed tears. Tantalus, in spite of his thirst, stopped for a moment his efforts for water, Ixion's wheel stood still, the vulture ceased to tear the giant's liver, the daughters of Danaus rested from their task of drawing water in a sieve, and Sisyphus sat on his rock to listen. Then for the first time, it is said, the cheeks of the Furies were wet with tears. Proserpine could not resist, and Pluto himself gave way. Eurydice was called. She came from among the new-arrived ghosts, limping with her wounded foot. Orpheus was permitted to take her away with him on one condition, that he should not turn around to look at her till they should have reached the upper air. Under this condition they proceeded on their way, he leading, she following, through passages dark and steep, in total silence, till they had nearly reached the outlet into the cheerful upper world, when Orpheus, in a moment of forgetfulness, to assure himself that she was still following, cast a glance behind him, when instantly she was borne away. Stretching out their arms to embrace each other, they grasped only the air! Dying now a second time, she yet cannot reproach her husband, for how can she blame his impatience to behold her? "Farewell," she said, "a last farewell"—and was hurried away, so fast that the sound hardly reached his ears.

Orpheus endeavored to follow her, and besought permission to return and try once more for her release; but the stern ferryman repulsed him and refused passage. Seven days he lingered about the brink, without food or sleep; then bitterly accusing of cruelty the powers of Erebus, he sang his complaints to the rocks and mountains, melting the hearts of tigers and moving the oaks from their stations. He held himself aloof from womankind, dwelling constantly on the recollection of his sad mischance. The Thracian maidens tried their best to captivate him, but he repulsed their advances. They bore with him as long as they could; but finding him insensible one day, excited by the rites of Bacchus, one of them exclaimed, "See yonder our despiser!" and threw at him her javelin. The weapon, as soon as it came within the sound of his lyre, fell harmless at his feet. So did also the stones that they threw at him. But the women raised a scream and drowned the voice of the music, and then the missiles reached him and soon were stained with his blood. The maniacs tore him limb from limb, and threw his head and his lyre into the river Hebrus, down which they floated, murmuring sad music, to which the shores responded a plaintive symphony. The Muses gathered up the fragments of his body and buried them at Libethra, where the nightingale is said to sing over his grave more sweetly than in any other part of Greece. His lyre was placed by Jupiter among the stars. His shade passed a second time to Tartarus, where he sought out his Eurydice and embraced her with eager arms. They roam the happy fields together now, sometimes he leading, sometimes she; and Orpheus gazes as much as he will upon her, no longer incurring a penalty for a thoughtless glance.

The Art of Courtly Love

Andreas Capellanus

In this thirteenth-century classic from the High Age of Chivalry, The Art of Courtly Love, *Andreas Capellanus diagnoses the sweet suffering of love. A man's love makes him conscious of his imperfections in his beloved's eyes, and gives him the strongest motive to overcome them.*

Love is a certain inborn suffering derived from the sight of and excessive meditation upon the beauty of the opposite sex, which causes each one to wish above all things the embraces of the other and by common desire to carry out all of love's precepts in the other's embrace.

That love is suffering is easy to see, for before the love becomes equally balanced on both sides there is no torment greater, since the lover is always in fear that his love may not gain its desire and that he is wasting his efforts. He fears, too, that rumors of it may get abroad, and he fears everything that might harm it in any way, for before things are perfected a slight disturbance often spoils them. If he is a poor man, he also fears that the woman may scorn his poverty; if he is ugly, he fears that she may despise his lack of beauty or may give her love to a more handsome man; if he is rich, he fears that his parsimony in the past may stand in his way. To tell the truth, no one can number the fears of one single lover. This kind of love, then, is a suffering which is felt by only one of the persons and may be called "single love." But even after both are in love the fears that arise are just as great, for each of the lovers fears that what he has acquired with so much effort may be lost through the effort of someone else, which is certainly much worse for a man than if, having no hope, he sees that his efforts are accomplishing nothing, for it is worse to lose the things you are seeking than to be deprived of a gain you merely hope for. The lover fears, too, that he may offend his loved one in some way; indeed he fears so many things that it would be difficult to tell them.

Now it is the effect of love that a true lover cannot be degraded with any avarice. Love causes a rough and uncouth man to be distinguished for his handsomeness; it can endow a man even of the humblest birth with nobility of character; it blesses the proud with humility; and the man in love becomes accustomed to performing many services gracefully for everyone. O what a wonderful thing is love, which makes a man shine with so many virtues and teaches everyone, no matter who he is, so many good traits of character! There is another thing about love that we should not praise in few words: it adorns a man, so to speak, with the virtue of chastity, because he who shines with the light of one love can hardly think of embracing another woman, even a beautiful one. For when he thinks deeply of his beloved, the sight of any other woman seems to his mind rough and rude.

We must now see what persons are fit to bear the arms of love. You should know that everyone of sound mind who is capable of doing the work of Venus may be wounded by one of Love's arrows unless prevented by age, or blindness, or excess of passion.

An excess of passion is a bar to love, because there are men who are slaves to such passionate desire that they cannot be held in the bonds of love—men who, after they have thought long about some woman, straightway desire her embraces, and they forget about the services they have received from their first love and they feel no gratitude for them. Men of this kind lust after every woman they see; their love is like that of a shameless dog. They should rather, I believe, be compared to asses, for they are moved only by that low nature which shows that men are on the level of the other animals rather than by that true nature which sets us apart from all the other animals by the difference of reason.

Love and Self-Perfection

From Baldesar Castiglione,
The Book of the Courtier

Perhaps nowhere is the ideal of manliness as courtliness better explored than in Castiglione's sixteenth-century Renaissance classic The Book of the Courtier. *According to Cesare, one of the characters in the dialogue, a man will perfect all the virtues in himself in order to prove himself worthy to the lady he loves. Hence, there is no better indı cement to goodness than romantic passion.*

Then messer Cesare said:

"The things that my lord Magnifico and I have said in praise of women, and many others too, were very well known and hence superfluous.

"Who does not know that without women we can feel no contentment or satisfaction throughout this life of ours, which but for them would be rude and devoid of all sweetness and more savage than that of wild beasts? Who does not know that women alone banish from our hearts all vile and base thoughts, vexations, miseries, and those turbid melancholies that so often are their fellows? And if you will consider well the truth, we shall also see that in our understanding of great matters women do not hamper our wits but rather quicken them, and in war make men fearless and brave beyond measure. And certainly it is impossible for vileness ever again to rule in a man's heart where once the flame of love has entered; for whoever loves desires always to make himself as lovable as he can, and always fears lest some disgrace befall him that may make him be esteemed lightly with her by whom he desires to be esteemed highly. Nor does he stop at risking his life a thousand times a day to show himself worthy of her love: hence whoever could form an army of lovers and have them fight in the presence of the ladies of their love, would conquer all the world, unless there were opposed to it another army similarly in love. And be well assured that Troy's ten years' resistance against all Greece proceeded from naught else but a few lovers, who on sallying forth to battle, armed themselves in the presence of their women; and often these women helped them and spoke some word to them at leaving, which inflamed them and made them more than men. Then in battle they knew that they were watched by their women from the walls and towers; wherefore it seemed to them that every act of hardihood they performed, every proof they gave, won them their women's praise, which was the greatest reward they could have in the world.

"Do you not know that the origin of all the graceful exercises that give pleasure in the world is to be ascribed to none other than to women? Who learns to dance and caper gallantly for aught else than to please women? Who studies the sweetness of music for other cause than this? Who tries to compose verses, in the vernacular at least, unless to express those feelings that are inspired by women? Think how many very noble poems we should be deprived of, both in the Greek tongue and in the Latin, if women had been lightly esteemed by the poets. But to pass all the others by, would it not have been a very great loss if messer Francesco Petrarch, who so divinely wrote his loves in this language of ours, had turned his mind solely to things Latin, as he would have done if the love of madonna Laura had not sometimes drawn him from them? I do not name you the bright geniuses now on earth and present here, who every day put forth some noble fruit and yet choose their subject only from the beauties and virtues of women.

"You see that Solomon, wishing to write mystically of things lofty and divine, to cover them with a graceful veil composed a fervent and tender dialogue between a lover and his sweetheart, deeming that he could not here below find any similitude more apt and befitting things divine than love for women; and in this way he tried to give us a little of the savour of that divinity which he both by knowledge and by grace knew better than the rest.

"Hence there was no need, my lord Gaspar, to dispute about this, or at least so wordily: but by gainsaying the truth you have prevented us from hearing a thousand other fine and weighty matters concerning the perfection of the Court Lady."

My lord Gaspar replied:

"I believe nothing more is left to say; yet if you think that my lord Magnifico has not adorned her with enough good qualities, the fault lay not with him, but with the one who arranged that there are not more virtues in the world; for the Magnifico gave her all there are."

My lady Duchess said, laughing:

"You shall now see that my lord Magnifico will find still others."

The Rules of Love

From Andreas Capellanus,
The Art of Courtly Love

During the High Middle Ages, people began to write more openly about the purely sensual side of love. Knightly chivalry gave way to the peace-time refinement, luxury, and etiquette of court life. Ladies were won now not so much by fighting in battle or winning a jousting match, as by an elaborate courtship involving exquisite manners, wit, and conversation. Even so, love was not reduced to carnal self-indulgence: the longing for an unattainable love was thought to stimulate finer and nobler passions than easy success. Romantic fidelity was hailed as a superior way of life to the indulgence of every passing carnal whim—although one could have more than one such romance! In The Art of Courtly Love, *Capellanus provides us with thirty-one simple rules for sublime longing and torment.*

I. Marriage is no real excuse for not loving.
II. He who is not jealous cannot love.
III. No one can be bound by a double love.
IV. It is well known that love is always increasing or decreasing.
V. That which a lover takes against his will of his beloved has no relish.
VI. Boys do not love until they arrive at the age of maturity.
VII. When one lover dies, a widowhood of two years is required of the survivor.
VIII. No one should be deprived of love without the very best of reasons.
IX. No one can love unless he is impelled by the persuasion of love.
X. Love is always a stranger in the home of avarice.
XI. It is not proper to love any woman whom one should be ashamed to seek to marry.
XII. A true lover does not desire to embrace in love anyone except his beloved.
XIII. When made public, love rarely endures.

XIV.   The easy attainment of love makes it of little value; difficulty of attainment makes it prized.

XV.   Every lover regularly turns pale in the presence of his beloved.

XVI.   When a lover suddenly catches sight of his beloved, his heart palpitates.

XVII. A new love puts to flight an old one.

XVIII. Good character alone makes any man worthy of love.

XIX.   If love diminishes, it quickly fails and rarely revives.

XX.   A man in love is always apprehensive.

XXI.   Real jealousy always increases the feeling of love.

XXII. Jealousy, and therefore love, are increased when one suspects his beloved.

XXIII. He whom the thought of love vexes, eats and sleeps very little.

XXIV. Every act of a lover ends in the thought of his beloved.

XXV.   A true lover considers nothing good except what he thinks will please his beloved.

XXVI. Love can deny nothing to love.

XXVII. A lover can never have enough of the solaces of his beloved.

XXVIII. A slight presumption causes a lover to suspect his beloved.

XXIX. A man who is vexed by too much passion usually does not love.

XXX.   A true lover is constantly and without intermission possessed by the thought of his beloved.

XXXI. Nothing forbids one woman being loved by two men or one man by two women.

Love and Valor

From Thomas Bulfinch, Bulfinch's Mythology

Love inspired Sir Lancelot to great deeds.

Sir Lancelot of the Lake, in all tournaments and jousts and deeds of arms, both for life and death, passed all other knights, and was never overcome, except it were by treason or enchantment; and he increased marvelously in worship, wherefore Queen Guenever had him in great favor, above all other knights. And for certain he loved the queen again above all other ladies; and for her he did many deeds of arms, and saved her from peril through his noble chivalry.

Older Men Make Better Lovers

From Baldesar Castiglione,
The Book of the Courtier

Whereupon messer Pietro, having first remained silent awhile, then settled himself a little as if about to speak of something important, and spoke thus:

"My Lords, in order to prove that old men can love not only without blame but sometimes more happily than young men, it will be needful for me to make a little discourse to explain what love is, and in what consists the happiness that lovers may enjoy. So I pray you hear me with attention, for I hope to make you see that there is no man for whom it is not becoming to be in love, even though he were fifteen or twenty years older than my lord Morello."

And then after some laughter, messer Pietro continued:

"Seized with desire to enjoy beauty as something good, if the soul allows herself to be guided by the judgment of sense, she runs into very grievous errors, and judges that the body wherein the beauty is seen is the chief cause of it; and hence, in order to enjoy that beauty, she deems it necessary to join herself as closely to that body as she can; which is false: and accordingly, whoever thinks to enjoy the beauty by possessing the body deceives himself, and is moved, not by true perception through reasonable choice, but by false opinion through sensual appetite: wherefore the pleasure also that results therefrom is necessarily false and vicious.

"Hence all those lovers who satisfy their unchaste desires with the women whom they love, run into one of two errors: for as soon as they have attained the end desired, they either feel satiety and tedium, or hate the beloved object as if appetite repented its error and perceived the deceit practised upon it by the false judgment of sense, which made it believe evil to be good.

"Such lovers as these, therefore, love most unhappily; for either they never attain their desires (which is great unhappiness), or if they do attain thereto, they find they have attained their woe, and finish their miseries with other miseries still greater; because even in the beginning and midst of their love naught else is ever felt but anguish, torments, sorrows, sufferings, toils. So that to be pale, melancholy, in continual tears and sighs, to be sad, to be ever silent or lamenting, to long for death, in short, to be most unhappy, are the conditions that are said to befit lovers.

"Hence it nearly always happens that young men are wrapped in this love which is sensual and wholly rebellious to reason, and thus they become unworthy to enjoy the graces and benefits which love bestows upon its true subjects; nor do they feel any pleasures in love beyond those which the unreasoning animals feel, but anguish far more grievous.

"This premise being admitted then,—and it is most true,—I say that the contrary happens to those who are of maturer age. For if such as these (when the soul is already less weighed down by bodily heaviness and when the natural heat begins to become tepid) are inflamed by beauty and turn thereto a desire guided by rational choice,—they are not deceived, and possess beauty perfectly. Therefore their possession of it always brings them good; because beauty is good, and hence true love of beauty is most good and holy, and always works for good in the mind of those who restrain the perversity of sense with the bridle of reason; which the old can do much more easily than the young.

"Hence it is not beyond reason to say further that the old can love without blame and more happily than the young; taking this word old, however, not in the sense of decrepit, nor when the bodily organs have already become so weak that the soul cannot perform its functions through them, but when our knowledge is at its true prime.

"I will not refrain from saying also this: which is, that I think that although sensual love is evil at every age, yet in the young it deserves excuse, and is perhaps in a measure permitted. For although it gives them anguish, dangers, toils, and those woes that have been told, still there are many who, to win the favour of the ladies of their love, do worthy acts, which (although not directed to a good end) are intrinsically good; and thus from that mass of bitterness they extract a little sweet, and through the adversities which they endure they at last perceive their error. Hence, just as I deem those youths divine who control their appetites and love in reason, so I excuse those who allow themselves to be overcome by sensual love, to which they are so strongly inclined by human frailty: provided they show therein gentleness, courtesy and worth, and the other noble qualities of which these gentlemen have told; and provided that when they are no longer of youthful age, they abandon it altogether, shunning this sensual desire as it were the lowest rung of the ladder by which true love can be attained."

Having thus far spoken, with such vehemence that he almost seemed transported and beside himself, Bembo remained silent and motionless, keeping his eyes towards heaven, as if wrapped in ecstasy; when my lady Emilia, who with the others had been listening most attentively to his discourse, took him by the border of his robe, and shaking him a little, said:

"Have a care, messer Pietro, th ɪt with these thoughts your soul, also, does not forsake your body."

"My Lady," replied messer Pietro, "that would not be the first miracle that love has wrought upon me."

Love or Wisdom?

Francis Bacon

A twist on the formula: It is impossible to love and be wise, says Bacon in his essay Of Love, *because such excess drains our energies from life's serious business.*

The stage is more beholding to love than the life of man. For as to the stage, love is ever a matter of comedies, and now and then of tragedies, but in life it doth much mischief, sometimes like a syren, sometimes like a fury. You may observe that amongst all the great and worthy persons (whereof the memory remaineth, either ancient or recent) there is not one that hath been transported to the mad degree of love, which shews that great spirits and great business do keep out this weak passion. You must except nevertheless Marcus Antonius, the half partner of the empire of Rome, and Appius Claudius, the decemvir and lawgiver; whereof the former was indeed a voluptuous man, and inordinate, but the latter was an austere and wise man; and therefore it seems (though rarely) that love can find entrance not only into an open heart, but also into a heart well fortified, if watch be not well kept. This passion hath his floods in the very times of weakness, which are great prosperity and great adversity, though this latter hath been less observed, both which times kindle love, and make it more fervent, and therefore shew it to be the child of folly. They do best, who if they cannot but admit love yet make it keep quarter, and sever it wholly from their serious affairs and actions of life, for if it check once with business, it troubleth men's fortunes, and maketh men that they can no ways be true to their own ends.

Love or Duty?

From Xenophon, The Education of Cyrus

Is it possible for a man to do his duty if he is distracted by erotic passion? Cyrus the Great's young lieutenant Araspas contends that a man can fall madly in love but compartmentalize his feelings so as to carry out his duties efficiently. The older Cyrus is not so sure. Eros enslaves a man and makes him lovesick so that he can't get anything useful accomplished. Better to avoid such entanglements! From a work by Xenophon, the celebrated Athenian general and student of Socrates.

And when he received this commission, Araspas asked: "And have you seen the lady, Cyrus, whom you give into my keeping?"

"No, by Zeus," said Cyrus; "not I."

"But I have," said the other. "And let me tell you, Cyrus," said he, "it seemed to me, as it did to all the rest who saw her, that there never was so beautiful a woman of mortal birth in Asia. But," he added, "you must by all means see her for yourself."

"No by Zeus," said Cyrus; "and all the less, if she is as beautiful as you say."

"Why so?" asked the young man.

"Because," said he, "if now I have heard from you that she is beautiful and am inclined just by your account of her to go and gaze on her, when I have no leisure, I am afraid that she will herself much more readily persuade me to come again to gaze on her. And in consequence of that I might sit there, in neglect of my duties, idly gazing upon her."

"Why Cyrus," said the young man breaking into a laugh, "you do not think, do you, that human beauty is able to compel a man against his will to act contrary to his own best interest? Why," said he, "if that were natural, it would compel us all alike. Do you see," said he, "how fire burns all alike. That is its nature. But of beautiful things we love some and some we do not; and one loves one, another another; for it is a matter of will and each one loves what he wishes."

"How then, pray," said Cyrus, "if falling in love is a matter of will is it not possible for any one to stop whenever he wishes? But I have seen people in tears of sorrow because of love and in slavery to the objects of their love, even though they believed before they fell in love that slavery is a great evil; I have seen them give those objects of their love many things that they could ill afford to part with; and I have seen people praying to be delivered from love just as from any other disease, and, for all that, unable to be delivered from it, but fettered by a stronger necessity than if they had been fettered with shackles of iron. At any rate, they surrender themselves to those they love to perform for them many services blindly. And yet, in spite of all their misery, they do not attempt to run away, but even guard their darlings to keep them from running away."

"Yes," the young man answered, "there are some who do so; but such are wretched weaklings, the beautiful do not compel humans to fall in love with them nor to desire that which they should not, but there are some miserable apologies for men who are slaves to all sorts of passions, I think, and then they blame love. But the good, though they also have a desire for money and good horses and beautiful women, have the power to let all that alone so as not to touch anything beyond the limit of what is just. At any rate," he added, "I have seen this lady and though she seemed to me surpassingly beautiful, still I am here with you, I practice horsemanship, and I do everything else that it is my duty to do."

"Aye, by Zeus," said Cyrus; "for you came away perhaps in less time than love takes, as its nature is, to get a man ensnared. For, you know, it is possible for a man to put his finger in the fire and not be burned at once, and wood does not burst at once into flame; still, for my part, I neither put my hand into the fire nor look upon the beautiful, if I can help it. And I advise you, too, Araspas," said he, "not to let your eyes linger upon the fair; for fire, to be sure, burns only those who touch it, but beauty insidiously kindles a fire even in those who gaze upon it from afar, so that they are inflamed with eros."

"Never fear, Cyrus," said he, "even if I never cease to look upon her, I shall never be so overcome as to do anything that I ought not."

"Your proposals," said he, "are most excellent. Keep her then, as I bid you, and take good care of her."

Now, he wished to send someone as a spy into Lydia to find out what the Assyrian was doing, and it seemed to him that Araspas, the guardian of the beautiful woman, was the proper person to go on this mission. Now Araspas's case had taken a turn like this: he had fallen in love with the lady and could not resist the impulse to approach her with amorous proposals. But she repulsed his advances and was true to her husband, although he was far away, for she loved him devotedly. Still, she did not accuse Araspas to Cyrus, for she shrank from making trouble between friends. But when Araspas, thinking that he should thus further the attainment of his desires, threatened the woman that he would use force if she would not submit willingly, then in fear of outrage the lady no longer kept it secret but sent her eunuch to Cyrus with instructions to tell him the whole story.

When Cyrus heard it, he laughed outright at the man who had claimed to be superior to the passion of love; and he sent Artabazus back with the eunuch and bade him warn Araspas not to lay violent hands upon such a woman; but if he could win her consent, he himself would interpose no objection.

So, when Artabazus came to Araspas, he rebuked him severely, saying that the woman had been given to him in trust; and he dwelt upon his ungodliness, sinfulness, and sensuality, until Araspas shed bitter tears of contrition and was overwhelmed with shame and frightened to death lest Cyrus should punish him.

So, when Cyrus learned of this, he sent for him and had a talk with him in private. "I see, Araspas," said he, "that you are afraid of me and terribly overcome with shame. Do not feel that way, pray; for I have heard say that even gods are victims of love; and as for mortals, I know that even some who are considered very discreet have suffered from love. And I had too poor an opinion of myself to suppose that I should have the strength of will to be thrown in contact with beauty and be indifferent to it. Besides, I am myself responsible for your condition, for it was I that shut you up with this irresistible creature."

"Aye, Cyrus," said Araspas, interrupting him, "you are in this, just as in everything else, gentle and forgiving of human errors. Other men make me ready to sink with my shame; for ever since the report of my fall got out, my enemies have been exulting over me, while my friends come to me and advise me to keep out of the way, for fear that you punish me for committing so great a wrong."

"Let me tell you then, Araspas," said Cyrus, "that by reason of this very report which people have heard in regard to you, you are in a position to do me a very great favor and to be of great assistance to our allies."

"Would that some occasion might arise," answered Araspas, "in which I could be of service to you."

"If, then," said the other, "under pretense that you were fleeing from me you would go over into the enemy's country, I believe they would trust you."

"Aye, by Zeus," said Araspas, "and I know that even with my friends I could start the story that I was running away from you."

"Then you would return to us," said he, "with full information about the enemy's condition and plans. And I suppose that because of their trusting you they would make you a participant in their discussions and counsels, so that not a single thing that we wish to know would be hidden from you."

"Depend upon it," said he, "I will start at once; and one of the circumstances that will gain my story credence will be the appearance that I have run away because I was likely to be punished by you."

"And will you be able to give up the beautiful Panthea?" asked Cyrus.

"Yes, Cyrus," said he; "for I evidently have two souls. I have now worked out this doctrine of philosophy in the school of that crooked sophist, Eros. For if the soul is one, it is not both good and bad at the same time, neither can it at the same time desire the right and the wrong, nor at the same time both will and not will to do the same things; but it is obvious that there are two souls, and when the good one prevails, what is noble is done; but when the bad one gains the ascendency, what is shameful is attempted. And now, since she has taken you to be her ally, it is the good soul that has gained the mastery, and that completely."

Lancelot and Guenever

From Thomas Bulfinch,
Bulfinch's Mythology

The conflict between the love of Sir Lancelot and Queen Guenever and their duty to their king leads to tragedy for them and for the kingdom.

So after the quest of the Holy Grail was fulfilled, and all the knights who were left alive were come again to the Table Round, there was great joy in the court, and especially King Arthur and Queen Guenever made great joy of the remnant that were come home, and passing glad were the king and the queen of Sir Lancelot and of Sir Bohort, for they had been passing long away in the quest of the Holy Grail.

Then Sir Lancelot began to resort unto Queen Guenever again, and forgot the promise that he made in the quest; so that many in the court spoke of it, and in especial Sir Agrivain, Sir Gawain's brother, for he was ever open-mouthed. So it happened Sir Gawain and all his brothers were in King Arthur's chamber, and then Sir Agrivain said thus openly, "I marvel that we all are not ashamed to see and to know so noble a knight as King Arthur so to be shamed by the conduct of Sir Lancelot and the queen." Then spoke Sir Gawain, and said, "Brother, Sir Agrivain, I pray for you and charge you move not such matters any more before me for be ye assured I will not be of your counsel." "Neither will we," said Sir Gaheris and Sir Gareth. "Then will I," said Sir Modred. "I doubt you not, " said Sir Gawain, "for to all mischief ever were ye prone; yet I would that ye left all this, for I know what will come of it." "Fall of it what may fall," said Sir Agrivain, "I will disclose it to the king." With that King Arthur came to them. "Now, brothers, hold your peace," said Sir Gawain.

"We will not," said Sir Agrivain. Then said Sir Gawain, "I will not hear your tales, nor be of your counsel." "No more will I," said Sir Gareth and Sir Gaheris, and they departed, making great sorrow.

Then Sir Agrivain told the king all that was said in the court of the conduct of Sir Lancelot and the queen, and it grieved the king very much. But he would not believe it to be true without proof. So

Sir Agrivain laid a plot to entrap Sir Lancelot and the queen, intending to take them together unawares. Sir Agrivain and Sir Modred led a party for this purpose, but Sir Lancelot escaped from them having slain Sir Agrivain and wounded Sir Modred. Then Sir Lancelot hastened to his friends, and told them what had happened, and withdrew with them to the forest; but he left spies to bring him tidings of whatever might be done.

So Sir Lancelot escaped, but the queen remained in the king's power, and Arthur could no longer doubt of her guilt. And the law was such in those days that they who committed such crimes, of whatever estate or condition they were, must be burned to death, and so it was ordained for Queen Guenever. Then said King Arthur to Sir Gawain, "I pray you make you ready, in your best armor, with your brethren, Sir Gaheris and Sir Gareth, to bring my queen to the fire, there to receive her death." "Nay, my most noble lord," said Sir Gawain, "that will I never do; for know thou well, my heart will never serve me to see her die, and it shall never be said that I was of your counsel in her death." Then the king commanded Sir Gaheris and Sir Gareth to be there, and they said, "We will be there, as ye command us, sire, but in peaceable wise, and bear no armor upon us."

So the queen was led forth, and her priest was brought to her to shrive her, and there was weeping and wailing of many lords and ladies. And one went and told Sir Lancelot that the queen was led forth to her death. Then Sir Lancelot and the knights that were with him fell upon the troop that guarded the queen, and dispersed them, and slew all who withstood them. And in the confusion Sir Gareth and Sir Gaheris were slain, for they were unarmed and defenseless. And Sir Lancelot carried away the queen to his castle of La Joyeuse Garde.

Then there came one to Sir Gawain and told him how that Sir Lancelot had slain the knights and carried away the queen. "O Lord, defend my brethren!" said Sir Gawain. "Truly," said the man, "Sir Gareth and Sir Gaheris are slain." "Alas!" said Sir Gawain, "now is my joy gone." And then he fell down and swooned, and long he lay there as if he were dead.

When he arose out of his swoon Sir Gawain ran to the king, crying, "O King Arthur, mine uncle, my brothers are slain." Then the king and he both wept. "My king, my lord, and mine uncle," said Sir Gawain, "bear witness now that I make you a promise that I shall hold by my knighthood, that from this day I will never fail Sir Lancelot until the one of us have slain the other. I will seek Sir

Lancelot throughout seven kings' realms, but I shall slay him or he shall slay me."

Dido and Aeneas

From Thomas Bulfinch,
Bulfinch's Mythology

The exiled Trojan hero Aeneas must renounce his love in order to fulfill his destiny.

Dido received the illustrious exiles with friendliness and hospitality. "Not unacquainted with distress," she said, "I have learned to succor the unfortunate." The queen's hospitality displayed itself in festivities at which games of strength and skill were exhibited. The strangers contended for the palm with her own subjects, on equal terms, the queen declaring that whether the victor were "Trojan or Tyrian should make no difference to her." At the feast which followed the games, Aeneas gave at her request a recital of the closing events of the Trojan history and his own adventures after the fall of the city. Dido was charmed with his discourse and filled with admiration of his exploits. She conceived an ardent passion for him, and he for his part seemed well content to accept the fortunate chance which appeared to offer him at once a happy termination of his wanderings, a home, a kingdom, and a bride. Months rolled away in the enjoyment of pleasant intercourse, and it seemed as if Italy and the empire destined to be founded on its shores were alike forgotten. Seeing which, Jupiter despatched Mercury with a message to Aeneas recalling him to a sense of his high destiny and commanding him to resume his voyage.

Aeneas parted from Dido, though she tried every allurement and persuasion to detain him. The blow to her affection and her pride was too much for her to endure, and when she found that he was gone, she mounted a funeral pile which she had caused to be erected, and having stabbed herself was consumed with the pile. The flames rising over the city were seen by the departing Trojans, and, though the cause was unknown, gave to Aeneas some intimation of the fatal event.

Breaking Up Is Hard to Do

From Plato, Symposium

According to the comic poet Aristophanes, as he appears in the Symposium, *men and women were once single beings, rolling around like Cheerios and perfectly happy; the gods split us into male and female halves to punish us for our arrogance. Today, when a man and woman fall in love, each is yearning for that missing half.*

Love is, of all the gods the best friend of men, the helper and the healer of the ills which are the great impediment to the happiness of the race. I will try to describe his power to you, and you shall teach the rest of the world what I am teaching you. In the first place, let me treat of the nature of man and what has happened to it; for the original human nature was not like the present, but different. The sexes were not two as they are now, but originally three in number; there was man, woman, and the union of the two, having a name corresponding to this double nature, which had once a real existence, but is now lost, and the word "Androgynous" is only preserved as a term of reproach. In the second place, the primeval man was round, his back and sides forming a circle; and he had four hands and four feet, one head with two faces, looking opposite ways, set on a round neck and precisely alike; also four ears, two privy members, and the remainder to correspond. He could walk upright as men now do, backwards or forwards as he pleased and he could also roll over and over at a great pace, turning on his four hands and four feet, eight in all, like tumblers going over and over with their legs in the air; this was when he wanted to run fast. Now the sexes were three, and such as I have described them; because the sun, moon, and earth are three; and the man was originally the child of the sun, the woman of the earth, and the man-woman of the moon, which is made up of sun and earth, and they were all round and moved round and round like their parents. Terrible was their might and strength, and the thoughts of their hearts were great, and they made an attack upon the gods; of them is told the tale of Otys and Ephialtes who, as Homer says, dared to scale heaven, and would have laid hands upon the gods. Doubt reigned in the celestial

councils. Should they kill them and annihilate the race with thun-
derbolts, as they had done the giants, then there would be an end of
the sacrifices and worship which men offered to them; but, on the
other hand, the gods could not suffer their insolence to be unre-
strained. At last, after a good deal of reflection, Zeus discovered a
way. He said: "Methinks I have a plan which will humble their pride
and improve their manners; men shall continue to exist, but I will
cut them in two and then they will be diminished in strength and
increased in numbers; this will have the advantage of making them
more profitable to us. They shall walk upright on two legs, and if
they continue insolent and will not be quiet, I will split them again
and they shall hop about on a single leg." He spoke and cut men in
two, like a sorb-apple which is halved for pickling, or as you might
divide an egg with a hair; and as he cut them one after another, he
bade Apollo give the face and the half of the neck a turn in order
that the man might contemplate the section of himself: he would
thus learn a lesson of humility. Apollo was also bidden to heal their
wounds and compose their forms. So he gave a turn to the face and
pulled the skin from the sides all over that which in our language is
called the belly, like the purses which draw in, and he made one
mouth at the centre, which he fastened in a knot (the same as which
is called the navel); he also moulded the breast and took out most
of the wrinkles, much as a shoemaker might smooth leather upon a
last; he left a few, however, in the region of the belly and navel, as a
memorial of the primeval state.

After the division the two parts of man, each desiring his other
half, came together, and throwing their arms about one another,
entwined in mutual embraces, longing to grow into one, they were
on the point of dying from hunger and self-neglect, because they
did not like to do anything apart; and when one of the halves died
and the other survived, the survivor sought another mate, man or
woman as we call them,—being the sections of entire men or
women,—and clung to that. They were being destroyed, when Zeus
in pity of them invented a new plan: he turned the parts of generation round to the front, for this had not been always their position,
and they sowed the seed no longer as hitherto like grasshoppers in
the ground, but in one another; and after the transposition the
male generated in the female in order that by the mutual embraces
of man and woman they might breed, and the race might continue;
or if man came to man they might be satisfied, and rest, and go
their ways to the business of life: so ancient is the desire of one
another which is implanted in us, reuniting our original nature,

making one of two, and healing the state of man. Each of us when separated, having one side only, like a flat fish, is but the indenture of a man, and he is always looking for his other half. Men who are a section of that double nature which was once called Androgynous are lovers of women; adulterers are generally of this breed, and also adulterous women who lust after men: the women who are a section of the woman do not care for men, but have female attachments; the female companions are of this sort. But they who are a section of the male follow the male, and while they are young, being slices of the original man, they hang about men and embrace them, and they are themselves the best of boys and youths, because they have the most manly nature. Some indeed assert that they are shameless, but this is not true; for they do not act thus from any want of shame, but because they are valiant and manly, and have a manly countenance, and they embrace that which is like them. And these when they grow up become our statesmen, and these only, which is a great proof of the truth of what I am saying. When they reach manhood they are lovers of youth, and are not naturally inclined to marry or beget children,—if at all, they do so only in obedience to the law; but they are satisfied if they may be allowed to live with one another unwedded; and such a nature is prone to love and ready to return love, always embracing that which is akin to him.

And when one of them meets with his other half, the actual half of himself, whether he be a lover of youth or a lover of another sort, the pair are lost in an amazement of love and friendship and intimacy, and will not be out of the other's sight, as I may say, even for a moment: these are the people who pass their whole lives together; yet they could not explain what they desire of one another. For the intense yearning which each of them has towards the other does not appear to be the desire of a lover's intercourse, but of something else which the soul of either evidently desires and cannot tell, and of which she has only a dark and doubtful presentiment. Suppose Hephaestus, with his instruments, were to come to the pair who are lying side by side and to say to them, "What do you people want of one another?" they would be unable to explain. And suppose further, that when he saw their perplexity he said: "Do you desire to be wholly one; always day and night to be in one another's company? For if this is what you desire, I am ready to melt you into one and let you grow together, so that being two you shall become one, and while you live a common life as if you were a single man, and after your death in the world below still be one departed soul instead of two—I ask whether this is what you lovingly desire, and whether you are satisfied to attain this?"—there is not a man of them who when he heard the proposal would deny or would not acknowledge that this meeting and melting into one another, this becoming one instead of two, was the very expression of his ancient need. And the reason is that human nature was originally one and we were a whole, and the desire and pursuit of the whole is called love.

Diana and Actaeon

From Thomas Bulfinch,
Bulfinch's Mythology

Among the lessons a man must learn: if you can't control your passions, they may devour you.

There was a valley thick enclosed with cypresses and pines, sacred to the huntress queen, Diana. In the extremity of the valley was a cave, not adorned with art, but nature had counterfeited art in its construction, for she had turned the arch of its roof with stones, as delicately fitted as if by the hand of man. A fountain burst out from one side, whose open basin was bounded by a grassy rim. Here the goddess of the woods used to come when weary with hunting and bathe her virgin limbs in the sparkling water.

One day, having repaired thither with her nymphs, she handed her javelin, her quiver, and her bow to one, her robe to another, while a third unbound the sandals from her feet. Then Crocale, the most skillful of them, arranged her hair, and Nephele, Hyale, and the rest drew water in capacious urns. While the goddess was thus employed in the labors of the toilet, behold Actaeon, having quitted his companions, and rambling without any especial object, came to the place, led thither by his destiny. As he presented himself at the entrance of the cave, the nymphs, seeing a man, screamed and rushed toward the goddess to hide her with their bodies. But she was taller than the rest and overtopped them all by a head. Such a color as tinges the clouds at sunset or at dawn came over the countenance of Diana thus taken by surprise. Surrounded as she was by her nymphs, she yet turned half away, and sought with a sudden impulse for her arrows. As they were not at hand, she dashed the water into the face of the intruder, adding these words: "Now go and tell, if you can, that you have seen Diana unappareled." Immediately a pair of branching stag's horns grew out of his head, his neck gained in length, his ears grew sharp-pointed, his hands became feet, his arms long legs, his body was covered with a hairy, spotted hide. Fear took the place of his former boldness, and the hero fled. He could not but admire his own speed; but when he saw his horns in the water, "Ah, wretched me!" he would have said, but no sound followed the effort. He groaned, and tears flowed down the face which had taken the place of his own. Yet his consciousness remained. What shall he do? Go home to seek the palace, or lie hid in the woods? The latter he was afraid, the former he was ashamed, to do. While he hesitated the dogs saw him. First Melampus, a Spartan dog, gave the signal with his bark, then Pamphagus, Dorceus, Lelaps, Theron, Nape, Tigris, and all the rest, rushed after him swifter than the wind. Over rocks and cliffs, through mountain gorges that seemed impracticable, he fled and they followed. Where he had often chased the stag and cheered on his pack, his pack now chased him, cheered on by his huntsmen. He longed to cry out, "I am Actaeon; recognize your master!" but the words came not at his will. The air resounded with the bark of the dogs. Presently one fastened on his back, another seized his shoulder. While they held their master, the rest of the pack came up and buried their teeth in his flesh. He groaned, not in a human voice, yet certainly not in a stag's, and falling on his knees, raised his eyes, and would have raised his arms in supplication, if he had had them. His friends and fellow-huntsmen cheered on the dogs, and looked everywhere for Actaeon, calling on him to join the sport. At the sound of his name he turned his head, and heard them regret that he should be away. He earnestly wished he was. He would have been well pleased to see the exploits of his dogs, but to feel them was too much. They were all around him, rending and tearing; and it was not till they had torn his life out that the anger of Diana was satisfied.

On Adultery

From Ovid, The Art of Love

Not much has changed on this score since the Roman love poet Ovid (43 B.C.–17 A.D.).

So, that husband of yours is going to be at the party—
Well, I hope he chokes; let him drop dead, who cares?
How am I going to act?—just stare at the girl I'm in love with,
Be just one more guest, let someone else feel your breast,
Let someone else put his arms around you whenever he wants to.
Sit at your side, rub knees, lean on your shoulder a bit?
I can believe what they say of the brawls of the Lapiths and
    Centaurs
Over the fair-haired girl, after the wine went round.
I do not live in the woods, and my members are not like a horse's,
Still I'll be having a time keeping my hands to myself.
Learn what you have to do, and please pay careful attention:
Get there before he does—not that that does any good.
Anyway, get there before him, and when he reclines, you beside
    him,
Modestly on the couch, give my foot just a touch,
Watch me for every nod, for every facial expression,
Catch my signs and return them, never saying a word.
I can talk with my eyebrows and spell out words with my fingers,
I can make you a sign, dipping my finger in wine.
When you think of the tumbles we've had in the hay together,
Touch your cheek with your hand; then I will understand.
If you're a little bit cross with the way I may be behaving,
Let your fingertip rest light on the lobe of an ear.
If, on the other hand, what I am saying should please you,
Darling, keep turning your ring; symbol enough that will be.
Fold your hands on the table, as people do when they're
    praying—
That means you wish him bad luck, yes, and a lot of it, too.
When he mixes your wine, let him drink it himself; so inform him:

Quietly speak to the boy, ask for the kind you enjoy.
When you pass him the cup, let me have a sip as it goes by;
Where you drank I will touch that part first with my lips.
Don't accept any food from a dish that he has first tasted;
Keep his arms from your neck; don't lay your head on his chest;
Don't let his fingers grope in the neck of your dress or your
    bosom;
More than everything else, don't let him kiss you at all.
Don't you kiss him either; you do, and you'll have me announcing
"Hands off there! She's mine"—and then I'll reach out for my
    claim.

I would not dare to defend my absolute absence of morals;
I would not smother my faults under a blanket of lies.
No: I own up; I confess, if any confession can help me;
Wailing *My grievous fault,* how I lash out at my sins!
I hate what I am, and yet, for all my desiring,
Cannot be anything else—what a misfortune to bear!
Borne along like a ship tossed on tempestuous waters,
Out of control, I lack willpower to keep me aright.
There is no definite One whose beauty drives me to frenzy;
No: there are hundreds, almost, keeping me always in love.

Apollo and Daphne

From Thomas Bulfinch,
Bulfinch's Mythology

A god lusts for what he cannot have, but ends up doing a good deed.

Daphne was Apollo's first love. It was not brought about by
accident, but by the malice of Cupid. Apollo saw the boy playing
with his bow and arrows; and being himself elated with his recent
victory over Python, he said to him, "What have you to do with warlike weapons, saucy boy? Leave them for hands worthy of them.
Behold the conquest I have won by means of them over the vast ser-
pent who stretched his poisonous body over acres of the plain! Be

content with your torch, child, and kindle up your flames, as you call them, where you will, but presume not to meddle with my weapons." Venus's boy heard these words, and rejoined, "Your arrows may strike all things else, Apollo, but mine shall strike you." So saying, he took his stand on a rock of Parnassus, and drew from his quiver two arrows of different workmanship, one to excite love, the other to repel it. The former was of gold and sharp pointed, the latter blunt and tipped with lead. With the leaden shaft he struck the nymph Daphne, the daughter of the river god Peneus, and with the golden one Apollo, through the heart. Forthwith the god was seized with love for the maiden, and she abhorred the thought of loving. Her delight was in woodland sports and in the spoils of the chase. Many lovers sought her, but she spurned them all, ranging the woods, and taking no thought of Cupid nor of Hymen. Her father often said to her, "Daughter, you owe me a son-in-law; you owe me grandchildren." She, hating the thought of marriage as a crime, with her beautiful face tinged all over with blushes, threw her arms around her father's neck, and said, "Dearest father, grant me this favor, that I may always remain unmarried, like Diana." He consented, but at the same time said, "Your own face will forbid it."

Apollo loved her, and longed to obtain her; and he who gives oracles to all the world was not wise enough to look into his own fortunes. He saw her hair flung loose over her shoulders, and said, "If so charming is disorder, what would it be if arranged?" He saw her eyes bright as stars; he saw her lips, and was not satisfied with only seeing them. He admired her hands and arms, naked to the shoulder, and whatever was hidden from view he imagined more beautiful still. He followed her; she fled, swifter than the wind, and delayed not a moment at his entreaties. "Stay," said he, "daughter of Peneus; I am not a foe. Do not fly me as a lamb flies the wolf, or a dove the hawk. It is for love I pursue you. You make me miserable, for fear you should fall and hurt yourself on these stones, and I should be the cause. Pray run slower, and I will follow slower. I am no clown, no rude peasant. Jupiter is my father, and I am lord of Delphos and Tenedos, and know all things, present and future. I am the god of song and the lyre. My arrows fly true to the mark; but, alas! An arrow more fatal than mine has pierced my heart! I am the god of medicine, and know the virtues of all healing plants. Alas! I suffer a malady that no balm can cure!"

And the nymph continued her flight and left his plea half uttered. And even as she fled she charmed him. The wind blew her garments, and her unbound hair streamed loose behind her. The god grew impatient to find his wooings thrown away, and, sped by Cupid, gained upon her in the race. It was like a hound pursuing a hare, with open jaws ready to seize, while the feebler animal darts forward, slipping from the very grasp. So flew the god and the virgin—he on the wings of love, and she on those of fear. The pursuer is the more rapid, however, and gains upon her, and his panting breath blows upon her hair. Her strength begins to fail, and, ready to sink, she calls upon her father, the river god: "Help me, Peneus! Open the earth to enclose me, or change my form, which has brought me into this danger!" Scarcely had she spoken when a stiffness seized all her limbs; her bosom began to be enclosed in a tender bark; her hair became leaves; her arms became branches; her foot stuck fast in the ground, as a root; her face became a treetop, retaining nothing of its former self but its beauty. Apollo stood amazed. He touched the stem, and felt the flesh tremble under the new bark. He embraced the branches, and lavished kisses on the wood. The branches shrank from his lips. "Since you cannot be my wife," said he, "thou shall assuredly be my tree. I will wear you for my crown; I will decorate with you my harp and my quiver; and when the great Roman conquerors lead up the triumphal pomp to the Capitol, you shall be woven into wreaths for their brows. And, as eternal youth is mine, you also shall be always green, and your leaf know no decay." The nymph, now changed into a Laurel tree, bowed its head in grateful acknowledgment.

The Narcissist

From Thomas Bulfinch,
Bulfinch's Mythology

What happens when a beautiful young man falls in love with himself? The lady he spurns gives him a taste of his own medicine. He ends up jilting himself!

Echo was a beautiful nymph, fond of the woods and hills, where she devoted herself to woodland sports. She was a favorite of Diana, and attended her in the chase. But Echo had one failing; she was fond of talking, and whether in chat or argument, would have the last word. One day Juno was seeking her husband, who, she had reason to fear, was amusing himself among the nymphs. Echo by her talk contrived to detain the goddess till the nymphs made their escape. When Juno discovered it, she passed sentence upon Echo in these words: "You shall forfeit the use of that tongue with which you have cheated me, except for that one purpose you are so fond of—*reply*. You shall still have the last word, but no power to speak first."

This nymph saw Narcissus, a beautiful youth, as he pursued the chase upon the mountains. She loved him and followed his footsteps. O how she longed to address him in the softest accents, and win him to converse! But it was not in her power. She waited with impatience for him to speak first, and had her answer ready. One day the youth, being separated from his companions, shouted aloud, "Who's here?" Echo replied, "Here." Narcissus looked around, but seeing no one, called out, "Come." Echo answered, "Come." As no one came, Narcissus called again, "Why do you shun me?" Echo asked the same question. "Let us join one another," said the youth. The maid answered with all her heart in the same words, and hastened to the spot, ready to throw her arms about his neck. He started back, exclaiming, "Hands off! I would rather die than you should have me!" "Have me," said she; but it was all in vain. He left her, and she went to hide her blushes in the recesses of the woods. From that time forth she lived in caves and among mountain cliffs. Her form faded with grief, till at last all her flesh shrank away. Her bones were changed into rocks and there was nothing left of her but her voice. With that she is still ready to reply to anyone who calls her, and keeps up her old habit of having the last word.

Narcissus's cruelty in this case was not the only instance. He shunned all the rest of the nymphs, as he had done poor Echo. One day a maiden who had in vain endeavored to attract him uttered a prayer that he might some time or other feel what it was to love and meet no return of affection. The avenging goddess heard and granted the prayer.

There was a clear fountain, with water like silver, to which the shepherds never drove their flocks, nor the mountain goats resorted, nor any of the beasts of the forests; neither was it defaced with fallen leaves or branches; but the grass grew fresh around it, and the rocks sheltered it from the sun. Hither came one day the youth, fatigued with hunting, heated and thirsty. He stooped down to drink, and saw his own image in the water; he thought it was some beautiful water-spirit living in the fountain. He stood gazing with admiration at those bright eyes, those locks curled like the locks of Bacchus or Apollo, the rounded cheeks, the ivory neck, the parted lips, and the glow of health and exercise over all. He fell in love with himself. He brought his lips near to take a kiss; he plunged his arms in to embrace the beloved object. It fled at the touch, but returned again after a moment and renewed the fascination. He could not tear himself away; he lost all thought of food or rest, while he hovered over the brink of the fountain gazing upon his own image. He talked with the supposed spirit: "Why, beautiful being, do you shun me? Surely my face is not one to repel you. The nymphs love me, and you yourself look not indifferent upon me. When I stretch forth my arms you do the same; and you smile upon me and answer my beckonings with the like." His tears fell into the water and disturbed the image. As he saw it depart, he exclaimed, "Stay, I entreat you! Let me at least gaze upon you, if I may not touch you." With this, and much more of the same kind, he cherished the flame that consumed him, so that by degrees he lost his color, his vigor, and the beauty which formerly had so charmed the nymph Echo. She kept near him, however, and when he exclaimed, "Alas! Alas!" she answered him with the same words. He pined away and died; and when his shade passed the Stygian River, it leaned over the boat to catch a look of itself in the waters. The nymphs mourned for him, especially the water-nymphs; and when they smote their breasts Echo smote hers also. They prepared a funeral pile and would have burned the body, but it was nowhere to be found; but in its place a flower, purple within and surrounded with white leaves, which bears the name and preserves the memory of Narcissus.

MANLINESS TOWARD WOMEN

Never Use Force Against a Woman

From Sir Thomas Malory,
Le Morte D'Arthur

Now we turn unto Sir Lancelot who rode with the damosel on a fair highway.

"Sir," said the damosel, "here by this way lurks a knight who distresses all ladies and gentlewomen; at the least he robbeth them or lieth by them."

"What?" said Sir Lancelot. "Is he a thief and a knight, and a ravisher of women? He doth shame unto the Order of Knighthood, contrary to his oath. It is a pity that he liveth! But fair damosel, ye shall ride on ahead by yourself and I will keep myself under cover. If he troubles you or distresses you, I shall be your rescue and teach him to be ruled as a knight."

So the maiden rode on by the way at a soft ambling pace; within a while that knight came out on horseback, out of the wood and his page with him. He pulled the damosel from her horse, and then she cried out. With that, Lancelot came as fast as he might till he reached the knight, saying, "Oh, thou false knight and traitor unto knighthood, who taught thee to distress ladies and gentlewomen?"

When the knight saw Sir Lancelot thus rebuking him he answered not, but drew his sword and rode unto Sir Lancelot. Sir Lancelot threw his spear from him, drew out his sword, and struck the knight such a buffet on the helmet that he split his head and neck unto the throat.

"Now thou hast thy payment which long thou hast deserved!"

"That is truth," said the damosel, "for just as Tarquine watched to destroy good knights, so did this knight lie in wait to destroy and distress ladies."

Every Man Thinketh His Own Lady Fairest

From Sir Thomas Malory,
Le Morte D'Arthur

A fight over Queen Guenever is narrowly avoided.

Sir Lamorak asked Sir Melyagaunt why he loved Queen Guenever, "for I was not far from you when you made your complaint by the chapel."

"Did ye so?" said Sir Melyagaunt. "Then I will abide by it. I love Queen Guenever."

"What will ye do about it?"

"I will prove and make it good that she is the fairest lady of most beauty in the world."

"As to that," said Sir Lamorak, "I say nay thereto. For Queen Morgause of Orkney, mother to Sir Gawain, is the fairest queen and lady who beareth the life."

"That is not so," said Sir Melyagaunt. "And that I will prove with my hands upon thy body!"

"Will ye so?" said Sir Lamorak. "And in a better quarrel I look not to fight."

Then they parted each from the other in great wrath, and they came riding together as if it had been thunder; each smote the other so sorely that their horses fell backward to the earth. Then they left their horses, dressed their shields, and drew their swords. They hurtled together like wild boars, and thus they fought a great while. For Sir Melyagaunt was a good man and of great might, but Sir Lamorak was too strong for him and put him always back; but each had wounded the other sorely. As they stood thus fighting, by fortune Sir Lancelot and Sir Bleoberys came riding by. Sir Lancelot rode between them and asked them for what cause they fought together, "and ye are both knights of King Arthur."

"Sir," said Melyagaunt, "I shall tell you for what cause we do this battle. I praised my lady Queen Guenever and said she was the fairest lady of the world. But Sir Lamorak said nay thereto, for he said Queen Morgause of Orkney was fairer than she and of more beauty."

"Ah," said Sir Lancelot, "Sir Lamorak, why sayest thou so? It is not thy part to dispraise thy princess when thou art under her obeisance, as we all are." Therewith he alighted on foot and said, "For this quarrel make thee ready. I will prove upon thee that Queen Guenever is the fairest lady and most of beauty in the world."

"Sir," said Sir Lamorak, "I am loath to have ado with you in this quarrel, for every man thinketh his own lady fairest; and though I praise the lady that I love most, ye should not be wroth. For though my lady Queen Guenever is fairest in your eye, wit ye well Queen Morgause is fairest in my eye; so every knight thinketh his own lady fairest. And wit ye well, sir, ye are the man in the world—except Sir Tristram—with whom I am most loath to have ado. But if ye must needs fight with me, I shall endure you as long as I may."

Then Sir Bleoberys spoke and said, "My lord Sir Lancelot, I knew you never so misadvised as ye are now, for Sir Lamorak sayeth to you but reason, and knightly. For I assure you I have a lady and methinketh that she is the fairest lady of the world. Would this be a great reason that ye should be wroth with me for such language? Well ye know that Sir Lamorak is as noble a knight as any I know living, and he hath ever owed you and us all good will. Therefore, I pray you, be good friends."

Then Sir Lancelot said unto Sir Lamorak, "I pray you, forgive me my offense and evil will. And if I was misadvised, I will make amends."

"Sir," said Sir Lamorak, "the amends are soon made between you and me."

Stalkers Beware!

From Sir Thomas Malory,
Le Morte D'Arthur

Camping outside the gate of a woman who doesn't want you is not only shameful but stupid—and dangerous.

"Sir," said the Damosel Lynet unto Sir Beaumains, "now ye should be strong and quick, for yonder is your deadly enemy. And at yonder window is my lady, my sister Dame Lyones."

"Where?" said Beaumains.

"Yonder," said the damosel and pointed with her finger.

"That is truth," said Beaumains. "She seemeth from afar the fairest lady that I ever looked upon. And truly I ask no better quarrel than now to do battle. For she shall be my lady, and for her I will fight." He looked steadily up to the window with glad countenance, and the Lady Lyones made a curtsy to him down to the earth, holding up both her hands.

With that, the Red Knight of the Red Lands called to Sir Beaumains, "Leave, sir knight, thy beholding and look at me, I counsel thee. For I warn thee well she is my lady and for her I have done many strong battles."

"If thou have done so," said Beaumains, "it seems to me it was but wasted labor, for she loveth not thy fellowship. And for thou to love one who loveth not thee is but great folly. If I understood that she were not glad of my coming, I would take thought ere I did battle for her. But I understand from the siege before this castle that she wishes to forgo thy fellowship. Therefore wit thou well, thou Red Knight of the Red Lands, I love her and will rescue her, or else I will die."

"Sayest thou that?" said the Red Knight. "It seems to me that in reason thou ought to be warned by the knights whom thou sawest hanging upon yonder trees."

"Fie, for shame," said Beaumains, "that ever thou shouldest say so or do such evil, for in that thou shamest thyself and all knighthood. And thou may be sure no lady will love thee who knoweth thy wicked customs. And now thou thinkest that the sight of these hanged knights should frighten me? Nay, truly not so. That shameful sight causeth me to have courage and hardiness against thee, much more than I would have had against thee if thou were a wellruled knight."

The Death of Robin Hood

From Thomas Bulfinch,
Bulfinch's Mythology

Robin Hood returned to Sherwood Forest, and there met his death. For one day, being wounded in a fight, he fled out of the battle with Little John. And being at some distance, Robin Hood said to his lieutenant, "Now truly I cannot shoot even one shot more, for the arrows will not fly. For I am sore wounded. So I will go to my cousin, the abbess, who dwells near here in Kirkley Hall, and she shall bleed me, that I may be well again." So Robin Hood left Little John, and he went his way to Kirkley; and reaching the Hall, his strength nearly left him, yet he knocked heavily at the door. And his cousin came down first to let him in. And when she saw him she knew that it was her cousin Robin Hood, and she received him with a joyful face. Then said Robin, "You see me, my cousin, how weak I am. Therefore I pray you to bleed me, that I may be whole again." And his cousin took him by the hand, and led him into an upper room, and laid him on a bed, and she bled him. But the treacherous woman tied not up the vein again, but left him so that his life began to flow from him. And he, finding his strength leaving him, thought to escape; but he could not, for the door was locked, and the casement window was so high that he might not leap down from it. Then, knowing that he must die, he reached forth his hand to his bugle horn, which lay by him on the bed. And setting the horn to his mouth, he blew weakly, though with all his strength, three blasts upon it. And Little John, as he sat under the tree in the greenwood, heard his blowing, and he said, "Now must Robin be near death, for his blast is very weak."

And he got up and ran to Kirkley Hall as fast as he might. And coming to the door, he found it locked; but he broke it down, and so came to Robin Hood. And coming to the bed, he fell upon his knees and said, "Master, I beg a boon of thee—that thou lettest me burn down Kirkley Hall and all the nunnery." "Nay," quoth Robin Hood; "nay, I cannot grant you your boon; for never in my life did I hurt woman, or man in woman's company, nor shall it be done when I die. But for me, give me my long bow, and I will let fly an arrow, and where you shall find the arrow, there bury me. And make my grave long and broad, that I may rest easily; and place my head upon a green sod, and place my bow at my side." And these words Little John readily promised him, so that Robin Hood was pleased. And they buried him as he had asked, an arrow-shot from Kirkley Hall.

Revenge Against Women Is Shameful

From Sir Thomas Malory,
Le Morte D'Arthur

Sir Lancelot rode in many wild ways throughout the moors and marshes, and as he rode in a valley he saw a knight chasing a lady with a naked sword in order to slay her. But just as this knight would have slain this lady, she cried to Sir Lancelot and prayed him to rescue her. When he saw that mischief, he took his horse and rode between them, saying, "Knight, fie, for shame! Why wilt thou slay this lady? Thou dost shame unto thee and all knights."

"What hast thou to do between me and my wife?" said the knight. "I will slay her despite my head."

"That shall ye not," said Sir Lancelot, "for instead we two will have ado together."

"Sir Lancelot," said the knight, "thou dost not thy part, for this lady hath betrayed me."

"It is not so," said the lady. "Truly he sayeth wrong about me. Because I love and cherish my cousin-germane, he is jealous; but as I shall answer to God, there was never sin between us. But, sir, as thou art called the most worshipful knight of the world I require thee of true knighthood to help me and save me. For whatsoever he says, he will slay me; he is without mercy."

"Have ye no fear," said Lancelot. "It shall not lie in his power."

"Sir," said the knight, "in your sight I will be ruled as ye will have me."

So Sir Lancelot rode with the knight on one side and the lady on the other. They had ridden only a short while when the knight bade Sir Lancelot turn and look behind him, and said, "Sir, yonder come men of arms riding after us."

So Sir Lancelot turned and suspected no treason. But therewith the knight went to his lady's side, and suddenly he cut off her head. When Sir Lancelot had spied what he had done, he said, "Traitor, thou hast shamed me forever!" And suddenly he alighted from his horse and pulled out his sword to slay the knight. But therewith he fell flat to the earth and gripped Sir Lancelot by the thighs and cried mercy.

"Fie on thee!" said Sir Lancelot. "Thou shameful knight, thou maist have no mercy; therefore arise and fight with me."

"Nay," said the knight, "I will never arise till ye grant me mercy."

"Now I will offer thee fairly," said Lancelot. "I will unarm myself to my shirt, and I will have nothing upon me but my shirt and my sword in my hand. Then if thou canst slay me, thou art quit forever."

"Nay, sir, that will I never do."

"Well," said Sir Lancelot, "take this lady and her head and bear them with thee. And here thou shalt swear upon my sword to bear them always upon thy back and never to rest till thou come to Queen Guenever."

"Sir," said he, "that I will do, by the faith of my body."

"Now," said Lancelot, "tell me, what is your name?"

"Sir, my name is Pedyvere."

"In a shameful hour thou were born," said Lancelot.

What Women *Really* Want in a Man

From Thomas Bulfinch,
Bulfinch's Mythology

In this tale, Sir Gawain performs the ultimate act of chivalry.

Once upon a time King Arthur held his court in merry Carlisle, when a damsel came before him and craved a boon. It was for vengeance upon a knight, who had made her lover captive and despoiled her of her lands. King Arthur commanded to bring him his sword, Excalibar, and to saddle his steed, and rode forth without delay to right the lady's wrong. Ere long he reached the castle of the grim baron, and challenged him to the conflict. But the castle stood on magic ground, and the spell was such that no knight could tread thereon but straight his courage fell and his strength decayed. King Arthur felt the charm, and before a blow was struck his sturdy limbs lost their strength, and his head grew faint. He was fain to yield himself prisoner to the churlish knight, who refused to release him except upon condition that he should return at the end of a year, and bring a true answer to the question, "What thing is it which women most desire?" or in default thereof surrender himself and his lands. King Arthur accepted the terms, and gave his oath to return at the time appointed. During the year the king rode east, and he rode west, and inquired of all whom he met what thing it was which all women most desire. Some told him riches; some pomp and state; some mirth; some flattery; and some a gallant knight. But in the diversity of answers he could find no sure dependence. The year was well nigh spent when, one day, as he rode thoughtfully through a forest, he saw sitting beneath a tree a lady of such hideous aspect that he turned away his eyes and when she greeted him in seemly sort made no answer. "What wretch art thou," the lady said, "that will not speak to me? It may chance that I may resolve thy doubts, though I be not fair of aspect." "If thou wilt do so," said King Arthur, "choose what reward thou wilt, thou grim lady, and it shall be given thee." "Swear me this upon thy faith," she said, and Arthur swore it. Then the lady told him the secret, and demanded her reward, which was that the king should find some fair and courtly knight to be her husband.

King Arthur hastened to the grim baron's castle and told him one by one all the answers which he had received from his various advisers, except the last, and not one was admitted as the true one. "Now yield thee, Arthur," the giant said, "for thou hast not paid thy ransom, and thou and thy lands are forfeited to me." Then King Arthur said:

"Yet hold thy hand, thou proud baron,
I pray thee hold thy hand.
And give me leave to speak once more,
In rescue of my land.
This morn, as I came over a moor,
I saw a lady set,
Between an oak and a green holly,
All clad in red scarlet.

She says *all women would have their will*
This is their chief desire;
Now yield, as thou art a baron true,
That I have paid my hire."

"It was my sister that told thee this," the churlish baron exclaimed. "Vengeance light on her! I will some time or other do her as ill a turn."

King Arthur rode homeward, but not light of heart; for he remembered the promise he was under to the loathly lady to give her one of his young and gallant knights for a husband. He told his grief to Sir Gawain, his nephew, and he replied, "Be not sad, my lord, for I will marry the loathly lady." King Arthur replied:

"Now nay, now nay, good Sir Gawain,
My sister's son ye be;
The loathly lady's all too grim,
And all too foule for thee."

But Gawain persisted, and the king at last, with sorrow of heart, consented that Gawain should be his ransom. So, one day, the king and his knights rode to the forest, met the loathly lady, and brought her to the court. Sir Gawain stood the scoffs and jeers of his companions as he best might, and the marriage was solemnized, but not with the usual festivities.

"There was no joye, ne fest at alle;
There n'as but hevinesse and mochel sorwe,
For prively he wed her on the morwe,
And all day after hid him as an owle,
So wo was him his wife loked so foule!"

When night came, and they were alone together, Sir Gawain could not conceal his aversion; and the lady asked him why he sighed so heavily, and turned away his face. He candidly confessed it was on account of three things, her age, her ugliness, and her low degree. The lady, not at all offended, replied with excellent arguments to all his objections. She showed him that with age is discretion, with ugliness security from rivals, and that all true gentility depends, not upon the accident of birth, but upon the character of the individual.

Sir Gawain made no reply; but, turning his eyes on his bride, what was his amazement to perceive that she wore no longer the unseemly aspect that had so distressed him. She then told him that the form she had worn was not her true form, but a disguise imposed upon her by a wicked enchanter, and that she was condemned to wear it until two things should happen; one, that she should obtain some young and gallant knight to be her husband. This having been done, one half of the charm was removed. She was now at liberty to wear her true form for half the time, and she bade him choose whether he would have her fair by day and ugly by night, or the reverse. Sir Gawain would fain have had her look her best by night, when he alone should see her, and show her repulsive visage, if at all, to others. But she reminded him how much more pleasant it would be to her to wear her best looks in the throng of knights and ladies by day. Sir Gawain yielded, and gave up his will to hers. This alone was wanting to dissolve the charm. The lovely lady now with joy assured him that she should change no more; but as she now was so would she remain by night as well as by day.

"Sweet blushes stayned her rud-red cheek,
Her eyen were black as sloe,
The ripening cherrye swelled her lippe,
And all her neck was snow.
Sir Gawain kist that ladye faire
Lying upon the sheete,
And swore, as he was true knight,
The spice was never so swete."

Stick Your Neck Out
and Close Your Eyes

From Geoffrey Chaucer,
The Canterbury Tales

Chanticleer the rooster tries to recover his hen's good opinion after being frightened by his dream of a fox. From the classic of early English poetry.

"Alas!" said she, "fie upon your timidness!
"Alas!" said she, "for, by that God above,
Now have you lost my heart and all my love.
I cannot love a coward, by my faith!
For certainly, whatever any woman says,
We all desire, if it might be,
To have husbands hardy, wise and free,
And discreet, not a niggard, nor a fool,
Nor one that is terrified of every tool,
Nor a boaster, by that God above!
How dare you say, for shame, to your love
That anything might make you afraid?
Have you no man's heart, but have a beard?
Alas! and are you afraid of dreams?"

And with that word he flew down from the beams,
For it was day, and so did his hens all,
And with a cluck, he began to call
For he had found some corn which lay in the yard.

Regal he was, he was no more afraid.
He feathered Pertelot twenty times,
And trod her just as often, before it was nine.
He looked as if he were a grim lion,
And on his toes he roamed up and down,
He deigned not to put his foot upon the ground.
He clucks whenever he finds some corn,
And then to him, run his wives all.
Thus regal, as a prince is in his hall.

This Chanticleer stood high upon his toes,
Stretching his neck, and held his eyes closed,
And began to crow loudly for the occasion
Master Russell, the fox, sprang up at once,
And by the throat seized Chanticleer,
And on his back toward the wood him bore,
For, as yet, no man pursued.
O destiny, that may not be eschewed!
Alas, that Chanticleer flew from the beams!
Alas, his wife thought nothing of dreams!

Can a Businessman Make a Good Lover?

From Andreas Capellanus,
The Art of Courtly Love

The Man says: "I know well that Love is not in the habit of differentiating men with titles of distinction, but that he obligates all equally to serve in his army, making no exceptions for beauty or birth and making no distinctions of sex or of inequality of family, considering only this, whether anybody is fit to bear Love's armor. Love is a thing that copies Nature herself, and so lovers ought to make no more distinction between classes of men than Love himself does. Just as love inflames men of all classes, so lovers should draw no distinctions of rank, but consider only whether the man who asks for love has been wounded by Love. Supported by this unanswerable argument, I may select for my beloved any woman I choose so long as I have no depravity of character to debase me."

The Woman says: "Who are you that ask for such great gifts? I know well enough what you look like, and the family you come from is obvious. But where can one find greater effrontery than in a man who for the space of a whole week devotes all his efforts to the various gains of business and then on the seventh day, his day of rest, tries to enjoy the gifts of love and to dishonor Love's commands and confound the distinctions of classes established among men from of old? It is not without cause or reason that this distinction of rank has been found among men from the very beginning; it is so that every man will stay within the bounds of his own class and be content with all things therein and never presume to arrogate to himself the things that were naturally set aside as belonging to a higher class, but will leave them severely alone. Who are you, then, to try to defile such ancient statutes and under the pretense of love to attempt to subvert the precepts of our ancestors and so presumptuously go beyond the limits of your own class?"

The Man says: "Although I am repulsed by what you say, still as long as I live I shall not give up the idea of your love, because even if I am never to get the result I hope for, the mere hope I have gained from the greatness of my heart will cause my body to lead a tranquil life, and ultimately, perhaps, God will put into your mind a cure for my pain."

The Woman says: "May God give you reward suited to your effort."

The Man says: "That word alone shows me that my hope is bearing fruit, and I pray to God that you may always be interested in the care of my health and that my sails may find a quiet haven."

Sigh No More, Ladies

From William Shakespeare,
Much Ado About Nothing

Sigh no more, ladies, sigh no more!
Men were deceivers ever,
One foot in sea, and one on shore;
To one thing constant never.
Then sigh not so,
But let them go,
And be you blithe and bonny,
Converting all your sounds of woe
Into Hey nonny, nonny.
Sing no more ditties, sing no moe,
Of dumps so dull and heavy!
The fraud of men was ever so,
Since summer first was leavy.
Then sigh not so, &c.

Pyramus and Thisbe

From Thomas Bulfinch,
Bulfinch's Mythology

A tragic error leads to an immortal love.

Pyramus was the handsomest youth, and Thisbe the fairest maiden, in all Babylonia, where Semiramis reigned. Their parents occupied adjoining houses; and neighborhood brought the young people together, and acquaintance ripened into love. They would gladly have married, but their parents forbade. One thing, however, they could not forbid—that love should glow with equal ardor in the bosoms of both. They conversed by signs and glances, and the fire burned more intensely for being covered up. In the wall that parted the two houses there was a crack, caused by some fault in the structure. No one had remarked it before, but the lovers discovered it. What will not love discover! It afforded a passage to the voice; and tender messages used to pass backward and forward through the gap. As they stood, Pyramus on this side, Thisbe on that, their breaths would mingle. "Cruel wall," they said, "why do you keep two lovers apart? But we will not be ungrateful. We owe you, we confess, the privilege of transmitting loving words to willing ears." Such words they uttered on different sides of the wall; and when night came and they must say farewell, they pressed their lips upon the wall, she on her side, he on his, as they could come no nearer.

Next morning, when Aurora had put out the stars, and the sun had melted the frost from the grass, they met at the accustomed spot. Then, after lamenting their hard fate, they agreed that next night, when all was still, they would slip away from the watchful eyes, leave their dwellings and walk out into the fields; and to insure a meeting, repair to a well-known edifice standing outside the city's bounds, called the Tomb of Ninus, and that the one who came first should await the other at the foot of a certain tree. It was a white mulberry tree, and stood near a cool spring. All was agreed on, and they waited impatiently for the sun to go down beneath the waters and night to rise up from them. Then cautiously Thisbe stole forth, unobserved by the family, her head covered with a veil, made her way to the monument and sat down under the tree. As she sat alone in the dim light of the evening she descried a lioness, her jaws reeking with recent slaughter, approaching the fountain to slake her thirst. Thisbe fled at the sight, and sought refuge in the hollow of a rock. As she fled she dropped her veil. The lioness after drinking at the spring turned to retreat to the woods, and seeing the veil on the ground, tossed and rent it with her bloody mouth.

Pyramus, having been delayed, now approached the place of meeting. He saw in the sand the footsteps of the lion, and the color fled from his cheeks at the sight. Presently he found the veil all rent and bloody. "O hapless girl," said he, "I have been the cause of thy death! Thou, more worthy of life than I, hast fallen the first victim. I will follow. I am the guilty cause, in tempting thee forth to a place of such peril, and not being myself on the spot to guard thee. Come forth, ye lions, from the rocks, and tear this guilt body with your teeth." He took up the veil, carried it with him to the appointed tree, and covered it with kisses and with tears. "*My* blood also shall stain your texture," said he, and drawing his sword plunged it into his heart. The blood spurted from the wound, and tinged the white mulberries of the tree all red; and sinking into the earth reached the roots, so that the red color mounted through the trunk to the fruit.

By this time Thisbe, still trembling with fear, yet wishing not to disappoint her love, stepped cautiously forth, looking anxiously for the youth, eager to tell him the danger she had escaped. When she came to the spot and saw the changed color of the mulberries she doubted whether it was the same place. While she hesitated she saw the form of one struggling in the agonies of death. She started back, a shudder ran through her frame as a ripple on the face of the still water when a sudden breeze sweeps over it. But as soon as she recognized her lover, she screamed and beat her breast, embracing the lifeless body, pouring tears into its wounds, and imprinting kisses on the cold lips. "O Pyramus," she cried, "what has done this? Answer me, Pyramus, it is your own Thisbe that speaks. Hear me, dearest, and lift that drooping head!" At the name of Thisbe Pyramus opened his eyes, then closed them again. She saw her veil stained with blood and the scabbard empty of its sword. "Thy own hand has slain thee, and for my sake," she said. "I too can be brave for once, and my love is as strong as thine. I will follow thee in death, for I have been the cause; and death which alone could part us shall not prevent my joining thee. And ye, unhappy parents of us both, deny us not our united request. As love and death have joined us, let one tomb contain us. And thou, tree, retain the marks of slaughter. Let thy berries still serve for memorials of our blood." So saying she plunged the sword into her breast. Her parents ratified her wish, the gods also ratified it. The two bodies were buried in one sepulcher, and the tree ever after brought forth purple berries, as it does to this day.

Emile and Sophy

From Jean-Jacques Rousseau, Emile

Beginning with Rousseau (1712–1778), the Romantic writers tried to restore the chivalric conception of love to compensate for an increasingly materialistic, self-interested modern age. In Rousseau's Emile, *the young man of the title perfects his own character through his devotion to Sophy, a young woman he admires from afar. In her, he sees the virtues that he wishes to cultivate in himself, and his longing to be worthy of Sophy, to be esteemed by her, gives him the impetus to strive harder to perfect himself. For her part, Sophy has always hoped to meet a young man like Homer's Telemachus. The flat-souled young men of the bourgeois era don't interest her; she is looking for a young hero, and in Emile she believes she may have found him.*

All women would be alike to a man who had no idea of virtue or beauty, and the first comer would always be the most charming. Love does not spring from nature, far from it; it is the curb and law of her desires; it is love that makes one sex indifferent to the other, the loved one alone excepted.

We wish to inspire the preference; we feel love must be mutual. To be loved we must be worthy of love; to be preferred we must be more worthy than the rest, at least in the eyes of our beloved. Hence we begin to look around among our fellows; we begin to compare ourselves with them, there is emulation, rivalry, and jealousy. A heart full to overflowing loves to make itself known; from the need of a mistress there soon springs the need of a friend. He who feels how sweet it is to be loved, desires to be loved by everybody; and there could be no preferences if there were not many that fail to find satisfaction. With love and friendship there begin dissensions, enmity, and hatred. I behold deference to other people's opinions enthroned among all these diverse passions, and foolish mortals, enslaved by her power, base their very existence merely on what other people think.

The first sentiment of which the well-trained youth is capable is not love but friendship. The first work of his rising imagination is to make known to him his fellows; the species affects him before the sex. Here is another advantage to be gained from prolonged innocence; you may take advantage of his dawning sensibility to sow the first seeds of humanity in the heart of the young adolescent. This advantage is all the greater because this is the only time in his life when such efforts may be really successful.

Do you desire to stimulate and nourish the first stirrings of awakening sensibility in the heart of a young man, do you desire to incline his disposition toward kindly deed and thought, do not cause the seeds of pride, vanity, and envy to spring up in him through the misleading picture of the happiness of mankind; do not show him to begin with the pomp of courts, the pride of palaces, the delights of pageants; do not take him into society and into brilliant assemblies; do not show him the outside of society till you have made him capable of estimating it at its true worth. To show him the world before he is acquainted with men is not to train him but to corrupt him; not to teach, but to mislead.

By nature men are neither kings, nobles, courtiers, nor millionaires. All men are born poor and naked, all are liable to the sorrows of life, its disappointments, its ills, its needs, its suffering of every kind; and all are condemned at length to die. This is what it really means to be a man, this is what no mortal can escape. Begin then with the study of the essentials of humanity, that which really constitutes mankind.

I will go further and maintain that virtue is no less favorable to love than to other rights of nature, and that it adds as much to the power of the beloved as to that of the wife or mother. There is no real love without enthusiasm, and no enthusiasm without an object of perfection real or supposed, but always present in the imagination. What is there to kindle the hearts of lovers for whom this perfection is nothing, for whom the loved one is merely the means to sensual pleasure? Nay, not thus is the heart kindled, not thus does it abandon itself to those sublime transports which form the rapture of lovers and the charm of love. Love is an illusion, I grant you, but its reality consists in the feelings it awakes, in the love of true beauty which it inspires. That beauty is not to be found in the object of our affections, it is the creation of our illusions. What matter! Do we not still sacrifice all those baser feelings to the imaginary model? And we still feed our hearts on the virtues we attribute to the beloved, we still withdraw ourselves from the baseness of human nature. What lover is there who would not give his life for his mistress? What gross and sensual passion is there in a man who is willing to die? We scoff at the knights of old; they knew the meaning of love; we know nothing but debauchery. When the teachings of romance began to seem ridiculous, it was not so much the work of reason as of immorality.

Sophy loves virtue; this love has come to be her ruling passion; she loves virtue because there is nothing fairer in itself, she loves it because it is a woman's glory and because a virtuous woman is little lower than the angels; she loves virtue as the only road to real happiness, because she sees nothing but poverty, neglect, unhappiness, shame, and disgrace in the life of a bad woman; she loves virtue because it is dear to her revered father and to her tender and worthy mother; they are not content to be happy in their own virtue, they desire hers; and she finds her chief happiness in the hope of making them happy. All these feelings inspire an enthusiasm which stirs her heart and keeps all its budding passions in subjection to this noble enthusiasm. Sophy will be chaste and good till her dying day; she has vowed it in her secret heart, and not before she knew how hard it would be to keep her vow; she made this vow at a time when she should have revoked it had she been the slave of her senses.

Sophy is not so fortunate as to be a charming French woman, cold-hearted and vain, who would rather attract attention than give pleasure, who seeks amusement rather than delight. She suffers from a consuming desire for love; it even disturbs and troubles her heart in the midst of festivities; she has lost her former liveliness and her taste for merry games; far from being afraid of the tedium of solitude she desires it. Her thoughts go out to him who will make solitude sweet to her. She finds strangers tedious, she wants a lover, not a circle of admirers. She would rather give pleasure to one good man than be a general favorite, or win that applause of society which lasts but a day and tomorrow is turned to scorn.

Husband and wife should choose each other. A mutual liking should be the first bond between them. They should follow the guidance of their own eyes and heads; when they are married their first duty will be to love one another, and as love and hatred do not depend on ourselves, this duty brings another with it, and they must begin to love each other before marriage. That is the law of nature, and no power can abrogate it; those who have fettered it by so many legal restrictions have given heed rather to the outward show of order than to the happiness of marriage or the morals of the citizen. You see, my dear Sophy, we do not preach a harsh morality. It tends to make you your own mistress and to make us leave the choice of your husband to yourself.

Sophy was in love with Telemachus, and loved him with a passion which nothing could cure. When her father and mother became aware of her infatuation, they laughed at it and tried to cure her by reasoning with her. They were mistaken, reason was not altogether on their side; Sophy had her own reason and knew how to use it. Many a time did she reduce them to silence by turning their own arguments against them, by showing them that it was all their own fault for not having trained her to suit the men of that century; that she would be compelled to adopt her husband's way of thinking or he must adopt hers, that they had made the former course impossible by the way she had been brought up, and that the latter was just what she wanted. "Give me," said she, "a man who holds the same opinions as I do, or one who will be willing to learn them from me, and I will marry him; but until then, why do you scold me? Pity me; I am miserable, but not mad. Is the heart controlled by the will? Did my father not ask that very question? Is it my fault if I love what has no existence? I am no visionary; I desire no prince, I seek no Telemachus, I know he is only an imaginary person; I seek someone like him. And why should there be no such person, since there is such a person as I, I who feel that my heart is like his? No, let us not wrong humanity so greatly, let us not think that an amiable and virtuous man is a figment of the imagination. He exists, he lives."

• • •

At the name of Sophy you would have seen Emile give a start. His attention is arrested by this dear name, and he awakes all at once and looks eagerly at one who dares to bear it. "Sophy! Are you the Sophy whom my heart is seeking? Is it you that I love?" He looks at her; he watches her with a sort of fear and self-distrust. The face is not quite what he pictured; he cannot tell whether he likes it more or less. He studies every feature, he watches every movement, every gesture; he has a hundred fleeting interpretations for them all; he would give half his life if she would but speak. He looks at me anxiously and uneasily; his eyes are full of questions and reproaches. His every glance seems to say, "Guide me while there is yet time; if my heart yields itself and is deceived, I shall never get over it."

Consider my Emile over twenty years of age, well formed, well developed in mind and body, strong, healthy, active, skillful, robust, full of sense, reason, kindness, humanity, possessed of good morals and good taste, loving what is beautiful, doing what is good, free from the sway of cruel passions, released from the tyranny of popular prejudices, but subject to the law of wisdom, and easily guided by the voice of a friend; gifted with so many useful and pleasant accomplishments, caring little for wealth, able to earn a living with his own hands, and not afraid of lacking bread, whatever may come. Behold him in the intoxication of a growing passion; his heart opens to the first beams of love; its pleasant fancies reveal to him a whole world of new delights and enjoyments; he loves a sweet woman, whose character is even more delightful than her person; he hopes, he expects the reward which he deserves.

Their first attachment took its rise in mutual affection, in community of honorable feelings; therefore this affection is lasting. It abandons itself, with confidence, with reason, to the most delightful madness, without fear, regret, remorse, or any other disturbing thought, but that which is inseparable from all happiness. What lacks there yet? Behold, inquire, imagine what still is lacking, that can be combined with present joys. Every happiness which can exist in combination is already present; nothing could be added without taking away from what there is; he is as happy as man can be. Shall I choose this time to cut short so sweet a period: Shall I disturb such pure enjoyment? The happiness he enjoys is my life's reward. What could I give that could outweigh what I should take away? Even if I set the crown to his happiness I should destroy its greatest charm. That supreme joy is a hundredfold greater in anticipation than in possession; its savor is greater while we wait for it then when it is ours. O worthy Emile! Love and be loved! Prolong your enjoyment before it is yours; rejoice in your love and in your innocence, find your paradise upon earth, while you await your heaven. I shall not cut short this happy period of life. I will draw out its enchantments, I will prolong them as far as possible. Alas! It must come to an end and that soon; but it shall at least linger in your memory, and you will never repent of its joys.

The Sorrows of Youth

From Johann Wolfgang von Goethe,
The Sorrows of Young Werther

Goethe's novel is nearly perfect in its depiction of a troubled young man wholly absorbed in romantic passion. Werther longs for a woman he knows he cannot have, and it destroys him. An early classic of Romanticism by the famed philosopher and poet (1775).

Why don't I write to you? You ask me that though you are also numbered among the scholars! You should be able to divine that I am well, and indeed—in short, I have met someone in whom my heart is interested. I have—I do not know.

To tell you in proper order how it happened that I made the acquaintance of one of the most charming of beings will be no easy matter; I am content and happy, so am not likely to be a satisfactory narrator.

An angel! By Heaven, everybody says that of his mistress! Doesn't he? And yet I am incapable of telling you how perfect she is, or why she is perfect, enough, she has taken complete possession of my mind.

So much naivety combined with such intelligence, such kindness and such resolve, such tranquillity of soul in such an active life.

This is all hopeless twaddle that I am saying about her, mere abstractions which fail to express a single feature of her real self. Another time—no, not another time, I will tell you now, immediately. If I don't do it now, I never shall. For, between ourselves, since I began this letter I have been three times on the verge of laying down my pen, saddling my horse and riding off though I vowed early this morning that I would not—and yet every minute I go to the window to see how high the sun stands . . .

I could not help it, I had to go out to her. I am back once more, Wilhelm, and will eat my supper and finish this letter. How it enraptures my soul to see her among the dear happy children, her eight brothers and sisters.

If I continue like this, you will be no wiser at the end than you were at the beginning, so listen, I will force myself to give you details.

I wrote to you recently that I had made the acquaintance of the bailiff S., and that he had invited me to come and visit him soon at his hermitage, or rather his little kingdom. I neglected to do so and would perhaps never have gone, if there had not been revealed to me by accident the treasure concealed in that tranquil spot.

The young people here had arranged a ball in the country, and I gladly agreed to go. I offered my escort to a nice, good-looking, but not otherwise interesting girl in this town, and it was settled that I was to hire a coach to drive out to the scene of the festivities with my partner and her cousin, and that we were to pick up Charlotte S. on the way. "You will make the acquaintance of a beautiful girl," my partner said, as we drove through a broad avenue in the wood toward the hunting lodge. "Take care," her cousin added, "that you don't fall in love." "What do you mean," I asked. "She is already betrothed," the former replied, "to a very worthy man who has gone to put his affairs in order after his father's death and to apply for an important post." The information did not interest me particularly.

The sun was still a quarter of an hour from the hilltop when we reached the lodge gate; it was very sultry and the ladies expressed their anxiety lest we should be overtaken by a storm which we could see gathering in heavy, whitish-gray little clouds round the horizon. I relieved their fears by pretending to a knowledge of the weather, though I began myself to have a foreboding that our festivities would be interrupted.

I had alighted, and a maid who came to the gate begged us to wait a moment, Mamselle Lotthe would be with us straightway. I went across the courtyard to the well-built house and, when I had ascended the steps in front and entered at the door, I caught sight of the most charming scene that I have ever witnessed. In the entrance hall there swarmed six children, from two to eleven years of age, round a handsome girl of middle height, who wore a simple white frock with pink bows on the breast and arms. She was holding a loaf of black bread and cutting a slice for each of the children round her in proportion to its age and appetite, offering it with such an amiable air and each one crying "Thank you!" so artlessly, after he had stretched his little hands up as high as he could before his slice was cut, and then springing away contentedly with his supper or, if he was of a quieter nature, walking tranquilly toward the gate to see the strangers and the coach in which their Lotte was to drive away. "I beg your pardon," she said, "for giving you the trouble of coming in and making the ladies wait. While I was dressing and making all sorts of arrangements for the house in my absence, I forgot to give my children their supper, and they won't have their bread cut by anyone but me." I paid her some harmless compliment while my whole soul was absorbed in the contemplation of her figure, her voice, her bearing, and I had just time to recover from my surprise when she ran into the room to fetch her gloves and fan. The children kept at a little distance, casting sidelong glances at me, and I went up to the youngest who was a most pleasant-looking child. He had just drawn back when Lotte appeared in the doorway and said, "Louis shake hands with your cousin." The boy did so with a very frank air, and I could not refrain from kissing him heartily in spite of his dirty little nose. "Cousin?" I said, as I offered her my hand. "Do you consider that I deserve the happiness of being related to you?" "Oh!" she said, with a roguish smile, "our circle of cousins is very extensive, and I should be very sorry if you were the least worthy among them." As we went she ordered Sophie, the next oldest sister to herself, a girl of about eleven, to keep an eye on the little ones, and greet their father when he came back from his ride. The little ones she admonished to obey their sister Sophie as they would herself, and some of them expressly promised to do so. A pert little blonde, however, of about six years, said, "But it isn't you, after all, Lottchen! We like you better." The two eldest boys had climbed up behind the coach, and at my request she allowed them to travel with us until we reached the edge of the wood, so long as they promised not to tease each other and to hold on firmly.

Hardly had we fitted ourselves in and the ladies greeted one another, each in turn expressing her views abut the others' costumes, particularly bonnets, and duly passing in review the company that they expected to meet, when Lotte stopped the coach for her brothers to descend; they asked to kiss her hand once more and the older one did so with all the delicacy that could be expected of a boy of fifteen, the other with impetuousness and levity. She bade them give her love once more to the little ones, and the coach rolled on.

The cousin enquired whether she had finished the book she had recently sent her. "No," said Lotte.

"I do not like it; you can have it back. The one you sent me before was no better." When I asked what the books were, I was amazed at her reply. There was so much character in all she said, and with every word I discovered fresh charms, saw new flashes of intelligence lighting up her features, which appeared gradually to brighten with pleasure because she felt that I understood her.

"When I was younger," she said, "I liked nothing so much as

novels. Heaven knows I felt happy when I could sit in some corner on Sundays and share with my whole heart the fortune or distress of some Miss Jenny. Nor do I deny that this kind of romance still has some charm for me. But since I now seldom have time for a book, it must be suited to my taste. And the author I most prefer is the one in whom I find my own world again, who describes happenings such as I see around me and yet whose story I find as interesting, as sympathetic as my own domestic existence, which is, to be sure, not a Paradise, but nevertheless on the whole a source of inexpressible bliss."

I did my best to conceal my emotions at these words. I was not, it is true, very successful, for when I heard her speak incidentally, but with such truth, about the Vicar of Wakefield and about—, I lost my control and told her everything that forced itself to my lips, and only noticed after some time, when Lotte directed her remarks to the others, that these had been sitting there the whole time with wide-open eyes, as though they were not there at all. The cousin looked at me more than once with a mocking air, which however was of little consequence to me.

The conversation turned upon the pleasure of dancing. "If this passion is a fault," said Lotte, "I willingly confess I know nothing that excels dancing. And when I have something on my mind and drum out a quadrille on my squeaky old harpsichord, then everything is all right again."

How I gazed into her black eyes as she spoke, how her vivacious lips and her fresh, lively mien drew my whole soul on, how totally absorbed I became in the glorious feeling of listening to her, so that I often did not even hear the words by which she expressed herself! Of this you can have some idea, since you know me. In short, I descended from the coach as though in a dream when we came to a halt in front of the summer house, and I was still so immersed in dreams amid the darkling world around me that I hardly noticed the music which was wafted down to us from the brightly lit hall.

The Age of Innocence

Edith Wharton

The delicacy of courtly love still surfaces in the more pragmatic world of American democracy. Edith Wharton's 1921 novel The Age of Innocence *is an unforgettable story of a respectable young man's unfulfilled passion for a not-quite-respectable European lady of American origins, Countess Olenska.*

That evening, after Mr. Jackson had taken himself away, and the ladies had retired to their chintz-curtained bedroom, Newland Archer mounted thoughtfully to his own study. A vigilant hand had, as usual, kept the fire alive and the lamp trimmed; and the room, with its rows and rows of books, its bronze and steel statuettes of "The Fencers" on the mantelpiece and its many photographs of famous pictures, looked singularly homelike and welcoming.

As he dropped into his armchair near the fire his eyes rested on a large photograph of May Welland, which the young girl had given him in the first days of their romance, and which had now displaced all the other portraits on the table. With a new sense of awe he looked at the frank forehead, serious eyes and gay innocent mouth of the young creature whose soul's custodian he was to be. That terrifying product of the social system he belonged to and believed in, the young girl who knew nothing and expected everything, looked back at him like a stranger through May Welland's familiar features; and once more it was borne in on him that marriage was not the safe anchorage he had been taught to think, but a voyage on uncharted seas.

The case of the Countess Olenska had stirred up old settled convictions and set them drifting dangerously through his mind. His own exclamation: "Women should be free—as free as we are," struck to the root of a problem that it was agreed in his world to regard as nonexistent. "Nice" women, however wronged, would never claim the kind of freedom he meant, and generous-minded men like himself were therefore—in the heat of argument—the more chivalrously ready to concede it to them. Such verbal generosities were in fact only a humbugging disguise of the inexorable conventions that tied things together and bound people down to the old pattern. But here he has pledged to defend, on the part of his betrothed's cousin, conduct that, on this own wife's part, would justify him in calling down on her all the thunders of Church and State. Of course the dilemma was purely hypothetical; since he wasn't a blackguard Polish nobleman, it was absurd to speculate what his wife's rights would be if he *were*. But Newland Archer was too imaginative not to feel that, in his case and May's, the tie might gall for reasons far less gross and palpable. What could he and she really know of each other, since it was his duty, as a "decent" fellow, to conceal his past from her, and hers, as a marriageable girl, to have no past to conceal? What if, for some one of the subtler reasons that would tell with both of them, they should tire of each other, misunderstand or irritate each other? He reviewed his friends' marriages—the supposedly happy ones—and saw none that answered, even remotely, to the passionate and tender comradeship which he pictured as his permanent relation with May Welland. He perceived that such a picture presupposed, on her part, the experience, the versatility, the freedom of judgment, which she had been carefully trained not to possess; and with a shiver of foreboding he saw his marriage becoming what most of the other marriages about him were: a dull association of material and social interests held together by ignorance on the one side and hypocrisy on the other. Lawrence Lefferts occurred to him as the husband who had most completely realized this enviable ideal. As became the high priest of form, he had formed a wife so completely to his own convenience that, in the most conspicuous moments of his frequent love affairs with other men's wives, she went about in smiling unconsciousness, saying that "Lawrence was so frightfully strict"; and had been known to blush indignantly, and avert her gaze, when someone alluded in her presence to the fact that Julius Beaufort (as became a "foreigner" of doubtful origin) had what was known in New York as "another establishment."

Archer tried to console himself with the thought that he was not quite such an ass as Larry Lefferts, nor May such a simpleton as poor Gertrude; but the difference was after all one of intelligence and not of standard. In reality they all lived in a kind of hieroglyphic world, where the real thing was never said or done or even thought, but only represented by a set of arbitrary signs; as when Mrs. Welland, who knew exactly why Archer had pressed her to announce her daughter's engagement at the Beaufort ball (and had indeed expected him to do no less), yet felt obliged to simulate reluctance, and the air of having had her hand forced, quite as, in the books on Primitive Man that people of advanced culture were beginning to read, the savage bride is dragged with shrieks from her parents' tent.

The result, of course, was that the young girl who was the center of this elaborate system of mystification remained the more inscrutable for her very frankness and assurance. She was frank, poor darling, because she had nothing to conceal, assured because she knew of nothing to be on her guard against; and with no better preparation than this, she was to be plunged overnight into what people evasively called "the facts of life."

The young man was sincerely but placidly in love. He delighted in the radiant good looks of his betrothed, in her health, her horsemanship, her grace and quickness at games, and the shy interest in books and ideas that she was beginning to develop under his guidance. (She had advanced far enough to join him in ridiculing the "Idyls of the King," but not to feel the beauty of "Ulysses" and the "Lotus Eaters.") She was straightforward, loyal and brave; she had a sense of humor (chiefly proved by her laughing at *his* jokes); and he suspected, in the depths of her innocently gazing soul, a glow of feeling that it would be a joy to waken. But when he had gone the brief round of her he returned discouraged by the thought that all this frankness and innocence were only an artificial product. Untrained human nature was not frank and innocent; it was full of the twists and defenses of an instinctive guile. And he felt himself oppressed by this creation of factitious purity, so cunningly manufactured by a conspiracy of mothers and aunts and grandmothers and long-dead ancestresses, because it was supposed to be what he wanted, what he had a right to, in order that he might exercise his lordly pleasure in smashing it like an image made of snow.

There was a certain triteness in these reflections: they were those habitual to young men on the approach of their wedding day. But they were generally accompanied by a sense of compunction and self-abasement of which Newland Archer felt no trace. He could not deplore (as Thackeray's heroes so often exasperated him by doing) that he had not a blank page to offer his bride in exchange for the unblemished one she was to give to him. He could not get away from the fact that if he had been brought up as she had they would have been no more fit to find their way about than the Babes in the Wood; nor could he, for all his anxious citations, see any honest reason (any, that is, unconnected with his own momentary pleasure, and the passion of masculine vanity) why his bride should not have been allowed the same freedom of experience as himself.

Such questions, at such an hour, were bound to drift through his mind; but he was conscious that their uncomfortable persistence and precision were due to the inopportune arrival of the Countess Olenska. Here he was, at the very moment of his betrothal—a moment for pure thoughts and cloudless hopes—pitchforked into a coil of scandal which raised all the special problems he would have preferred to let lie. "Hang Ellen Olenska!" he grumbled, as he covered his fire and began to undress. He could not really see why her fate should have the least bearing on his; yet he dimly felt that he had only just begun to measure the risks of the championship which his engagement had forced upon him.

Years after their flirtation with having an affair, having succumbed to the expectations of his family and class and made a good marriage, Newland Archer visits Paris with his son and considers visiting the Countess. He makes it to her building, but cannot bring himself to go up. After all these years of wondering if he made the right decision, he realizes the memory of what might have been is more beautiful than the reality.

Newland Archer, looking out of his hotel window at the stately gaiety of the Paris streets, felt his heart beating with the confusion and eagerness of youth.

It was long since it had thus plunged and reared under his widening waistcoat, leaving him, the next minute, with an empty breast and hot temples. He wondered if it was thus that his son's conducted itself in the presence of Miss Fanny Beaufort—and decided that it was not. "It functions as actively, no doubt, but the rhythm is different," he reflected, recalling the cool composure with which the young man had announced his engagement, and taken for granted that his family would approve.

"The difference is that these young people take it for granted that they're going to get whatever they want, and that we almost always took it for granted that we shouldn't. Only, I wonder—the thing one's so certain of in advance: can it ever make one's heart beat as wildly?"

It was the day after their arrival in Paris, and the spring sunshine held Archer in his open window, above the wide silvery prospect of the Place Vendome. One of the things he had stipulated—almost the only one—when he had agreed to come abroad with Dallas, was that, in Paris, he shouldn't be made to go to one of the new-fangled "palaces."

"Oh, all right—of course," Dallas good-naturedly agreed. "I'll take you to some jolly old-fashioned place—the Bristol say—" leaving his father speechless at hearing that the century-long home of kings and emperors was now spoken of as an old-fashioned inn, where one went for its quaint inconveniences and lingering local color.

Archer had pictured often enough, in the first impatient years, the scene of his return to Paris; then the personal vision had faded, and he had simply tried to see the city as the setting of Madame Olenska's life. Sitting alone at night in his library, after the household had gone to bed, he had evoked the radiant outbreak of spring down the avenues of horse-chestnuts, the flowers and statues in the public gardens, the whiff of lilacs from the flower-carts, the majestic roll of the river under the great bridges, and the life of art and study and pleasure that filled each mighty artery to bursting. Now the spectacle was before him in its glory, and as he looked out on it he felt shy, old-fashioned, inadequate: a mere gray speck of a man compared with the ruthless magnificent fellow he had dreamed of being. . . .

Dallas's hand came down cheerily on his shoulder. "Hullo, Father: this is something like, isn't it?" They stood for a while looking out in silence, and then the young man continued: "By the way, I've got a message for you: the Countess Olenska expects us both at half-past five."

He said it lightly, carelessly, as he might have imparted any casual item of information, such as the hour at which their train was to leave for Florence the next evening. Archer looked at him, and thought he saw in his gay young eyes a gleam of his great-grandmother Mingott's malice.

"Oh, didn't I tell you?" Dallas pursued. "Fanny made me swear to do three things while I was in Paris: get her the score of the last Debussy songs, go to the Grand-Guignol, and see Madame Olenska. You know she was awfully good to Fanny when Mr. Beaufort sent her over from Buenos Aires to the Assomption. Fanny hadn't any friends in Paris, and Madame Olenska used to be kind to her and trot her about on holidays. I believe she was a great friend of the first Mrs. Beaufort's. And she's our cousin, of course. So I rang her up this morning before I went out, and told her you and I were here for two days and wanted to see her."

Archer continued to stare at him. "You told her I was here?"

"Of course—why not?" Dallas's eyebrows went up whimsically. Then, getting no answer, he slipped his arm through his father's with a confidential pressure.

"I say, Father: what was she like?"

Archer felt his color rise under his son's unabashed gaze.

"Come, own up: you and she were great pals, weren't you? Wasn't she most awfully lovely?"

"Lovely? I don't know. She was different."

"Ah—there you have it! That's what it always comes to, doesn't it? When she comes, *she's different*—and one doesn't know why. It's exactly what I feel about Fanny."

His father drew back a step, releasing his arm. "About Fanny? But, my dear fellow—I should hope so! Only I don't see—"

"Dash it, Dad, don't be prehistoric. Wasn't she—once—your Fanny?"

Dallas belonged body and soul to the new generation. He was the firstborn of Newland and May Archer, yet it had never been possible to inculcate in him even the rudiments of reserve. "What's the use of making mysteries? It only makes people want to nose 'em out," he always objected when enjoined to discretion. But Archer, meeting his eyes, saw the filial light under their banter.

"My Fanny—?"

"Well, the woman you'd have chucked everything for: only you didn't," continued his surprising son.

"I didn't," echoed Archer with a kind of solemnity.

"No: you date, you see, dear old boy. But Mother said . . . "

"Your mother?"

"Yes: the day before she died. It was when she sent for me alone—you remember? She said she knew we were safe with you, and always would be, because once, when she asked you to, you'd given up the thing you most wanted."

Archer received this strange communication in silence. His eyes remained unseeingly fixed on the thronged sunlit square below the window. At length he said in a low voice: "She never asked me."

"No. I forgot. You never did ask each other anything, did you? And you never told each other anything. You just sat and watched each other, and guessed at what was going on underneath. A deaf-and-dumb asylum, in fact. Well, I back your generation for knowing more about each other's private thoughts than we ever have time to find out about our own. I say, Dad," Dallas broke off, "you're not angry with me? If you are, let's make it up and go and lunch at Henri's. I've got to rush out to Versailles afterward."

Archer did not accompany his son to Versailles. He preferred
to spend the afternoon in solitary roamings through Paris. He had
to deal all at once with the packed regrets and stifled memories of
an inarticulate lifetime.

After a little while he did not regret Dallas's indiscretion. It
seemed to take an iron band from his heart to know that, after all,
someone had guessed and pitied. . . . And that it should have been
his wife moved him indescribably. Dallas, for all his affectionate
insight, would not have understood that. To the boy, no doubt, the
episode was only a pathetic instance of vain frustration, of wasted
forces. But was it really no more? For a long time Archer sat on a
bench in the Champs Elysees and wondered, while the stream of
life rolled by. . . .

A few streets away, a few hours away, Ellen Olenska waited. She
had never gone back to her husband, and when he had died, some
years before, she had made no change in her way of living. There
was nothing now to keep her and Archer apart—and that afternoon he was to see her.

He got up and walked across the Place de la Concorde and the
Tuileries gardens to the Louvre. She had once told him that she
often went there, and he had a fancy to spend the intervening time
in a place where he could think of her as perhaps having lately
been. For an hour or more he wandered from gallery to gallery
through the dazzle of afternoon light, and one by one the pictures
burst on him in their half-forgotten splendor, filling his soul with
the long echoes of beauty. After all, his life had been too
starved. . . .

Suddenly, before an effulgent Titian, he found himself saying:
"But I'm only fifty-seven—" and then he turned away. For such summer dreams it was too late; but surely not of a quiet harvest of
friendship, of comradeship, in the blessed hush of her nearness.

He went back to the hotel, where he and Dallas were to meet;
and together they walked again across the Place de la Concorde
and over the bridge that leads to the Chamber of Deputies.

Dallas, unconscious of what was going on in his father's mind,
was talking excitedly and abundantly of Versailles. He had had but
one previous glimpse of it, during a holiday trip in which he had
tried to pack all the sights he had been deprived of when he had
had to go with the family to Switzerland; and tumultuous enthusiasm and cocksure criticism tripped each other up on his lips.

As Archer listened, his sense of inadequacy and inexpressive-
ness increased. The boy was not insensitive, he knew; but he had

the facility and self-confidence that came of looking at fate not as a master but as an equal. "That's it: they feel equal to things—they know their way about," he mused, thinking of his son as the spokesman of the new generation which had swept away all the old landmarks, and with them the sign-posts and the danger-signal.

Suddenly Dallas stopped short, grasping his father's arm. "Oh, by Jove," he exclaimed.

They had come out into the great tree-planted space before the Invalides. The dome of Mansart floated ethereally above the budding trees and the long gray front of the building: drawing up into itself all the rays of afternoon light, it hung there like the visible symbol of the race's glory.

Archer knew that Madame Olenska lived in a square near one of the avenues radiating from the Invalides; and he had pictured the quarter as quiet and almost obscure, forgetting the central splendor that lit it up. Now, by some queer process of association, that golden light became for him the pervading illumination in which she lived. For nearly thirty years, her life—of which he knew so strangely little—had been spent in this rich atmosphere that he already felt to be too dense and yet too stimulating for his lungs. He thought of the theaters she must have been to, the pictures she must have looked at, the sober and splendid old houses she must have frequented, the people she must have talked with, the incessant stir of ideas, curiosities, images, and associations thrown out by an intensely social race in a setting of immemorial manners; and suddenly he remembered the young Frenchman who had once said to him: "Ah, good conversation—there is nothing like it, is there?"

Archer had not seen M. Riviere, or heard of him, for nearly thirty years; and that fact gave the measure of his ignorance of Madame Olenska's existence. More than half a lifetime divided them, and she had spent the long interval among people he did not know, in a society he but faintly guessed at, in conditions he would never wholly understand. During that time he had been living with his youthful memory of her; but she had doubtless had other and more tangible companionship. Perhaps she too had kept her memory of him as something apart; but if she had, it must have been like a relic in a small dim chapel, where there was not time to pray every day. . . .

They had crossed the Place des Invalides, and were walking down one of the thoroughfares flanking the building. It was a quiet quarter, after all, in spite of its splendor and its history; and the fact gave one an idea of the riches Paris had to draw on, since such scenes as this were left to the few and the indifferent.

The day was fading into a soft sun-shot haze, pricked here and there by a yellow electric light, and passers were rare in the little square into which they had turned. Dallas stopped again, and looked up.

"It must be here," he said, slipping his arm through his father's with a movement from which Archer's shyness did not shrink; and they stood together looking up at the house.

It was a modern building, without distinctive character, but many-windowed, and pleasantly balconied up its wide cream-colored front. On one of the upper balconies, which hung well above the rounded tops of the horse-chestnuts in the square, the awnings were still lowered, as though the sun had just left it.

"I wonder which floor—?" Dallas conjectured and moving toward the *porte-cochere* he put his head into the porter's lodge, and came back to say, "The fifth. It must be the one with the awnings."

Archer remained motionless, gazing at the upper windows as if the end of their pilgrimage had been attained.

"I say, you know, it's nearly six," his son at length reminded him.

The father glanced away at an empty bench under the trees.

"I believe I'll sit there a moment," he said.

"Why—aren't you well?" his son exclaimed.

"Oh, perfectly. But I should like you, please, to go up without me."

Dallas paused before him, visibly bewildered. "But, I say, Dad: do you mean you won't come up at all?"

"I don't know," said Archer slowly.

"If you don't she won't understand."

"Go, my boy; perhaps I shall follow you."

Dallas gave him a long look through the twilight.

"But what on earth shall I say?"

"My dear fellow, don't you always know what to say?" his father rejoined with a smile.

"Very well. I shall say you're old-fashioned, and prefer walking up the five flights because you don't like lifts."

His father smiled again. "Say I'm old-fashioned: that's enough."

Dallas looked at him again, and then, with an incredulous gesture, passed out of sight under the vaulted doorway.

Archer sat down on the bench and continued to gaze at the

awninged balcony. He calculated the time it would take his son to be carried up in the lift to the fifth floor, to ring the bell, and be admitted to the hall, and then ushered into the drawing room. He pictured Dallas entering that room with his quick assured step; and his delightful smile, and wondered if the people were right who said that his boy "took after him."

Then he tried to see the persons already in the room—for probably at that sociable hour there would be more than one—and among them a dark lady, pale and dark, who would look up quickly, half rise, and hold out a long thin hand with three rings on it. . . . He thought she would be sitting in a sofa-corner near the fire, with azaleas banked behind her on a table.

"It's more real to me here than if I went up," he suddenly heard himself say; and the fear lest that last shadow of reality should lose its edge kept him rooted to his seat as the minutes succeeded each other.

He sat for a long time on the bench in the thickening dusk, his eyes never turning from the balcony. At length a light shone through the windows, and a moment later a man-servant came out on the balcony, drew up the awnings, and closed the shutters.

At that, as if it had been the signal he waited for, Newland Archer got up slowly and walked back alone to his hotel.

2

THE GENTLEMAN

WHAT DOES IT MEAN TO BE A GENTLEMAN? MOST OF US WOULD associate the idea with a certain standard of exterior refinement. A gentleman dresses well, has perfect, unobtrusive manners. He is urbane, an excellent conversationalist, and can put others at their ease. He is well informed about art, literature, music, and current events. True gentlemen are often said to exhibit the signs of good "breeding"—an old-fashioned word that historically had as much to do with innate character and instinct as with class or inherited privilege. Traditional interpreters of manliness, as the readings in this section make very clear, have always pointed to signs of natural ability and refinement, rather than background, as the hallmarks of a gentleman.

A gentleman, then, is one who knows, in any circumstances, just how to act. His dress, bearing, and knowledge are worn lightly, never ostentatiously. A gentleman does not call attention to himself by flaunting his superiority. In conversation, for example, he will say something if he has something worthwhile to contribute; yet if he happens to be an expert on any given topic, he will never resort to showing off. Confidence, self-assurance, modesty, and consideration are equally apportioned in his character, and in the end his quiet, judicious contributions will leave his companions duly impressed.

Gentlemanliness, in short, is about what's on the inside, not on the outside. True gentlemanliness should not be confused with mere surface polish, foppery, flattery, or dandyism. A man may be genteel, Samuel Johnson observed, and yet immoral: "Many of his vices may be committed very genteelly, a man may debauch his friend's wife most genteely, he may cheat at cards most genteelly." It is important to distinguish between the true gentleman and his counterfeit, the man of shallow charm or sophistication. The counterfeit gentleman is nothing but surfaces, while a true gentleman's outward graciousness stems from inward virtues of mind and temperament. In this section, readers can sample a wide variety of commentary on the gentlemanly character, and how this character reveals itself in conduct.

Edmund Burke has described a gentleman as one who possesses a "most perfect vigor" and maturity in thought, and who actively cultivates in himself thoughts of kindness, generosity, and honesty. To this, Ralph Waldo Emerson adds that a gentleman is a creature of sense, of grace, of accomplishment, and of social power. Though the true gentleman is commonly a man of cultivation and learning, in the end neither intellect nor education alone will carry the day: Even the most brilliant scientists or philosophers can be callous or selfish, faithless or even ruthless. As Daniel Defoe puts it, "A man that understands everybody is understood by nobody." The intellect that develops entirely on its own, without guidance from sentiment or character, runs the risk of becoming detached, cold, even inhuman. That is why Aristotle, in the *Nicomachean Ethics,* stresses that a virtuous man needs friends with whom he can cooperate in some honorable enterprise. A gentleman is generous in recognizing the merits of his friends, and he wants friends whose honor is worth having.

Finally, a gentleman is "gentle" not merely in the sense of gracious bearing and a soft-spoken presence, but in the deeper sense of compassion for those who suffer. As Thomas Dekker wrote in 1604, he is patient, humble, and of tranquil spirit. Perhaps this aspect of manliness is best summed up by Cardinal Newman, who included in *The Idea of a University* an observation compelling in its simplicity and difficult to deny: "It is almost the definition of a gentleman," he writes, "that he is one who never inflicts pain."

A WELL-BRED MAN

Austen on Gentlemanliness

From Jane Austen, Emma

In Jane Austen's 1816 novel, Emma Woodhouse and her protégé Harriet Smith discuss the merits and drawbacks of the different varieties of gentleman. Emma believes Harriet is too good to marry a young farmer, Robert Martin. He isn't a gentleman like Emma's friend Mr. Knightley. Won't she find a farmer's life too narrow and uncultured? Emma believes a clergyman, Mr. Elton, is the right match for Harriet. When Robert Martin sends Harriet a letter of proposal, Emma persuades her to turn him down. But Mr. Knightley reproaches Emma for her meddling and snobbery.

They met Mr. Martin the very next day, as they were walking on the Donwell road. He was on foot, and after looking very respectfully at her, looked with most unfeigned satisfaction at her companion. Emma was not sorry to have such an opportunity of survey; and walking a few yards forward, while they talked together, soon made her quick eye sufficiently acquainted with Mr. Robert Martin. His appearance was very neat, and he looked like a sensible young man, but his person had no other advantage; and when he came to be contrasted with gentlemen, she thought he must lose all the ground he had gained in Harriet's inclination. Harriet was not insensible of manner; she had voluntarily noticed her father's gentleness with admiration as well as wonder. Mr. Martin looked as if he did not know what manner was.

They remained but a few minutes together, as Miss Woodhouse must not be kept waiting; and Harriet then came running to her with a smiling face, and in a flutter of spirits, which Miss Woodhouse hoped very soon to compose.

"Only think of our happening to meet him! How very odd! It was quite a chance, he said, that he had not gone round by Randalls. He did not think we ever walked this road. He thought we walked toward Randalls most days. He has not been able to get the 'Romance of the Forest' yet. He was so busy the last time he was at Kingston that he quite forgot it, but he goes again tomorrow. So very odd we should happen to meet! Well, Miss Woodhouse, is he like what you expected? What do you think of him? Do you think him so very plain?"

"He is very plain, undoubtedly—remarkably plain: but that is nothing, compared with his entire want of gentility. I had no right to expect much, and I did not expect much; but I had no idea that he could be so very clownish, so totally without air. I had imagined him, I confess, a degree or two nearer gentility."

"To be sure," said Harriet, in a mortified voice, "he is not so genteel as real gentlemen."

"I think, Harriet, since your acquaintance with us, you have been repeatedly in the company of some, such very real gentlemen, that you must yourself be struck with the difference in Mr. Martin. At Hartfield you have had very good specimens of well-educated, well-bred men. I should be surprised if, after seeing them, you could be in company with Mr. Martin again without perceiving him to be a very inferior creature—and rather wondering at yourself for having ever thought him at all agreeable before. Do not you begin to feel that now? Were not you struck? I am sure you must have been struck by his awkward look and abrupt manner—and the uncouthness of a voice, which I heard to be wholly unmodulated as I stood here."

"Certainly, he is not like Mr. Knightley. He has not such a fine air and way of walking as Mr. Knightley. I see the difference plain enough. But Mr. Knightley is so very fine a man!"

"Mr. Knightley's air is so remarkably good, that it is not fair to compare Mr. Martin with *him*. You might not see one in a hundred, with *gentleman* so plainly written as in Mr. Knightley. But he is not the only gentleman you have been lately used to. What say you to Mr. Weston and Mr. Elton? Compare Mr. Martin with either of *them*. Compare their manner of carrying themselves; of walking; of speaking; of being silent. You must see the difference."

"Oh, yes! There is a great difference. But Mr. Weston is almost an old man. Mr. Weston must be between forty and fifty."

"Which makes his good manners the more valuable. The older a person grows, Harriet, the more important it is that their manners should not be bad—the more glaring and disgusting any loudness, or coarseness, or awkwardness become. What is passable in youth, is detestable in later age. Mr. Martin is now awkward and abrupt; what will he be at Mr. Weston's time of life?"

"There is no saying, indeed!" replied Harriet, rather solemnly.

"But there may be pretty good guessing. He will be a completely gross, vulgar farmer—totally inattentive to appearances, and thinking of nothing but profit and loss."

"Will he, indeed? that will be very bad."

"How much his business engrosses him already, is very plain from the circumstance of his forgetting to inquire for the book you recommended. He was a great deal too full of the market to think of anything else—which is just as it should be, for a thriving man. What has he to do with books? And I have no doubt that he *will* thrive and be a very rich man in time—and his being illiterate and coarse need not disturb *us*."

"I wonder he did not remember the book" was all Harriet's answer, and spoken with a degree of grave displeasure which Emma thought might be safely left to itself. She, therefore, said no more for some time. Her next beginning was,

"In one respect, perhaps, Mr. Elton's manners are superior to Mr. Knightley's or Mr. Weston's. They have more gentleness. They might be more safely held up as a pattern. There is an openness, a quickness, almost a bluntness in Mr. Weston, which everybody likes in *him* because there is so much good humor with it—but that would not do to be copied. Neither would Mr. Knightley's downright, decided, commanding sort of manner—though it suits *him* very well; his figure and look, and situation in life seem to allow it; but if any young man were to set about copying him, he would not be sufferable. On the contrary, I think a young man might be very safely recommended to take Mr. Elton as a model. Mr. Elton is good humored, cheerful, obliging, and gentle. He seems to me to be grown particularly gentle of late. I do not know whether he has any design of ingratiating himself with either of us, Harriet, by additional softness, but it strikes me that his manners are softer than they used to be. If he means anything, it must be to please you. Did not I tell you what he said of you the other day?"

She then repeated some warm personal praise which she had drawn from Mr. Elton, and now did full justice to; and Harriet blushed and smiled, and said she had always thought Mr. Elton very agreeable.

Mr. Elton was the very person fixed on by Emma for driving the young farmer out of Harriet's head. She thought it would be an excellent match; and only too palpably desirable, natural, and probable, for her to have much merit in planning it. She feared it was what everybody else must think of and predict. It was not likely, however, that anybody should have equaled her in the date of the plan, as it had entered her brain during the very first evening of Harriet's coming to Hartfield. The longer she considered it, the greater was her sense of its expediency. Mr. Elton's situation was most suitable, quite the gentleman himself, and without low connections; at the same time not of any family that could fairly object to the doubtful birth of Harriet. He had a comfortable home for her, and Emma imagined a very sufficient income; for though the vicarage of Highbury was not large, he was known to have some independent property; and she thought very highly of him as a good-humored, well-meaning, respectable young man, without any deficiency of useful understanding or knowledge of the world.

She had already satisfied herself that he thought Harriet a beautiful girl, which she trusted, with such frequent meetings at Hartfield, was foundation enough on his side; and on Harriet's, there could be little doubt that the idea of being preferred by him would have all the usual weight and efficacy. And he was really a very pleasing young man, a young man whom any woman not fastidious might like.

The very day of Mr. Elton's going to London produced a fresh occasion for Emma's services toward her friend. Harriet had been at Hartfield, as usual, soon after breakfast; and after a time, had gone home to return again to dinner: she returned, and sooner than had been talked of, and with an agitated, hurried look announcing something extraordinary to have happened which she was longing to tell. Half a minute brought it all out. She had heard, as soon as she got back to Mrs. Goddard's, that Mr. Martin had been there an hour before, and finding she was not at home, nor particularly expected, had left a little parcel for her from one of his sisters, and gone away; and on opening this parcel, she had actually found, besides the two songs which she had lent Elizabeth to copy, a letter to herself; and this letter was from him, from Mr. Martin, and contained a direct proposal of marriage. "Who could have thought it! She was so surprised she did not know what to do. Yes, quite a proposal of marriage; and a very good letter, at least she thought so. And he wrote as if he really loved her very much—but she did not know—and so, she was come as fast as she could to ask Miss Woodhouse what she should do." Emma was half ashamed of her friend for seeming so pleased and so doubtful.

"Upon my word," she cried, "the young man is determined not to lose anything for want of asking. He will connect himself well if he can."

"Will you read the letter?" cried Harriet. "Pray do. I'd rather you would."

Emma was not sorry to be pressed. She read, and was surprised. The style of the letter was much above her expectation. There were not merely no grammatical errors, but as a composition it would not have disgraced a gentleman; the language, though plain, was strong and unaffected, and the sentiments it conveyed very much to the credit of the writer. It was short, but expressed good sense, warm attachment, liberality, propriety, even delicacy of feeling. She paused over it, while Harriet stood anxiously watching for her opinion, with a "Well, well," and was at last forced to add, "Is it a good letter? Or is it too short?"

"Yes, indeed, a very good letter," replied Emma rather slowly— "so good a letter, Harriet, that everything considered, I think one of his sisters must have helped him. I can hardly image the young man whom I saw talking with you the other day could express himself so well, if left quite to his own powers, and yet it is not the style of a woman; no, certainly, it is too strong and concise; not diffuse enough for a woman. No doubt he is a sensible man, and I suppose may have a natural talent for—thinks strongly and clearly—and when he takes a pen in hand, his thoughts naturally find proper words. It is so with some men. Yes, I understand the sort of mind. Vigorous, decided, with sentiments to a certain point, not coarse. A better written letter, Harriet (returning it), than I had expected."

"Well," said the still waiting Harriet;—"well—and—and what shall I do?"

"Dear affectionate creature! —*You* banished to Abbey-Mill Farm!—*You* confined to the society of the illiterate and vulgar all your life! I wonder how the young man could have the assurance to ask it. He must have a pretty good opinion of himself."

"I do not think he is conceited either, in general," said Harriet, her conscience opposing such censure; "at least he is very good natured, and I shall always feel much obliged to him, and have a great regard for—but that is quite a different thing from— and you know, though he may like me, it does not follow that I should—and certainly I must confess that since my visiting here I have seen people—and if one comes to compare them, person and manners, there is no comparison at all, *one* is so very handsome and agreeable. However, I do really think Mr. Martin a very amiable young man, and have a great opinion of him; and his being so attached to me—and his writing such a letter—but as to leaving you, it is what I would not do upon any consideration."

"Thank you, thank you, my own sweet little friend. We will not be parted. A woman is not to marry a man merely because she is asked, or because he is attached to her, and can write a tolerable letter."

"Oh! No; and it is but a short letter too."

Emma felt the bad taste of her friend, but let it pass with a "very true; and it would be a small consolation to her, for the clownish manner which might be offending her every hour of the day, to know that her husband could write a good letter."

Mr. Knightley tells Emma that Robert Martin is the right match for Harriet. He is in for a shock.

"Robert Martin is the man. Her visit to Abbey-Mill, this summer, seems to have done his business. He is desperately in love and means to marry her."

"He is very obliging," said Emma; "but is he sure that Harriet means to marry him?"

"Well, well, means to make her an offer then. Will that do? He came to the Abbey two evenings ago, on purpose to consult me about it. He knows I have a thorough regard for him and all his family. And, I believe, considers me as one of his best friends. He came to ask me whether I thought it would be imprudent in him to settle so early; whether I thought her too young: in short, whether I approved his choice altogether; having some apprehension perhaps of her being considered (especially since *your* making so much of her) as in a line of society above him. I was very much pleased with all that he said. I never hear better sense from anyone than Robert Martin. He always speaks to the purpose; open, straightforward, and very well judging. He told me everything; his circumstances and plans, and what they all proposed doing in the event of his marriage. He is an excellent young man, both as son and brother. I had no hesitation in advising him to marry. He proved to me that he could afford it; and that being the case, I was convinced he could not do better. I praised the fair lady too, and altogether sent him away very happy. If he had never esteemed my opinion before, he would have thought highly of me then; and, I daresay, left the house thinking me the best friend and counselor man ever had. This happened the night before last. Now, as we may fairly suppose, he would not allow much time to pass before he spoke to the lady, and as he does not appear to have spoken yesterday, it is not unlikely that he should be at Mrs. Goddard's today;

and she may be detained by a visitor, without thinking him at all a tiresome wretch."

"Pray, Mr. Knightley," said Emma, who had been smiling to herself through a great part of this speech, "how do you know that Mr. Martin did not speak yesterday?"

"Certainly," replied he, surprised, "I do not absolutely know it; but it may be inferred. Was not she the whole day with you?"

"Come," said she, "I will tell you something, in return for what you have told me. He did speak yesterday—that is, he wrote and was refused."

This was obliged to be repeated before it could be believed and Mr. Knightley actually looked red with surprise and displeasure, as he stood up, in tall indignation, and said,

"Then she is a greater simpleton than I ever believed her. What is the foolish girl about?"

"Oh! To be sure," cried Emma, "it is always incomprehensible to a man that a woman should ever refuse an offer of marriage. A man always imagines a woman to be ready for anybody who asks her."

"Nonsense! A man does not imagine any such thing. But what is the meaning of this? Harriet Smith refuse Robert Martin? Madness, if it is so; but I hope you are mistaken."

"I saw her answer, nothing could be clearer."

"You saw her answer! You wrote her answer too. Emma, this is your doing. You persuaded her to refuse him."

"And if I did (which, however, I am far from allowing), I should not feel that I had done wrong. Mr. Martin is a very respectable young man, but I cannot admit him to be Harriet's equal and am rather surprised indeed that he should have ventured to address her. By your account, he does seem to have had some scruples. It is a pity that they were ever got over."

"Not Harriet's equal!" exclaimed Mr. Knightley loudly and warmly; and with calmer asperity, added, a few moments afterward, "No, he is not her equal indeed, for he is as much her superior in sense as in situation. Emma, your infatuation about that girl blinds you. What are Harriet Smith's claims, either of birth, nature, or education, to any connection higher than Robert Martin? She is the natural daughter of nobody knows whom, with probably no settled provision at all, and certainly no respectable relations. She is known only as parlor-boarder at a common school. She is not a sensible girl, nor a girl of any information. She has been taught nothing useful, and is too young and too simple to have acquired anything herself. At her age she can have no experience, and with her little wit, is not very likely ever to have any that can avail her. She is pretty, and she is good tempered, and that is all. My only scruple in advising the match was on his account, as being beneath his deserts, and a bad connection for him. I felt that, as to fortune, in all probability he might do much better; and that as to a rational companion or useful helpmate, he could not do worse. But I could not reason so to a man in love, and was willing to trust to there being no harm in her, to her having that sort of disposition, which, in good hands, like his, might be easily led aright and turn out very well. The advantage of the match I felt to be all on her side; and had not the smallest doubt (nor have I now) that there would be a general cry-out upon her extreme good luck. Even *your* satisfaction I made sure of. It crossed my mind immediately that you would not regret your friend's leaving Highbury, for the sake of her being settled so well. I remember saying to myself, 'Even Emma, with all her partiality for Harriet, will think this a good match.'"

"I cannot help wondering at your knowing so little of Emma as to say such a thing. What! Think a farmer (and with all his sense and all his merit Mr. Martin is nothing more) a good match for my intimate friend! Not regret her leaving Highbury for the sake of marrying a man whom I could never admit as an acquaintance of my own! I wonder you should think it possible for me to have such feelings. I assure you mine are very different. I must think your statement by no means fair. You are not just to Harriet's claims. They would be estimated very differently by others as well as myself; Mr. Martin may be the richest of the two, but he is undoubtedly her inferior as to rank in society. The sphere in which she moves is much above his. It would be a degradation."

"A degradation to illegitimacy and ignorance, to be married to a respectable, intelligent gentleman-farmer!"

"As to the circumstances of her birth, though in a legal sense she may be called Nobody, it will not hold in common sense. She is not to pay for the offense of others, by being held below the level of those with whom she is brought up. There can scarcely be a doubt that her father is a gentleman—and a gentleman of fortune.—Her allowance is very liberal; nothing has ever been grudged for her improvement or comfort. That she is a gentleman's daughter, is indubitable to me; that she associates with gentlemen's daughters, no one, I apprehend, will deny. She is superior to Mr. Robert Martin."

"Whoever might be her parents," said Mr. Knightley, "whoever may have had the charge of her, it does not appear to have been any part of their plan to introduce her into what you would call good society. After receiving a very indifferent education she is left in Mrs. Goddard's hands to shift as she can; to move, in short, in Mrs. Goddard's line, to have Mrs. Goddard's acquaintance. Her friends evidently thought this good enough for her; and it *was* good enough. She desired nothing better herself. Till you chose to turn her into a friend, her mind had no distaste for her own set, nor any ambition beyond it. She was as happy as possible with the Martins in the summer. She had no sense of superiority then. If she has it now, you have given it. You have been no friend to Harriet Smith, Emma. Robert Martin would never have proceeded so far, if he had not felt persuaded of her not being disinclined to him. I know him well. He has too much real feeling to address any woman on the haphazard of selfish passion. And as to conceit, he is the furthest from it of any man I know. Depend upon it he had encouragement."

It was most convenient to Emma not to make a direct reply to his assertion; she chose rather to take up her own line of the subject again.

"You are a very warm friend to Mr. Martin; but, as I said before, are unjust to Harriet. Harriet's claims to marry well are not so contemptible as you represent them. She is not a clever girl, but she has better sense than you are aware of, and does not deserve to have her understanding spoken of so slightingly. Waiving that point, however, and supposing her to be, as you describe her, only pretty and good natured, let me tell you, that in the degree she possesses them, they are not trivial recommendations to the world in general, for she is, in fact, a beautiful girl, and must be thought so by ninety-nine people out of a hundred; and till it appears that men are much more philosophic on the subject of beauty than they are generally supposed; till they do fall in love with well-informed minds instead of handsome faces, a girl, with such loveliness as Harriet, has a certainty of being admired and sought after, of having the power of choosing from among many, consequently a claim to be nice. Her good nature, too, is not so very slight a claim, comprehending, as it does, real, thorough sweetness of temper and manner, a very humble opinion of herself, and a great readiness to be pleased with other people. I am very much mistaken if your sex in general would think such beauty, and such temper, the highest claims a woman could possess."

"Upon my word, Emma, to hear you abusing the reason you have, is almost enough to make me think so too. Better be without sense, than misapply it as you do."

A Gentleman Avoids Vulgarity

From Lord Chesterfield,
The Letters of Lord Chesterfield to His Son

Lord Chesterfield's letters show us how a father can combine affection for his son with demanding standards of decency, learning, and manners. Chester-field (1694–1773), who never intended these letters to be seen by others, achieved posthumous fame upon their publication by his son's widow.

A vulgar man is captious and jealous; eager and impetuous about trifles. He suspects himself to be slighted, thinks everything that is said is meant at him; if the company happens to laugh, he is persuaded they laugh at him; he grows angry and testy, says something very impertinent, and draws himself into a scrape, by showing what he calls a proper spirit, and asserting himself. A man of fashion does not suppose himself to be either the sole or principal object of the thoughts, looks, or words of the company; and never suspects that he is either slighted or laughed at, unless he is conscious that he deserves it. And if (which very seldom happens) the company is absurd or ill-bred enough to do either, he does not care two-pence, unless the insult be so gross and plain as to require satisfaction of another kind. As he is above trifles, he is never vehement and eager about them; and, wherever they are concerned, rather acquiesces than wrangles. A vulgar man's conversation always savors strongly of the lowness of his education and company. It turns chiefly upon his domestic affairs, his servants, the excellent order he keeps in his own family, and the little anecdotes of the neighborhood; all which he relates with emphasis, as interesting matters. He is a man gossip.

There is an incontinency of friendship among young fellows, who are associated by their mutual pleasures only, which has, very frequently, bad consequences. A parcel of warm hearts and inexperienced heads, heated by convivial mirth, and possibly a little too much wine, vow, and really mean at the time, eternal friendship to each other, and indiscreetly pour out their whole souls in common, and without the least reserve. These confidences are as indiscreetly repealed as they were made: for new pleasures and new places soon dissolve this ill-cemented connection; and then very ill uses are made of these rash confidences. Bear your part, however, in young companies; nay, excel if you can in all the social and convivial joy and festivity that become youth. Trust them with your love-tales, if you please, but keep your serious views secret. Trust those only to some tried friend more experienced than yourself, and who, being in a different walk of life from you, is not likely to become your rival; for I would not advise you to depend so much upon the heroic virtue of mankind as to hope or believe that your competitor will ever be your friend, as to the object of that competition.

There is nothing so delicate as your moral character, and nothing which it is your interest so much to preserve pure. Should you be suspected of injustice, malignity, perfidy, lying, etc., all the parts and knowledge in the world will never procure you esteem, friendship, or respect. A strange concurrence of circumstances has sometimes raised very bad men to high stations; but they have been raised like criminals to a pillory, where their persons and their crimes, by being more conspicuous, are only the more known, the more detested, and the more pelted and insulted. If, in any case whatsoever, affectation and ostentation are pardonable, it is in the case of morality; though, even there, I would not advise you to a pharisaical pomp of virtue. But I will recommend to you a most scrupulous tenderness for your moral character, and the utmost care not to say or do the least thing that may, ever so slightly, taint it. Show yourself, upon all occasions, the advocate, the friend, but not the bully, of Virtue.

Many people lose a great deal of their time by laziness; they loll and yawn in a great chair, tell themselves that they have not time to begin anything then, and that it will do as well another time. This is a most unfortunate disposition, and the greatest obstruction to both knowledge and business. At your age, you have no right nor claim to laziness as I have, if I please, being *emeritus*. You are but just listed in the world, and must be active, diligent, indefatigable. If ever you propose commanding with dignity, you must serve up to it with diligence. Never put off till tomorrow what you can do today.

The Sun King

From the Duke of Saint-Simon,
The Memoirs of the Duke of Saint-Simon

Not without flaws, Louis XIV nevertheless displayed great refinement of manners. From a secret diary of the Sun King's court by Louis de Rouvroy, Duc de Saint Simon (1675–1755), published posthumously in 1829.

At twenty-three years of age he entered the great world as King, under the most favorable auspices. His ministers were the most skillful in all Europe; his generals the best; his Court was filled with illustrious and clever men, formed during the troubles which had followed the death of Louis XIII.

Louis XIV was made for a brilliant Court. In the midst of other men, his figure, his courage, his grace, his beauty, his grand mien, even the tone of his voice and the majestic and natural charm of all his person, distinguished him till his death as the King Bee, and showed that if he had only been born a simple private gentlemen, he would equally have excelled in fêtes, pleasures, and gallantry, and would have had the greatest success in love. The intrigues and adventures which early in life he had been engaged in—when the Comtesse de Soissons lodged at the Tuileries, as superintendent of the Queen's household, and was the center figure of the Court group—had exercised an unfortunate influence upon him: he received those impressions with which he could never after successfully struggle. From this time, intellect, education, nobility of sentiment, and high principle, in others, became objects of suspicion to him, and soon of hatred. The more he advanced in years the more this sentiment was confirmed in him. He wished to reign by himself. His jealousy on this point unceasingly became weakness.

Never did man give with better grace than Louis XIV, or augmented so much, in this way, the price of his benefits. Never did man sell to better profit his words, even his smiles, nay, his looks. Never did disobliging words escape him; and if he had to blame, to reprimand, or correct, which was very rare, it was nearly always with goodness, never, except on one occasion (the admonition of Courtenvaux, related in its place), with anger or severity. Never was man so naturally polite, or of a politeness so measured, so graduated, so adapted to person, time, and place. Toward women his politeness was without parallel.

The Importance of Good Grooming and Good Company

From Lord Chesterfield,
The Letters of Lord Chesterfield to His Son

I must remind you that it will be to very little purpose for you to frequent good company, if you do not conform to, and learn, their manners; if you are not attentive to please, and well bred, with the easiness of a man of fashion. As you must attend to your manners, so you must not neglect your person; but take care to be very clean, well dressed, and genteel; to have no disagreeable attitudes, nor awkward tricks, which many people use themselves to, and then cannot leave them off. Do you take care to keep your teeth very clean, by washing them constantly every morning, and after every meal? This is very necessary, both to preserve your teeth a great while, and to save you a great deal of pain. Mine have plagued me long, and are now falling out, merely for want of care when I was your age.

The next thing to the choice of your friends, is the choice of your company. Endeavor, as much as you can, to keep company with people above you. There you rise, as much as you sink with people below you; for (as I have mentioned before) you are, whatever the company you keep is. Do not mistake, when I say company above you, and think that I mean with regard to their birth; that is the least consideration: but I mean with regard to their merit, and the light in which the world considers them.

The Boor

From Theophrastus, The Characters

Student of Aristotle and an illustrious teacher and scholar in his own right, Theophrastus (372–288 B.C.) gives us a rich diagnosis of human baseness in The Characters.

Boorishness would appear to be an unseemly lack of cultured behavior. Your typical boor will walk into a public assembly after eating a garlic mixture and claim that it smells every bit as good as myrrh. In addition, he wears shoes two sizes too large and talks in a loud voice. Also, he will not trust family or friends but instead asks the servants what they think about any really important question; and out on the farm he treats the hired men to a full description of everything that went on in the town meeting.

He will sit, moreover, with his clothes tucked far above the knee so that he leaves himself exposed. Nothing else in town makes any impression on him, but at the sight of a cow or donkey or goat in the street he stands gawking. And when he fetches food from the pantry shelf he takes a bite of it every time; or if he has a drink he gulps it down. Besides that, he tries to seduce the kitchen-maid when nobody's around, and then helps her grind meal for himself and the servants. He eats his breakfast and pitches hay to the oxen at the same time, too. What's more, he answers your knock himself; and when he comes to the door he will call the dog, take him by the muzzle, and tell you, "Here's the fellow who watches our house and yard."

Again, when somebody tries to give him a coin in payment he says it's worn too thin and demands another. Or if he has let a neighbor borrow his plow or sickle, or a sack or basket, spends a sleepless night thinking about them. Or on his way into town he will ask the first person he meets how hides and salt fish were selling, and whether it's market-day. He can't wait, either, to announce that he means to get his hair cut in town and bring back some salt fish from Archias's, seeing as how it's right on the way. He sings in the public bath-house, besides, and hammers hobnails into his shoes.

The Art of Good Manners

Jonathan Swift,
On Good Manners and Good Breeding

This essay by the famed Irish-born satirist (1667–1775) is a good example of his sometimes ferocious irony.

Good manners is the art of making those people easy with whom we converse.

Whoever makes the fewest persons uneasy is the best bred in the company.

As the best law is founded upon reason, so are the best manners. And as some lawyers have introduced unreasonable things into common law, so likewise many teachers have introduced absurd things into common good manners.

One principal point of this art is to suit our behavior to the three several degrees of men; our superiors, our equals, and those below us.

For instance, to press either of the two former to eat or drink is a breach of manners; but a farmer or tradesman must be thus treated, or else it will be difficult to persuade them that they are welcome.

Pride, ill nature, and want of sense are the three great sources of ill manners; without some one of these defects, no man will behave himself ill for want of experience; or of what, in the language of fools, is called knowing the world.

I defy anyone to assign an incident wherein reason will not direct us what we are to say or do in company, if we are not misled by pride or ill nature.

Therefore I insist that good sense is the principal foundation of good manners but because the former is a gift which very few among mankind are possessed of, therefore all the civilized nations of the world have agreed upon fixing some rules for common behavior, best suited to their general customs, or fancies, as a kind of artificial good sense, to supply the defects of reason. Without which the gentlemanly part of dunces would be perpetually at cuffs, as they seldom fail when they happen to be drunk, or engaged in squabbles about women or play. And, God be thanked, there hardly happens a duel in a year, which may not be imputed to one of those three motives. Upon which account, I should be exceedingly sorry to find the legislature make any new laws against the practice of dueling; because the methods are easy and many for a wise man to avoid a quarrel with honor, or engage in it with innocence. And I can discover no political evil in suffering bullies, sharpers, and rakes to rid the world of each other by a method of their own; where the law hath not been able to find an expedient.

As the common forms of good manners were intended for regulating the conduct of those who have weak understandings; so they have been corrupted by the persons for whose use they were contrived. For these people have fallen into a needless and endless way of multiplying ceremonies, which have been extremely troublesome to those who practice them, and insupportable to everybody else: insomuch that wise men are often more uneasy at the overcivility of these refiners, than they could possibly be in the conversations of peasants or mechanics.

I have seen a duchess fairly knocked down, by the precipitancy of an officious coxcomb running to save her the trouble of opening a door. I remember, upon a birthday at court, a great lady was utterly desperate by a dish of sauce let fall by a page directly upon her headdress and brocade, while she gave a sudden turn to her elbow upon some point of ceremony with the person who sat next her. Monsieur Buys, the Dutch envoy, whose politics and manners were much of a size, brought a son with him, about thirteen years old, to a great table at court. The boy and his father, whatever they put on their plates, the first offered round in order, to every person in the company; so that we could not get a minute's quiet during the whole dinner. At last their two plates happened to encounter, and with so much violence, that, being china, they broke in twenty pieces, and stained half the company with wet sweetmeats and cream.

I make a difference between good manners and good breeding; although, in order to vary my expression, I am sometimes forced to confound them. By the first, I only understand the art of remembering and applying certain settled forms of general behavior. But good breeding is of a much larger extent; for besides an uncommon degree of literature sufficient to qualify a gentleman for reading a play, or a political pamphlet, it takes in a great compass of knowledge; no less than that of dancing, fighting, gaming, making the circle of Italy, riding the great horse, and speaking

French; not to mention some other secondary, or subaltern accomplishments, which are more easily acquired. So that the difference between good breeding and good manners lies in this, that the former cannot be attained to by the best understandings, without study and labor; whereas a tolerable degree of reason will instruct us in every part of good manners, without other assistance.

Ignorance of forms cannot properly be styled ill manners; because forms are subject to frequent changes; and consequently, being not founded upon reason, are beneath a wise man's regard. Besides, they vary in every country; and after a short period of time, very frequently in the same; so that a man who travels, must needs be at first a stranger to them in every court through which he passes; and perhaps at his return, as much a stranger in his own; and after all, they are easier to be remembered or forgotten than faces or names.

Indeed, among the many impertinencies that superficial young men bring with them from abroad, this bigotry of forms is one of the principal, and more prominent than the rest; who look upon them not only as if they were matters capable of admitting of choice, but even as points of importance; and are therefore zealous on all occasions to introduce and propagate the new forms and fashions they have brought back with them. So that, usually speaking, the worst-bred person in the company is a young traveler just returned from abroad.

A Club Man

From Sir Richard Steele,
The Spectator Club

Male bonding has a long history. Poet, playwright, politician, and wit, Sir Richard Steele is best known for founding the Tatler *in 1711, a journal of social, moral, and literary observation from which this essay is taken.*

The first of our society is a gentleman of Worcestershire, of an ancient descent, a baronet, his name Sir Roger de Coverley. His great-grandfather was inventor of that famous country-dance which is called after him. All who know that shire are very well acquainted with the parts and merits of Sir Roger. He is a gentleman that is very singular in his behavior, but his singularities proceed from his good sense, and are contradictions to the manners of the world, only as he thinks the world is in the wrong. However, this humor creates him no enemies, for he does nothing with sourness or obstinacy; and his being unconfined to modes and forms makes him but the readier and more capable to please and oblige all who know him. When he is in town he lives in Soho Square. It is said he keeps himself a bachelor by reason he was crossed in love by a perverse beautiful widow of the next county to him. Before this disappointment, Sir Roger was what you call a fine gentleman, had often supped with my Lord Rochester and Sir George Etherege, fought a duel upon his first coming to town, and kicked bully Dawson in a public coffeehouse for calling him youngster. But being ill-used by the above-mentioned widow, he was very serious for a year and a half; and though, his temper being naturally jovial, he at last got over it, he grew careless of himself and never dressed afterward. He continues to wear a coat and doublet of the same cut that were in fashion at the time of his repulse, which, in his merry humors, he tells us, has been in and out twelve times since he first wore it. It is said Sir Roger grew humble in his desires after he had forgot his cruel beauty, insomuch that it is reported he has frequently offended with beggars and gypsies; but this is looked upon, by his friends, rather as matter of raillery than truth. He is now in his fifty-sixth year, cheerful, gay, and hearty; keeps a good house both in town and country; a great lover of mankind; but there is such a mirthful cast in his behavior, that he is rather beloved than esteemed. His tenants grow rich, his servants look satisfied, all the young women profess love to him, and the young men are glad of his company.

Gentlemanly Reserve

From William Shenstone, On Reserve

Although such beliefs are not much in fashion today, our ancestors believed reserve was essential to gentlemanly behavior. The essays of William Shen-

stone (1714–1763) were celebrated for their stylistic grace and discriminating judgment.

There would not be any absolute necessity for reserve, if the world were honest: yet, even then, it would prove expedient. For, in order to attain any degree of deference, it seems necessary that people should imagine you have more accomplishments than you discover.

A person who would secure to himself great deference will, perhaps, gain his point by silence as effectually as by anything he can say.

To be, however, a niggard of one's observation is so much worse than to hoard up one's money, as the former may be both imparted and retained at the same time.

Virtues, like essences, lose their fragrance when exposed. They are sensitive plants, which will not bear too familiar approaches.

Let us be careful to distinguish modesty, which is ever amiable, from reserve, which is only prudent. A man is hated sometimes for pride, when it was an excess of humility gave the occasion.

What is often termed shyness is nothing more than refined sense, and an indifference to common observations.

The reserved man's intimate acquaintance are, for the most part, fonder of him than the persons of a more affable character, *i.e.,* he pays them a greater compliment than the other can do his, as he distinguishes them more.

The most reserved of men, who would not exchange two syllables together in an English coffeehouse, should they meet at Ispahan, would drink sherbet and eat a mess of rice together.

The man of show is vain: the reserved man is proud more properly. The one has greater depth: the other a more lively imagination. The one is more frequently respected: the other more generally beloved. The one a Cato; the other a Caesar.

The reserved man should drink double glasses.

Prudent men lock up their motives; letting familiars have a key to their heart as to their garden.

A reserved man is in continual conflict with the social part of his nature; and even grudges himself the laugh into which he is sometimes betrayed.

"Seldom he smiles—
And smiles in such a sort as he disdained
Himself—that could be moved to smile at anything."

The Ugly Club

From Sir Richard Steele, The Ugly Club

Not every man can be a "hunk": Homely men must make the best of it. They have nowhere to go but up.

Since our persons are not of our own making, when they are such as appear defective or uncomely, it is, methinks, an honest and laudable fortitude to dare to be ugly; at least to keep ourselves from being abashed with a consciousness of imperfections which we cannot help, and in which there is no guilt. I would not defend a haggard beau for passing away much time at a glass, and giving softness and languishing graces to deformity: all I intend is, that we ought to be contented with our countenance and shape, so far as never to give ourselves an uneasy reflection on that subject. It is to the ordinary people, who are not accustomed to make very proper remarks on any occasion, matter of great jest if a man enters with a prominent pair of shoulders into an assembly, or is distinguished by an expansion of mouth, or obliquity of aspect. It is happy for a man that has any of these oddnesses about him, if he can be as merry upon himself as others are apt to be upon that occasion. When he can possess himself with such a cheerfulness, women and children, who are at first frightened at him, will afterward be as much pleased with him. As it is barbarous in others to rally him for natural defects, it is extremely agreeable when he can jest upon himself for them.

MANLY CHARACTER AND CONDUCT

The Rules of Harvard College (1643)

Who could pass this SAT today?

1. When any scholar is able to understand Tully or such like classical author *extempore,* and make and speak true Latin in verse and prose, *suo ut aiunt marte,* and decline perfectly the paradigms of nouns and verbs in the Greek tongue: let him then, and not before, be capable of admission into the College.

2. Let every student be plainly instructed and earnestly pressed to consider well, the main end of his life and studies is, "to know God and Jesus Christ which is eternal life," John 17:3, and therefore to lay Christ in the bottom, as the only foundation of all sound knowledge and learning.

And seeing the Lord only giveth wisdom, let everyone seriously set himself by prayer in secret to seek it of Him, Prov. 2:3.

3. Everyone shall so exercise himself in reading the scriptures twice a day, that he shall be ready to give such an account of his proficiency therein, both in theoretical observations of the language, and logic, and in practical and spiritual truths, as his tutor shall require, according to his ability; seeing "the entrance of the Word giveth light, it giveth understanding to the simple," Psalm 119:130.

4. That they, eschewing all profanation of God's name, attributes, word, ordinances, and times of worship, do study with good conscience, carefully to retain God, and the love of His truth in their minds. Else, let them know, that (notwithstanding their learning) God may give them up "to strong delusions," and in the end "to a reprobate mind," 2 Thes. 2:11, 12; Rom. 1:28.

5. That they studiously redeem the time; observe the general hours appointed for all the students, and the special hours for their own classes; and then diligently attend the lectures, without any dis-

turbance by word or gesture. And if in anything they doubt, they shall inquire, as of their fellows, so (in the case of "nonsatisfaction"), modestly of their tutors.

6. None shall, under any pretense whatsoever, frequent the company and society of such men as lead an unfit and dissolute life.

Nor shall any without his tutor's leave, or (in his absence) the call of parents or guardians, go abroad to other towns.

7. Every scholar shall be present in his tutor's chamber at the seventh hour in the morning, immediately after the sound of the bell, at his opening the scripture and prayer; so also at the fifth hour at night, and then give account of his own private reading, as aforesaid in particular the third, and constantly attend lectures in the hall at the hours appointed. But if any (without necessary impediment) shall absent himself from prayer or lectures, he shall be liable to admonition, if he offend above once a week.

8. If any scholar shall be found to transgress any of the laws of God, or the school, after twice admonition, he shall be liable, if not *adultus,* to correction; if *adultus,* his name shall be given up to the overseers of the College, that he may be admonished at the public monthly act.

Pride and Prejudice

From Jane Austen,
Pride and Prejudice

Sometimes women are the best authority on what it means to be a man. In Jane Austen's Pride and Prejudice, *when Mr. Darcy first proposes marriage to Elizabeth Bennet, she angrily rejects the gesture for its conspicuous lack of chivalry and even simple politeness, both of which are consumed by his intolerable pride. To Elizabeth, Mr. Darcy appears to believe he would be doing her a favor to marry her. Her antipathy is deepened by what she percieves to be Darcy's obstruction of her sister's relationship with his friend Mr. Bingley, and his apparent injustice to Mr. Wickham.*

When they were gone, Elizabeth, as if intending to exasperate herself as much as possible against Mr. Darcy, chose for her employment the examination of all the letters which Jane had written to her since her being in Kent. They contained no actual complaint, nor was there any revival of past occurrences, or any communication of present suffering. But in all, and in almost every line of each, there was a want of that cheerfulness which had been used to characterize her style and which, proceeding from the serenity of a mind at ease with itself, and kindly disposed toward everyone, had been scarcely ever clouded. Elizabeth noticed every sentence conveying the idea of uneasiness, with an attention which it had hardly received on the first perusal. Mr. Darcy's shameful boast of what misery he had been able to inflict, gave her a keener sense of her sister's sufferings. It was some consolation to think that his visit to Rosings was to end on the day after the next, and a still greater, that in less than a fortnight she should herself be with Jane again, and enabled to contribute to the recovery of her spirits, by all that affection could do.

She could not think of Darcy's leaving Kent, without remembering that his cousin was to go with him; but Colonel Fitzwilliam had made it clear that he had no intentions at all, and agreeable as he was, she did not mean to be unhappy about him.

While settling this point, she was suddenly roused by the sound of the doorbell, and her spirits were a little fluttered by the idea of its being Colonel Fitzwilliam himself, who had once before called late in the evening, and might now come to enquire particularly after her. But this idea was soon banished, and her spirits were very differently affected, when, to her utter amazement, she saw Mr. Darcy walk into the room. In a hurried manner he immediately began an enquiry after her health, imputing his visit to a wish of hearing that she were better. She answered him with cold civility. He sat down for a few moments, and then getting up walked about the room. Elizabeth was surprised, but said not a word. After a silence of several minutes he came toward her in an agitated manner, and thus began,

"In vain have I struggled. It will not do. My feelings will not be repressed. You must allow me to tell you how ardently I admire and love you."

Elizabeth's astonishment was beyond expression. She stared, colored, doubted, and was silent. This he considered sufficient encouragement, and the avowal of all that he felt and had long felt for her, immediately followed. He spoke well, but there were feelings besides those of the heart to be detailed, and he was not more eloquent on the subject of tenderness than of pride. His sense of her inferiority—of its being a degradation—of the family obstacles which judgment had always opposed to inclination, were dwelt on with a warmth which seemed due to the consequence he was wounding, but was very unlikely to recommend his suit.

In spite of her deeply rooted dislike, she could not be insensible to the compliment of such a man's affection, and though her intentions did not vary for an instant, she was at first sorry for the pain he was to receive; till, roused to resentment by his subsequent language, she lost all compassion in anger. She tried, however, to compose herself to answer him with patience, when he should have done. He concluded with representing to her the strength of that attachment which, in spite of all his endeavors, he had found impossible to conquer; and with expressing his hope that it would now be rewarded by her acceptance of his hand. As he said this, she could easily see that he had no doubt of a favorable answer. He *spoke* of apprehension and anxiety, but his countenance expressed real security. Such a circumstance could only exasperate further, and when he ceased, the color rose into her cheeks, and she said,

"In such cases as this, it is, I believe, the established mode to express a sense of obligation for the sentiments avowed, however unequally they may be returned. It is natural that obligation should be felt, and if I could *feel* gratitude, I would now thank you. But I cannot—I have never desired your good opinion, and you have certainly bestowed it most unwillingly. I am sorry to have occasioned pain to anyone. It has been most unconsciously done, however, and I hope will be of short duration. The feelings which, you tell me, have long prevented the acknowledgment of your regard, can have little difficulty in overcoming it after this explanation."

Mr. Darcy, who was leaning against the mantlepiece with his eyes fixed on her face, seemed to catch her words with no less resentment than surprise. His complexion became pale with anger, and the disturbance of his mind was visible in every feature. He was struggling for the appearance of composure, and would not open his lips, till he believed himself to have attained it. The pause was to Elizabeth's feelings dreadful. At length, in a voice of forced calmness, he said,

"And this is all the reply which I am to have the honor of expecting! I might, perhaps, wish to be informed why, with so little *endeavor* at civility, I am thus rejected. But it is of small importance."

"I might as well enquire," replied she, "why with so evident a design of offending and insulting me, you chose to tell me that you liked me against your will, against your reason, and even against your character? Was not this some excuse for incivility, if I *was* uncivil? But I have other provocations. You know I have. Had not my own feelings decided against you, had they been indifferent, or had they even been favorable, do you think that any consideration would tempt me to accept the man, who has been the means of ruining, perhaps forever, the happiness of a most beloved sister?"

As she pronounced these words, Mr. Darcy changed color; but the emotion was short, and he listened without attempting to interrupt her while she continued.

"I have every reason in the world to think ill of you. No motive can excuse the most unjust and ungenerous part you acted *there*. You dare not, you cannot deny that you have been the principal, if not the only means of dividing them from each other, of exposing one to the censure of the world for caprice and instability, the other to its derision for disappointed hopes, and involving them both in misery of the acutest kind."

She paused, and saw with no slight indignation that he was listening with an air which proved him wholly unmoved by any feeling of remorse. He even looked at her with a smile of affected incredulity.

"Can you deny that you have done it?" she repeated.

With assumed tranquillity he then replied, "I have no wish of denying that I did everything in my power to separate my friend from your sister, or that I rejoice in my success. Toward *him* I have been kinder than toward myself."

Elizabeth disdained the appearance of noticing this civil reflection, but its meaning did not escape, nor was it likely to conciliate her.

"But it is not merely this affair," she continued, "on which my dislike is founded. Long before it had taken place, my opinion of you was decided. Your character was unfolded in the recital which I received many months ago from Mr. Wickham. On this subject, what can you have to say? In what imaginary act of friendship can you here defend yourself? Or under what misrepresentation, can you here impose upon others?"

"You take an eager interest in that gentleman's concerns," said Darcy in a less tranquil tone, and with a heightened color.

"Who that knows what his misfortunes have been, can help feeling an interest in him?"

"His misfortunes!" repeated Darcy contemptuously; "yes, his misfortunes have been great indeed."

"And of your infliction," cried Elizabeth with energy. "You have reduced him to his present state of poverty, comparative poverty. You have withheld the advantages, which you must know to have been designed for him. You have deprived the best years of his life, of that independence which was no less his due than his desert. You have done all this! And yet you can treat the mention of his misfortunes with contempt and ridicule."

"And this," cried Darcy, as he walked with quick steps across the room, "is your opinion of me! This is the estimation in which you hold me! I thank you for explaining it so fully. My faults, according to this calculation, are heavy indeed! But perhaps," added he, stopping in his walk, and turning toward her, "these offenses might have been overlooked, had not your pride been hurt by my honest confession of the scruples that had long prevented my forming any serious design. These bitter accusations might have been suppressed, had I with greater policy concealed my struggles, and flattered you into the belief of my being impelled by unqualified, unalloyed inclination; by reason, by reflection, by everything. But disguise of every sort is my abhorrence. Nor am I ashamed of the feelings I related. They were natural and just. Could you expect me to rejoice in the inferiority of your connections? To congratulate myself on the hope of relations, whose condition in life is so decidedly beneath my own?"

Elizabeth felt herself growing more angry every moment; yet she tried to the utmost to speak with composure when she said,

"You are mistaken, Mr. Darcy, if you suppose that the mode of your declaration affected me in any other way, than as it spared me the concern which I might have felt in refusing you, had you behaved in a more gentleman-like manner."

She saw him start at this, but he said nothing, and she continued,

"You could not have made me the offer of your hand in any possible way that would have tempted me to accept it."

Again his astonishment was obvious; and he looked at her with an expression of mingled incredulity and mortification. She went on.

"From the very beginning, from the first moment I may almost say, of my acquaintance with you, your manners impressing me with the fullest belief of your arrogance, your conceit, and your selfish disdain of the feelings of others, were such as to form that groundwork of disapprobation, on which succeeding events have built so immovable a dislike; and I had not known you a month before I felt that you were the last man in the world whom I could ever be prevailed on to marry."

"You have said quite enough, madam. I perfectly comprehend your feelings, and have now only to be ashamed of what my own have been. Forgive me for having taken up so much of your time, and accept my best wishes for your health and happiness."

And with these words he hastily left the room, and Elizabeth heard him the next moment open the front door and quit the house.

The tumult of her mind was now painfully great. She knew not how to support herself, and from actual weakness sat down and cried for half an hour. Her astonishment, as she reflected on what had passed, was increased by every review of it. That she should receive an offer of marriage from Mr. Darcy! That he should have been in love with her for so many months! So much in love as to wish to marry her in spite of all the objections which had made him prevent his friend's marrying her sister, and which must appear at least with equal force in his own case, was almost incredible! It was gratifying to have inspired unconsciously so strong an affection. But his pride, his abominable pride, his shameless avowal of what he had done with respect to Jane, his unpardonable assurance in acknowledging, though he could not justify it, and the unfeeling manner in which he had mentioned Mr. Wickham, his cruelty toward whom he had not attempted to deny, soon overcame the pity which the consideration of his attachment had for a moment excited.

She continued in very agitating reflections till the sound of Lady Catherine's carriage made her feel how unequal she was to encounter Charlotte's observation, and hurried her away to her room.

When Darcy proposes for a second time, both he and Elizabeth acknowledge the faults they displayed during his first proposal. Each has shown a measure of pride and prejudice alike toward the other. Darcy, moreover, has redeemed himself by proving correct in his low opinion of Mr. Wickham, and by helping the Bennetts deal with the scandal of Wickham's elopement with Elizabeth's foolish younger sister, Lydia.

The gentlemen arrived early; and, before Mrs. Bennet had time to tell him of their having seen his aunt, of which her daughter sat in momentary dread, Bingley, who wanted to be alone with Jane, proposed their all walking out. It was agreed to. Mrs. Bennet was not in the habit of walking, Mary could never spare time, but the remaining five set off together. Bingley and Jane, however, soon allowed the others to outstrip them. They lagged behind, while Elizabeth, Kitty, and Darcy, were to entertain each other. Very little was said by either; Kitty was too much afraid of him to talk; Elizabeth was secretly forming a desperate resolution; and perhaps he might be doing the same.

They walked toward the Lucases, because Kitty wished to call upon Maria; and as Elizabeth saw no occasion for making it a general concern, when Kitty left them, she went boldly on with him alone. Now was the moment for her resolution to be executed, and, while her courage was high, she immediately said,

"Mr. Darcy, I am a very selfish creature; and, for the sake of giving relief to my own feelings, care not how much I may be wounding yours. I can no longer help thanking you for your unexampled kindness to my poor sister. Ever since I have known it, I have been most anxious to acknowledge to you how gratefully I feel it. Were it known to the rest of my family, I should not have merely my own gratitude to express."

"I am sorry, exceedingly sorry," replied Darcy, in a tone of surprise and emotion, "that you have ever been informed of what may, in a mistaken light, have given you uneasiness. I did not think Mrs. Gardiner was so little to be trusted."

"You must not blame my aunt. Lydia's thoughtlessness first betrayed to me that you had been concerned in the matter; and, of course, I could not rest till I knew the particulars. Let me thank you again and again, in the name of all my family, for that generous compassion which induced you to take so much trouble, and bear so many mortifications, for the sake of discovering them."

"If you *will* thank me," he replied, "let it be for yourself alone. That the wish of giving happiness to you, might add force to the other inducements which led me on, I shall not attempt to deny. But your *family* owe me nothing. Much as I respect them, I believe, I thought only of *you*."

Elizabeth was too much embarrassed to say a word. After a short pause, her companion added, "You are too generous to trifle with me. If your feelings are still what they were last April, tell me so at once. *My* affections and wishes are unchanged, but one word from you will silence me on this subject forever."

Elizabeth, feeling all the more than common awkwardness and anxiety of his situation, now forced herself to speak; and immediately, though not very fluently, gave him to understand, that her sentiments had undergone so material a change, since the period to which he alluded, as to make her receive with gratitude and pleasure, his present assurances. The happiness which this reply produced, was such as he had probably never felt before; and he expressed himself on the occasion as sensibly and as warmly as a man violently in love can be supposed to do. Had Elizabeth been able to encounter his eye, she might have seen how well the expression of heartfelt delight, diffused over his face, became him; but, though she could not look, she could listen, and he told her of feelings, which, in proving of what importance she was to him, made his affection every moment more valuable.

They walked on, without knowing in what direction. There was too much to be thought, and felt, and said, for attention to any other objects. She soon learned that they were indebted for their present good understanding to the efforts of his aunt, who *did* call on him in her return through London, and there relate her journey to Longbourn, its motive, and the substance of her conversation with Elizabeth; dwelling emphatically on every expression of the latter, which, in her ladyship's apprehension, peculiarly denoted her perverseness and assurance, in the belief that such a relation must assist her endeavors to obtain that promise from her nephew, which *she* had refused to give. But, unluckily for her ladyship, its effect had been exactly contrariwise.

"It taught me to hope," said he, "as I had scarcely ever allowed myself to hope before. I knew enough of your disposition to be certain, that, had you been absolutely, irrevocably decided against me, you would have acknowledged it to Lady Catherine, frankly and openly."

Elizabeth colored and laughed as she replied, "Yes, you know enough of my *frankness* to believe me capable of *that*. After abusing you so abominably to your face, I could have no scruple in abusing you to all your relations."

"What did you say of me, that I did not deserve? For, though your accusations were ill founded, formed on mistaken premises, my behavior to you at the time, had merited the severest reproof. It was unpardonable. I cannot think of it without abhorrence."

"We will not quarrel for the greater share of blame annexed to that evening," said Elizabeth. "The conduct of neither, if strictly examined, will be irreproachable; but since then, we have both, I hope, improved in civility."

"I cannot be so easily reconciled to myself. The recollection of what I then said, of my conduct, my manners, my expressions dur-

ing the whole of it, is now, and has been many months, inexpress-
ibly painful to me. Your reproof, so well applied, I shall never forget: 'had you behaved in a more gentleman-like manner.' These
were your words. You know not, you can scarcely conceive, how
they have tortured me; though it was some time, I confess, before I
was reasonable enough to allow their justice."

"I was certainly very far from expecting them to make so
strong an impression. I had not the smallest idea of their being
ever felt in such a way."

"I can easily believe it. You thought me then devoid of every
proper feeling, I am sure you did. The turn of your countenance I
shall never forget, as you said that I could not have addressed you
in any possible way, that would induce you to accept me."

"Oh! Do not repeat what I then said. These recollections will
not do at all. I assure you, that I have long been most heartily
ashamed of it."

Darcy mentioned his letter. "Did it," said he, "did it *soon* make
you think better of me? Did you, on reading it, give any credit to its
contents?"

She explained what its effect on her had been, and how gradually all her former prejudices had been removed.

"I knew," said he, "that what I wrote must give you pain, but it
was necessary. I hope you have destroyed the letter. There was one
part especially, the opening of it, which I should dread your having
the power of reading again. I can remember some expressions
which might justly make you hate me."

"The letter shall certainly be burned, if you believe it essential
to the preservation of my regard; but, though we have both reason
to think my opinions not entirely unalterable, they are not, I hope,
quite so easily changed as that implies."

"When I wrote that letter," replied Darcy, "I believed myself
perfectly calm and cool, but I am since convinced that it was written in a dreadful bitterness of spirit."

"The letter, perhaps, began in bitterness, but it did not end so.
The adieu is charity itself. But think no more of the letter. The feelings of the person who wrote, and the person who received it, are
now so widely different from what they were then, that every
unpleasant circumstance attending it, ought to be forgotten. You
must learn some of my philosophy. Think only of the past as its
remembrance gives you pleasure."

"I cannot give you credit for any philosophy of the kind. *Your* retrospections must be so totally void of reproach, that the contentment arising from them, is not of philosophy, but what is much better, of ignorance. But with *me*, it is not so. Painful recollections will intrude, which cannot, which ought not to be repelled. I have been a selfish being all my life, in practice, though not in principle. As a child I was taught what was *right*, but I was not taught to correct my temper. I was given good principles, but left to follow them in pride and conceit. Unfortunately an only son (for many years an only *child*), I was spoiled by my parents, who though good themselves (my father particularly, all that was benevolent and amiable), allowed, encouraged, almost taught me to be selfish and overbearing, to care for none beyond my own family circle, to think meanly of all the rest of the world, to *wish* at least to think meanly of their sense and worth compared with my own. Such I was, from eight to eight-and-twenty; and such I might still have been but for you, dearest, loveliest Elizabeth! What do I not owe you! You taught me a lesson, hard indeed at first, but most advantageous. By you, I was properly humbled. I came to you without a doubt of my reception. You shewed me how insufficient were all my pretensions to please a woman worthy of being pleased."

"Had you then persuaded yourself that I should?"

"Indeed I had. What will you think of my vanity? I believed you to be wishing, expecting my addresses."

"My manners must have been in fault, but not intentionally I assure you. I never meant to deceive you, but my spirits might often lead me wrong. How you must have hated me after *that* evening."

"Hate you! I was angry perhaps at first, but my anger soon began to take a proper direction."

"I am almost afraid of asking what you thought of me; when we met at Pemberley. You blamed me for coming?"

"No indeed; I felt nothing but surprise."

"Your surprise could not be greater than *mine* in being noticed by you. My conscience told me that I deserved no extraordinary politeness, and I confess that I did not expect to receive *more* than my due."

"My object *then*," replied Darcy, "was to shew you, by every civility in my power, that I was not so mean as to resent the past; and I hoped to obtain your forgiveness, to lessen your ill opinion, by letting you see that your reproofs had been attended to."

Do Not Be a Rake

From Lord Chesterfield,
The Letters of Lord Chesterfield to His Son

An uninterrupted life of pleasures is as insipid as contemptible. Some hours given every day to serious business, must whet both the mind and the senses, to enjoy those of pleasure. A surfeited glutton, an emaciated sot, and an enervated rotten whoremaster never enjoy the pleasures to which they devote themselves; they are only so many human sacrifices to false gods. The pleasures of low life are all of this mistaken, merely sensual, and disgraceful nature; whereas those of high life, and in good company (though possibly in themselves not more moral), are more delicate, more refined, less dangerous, and less disgraceful; and, in the common course of things, not reckoned disgraceful at all. In short, pleasure must not, nay, cannot, be the business of a man of sense and character; but it may be, and is, his relief, his reward.

Nothing sinks a young man into low company, both of women and men, so surely as timidity, and diffidence of himself. If he thinks that he shall not, he may depend upon it, he will not please. But with proper endeavors to please, and a degree of persuasion that he shall, it is almost certain that he will. How many people does one meet with everywhere, who with very moderate parts, and very little knowledge, push themselves pretty far, singly by being sanguine, enterprising, and persevering? They will take no denial from man or woman; difficulties do not discourage them; repulsed twice or thrice, they rally, they charge again, and nine times in ten prevail at last. The same means will much sooner, and more certainly, attain the same ends, with your parts and knowledge. You have a fund to be sanguine upon, and good forces to rally. In business (talents supposed) nothing is more effectual, or successful, than a good, though concealed, opinion of one's self, a firm resolution, and an unwearied perseverance. None but madmen attempt impossibilities; and whatever is possible, is one way or another to be brought about. If one method fails, try another, and suit your methods to the characters you have to do with.

Having mentioned the word rake, I must say a word or two

more on that subject, because young people too frequently, and always fatally, are apt to mistake that character for that of a man of pleasure; whereas, there are not in the world two characters more different. A rake is a composition of all the lowest, most ignoble, degrading, and shameful vices; they all conspire to disgrace his character and to ruin his fortune; while wine and the pox contend which shall soonest and most effectually destroy his constitution. A dissolute, flagitious footman or porter makes full as good a rake as a man of the first quality. By the bye, let me tell you that in the wildest part of my youth I never was a rake, but on the contrary, always detested and despised the character.

For, as I have often formerly observed to you, nobody but a father can take the liberty to reprove a young fellow grown up, for those kind of inaccuracies and improprieties of behavior. The most intimate friendship, unassisted by the paternal superiority, will not authorize it. I may truly say, therefore, that you are happy in having me for a sincere, friendly, and quick-sighted monitor. Nothing will escape me; I shall pry for your defects, in order to correct them, as curiously as I shall seek for your perfections, in order to applaud and reward them; with this difference only, that I shall publicly mention the latter, and never hint at the former, but in a letter to, or a *tête-à-tête* with you.

John Grey, the Worthy Man

From Anthony Trollope,
Can You Forgive Her?

Alice Vavasor has a problem. A man with no character flaws of any kind whatsoever has proposed marriage. Trollope's 1864 novel chronicles Alice's vacillations between two suitors—the somewhat too flawless John Grey and her charming but unreliable cousin, George Vavasor.

Mr. Grey's answer to Alice Vavasor's letter, which was duly sent by return of post and duly received on the morning after Lady Macleod's visit, may perhaps be taken as giving a sample of his worthiness. It was dated from Nethercoats, a small countryhouse in Cambridgeshire which belonged to him, at which he already spent much of his time, and at which he intended to live altogether after his marriage.

> *Nethercoats, June, 186–*
>
> *Dearest Alice,*
>
>   *I am glad you have settled your affairs, foreign affairs, I mean, so much to your mind. As to your home affairs they are not, to my thinking, quite so satisfactorily arranged. But as I am a party interested in the latter my opinion may perhaps have an undue bias. Touching the tour, I quite agree with you that you and Kate would have been uncomfortable alone. It's a very fine theory, that of women being able to get along without men as well as with them; but, like other fine theories, it will be found very troublesome by those who first put it in practise. Gloved hands, petticoats, feminine softness, and the general homage paid to beauty, all stand in the way of success. These things may perhaps someday be got rid of, and possibly with advantage; but while young ladies are still encumbered with them a male companion will always be found to be a comfort. I don't quite know whether your cousin George is the best possible knight you might have chosen. I should consider myself to be infinitely preferable, had my going been upon the cards. Were you in danger of meeting Paynim foes, he, no doubt, would kill them off much quicker than I could do, and would be much more serviceable in liberating you from the dungeons of oppressors, or even from stray tigers in the Swiss forests. But I doubt his being punctual with the luggage. He will want you or Kate to keep the accounts, if any are kept. He will be slow in getting you glasses of water at the railway stations, and will always keep you waiting at breakfast. I hold that a man with two ladies on a tour should be an absolute slave to them, or they will not fully enjoy themselves. He should simply be an upper servant, with the privilege of sitting at the same table with his mistresses. I have my doubts as to whether your cousin is fit for the place; but, as to myself, it is just the thing that I was made for. Luckily, however, neither you nor Kate are without wills of your own, and perhaps you may be able to reduce Mr. Vavasor to obedience.*
>
>   *As to the home affairs I have very little to say here, in this letter. I shall of course run up and see you before you start, and shall probably stay a week in town. I know I ought not to do so, as it will be a week of idleness, and yet not a week of happiness. I'd sooner have an hour with you in the country than a whole day in London. And I always feel in town that I've too much to do to allow of my doing anything. If it were sheer idleness I could enjoy it, but it is a feverish idle-*

*ness, in which one is driven here and there, expecting some gratifica-
tion which not only never comes, but which never even begins to come.
I will, however, undergo a week of it, say the last seven days of this
month, and shall trust to you to recompense me by as much of yourself
as your town doings will permit.*

*And now again as to those home affairs. If I say nothing now I
believe you will understand why I refrain. You have cunningly just
left me to imply, from what you say, that all my arguments have been
of no avail; but you do not answer them, or even tell me that you
have decided. I shall therefore imply nothing, and still trust to my personal eloquence for success. Or rather not trust—not trust, but hope.*

*The garden is going on very well. We are rather short of water,
and therefore not quite as bright as I had hoped; but we are preparing
with untiring industry for future brightness. Your commands have
been obeyed in all things, and Morrison always says, "The mistress
didn't mean this," or "The mistress did intend that." God bless the
mistress is what I now say, and send her home, to her own home, to
her flowers, and her fruit, and her house, and her husband, as soon
as may be, with no more of these delays which are to me so grievous,
and which seem to me to be so unnecessary. That is my prayer.*

Yours ever and always,

J.G.

"I didn't give commands," Alice said to herself, as she sat with
the letter at her solitary breakfast-table. "He asked me how I liked
the things, and of course I was obliged to say. I was obliged to seem
to care, even if I didn't care." Such were her first thoughts as she
put the letter back into its envelope, after reading it the second
time. When she opened it, which she did quickly, not pausing a
moment lest she should suspect herself of fearing to see what
might be its contents, her mind was full of that rebuke which her
aunt had anticipated, and which she had almost taught herself to
expect. She had torn the letter open rapidly, and had dashed at its
contents with quick eyes. In half a moment she had seen what was
the nature of the reply respecting the proposed companion of her
tour, and then she had completed her reading slowly enough. "No;
I gave no commands," she repeated to herself, as though she might
thereby absolve herself from blame in reference to some possible
future accusations, which might perhaps be brought against her
under certain circumstances which she was contemplating.

Then she considered the letter bit by bit, taking it backward,
and sipping her tea every now and then amidst her thoughts. No;

she had no home, no house, there. She had no husband; not as yet. He spoke of their engagement as though it were a betrothal, as betrothals used to be of yore; as though they were already in some sort married. Such betrothals were not made nowadays. There still remained, both to him and to her, a certain liberty of extricating themselves from this engagement. Should he come to her and say that he found that their contemplated marriage would not make him happy, would not she release him without a word of reproach? Would not she regard him as much more honorable in doing so than in adhering to a marriage which was distasteful to him? And if she would so judge him, judge him and certainly acquit him, was it not reasonable that she under similar circumstances should expect a similar acquittal? Then she declared to herself that she carried on this argument within her own breast simply as an argument, induced to do so by that assertion on his part that he was already her husband, that his house was even now her home. She had no intention of using that power which was still hers. She had no wish to go back from her pledged word.

She thought that she had no such wish. She loved him much, and admired him even more than she loved him. He was noble, generous, clever, good, so good as to be almost perfect; nay, for aught she knew he was perfect. Would that he had some faults! Would that he had! Would that he had! How could she, full of faults as she knew herself to be, how could she hope to make happy a man perfect as he was! But then there would be no doubt as to her present duty. She loved him, and that was everything. Having told him that she loved him, and having on that score accepted his love, nothing but a change in her heart toward him could justify her in seeking to break the bond which bound them together. She did love him, and she loved him only.

But she had once loved her cousin. Yes, truly it was so. In her thoughts she did not now deny it. She had loved him, and was tormented by a feeling that she had had a more full delight in that love than in this other that had sprung up subsequently. She had told herself that this had come of her youth; that love at twenty was sweeter than it could be afterward. There had been a something of rapture in that earlier dream which could never be repeated, which could never live, indeed, except in a dream. Now, now that she was older and perhaps wiser, love meant a partnership, in which each partner would be honest to the other, in which each would wish and strive for the other's welfare, so that thus their joint welfare might be insured. Then, in those early girlish days, it had meant a total abnegation of self. The one was of earth, and therefore possible. The other had been a ray from heaven, and impossible, except in a dream.

And she had been mistaken in her first love. She admitted that frankly. He whom she had worshiped had been an idol of clay, and she knew that it was well for her to have abandoned that idolatry. He had not only been untrue to her, but, worse than that, had been false in excusing his untruth. He had not only promised falsely, but had made such promises with a deliberate, premeditated falsehood. And he had been selfish, coldly selfish, weighing the value of his own low lusts against that of her holy love. She had known this, and had parted from him with an oath to herself that no promised contrition on his part should ever bring them again together. But she had pardoned him as a man, though never as a lover, and had bade him welcome again as a cousin and as her friend's brother. She had again become very anxious as to his career, not hiding her regard, but professing that anxiety aloud. She knew him to be clever, ambitious, bold, and she believed even yet, in spite of her own experience, that he might not be bad at heart. Now, as she told herself that in truth she loved the man to whom her troth was plighted, I fear that she almost thought more of that other man from whom she had torn herself asunder.

"Why should he find himself unhappy in London?" she said, as she went back to the letter. "Why should he pretend to condemn the very place which most men find the fittest for all their energies? Were I a man, no earthly consideration should induce me to live elsewhere. It is odd how we differ in all things. However brilliant might be his own light, he would be contented to hide it under a bushel!"

And at last she recurred to that matter as to which he had been so anxious when she first opened her lover's letter. It will be remembered how assured she had expressed herself that Mr. Grey would not condescend to object to her traveling with her cousin. He had not so condescended. He had written on the matter with a pleasant joke, like a gentleman as he was, disdaining to allude to the past passages in the life of her whom he loved, abstaining even from expressing anything that might be taken as a permission on his part. There had been in Alice's words, as she told him of their proposed plan, a something that had betrayed a tremor in her thoughts. She had studiously striven so to frame her phrases that her tale might be told as any other simple statement, as though there had been no trembling in her mind as she wrote. But she had failed, and she knew that she had failed. She had failed; and he had read all her effort and all her failure. She was quite conscious of this; she felt it thoroughly: and she knew that he was noble and a gentleman to the last drop of his blood. And yet—yet—yet there was almost a feeling of disappointment in that he had not written such a letter as Lady Macleod had anticipated.

During the next week Lady Macleod still came almost daily to Queen Anne Street, but nothing further was said between her and Miss Vavasor as to the Swiss tour; nor were any questions asked about Mr. Grey's opinion on the subject. The old lady of course discovered that there was no quarrel, or, as she believed, any probability of a quarrel; and with that she was obliged to be contented. Nor did she again on this occasion attempt to take Alice to Lady Midlothian's. Indeed, their usual subjects of conversation were almost abandoned, and Lady Macleod's visits, though they were as constant as heretofore, were not so long. She did not dare to talk about Mr. Grey, and because she did not so dare, was determined to regard herself as in a degree ill-used. So she was silent, reserved, and fretful. At length came the last day of her London season, and her last visit to her niece. "I would come because it's my last day," said Lady Macleod; "but really I'm so hurried, and have so many things to do, that I hardly know how to manage it."

"It's very kind," said Alice, giving her aunt an affectionate squeeze of the hand.

"I'm keeping the cab, so I can just stay twenty-five minutes. I've marked the time accurately, but I know the man will swear it's over the half-hour."

"You'll have no more trouble about cabs, Aunt, when you are back in Cheltenham."

"The flies are worse, my dear. I really think they're worse. I pay the bill every month, but they've always one down that I didn't have. It's the regular practice, for I've had them from all the men in the place."

"It's hard enough to find honest men anywhere, I suppose."

"Or honest women either. What do you think of Mrs. Green wanting to charge me for an extra week, because she says I didn't give her notice till Tuesday morning? I won't pay her, and she may stop my things if she dares. However, it's the last time. I shall never come up to London again, my dear."

"Oh, Aunt, don't say that!"

"But I do say it, my dear. What should an old woman like me

do, trailing up to town every year, merely because it's what people choose to call the season."

"To see your friends, of course. Age doesn't matter when a person's health is so good as yours."

"If you knew what I suffer from lumbago, though I must say coming to London always does cure that for the time. But as for friends! Well, I suppose one has no right to complain when one gets to be as old as I am; but I declare I believe that those I love best would sooner be without me than with me."

"Do you mean me, Aunt?"

"No, my dear, I don't mean you. Of course my life would have been very different if you could have consented to remain with me till you were married. But I didn't mean you. I don't know that I meant anyone. You shouldn't mind what an old woman like me says."

"You're a little melancholy because you're going away."

"No, indeed. I don't know why I stayed the last week. I did say to Lady Midlothian that I thought I should go on the twentieth; and, though I know that she knew that I really didn't go, she has not once sent to me since. To be sure they've been out every night; but I thought she might have asked me to come and lunch. It's so very lonely dining by myself in lodgings in London."

"And yet you never will come and dine with me."

"No, my dear; no. But we won't talk about that. I've just one word more to say. Let me see. I've just six minutes to stay. I've made up my mind that I'll never come up to town again, except for one thing."

"And what's that, Aunt?" Alice, as she asked the question, well knew what that one thing was.

"I'll come for your marriage, my dear. I do hope you will not keep me long waiting."

"Ah! I can't make any promise. There's no knowing when that may be."

"And why should there be no knowing? I always think that when a girl is once engaged the sooner she's married the better. There may be reasons for delay on the gentleman's part."

"There very often are, you know."

"But, Alice, you don't mean to say that Mr. Grey is putting it off?"

Alice was silent for a moment, during which Lady Macleod's face assumed a look of almost tragic horror. Was there something wrong on Mr. Grey's side of which she was altogether unaware?

Alice, though for a second or two she had been guilty of a slight playful deceit, was too honest to allow the impression to remain. "No Aunt," she said; "Mr. Grey is not putting it off. It has been left to me to fix the time."

"And why don't you fix it?"

"It is such a serious thing! After all it is not more than four months yet since I—I accepted him. I don't know that there has been any delay."

"But you might fix the time now, if he wishes it."

"Well, perhaps I shall, some day, Aunt. I'm going to think about it, and you mustn't drive me."

"But you should have some one to advise you, Alice."

"Ah! That's just it. People always do seem to think it so terrible that a girl should have her own way in anything. She mustn't like anyone at first; and then, when she does like someone, she must marry him directly she's bidden. I haven't much of my own way at present; but you see, when I'm married I shan't have it at all. You can't wonder that I shouldn't be in a hurry."

"I am not advocating anything like hurry, my dear. But, goodness gracious me! I've been here twenty-eight minutes, and that horrid man will impose upon me. Good-bye; God bless you! Mind you write." And Lady Macleod hurried out of the room more intent at the present moment upon saving her sixpence than she was on any other matter whatsoever.

And then John Grey came up to town, arriving a day or two after the time that he had fixed. It is not, perhaps, improbable that Alice had used some diplomatic skill in preventing a meeting between Lady Macleod and her lover. They both were very anxious to obtain the same object, and Alice was to some extent opposed to their views. Had Lady Macleod and John Grey put their forces together she might have found herself unable to resist their joint endeavors. She was resolved that she would not at any rate name any day for her marriage before her return from Switzerland; and she may therefore have thought it wise to keep Mr. Grey in the country till after Lady Macleod had gone, even though she thereby cut down the time of his sojourn in London to four days. On the occasion of that visit Mr. Vavasor did a very memorable thing. He dined at home with the view of welcoming his future son-in-law. He dined at home, and asked, or rather assented to Alice's asking, George and Kate Vavasor to join the dinner-party. "What an auspicious omen for the future nuptials!" said Kate, with her little sarcastic smile. "Uncle John dines at home, and Mr. Grey joins in the dissipation of a dinner-party. We shall all be changed soon, I suppose, and George and I will take to keeping a little cottage in the country."

"Kate," said Alice, angrily, "I think you are about the most unjust person I ever met. I would forgive your raillery, however painful it might be, if it were only fair."

"And to whom is it unfair on the present occasion; to your father?"

"It was not intended for him."

"To yourself?"

"I care nothing as to myself; you know that very well."

"Then it must have been unfair to Mr. Grey."

"Yes; it was Mr. Grey whom you meant to attack. If I can forgive him for not caring for society, surely you might do so."

"Exactly; but that's just what you can't do, my dear. You don't forgive him. If you did you might be quite sure that I should say nothing. And if you choose to bid me hold my tongue I will say nothing. But when you tell me all your own thoughts about this thing you can hardly expect but that I should let you know mine in return. I'm not particular; and if you are ready for a little good, wholesome, useful hypocrisy, I won't balk you. I mayn't be quite so dishonest as you call me, but I'm not so wedded to truth but what I can look, and act, and speak a few falsehoods if you wish it. Only let us understand each other."

"You know I wish for no falsehood, Kate."

"I know it's very hard to understand what you do wish. I know that for the last year or two I have been trying to find out your wishes, and, upon my word, my success has been very indifferent. I suppose you wish to marry Mr. Grey, but I'm by no means certain. I suppose the last thing on earth you'd wish would be to marry George."

"The very last. You're right there at any rate."

"Alice! Sometimes you drive me too hard; you do, indeed. You make me doubt whether I hate or love you most. Knowing what my feelings are about George, I cannot understand how you can bring yourself to speak of him to me with such contempt!" Kate Vavasor, as she spoke these words, left the room with a quick step, and hurried up to her own chamber. There Alice found her in tears, and was driven by her friend's real grief into the expression of an apology, which she knew was not properly due from her. Kate was acquainted with all the circumstances of that old affair between her

brother and Alice. She had given in her adhesion to the propriety
of what Alice had done. She had allowed that her brother George's
behaviors had been such as to make any engagement between
them impossible. The fault, therefore, had been hers in making
any reference to the question of such a marriage. Nor had it been
by any means her first fault of the same kind. Till Alice had become
engaged to Mr. Grey she had spoken of George only as her brother,
or as her friend's cousin, but now she was constantly making allusion to those past occurrences, which all of them should have
striven to forget. Under these circumstances was not Lady Macleod
right in saying that George Vavasor should not have been accepted
as a companion for the Swiss tour?

The little dinner-party went off very quietly; and if no other
ground existed for charging Mr. Grey with London dissipation
than what that afforded, he was accused most unjustly. The two
young men had never before met each other; and Vavasor had
gone to his uncle's house, prepared not only to dislike but to
despise his successor in Alice's favor. But in this he was either disappointed or gratified, as the case may be. "He has plenty to say for
himself," he said to Kate on his way home.

"Oh yes; he can talk."

"And he doesn't talk like a prig either, which was what I
expected. He's uncommonly handsome."

"I thought men never saw that in each other. I never see it in
any man."

"I see it in every animal—in men, women, horses, dogs, and
even pigs. I like to look on handsome things. I think people always
do who are ugly themselves."

"And so you're going into raptures in favor of John Grey."

"No, I'm not. I very seldom go into raptures about anything.
But he talks in the way I like a man to talk. How he bowled my
uncle over about those actors; and yet if my uncle knows anything
about anything it is about the stage twenty years ago." There was
nothing more said then about John Grey; but Kate understood her
brother well enough to be aware that this praise meant very little.
George Vavasor spoke sometimes from his heart, and did so more
frequently to his sister than to any one else; but his words came
generally from his head.

On the day after the little dinner in Queen Anne Street, John
Grey came to say good-bye to his betrothed; for his betrothed she certainly was, in spite of those very poor arguments which she had used
in trying to convince herself that she was still free if she wished to

claim her freedom. Though he had been constantly with Alice during the last three days, he had not hitherto said anything as to the day of their marriage. He had been constantly with her alone, sitting for hours in that ugly green drawing-room, but he had never touched the subject. He had told her much of Switzerland, which she had never yet seen but which he knew well. He had told her much of his garden and house, whither she had once gone with her father, whilst paying a visit nominally to the colleges at Cambridge. And he had talked of various matters, matters bearing in an immediate way upon his own or her affairs; for Mr. Grey was a man who knew well how to make words pleasant; but previous to this last moment he had said nothing on that subject on which he was so intent.

"Well, Alice," he said, when the last hour had come, "and about that question of home affairs?"

"Let us finish off the foreign affairs first."

"We have finished them; haven't we?"

"Finished them! Why we haven't started yet."

"No; you haven't started. But we've had this discussion. Is there any reason why you'd rather not have this thing settled?"

"No, no special reason."

"Then why not let it be fixed? Do you fear coming to me as my wife?"

"No."

"I cannot think that you repent your goodness to me."

"No; I don't repent it; what you call my goodness? I love you too entirely for that."

"My darling!" And now he passed his arm round her waist as they stood near the empty fireplace. "And if you love me . . . "

"I do love you."

"Then why should you not wish to come to me?"

"I do wish it. I think I wish it."

"But, Alice, you must have wished it altogether when you consented to be my wife."

"A person may wish for a thing altogether, and yet not wish for it instantly."

"Instantly! Come; I have not been hard on you. This is still June. Will you say the middle of September, and we shall still be in time for warm pleasant days among the lakes? Is that asking for too much?"

"It is not asking for anything."

"Nay, but it is, love. Grant it, and I will swear that you have granted me everything."

She was silent, having things to say but not knowing in what words to put them. Now that he was with her she could not say the things which she had told herself that she would utter to him. She could not bring herself to hint to him that his views of life were so unlike her own, that there could be no chance of happiness between them, unless each could strive to lean somewhat toward the other. No man could be more gracious in word and manner than John Grey; no man more chivalrous in his carriage toward a woman; but he always spoke and acted as though there could be no question that his manner of life was to be adopted, without a word or thought of doubting, by his wife. When two came together, why should not each yield something, and each claim something? This she had meant to say to him on this day; but now that he was with her she could not say it.

"John," she said at last, "do not press me about this till I return."

"But then you will say the time is short. It would be short then."

"I cannot answer you now; indeed, I cannot. That is I cannot answer in the affirmative. It is such a solemn thing."

"Will it ever be less solemn, dearest?"

"Never, I hope never."

He did not press her further then, but kissed her and bade her farewell.

The Knight

From Geoffrey Chaucer, The Canterbury Tales

A knight there was, and that a worthy man,
That from the time he first began
To ride out, he loved chivalry,
Truth and honor, generosity and courtesy.
Full worthy was he in his lord's wars
And to them he had ridden, no man farther,

As well in Christiandom as in heathenness,
And ever honored for his worthiness.

And always he had the highest praise,
And though that he were worthy, he was wise,
And bore himself as meekly as a maid.
He never yet a vile thing said
In all his life to anyone of any kind.
He was a truly perfect, gentle knight.

Honor and Reputation

From Francis Bacon, Essays

From Bacon's essay, Of Honor and Reputation.

The winning of honor is but the revealing of a man's virtue and worth without disadvantage. For some in their actions do woo and affect honor and reputation, which sort of men are commonly much talked of, but inwardly little admired. And some, contrariwise, darken their virtue in the shew of it, so as they be undervalued in opinion. If a man perform that which hath not been attempted before, or attempted and given over, or hath been achieved, but not with so good circumstance, he shall purchase more honor than by effecting a matter of greater difficulty or virtue, wherein he is but a follower. If a man so temper his actions as in some one of them he doth content every faction or combination of people, the music will be the fuller. A man is an ill husband of his honor that entereth into any action, the failing wherein may disgrace him more than the carrying of it through can honor him. Honor that is gained and broken upon another hath the quickest reflexion, like diamonds cut with facets. And therefore let a man contend to excel any competitors of his in honor, in outshooting them, if he can, in their own bow.

Temperance

From Baldesar Castiglione, The Book of the Courtier

A gentleman must possess all the virtues: prudence, justice, liberality, magnif-icence, honor, gentleness, pleasantness, and affability. Temperance, according to Ottaviano, is the basis for them all.

My lord Ottaviano was continuing his discourse further, but the Magnifico Giuliano interrupted him and said:

"If I heard rightly, my lord Ottaviano, you said that continence is an imperfect virtue because it has a grain of passion in it. But when there is a struggle waging in our minds between reason and appetite, I think that the virtue which battles and gives reason the victory, ought to be esteemed more perfect than that which con-quers without opposition of lust or passion; for there the mind seems not to abstain from evil by force of virtue, but to refrain from doing evil because it has no inclination thereto."

Then my lord Ottaviano said:

"Which captain would you deem of greater worth, the one who fighting openly puts himself in danger and yet conquers the enemy, or the one who by his ability and skill deprives them of their strength, reducing them to such straits that they cannot fight, and thus conquers them without any battle or danger whatever?"

"The one," said the Magnifico Giuliano, "who more safely con-quers is without doubt more to be praised, provided this safe vic-tory of his does not proceed from the cowardice of the enemy."

My lord Ottaviano replied:

"You have judged rightly; and hence I tell you that continence may be likened to a captain who fights manfully, and although the enemy be strong and powerful, still conquers them, albeit not with-out great difficulty and danger. While temperance unperturbed is like that captain who conquers and rules without opposition, and having not only abated but quite extinguished the fire of lust in the mind where she abides, like a good prince in time of civil strife, she destroys her seditious enemies within, and gives reason the sceptre and whole dominion.

"Thus this virtue does not compel the mind, but infusing it by very gentle means with a vehement belief that inclines it to right-eousness, renders it calm and full of rest, in all things equal and well measured, and disposed on every side by a certain self-accord which adorns it with a tranquillity so serene that it is never ruffled, and becomes in all things very obedient to reason and ready to turn its every act thereto and to follow wherever reason may wish to lead it, without the least unwillingness; like a tender lambkin, which always runs and stops and walks near its mother, and moves only with her.

"This virtue, then, is very perfect and especially befitting to princes, because from it spring many others."

Then messer Cesare Gonzaga said:

"I do not know what virtues befitting to a lord can spring from this temperance, if it is the one which removes the passions from the mind, as you say. Perhaps this would be fitting in a monk or hermit; but I am by no means sure whether it would befit a prince (who was magnanimous, liberal and valiant in arms) never to feel, whatever might be done to him, either wrath or hate or good will or scorn or lust or passion of any kind, and whether he could without this wield authority over citizens or soldiers."

My lord Ottaviano replied:

"I did not say that temperance wholly removes and uproots the passions from the human mind, nor would it be well to do this, for even the passions contain some elements of good; but it reduces to the sway of reason that which is perverse in our passions and resistant to right. Therefore it is not well to extirpate the passions altogether, in order to be rid of disturbance; for this would be like making an edict that no one must drink wine, in order to be rid of drunkenness, or forbidding everyone to run, because in running we sometimes fall. You know that those who tame horses do not keep them from running and leaping, but would have them do so seasonably and in obedience to the rider.

"Thus, when moderated by temperance, the passions are help-ful to virtue, like the wrath that aids strength, hatred of evil-doers aids justice, and likewise the other virtues are aided by the passions; which, if they were wholly removed, would leave reason very weak and languid, so that it could effect little, like the master of a vessel abandoned by the winds in a great calm.

"Now do not marvel, messer Cesare, if I have said that many other virtues are born of temperance, for when a mind is attuned to this harmony, it then through reason easily receives true strength, which makes it bold, and safe from every peril, and almost superior to human passions. Nor is this less true of justice (unspotted virgin, friend of modesty and good, queen of all the other virtues), because she teaches us to do that which it is right to do, and to shun that which it is right to shun; and therefore she is most perfect, because the other virtues perform their works through her, and because she is helpful to whomsoever possesses her, both to himself and to others: without whom (as it is said) Jove himself could not rule his kingdom rightly. Magnanimity also follows these and enhances them all; but she cannot stand alone, for whoever has no other virtue, cannot be magnanimous. Then the guide of these virtues is foresight, which consists in a certain judgment in choosing well. And in this happy chain are joined liberality, magnificence, thirst for honour, gentleness, pleasantness, affability and many others which there is not now time to name.

"But if our Courtier will do that which we have said, he will find them all in his prince's mind, and will daily see spring therefrom beautiful flowers and fruits, such as all the delightful gardens in the world do not contain."

The Man Without Moral Feeling

From Theophrastus, The Characters

Lack of moral feeling is willingness to do or say what is disgraceful. The man without moral feeling is the kind who will take an oath with no sense of responsibility, since he does not mind letting himself in for hard words or even downright abuse. By nature he is a base kind of person, lacking the most elementary sense of decency and capable of absolutely anything. Dead sober, he will do a belly dance when he is supposed to be part of a comic chorus; and at a puppet show he goes around collecting the penny admission from everybody and arguing with pass-holders who think they have a right to watch free. Very likely he runs a shady hotel or a whorehouse, too, or collects taxes. Town crier, gambler, cook—no trade is too disgraceful for this fellow. He leaves his mother without support in her old age; he gets hauled into court for petty theft and knows the inside of the town jail better than his own house.

[This man also seems to be the sort who gets a crowd around

him and lectures his listeners in a loud, cracked voice, trading arguments and abuse. And some of them arrive in the middle of his tirade, while others leave without bothering to hear it all; but he obliges with a summary of whatever is left out, convinced that there's no occasion so proper for a display of his lack of moral feeling as when he has an audience.]

In court, moreover, he is capable of playing any role: defendant, plaintiff, or witness. Sometimes he gets out of testifying by swearing ignorance; or he may appear in court as a witness, with stacks of evidence inside his coat and whole handfuls of documents. He knows a good many rascals, and he will not disqualify even the worst of them from high office. More than that, he lends money to these fellows the moment they ask for the loan—collecting interest, to be sure, at a rate of three obols in twelve, not yearly or monthly but daily. He gets the interest from their businesses, too, and makes the rounds of bakers and fishmongers with the money stuffed into his cheek.

[They are a troublesome lot, always ready with an insult and talking so loudly that the market-place and the shops echo.]

Practice Makes Perfect

From John Locke, Of Practice and Habits

John Locke (1632–1704) was perhaps the single most influential English philosopher. His views on individual liberty, religious tolerance, and liberal education were influential in America as well.

We are born with faculties and powers capable almost of anything, such at least as would carry us further than can be easily imagined; but it is only the exercise of those powers which gives us ability and skill in anything, and leads us towards perfection.

A middle-aged ploughman will scarce ever be brought to the carriage and language of a gentleman, though his body be as well proportioned, and his joints as supple, and his natural parts not any way inferior. The legs of a dancing-master, and the fingers of a musician, fall as it were naturally, without thought or pains, into regular and admirable motions. Bid them change their parts, and they will in vain endeavor to produce like motions in the members not used to them, and it will require length of time and long practice to attain but some degrees of a like ability. What incredible and astonishing actions do we find rope-dancers and tumblers bring their bodies to! Not but that sundry in almost all manual arts are as wonderful; but I name those which the world takes notice of for such, because, on that very account, they give money to see them. All these admired motions, beyond the reach, and almost the conception, of unpracticed spectators, are nothing but the mere effects of use and industry in men whose bodies have nothing different in them from those of the amazed lookers-on.

As it is in the body, so it is in the mind; practice makes it what it is: and most, even of those excellencies which are looked on as natural endowments, will be found, when examined into more narrowly, to be the product of exercise, and to be raised to that pitch only by repeated actions. Some men are remarked for pleasantness in raillery; others for apologues and apposite diverting stories. This is apt to be taken for the effect of pure nature, and that the rather, because it is not got by rules; and those who excel in either of them never purposely set themselves to the study of it as an art to be learned. But yet it is true that at first some lucky hit which took with somebody, and gained him commendation, encouraged him to try again, inclined his thoughts and endeavors that way, till at last he insensibly got a facility in it without perceiving how; and that is attributed wholly to nature, which was much more the effect of use and practice. I do not deny that natural disposition may often give the first rise to it; but that never carries a man far without use and exercise, and it is practice alone that brings the powers of the mind, as well as those of the body, to their perfection.

On Friendship

From Aristotle, The Nicomachean Ethics

A gentleman takes pleasure in the esteem of a friend whom he esteems in return.

The duties which we owe to our friends seem analogous to those which each individual willingly pays to himself. We ought, it is said, to wish their good, or what appears to us to be such, and to promote it to our best ability, merely on their own account. With this kind of disinterested affection mothers are animated towards their children, and those friends towards each other, between whom some disgust has arisen which, though it interrupts their intercourse, does not destroy their mutual kindness. Others say that friends must spend much of their time together, have the same inclinations and pursuits, and sympathize with each other in their joy as well as in their sorrow. On whichever or how many soever of those conditions friendship principally depends, we shall find that all of them belong to the affections by which a good man is animated towards himself; and by which all men are animated in proportion as they either approximate, or only think they approximate, to an honorable and praiseworthy character; which, in questions concerning human nature, is justly considered as the sole unerring standard. The virtuous man only is at peace within himself, since all the powers of his mind are actuated by the same motives, and conspire to the same end: always aiming at good, real and intrinsic, the good of his intellectual part. To him existence is a benefit, which he earnestly wishes may be preserved, especially the existence of the thinking principle within him, which is peculiarly himself; for every individual strives after its own good, real or apparent, which in the virtuous man only coincide: but could an individual love its change into something quite different from itself, the good of the latter would be to the former a matter of slight concern. In Deity all goods are accumulated, because he is ever and invariably that which he is; and in man the thinking principle is the part that is properly and permanently himself. He who pursues the good of his mind is pleased in his own company, being delighted with the recollection of the past as well as animated with the prospect of the future; and having ever at command innumerable speculations, in which he exercises himself with the most exquisite pleasure. Both his joys and his sorrows are respectively consistent with themselves, since they invariably proceed from fixed and regular causes; for he does not delight at one time in what will excite his repentance at another; and thus harmonized within his own breast, he is similarly affected towards his friend, whom he considers as a second self; and his sympathy for whom, when it reaches the highest perfection, resembles that internal concord which is experienced in his own mind, when the various principles of his nature coalesce into one movement, and flow in the same homogeneous stream of virtuous energy.

Yet many men of very irregular lives seem to be highly satisfied with themselves. Is this because they mistake their own characters? It should seem so, since the complete villain is always visibly at variance with himself; and all others are similarly affected in proportion to their progress in wickedness; willing one thing, yet desiring and preferring another as those who allow themselves to be subdued by vicious pleasure, and who may be said, with their eyes open, to rush into voluntary destruction. In the same manner others, through laziness or cowardice, avoid that conduct which they know most likely to promote their happiness. When men proceed to the last stage of depravity, they become as odious to themselves as they are detestable to others, and therefore often destroy their own lives; and even before they arrive at this deplorable condition, they fly from and avoid themselves; preferring any kind of society to that of their own reflections; the past crimes which haunt their memory, and the meditated guilt which is continually occurring to their fancy. As they have nothing in them that is amiable, they cannot be the objects of their own love. Neither their joys nor their sorrows are consistent. Their whole soul is in sedition, distracted between contending principles, the pleasure of one giving pain to another; and when the worst principle prevails, a foundation is laid for the bitterest remorse. If such be the wretchedness of wickedness, how strenuously ought we to exert ourselves to become good men, that we may live in friendship with ourselves, and be worthy of the friendship of others!

The Lover of Bad Company

From Theophrastus, The Characters

Love of bad company and rascally behavior is a passion for the vicious. It makes the kind of man who imagines that he will find out what life is really about and become a terror if he associates with people convicted of crimes against the state. Or when you describe somebody as respectable this fellow will reply, "So it would appear . . ." and then go on to argue that really nobody can claim respectability—people are all alike. A remark like "What a respectable man so-and-so is" he turns into a joke.

Moreover it's the rascal, he argues, who turns out to be the real gentleman if you put him to the test. Some of what you hear about such men is true, he admits, but other things aren't. "They're clever and good-natured, the kind who won't let a friend down," he maintains; and he champions anyone like this with all his might as the most capable person he ever met. In addition, he listens sympathetically whenever a rascal is bing prosecuted in a court of law or called on to make a public defence of his record. "Remember, you're trying the case, not the man," he will say to the jury every time; and he calls the defendant a watchdog of the people's interests, on the look-out against lawbreakers. "We won't have anybody left to worry about good government," he adds, "if we don't stand by fellows like this."

You also find him playing the protector of worthless men, or trying to get a jury packed for dirty work in the courtroom. And if he is called in to give an individual opinion, he puts the arguments of the opposing sides in an unfavorable light.

It could be said generally that sympathy with rascally behavior represents the next thing to rascality itself; and there is some truth in the old saying about birds of a feather.

3

THE WISE MAN

Few thoughtful people would contest the notion that manliness includes, indeed requires, a quotient of wisdom. But the connection between the two is elusive and has sparked a lively and even fierce debate over the centuries. What do we mean by wisdom? The abstract, purely intellectual rigor of academia? The grand contemplative speculations and metaphysical doctrines of philosophers from Plato to Hegel? The search by natural scientists for ever greater clarity about the universe, the beautiful complexities of pure mathematics, the jeweler's-eye precision of the logician? Or is wisdom something deeper, more universal?

The readings in this section examine the question of wisdom from many perspectives. It may be helpful to keep in mind that the word *wise* suggests a different human quality from the intellectual connotations of words like *brilliant* or *smart*. As Aristotle tells us, a young man can be a brilliant metaphysician or mathematician, and yet lack enough experience of the world to be wise in civic affairs, family relations, and ethical behavior. Wisdom—as opposed to braininess or brilliance—suggests character tested and tempered by time, challenged by adversity and fortified by the earned insights of experience. The best recipe for happiness, Aristotle concludes, involves a balance of contemplative and active virtues—a teaching that weaves a golden thread throughout every period of reflection on the meaning of manliness.

It is this broader kind of wisdom that we explore in this section: what it means to be wise in the affairs of one's fellow citizens, but also what it means for a man to embark on an *inner* journey of self-awareness and spiritual evolution, reflecting on life's hardships and disappointments, reversals and rewards.

It was Cato who observed that wise men learn more from fools than fools do from wise men, for wise men can avoid the errors of fools while fools rarely profit from the examples of the wise. This sharp distinction between the wise and the foolish does not sit well with our democratic instincts, but it is often amply justified by everyday experience. Men we know to be wise learn from every source available in life: from their elders, from their peers, from family and loved ones—above all, they learn by example. A wise man is cautious and deliberate, reserving judgment and taking nothing for granted. Among his qualities are a commitment to open-mindedness and an ability to look beyond the conventional wisdom of the status quo. As Thoreau put it, "The wisest man preaches no doctrines, he has no scheme, he sees no rafter, not even a cobweb, against the heavens. It is clear sky." Wisdom has more to do with an appetite to learn than with a blind faith in one's own judgment; the wise man never mistakes his opinion for a fixed and unalterable truth. In this sense, wisdom is intrinsically connected with intellectual modesty. As Thomas Jefferson wrote (echoing Socrates), a wise man is the best expert on his own weaknesses and failings, for he recognizes how little he truly knows.

THE WISE MAN OF AFFAIRS

Where Do You Shop for Wisdom?

From Diogenes Laertius,
Lives of the Philosophers

Xenophon, son of Gryllus, was an Athenian citizen and belonged to the deme Erchia. He was an extremely handsome man, yet possessed an unusual modesty. There is a story that once Socrates on meeting him in a narrow passage stretched out his stick, barring his way, and asked him where different kinds of food might be bought. When Xenophon answered, Socrates asked another question, "And where do men become good and honorable?" Xenophon was too puzzled to reply. "Then follow me," said Socrates, "and learn." Thence forward Xenophon was a pupil of Socrates.

My Son, Be Admonished!

From Ecclesiastes (11:9–12; 12)

Rejoice, O young man, in thy youth; and let thy heart cheer thee in the days of thy youth, and walk in the ways of thine heart, and in the sight of thine eyes: but know thou, that for all these things God will bring thee into judgment. Therefore remove sorrow from thy heart, and put away evil from thy flesh: for youth and the prime of life are vanity. Remember also thy Creator in the days of thy youth, or ever the evil days come, and the years draw nigh, when thou shalt say, I have no pleasure in them; or ever the sun, and the light, and the moon, and the stars, be darkened, and the clouds return after the rain: in the day when the keepers of the house shall tremble, and the strong men shall bow themselves, and the grinders cease because they are few, and those that look out of the windows be darkened, and the doors shall be shut in the street; when the sound of the grinding is low, and one shall rise up at the voice of a bird, and all the daughters of music shall be brought low; yea, they shall be afraid of *that which is high,* and terrors *shall be* in the way; and the almond tree shall blossom, and the grasshopper shall be a burden, and the caper-berry shall fail: because man goeth to his long home, and the mourners go about the streets: or ever the silver cord be loosed, or the golden bowl be broken, or the Pitcher be broken at the fountain, or the wheel broken at the cistern; and the dust return to the earth as it was, and the spirit return unto God who gave it. Vanity of vanities, saith the Preacher; all is vanity.

And furthermore, my son, be admonished: of making many books there is no end; and much study is a weariness of the flesh. *This is* the end of the matter; all hath been heard: fear God, and keep his commandments; for this is the whole *duty* of man. For God shall bring every work into judgment, with every hidden thing, whether it be good or whether it be evil.

How Should a Young Man Live?

From Plato, The Republic

How should a young man live? Should he devote himself to justice, modera-
tion and the other virtues? Or should he get all the pleasures he can out of
life—limitless sex, wealth, power, and glory? In Plato's Republic, *we see*
two promising young men, Glaucon and Adeimantos—the brothers of
Plato—wrestling with this dilemma, as common to teenagers then as it is
now. According to Glaucon, some influential thinkers argue that justice is
only an artificial convention to protect the weak from the strong. By con-
trast, exploiting and taking advantage of others is the natural way for a
man to live if he has the brains and guts to get away with it. The proof: Give
any so-called law-abiding citizen a magic ring that would make him invisi-
ble, and he would immediately begin living "naturally" by plundering and
ravishing everyone in sight. If people weren't afraid of being caught for
breaking the law, in other words, everyone would do it. Glaucon challenges
Socrates: Prove that justice really is a happier life than a life of tyrannical
pleasure, not just something we do because we're slaves of convention.

"I am perplexed when I hear the voices of Thrasymachus and
myriads of others dinning in my ears; and, on the other hand, I
have never yet heard the superiority of justice to injustice maintained by anyone in a satisfactory way. I want to hear justice praised
in respect of itself; then I shall be satisfied, and you are the person
from whom I think that I am most likely to hear this; and therefore
I will praise the unjust life to the utmost of my power, and my manner of speaking will indicate the manner in which I desire to hear
you too praising justice and censuring injustice. Will you say
whether you approve of my proposal?"

"Indeed I do; nor can I imagine any theme about which a man
of sense would oftener wish to converse."

"I am delighted," he replied, "to hear you say so, and shall begin
by speaking, as I proposed, of the nature and origin of justice.

"They say that to do injustice is, by nature, good; to suffer
injustice, evil; but that the evil is greater than the good. And so
when men have both done and suffered injustice and have had
experience of both, not being able to avoid the one and obtain the

other, they think that they had better agree among themselves to have neither; hence there arise laws and mutual covenants; and that which is ordained by law is termed by them lawful and just. This they affirm to be the origin and nature of justice; it is a mean or compromise between the best of all, which is to do injustice and not be punished, and worst of all, which is to suffer injustice without the power of retaliation; and justice being at a middle point between the two, is tolerated not as a good, but as the lesser evil, and honored by reason of the inability of men to do injustice. For no man who is worthy to be called a man would ever submit to such an agreement if he were able to resist; he would be mad if he did. Such is the received account, Socrates, of the nature and origin of justice.

"Now that those who practice justice do so involuntarily and because they have not the power to be unjust will best appear if we imagine something of this kind: having given both to the just and the unjust power to do what they will, let us watch and see whither desire will lead them; then we shall discover in the very act the just and unjust man to be proceeding along the same road, following their interest, which all natures deem to be their good, and are only diverted into the path of justice by the force of law. The liberty which we are supposing may be most completely given to them in the form of such a power as is said to have been possessed by Gyges the ancestor of Croesus the Lydian. According to the tradition, Gyges was a shepherd in the service of the king of Lydia; there was a great storm, and an earthquake made an opening in the earth at the place where he was feeding his flock. Amazed at the sight, he descended into the opening, where, among other marvels, he beheld a hollow brazen horse, having doors, at which he stooping and looking in saw a dead body of stature, as appeared to him, more than human, and having nothing on but a gold ring; this he took from the finger of the dead and reascended. Now the shepherds met together, according to custom, that they might send their monthly report about the flocks to the king; into their assembly he came having the ring on his finger, and as he was sitting among them he chanced to turn the collet of the ring inside his hand, when instantly he became invisible to the rest of the company and they began to speak of him as if he were no longer present. He was astonished at this, and again touching the ring he turned the collet outward and reappeared; he made several trials of the ring, and always with the same result–when he turned the collet inward he became invisible, when outward he reappeared. Where-

upon he contrived to be chosen one of the messengers who were
sent to the court; where as soon as he arrived he seduced the
queen, and with her help conspired against the king and slew him,
and took the kingdom. Suppose now that there were two such
magic rings, and the just put on one of them and the unjust the
other; no man can be imagined to be of such an iron nature that
he would stand fast in justice. No man would keep his hands off
what was not his own when he could safely take what he liked out of
the market, or go into houses and lie with anyone at his pleasure,
or kill or release from prison whom he would, and in all respects be
like a God among men. Then the actions of the just would be as the
actions of the unjust; they would both come at last to the same
point. And this we may truly affirm to be a great proof that a man is
just, not willingly or because he thinks that justice is any good to
him individually, but of necessity, for whenever anyone thinks that
he can safely be unjust, then he is unjust. For all men believe in
their hearts that injustice is far more profitable to the individual
than justice, and if a man argues as I have been supposing, he will
say that they are right. If you could imagine anyone obtaining this
power of becoming invisible, and never doing any wrong or touching what was another's, he would be thought by the lookers-on to
be a most wretched idiot, although they would praise him to one
another's faces, and keep up appearances with one another from a
fear that they too might suffer injustice. Enough of this.

"Now, if we are to form a real judgment of the life of the just
and unjust, we must isolate them; there is no other way; and how is
the isolation to be effected? I answer: Let the unjust man be
entirely unjust and the just man entirely just; nothing is to be taken
away from either of them, and both are to be perfectly furnished
for the work of their respective lives. First, let the unjust be like
other distinguished masters of craft; like the skillful pilot or physician, who knows intuitively his own powers and keeps within their
limits, and who, if he fails at any point, is able to recover himself. So
let the unjust make his unjust attempts in the right way, and lie hidden if he means to be great in his injustice (he who is found out is
nobody): for the highest reach of injustice is: to be deemed just
when you are not. Therefore I say that in the perfectly unjust man
we must assume the most perfect injustice; there is to be no deduc-
tion, but we must allow him while doing the most unjust acts, to
have acquired the greatest reputation for justice. If he has taken a
false step he must be able to recover himself; he must be one who
can speak with effect, if any of his deeds come to light, and who can

force his way where force is required by his courage and strength, and command of money and friends. And at his side let us place the just man in his nobleness and simplicity, wishing, as Aeschylus says, to be and not to seem good. There must be no seeming, for if he seem to be just he will be honored and rewarded, and then we shall not know whether he is just for the sake of justice or for the sake of honors and rewards; therefore, let him be clothed in justice only, and have no other covering; and he must be imagined in a state of life the opposite of the former. Let him be the best of men, and let him be thought the worst; then he will have been put to the proof; and we shall see whether he will be affected by the fear of infamy and its consequences. And let him continue thus to the hour of death; being just and seeming to be unjust. When both have reached the uttermost extreme, the one of justice and the other of injustice, let judgment be given which of them is the happier of the two."

"Heavens! My dear Glaucon," I said, "how energetically you polish them up for the decision, first one and then the other, as if they were two statues."

"I do my best," he said. "And now that we know what they are like there is no difficulty in tracing out the sort of life which awaits either of them. This I will proceed to describe; but as you may think the description a little too coarse, I ask you to suppose, Socrates, that the words which follow are not mine. Let me put them into the mouths of the eulogists of injustice: They will tell you that the just man who is thought unjust will be scourged, racked, bound—will have his eyes burned out; and, at last, after suffering every kind of evil, he will be impaled: Then he will understand that he ought to seem only, and not to be, just; the words of Aeschylus may be more truly spoken of the unjust than of the just. For the unjust is pursuing a reality; he does not live with a view to appearances—he wants to be really unjust and not seem only:

'His mind has a soil deep and fertile,
Out of which spring his prudent counsels.'

"In the first place, he is thought just, and therefore rules in the city; he can marry whom he will, and give in marriage to whom he will; also he can trade and deal where he likes, and always to his own advantage, because he has no misgivings about injustice; and at every contest, whether in public or private, he gets the better of his antagonists, and gains at their expense, and is rich, and out of

his gains he can benefit his friends, and harm his enemies; moreover, he can offer sacrifices, and dedicate gifts to the gods abundantly and magnificently, and can honor the gods or any man
whom he wants to honor in a far better style than the just, and
therefore he is likely to be dearer than they are to the gods. And
thus, Socrates, gods and men are said to unite in making the life of
the unjust better than the life of the just."

Daedalus and Icarus

From Thomas Bulfinch,
Bulfinch's Mythology

*The ancient legend of Daedalus and his son Icarus, who flew too high.
Scientific and technical knowledge can bring great rewards, but unless governed by moderation, they can also bring destruction.*

The labyrinth from which Theseus escaped by means of the
clew of Ariadne was built by Daedalus, a most skillful artificer. It was
an edifice with numberless winding passages and turnings opening
into one another, and seeming to have neither beginning nor end,
like the River Maeander, which returns on itself, and flows now
onward, now backward, in its course to the sea. Daedalus built the
labyrinth for King Minos, but afterward lost the favor of the king,
and was shut up in a tower. He contrived to make his escape from
his prison, but could not leave the island by sea, as the king kept
strict watch on all the vessels, and permitted none to sail without
being carefully searched. "Minos may control the land and sea,"
said Daedalus, "but not the regions of the air. I will try that way." So
he set to work to fabricate wings for himself and his young son
Icarus. He wrought feathers together, beginning with the smallest
and adding larger, so as to form an increasing surface. The larger
ones he secured with thread and the smaller with wax, and gave the
whole a gentle curvature like the wings of a bird. Icarus, the boy,
stood and looked on, sometimes running to gather up the feathers
which the wind had blown away, and then handling the wax and
working it over with his fingers, by his play impeding his father in
his labors. When at last the work was done, the artist, waving his

wings, found himself buoyed upward, and hung suspended, poising himself on the beaten air. He next equipped his son in the same manner and taught him how to fly, as a bird tempts her young ones from the lofty nest into the air. When all was prepared for flight he said, "Icarus, my son, I charge you to keep at a moderate height, for if you fly too low the damp will clog your wings, and if too high the heat will melt them. Keep near me and you will be safe." While he gave him these instructions and fitted the wings to his shoulders, the face of the father was wet with tears, and his hands trembled. He kissed the boy, not knowing that it was for the last time. Then rising on his wings, he flew off, encouraging him to follow, and looked back from his own flight to see how his son managed his wings. As they flew the ploughman stopped his work to gaze, and the shepherd leaned on his staff and watched them, astonished at the sight, and thinking they were gods who could thus cleave the air.

They passed Samos and Delos on the left and Lebynthos on the right, when the boy, exulting in his career, began to leave the guidance of his companion and soar upward as if to reach heaven. The nearness of the blazing sun softened the wax which held the feathers together, and they came off. He fluttered with his arms, but no feathers remained to hold the air. While his mouth uttered cries to his father, it was submerged in the blue waters of the sea, which henceforth was called by his name. His father cried, "Icarus, Icarus, where are you?" At last he saw the feathers floating on the water, and bitterly lamenting his own arts, he buried the body and called the land Icaria in memory of his child. Daedalus arrived safe in Sicily, where he built a temple to Apollo, and hung up his wings, an offering to the god.

The Man of Discipline

From The Bhagavad-Gita

In this great Hindu poem of the first century A.D. *King Arjuna, about to lead his army into battle, despairs of finding a reason to perform his earthly duties when religion teaches us to flee the world for a higher realm of perfec-*

tion. Although most of this anthology is from Western sources, there are equally rich traditions of manly virtue in non-Western civilizations.

Why go to war or govern if the world of mortals is an illusion? The great god Krishna suspends time on the eve of the battle as Arjuna is paralyzed by these doubts. There must be a balance, Lord Krishna teaches, between our duties in life and the perfection of our inner selves through renouncing worldly ambition and willfulness.

Doing our duty without regard for the rewards both helps us to shed our worldly selves and to fulfill our worldly duties.

Krishna:
Therefore, whoever does work rightful to do,
Not seeking gain from work, that man, O Prince!
Is Renouncer and man of holy discipline—both in one.
And he is neither who does not light the flame
Of sacrifice, nor sets his hands to work.

Regard as a true Renouncer he who makes
Worship by work, for he who renounces not,
Works not with Holy Discipline. So it is well said:
"By works the votary rises to faith,
And sainthood is the ceasing from all works;"
Because the perfect self-disciplined worker acts—but acts
Unmoved by passions and unbound by deeds,
Setting result aside.

Let each man raise
Himself by Soul, but not by trampling down his Self,
For Soul, which is Self's friend, can become Self's enemy.
Soul is Self's friend when Self controls itself,
But Self becomes Soul's enemy if Soul's own Self
Hates Self as not part of itself.

The sovereign soul
Of he who lives self-governed and at peace
Is centered in itself, impartial alike to
Pleasure and pain; heat and cold; glory and shame.
He is a man of holy discipline, glad
With joy of light and truth; dwelling apart
Upon a peak, with senses subjugated.
To him a clod of earth, a rock, and glistening gold

Show all as one. By this sign he is known:
Being of equal grace to comrades, friends,
Chance-comers, strangers, lovers, enemies,
Aliens and kinsmen; loving all alike,
Evil or good.

Sequestered, he should sit,
Steadfastly meditating, solitary,
His thoughts controlled, his passions put away,
Rid of possessions. Let him abide
In a fair, still spot—not too much raised,
Nor yet too low—His goods:
A cloth, a deerskin, and the grass.
There, focusing his mind upon The One,
Restraining heart and senses, silent and calm,
Let him accomplish self-discipline and achieve
Pureness of soul, holding immovable
Body and neck and head, his gaze absorbed
Upon the tip of his nose, oblivious to all around him,
Tranquil in spirit, free of fear, intent
Upon his vow of chastity, devout,
Musing on Me, lost in the thought of Me.
That man of self-discipline, so devoted, so controlled,
Comes to the peace beyond,—My peace, the peace
Of high Nirvana!

But for earthly needs,
Piety is not his who fasts too much
Or feasts too much, nor his who sleeps away
An idle mind; nor his who wears himself down,
Wasting his strength in vigils. Nay! Arjuna! Call
That the true piety which most removes
Earthly aches and ills, where one is moderate
In eating and in resting, and in sport;
Moderate in wish and in act; sleeping early,
Waking early for duty.

When a man,
So living, centers on his soul, his thought
Tightly restrained—untouched within
By stress of sense—then he achieves true discipline. See!
Like an unwavering lamp which burns sheltered from the wind;

Such is the steadiness of the disciplined mind
Freed from the storms of sense and burning bright to Heaven.
When mind broods calmly, soothed with holy discipline;
When Self contemplates Self, and in itself
Has comfort; when it knows the nameless joy
Beyond all scope of sense, revealed to soul—
Only to soul! and, knowing, wavers not,
True to the farther Truth; when, holding this,
It deems no other treasure comparable,
But, harbored there, cannot be stirred or shook
By any gravest grief, call that state "peace,"
That happy severance from suffering; call that man
The perfect man of self-discipline.

Steadfastly the will
Must toil thereto, until its efforts end in ease,
And thought has passed from thinking. Shaking off
All longings bred by dreams of fame and gain,
Shutting the doorways of the senses, closed
With watchful guard; so, step by step, he comes
To the gift of peace assured and heart calmed,
When the mind dwells self-wrapped, and the soul broods
Unencumbered. But as often as the heart
Breaks—wild and wavering—from control, so often
Let him re-curb it, let him rein it back in
To the soul's mastery; for perfect bliss
Grows only in the bosom tranquillized,
The spirit passionless, purged from offence,
Vowed to the Infinite. He who thus vows
His soul to the Supreme Soul, quitting sin,
Passes unhindered to the endless bliss
Of unity with Brahma. He so vowed,
So blended, sees the Life-Soul resident
In all things living, and all living things
In that Life-Soul contained. And whoever thus
Discerns Me in all, and all in Me,
I never let him go; nor does he loosen his
Hold upon Me; but, dwell he where he may,
Whatever his life, in Me he dwells and lives,
Because he knows and worships Me, I who dwell
In all which lives, and cleaves to me in all.
Arjuna! If a man sees everywhere—

Taught by his own similitude to all—one Life
One Essence in the Evil and the Good,
Behold in him a man of holy discipline, yes! well perfected!

The Value of Study

From Francis Bacon, Essays

Studies serve for delight, for ornament, and for ability. Their chief use for delight, is in privateness and retiring; for ornament, is in discourse; and for ability, is in the judgment and disposition of business. For expert men can execute, and perhaps judge of particulars, one by one; but the general counsels, and the plots and marshaling of affairs, come best, from those that are learned. To spend too much time in studies is sloth; to use them too much for ornament, is affectation; to make judgment wholly by their rules, is the humor of a scholar. They perfect nature, and are perfected by experience: for natural abilities are like natural plants, that need pruning, by study; and studies themselves, do give forth directions too much at large, except they be bounded in by experience. Crafty men condemn studies, simple men admire them, and wise men use them; for they teach not their own use; but that is a wisdom without them, and above them, won by observation. Read not to contradict and confute; nor to believe and take for granted; nor to find talk and discourse; but to weigh and consider. Some books are to be tasted, others to be swallowed, and some few to be chewed and digested; that is, some books are to be read only in parts; others to be read, but not curiously; and some few to be read wholly, and with diligence and attention. Reading maketh a full man; conference a ready man; and writing an exact man. And therefore, if a man write little, he had need have a great memory; if he confer little, he had need have a present wit: and if he read little, he had need have much cunning, to seem to know, that he doth not.

Why a Man Must Be Liberally Educated If He Is to Gain Eternal Fame

From Baldesar Castiglione, The Book of the Courtier

"And if I were speaking with them, or with others who had an opinion contrary to mine, I should strive to show them how useful and necessary letters are to our life and dignity, having indeed been granted by God to men as a crowning gift. Nor should I lack instances of many excellent commanders of antiquity, who all added the ornament of letters to the valour of their arms.

"Thus you know Alexander held Homer in such veneration that he always kept the Iliad by his bedside; and he devoted the greatest attention not only to these studies but to philosophical speculation under Aristotle's guidance. Alcibiades enlarged his natural aptitudes and made them greater by means of letters and the teachings of Socrates. The care that Caesar gave to study is also attested by the surviving works that he divinely wrote. It is said that Scipio Africanus always kept in his hand the works of Xenophon, wherein the perfect king is portrayed under the name of Cyrus. I could tell you of Lucullus, Sulla, Pompey, Brutus, and many other Romans and Greeks; but I will merely remind you that Hannibal, the illustrious commander,—although fierce by nature and a stranger to all humanity, faithless and a despiser of both men and gods,—yet had knowledge of letters and was conversant with the Greek language; and if I mistake not, I once read that he even left a book composed by him in Greek.

"However it is superfluous to tell you this, for I well know that you all see how wrong the French are in thinking that letters are injurious to arms. You know that glory is the true stimulus to great and hazardous deeds of war, and whoso is moved thereto by gain or other motive, besides doing nothing good, deserves not to be called a gentleman, but a base trafficker. And true glory is that which is preserved in the sacred treasure-house of letters, as everyone may understand except those unfortunates who have never enjoyed them.

"What soul is there so abject, timid and humble, that when he reads the deeds of Caesar, Alexander, Scipio, Hannibal, and many others, is not inflamed by an ardent desire to be like them, and does not make small account of this frail two days' life, in order to win the almost eternal life of fame, which in spite of death makes him live in far greater glory than before? But he who does not feel the delight of letters, cannot either know how great is the glory they so long preserve, and measures it by the life of one man or two, because his memory runs no further. Hence he cannot esteem this short-lived glory so much as he would that almost eternal glory if knowledge of it were unhappily not denied him, and as he does not esteem it so much, we may reasonably believe that he will not run such danger to pursue it as one who knew it would."

Men's Happiness or Misery Is Mostly of Their Own Making

From John Locke, Some Thoughts Concerning Education

A sound mind in a sound body is a short but full description of a happy state in this world. He that has these two has little more to wish for, and he that wants either of them will be but little the better for anything else. Men's happiness or misery is most part of their own making. He whose mind directs not wisely will never take the right away, and he whose body is crazy and feeble will never be able to advance in it. I confess there are some men's constitutions of body and mind so vigorous and well framed by nature that they need not much assistance from others, but by the strength of their natural genius, they are from their cradles carried toward what is excellent; and by the privilege of their happy constitutions, are able to do wonders. But examples of this kind are but few, and I think I may say, that of all the men we meet with, nine parts of ten are what they are, good or evil, useful or not, by their education. It is that which makes the great difference in mankind. The little or almost insensible impressions on our tender infancies have very important and lasting consequences. And there it is, as in the fountains of some rivers, where a gentle application of the hand turns the flexible waters into channels, that make them take quite contrary courses; and by this little direction, given them at first in the source, they receive different tendencies, and arrive at last at very remote and distant places.

The great work of a governor is to fashion the carriage, and form the mind; to settle in his pupil good habits, and the principles of virtue and wisdom; to give him by little and little a view of mankind, and work him into a love and imitation of what is excellent and praiseworthy; and in the prosecution of it, to give him vigor, activity, and industry. The studies which he sets him upon are but as it were the exercises of his faculties and employment of his time, to keep him from sauntering and idleness, to teach him application, and accustom him to take pains, and to give him some little taste of what his own industry must perfect.

The Contemplative Man
and the Active Man

From Aristotle,
The Nicomachean Ethics

The best recipe for happiness, Aristotle concludes in the Nicomachean Ethics, *is the right balance of active and contemplative virtues—contemplation is nobler, but the life of an active citizen can achieve happiness in its own right. With this hierarchy of virtues, Aristotle crystallizes a teaching that weaves throughout every period of reflection on the meaning of manliness, stretching through medieval chivalry and the Renaissance gentleman down to the present.*

Of all human things, habitual energies of virtue are the most stable; they are more permanent than even the sciences; and of the virtues themselves, the most valuable are the firmest; forming the continual meditation and delight of those whom they adorn. For this reason, they alone are not liable to be forgotten or lost; but are an immovable property in the thoughts and life of a good man; who, whatever may befall him, will behave gracefully; approving his conduct exact, square, and blameless. Slight misfortunes are unable to shake his well-balanced happiness; but, in the use of a great prosperity, his excellence will shine more conspicuous: and when persecuted by painful and afflicting calamity, which not only impedes his present exertions but darkens his future prospects, his worth will irradiate the gloom, while he resists and surmounts the severest sufferings, not by stupid insensibility, but by generous magnanimity; for, if our own actions be the sovereign arbiters of our lot, a virtuous man can never be wretched; because he will never render himself an object either of hatred or contempt. Of the circumstances in which he is placed, he will always make the best and most honorable use; as a good general, and a good artist, employs the forces, and the materials, with which they are respectively entrusted, always to the best advantage. A happiness, founded on such a basis, can never sink into misery; although it must be shaken by tragic misfortunes, from which it will not soon recover its natural state. Yet, in consequence of virtuous exertions, continued through a sufficient length of time, a good man, competently furnished with the accommodations of life, will resume his wonted serenity; and may be pronounced happy, notwithstanding the vicissitudes to which he is still exposed; at least possessed of such happiness as is consistent with the condition of humanity.

Happiness, then, cannot consist in mere recreative pastime; for it is absurd to think that all our serious exertions and strenuous labors should terminate in so frivolous an end. We do not labor that we may be idle; but, as Anarchis justly said, we are idle that we may labor with more effect; that is, we have recourse to sports and amusements as refreshing cordials after contentious exertions, that, having reposed in such diversions for a while, we may recommence our labors with increased vigor. The weakness of human nature requires frequent remissions of energy; but these rests and pauses are only the better to prepare us for enjoying the pleasures of activity. The amusements of life, therefore, are but preludes to its business, the place of which they cannot possibly supply; and its happiness, because its business, consists in the exercise of those virtuous energies which constitute the worth and dignity of our nature. Inferior pleasures may be enjoyed by the fool and the slave as completely as by the hero or the sage. But who will ascribe the happiness of a man to him, who by his character and condition, is disqualified for manly pursuits?

If happiness consists in virtuous energies, the greatest human happiness must consist in the exercise of the greatest virtue in man, which must be the virtue or perfection of his best part, whether this be intellect, or whatever principle it be, that is destined to command and bear sway; having knowledge of things beautiful and divine, as being either divine itself, or at least that principle in us which most approximates to divinity. The greatest human happiness, then, is theoretic and intellectual, which well accords with the properties which we formerly found, by investigation, to be essentially inherent in that most coveted object. The intellect is the best principle in man; its energies are the strongest, and the objects about which it is conversant are far the most sublime. The energies of intellect are also the longest and most continuous, since we can persevere in theorizing and thinking much longer than in performing any action whatever. Pleasure, it was observed, must be an ingredient in happiness; but contemplative wisdom offers pleasures the most admirable in purity and stability, and the pleasures of knowledge continually increase in proportion to our improvement in it; certainty concerning the sublimest truths affording still higher delight in proportion to the intense efforts of intellect by which they were discovered. That all-sufficiency, which we remarked as a property of happiness, belongs to intellectual energies more than to any other; for though the sage, as well as the moralist or the patriot, stands in need of bodily accommodations, yet in exerting his highest excellencies he is not like them dependent on fortune, both for his objects and his instruments; for objects towards whom he may exercise his virtues, and instruments which may enable him to effectuate his ends. Even unassisted and alone, though perhaps better with assistants, he can still think and theorize, possessing in the energies of his own mind the purest and most independent enjoyments. These enjoyments are valuable peculiarly on their own account, since they terminate completely in themselves; whereas all practical virtue has, beside the practice itself, some distinct and separate end in view. The tranquillity of leisure is naturally more agreeable than the bustle of business; we toil for the sake of quiet, and make war for the sake of peace.

The Dream of Scipio

From Cicero, On the Commonwealth

Cicero's On the Commonwealth *beautifully expresses the classical ideal of manliness. The Roman statesman and general Scipio Africanus the Younger is a brilliant success in public life, but reserves his greatest respect for the life of learning. In his formulation, to be a man is not only to be vigorous in service of the common good, but to be refined, gracious, and learned, familiar with the sublime beauties of art, music, and philosophy. In the magnificent Dream of Scipio, the noble Roman is given a vision of the afterlife in which eternal celestial bliss is the reward of serving one's country, parents, and kindred here on earth.*

Maurus Tullius Cicero (106–43 B.C.) was one of the greatest men of the Roman Republic. As a statesman, he defended constitutional government against the despotic ambitions of Julius Caesar. His philosophical and oratorical writings are among the most influential in European history.

After my arrival in Africa—where, as you know, I served under Manius Manilius as military tribune of the fourth legion—my first desire was to meet King Masinissa, who, for very good reasons, was a close friend of our family. When I met him, the aged prince embraced me and burst into tears. After a brief space he looked up into the sky and said: "To thee, O mighty Sun, and to you, ye other dwellers in heaven, I give thanks because, ere I depart this life, I behold in my kingdom and within this palace Publius Cornelius Scipio whose very name gives me new life. So constantly does my heart muse on the memory of his grandfather, that excellent man and invincible general." Then I questioned him about his kingdom, and he asked me about the condition of our commonwealth; and we spent the day together in lengthy conversation.

I was then entertained with princely splendor, and we prolonged our discussion late into the night. For the venerable man spoke of nothing except Africanus, and recalled not only all that he had done but even all that he had said. I was exhausted both by my journey and by the lateness of the hour. Accordingly, when we separated to retire, a deeper sleep than usual took me in its embrace. What ensued had its origin, I suppose, in the matter of our conver-

sation. For quite regularly the subjects of our thought and discourse suggest our dreams, as Ennius writes that he dreamed of
Homer, who no doubt was frequently the theme of his waking
thought and conversation. Thus it happened that Africanus
appeared to me, in a form which was more familiar from his death
mask than from the man himself. When I recognized him, I confess
that I was stricken with fear. But he said, "Be calm, Scipio; banish
your fears, and inscribe my words in your memory."

"Do you see that city?" From a lofty station, bright and glittering and filled with stars, he pointed out Carthage. "Do you see that
city which I forced to obey the Roman people, but which now
begins anew those ancient wars and cannot be at peace? Although
you who now come to besiege it are as yet hardly a soldier, in three
years you will be consul and will overthrow it, and the cognomen
which now you inherit from me you will then have won for yourself
by your own achievements. After you have destroyed Carthage, celebrated your triumph, been censor, and traveled on an embassy
through Egypt, Syria, Asia and Greece, a second time you will be
chosen consul, though absent from Rome, and by destroying
Numanthia you will bring to a close Rome's greatest war. But when
you have been borne to the Capitol in your triumphal chariot, you
will find the commonwealth thrown into utter confusion by the
designs of my grandson."

"Then, Africanus, you must show to your country the light of
your courage, your character, and your wisdom. But I see, as it
were, the course of your destiny then becoming uncertain. For
when your life has passed through eight times seven yearly revolutions of the sun, and when these two numbers, seven and eight—
each of which is considered perfect for a special reason—have by
their natural cycle completed the span allotted you by destiny, then
to you alone, because of your renown, the whole state will turn. On
you the senate, all patriotic citizens, the allies, and the Latins will
fix their eyes. On you alone the safety of the state will rest. In a
word, you must be dictator and must set the state in order—if only
you escape the godless hands of your kindred."

At an exclamation from Laelius and at the deeper groans of the
others, Scipio gently smiled. "Hush," said he, "pray, do not break my
slumber. Hear yet a little longer what remains for me to tell."

"Yet Africanus, that you may be more zealous in guarding your
country, be assured of this: All men who have saved or benefited
their native land, or have enhanced its power, are assigned an especial place in heaven where they may enjoy a life of eternal bliss. For

the supreme god who rules the entire universe finds nothing, at least among earthly objects, more pleasing than the societies and groups of men, united by law and right, which are called states. The rulers and saviors of states set forth from that place and to that place return."

At these words I was greatly frightened, less by fear of death than by the thought of treachery at the hands of my kindred. Nevertheless, I asked Africanus whether he and my father Paulus and the others whom we supposed dead were still living. "In truth, he replied, "only those are alive who have escaped the bondage of the flesh as from a prison, while that which you call life is in reality death. Do you not behold your father Paulus coming toward you?" When I saw him, I poured forth a flood of tears, but Paulus embraced me and bade me not to weep.

As soon as I mastered my tears and regained the power of speech, I said, "O father most excellent and holy, since true life is here, as Africanus tells me, why, I ask you, do I linger upon earth? Why may I not hasten to come to you?" "That may not be," he replied, "for, until God, to whom belongs this whole world before your eyes, shall free you from the body's prison, you may not enter this place. For the human race was born subject to the condition that they should guard the sphere which you see in the center of the heavens and which is called earth. To them souls were given, drawn from those eternal fires which you name constellations and stars. These heavenly bodies are round like spheres. They are quickened by divine intelligences and complete their cycles and rotations with wonderful swiftness. For this reason, Publius, you and all loyal men must retain the soul in its fleshly prison, and unless he who has bestowed the soul upon you so commands, you must not abandon human life, lest you seem to have deserted the earthly tasks imposed by God.

"But even as your grandfather here before you, even as I who begot you, so do you, Scipio, cultivate justice and loyalty, which is a noble spirit when shown toward parents and kindred, but noblest when shown toward your country. Such a life is the way to heaven and to the company of those whose life on earth is done and who released from the body, inhabit the region which you behold, and which, after the Greeks, you name the Milky Way."

The place was a glittering circle that shone with exceeding brilliance in the midst of fiery stars. As I gazed down from it all other objects seemed dazzling and wonderful. There were stars which we have never seen from this earth of ours, and all of them had magnitudes such as we have never supposed to exist. The smallest of them was situated most remote from the heaven (of the fixed stars) and nearest to the earth, and shone with borrowed light. Moreover, the stars appeared so small that I felt ashamed of our empire, by which we cover a point, as it were, upon its surface.

Since I was observing the earth more intently than aught else, Africanus said, "How long, I ask you, will your thoughts be fixed upon the earth? Do you not perceive the heavenly spaces into which you have come? The universe is formed of nine circles or spheres, as we should more properly call them. One of these is the heaven (of the fixed stars); it is on the exterior of the universe, embracing all the other orbs, and is the supreme god himself who constrains and includes the remaining spheres. In it are placed the eternal courses of the rolling stars. Beneath this outer circle are the seven orbs which revolve in a direction opposite to that of the heavens. The outermost of these spheres belongs to the planet which men on earth call Saturn. The next is the luminary called Jupiter, benign and propitious to the human race, and next the ruddy star, feared by earth, which you call Mars. Below Mars comes the sun, which holds almost the mid-region (between the earth and the heavens) and is the leader, chief, and director of the other stars, and the mind which keeps the universe in balance. Such is his greatness that he encompasses and fills the whole world with his light. In the sun's train, like comrades, follow the spheres of Venus and Mercury. The lowest globe carries the moon, which is kindled by the rays of the sun. All below the moon is mortal and transitory, except the souls which the gods have bestowed on man, while all above the moon is immortal. The earth, which occupies the ninth position, is the center of the universe. It does not move, it is the lowest of the spheres, and all heavy bodies are swept to it by gravity."

When I recovered from the astonishment with which I was gazing upon this spectacle, I asked, "What is this mighty yet delightful sound which fills my ears?" "That," he replied, "is the melody produced by the swift movement of the spheres themselves."

Though I was filled with awe at the celestial harmonies, I kept turning my eyes constantly toward the earth. "I see," said Africanus, "that you still contemplate the abode and home of man. If the earth appears insignificant to you—as indeed it is—ever lift up your eyes to these heavenly realms and despise the concerns of men. For what fame can you win among men or what renown worthy of your striving?"

"If, then, you give up the hope of returning to this place where all blessings await great and distinguished men, how puerile is the renown conferred by man, lasting as it does for only a small portion of a single year! But if you wish to look on high and to contemplate this abode and eternal home, you will not yield to the flattery of the rabble or set your hopes upon the rewards that men may give. Excellence itself, by its own inherent charm, must draw you toward true glory. What others say about you must be their concern; nothing will prevent their talking. All that they may say, however, is confined to the narrow limits you perceive; it is never lasting in the case of any man, but is obscured when men die and is blotted out when posterity forgets."

After he had spoken thus, I answered: "Since, Africanus, there is, as it were, a path which leads to heaven and which lies open to men who have earned their country's gratitude, I shall strive for so glorious a reward even more earnestly than I have. And yet from boyhood I have followed in my father's footsteps and in yours and have not tarnished your glory." "Strive earnestly," he replied, "and be assured that only this body of yours, and not your real self, is mortal. For you are not the mere physical form that you appear to be; but the real man is the soul and not that physical body which men can point to. Know, then, that your true nature is divine, if indeed it is a divine principle which lives, feels, remembers, and foresees, and which rules, guides, and activates the body beneath its sway, even as the supreme god directs the universe. And as the world, which is in part mortal, is stirred to motion by God Himself, who lives forever, so the frail body is quickened by an immortal soul.

"Now the noblest concerns of the soul have to do with the security of your country, and the soul which is employed and disciplined in such pursuits will fly more speedily to this abode, its natural home. This journey it will make the swifter, if it looks abroad, while still imprisoned in the flesh, and if, by meditating upon that which lies beyond it, it divorces itself as far as may be from the body. For the souls of men who have surrendered themselves to carnal delights, who have made themselves as it were slaves of the passions, and who have been prompted by lust to violate the laws of gods and men, wander about near the earth itself, after their escape from the body, and do not return hither until they have been driven about for many ages."

He departed; I awoke from sleep.

A Man of Principles

From John Locke, Of Principles

It is not unusual to see men rest their opinions upon foundations that have no more certainty nor solidity than the propositions built on them, and embraced for their sake. Such foundations are these, and the like, namely: The founders or leaders of my party are good men, and therefore their tenets are true; it is the opinion of a sect that is erroneous, therefore it is false; it hath been long received in the world, therefore it is true; or, it is new, and therefore false.

There is not any who pretends to the least reason, but when any of these his false maxims are brought to the test, must acknowledge them to be fallible, and such as he will not allow in those that differ from him; and yet, after he is convinced of this, you shall see him go on in the use of them, and the very next occasion that offers, argue again upon the same grounds. Would one not be ready to think that men are willing to impose upon themselves, and mislead their own understanding, who conduct them by such wrong measures, even after they see they cannot be relied on? But yet, they will not appear so blamable as may be thought at first sight; for I think there are a great many that argue thus in earnest, and do it not to impose on themselves or others. They are persuaded of what they say, and think there is weight in it, though, in a like case, they have been convinced there is none; but men would be intolerable to themselves, and contemptible to others, if they should embrace opinions without any ground, and hold what they could give no manner of reason for. True or false, solid or sandy, the mind must have some foundation to rest itself upon; and, as I have remarked in another place, it no sooner entertains any proposition, but it presently hastens to some hypothesis to bottom it on: till then it is unquiet and unsettled. So much do our own very tempers dispose us to a right use of our understandings, if we would follow as we should the inclinations of our nature.

What, then, should be done in the case? I answer, we should always remember that the faculties of our souls are improved and made useful to us, just after the same manner as our bodies are. Would you have a man write or paint, dance or fence well, or perform any other manual operation dexterously and with ease, let him have never so much vigor and activity, suppleness and address, naturally, yet nobody expects this from him unless he has been used to it, and has employed time and pains in fashioning and forming his hand, or outward parts, to these motions. Just so it is in the mind—would you have a man reason well, you must use him to it betimes, exercise his mind in observing the connection of ideas, and following them in train. Nothing does this better than mathematics, which, therefore, I think, should be taught all those who have the time and opportunity; not so much to make them mathematicians, as to make them reasonable creatures; for though we all call ourselves so, because we are born to it, if we please, yet we may truly say, nature gives us but the seeds of it; we are born to be, if we please, rational creatures, but it is use and exercise only that make us so, and we are indeed so no further than industry and application have carried us.

How a Grown Man Should Live

From Plato, The Republic

Socrates's answer to how man should live is as profound as it is simple. The passions must be governed by a well-ordered soul, and a well-ordered soul parallels a well-ordered city. Civic-spiritedness is higher than economic productivity, and both must be governed by wisdom. There can be no conflict between virtue and happiness. Virtue cannot be enforced, it must be satisfying. Happiness cannot be a life of degraded hedonism. If a man is moderate, he will be spared the toil and pain of gratifying endless and unlimited desires, and in this way happier than a tyrant or hedonist. The aim of education is to cultivate the soul so that it mirrors the beautiful harmony and orderly proportionality of the cosmos. A man should not aspire merely to master others, but should turn his ambition inward and master his own unruly impulses. If we believe the world as a whole is orderly and intelligible, we will behave in the same way. If we believe the world is chaotic and irrational, we will in turn be governed by impulse and passion. The issue of

the attitude of the epic poets is brought into focus here: it is contended that
their world is one of irrational chance—a world of absurdity. As a result, a
figure like Achilles careens between extremes of frenzied daring and hopeless-
ness. Achilles must be replaced, it is argued, with a new model for young
men: a moderate Guardian of the common good, whose gracious repose and
consistency mirror the rationality of the cosmic order. Being a guardian
probably isn't as much fun as being the wild, moody, beautiful and charis-
matic demi-god of youth Achilles. But, while Socratic manliness may not
match the glorious excesses of Achilles's daring, neither does it lead to the
adolescent self-pity, fury, and pointless aggression of his lot. Under
Socrates's influence, "courage"—which in ancient Greek was literally a syn-
onym for "manliness"—becomes primarily a quality of soul, mind, and
will, not of brute strength or martial prowess.

We must beg Homer and the other poets not to be angry if we
strike out these and similar passages, not because they are unpoeti-
cal, or unattractive to the popular ear, but because the greater the
poetical charm of them, the less are they meet for the ears of boys
and men who are meant to be free, and who should fear slavery
more than death.

Then we will once more entreat Homer and the other poets
not to depict Achilles, who is the son of a goddess, first lying on his
side, then on his back, and then on his face; then starting up and
sailing in a frenzy along the shores of the barren sea; now taking
the sooty ashes in both his hands and pouring them over his head,
or weeping and wailing in the various modes which Homer has
delineated.

Loving Homer as I do, I hardly like to say that in attributing
these feelings to Achilles, or in believing that they are truly attributed to him, he is guilty of downright impiety. As little can I believe
the narrative of his insolence to Apollo, where he says,

"Thou hast wronged me, O far-darter, most abominable of
deities. Verily I would be even with thee, if I had only the
power,"

or his insubordination to the river-god, on whose divinity he is
ready to lay hands; or his offering to the dead Patroclus of his own
hair, which had been previously dedicated to the other river-god
Spercheius, and that he actually performed this vow; or that he
dragged Hector round the tomb of Patroclus, and slaughtered the

captives at the pyre; of all this I cannot believe that he was guilty, any more than I can allow our citizens to believe that he, the wise Cheiron's pupil, the son of a goddess and of Peleus who was the gentlest of men and third in descent from Zeus, was so disordered in his wits as to be at one time the slave of two seemingly inconsistent passions, meanness, not untainted by avarice, combined with overweening contempt of gods and men.

If I am not mistaken, we shall have to say that about men poets and storytellers are guilty of making the gravest misstatements when they tell us that wicked men are often happy, and the good miserable; and that injustice is profitable when undetected, but that justice is a man's own loss and another's gain—these things we shall forbid them to utter, and command them to sing and say the opposite.

Suppose, that a just and good man in the course of a narration comes on some saying or action of another good man,—I should imagine that he will like to impersonate him, and will not be ashamed of this sort of imitation: he will be most ready to play the part of the good man when he is acting firmly and wisely; in a less degree when he is overtaken by illness or love or drink, or has met with any other disaster. But when he comes to a character which is unworthy of him, he will not make a study of that; he will disdain such a person, and will assume his likeness, if at all, for a moment only when he is performing some good action; at other times he will be ashamed to play a part which he has never practiced, nor will he like to fashion and frame himself after the baser models; he feels the employment of such an art, unless in jest, to be beneath him, and his mind revolts at it.

A WISE MAN WITHIN

The Child Is Father of the Man

William Wordsworth

From the quintessential Romantic poet (1770–1850).

My heart leaps up when I behold
A rainbow in the sky:
So was it when my life began;
So is it now I am a man;
So be it when I shall grow old,
Or let me die!
The child is father of the man;
And I could wish my days to be
Bound each to each by natural piety.

The Painful Path to Manhood

From St. Augustine, Confessions

In the Confessions, *St. Augustine describes his upbringing, education, and search for a successful occupation and marriage. In all these pursuits, he laments, he was motivated by fleshly longings and a vain craving for worldly distinction. Through a painful process of inner deepening, he gradually came to realize how shallow was the world's definition of happiness and success in comparison with the true inner repose offered by faith in God.*

Born in 345 A.D. in the Roman providence of Numidia, Augustine became the Bishop of Hippo and the author of timeless works of Christian reflection.

My God, what miseries and mockeries I experienced at that age! I was told that in order to get ahead in the world, a boy my age should be obedient and achieve excellence in the arts of language and rhetoric. For this would gain me reputation among men, and deceitful riches! So I was sent to school to get learning. Little did I know what profit I might gain from it, wretch that I was. But if I neglected my studies, I was soon beaten for it. For this form of discipline was recommended by our ancestors. Those who had passed the same way before us, laid out this troublesome course for us, which we were forced to follow in our turn, thus multiplying the labor and sorrow of the sons of Adam.

Yet we observed, Oh Lord, that some men prayed to you, and we learned from them to think of you, insofar as we could understand, as some Great One who—although not perceived by our senses—was able to both hear and help us. Though still a boy, I began to pray to you, my Help and Refuge. Even then, I wore out my tongue in praying to you. Although still a little boy, I prayed to you with great devotion that I would not be beaten at school. And when you did not hear my prayers—which were folly, although I did not think so then—my punishments, which I then thought were my greatest and most grievous affliction, were laughed at by my elders, yes, and by my own parents who wished that no harm befall me. Is there any man, Oh Lord, of such great spirit, attached to you with such devotion, that he can fear those racks and hooks and other instruments of torture so little—to avoid which men all over the world pray to you with so much fear—that he can laugh at those who most bitterly fear them, as our parents laughed at those tortures which we school boys suffered at the hands of our masters? Is there any man, I say, whose devotion is so strong? For otherwise, even callous indifference might be enough.

We were just as much afraid of the strap and prayed just as earnestly to escape it, as others have prayed to escape torture. But for all our fears, we played truant all too often, either in writing or reading or thinking about our lessons less than was required. It was not, Oh Lord, that we lacked either memory or capacity (of which it had pleased you to give us enough for our age). It was that our minds were set upon playing, for which we were beaten by those same masters who were doing much the same thing themselves. But older people's idleness is called "business." When children do the same thing, these same men must punish them. Yet no one pities either the children or the men, or both. However, perhaps some impartial judge might think that it was just for me to be beaten for playing ball when I was a boy, because playing that sport was distracting me from my studies, with the consequence of my playing the fool all the more unbecomingly when I became a man. Is this not what my master who beat me did, when, if thwarted by another school master over some trifling matter, was soon more racked by rage and envy toward him, than I was when I lost a tennis match to my playfellow?

I will now call to mind my impurities and the carnal corruptions of my soul, which I passed over before, not because I love them, Oh my God. I do it for love of your love, repeating in the very bitterness of my memories my most wicked ways, so that only you may grow sweet to me. Your sweetness is never deceptive, but is happy and secure! I remember myself in my broken condition, in which I was torn to pieces, when turning away from you alone, I squandered myself away on vanities.

In my youth, I even burned to take my fill of hell. I even dared to grow wild with various shady loves. My beauty withered away. I even stank in your eyes. But all this while I was pleased with myself and desired to please the eyes of men.

What was it that I delighted in but to love and be loved? But I did not restrict my love to the moderation of one mind loving another, which is the bright path of friendship. But out of the foul desirousness of my flesh, mists and delusions of youth reeked up, which so obscured and overcast my heart that I could not distinguish the beauty of pure affection from the fog of impure lust. Both boiled confusedly within me, and my youthful instability swept me away over the precipice of impure desires, and drenched me over head and ears in the whirlpool of wicked impurities. All this time, your anger with me grew, and I knew it not. By now I had grown deaf from the continual clanking of the chains of my mortality: your punishment for the pride in my soul. I strayed further from you, and you let me go. I was tumbled up and down. I was even split and poured out. Yes, and I boiled over in my fornications, and you remained silent. Oh my tardy Joy! You remained silent then, and I wandered still further and further from you, sowing more and more fruitless seeds of sorrow with proud dejection and untried weariness.

Wretch that I was, I seethed with wickedness and still pursued the violent course of my own stream, forsaking you utterly. I broke all your laws, but did not escape your lashes, for what mortal can avoid them? For you were with me at every turn—mercifully angry, and flavoring all my unlawful pleasures with most bitter discontent—in order to lead me to seek pleasures that are not accompanied by discontent. I could not find any, except for you, Oh Lord: you who teach your commandments through pain and wound us so that you may heal us, yes, and slay us so that we may not die away from you. Where was I, how far was I banished from the delights of your house in the sixteenth year of the age of my flesh? At that age, the madness of raging lust—in which human shamelessness takes too much liberty despite being forbidden by your laws—exercised such supreme domination over me that I put all my efforts into it. My parents took no care to save me from ruin, by marriage. All they cared about was that I learn to make a powerful speech and prove a most persuasive speaker.

I desired honours, wealth and marriage, and you laughed at me. From these desires I suffered most bitter hardships. You were all the more gracious to me, the less you allowed anything but you to seem sweet to me. Behold now my heart, Oh Lord, who wills that I remember this, so that I might confess it to you now. Let my soul cling tightly to you, for you have freed it from the tight-clinging snare of death. How wretched I was then! You probed my wound to the quick, so that forsaking all other things, I might turn to you who are above all.

You did this, I say, so that I might turn and be healed, for without you all things would turn to nothing. Therefore, how miserable I was! How you dealt with me, to make me aware of my misery! The same day that I was preparing a speech in praise of the Emperor, in which I was to deliver many lies, and be applauded for my lies, even by those who knew that I lied. Walking along one of the streets of Milan, while my heart panted with these cares and boiled again with the feverishness of these consuming thoughts, I observed a poor beggar. I believe he was half drunk and with a belly full of food, for he was joyous and merry. I looked at him sadly, however, and spoke to my friends who were with me about the many sorrows brought about by our own madness. For the goal of all our efforts is nothing but to gain joy without care. Yet the efforts I labored under then, goaded by the spurs of desire, only increased the burden of my own unhappiness which I dragged along behind me, and increased by dragging. That beggar had already reached that joy which we, perhaps, might never reach at all. For what he had gained by means of a few coins he had begged, I was still scheming for by many a tortuous twisting and turning. Namely, to know the joy of a temporary happiness.

In truth, that beggar did not enjoy true happiness. But I, with my ambitious designs, chased after a happiness more uncertain still. For he was merry, but I was perplexed; he was without care but I was full of fears. But if someone had asked me whether I would rather be merry or fearful, I would answer, merry. Again, if I were asked whether I would rather be in that beggar's shoes or in my own? At that time I would have chosen my own, although I was overwhelmed with cares and fears. Was this out of perversity? Was it for any true reason? For I ought not to prefer myself over that beggar because I was more learned than he, seeing that my learning did not make me happy. Instead, I sought to please others with it: not to instruct them, but merely to delight them. For this reason you broke even my bones with the rod of your correction.

Youth

From John Woolman, Journal

John Greenleaf Whittier called this Quaker's account of his search for God "a classic of the inner life." John Woolman (1720–1772) traveled the New England colonies for thirty years, preaching the Quaker faith and advocating temperance and the abolition of slavery.

I have often felt a motion of love to leave some hints of my experience of the goodness of God; and pursuant thereto, in the thirty-sixth year of my age, I begin this work.

I was born in Northampton, in Burlington county, in West Jersey, in the year of our Lord 1720; and before I was seven years old I began to be acquainted with the operations of divine love. Through the care of my parents, I was taught to read near as soon as I was capable of it; and as I went from school one seventh-day, I remember, while my companions went to play by the way, I went forward out of sight, and setting down, I read the twenty-second chapter of the Revelations: "He showed me a pure river of water of life, clear as crystal, proceeding out of the throne of God and of the lamb," etc.; and in the reading of it, my mind was drawn to seek after that pure habitation, which I then believed God had prepared for His servants. The place where I sat, and the sweetness that attended my mind, remain fresh in my memory.

This, and the like gracious visitations, had that effect upon me, that when boys used ill language, it troubled me, and through the continued mercies of God, I was preserved from it. The pious instructions of my parents were often fresh in my mind when I happened to be among wicked children, and were of use to me.

My parents, having a large family of children, used frequently, on first days after meeting, to put us to read in the holy scriptures, or some religious books, one after another, the rest sitting by without much conversation; which I have since often thought was a good practice. From what I had read, I believed there had been in past ages, people who walked in uprightness before God in a degree exceeding any that I knew, or heard of, now living; and the apprehension of there being less steadiness and firmness amongst people in this age than in past ages, often troubled me while I was still young.

I had a dream about the ninth year of my age as follows: I saw the moon rise near the West, and run a regular course Eastward, so swift that in about a quarter of an hour, she reached our meridian, when there descended from her a small cloud on direct line to the earth, which lighted on a pleasant green about twenty yards from the door of my father's house (in which I thought I stood) and was immediately turned into a beautiful green tree. The moon appeared to run on with equal swiftness, and soon set in the East, at which time the sun arose at the place where it commonly doth in the summer, and shining with full radiance in a serene air, it appeared as pleasant a morning as ever I saw.

All this time I stood still in the door, in an awful frame of mind, and I observed that as heat increased by the rising sun, it wrought so powerfully on the little green tree, that the leaves gradually withered, and before noon it appeared dry and dead. There then appeared a being, small of size, moving swift from the North Southward, called a sun worm.

(Though I was a child, this dream was instructive to me.)

Another thing remarkable in my childhood was, that once, as I went to a neighbor's house, I saw, on the way, a robin sitting on her nest; and as I came near she went off, but having young ones, flew about, and with many cries expressed her concern for them. I stood and threw stones at her, till one striking her, she fell down dead. At first I was pleased with the exploit, but after a few minutes was seized with horror, as having in a sportive way killed an innocent creature while she was careful for her young. I beheld her lying dead, and thought those young ones for which she was so careful must now perish for want of their dam to nourish them; and after some painful considerations on the subject, I climbed up the tree, took all the young birds, and killed them—supposing that better than to leave them to pine away and die miserably: and believed in this case, that scripture proverb was fulfilled, "The tender mercies of the wicked are cruel." I then went on my errand, but, for some hours, could think of little else but (the cruelties I had committed, and was much troubled).

Thus He, whose tender mercies are over all His works, hath placed that in the human mind, which incites to exercise goodness toward every living creature, and this singly attended to, people become tender-hearted and sympathizing; but being frequently and totally rejected, the mind shuts itself up in a contrary disposition.

About the twelfth year of my age, my father being abroad, my mother reproved me for some misconduct, to which I made an undutiful reply; and the next first-day, as I was with my father returning from meeting, he told me he understood I had behaved amiss to my mother, and advised me to be more careful in future. I knew myself blamable, and in shame and confusion remained silent. Being thus awakened to a sense of wickedness, I felt remorse in my mind, and getting home, I retired and prayed to the Lord to forgive me; and I do not remember that I ever, after that, spoke unhandsomely to either of my parents, however foolish in some other things.

Having attained the age of sixteen, I began to love wanton company: and though I was preserved from profane language or scandalous conduct, still I perceived a plant in me which produced such wild grapes. Yet my merciful Father forsook me not utterly, but at times, through His grace, I was brought seriously to consider my ways; and the sight of my backsliding affected me with sorrow: but for want of rightly attending to the reproofs of instruction, vanity was added to vanity, and repentance. Upon the whole, my mind was more and more alienated from the truth, and I hastened toward destruction. While I meditate on the gulf toward which I traveled, and reflect on my youthful disobedience, my heart is affected with sorrow.

I was now led to look seriously at the means by which I was drawn from the pure truth, and I learned this: that if I would live in the life which the faithful servants of God lived in, I must not go into company as heretofore, in my own will; but all the cravings of sense must be governed by a divine principle. In times of sorrow and abasement, these instructions were sealed upon me, and I felt the power of Christ prevail over all selfish desires, so that I was preserved in a good degree of steadiness; and being young and believing at that time that a single life was best for me, I was strengthened to keep from such company as had often been a snare to me.

As I lived under the cross, and simply followed the openings of truth, my mind from day to day was more enlightened; my former acquaintance were left to judge of me as they would, for I found it safest for me to live in private and keep these things sealed up in my own breast. While I silently ponder on that change which was wrought in me, I find no language equal to it, not any means to convey to another a clear idea of it. I looked upon the works of God in this visible creation, and an awfulness covered me: my heart was tender and often contrite, and a universal love to my fellow creatures increased in me. This will be understood by such who have trodden in the same path.

The Four Ages of Man

W. B. Yeats

From the great Irish symbolist poet (1865–1939).

He with body waged a fight,
But body won; it walks upright.

Then he struggled with the heart;
Innocence and peace depart.

Then he struggled with the mind;
His proud heart he left behind.

Now his wars on God begin;
At stroke of midnight God shall win.

Reflections on a Man's Success

William James, The Varieties of Religious Experience

In The Varieties of Religious Experience, *the American Pragmatic philosopher William James (1842–1910) reflects on how a man who builds his sense of self on his successes and accomplishments will inevitably look back on his life and be disappointed. To illustrate, James cites Martin Luther and Goethe as they looked back on their respective lives.*

To begin with, how *can* things so insecure as the successful experiences of this world afford a stable anchorage? A chain is no stronger than its weakest link, and life is after all a chain. In the healthiest and most prosperous existence, how many links of illness, danger, and disaster are always interposed? Unsuspectedly from the bottom of every fountain of pleasure, as the old poet said, something bitter rises up: a touch of nausea, a falling dead of the delight, a whiff of melancholy, things that sound a knell, for fugitive as they may be, they bring a feeling of coming from a deeper region and often have an appalling convincingness. The buzz of life ceases at their touch as a piano-string stops sounding when the damper fall upon it.

Of course the music can commence again—and again and again—at intervals. But with this the healthy-minded consciousness is left with an irremediable sense of precariousness. It is a bell with a crack; it draws its breath on sufferance and by an accident.

Even if we suppose a man so packed with healthy-mindedness as never to have experienced in his own person any of these sobering intervals, still, if he is a reflecting being, he must generalize and class his own lot with that of others; and, in doing so, he must see that his escape is just a lucky chance and no essential difference. He might just as well have been born to an entirely different fortune. And then indeed the hollow security! What kind of a frame of things is it of which the best you can say is, "Thank God, it has let me off clear this time!" Is not its blessedness a fragile fiction? Is not your joy in it a very vulgar glee, not much unlike the snicker of any rogue at his success? If indeed it were all success, even on such terms as that! But take the happiest man, the one most envied by the world, and in nine cases out of ten his inmost consciousness is one of failure. Either his ideals in the line of his achievements are pitched far higher than the achievement themselves, or else he has secret ideals of which the world knows nothing, and in regard to which he inwardly knows himself to be found wanting.

When such a conquering optimist as Goethe can express himself in this wise, how must it be with less successful men?

"I will say nothing," writes Goethe in 1824, "against the course of my existence. But at bottom it has been nothing but pain and burden, and I can affirm that during the whole of my 75 years, I have not had four weeks of genuine well-being. It is but the perpetual rolling of a rock that must be raised up again forever."

What single-handed man was ever on the whole as successful as Luther? yet when he had grown old, he looked back on his life as if it were an absolute failure.

"I am utterly weary of life. I pray the Lord will come forthwith and carry me hence. Let him come, above all, with his last Judgment: I will stretch out my neck, the thunder will burst forth, and I shall be at rest." —And having a necklace of white agates in his hand at the time he added: "O God, grant that it may come without delay. I would readily eat up this necklace today, for the Judgment to come tomorrow." —The Electress Dowager, one day when Luther was dining with her, said to him: "Doctor, I wish you may live forty years more, I would give up my chance of Paradise."

Failure, then, failure! So the world stamps us at every turn. We strew it with our blunders, our misdeeds, our lost opportunities, with all the memorials of our inadequacy to our vocation. And with what a damning emphasis does it then blot us out! No easy fine, no mere apology or formal expiation, will satisfy the world's demands, but every pound of flesh exacted is soaked with all its blood. The subtlest forms of suffering known to man are connected with the poisonous humiliations incidental to these results.

And they are pivotal human experiences. A process so ubiquitous and everlasting is evidently an integral part of life. "There is indeed one element in human destiny," Robert Louis Stevenson writes, "that not blindness itself can controvert: whatever else we are intended to do, we are not intended to succeed; failure is the fate allotted." And our nature being thus rooted in failure, is it any wonder that theologians should have held it to be essential, and thought that only through the personal experience of humiliation which it engenders the deeper sense of life's significance is reached?

All natural goods perish. Riches take wings; fame is a breath; love is a cheat; youth and health and pleasure vanish. Can things whose end is always dust and disappointment be the real goods which our souls require? Back of everything is the great specter of universal death, the all-encompassing blackness:

In short, life and its negation are beaten up inextricably together. But if the life be good, the negation of it must be bad. Yet the two are equally essential facts of existence; and all natural happiness thus seems infected with a contradiction. The breath of the sepulcher surrounds it.

A Man Must Stand Erect

From Marcus Aurelius, Meditations

For the great Roman emperor and stoic philosopher Marcus Aurelius, "a man must stand erect, not be kept erect by others." Happiness comes from understanding that a virtuous soul participates in eternity, while everything else—power, riches, prestige—vanish with our mortal shells. True strength is the inner strength of self-mastery. A man who knows this will neither be intoxicated by his earthly authority nor overwhelmed by its frustrations and failures.

Begin the morning by saying to thyself, I shall meet with the busybody, the ungrateful, arrogant, deceitful, envious, unsocial. All these things happen to them by reason of their ignorance of what is good and evil. But I who have seen the nature of the good that it is beautiful, and of the bad that it is ugly, and the nature of him who does wrong, that it is akin to me, not (only) of the same blood or seed, but that it participates in (the same) intelligence and (the same) portion of the divinity, I can neither be injured by any of them, for no one can fix on me what is ugly, nor can I be angry with my kinsman, nor hate him. For we are made for cooperation, like feet, like hands, like eyelids, like the rows of the upper and lower teeth. To act against one another then is contrary to nature; and it is acting against one another to be vexed and to turn away.

Whatever this is that I am, it is a little flesh and breath, and the ruling part. Throw away thy books; no longer distract thyself: it is not allowed; but as if thou was now dying, despise the flesh; it is blood and bones and a network, a contexture of nerves, veins, and arteries. See the breath also, what kind of a thing it is, air and not always the same, but every moment sent out and again sucked in. The third then is the ruling part: consider thus: Thou art an old man; no longer let this be a slave, no longer be pulled by the strings like a puppet to unsocial movements, no longer be either dissatisfied with thy present lot, or shrink from the future.

All that is from the gods is full of providence. That which is from fortune is not separated from nature or without an interweaving and involution with the things which are ordered by providence. From thence all things flow; and there is besides necessity, and that which is for the advantage of the whole universe, of which thou art a part. But that is good for every part of nature which the nature of the whole brings, and what serves to maintain this nature. Now the universe is preserved, as by the changes of the elements so by the changes of things compounded of the elements. Let these principles be enough for thee, let them always be fixed opinions. But cast away the thirst after books, that thou mayest not die murmuring, but cheerfully, truly, and from thy heart thankful to the gods.

Remember how long thou hast been putting off these things, and how often thou hast received an opportunity from the gods, and yet dost not use it. Thou must now at last perceive of what universe thou are a part, and of what administrator of the universe thy existence is a efflux, and that a limit of time is fixed for thee, which if thou dost not use for clearing away the clouds from thy mind, it will go and thou wilt go, and it will never return.

Every moment think steadily as a Roman and a man to do what thou hast in hand with perfect and simple dignity, and feeling of affection, and freedom, and justice; and to give thyself relief from all other thoughts. And thou wilt give thyself relief, if thou doest every act of thy life as if it were the last, laying aside all carelessness and passionate aversion from the commands of reason, and all hypocrisy, and self-love, and discontent with the portion which has been given to thee.

Since it is possible that thou mayest depart from life this very moment, regulate every act and thought accordingly. But to go away from among men, if there are gods, is not a thing to be afraid of, for the gods will not involve thee in evil; but if indeed they do not exist, or if they have no concern about human affairs, what is it to me to live in a universe devoid of gods or devoid of providence? But in truth they do exist, and they do care for human things, and they have put all the means in man's power to enable him not to fall into real evils. And as to the rest, if there was anything evil, they would have provided for this also, that it should be altogether in a man's power not to fall into it. Now that which does not make a man worse, how can it make a man's life worse? But neither through ignorance, nor having the knowledge, but not the power to guard against or correct these things, is it possible that the nature of the universe has overlooked them; nor is it possible that it has made so great a mistake, either through want of power or want of skill, that good and evil should happen indiscriminately to the good and the bad. But death certainly, and life, honor and dishonor, pain and pleasure, all these things equally happen to good men and bad, being things which make us neither better nor worse. Therefore they are neither good nor evil.

Of human life the time is a point, and the substance is in a flux, and the perception dull, and the composition of the whole body subject to putrefaction, and the soul a whirl, and fortune hard to divine, and fame a thing devoid of judgment. And, to say all in a word, everything which belongs to the body is a stream, and what belongs to the soul is a dream and vapor, and life is a warfare and a stranger's sojourn, and after-fame is oblivion. What then is that which is able to conduct a man? One thing and only one, philosophy.

Intimations of Immortality from Recollections of Childhood

William Wordsworth

The child is father of the man;
And I could wish my days to be
Bound each to each by natural piety.

I

There was a time when meadow, grove, and stream,
The earth, and every common sight,
To me did seem
Apparelled in celestial light,
The glory and the freshness of a dream.
It is not now as it hath been of yore;—
Turn whersoe'er I may,
By night or day,
The things which I have seen I now can see no more.

II

The Rainbow comes and goes,
And lovely is the rose,
The moon doth with delight
Look round her when the heavens are bare,
Waters on a starry night
Are beautiful and fair;
The sunshine is a glorious birth;
But yet I know, where'er I go,
That there hath past away a glory from the earth.

III

Now, while the birds thus sing a joyous song,
And while the young lambs bound
As to the tabor's sound,
To me alone there came a thought of grief:
A timely utterance gave that thought relief,
And I again am strong:
The cataracts blow their trumpets from the steep;
No more shall grief of mine the season wrong;
I hear the echoes through the mountains throng,
The winds come to me from the fields of sleep,
And all the earth is gay;
Land and sea
Give themselves up to jollity,

And with the heart of May
Doth every beast keep holiday;
Thou child of joy,
Shout round me, let me hear thy shouts, thou happy
shepherd-boy!

IV

Ye blessed creatures, I have heard the call
Ye to each other make; I see
The heavens laugh with you in your jubilee;
My heart is at your festival,
My head hath its coronal,
The fulness of your bliss, I feel—I feel it all.
Oh evil day! if I were sullen
While earth herself is adorning,
This sweet May-morning,
And the children are culling
On every side,
In a thousand valleys far and wide,
Fresh flowers; while the sun shines warm,
And the babe leaps up on his mother's arm:—
I hear, I hear, with joy, I hear!
—But there's a tree, of many, one,
A single field which I have looked upon,
Both of them speak of something that is gone:
The pansy at my feet
Doth the same tale repeat:
Whither is fled the visionary gleam?
Where is it now, the glory and the dream?

V

Our birth is but a sleep and a forgetting:
The soul that rises with us, our life's star,
Hath had elsewhere its setting,
And cometh from afar:
Not in entire forgetfulness,
And not in utter nakedness,
But trailing clouds of glory do we come

From God, who is our home:
Heaven lies about us in our infancy!
Shades of the prison-house begin to close
Upon the growing boy,
But he beholds the light, and whence it flows,
He sees it in his joy;
The youth, who daily farther from the east
Must travel, still is nature's priest,
And by the vision splendid
Is on his way attended;
At length the man perceives it die away,
And fade into the light of common day.

VI

Earth fills her lap with pleasures of her own;
Yearnings she hath in her own natural kind,
And, even with something of a mother's mind,
And no unworthy aim,
The homely nurse doth all she can
To make her foster-child, her inmate man,
Forget the glories he hath known,
And that imperial palace whence he came.

VII

Behold the child among his new-born blisses,
A six years' darling of a pigmy size!
See, where 'mid work of his own hand he lies,
Fretted by sallies of his mother's kisses,
With light upon him from his father's eyes!
See, at his feet, some little plan or chart,
Some fragment from his dream of human life,
Shaped by himself with newly-learned art;
A wedding or a festival,
A mourning or a funeral;
And this hath now his heart,
And unto this he frames his song:
Then will he fit his tongue
To dialogues of business, love, or strife;

But it will not be long
Ere this be thrown aside,
And with new joy and pride
The little actor cons another part;
Filling from time to time his "humorous stage"
With all the persons, down to palsied age,
That life brings with her in her equipage;
As if his whole vocation
Were endless imitation.

VIII

Thou, whose exterior semblance doth belie
Thy soul's immensity;
Thou best philosopher, who yet dost keep
Thy heritage, thou eye among the blind,
That, deaf and silent, read'st the eternal deep,
Haunted for ever by the eternal mind,—
Mighty prophet! Seer blest!
On whom those truths do rest,
Which we are toiling all our lives to find,
In darkness lost, the darkness of the grave;
Thou, over whom thy immortality
Broods like the day, a master o'er a slave,
A presence which is not to be put by;
Thou little child, yet glorious in the might
Of heaven-born freedom on thy being's height,
Why with such earnest pains dost thou provoke
The years to bring the inevitable yoke,
Thus blindly with thy blessedness at strife?
Full soon thy soul shall have her earthly freight,
And custom lie upon thee with a weight,
Heavy as frost, and deep almost as life!

IX

O joy! that in our embers
Is something that doth live,
That nature yet remembers
What was so fugitive!

The thought of our past years in me doth breed
Perpetual benediction: not indeed
For that which is most worthy to be blest;
Delight and liberty, the simple creed
Of childhood, whether busy or at rest,
With new-fledged hope still fluttering in his breast:—
Not for these I raise
The song of thanks and praise;
But for those obstinate questionings
Of sense and outward things,
Fallings from us, vanishings;
Blank misgivings of a creature
Moving about in worlds not realised,
High instincts before which our mortal nature
Did tremble like a guilty thing surprised:
But for those first affections,
Those shadowy recollections,
Which, be they what they may,
Are yet the fountain-light of all our day,
Are yet a master-light of all our seeing;
Uphold us, cherish, and have power to make
Our noisy years seem moments in the being
Of the eternal silence: truths that wake,
To perish never:
Which neither listlessness, nor mad endeavour,
Nor man nor boy,
Nor all that is at enmity with joy,
Can utterly abolish or destroy.
Hence in a season of calm weather
Though inland far we be,
Our souls have sight of that immortal sea
Which brought us hither,
Can in a moment travel thither,
And see the children sport upon the shore,
And hear the mighty waters rolling evermore.

X

Then sing, ye birds, sing, sing a joyous song!
And let the young lambs bound
As to the tabor's sound!

We in thought will join your throng,
Ye that pipe and ye that play,
Ye that through your hearts to-day
Feel the gladness of the May!
What though the radiance which was once so bright
Be now for ever taken from my sight,
Though nothing can bring back the hour
Of splendour in the grass, of glory in the flower;
We will grieve not, rather find
Strength in what remains behind;
In the primal sympathy
Which having been must ever be;
In the soothing thoughts that spring
Out of human suffering;
In the faith that looks through death,
In years that bring the philosophic mind.

XI

And O, ye fountains, meadows, hills, and groves,
Forebode not any severing of our loves!
Yet in my heart of hearts I feel your might;
I only have relinquished one delight
To live beneath your more habitual sway.
I love the brooks which down their channels fret,
Even more than when I tripped lightly as they;
The innocent brightness of a new-born day
Is lovely yet;
The clouds that gather round the setting sun
Do take a sober colouring from an eye
That hath kept watch o'er man's mortality;
Another race hath been, and other palms are won.
Thanks to the human heart by which we live,
Thanks to its tenderness, its joys, and fears,
To me the meanest flower that blows can give
Thoughts that do often lie too deep for tears.

Death Is Not to Be Feared

Desiderius Erasmus,
The Education of a Christian Prince

At once learned humanist and devout Christian, Erasmus of Rotterdam (1466–1530) was a Renaissance thinker of enormous depth and breadth, from theology to education, statesmanship, and humor.

The tutor should first see that his pupil loves and honors virtue as the finest quality of all, the most felicitous, the most fitting a prince; and that he loathes and shuns moral turpitude as the foulest and most terrible of things. Lest the young prince be accustomed to regard riches as an indispensable necessity, to be gained by right or wrong, he should learn that those are not true honors which are commonly acclaimed as such. True honor is that which follows on virtue and right action of its own will. The less affected it is, the more it redounds to fame. The low pleasures of the people are so far beneath a prince, especially a Christian prince, that they hardly become any man. There is another kind of pleasure which will endure, genuine and true, all through life. Teach the prince that nobility, statues, wax masks, family-trees, all the pomp of heralds, over which the great mass of people stupidly swell with pride, are only empty terms unless supported by deeds worth while. The prestige of a prince, his greatness, his majesty, must be not developed and preserved by fortune's wild display, but by wisdom, solidarity, and good deeds.

Death is not to be feared, nor should we wail when it comes to others, unless it was a foul death. The happiest man is not the one who has lived the longest, but the one who has made the most of his life. The span of life should be measured not by years but by our deeds well performed. Length of life has no bearing on a man's happiness. It is how well he lived that counts. Surely virtue is its own reward. It is the duty of a good prince to consider the welfare of his people, even at the cost of his own life if need be. But that prince does not really die who loses his life in such a cause. All those things which the common people cherish as delightful, or revere as excel-

lent, or adopt as useful, are to be measured by just one standard—
worth. On the other hand, whatever things the common people
object to as disagreeable, or despise as lowly, or shun as pernicious,
should not be avoided unless they are bound up with dishonor.

The True Spirit of Man

From The Bhagavad-Gita

Krishna:
Men call the tree of life,—the Banyan-tree,—
Which has its branches beneath, its roots above,—
the ever-holy tree. Yes! for its leaves
Are green and waving hymns which whisper Truth!
Whoever knows the tree of life, knows holy lore.

Its branches shoot to heaven and sink to earth,
Like the deeds of men, which take their birth
From qualities: its silver sprays and blooms,
And all the eager verdure of its girth
Leap to quick life at the kiss of sun and air,
As men's lives quicken to the fair temptations
Of wooing sense: its hanging rootlets seek
The soil beneath, helping to hold it there

As actions wrought amid this world of men
Bind them by ever-tightening bonds again.
If you know well the teaching of the Tree,
What its shape says; and whence it springs; and, then

How it must end, and all the ills of it,
You would sharpen the ax of sharp Detachment,
And sever the clinging snaky roots, and lay
This tree of sense-life low,—to set

New growths upspringing to that happier sky,—
Which those who reach shall have no day to die,
Nor fade away, nor fall—to Him, I mean,
FATHER and FIRST, Who made the mystery

Of old Creation; for to Him come those
Who break away from passing and from dreams;
Who part the bonds constraining them to flesh,
And—worshipping always Him, the Highest—

No longer grow at the mercy of whatever breeze
Of summer pleasure stirs the sleeping trees,
Whatever blast of tempest tears them, bough and stem:
To the eternal world pass such as these!

Another Sun gleams there! another Moon!
Another Light,—not Dusk, nor Dawn, nor Noon—
They who once behold it return no more;
They have attained My rest, life's Utmost boon!

When, in this world of manifested life,
The undying Spirit, setting forth from Me,
Takes on form, it draws to itself
From Being's storehouse,—which contains all,—
Senses and intellect both. The Sovereign Soul
Thus entering the flesh, or quitting it,
Gathers these up, as the wind gathers scents,
Blowing above the flower beds. Ear and Eye,
And Touch and Taste, and Smelling, these it takes,—
Yes, and a sentient mind;—linking itself
To sense-things so.

The unenlightened ones
Do not perceive Spirit when he goes or comes,
Nor when he takes his pleasure in the form,
Conjoined with these qualities; but those see plain
Who have the eyes to see. Holy souls see Spirit
When they strive to see. Enlightened, they perceive
That Spirit in themselves; but foolish ones,
without holy discipline,
Even though they strive, discern not, having hearts
Unkindled, ill-informed!

Know, too, from Me
Shines the gathered glory of the suns
Which lighten all the world: from Me the moons
Draw silvery beams, and fire draws fierce loveliness.
I penetrate the clay, and lend all shapes
Their living force; I glide into the plant—
Root, leaf, and bloom—to make the woodlands green
With springing sap. Becoming vital warmth,
I glow in glad, respiring frames, and pass,
With outward and with inward breath, to feed
The body with all nourishment.

For in this world
Being is twofold: the Divided, one;
The Undivided, one. All things that live
Are "the Divided." That which sits apart, is
"The Undivided."

Higher still is He,
The Highest, holding all, whose Name is LORD,
The Eternal, Sovereign, First! Who fills all worlds,
Sustaining them. And—dwelling thus beyond
Divided being and Undivided—I
Am called by men and by holy lore, Life Supreme,
The TRUE SPIRIT OF MAN.

Who knows Me thus,
With mind unclouded, knows all, dear Prince!
And with his whole soul forever worships Me.

Now is the sacred, secret Mystery
Declared to thee! Whoever comprehends this
Has wisdom! He is freed from works, in bliss!

The Two Paths

St. Augustine, The City of God

Not everyone admired the classical ideal of wisdom. With Christianity came new beliefs about man's foremost duties. Godliness and humility became far more important than a concern with worldly success and intellect. The classical ideal of manhood had subordinated civic virtue to the life of the mind in a harmonious hierarchy, but in The City of God, *St. Augustine insists one must choose between two irreconcilable ways of life—the city of the flesh and the city of the spirit. A life devoted to worldly ambition, he claims, is vain, exploitive, arrogant, and restless. A life devoted to God is moderate, modest, peaceable, and allows a man to be at peace with himself. Faith becomes the new model for manliness. Being a Stoic is preferable to being a hedonist, but both schools of thought are mistaken in believing that wisdom and happiness are possible though man's efforts alone, without faith in God.*

Is it reasonable and wise to glory in the extent and greatness of the empire when you can in no way prove that there is any real happiness in men perpetually living amid the horrors of war, perpetually wading in blood?—Does it matter whether it is the blood of their fellow citizens or the blood of their enemies? It is still human blood, in men perpetually haunted by the gloomy specter of fear and driven by murderous passions. The happiness arising from such conditions is a thing of glass, of mere glittering brittleness. One can never shake off the horrible dread that it may suddenly shiver into fragments.

In order to be perfectly clear on this point, we must not be carried away by hollow verbal blasts and allow our judgment to be confused by the high-sounding words of prattlers about nations, kingdoms, and provinces. Let us imagine two individuals—for each man, like a letter in a word, is an integral part of a city or of a kingdom, however extensive. Of these two men, let us suppose that one is poor, or, better, in moderate circumstances; the other, extremely wealthy. But, our wealthy man is haunted by fear, heavy with cares, feverish with greed, never secure, always restless, breathless from endless quarrels with his enemies. By these miseries, he adds to possessions beyond measure, but he also piles up for himself a mountain of distressing worries. The man of modest means is content with a small and compact patrimony. He is loved by his own, enjoys the sweetness of peace in his relations with kindred, neighbors, and friends, is religious and pious, of kindly disposition, healthy in body, self-restrained, chaste in morals, and at peace with his conscience.

I wonder if there is anyone so senseless as to hesitate over which of the two to prefer. What is true of these two individuals is likewise true of two families, two nations, two kingdoms; the analog holds in both cases. If we apply it with care and correct our judgment accordingly, it will be easy to see on which side lies folly and on which true happiness.

Hence, if the true God is adored, and if He is given the service of true sacrifice and of an upright life, then it is beneficial for good men to extend their empire far and wide and to rule for a long time. This is beneficial, not so much for themselves as for their subjects. Fear of God, and uprightness, God's great gifts, are enough for the true happiness of rulers, since this will enable them to spend this life well and thus win life eternal. On this earth, therefore, rule by good men is a blessing bestowed, not so much on themselves as upon mankind. But the rule of wicked men brings greater harm to themselves, since they ruin their own souls by the greater ease with which they can do wrong.

As for their subjects, only their own villainy can harm them. For, whatever injury wicked masters inflict upon good men is to be regarded, not as a penalty for wrongdoing, but as a test for their virtues. Thus, a good man, though a slave, is free; but a wicked man, though a king, is a slave. For he serves, not one man alone, but what is worse, as many masters as he has vices. For, it is in reference to vice that the Holy Scripture says: "For by whom a man is overcome, of the same also he is the slave."

In the absence of justice, what is sovereignty but organized brigandage? For, what are bands of brigands but petty kingdoms? They also are groups of men, under the rule of a leader, bound together by a common agreement, dividing their booty according to a settled principle. And even though a crooked world came to admit that men should be honored only according to merit, even humans' honor would be of no great value. It is smoke that weighs nothing. The reward of the saints is altogether different. They were men who, while on earth, suffered reproaches for the City of God which is so much hated by the lovers of this world. That City is eternal. There, no one is born because no one dies. There, there reigns that true and perfect happiness which is not a goddess, but a gift of God—toward whose beauty we can but sigh in our pilgrimage on earth, though we hold the pledge of it by faith. In that City, the sun does not "rise upon the good and bad" for the Sun of Justice cherishes the good alone. There, where the Truth is a treasure shared by all, there is no need to pinch the poor to fill the coffers of the state.

When it is considered how short is the span of human life, does it really matter to a man whose days are numbered what government he must obey, so long as he is not compelled to act against God or his conscience?

Those philosophers who regard virtue as the ultimate human good try to make those others feel ashamed of themselves who think highly enough of the virtues, but who subordinate them to physical pleasure, making pleasure an end in itself and virtues merely a means to this end. They do this by picturing Pleasure enthroned like a high-born queen, surrounded by ministering virtues who watch her every nod, ready to do whatever she bids them. Thus, she bids Prudence to examine carefully in what way Pleasure may be both supreme and safe. She commands Justice to render whatever services she can in the interest of friendships which are necessary for bodily comfort and to avoid doing wrong, lest pleasure might be jeopardized by the breaking of laws. She bids Fortitude keep her mistress, Pleasure, very much in mind, so that, when the body suffers some affliction, short of death, the memory of former pleasures may mitigate the pangs of present pain. She orders Temperance to take just so much of food or of other pleasant things that health may not be endangered by any excess, or Pleasure (which, for the Epicureans, is mainly a matter of bodily health) be seriously checked.

Thus, the virtues with all the glory of their dignity are made to minister to Pleasure, like the servants of an imperious but ill-famed mistress. The Stoics are right when they say that no picture could be more ugly and ignominious and difficult for good people to look at than this. But I do not see how the picture becomes much more beautiful if we imagine the virtues ministering to human glory. For, if Glory is not exactly a lovely lady, she has a certain vanity and inanity about her. Certainly, it ill becomes the gravity and solidity of the virtues to be her servants; so that, apart from pleasing men and serving their vainglory, Prudence should make no provision, Justice should share nothing. Ugly as this picture is, it fits those self-complacent and seeming philosophers who, in the guise of despising glory, pay no heed to what others think. Their virtue, if they have any, is just as much a slave to glory.

The Myth of the Cave

From Plato, The Republic

Perhaps the single most powerful and influential allegory for the soul's ascent from the darkness of passion and prejudice to the sunlight of wisdom: Socrates teaches young Glaucon to prefer the enduring pleasures of the mind to the empty pleasures of tyranny.

"And now," I said, "let me show in a figure how far our nature is enlightened or unenlightened: Behold! Human beings living in an underground den, which has a mouth open toward the light and reaching all along the den; here they have been from their childhood, and have their legs and necks chained so that they cannot move, and can only see before them, being prevented by the chains from turning round their heads. Above and behind them a fire is blazing at a distance, and between the fire and the prisoners there is a raised way; and you will see, if you look, a low wall built along the way, like the screen which marionette players have in front of them, over which they show the puppets."

"I see."

"And do you see," I said, "men passing along the wall all sorts of vessels, and statues and figures of animals made of wood and stone and various materials, which appear over the wall? Some of them are talking, others silent."

"You have shown me a strange image, and they are strange prisoners."

"Like ourselves," I replied; "and they see only their own shadows, or the shadows of one another, which the fire throws on the opposite wall of the cave?"

"True," he said; "how could they see anything but the shadows if they were never allowed to move their heads?"

"And of the objects which are being carried in like manner they would only see the shadows?"

"Yes," he said.

"And if they were able to converse with one another, would they not suppose that they were naming what was actually before them?"

"Very true."

"And suppose further that the prison had an echo which came from the other side, would they not be sure to fancy when one of the passers-by spoke that the voice which they heard came from the passing shadow?"

"No question," he replied.

"To them," I said, "the truth would be literally nothing but the shadows of the images."

"That is certain."

"And now look again, and see what will naturally follow if the prisoners are released and disabused of their error. At first, when any of them is liberated and compelled suddenly to stand up and turn his neck round and walk and look toward the light, he will suffer sharp pains; the glare will distress him, and he will be unable to see the realities of which in his former state he had seen the shadows; and then conceive someone saying to him, that what he saw before was an illusion, but that now, when he is approaching nearer to being and his eye is turned toward more real existence, he has a clearer vision, what will be his reply? And you may further imagine that his instructor is pointing to the objects as they pass and requiring him to name them, will he not be perplexed? Will he not fancy that the shadows which he formerly saw are truer than the objects which are now shown to him?"

"Far truer."

"And if he is compelled to look straight at the light, will he not have a pain in his eyes which will make him turn away to take refuge in the objects of vision which he can see, and which he will conceive to be in reality clearer than the things which are now being shown to him?"

"True," he said.

"And suppose once more, that he is reluctantly dragged up a steep and rugged ascent, and held fast until he is forced into the presence of the sun himself, is he not likely to be pained and irritated? When he approaches the light his eyes will be dazzled, and he will not be able to see anything at all of what are now called realities."

"Not all in a moment," he said.

"He will require to grow accustomed to the sight of the upper world. And first he will see the shadows best, next the reflections of men and other objects in the water, and then the objects themselves; then he will gaze upon the light of the moon and the stars and the spangled heaven; and he will see the sky and the stars by night better than the sun or the light of the sun by day?"

"Certainly."

"Last of all he will be able to see the sun, and not mere reflections of him in the water, but he will see him in his own proper place, and not in another; and he will contemplate him as he is.

"This entire allegory," I said, "you may now append, dear Glaucon, to the previous argument; the prison-house is the world of sight, the light of the fire is the sun, and you will not misapprehend me if you interpret the journey upward to be the ascent of the soul into the intellectual world according to my poor belief, which, at your desire, I have expressed—whether rightly or wrongly God knows. But, whether true or false, my opinion is that in the world of knowledge the idea of good appears last of all, and is seen only with an effort; and, when seen, is also inferred to be the universal author of all things beautiful and right, parent of light and of the lord of light in this visible world, and the immediate source of reason and truth in the intellectual; and that this is the power upon which he who would act rationally either in public or private life must have his eye fixed."

"I agree," he said, "as far as I am able to understand you."

Levin Wonders About the Meaning of Life

From Leo Tolstoy, Anna Karenina

There are quiet heroes of peace as well as heroes of war, and perhaps the former are more impressive. In this moving scene from Tolstoy's Anna Karenina *(1876), Levin is plunged by the death of his beloved brother into wondering what meaning his life has as a man. He concludes that the philosophy and theology he learned as a young man amount to little more than vanity and conceit. Instead, he realizes that it is his daily obligations as a husband and a father that give his life meaning—his duty to his wife and children, to their extended families, and to the people who work for him.*

From the moment when, at the sight of his dying brother, Levin had for the first time looked at the questions of life and death through his new convictions, as he called them, convictions which, in the period between his twentieth and thirty-sixth year had imperceptibly taken the place of his childish beliefs, he had become horrified, not so much at death, as at life, without the least conception whence it came, what it was for, and what it meant. The organism, its dissolution, the indestructibility of matter, the law of the conservation of energy, evolution, were the words that had taken the place of his former beliefs. These words and the conceptions they stood for satisfied his mental requirements, but they gave him nothing for life, and he suddenly began to feel himself in the position of a man who has given up his fur coat in exchange for a gauze garment, and at the first approach of the frost realizes that he is little better than naked, and must inevitably die a painful death.

Levin continued to live as before, but was constantly tormented on account of his ignorance. He had a vague feeling that what he called his convictions was not only ignorance, but that it actually stood in the way of the knowledge that he needed.

In the early days of his marriage his new joys and duties had completely drowned these thoughts, but later, after his wife's confinement, when he had lived in Moscow without occupation, the question began to present itself more and more frequently, demanding a solution.

It presented itself in this way: "If I do not accept the explanation offered me by Christianity on the problem of my existence, where shall I find others?" He scrutinized the whole arsenal of his scientific convictions and found no answer whatsoever to this question. He was in the position of a man who seeks to find food in a toy shop or a gun shop.

Involuntarily and unconsciously he sought now in every book, in every conversation, in every person he met, some sympathy with the subject that absorbed him.

What surprised and puzzled him most was the fact that the majority of men of his circle, who had, like himself, substituted science for religion, did not experience the least moral suffering, and were perfectly contented and happy. Were they sincere, or did science give them a clearer answer to these troublesome questions? And he took to studying these men and books that might contain the solution that he desired.

He discovered that he had made a gross error in taking up the idea of his university friends, that religion had outlived its day and no longer existed. The best people he knew were believers—the old prince, Lvov, for whom he had taken such a liking, Sergei

Ivanovitch, all the women, including his wife, who believed, just as he had done when he was a child, nine-tenths of the Russian people—the part of the nation whose lives inspired him with the greatest respect, were believers.

Another strange thing was that, as he read many books, he became convinced that the materialists whose opinions he shared did not attach any importance to these questions. Far from explaining them, they set them aside and took up others of no interest to him, such as, for instance, the evolution of organisms, the mechanical explanation of the soul, and so forth.

Moreover, during his wife's illness an extraordinary event had occurred. He, an unbeliever, had prayed fervently, in full faith. But as soon as the danger was over he was unable to give that spiritual experience any place in his life.

He could not admit that he had known the truth then and was mistaken now, for the moment he began to think of it calmly everything went to pieces. Nor could he admit that he had been mistaken then, for he thought too highly of that experience, and if he assumed it to have been a weakness, he was defiling those precious moments. He was in painful discord with himself, and strained all his mental powers in order to put himself right.

There were days when these thoughts tormented him more than others, but they never left him entirely. The more he read and thought, the further he felt himself from the aim he was pursuing.

Having convinced himself that he could get no answer from the materialists, he turned to Plato, Spinoza, Kant, Schelling, Hegel, Schopenhauer—all those philosophers who did not give a materialistic explanation of life.

The ideas seemed to him fruitful, particularly as a refutation of the materialistic teaching, but the moment he reflected on the solution of the important question, he found the same thing repeated again and again. Following the definition given to obscure words such as spirit, will, freedom, substance, and purposely allowing himself to be caught in the word-trap, he seemed to understand something, but he need only forget the artificial chain of thoughts and return to what satisfied him, and the whole edifice fell to pieces like a house of cards.

When reading Schopenhauer one day he substituted the word "love" for "will," and for a short time this new philosophy consoled him, but even that fell like the rest when dissected and brought into the domain of real life.

His brother advised him to read the theological works of Hor-niakov, and the second volume, in spite of its polemical, brilliant, elegant style, which at first repelled him, impressed him deeply by its Church doctrine. He was struck by the idea that the attainment of divine truth was not given to one man, but to the totality of men, embodied in the Church. He rejoiced at the thought that it was eas-ier to believe in an existing, living church embracing all the creeds of men with God at its head, than to begin with some distant, mys-terious, unknown God.

Later, when he read a history of the Church by a Catholic writer, and another by a Greek Orthodox writer, and saw that both Churches, infallible in their essence, denied each other, he was again disappointed in Horniakov's doctrine, and this structure, too, fell to pieces just as the philosophical teachings had done.

The spring was a most difficult time for Levin, and he lived through some terrible moments.

"Without knowing who I am and why I am here life is impossi-ble. And I cannot know it, consequently I cannot live," he would say to himself.

"In endless time and space, in the infinitude of matter, an organic bubble separated itself, will hold together a while, and burst. And that bubble am I."

It was an agonizing untruth, but it was the result of centuries of labor of the human mind in that direction.

It was the last belief on which was reared all human inquiry, in all its branches. It was the reigning conviction, and Levin had invol-untarily adopted it out of all other explanations, as being the most clear.

But it was only an untruth—a cruel sarcasm of some evil power, impossible to submit to.

It was necessary to free oneself from that power, and each man held his liberation in his own hands. There was only one means to do this, and that was death.

And though in good health and happily married, Levin was several times so near to killing himself that he had to hide a rope so as not to hang himself, and would not go out with a gun for fear of shooting himself.

But he did neither the one nor the other, and still continued living.

When Levin puzzled over what he was and where he came from, he found no answer and fell into despair, but when he ceased worrying about it he seemed to know definitely why he was there, and acted accordingly. Latterly his life had even assumed a more definite purpose than before.

On his return to the country at the beginning of June, he returned also to his customary occupations. The farm, his relations with the peasants and the neighboring gentry, his home affairs, his brother's and sister's affairs, his relation with his wife and her relatives, his care for the child, the new bee-keeping that had fascinated him since the spring, and a hundred other things, absorbed all his time.

These matters interested him not because he justified them by some general principle as he had done formerly; on the contrary, having become disenchanted by the failure of his various undertakings for the common good, he now busied himself for no other reason than because it seemed to him that he could not do otherwise.

Formerly, whenever he had tried to do anything for the good of humanity, for Russia, for the village, he had observed that the idea itself was agreeable, but the work senseless. There was no full conviction that it was absolutely necessary, and from at first appearing great, it grew smaller and smaller, until it reached the point of impossibility. Since his marriage, however, he had begun to confine his life more strictly to himself, and though he no longer experienced the same joy at the thought of his activity, he felt more certain of its usefulness, saw that it proceeded much better than before, and that it grew larger instead of smaller.

Almost against his will he buried himself deeper and deeper into the soil, so that he could not get out of it without opening a furrow.

To live as his father and grandfathers had lived, to carry out their work so as to hand it on to his children, seemed to him a plain duty. It was as necessary as eating when one is hungry. And for that, just as one had to prepare a meal, one had to keep the farm at Pokrovsky in such a manner as to make it profitable. Just as it was necessary to pay one's debts, so it was necessary to manage the estate in such a manner that when his son inherited it from him, he would be as grateful as Levin himself had been when he had received it from his grandfather. And so he looked after his cows, fields and manures, and planted forests.

He could not help attending to the affairs of Sergei Ivanovitch and his sister, and the peasants had become so accustomed to coming to him for advice that he had not the heart to cast them off. Then he had to see to the comforts of his sister-in-law and her children, whom he had invited to stay with them, and to that of his wife and child; he had to be with them at least a small part of the day.

Taken all together, Levin's life was fully occupied, yet it had no meaning for him whenever he thought of it.

Not only did Levin see clearly what it was he had to do, but he saw also how he must do it, and what part was of paramount importance.

He knew that it was necessary to hire laborers as cheaply as possible, but that he ought not to enslave them by advancing them money in order to get them below market price. There was no harm in selling peasants straw when they had no food for their cattle, but the wine and the dramshop had to be abolished, even though they brought in an income. Wood-stealing he would punish most severely, but he would take no fines for cattle driven on to his land, much to the disgust of his own herds.

Peter, who was paying a moneylender ten per cent a month, was to get a loan in order to save him, but no mercy was to be shown to those peasants who did not pay their rents. His bailiff was not to be forgiven for having delayed mowing a small meadow and thus losing the grass for nothing; on the other hand, the eighty acres where new trees had been planted were not to be mowed at all. No mercy was to be shown to a laborer who went away during working time because his father had died, no matter how much he was to be pitied, and he was to be paid less for the valuable time he had lost; at the same time, he could not refuse giving a monthly allowance to old, worthless servants.

Upon returning home he knew that he had to go to his wife even though some peasants had been waiting for him for hours, yet he would forego the pleasure of hiving a swarm of bees to talk to the peasants who came to find him at the apiary.

He did not know whether he was doing right or wrong, indeed he had ceased thinking about the question. He dreaded any reflection that would have given rise to doubts and obscured the clear and accurate view he had taken of his duties. But an infallible judge was ever present in his soul who decided which of two possible acts was the better one, and instantly let him know the moment he did not act as was proper.

Thus he lived, not knowing and not seeing the remotest possibility of knowing what he was and for what purpose he had been placed in the world. He was tormented by this ignorance to the extent of fearing suicide, yet at the same time was laying out for himself a definite path in life.

The day on which Sergei Ivanovitch reached Pokrovsky was one full of torment for Levin. It was at that hurried, busy season of the year when the peasantry put forth an extraordinary amount of effort and show an endurance quite unknown in any other conditions of life—an endurance that would be prized more highly were it not repeated every year, and if it did not produce such very simple results. Digging, sowing, mowing, reaping, harvesting, threshing—these are labors that seem simple and commonplace, but to accomplish them in the short time accorded by nature, every one, old and young, must set to work. For three or four weeks they must be content with the simplest fare, such as black bread, garlic, and kvas, and must haul the ricks at night and not get more than two or three hours' sleep a day. And this is done every year throughout the whole of Russia.

Having lived the greater part of his life in the country in close relations with the people, Levin always felt the electric feeling of this particular time communicate itself to him.

Early in the morning he went out to see the first sowing of the rye and the oats that were being hauled to the lots, and returning home, he drank his coffee with his wife and sister-in-law, and afterwards departed on foot to the outfarm, where they were to start a newly erected threshing-machine for the preparation of the seeds.

All that day while talking with his bailiff, the peasants, or at home with his wife, Dolly, the children, and his father-in-law, Levin kept thinking of the one and only thing that interested him at that time, in spite of all his farm cares. "What am I? where am I? and why am I?" he asked himself.

Standing in the cold-room of the newly thatched kiln, he watched the dust thrown off by the threshing-machine flying about in the air, the chaff settling down on the sunny grass, while the swallows took refuge under the roof and the laborers hurried about in the dark interior. A strange idea came into his head.

"What is this all done for?" he thought. "Why do I stand here compelling them to work? What makes them bustle so and try to show their zeal in my presence? Why does that old woman Matriona work so hard? I remember curing her once when she was struck down by a beam during a fire." He was looking at the haggard old woman who was trotting about on her sunburnt feet over the rough, uneven threshing floor, turning the grain over with a rake. "She recovered then, but to-day, or to-morrow, or in ten years, she will be dead and buried, and nothing will be left of her. And that pretty woman in the red blouse, who is so nimbly separating the grain from the chaff, will share the same fate. She, too, will be buried, and so will that horse," he thought, as he gazed at the piebald gelding that was breathing heavily through its dilated nostrils as it walked in the tread-mill. "The horse will be buried and so will Fiodor, the feeder, with his curly beard full of chaff and the shirt that is torn over the shoulder. And I, too, will be buried and nothing will be left. What is it all for?"

During these thoughts he kept a steady watch in order to calculate how much work they would do in an hour. He had to know that in order to fix the task of the day.

"An hour has nearly gone and they are only on the third rick," Levin thought. He walked over to the feeder, and raising his voice above the rumble of the machine, ordered him to feed it more evenly.

"You put too much at a time, Fiodor! You see, it catches and goes more slowly. Try and make it more even!"

Fiodor, his face black from perspiration and dust, shouted something in reply, but still did not do what Levin wanted him to.

Levin walked over to the drum, and pushing Fiodor aside began feeding it himself.

He worked until the peasant dinner hour, then went out of the kiln with the feeder, and stopped to talk to him at the yellow stack of cut rye.

The man came from a distant village, where Levin had once let land on the company system. Now it was let to the innkeeper.

Levin questioned Fiodor about this land, and asked whether Platon, a rich merchant of that village, would not take it for the coming year.

"The price is high, Konstantin Dmitritch; Platon cannot make it pay," the peasant replied, picking off the ears of rye from his perspiring bosom.

"But how does Kirillov make it pay?"

"Oh, Mityuha could make anything pay!" (Mityuha was a nickname the innkeeper was known by in the village.) "He will squeeze a fellow and get what he wants. He will not spare a Christian. As for Uncle Fokanitch" (thus he called Platon), "he is different. To some he gives on credit, and on others he loses. Sometimes he does not get back his own. He is a good man."

"But why doesn't he insist on getting his own?"

"People are different; one man lives for himself alone, like Mityuha, who only thinks of filling his belly, but Fokanitch is an honest man; he lives for his soul. He thinks of God."

"What do you mean by that? How does he live for his soul?" Levin almost shouted.

"It's quite simple, according to the truth, according to God's work. There are all kinds of people. Take yourself, for example, you would not hurt any one . . . "

"Yes, yes, good-bye!" Levin said, hastily, and turned away. He took his cane and walked rapidly towards the house, in a state of great agitation. The peasant's simple words about Fokanitch living for his soul, according to God's word, set a whole chain of thoughts whirling in his brain, blinding him with their light.

Levin walked along the highway with long strides, excited, not so much by his thoughts, as by his strange mental condition—a condition he had never experienced before.

The words uttered by the peasant were like an electric spark, that suddenly transformed and blended into a whole series of heterogeneous, impotent, disconnected thoughts, that had never ceased interesting him. They had been with him even when he had spoken to the peasant about the land.

He felt that something new was taking place in his soul, and though he did not yet know what it was, he felt a pleasurable excitement in the feeling.

"Not to live for oneself, but for God. For what God? Could any one have said anything more stupid? According to Fiodor one must live not for one's own needs, that is, for what we want, what we understand, but for some incomprehensible God whom nobody knows or can define. Well? Did I not understand the meaning of Fiodor's words? Did I doubt their justice? Did I find them senseless, incomprehensible, insignificant? I understood them just as Fiodor understood them. I understand them more clearly and fully than anything in life, and never have I doubted them, or could have doubted them. Not I alone, but everybody, the whole world understands them fully; in this alone men have no doubts, and are in complete accord. Fiodor said that Kirillovitch the innkeeper lives only for his stomach. That is comprehensible and sensible. All sensible people cannot help but live for their stomachs. And suddenly this same Fiodor says that it is bad to live for one's stomach, that one ought to live for truth, for God, and I understand him. And the millions of people who lived centuries back, and those who are living now, peasants, the poor in spirit, and the wise, those who have thought and written about it, those who say the same in their own simple language—all are agreed on this one point, and know what it is we should live for, and what is

good. With all people in common, I have one firm, indubitable piece
of knowledge—a knowledge that cannot be explained through reason, because it is beyond the sphere of reason, a knowledge that has
no causes and can have no effects. If good has a cause, it is no longer
good if it has an effect—rewards—it is again not good. Consequently
good must be beyond the law of cause and effect.

"I know this and we all know it.

"I wanted a miracle to convince me. But here it is, the only
possible, existing miracle, surrounding me on all sides, and I did
not even observe it! What greater miracle can there be?

"Is it possible that I have found the solution to everything? Is it
possible that all my sufferings have come to an end?" Levin asked
himself, as he continued on his way along the dusty road, oblivious
to heat and fatigue, with a sensation as though an old pain had suddenly left him. The sensation was so joyous that it seemed almost
incredible to him. He was so overcome by emotion that he was
unable to proceed, and leaving the road, he turned aside into the
forest. He took off his hat and sank down on the rich, luxurious
grass, under the shade of the aspens.

"Yes, I must consider it carefully," he thought, gazing at the
untrodden grass in front of him, and watching the movements of a
little green caterpillar that was climbing up a blade of couch-grass.
"What is it I have discovered?" he asked himself, bending another
blade of grass for the caterpillar to crawl on. "Why am I so pleased?
What have I discovered?

"Formerly I used to say that in my body, in this grass, in this
caterpillar, a transmutation of matter takes place according to physical, chemical, and physiological laws. And in all of us, in these
aspens, in the clouds, evolution is going on. Evolution from what,
to what? An eternal evolution and struggle? As if there could be any
direction and struggle in the infinite! And in spite of all the efforts
of my reason in that direction, until now, the meaning of life, the
meaning of my own impulses and strivings were not revealed to me.
Now I know that life consists in living for God, for the soul.

"I have not discovered anything; I have merely found what I
knew already. I have come to understand the power that gave me
life in the past, that gives me life in the present. I have freed myself
from deception and found the master."

He reviewed briefly the whole progress of his thoughts of the
last two years, thoughts that had first been aroused by the sight of
his sick, dying brother. Then, for the first time, had he clearly com-

prehended that for every man, and himself too, there was nothing
ahead but suffering, death, eternal oblivion. He had decided that it
was impossible to live thus, that it was necessary to explain life in a
more sane way or else shoot himself. But he had done neither the
one nor the other; he had continued to live, think, and feel. He
even married during that time, experienced many joys, and was
happy so long as he tried to shut his eyes to the meaning of life.

What did it mean? It meant that he was living well and thinking badly.

He had been living unconsciously on the spiritual truths he
had imbibed with his mother's milk, yet in his thoughts he had not
only refused to acknowledge them, but had cautiously avoided
them altogether.

Now it was clear to him that he could only live according to
the beliefs in which he had been brought up.

"What should I have been, how should I have passed my life
had it not been for those beliefs, had I not known that one must
live for God and not for one's own needs? I might have robbed,
lied, and killed. What are now the chief joys of my life would never
have existed for me." And try as he would he was unable to picture
to himself the bestial creature he would have been had he not
known what he was living for.

"I have been seeking an answer to my question, but reason
could not give it to me. It was life itself gave me the answer, through
my knowledge of good and bad. This knowledge I have not
acquired in any way; it was given me from the beginning, given me
because I could not get it anywhere.

"Where did it come from? Was it reason that told me it was
necessary to love my neighbor? It was told to me in my childhood,
and I gladly believed it, because it was already in my soul. Who discovered it? Not reason; reason discovered the theory of the struggle of existence and the law demanding that I should gratify my
own desires at the cost of others. To love my neighbor could not
have been discovered by reason, because it is unreasonable."

Levin recalled a recent scene between Dolly and her children.
When left alone one day the children began amusing themselves by
making raspberry jam in a tea-cup over a lighted candle, and throwing milk into each other's faces. Their mother, catching them in
the act, began scolding them before Levin. She tried to impress on
them the idea that what they were destroying had cost their elders
a large amount of labor, performed for their sakes, also saying that
if they broke the cups they would have nothing from which to

drink their tea, and that if they spilled the milk they would have nothing to eat, and would have to go hungry.

Levin was struck by the indifference and scepticism with which the children listened to their mother's words. They did not believe what she said, and were merely sorry to have their interesting game interrupted. They did not believe because they did not know the value of what they were playing with, and did not understand that they were destroying their own means of subsistence.

"That is all very well," they thought, "but these things are not so important, for they have always been and always will be. We needn't worry about that, that is all ready for us. We want to invent something new. It was quite a nice idea to make raspberry jam in a cup over a candle, and to pour milk into each other's mouths as from a fountain. It was very jolly, and not in any way worse than drinking it out of a cup.

"Are we not doing the same?" Levin thought. "Have I not done it by trying to discover the meaning of the forces of nature and human life through reason? And is not the same done by all philosophical theories that lead us by strange paths to the knowledge that we already have? Can we not see clearly in the development of the theory of any philosopher that he knows in advance, just as much as Fiodor did, what is the real meaning of life?

"If we were to let the children get things for themselves, make the dishes, milk the cows, and so forth, what would happen? They would starve, probably. In the same way if we were let loose with our passions and ideas, without any conception of a God, a Creator, of what is good or evil, we should only destroy just as the children do. For without the idea of a God we cannot build up anything.

"From whence did this joyful knowledge come to me, a knowledge that I have in common with the peasant Fiodor, which alone gives me peace of mind? Here am I, a Christian, brought up in the faith, surrounded by the blessings of Christianity, living upon these spiritual blessings without being conscious of them, and failing to understand them, destroying that by which I live. And the moment anything important in life occurs I run to Him as children run to their mother when they are cold and hungry.

"Yes, what I know has not come to me through reason, it has been given to me, revealed to me; I know it with my heart, by my faith in the teachings of the Church.

"The Church? The Church?" Levin repeated to himself as he rolled over on his other side and, leaning on his arm, looked away into the distance, beyond the cattle going down to the river.

"But can I believe in all that the Church teaches?" he said, in order to test himself, and bring up everything that might destroy his present feeling of security. He purposely brought to mind the part of the Church teaching that had seemed to him strange and had most alienated him. "Creation? Yes, how did I explain existence? By existence? By nothing? The devil, and sin? But how did I explain evil? The Redeemer? . . .

"But I know nothing, nothing, and cannot know other than what I have been told with the rest."

It seemed to him now that not one of these Church dogmas was inimical to the great objects of life—faith in God and goodness. On the contrary, all tended to produce the greatest of miracles; enabling the world with its millions of human beings, young and old, Lvov, Kitty, peasants, and kings, to comprehend the same great truths, so as to live the life of the soul—the only life that is worth living.

Lying on his back he looked up into the high, cloudless sky.

"Do I not know that that is endless space and not a vault of blue stretching over me? But however much I may strain my sight I can only see a vaulted dome; and in spite of my knowledge of infinite space I am unquestionably right when I see it like that, far more right than when I try to probe into the beyond."

Levin stopped thinking, and listened intently to the mysterious joyful voices that seemed to be talking about him.

"Is it faith?" he thought, afraid to believe his own happiness.

"My God, I thank thee!" he cried, swallowing the sobs that rose within him, and brushing the tears from his eyes.

4

THE FAMILY MAN

Perhaps there is no more complex set of relationships for a man than that of family life. At different stages and in different spheres of his life, a man relates to his family as a son, grandson, brother, cousin, nephew, husband, father, uncle, and grandfather. The demands and rewards, triumphs and heartbreaks of the web of family relationships are almost endless in their variety. In all the stages and spheres I've just listed, a boy and later a man can experience the most astonishing range of emotions—achingly intense love for a parent, spouse, child, or relation combined with feelings of disappointment, envy, betrayal, or rejection, and sorrow and grief should illness, pain, or misfortune befall any of those family members.

Family life, for these reasons, is a lifelong school for a man in developing his own inner resources, fortitude under adversity, compassion, understanding, and patience. Aristotle believed that the successful head of a household must possess what he termed "the proper art of household management"—the virtuous organization of the family to sustain it economically and, at a higher level, to raise children in partnership with their mother so as to prepare them for their future duties as citizens and family members. As G. K. Chesterton has observed, the family is the most demanding test of a man's freedom because it is the only situation that a man is more or less free to succeed at or bungle all on his own. For many men family life is the source of their chief satisfactions, and most men at some point find themselves contemplating the meaning of life in a larger religious or philosophical context chiefly as the result of the reversals, torments, and puzzles of family love.

Of course, the very reasons that family life offers such intense satisfactions can also make us bitter enemies of the institution. Because we are so vulnerable to the wounds that parents, spouses, and children can inflict on us, some men long to flee the responsibilities of family altogether. "Sacred family!" cries a character in one of Strindberg's plays, "the supposed home of all the virtues, where innocent children are tortured into their first falsehoods,

where wills are broken by parental tyranny, and self-respect smothered by crowded jostling egos." Some men find friendships outside
of the family more satisfying than blood ties because they can
choose a friend or lover freely, without the obligations implied by a
biological kinship. But for most men the family is, for better or
worse, their best shot at personal happiness; even the most presti-
gious and rewarding job is unlikely to give one a comparable feeling of inner contentment and peace.

Being the father of a family can be likened to governing the
affairs of a small, self-contained country. It requires great reserves
of prudence—an ability to alternate between reticence and candor,
and between exerting too much authority and too little. According
to the great French humanist Michel de Montaigne, governing a
private family is in fact hardly less challenging than governing a
whole kingdom—and even more complicated in our era, when we
are no likelier to accept a king in private life than in public. The
Chinese proverb puts it wisely: the family man should "govern his
family as you would cook a small fish—very carefully."

BOYS INTO MEN

Telemachus's Search for a Father

From Homer, The Odyssey

Homer's Odyssey *is a search within a search. While Odysseus is making his
slow way home from Troy, his son Telemachus embarks on a voyage of his
own to search for his missing father and bring him back. Spiritually as well
as literally, Telemachus is a fatherless young man searching for that missing
guide in his life. In the course of searching for his father, he becomes more
mature. By pursuing a father who, absent for twenty years, is really more of
an ideal for Telemachus than a flesh-and-blood reality, Telemachus raises
himself in the light of this ideal, trying to become the man he thinks his
father would want him to be. Both Odysseus and Telemachus are under the*

protection of Athena, the goddess of sage counsel. Her intelligence, subtlety, and curiosity mirror Odysseus's own. Her partnership with Odysseus and his son suggests a new vision of manliness, in which male and female traits deepen and temper each other.

Almost nothing is known of Homer, who may or may not have been born in the middle of the 9th century B.C. in Ionia. But the ancient Greeks firmly believed he was the author of both the Odyssey *and its companion poem, the* Iliad. *Their influence on Western literature is immeasurable.*

Early in the Odyssey, *young Telemachus laments the twenty-year absence of his father. How can the boy protect his mother Penelope from the rapacious suitors who are eating her out of house and home? Is he man enough to take on his adult responsibilities? He confides his worries to Athena, who appears in human guise at the palace.*

Now far the first to see Athene was godlike Telemachus, as he sat among the suitors, his heart deep grieving within him, imagining in his mind his great father, how he might come back and all throughout the house might cause the suitors to scatter, and hold his rightful place and be lord of his own possessions. With such thoughts, sitting among the suitors, he saw Athene and went straight to the forecourt, the heart within him scandalized that a guest should still be standing at the doors. He stood beside her and took her by the right hand, and relieved her of the bronze spear, and spoke to her and addressed her in winged words: "Welcome, stranger. You shall be entertained as a guest among us. Afterward, when you have tasted dinner, you shall tell us what your need is."

Then the haughty suitors came in, and all of them straightway took their places in order on chairs and along the benches, and their heralds poured water over their hands for them to wash with, and the serving maids brought them bread heaped up in the baskets, and the young men filled the mixing bowls with wine for their drinking. They put their hands to the good things that lay ready before them. But when they had put away their desire for eating and drinking, the suitors found their attention turned to other matters, the song and the dance; for these things come at the end of the feasting. A herald put the beautifully wrought lyre in the hands of Phemios, who sang for the suitors, because they made him. He played his lyre and struck up a fine song. Meanwhile Telemachus talked to Athene of the gray eyes, leaning his head close to hers, so that none of the others might hear him:

"Dear stranger, would you be scandalized at what I say to you? This is all they think of, the lyre and the singing. Easy for them, since without penalty they eat up the substance of a man whose white bones lie out in the rain and fester somewhere on the mainland, or roll in the wash of the breakers. If they were ever to see him coming back to Ithaka all the prayer of them all would be to be lighter on their feet instead of to be richer men for gold and clothing. As it is, he has died by an evil fate, and there is no comfort left for us, not even though someone among mortals tells us he will come back. His day of homecoming has perished."

"Now I have come," Athene replied. "They told me he was here in this country, your father, I mean. But no. The gods are impeding his passage. For no death on the land has befallen the great Odysseus, but somewhere, alive on the wide sea, he is held captive, on a sea-washed island, and savage men have him in their keeping, rough men, who somehow keep him back, though he is unwilling. Now, I will make you a prophecy, in the way the immortals put it into my mind, and as I think it will come out, though I am no prophet, nor do I know the ways of birds clearly. He will not long be absent from the beloved land of his fathers, even if the bonds that hold him are iron, but he will be thinking of a way to come back, since he is a man of many resources. But come now tell me this and give me an accurate answer. Are you, big as you are, the very child of Odysseus? Indeed, you are strangely alike about the head, the fine eyes, as I remember; we used to meet so often together before he went away to Troy, where others beside him and the greatest of the Argives went in their hollow vessels. Since that time I have not seen Odysseus nor has he seen me."

Then the thoughtful Telemachus said to her in answer: "See, I will accurately answer all that you ask me. My mother says indeed I am his. I for my part do not know. Nobody really knows his own father."

Now the suitors all through the shadowy halls were raising a tumult, and all prayed for the privilege of lying beside Penelope, until the thoughtful Telemachus began speaking among them:

"You suitors of my mother, overbearing in your rapacity, now let us dine and take our pleasure, and let there be no shouting. . . Then tomorrow let us all go to the place of assembly, and hold a session, where I will give you my forthright statement, that you go out of my palace and do your feasting elsewhere, eating up your own possessions, taking turns, household by household. But if you decide it is more profitable and better to go on, eating up one man's livelihood, without payment, then spoil my house. I will cry out to the gods everlasting in the hope that Zeus might somehow grant a reversal of fortunes. Then you may perish in this house, with no payment given."

The suitors, men from noble families, want Penelope to give Odysseus up for dead and marry one of them so as to preserve dynastic and social stability. Telemachus takes his complaint about them to the Assembly. The suitors threaten to usurp his father's rightful place. As son and heir, it is his duty to resist them.

"I have lost a noble father, one who was king once over you here, and was kind to you like a father; and now here is a greater evil, one which presently will break up the whole house and destroy all my livelihood. For my mother, against her will, is beset by suitors, own sons to the men who are greatest hereabouts. These shrink from making the journey to the house of her father Ikarios, so that he might take bride gifts for his daughter and bestow on her the one he wished, who came as his favorite; rather, all their days, they come and loiter in our house and sacrifice our oxen and our sheep and our fat goats and make a holiday feast of it and drink the bright wine recklessly. Most of our substance is wasted. We have no man here such as Odysseus was, to drive this curse from the household.

"We ourselves are not the men to do it; we must be weaklings in such a case, not men well seasoned in battle. I would defend myself if the power were in me. No longer are the things endurable that have been done, and beyond all decency my house has been destroyed. Even you must be scandalized and ashamed before the neighboring men about us, the people who live around our land; fear also the gods' anger, lest they, astonished by evil actions, turn against you. I supplicate you: by Zeus the Olympian and by Themis who breaks up the assemblies of men and calls them in session; let be, my friends, and leave me alone with my bitter sorrow to waste away; unless my noble father Odysseus at some time in anger did evil to the strong-greaved Achaians, for which angry with me in revenge you do me evil in setting these on me. But for me it would be far better for you to eat away my treasures and eat my cattle. If you were to eat them, there might be a recompense someday, for we could go through all the settlement, with claims made public asking for our goods again, until it was all regiven. But now you are heaping me with troubles I cannot deal with."

So he spoke in anger, and dashed to the ground the scepter in a stormburst of tears; and pity held all the people.

Educating Boys

From Michel de Montaigne, Essays

Don't make a boy "a prisoner to schooling," writes the great sixteenth-century French humanist, by cooping him up all day to learn by rote. Encourage him to relate his learning to life's grandeur and adversities, and let his experience of life and the company of others motivate him to learn more. The test of a boy's education is the goodness, justice, and prudence of his actions.

Let the tutor demand of him an account not only of the words of his lesson, but of their meaning and substance, and let him estimate the profit he has gained, not by the testimony of his memory, but of his life. Let him show what he has just learned from a hundred points of view, and adapt it to as many different subjects, to see if he has yet rightly taken it in and made it his own, taking stock of his progress according to Plato's disciplinary method.

Let his conscience and his virtue shine forth in his speech, and be guided solely by reason. Make him understand that to confess the error he discovers in his own reasoning, though he himself alone perceives it, is a mark of judgment and honesty, which are the chief qualities he aims at; that obstinacy and contention are vulgar qualities, most apparent in the basest minds; that to correct oneself and change one's mind, and in the heat of ardor to abandon a weak position, is a sign of strong, rare, and philosophical qualities.

He will sound the depths of every man: a neatherd, a mason, a passing stranger; he should utilize and borrow from each according to his wares, for everything is of use in the household; he will learn something even from the follies and weaknesses of others. By observing the graces and manners of each, he will plant in himself the seeds of emulation of the good, and contempt of the bad.

Suggest to his fancy an honest curiosity that will make him inquire into all things; he should see everything uncommon in his surroundings: a building, a fountain, a man, the scene of an ancient battle, the passage of Caesar or of Charlemagne.

For all those reasons I would not have this youth kept a prisoner; I would not hand him over to the melancholy humors of a hot-tempered schoolmaster. I would not break his spirit by keeping him, as some others do, to hard labor and the torture for fourteen or fifteen hours a day, like a porter. Nor should I think it well, if, in consequence of a disposition to solitude and melancholy, he were found to be addicted to a too close application to his books, to encourage that tendency in him: that renders them unfit for society and conversation, and diverts them from better occupations. How many men have I not seen in my time dulled by this injudicious avidity for learning! Carneades was so infatuated with it that he had no leisure to comb his hair and pare his nails.

He should not so much say his lesson, as do it. He should repeat it in his actions. We shall see if there is prudence in his enterprises, if there is goodness and justice in his behaviour, if there is judgment and grace in his speaking, manliness in his maladies, soberness in his play, temperance in his pleasures, indifference in his tastes, whether meat, fish, wine, or water, order in his economy.

For the rest, this education is to be conducted with a mild severity, contrary to the usual practice. Instead of making study attractive to children, they only suggest to their minds horrors and cruelties. Away with violence and compulsion! There is nothing to my mind more calculated to deaden and brutalize a generous nature. If you wish him to fear shame and chastisement do not harden him to them. Harden him to sweat and cold, wind and sun, and the dangers that he is to despise; wean him from all effeminacy and delicacy in clothing and bedding, in eating and drinking; accustom him to everything. Let him not be a pretty and namby-pamby youth, but a fresh and sturdy boy. As boy and man I have ever been of this belief and opinion, and am so still in my old age.

The Value of a Fair Fight

From Thomas Hughes,
Tom Brown's School Days

Tom Brown's School Days *(1881) is one of the best-loved accounts of how a boy grows into a man by experiencing the trials of homesickness and the rewards of fair play and friendship. Fighting isn't necessarily a bad thing, Tom learns, if you choose the right fight.*

Let those young persons who stomachs are not strong, or who think a good set-to with the weapons which God has given us all, an uncivilized, unchristian, or ungentlemanly affair, just skip this chapter at once, for it won't be to their taste.

It was not at all usual in those days for two School-house boys to have a fight. Of course there were exceptions, when some cross-grained hard-headed fellow came up who would never be happy unless he was quarreling with his nearest neighbors, or when there was some class-dispute, between the fifth-form and the fags for instance, which required blood-letting; and a champion was picked out on each side tacitly, who settled the matter by a good hearty mill. But for the most part the constant use of those surest keepers of the peace, the boxing-gloves, kept the School-house boys from fighting one another. Two or three nights in every week the gloves were brought out, either in the hall or fifth-form room; and every boy who was ever likely to fight at all knew all his neighbor's prowess perfectly well, and could tell to a nicety what chance he would have in a stand-up fight with any other boy in the house. But of course no such experience could be gotten as regarded boys in other houses; and as most of the other houses were more or less jealous of the School-house, collisions were frequent.

After all, what would life be without fighting, I should like to know? From the cradle to the grave, fighting, rightly understood, is the business, the real, highest, honestest, business of every son of man. Every one who is worth his salt has his enemies, who must be beaten, be they evil thoughts and habits in himself, or spiritual wickedness in high places, or Russians, or Border-ruffians, or Bill, Tom, or Harry, who will not let him live his life in quiet till he has thrashed them.

It is no good for Quakers, or any other body of men, to uplift their voices against fighting. Human nature is too strong for them, and they don't follow their own precepts. Every soul of them is doing his own piece of fighting, somehow and somewhere. The world might be a better world without fighting, for anything I know, but it wouldn't be our world; and therefore I am dead against crying peace when there is no peace, and isn't meant to be. I am as sorry as any man to see folk fighting the wrong people and the wrong things, but I'd a deal sooner see them doing that, than that they should have no fight in them.

As to fighting, keep out of it if you can, by all means. When the time comes, if it ever should, that you have to say "Yes" or "No" to a challenge to fight, say, "No" if you can—only take care you make it clear to yourselves why you say "No." It's a proof of the highest courage, if done from true Christian motives. It's quite right and justifiable, if done from a simple aversion to physical pain and danger. But don't say "No" because you fear a licking, and say or think it's because you fear God, for that's neither Christian nor honest. And if you do fight, fight it out; and don't give in while you can stand and see.

Telemachus Finds His Father

From Homer, The Odyssey

As he begins his journey in search of his father, Athena guides Telemachus to some of the legendary figures from the Trojan War. Hearing them talk about his father, Telemachus absorbs the heritage of the Iliad *and lessons of war that his father would otherwise have imparted to him. At first, Telemachus cannot believe his eyes when he finally sees his father back home. Then they fall into each other's arms weeping, man and boy reunited at last. Through the lessons of his travels and trials, as guided by Athena, Telemachus knows he has proven himself worthy of his long-lost father, an ideal he carried around in his heart during every moment of his journey.*

"Son of Laertes and seed of Zeus, resourceful Odysseus, it is time now to tell your son the story; no longer hide it, so that, contriving death and doom for the suitors, you may go to the glorious city. I myself shall not be long absent from you in my eagerness for the fighting."

So spoke Athene, and with her golden wand she tapped him. First she made the mantle and the tunic that covered his chest turn bright and clean; she increased his strength and stature. His dark color came back to him again, his jaws firmed, and the beard that grew about his chin turned black. Athene went away once more, having done her work, but Odysseus went back into the shelter. His beloved son was astonished and turned his eyes in the other direction, fearing this must be a god, and spoke aloud to him and addressed him in winged words:

"Suddenly you have changed, my friend, from what you were formerly; your skin is no longer as it was, you have other clothing.

Surely you are one of the gods who hold the high heaven. Be gracious, then: so we shall give you favored offerings and golden gifts that have been well wrought. Only be merciful."

Then in turn long-suffering great Odysseus answered him:

"No I am not a god. Why liken me to the immortals? But I am your father, for whose sake you are always grieving as you look for violence from others, and endure hardships."

So he spoke, and kissed his son, and the tears running down his cheeks splashed on the ground. Until now, he was always unyielding. But Telemachus, for he did not yet believe that this was his father, spoke to him once again in answer, saying:

"No, you are not Odysseus my father, but some divinity beguiles me, so that I must grieve the more and be sorry. For no man who was mortal could ever have so contrived it by his own mind alone, not unless some immortal, descending on him in person, were likely to make him a young or an old man. For even now you were an old man in unseemly clothing, but now you resemble one of the gods who hold wide heaven."

Then resourceful Odysseus spoke in turn and answered him:

"Telemachus, it does not become you to wonder too much at your own father when he is here, nor doubt him. No other Odysseus than I will ever come back to you. But here I am, and I am as you see me, and after hardships and suffering much I have come, in the twentieth year, back to my own country. But here you see the work of Athene, the giver of plunder, who turns me into whatever she pleases, since she can do this; and now she will make me look like a beggar, but then the next time like a young man, and wearing splendid clothes on my body; and it is a light thing for the gods who hold wide heaven to glorify any mortal man, or else to degrade him."

So he spoke, and sat down again, but now Telemachus folded his great father in his arms and lamented, shedding tears, and desire for mourning rose in both of them; and they cried shrill in a pulsing voice, even more than the outcry of birds.

The New Kid in Town

From Mark Twain,
The Adventures of Tom Sawyer

Writing as Mark Twain, Samuel Clemens (1835–1910) chronicles life in rural and frontier America with gentle humor and irony.

A new-comer of any age or either sex was an impressive curiosity in the poor little shabby village of St. Petersburg. This boy was well dressed, too—well dressed on a week-day. This was simply astounding. His cap was a dainty thing, his close buttoned blue cloth roundabout was new and natty, and so were his pantaloons. He had shoes on—and it was only Friday. He even wore a necktie, a bright bit of ribbon. He had a citified air about him that ate into Tom's vitals. The more Tom stared at the splendid marvel, the higher he turned up his nose at his finery and the shabbier and shabbier his own outfit seemed to him to grow. Neither boy spoke. If one moved, the other moved—but only sidewise, in a circle; they kept face to face and eye to eye all the time. Finally Tom said:
"I can lick you!"
"I'd like to see you try it."
"Well, I can do it."
"No, you can't, either."
"Yes I can."
"No you can't."
"I can."
"You can't."
"Can!"
"Can't!"
An uncomfortable pause. Then Tom said:
"What's your name?"
"'Tisn't any of your business, maybe."
"Well I 'low I'll *make* it my business."
"Well why don't you?"
"If you say much, I will."
"Much—much—*much*. There now."
"Oh, you think you're mighty smart, *don't* you?"

"I could lick you with one hand tied behind me, if I wanted to."

"Well why don't you *do* it? You *say* you can do it."

"Well I *will*, if you fool with me."

"Oh yes—I've seen whole families in the same fix."

"Smarty! You think you're *some*, now, *don't* you? Oh, what a hat!"

"You can lump that hat if you don't like it. I dare you to knock it off—and anybody that'll take a dare will suck eggs."

"You're a liar!"

"You're another."

"You're a fighting liar and dasn't take it up."

"Aw—take a walk!"

"Say—if you give me much more of your sass I'll take and bounce a rock off'n your head."

"Oh, of *course* you will."

"Well I *will*."

"Why don't you *do* it then? What do you keep *saying* you will for? Why don't you *do* it? It's because you're afraid."

"I ain't afraid."

"You are."

"I ain't."

"You are."

Another pause, and more eying and sidling around each other. Presently they were shoulder to shoulder. Tom said:

"Get away from here!"

"Go away yourself!"

"I won't."

"*I* won't either."

So they stood, each with a foot placed at an angle as a brace, and both shoving with might and main, and glowering at each other with hate. But neither could get an advantage. After struggling till both were hot and flushed, each relaxed his strain with watchful caution, and Tom said:

"You're a coward and a pup. I'll tell my big brother on you, and he can thrash you with his little finger, and I'll make him do it, too."

"What do I care for your big brother? I've got a brother that's bigger than he is—and what's more, he can throw him over that fence, too."

(Both brothers were imaginary.)

"That's a lie."

"*Your* saying so don't make it so."

Tom drew a line in the dust with his big toe, and said:

"I dare you to step over that, and I'll lick you till you can't stand up. Anybody that'll take a dare will steal sheep."

The new boy stepped over promptly, and said:

"Now you said you'd do it, now let's see you do it."

"Don't you crowd me now; you better look out."

"Well, you *said* you'd do it—why don't you do it?"

"By jingo! For two cents I *will* do it."

The new boy took two broad coppers out of his pocket and held them out with derision. Tom struck them to the ground. In an instant both boys were rolling and tumbling in the dirt, gripped together like cats; and for the space of a minute they tugged and tore at each other's hair and clothes, punched and scratched each other's noses, and covered themselves with dust and glory. Presently the confusion took form and through the fog of battle Tom appeared, seated astride the new boy, and pounding him with his fists.

"Holler 'nuff!" said he.

The boy only struggled to free himself. He was crying—mainly from rage.

"Holler 'nuff!"—and the pounding went on.

At last the stranger got out a smothered "'Nuff!" and Tom let him up and said:

"Now that'll learn you. Better look out who you're fooling with next time."

The new boy went off brushing the dust from his clothes, sobbing, snuffling and occasionally looking back and shaking his head and threatening what he would do to Tom the "next time he caught him out." To which Tom responded with jeers, and started off in high feather, and as soon as his back was turned the new boy snatched up a stone, threw it and hit him between the shoulders and then turned tail and ran like an antelope. Tom chased the traitor home, and thus found out where he lived. He then held a position at the gate for some time, daring the enemy to come outside, but the enemy only made faces at him through the window and declined. At last the enemy's mother appeared, and called Tom a bad, vicious, vulgar child, and ordered him away. So he went away, but he said he "lowed" to "lay" for that boy.

He got home pretty late, that night, and when he climbed cautiously in at the window, he uncovered an ambuscade, in the person of his aunt; and when she saw the state his clothes were in her resolution to turn his Saturday holiday into captivity at hard labor became adamantine in its firmness.

The Education of Cyrus

From Xenophon, The Education of Cyrus

The classical ideal of manhood called for a lifelong commitment to moral and intellectual education. One of the most famous accounts comes to us from Xenophon's Education of Cyrus, *an idealized account of the life of Cyrus the Great. In the Persian Republic, the boys were educated throughout all the stages of childhood and youth to prefer the common good to their own selfish desires. Xenophon says that special care must be taken during adolescence to teach boys self-control and keep them occupied all day long with their duties and games—"for this time of life, it seems, demands the most watchful care."*

He was educated in conformity with the laws of the Persians; and these laws appear in their care for the common weal not to start from the same point as they do in most states. For most states permit everyone to train his own children just as he will, and the older people themselves to live as they please; and then they command them not to steal and not to rob, not to break into anybody's house, not to strike a person whom they have no right to strike, not to commit adultery, not to disobey an officer, and so forth; and if a man transgress any one of these laws, they punish him. The Persian laws, however, begin at the beginning and take care that from the first their citizens shall not be of such a character as ever to desire anything improper or immoral; and the measures they take are as follows.

They have their so-called "Free Square," where the royal palace and other government buildings are located. The hucksters with their wares, their cries, and their vulgarities are excluded from this and relegated to another part of the city, in order that their tumult may not intrude upon the orderly life of the cultured. This square, enclosing the government buildings, is divided into four parts; one of these belongs to the boys, one to the youths, another to the men of mature years, and another to those who are past the age for military service. And the laws require them to come daily to their several quarters.

The boys go to school and spend their time in learning justice;

and they say that they go there for this purpose; just as in our country they say that they go to learn to read and write. And their officers spend the greater part of the day in deciding cases for them. For, as a matter of course, boys also prefer charges against one another, just as men do, of theft, robbery, assault, cheating, slander, and other things that might naturally come up; and when they discover anyone committing any of these crimes they punish him; and they punish also anyone whom they find accusing another falsely. And they bring one another to trial also charged with an offense for which people hate one another most but go to law least, namely, that of ingratitude; and if they know that anyone is able to return a favor and fails to do so, they punish him also severely. For they think that the ungrateful are likely to be most neglectful of their duty toward their gods, their parents, their country, and their friends; for it seems that shamelessness goes hand in hand with ingratitude; and it is that, we know, which leads the way to every moral wrong.

This, then, is what the boys do until they are sixteen or seventeen years of age, and after this they are promoted from the class of boys and enrolled among the young men.

Now the young men in their turn live as follows: for ten years after they are promoted from the class of boys they pass the nights about the government buildings. This they do for the sake of guarding the city and of developing their powers of self-control; for this time of life, it seems, demands the most watchful care.

An Early Critic of Rock Music?

From Jacopo Sadoleto,
On the Education of Boys

Born in 1477, this Renaissance humanist wrote an influential dialogue on educating boys.

What correctness or beauty can the music which is now in vogue possess? It has scarcely any real and stable foundation in word or thought. If it should have for its subject a maxim or proverb, it would obscure and hamper the sense and meaning by abruptly cutting and jerking the sounds in the throat—as though music were designed not to soothe and control the spirit, but merely to afford a base pleasure to the ears, mimicking the cries of birds and beasts, which we should be sorry to resemble. This is to turn soul into body, and weaken self-control. From this Plato most properly shrank in horror, and refused a place in his ideal state for such music as this. For when flaccid, feeble, sensual ideas are rendered in similar music, in kindred modulation of the voice, weakly yielding to lust, languishing in grief, or rushing in frenzied agitation toward the sudden passions of a disordered mind, what ruin to virtue, what wreckage of character, do you suppose, must ensue?

Bringing Up a Prince

From Desiderius Erasmus,
The Education of a Christian Prince

In this celebrated treatise, the Renaissance philosopher and man of letters stresses the importance of instilling good habits in a boy from the earliest age—especially when he is destined to rule a Kingdom.

There is no better time to shape and improve a prince than when he does not yet realize himself a prince. This time must be diligently employed, not only to the end that for a while he may be kept away from base associations, but also that he may be imbued with certain definite moral principles. If diligent parents raise with great care a boy who is destined to inherit only an acre or two, think how much interest and concern should be given to the education of one who will succeed not to a single dwelling, but to so many peoples, to so many cities, yea, to the world, either as a good man for the common gain of all, or an evil one, to the great ruination of all!

He should not be allowed to associate with whatever playmates appear, but only with those boys of good and modest character; he should be reared and trained most carefully and as becomes a gentleman. That whole crowd of wantons, hard drinkers, filthy-tongued fellows, especially flatterers, must be kept far from his sight and hearing while his mind is not yet fortified with precepts to the contrary. Since the natures of so many men are inclined toward the ways of evil, there is no nature so happily born that it cannot be corrupted by wrong training. What do you expect except a great fund of evil in a prince, who, regardless, of his native character (and a long line of ancestors does not necessarily furnish a mind, as it does a kingdom), is beset from his very cradle by the most inane opinions; is raised in the circle of senseless women; grows to boyhood among naughty girls, abandoned playfellows, and the most abject flatterers, among buffoons and mimes, drinkers and gamesters, and worse than stupid and worthless creators of wanton pleasures. In the company of all these he hears nothing, learns nothing, absorbs nothing except pleasures, amusements, arrogance, haughtiness, greed, petulance, and tyranny—and from this school he will soon progress to the government of his kingdom! Although each one of all the great arts is very difficult, there is none finer nor more difficult than that of ruling well. Why in the case of this one thing alone do we feel the need of no training, but deem it sufficient to have been born for it? To what end except tyranny do they devote themselves as men, who as boys played at nothing except as tyrants?

The teacher, into whose care the state has given its prince, shall give much careful thought to discover his leanings. Sometimes, too, at this early age it can be discovered by certain signs whether the prince is more prone to petulance or arrogance, to a desire for popularity or a thirst for fame, to licentiousness or dicing or greed, to defense or war, to rashness or tyranny. When he has found the prince's weak spot, there he should strengthen him with goodly doctrines and suitable teachings and try to lead into better ways a spirit still prone to follow. On the other hand, if he finds a nature prone to the good things of life, or at any rate to only those vices which are readily turned to virtue, e.g., ambition and prodigality, he should work the harder and assist advantages of nature with refinement. It is not enough just to hand out precepts to restrain the prince from vices or to incite him to a better course—they must be impressed, crammed in, inculcated, and in one way and another be kept before him, now by a suggestive thought, now by a fable, now by analogy, now by example, now by maxims, now by a proverb. They should be engraved on rings, painted on pictures, appended to the wreaths of honor, and, by using any other means by which that age can be interested, kept always before him. The deeds of famous men fire the minds of noble youths, but the opinions with which they become imbued is a matter of far greater importance, for from these sources the whole scheme of life is developed. In the case of a mere boy, we must immediately be on guard, to see that he gets only the virtuous and helpful ideas and that he be fortified as by certain efficacious drugs against the poisoned opinions of the common people. But if the prince happens to be somewhat tinged with the thoughts of the common people, then the first effort must be to rid him of them little by little, to weed out the seeds of trouble and replace them by wholesome ones.

A prince who is about to assume control of the state must be advised at once that the main hope of a state lies in the proper education of its youth. This Xenophon wisely taught in his *Cyropaedia*. Pliable youth is amenable to any system of training.

The Lion and the Mouse

Aesop

Recommended reading by Erasmus for a boy Prince. The Fables *are traditionally ascribed to Aesop, a Greek slave in the 6th century* B.C.

A Lion was awakened from sleep by a Mouse running over his face. Rising up in anger, he caught him and was about to kill him, when the Mouse piteously entreated, saying: "If you would only spare my life, I would be sure to repay your kindness." The Lion laughed and let him go. It happened shortly after this that the Lion was caught by some hunters, who bound him by strong ropes to the ground. The Mouse, recognizing his roar, came up, and gnawed the rope with his teeth, and setting him free, exclaimed: "You ridiculed the idea of my ever being able to help you, not expecting to receive from me any repayment of your favor; but now you know that it is possible for even a Mouse to confer benefits on a Lion."

It Is Held That Schools
Corrupt the Morals

From Quintillian, On Public and Private Instruction

*Marcus Fabius Quintillianus (born around 35 A.D.) was a celebrated profes-
sor of rhetoric, an attorney, and a personal tutor of the Emperor Domitian's
great-nephews. His reflections on educating boys are remarkable for their level-
headed and sympathetic understanding.*

It is held that schools corrupt the morals. It is true that this is
sometimes the case. But morals may be corrupted at home as well.
There are numerous instances of both, as there are also of the preservation of a good reputation under either circumstance. The nature
of the individual boy and the care devoted to his education make all
the difference. Given a natural bent toward evil or negligence in
developing and watching over modest behavior in early years, privacy
will provide equal opportunity for sin. The teacher employed at
home may be of bad character, and there is just as much danger in
associating with bad slaves as there is with immodest companions of
good birth. On the other hand if the natural bent be towards virtue,
and parents are not afflicted with a blind and torpid indifference, it
is possible to choose a teacher of the highest character (and those
who are wise will make this their first object), to adopt a method of
education of the strictest kind and at the same time to attach some
respectable man or faithful freedman to their son as his friend and
guardian, that his unfailing companionship may improve the character even of those who gave rise to apprehension.

Yet how easy were the remedy for such fears. Would that we did
not too often ruin our children's character ourselves! We spoil them
from the cradle. That soft upbringing, which we call kindness, saps all
the sinews both of mind and body. We rejoice if they say something
impudent, and words which we should not tolerate from the lips even
of an Alexandrian page are greeted with laughter and a kiss. We have
no right to be surprised. It was we that taught them: they hear us use
such words, they see our mistresses and minions; every dinner party
is loud with foul songs, and things are presented to their eyes of

which we should blush to speak. Hence springs habit, and habit in time becomes second nature. The poor children learn these things before they know them to be wrong. They become luxurious and effeminate, and far from acquiring such vices at schools, introduce them into the schools themselves.

The skilful teacher will make it his first care, as soon as a boy is entrusted to him, to ascertain his ability and character. The surest indication in a child is his power of memory. The characteristics of a good memory are twofold: it must be quick to take in and faithful to retain impressions of what it receives. The indication of next importance is the power of imitation: for this is a sign that the child is teachable: but he must imitate merely what he is taught, and must not, for example, mimic someone's gait or bearing or defects. For I have no hope that a child will turn out well who loves imitation merely for the purpose of raising a laugh. He who is really gifted will also above all else be good. For the rest, I regard slowness of intellect as preferable to actual badness. But a good boy will be quite unlike the dullard and the sloth. My ideal pupil will absorb instruction with ease and will even ask some questions; but he will follow rather than anticipate his teacher. Precocious intellects rarely produce sound fruit. By the precocious I mean those who perform small tasks with ease and, thus emboldened, proceed to display all their little accomplishments without being asked: but their accomplishments are only of the most obvious kind: they string words together and trot them out boldly and undeterred by the slightest sense of modesty. Their actual achievement is small, but what they can do they perform with ease. They have no real power and what they have is but of shallow growth: it is as when we cast seed on the surface of the soil: it springs up too rapidly, the blade apes the loaded ear, and yellows ere harvest time, but bears no grain. Such tricks please us when we contrast them with the performer's age, but progress soon stops and our admiration withers away.

Such indications once noted, the teacher must next consider what treatment is to be applied to the mind of his pupil. There are some boys who are slack, unless pressed on; others again are impatient of control: some are amenable to fear, while others are paralysed by it: in some cases the mind requires continued application to form it, in others this result is best obtained by rapid concentration. Give me the boy who is spurred on by praise, delighted by success and ready to weep over failure. Such a one must be encouraged by appeals to his ambition; rebuke will bite him to the quick; honor will be a spur, and there is no fear of his proving indolent.

Still, all our pupils will require some relaxation, not merely because there is nothing in this world that can stand continued strain (and even unthinking and inanimate objects are unable to maintain their strength, unless given intervals of rest), but because study depends on the good will of the student, a quality that cannot be secured by compulsion. Consequently, if restored and refreshed by a holiday they will bring greater energy to their learning and approach their work with greater spirit of a kind that will not submit to be driven. I approve of play in the young; it is a sign of a lively disposition; nor will you ever lead me to believe that a boy who is gloomy and in a continual state of depression is ever likely to show alertness of mind in his work, lacking as he does the impulse most natural to boys of his age. Such relaxation must not however be unlimited: otherwise the refusal to give a holiday will make boys hate their work, while excessive indulgence will accustom them to idleness. There are moreover certain games which have an educational value for boys, as for instance when they compete in posing each other all kinds of questions which they take turns asking. Games too reveal character in the most natural way, at least that is so if the teacher will bear in mind that there is no child so young as to be unable to learn to distinguish between right and wrong, and that the character is best moulded, when it is still guiltless of deceit and most susceptible to instruction: for once a bad habit has become engrained, it is easier to break than bend. There must be no delay, then, in warning a boy that his actions must be unselfish, honest, self-controlled, and we must never forget the words of Virgil,

"So strong is custom formed in early years."

Shame Is Good in a Boy

From Jacopo Sadoleto,
On the Education of Boys

A boy's ability to blush shows that he is capable of shame, therefore of virtue.

The blush is the pledge of a good disposition and of the virtue we look for in a boy, so that there seems much fitness in the saying

"He blushed—all's well." For shame itself is a habit of taking precaution against the occurrence of anything which may cause a blush: and while it is appropriate to any time of life, it is the chief grace of youth: nor should we be wrong in describing it as the averter of crime and the bulwark of temperance and virtue. And I would urge upon any parents, with whom my influence is likely to have weight, that they delay not to cherish and increase in their children this root of shame which nature has planted in their fresh minds. They can rely upon reaping a rich harvest for their pains. For though a sense of shame may not actually be virtue itself, it is the chief support to virtue: since it is the dread of an evil name and of disgrace: and this is a stern and vigilant guardian of virtue. So those who call shame a kind of divine timidity seem to me to get nearer the right definition of this emotion. It alone dreads the loss of that one well-nigh divine possession, which we win from high honor and office—to wit, our credit and good repute.

The Hare and the Tortoise

Aesop

A Hare one day ridiculed the short feet and slow pace of the Tortoise. The latter, laughing, said: "Though you be swift as the wind, I will beat you in a race." The Hare, deeming her assertion to be simply impossible, assented to the proposal; and they agreed that the Fox should choose the course, and fix the goal. On the day appointed for the race they started together. The Tortoise never for a moment stopped, but went on with a slow but steady pace straight to the end of the course. The Hare, trusting to his native swiftness cared little about the race, and lying down by the wayside, fell fast asleep. At last waking up, and moving as fast as he could, he saw the Tortoise had reached the goal, and was comfortably dozing after her fatigue.

The Duties and Education of Children

From Leon Battista Alberti,
On the Duties and Education of Children

A young man owes respect and gratitude to his father and elders. Thoughts from the Renaissance humanist and architect (1407–1472).

The young, then, must respect the old, especially their fathers, who well deserve it for their age and for many other reasons. From your father you have received life and instruction on how to acquire virtue. With his labor, solicitude, and zeal, your father has brought you to manhood and to that state and condition in which you find your-self. If you owe gratitude to those who help you when in need and mis-ery, you will certainly owe more to the one who, insofar as he could, did not let you want in the least. If you must share every thought, pos-session, and fortune with your friends and undergo inconveniences, hardships, and fatigue for those who love you, you certainly owe much more to your father, who loves you more than anyone else, and toward whom you have almost more obligations than to your very self. If your friends and acquaintances must enjoy a goodly part of your wealth and possessions, your father is entitled to much more, for you received your life, if not your wealth, from him; not only life, but your nourish-ment for so long a time, or if not your nourishment, your being and your name. It is the duty of the young, therefore, to share with their fathers and elders their every wish, thought, and plan and to ask coun-sel of many on everything, especially of those who, to our knowledge, love and cherish us more than others. They must listen to them will-ingly because of their prudence and experience and cheerfully follow the teachings of those who are older and wiser. Let the young not be slow in helping all elders in their age and weakness; they should hope that in their own old age they will receive from youth the same respect and kindness they themselves have shown their elders. Let them, therefore, be diligent and prompt in giving them comfort, pleasure, and rest in their tired old age. Let them not think there is any greater pleasure or happiness for the old than seeing their young virtuous and deserving of love. And I tell you there is no greater comfort for the old than to see that those in whom they have placed all their hopes and expectations, those for whom they have been ever solicitous and full of care, are esteemed, loved, and honored for their customs and virtues. Those men are happy who in their old age see their children entering upon a peaceful and honorable life. A peaceful life shall be the reward of men of irreproachable customs; an honorable one, that of virtuous men. Nothing so much as vice disturbs the life of mortals.

The Shepherd's Boy and Wolf

Aesop

A Shepherd-boy who watched a flock of sheep near a village, brought out the villagers three or four times by crying out, "Wolf! Wolf!" and when his neighbors came to help him, laughed at them for their pains. The Wolf, however, did truly come at last. The Shepherd-boy, now really alarmed, shouted in an agony of terror: "Pray, do come and help me; the Wolf is killing the sheep;" but no one paid any heed to his cries, nor rendered any assistance. The Wolf, having no cause of fear, took it easily, and lacerated or destroyed the whole flock.

There is no believing a liar, even when he speaks the truth.

The Right Kind of Boy: Brave and Tender

From Theodore Roosevelt, The Americanism of Theodore Roosevelt

Even though American democracy might weaken the authority of the father as paterfamilias, *Americans continued to think that manly pride, honor, and striving were important. Theodore Roosevelt (1858–1919)—writer, explorer, soldier, and President—was especially eloquent on the importance of manliness to a vigorous sense of citizenship and meritocracy. And yet,*

Roosevelt reserves his highest praise for the kind of manliness that combines tenderness with honor. In this we hear an echo of traditional notions of manly civility and refinement hearkening back to the ancients. For, although Roosevelt admires courage in battle and in the opening of the American frontier, he is even more admiring of the steadiness and affection of a good husband and father.

I want to see you game, boys; I want to see you brave and manly; and I also want to see you gentle and tender. In other words, you should make it your object to be the right kind of boys at home, so that your family will feel a genuine regret, instead of a sense of relief, when you stay away; and at the same time you must be able to hold your own in the outside world. You cannot do that if you have not manliness, courage in you. It does no good to have either or those two sets of qualities if you lack the other. I do not care how nice a little boy you are, how pleasant at home, if when you are out you are afraid of other little boys lest they be rude to you; for if so you will not be a very happy boy nor grow up a very useful man. When a boy grows up I want him to be of such a type that when somebody wrongs him he will feel a good, healthy desire to show the wrongdoers that he cannot be wronged with impunity. I like to have the man who is a citizen feel, when a wrong is done to the community by anyone, when there is an exhibition of corruption or betrayal of trust, or demagogy or violence, or brutality, not that he is shocked and horrified and would like to go home; but I want to have him feel the determination to put the wrongdoer down, to make the man who does wrong aware that the decent man is not only his superior in decency, but his superior in strength; not necessarily physical strength, but strength of character, the kind of strength that makes a good and forceful citizen.

The place in which each of you should try to be most useful is his own home, and each of you should wish for and should practice in order to have courage and strength, so that they can be used in protecting the gentle, in protecting the weak, against those who would wrong weakness and gentleness. The boy who will maltreat either a smaller child, a little boy or a little girl, or a dumb animal, is just about the meanest boy that you can find anywhere in the world. You should be brave and able to hold your own just because you should be able to put down such a bully. It should be your pride to be the champion of the weak. You will find a certain number of boys who have strength and who pride themselves in it, and who misuse it. The boy who will torture something harmless, who will oppress the boy or girl who is weak, or do wrong to those who cannot resist, almost always proves to have a weak streak in him, and not to have the stuff in him that would make him stand up to an equal foe under punishment. That boy has not real courage, real strength; and much though I dislike seeing a boy who is timid, who is afraid, who cannot hold his own, I dislike infinitely more, I abhor, the boy who uses strength and courage to oppress those who cannot help themselves.

The Value of a Boy's Friendships

From Thomas Hughes,
Tom Brown's School Days

Tom learns the importance of sharing his inner life with a trusted friend, East. He also grows into manliness by taking responsibility for a younger boy, Arthur—as the school's headmaster had always intended he should.

The fact is, that in the stage of his inner life at which Tom had lately arrived, his intimacy with and friendship for East could not have lasted if he had not made him aware of, and a sharer in, the thoughts that were beginning to exercise him. Nor indeed could the friendship have lasted if East had shown no sympathy with these thoughts; so that it was a great relief to have unbosomed himself, and to have found that his friend could listen.

Tom had always had a sort of instinct that East's levity was only skin-deep, and this instinct was a true one. East had no want of reverence for anything he felt to be real: but his was one of those natures that burst into what is generally called recklessness and impiety the moment they feel that anything is being poured upon them for their good, which does not come home to their inborn sense of right, or which appeals to anything like self-interest in them. Daring and honest by nature, and outspoken to an extent which alarmed all respectabilities, with a constant fund of animal health and spirits which he did not feel bound to curb in any way, he had gained for himself with the steady part of the School (including as well those who wished to appear steady as those who really were so), the character of a boy whom it would be dangerous to be intimate with; while his own hatred of everything cruel, or underhand, or false, and his hearty respect for what he could see to be good and true, kept off the rest.

Tom, besides being very like East in many points of character, had largely developed in his composition the capacity for taking the weakest side. This is not putting it strongly enough; it was a necessity with him; he couldn't help it any more than he could eating or drinking. He could never play on the strongest side with any heart at football or cricket, and was sure to make friends with any boy who was unpopular, or down on his luck.

Now though East was not what is generally called unpopular, Tom felt more and more every day, as their characters developed, that he stood alone, and did not make friends among their contemporaries, and therefore sought him out. Tom was himself much more popular, for his power of detecting humbug was much less acute, and his instincts were much more sociable. He was at this period of his life, too, largely given to taking people for what they gave themselves out to be; but his singleness of heart, fearfulness and honesty were just what East appreciated, and thus the two had been drawn into greater intimacy.

This intimacy had not been interrupted by Tom's guardianship of Arthur.

East had often, as has been said, joined them in reading the Bible; but their discussions had almost always turned upon the characters of the men and women of whom they read, and not become personal to themselves. In fact, the two had shrunk from personal religious discussion, not knowing how it might end; and fearful of risking a friendship very dear to both, and which they felt somehow, without quite knowing why, would never be the same, but either tenfold stronger or sapped at its foundation, after such a communing together.

What a bother all this explaining is! I wish we could get on without it. But we can't. However, you'll all find, if you haven't found it out already, that a time comes in every human friendship, when you must go down into the depths of yourself, and lay bare what is there to your friend, and wait in fear for his answer. A few moments may do it; and it may be (most likely will be, as you are English boys) that you never do it but once. But done it must be, if the friendship is to be worth the name. You must find what is there, at the very root and bottom of one another's hearts; and if you are at once there, nothing on earth can, or at least ought to sunder you.

East had remained lying down until Tom finished speaking, as if fearing to interrupt him; he now sat up at the table, and leaned his head on one hand, taking up a pencil with the other, and working little holes with it in the tablecover. After a bit he looked up, stopped the pencil and said, "Thank you very much, old fellow; there's no other boy in the house would have done it for me but you or Arthur. I can see well enough," he went on after a pause, "all the best big fellows look on me with suspicion; they think I'm a devil-may-care, reckless young scamp. So I am—eleven hours out of twelve—but not the twelfth. Then all our contemporaries worth knowing follow suit, of course; we're very good friends at games and all that, but not a soul of them but you and Arthur ever tried to break through the crust, and see whether there was anything at the bottom of me; and then the bad ones I won't stand, and they know that."

"I wonder where Arthur can be," said Tom at last, looking at his watch: "why, it's nearly half-past nine already."

"Oh, he is comfortably at supper with the eleven, forgetful of his oldest friends," said the master. "Nothing has given me greater pleasure," he went on, "than your friendship for him; it has been the making of you both."

"Of me, at any rate," answered Tom; "I should never have been here now but for him. It was the luckiest chance in the world that sent him to Rugby, and made him my chum."

"Why do you talk of lucky chances?" said the master; "I don't know that there are any such things in the world; at any rate there was neither luck nor chance in that matter."

Tom looked at him inquiringly, and he went on.

"Do you remember when the Doctor lectured you and East at the end of one half-year, when you were in the shell, and had been getting into all sorts of scrapes?"

"Yes, well enough," said Tom; "it was the half-year before Arthur came."

"Exactly so," answered the master. "Now, I was with him a few minutes afterward, and he was in great distress about you two. And, after some talk, we both agreed that you in particular wanted some object in the School beyond games and mischief; for it was quite clear that you never would make the regular school work your first object. And so the Doctor, at the beginning of the next half-year, looked out the best of the new boys, and separated you and East, and put the young boy into your study, in the hope that when you had somebody to lean on you, you would begin to stand a little steadier yourself, and get manliness and thoughtfulness. And I can assure you he has watched the experiment ever since with great satisfaction. Ah! not one of you boys will ever know the anxiety you have given him, or the care with which he has watched over every step in your school lives."

THE MANLY FATHER

I Have a Boy of Five Years Old

William Wordsworth

I have a boy of five years old;
His face is fair and fresh to see;
His limbs are cast in beauty's mould,
And dearly he loves me.

One morn we strolled on our dry walk,
Our quiet home all full in view,
And held such intermitted talk
As we are wont to do.

My thoughts on former pleasures ran;
I thought of Kilve's delightful shore,
Our pleasant home when spring began,
A long, long year before.

A day it was when I could bear
Some fond regrets to entertain;
With so much happiness to spare,
I could not feel a pain.

The green earth echoed to the feet
Of lambs that bounded through the glade,
From shade to sunshine, and as fleet
From sunshine back to shade.

Birds warbled round me—and each trace
Of inward sadness had its charm;
Kilve, thought I, was a favored place,
And so is Liswyn farm.

My boy beside me tripped, so slim
And graceful in his rustic dress!
And, as we talked, I questioned him,
In every idleness.

"Now tell me, had you rather be,"
I said, and took him by the arm,
"On Kilve's smooth shore, by the green sea,
Or here at Liswyn farm?"

In careless mood he looked at me,
While still I held him by the arm,
And said, "At Kilve I'd rather be
Than here at Liswyn farm."

"Now, little Edward, say why so:
My little Edward, tell me why."—
"I cannot tell, I do not know."—
"Why, this is strange," said I;

"For here are woods, hills smooth and warm:
There surely must some reason be
Why you would change sweet Liswyn farm
For Kilve by the green sea."

At this my boy hung down his head,
He blushed with shame, nor made reply;
And three times to the child I said,
"Why, Edward, tell me why?"

His head he raised—there was in sight
It caught his eye, he saw it plain—

Upon the house-top, glittering bright,
A broad and gilded vane.

Then did the boy his tongue unlock,
And eased his mind with this reply:
"At Kilve there was no weather-cock;
And that's the reason why."

O dearest, dearest boy! my heart
For better lore would seldom yearn,
Could I but teach the hundredth part
Of what from thee I learn.

Apply Yourself, My Boy

From Lord Chesterfield,
The Letters of Lord Chesterfield to His Son

Son, I would never want the fact that I could cut you off without a penny to influence in any way your behavior and your wish to please me.

Dear Boy,

I was very sorry that Mr. Maittaire did not give me such an account of you yesterday as I wished and expected. He takes so much pains to teach you, that he well deserves from you the returns of care and attention. Besides, pray consider, now that you have justly got the reputation of knowing much more than other boys of your age do, how shameful it would be for you to lose it, and to let other boys, that are now behind you, get before you. If you would but have attention, you have quickness enough to conceive, and memory enough to retain: but, without attention while you are learning, all the time you employ at your book is thrown away; and your shame will be the greater if you should be ignorant, when you had such opportunities of learning. An ignorant man is insignificant and contemptible; nobody cares for his company, and he can just be said to live, and that is all. There is a very pretty French epigram upon the death of such an ignorant, insignificant fellow; the sting of which is, that all that can be said of him is, that he was once alive, and that he is now dead.

Though I employ so much of my time in writing to you, I confess I have often my doubts whether it is to any purpose. I know how unwelcome advice generally is; I know that those who want it most, like it and follow it least; and I know, too, that the advice of parents, more particularly, is ascribed to the moroseness, the imperiousness, or the garrulity of old age. But then, on the other hand, I flatter myself, that as your own reason, though too young as yet to suggest much to you of itself, is, however, strong enough to enable you, both to judge of, and receive plain truths: I flatter myself (I say) that your own reason, young as it is, must tell you, that I can have no interest but yours in the advice I give you; and that, consequently, you will at least weigh and consider it well: in which case, some of it will, I hope, have its effect. Do not think that I mean to dictate as a parent; I only mean to advise as a friend, and an indulgent one too: and do not apprehend that I mean to check your pleasures; of which, on the contrary, I only desire to be the guide, not the censor. Let my experience supply your want of it, and clear your way, in the progress of your youth, of those thorns and briars which scratched and disfigured me in the course of mine. I do not, therefore, so much as hint to you, how absolutely dependent you are upon me; that you neither have, nor can have a shilling in the world but from me; and that, as I have no womanish weakness for your person, your merit must, and will, be the only measure of my kindness. I say, I do not hint these things to you, because I am convinced that you will act right, upon more noble and generous principles: I mean, for the sake of doing right, and out of affection and gratitude to me.

Pleasure is the rock which most young people split upon; they launch out with crowded sails in quest of it, but without a compass to direct their course, or reason sufficient to steer the vessel; for want of which, pain and shame, instead of Pleasure, are the returns of their voyage. Do not think that I mean to snarl at Pleasure, like a Stoic, or to preach against it, like a parson; no, I mean to point it out a great deal; and my only view is to hinder you from mistaking it.

A Father Pays Attention All the Time

From Leon Battista Alberti,
On the Duties and Education of Children

A boy needs to be paid attention to at every stage of his development. A father shouldn't be overly familiar or try to be his son's pal. But, by the same token, he can only maintain his authority through love, never through fear.

A father's duties do not consist solely in filling the granary and the cradle, as they say. The head of a family must be vigilant and observant above all. He must know all the family's acquaintances, examine all customs both within and without the house, and correct and mend the evil ways of any member of the family with words of reason rather than anger. He must use a father's authority rather than despotism, and counsel where it is of more value than commanding. He must be severe, firm, and stern when necessary, and he must always keep in mind the well-being, peace, and tranquillity of his entire family as the ultimate purpose of all his efforts and counsels for the guidance of the family in virtue and honor.

The head of the family must first of all be on the watch for the first sparks of vice to appear among his children's appetites and must put them out immediately if he does not wish to be compelled later to extinguish the flames of corrupt desire at greater cost, with sorrow and tears.

The proverb says that the right path must be taken where it begins. A father must see where his son is headed from the earliest age and must not allow him to proceed on an unsafe and little-praised path. He must not allow his sons to have their way against his wishes or become accustomed to dishonest ways. The father must always appear as a father; he must be severe, but not hateful, loving, but not too familiar. Let all fathers and elders remember that authority maintained through force is always less stable than that maintained through love. No fear can last forever; love is long enduring. Fear loses its power with time, but love grows from day to day. Who, then, is so mad as to believe that one must show himself strict and harsh in all things? Severity without humaneness breeds hatred, rather than authority. The more loving and free from harshness kindness is, the more benevolence and good will it acquires. Excessive curiosity in everything is not what I should call diligence; it resembles a tyrant's ways more than a father's. Austerity and harshness make one angry and scornful toward his elders more often than obedient. A noble spirit suffers when treated as a servant rather than as a son.

A Father's Parting Advice

From Thomas Hughes,
Tom Brown's School Days

Squire Brown's advice as he sends his son Tom off to school.

"And now, Tom, my boy," said the Squire, "remember you are going, at your own earnest request, to be chucked into this great school, like a young bear with all your troubles before you—earlier than we should have sent you perhaps. If schools are what they were in my time, you'll see a great many cruel blackguard things done, and hear a deal of foul bad talk. But never fear. You tell the truth, keep a brave and kind heart, and never listen to or say anything you wouldn't have your mother and sister hear, and you'll never feel ashamed to come home, or we to see you."

The allusion to his mother made Tom feel rather chokey, and he would have liked to have hugged his father well, if it hadn't been for the recent stipulation.

As it was, he only squeezed his father's hand, and looked bravely up and said, "I'll try, Father."

"I know you will, my boy. Is your money all safe?"

"Yes," said Tom, diving into one pocket to make sure.

"And your keys?" said the Squire.

"All right," said Tom, diving into the other pocket.

"Well then, good night. God bless you! I'll tell Boots to call you, and be up to see you off."

Tom was carried off by the chambermaid in a brown study, from which he was roused in a clean little attic by that buxom person calling him a little darling, and kissing him as she left the

room, which indignity he was too much surprised to resent. And
still thinking of his father's last words, and the look with which they
were spoken, he knelt down and prayed, that, come what might, he
might never bring shame or sorrow on the dear folk at home.

Indeed, the Squire's last words deserved to have their effect,
for they had been the result of much anxious thought. All the way
up to London he had pondered what he should say to Tom by way
of parting advice, something that the boy could keep in his head
ready for use. By way of assisting meditation, he had even gone the
length of taking out his flint and steel and tinder, and hammering
away for a quarter of an hour till he had manufactured a light for a
long Trichinopoli cheroot, which he silently puffed; to the no small
wonder of Coachee, who was an old friend, and an institution on
the Bath road; and who always expected a talk on the prospects and
doings, agricultural and social, of the whole country when he carried the Squire.

To condense the Squire's meditation, it was somewhat as follows: "I won't tell him to read his Bible and love and serve God; if
he don't do that for his mother's sake and teaching, he won't for
mine. Shall I go into the sort of temptations he'll meet with? No, I
can't do that. Never do for an old fellow to go into such things with
a boy. He won't understand me. Do him more harm than good, ten
to one. Shall I tell him to mind his work, and say he's sent to school
to make himself a good scholar? Well, but he isn't sent to school for
that—at any rate, not for that mainly. I don't care a straw for Greek
particles, or the digamma, no more does his mother. What is he
sent to school for? Well, partly because he wanted so to go. If he'll
only turn out a brave, helpful, truth-telling Englishman, and a gentleman, and a Christian, that's all I want," thought the Squire; and
upon this view of the case framed his last words of advice to Tom,
which were well enough suited to his purpose.

This Fair Child of Mine

William Shakespeare

When forty winters shall beseige thy brow
And dig deep trenches in thy beauty's field,
Thy youth's proud livery, so gazed on now,
Will be a tottered weed of small worth held:
Then being asked where all thy beauty lies,
Where all the treasures of thy lusty days,
To say within thine own deep-sunken eyes
Were an all-eating shame and thriftless praise.
How much more praise deserved thy beauty's use
If thou couldst answer, "This fair child of mine
Shall sum my count and make my old excuse,"
Proving his beauty by succession thine.
This were to be new made when thou art old
And see thy blood warm when thou feel'st it cold.

A Father Sets the Example

From Leon Battista Alberti, The Duties
and Education of Children

In The Duties and Education of Children, *Alberti stresses that a father
must serve as a model of the virtues for his children. In other words, practice
what you preach—don't expect your son to grow up well unless you exem-
plify the behavior you want from him. A father is entitled to a son's respect,
but he has to earn it. Your son will be good if he respects you and wants to
earn your affection by living up to the example you set for him.*

I do not deny that fathers, more than others, must strive with
their whole being, with all their diligence and wisdom, to make

their children honest and high-principled. They must do so because they will be rendering a service to them, since principles in a young man are not esteemed less than wealth. They will also bring honor to their house, their country, and themselves, for virtuous children bear witness to their fathers' diligence and honor them. If I am not mistaken, it is thought better for a country to have virtuous and honest citizens than rich and powerful ones. In truth, unprincipled children must be the cause of great sorrow to a sensitive father. This is not only because a father dislikes to see vice and wickedness in his child, but also because there can be no doubt that a son's dishonesty redounds to his father's shame. The more so in that everyone knows it is mainly up to the father to make the children honest, virtuous, and honorable. No one denies that fathers can accomplish as much as they wish with their children. A good horseman will make a horse gentle and obedient; a less skillful and diligent one could not even bridle the same horse. In the same way, a solicitous father will make his children modest and courteous. Those whose sons are wicked and lost in iniquity shall not avoid shame or escape blame for negligence.

It is a father's duty to test his sons' intellect in many ways. He must be alert and notice his sons' every act and indication, encouraging and praising the children when they are manly and good, and correcting them when lazy and dissolute. He must make them exercise according to their needs and at the proper time. It is said that it is harmful to engage in bodily exercise immediately after meals. To be active and become somewhat tired before eating does no harm, but it is not helpful to become extremely fatigued. To exercise one's intellect and spirit in the pursuit of virtue at any time and in any place and in all things has always been praiseworthy. Let fathers, then, consider this task not troublesome, but pleasant. You go hunting in the forest, tire yourself, sweat, spend the night in the cold and wind and the day in the sun and dust in order to see dogs run after animals and hunt them down. Is there any less pleasure in seeing two or more minds vie in the pursuit of virtue? Is it less useful for you to adorn your children with good habits and manners through your worthy and just efforts than to return home tired and hot with whatever game you have killed? Let fathers take pleasure, then, in inciting their sons to pursue virtue and fame. Let them encourage them to vie for honors. Let them praise the victor and enjoy having sons who are alert and thirst for well-deserved praise and honor.

How harmful do you think it is for the young to associate with a father who is ill-mannered, haughty, and bestial in words and deeds, who shouts and blusters, swears and blasphemes endlessly? He rages, and his children believe they should and can imitate the customs of their elders. This sort of dissolute fathers can have only one reason for not daring to punish their children in order to instill honesty and good habits in them. They are afraid that if their children grow up virtuous they will then reproach them for their vices, as is often the case. There are some who do not like to see in others the vices in which they themselves indulge: they stuff themselves, yet hate gluttons; they perjure themselves, yet scorn liars; they are obstinate in everything, yet they condemn the stubborn. For this reason they become excessively stern disciplinarians, punishing in their children those vices for which they themselves are infamous. They beat their children to give vent to their wrath and ill humor. These fathers are most unjust, for they do not first correct in themselves what they hate in others. To these one can say: "O foolish, mad fathers, how do you expect your little children not to have learned what you, with your hoary locks, have taught them by persisting in your vices?"

Son, What Have I Done to Deserve This?

From William Shakespeare, Henry IV, Part One

Shakespeare's Henry IV *presents a striking example of the familiar tension between the gravity of age and the impetuosity of youth, compounded by the tension between a father and a son who also happen to be the King of England and the heir to the throne. There could hardly be a better illustration of how a flawed relationship between a father and a son in private life can have profoundly important consequences for the wider sphere of society and politics. The scene begins with Henry asking his noblemen to leave the room so that he can have some private words with the Prince. Like a father taking his son to his room to upbraid him beyond the view of his friends and the rest of the family, Henry chastises Hal severely for being such a wastrel and* layabout. *His are the kind of words disappointed fathers have said to rebel-lious sons throughout history: What have I done to deserve this? Don't you have any feeling for me?*

King.   Lords, give us leave: the Prince of Wales and I
Must have some private conference; but be near at hand,
For we shall presently have need of you.
Exeunt Lords.
I know not whether God will have it so
For some displeasing service I have done,
That, in his secret doom, out of my blood
He'll breed revengement and a scourge for me;
But thou dost in thy passages of life
Make me believe that thou art only marked
For the hot vengeance and the rod of heaven
To punish my mistreadings. Tell me else,
Could such inordinate and low desires,
Such poor, such bare, such lewd, such mean attempts,
Such barren pleasures, rude society,
As thou art matched withal and grafted to,
Accompany the greatness of thy blood
And hold their level with thy princely heart?
Prince.   So please your Majesty, I would I could
Quit all offenses with as clear excuse
As well as I am doubtless I can purge
Myself of many I am charged withal.
Yet such extenuation let me beg
As, in reproof of many tales devised,
Which oft the ear of greatness needs must hear
By smiling pickthanks and base newsmongers,
I may, for some things true wherein my youth
Hath faulty wand'red and irregular
Find pardon on my true submission.
King.   God pardon thee! Yet let me wonder, Harry,
At thy affections, which do hold a wing
Quite from the flight of all thy ancestors.
Thy place in council thou hast rudely lost,
Which by thy young brother is supplied,
And art almost an alien to the hearts
Of all the court and princes of my blood.

The hope and expectation of thy time
Is ruined, and the soul of every man
Prophetically do forethink thy fall.
Had I so lavish of my presence been,
So common-hackneyed in the eyes of men,
So stale and cheap to vulgar company,
Opinion that did help me to the crown,
Had still kept loyal to possession
And left me in reputeless banishment,
A fellow of no mark nor likelihood.
By being seldom seen, I could not stir
But, like a comet, I was wond'red at;
That men would tell their children, "This is he!"
Others would say, "Where? Which is Bolingbroke?"
And then I stole all courtesy from heaven,
And dressed myself in such humility
That I did pluck allegiance from men's hearts,
Loud shouts and salutations from their mouths
Even in the presence of the crowned King.
Thus did I keep my person fresh and new,
My presence, like a robe pontifical,
Ne'er seen but wond'red at; and so my state,
Seldom but sumptuous, showed like a feast
And won by rareness such solemnity.
The skipping King, he ambled up and down
With shallow jesters and rash bavin wits,
Soon kindled and soon burnt; carded his state;
Mingled his royalty with cap'ring fools;
Had his great name profaned with their scorns
And gave his countenance, against his name,
To laugh at gibing boys and stand the push
Of every beardless vain comparative,
Grew a companion to the common streets,
Enfeoffed himself to popularity;
That, being daily swallowed by men's eyes,
They surfeited with honey and began
To loathe the taste of sweetness, whereof a little
More than a little is by much too much.
So, when he had occasion to be seen,
He was but as the cuckoo is in June,
Heard, not regarded—seen, but with such eyes
As, sick and blunted with community,

Afford no extraordinary gaze,
Such as is bent on sunlike majesty
When it shines seldom in admiring eyes;
but rather drowsed and hung their eyelids down,
Slept in his face, and rend'red such aspect
As cloudy men use to their adversaries,
Being with his presence glutted, gorged, and full.
And in that very line, Harry, standest thou;
For thou hast lost thy princely privilege
With vile participation. Not an eye
But is aweary of thy common sight,
Save mine, which hath desired to see thee more;
Which now doth that I would not have it do—
Make blind itself with foolish tenderness.
Prince. I shall hereafter, my thrice-gracious lord,
Be more myself.

*But the political dimension makes their private tension much graver. Henry
tells Hal: You are like Richard II, the unworthy ruler I deposed, while your
cousin Hotspur is like I was when I was your age. Your undignified, dishonorable way of life makes you unfit to succeed to the throne. In the
unkindest cut, Henry tells his son he isn't even sure that Hal won't desert to
the other side in the civil war with the Percys. Hal pleads with his father for
a chance to redeem himself—to prove to his father that he truly is his son.*

King.   For all the world,
As thou art to this hour was Richard then
When I from France set foot at Ravenspurgh;
And even as I was then is Percy now.
Now, by my scepter, and my soul to boot,
He hath more worthy interest to the state
Than thou the shadow of succession;
For of no right, nor color like to right,
He doth fill fields with harness in the realm,
Turns head against the lion's armed jaws.
Why, Harry, do I tell thee of my foes,
Which art my nearest and dearest enemy?
Thou that art like enough, through vassal fear,
Base inclination, and the start of spleen,
To fight against me under Percy's pay,

To dog his heels and curtsy at his frowns,
To show how much thou art degenerate.
Prince.   Do not think so, you shall not find it so.
And God forgive them that so much have swayed
Your Majesty's good thoughts away from me.
I will redeem all this on Percy's head
And, in the closing of some glorious day,
Be bold to tell you that I am your son.

On the Affection of Fathers
for Their Children

From Michel de Montaigne, Essays

The relation of children to their fathers is one of respect. Friendship is kept alive by communication, which, by reason of too great disparity, cannot exist between them, and would haply conflict with natural duties. For neither can all the secret thoughts of the father be communicated to his son, in order not to beget an unseemly familiarity, nor can the admonitions and corrections, which are among the first offices of friendship, be administered by the son to the father.

As concerning marriage, besides that it is a bargain to which only the entrance is free (its continuance being forced and constrained; and depending on something other than our will), a bargain moreover that is usually concluded to other ends, there supervene a thousand extraneous entanglements to unravel, sufficient to break the thread and disturb the course of a lively affection; whereas in friendship there is no traffic or business except with itself.

A father is indeed miserable who holds the affection of his children only through the need they have of his assistance, if that may be called affection. He should make himself worthy of respect by his virtue and abilities, and worthy of love by his kindness and gentle manners.

No old age can be so decrepit and musty in a person who has

lived an honorable life, but it should be revered, especially by his children, whose minds he should have trained to their duty by reason, not by want and the need that they have of him, nor by harshness and compulsion:

Do we wish to be loved by our children? Would we take from them all occasion to desire our death (although no cause for so dreadful a desire can be either right or excusable)? Let us reasonably furnish their lives with what is in our power. To do that we should not marry so young that our age will be almost confounded with theirs. For this inconvenience plunges us into many great difficulties.

I married at thirty-three, and concur in Aristotle's opinion, which is said to have recommended thirty-five.

A Roman Father

From Plutarch,
Lives of the Noble Greeks and Romans

Plutarch's lives of eminent Greeks and Romans abundantly illustrate the classical ideal of manliness. Cato the Elder, despite his famous moral rectitude, was also a loving husband and a good father. He expected much of his son, but because the boy had a delicate physique, he relaxed the physical requirements of his education. The boy rewarded his father's careful attention to his education and his understanding attitude by distinguishing himself in battle.

Cato was also a good father, an excellent husband to his wife, and an extraordinary household manager. And since he did not manage his affairs of this kind carelessly, or treat them as things of no importance, I think I ought to record a little further whatever was commendable in him in this regard. He married a wife whose nobility exceeded her wealth, being of the opinion that the rich and the high-born are equally haughty and proud, but that those of noble blood would be more ashamed of base behavior, and consequently more obedient to their husbands in all that was fitting and right. Cato said that a man who beat his wife or child laid violent hands on what was most sacred, and in his view a good husband was more worthy of praise than a great senator. He admired the ancient Socrates more than anything else for having lived a temperate and contented life in spite of having a wife who was a scold and children who were half-witted.

As soon as his son was born, unless Cato was occupied by the most urgent affairs of state, he would be on hand when his wife washed it and dressed it in its swaddling clothes. For she herself suckled it, and she often gave her breast to her servants' children, to produce in them, by suckling the same milk, a kind of brotherly love for her son. When their son began to mature, Cato himself would teach him to read, although he had a servant, a very good grammarian, called Chilo, who taught many others. But Cato thought it not fit, as he himself said, to have his son reprimanded by a slave, or pulled by the ears when found tardy in his lesson: nor would he have him owe to a servant the obligation of so great a thing as his learning. Cato himself, therefore, taught his son grammar, law, and his gymnastic exercises. Not only did he show him, as well, how to throw a dart, to fight in armor, and to ride, but also how to box and to endure both heat and cold, and to swim in the most rapid and rough rivers. Cato tells us that he wrote histories, in large letters, with his own hand, so that his son, without stirring out of the house, might learn to know about his countrymen and forefathers. He never said anything obscene in front of his son, no more than if he had been in the presence of the holy Vestal Virgins. Nor would he ever go into the bath with him, although this seems to have been the common custom of the Romans. In earlier times, sons-in-law used to avoid bathing with fathers-in-law, ashamed to see one another naked. But later on, having learned from the Greeks to strip before men, they have since taught the Greeks to do it even with the women themselves.

Thus, like an excellent piece of work, Cato formed and fashioned his son to virtue, and he never had occasion to find fault with him, since the boy was always eager and never docile. But because he proved to have too weak a constitution for undergoing hardships, Cato did not insist on requiring of him any very austere way of living. However, though delicate in health, he proved a stout man in the field, and behaved himself valiantly when Paulus Æmilius fought against Perseus. When his sword was struck from him by a blow, or rather slipped out of his hand by reason of its moistness, he so keenly resented it, that he turned to some of his friends about him, and taking them along with him again fell upon the enemy; and having by a long fight and such force cleared the place, at length found his sword among great heaps of arms, and the dead bodies of friends as well as enemies piled one upon the other. Upon which Paulus, his general, much commended the youth; and there is a letter of Cato's to his son, which highly praised his honorable eagerness for the recovery of his sword. Afterwards he married Tertia, Æmilius Paulus's daughter, and sister to Scipio. He was admitted into this family as much for his own worth as his father's. So Cato's care over his son's education was fittingly rewarded.

Fathers Must Earn Their Authority

From Jacopo Sadoleto,
On the Education of Boys

According to Sadoleto, a father must provide for his son a model of decency, learning, and good manners. He doesn't actually have to possess all the virtues he encourages in his son. But by setting an example, he can hope that his son will grow up to be a better man than himself—which all fathers naturally desire.

The next main principle in a child's training . . . is that a father, who desires to bring his son up as a good and noble man, should himself afford a pattern to be copied. No training can be better than that. In saying this I do not deny that there are many graces of life that ought daily to be increased in a child, though his father may not possess them: for example, letters and the pursuit and study of those Arts which are called Liberal, the knowledge of civil or ecclesiastical law, practice and understanding of war and military matters, it may be: for while a father may by the fault of his own father or of mere mischance be wholly ignorant of these matters, he should see that his son know something of them. For there is a natural desire common to all fathers, that they should leave sons better and more illustrious than themselves. And this comes from a natural love in every man, not more for his son than for himself, due to the deeply implanted, inborn craving to prolong our life, a craving by which we are swept on to the lust for immortality; and a father always feels himself to live again in his son and to pass into his own image.

Let this, then, be the first rule for parents in regard to their children if they desire to bring them to the best fruits of goodness—that what they long for their children to become, they must show themselves to be in their children's eyes.

Let the father then be a man of this sort: of well-balanced nature, his one vehement passion the pursuit of goodness and honor, eager to pour his whole soul through the channel of ears and eyes into the mind and spirit of his son.

Dignity, of course, must always be kept; a father should never let himself sink to the level of familiarity or become the boon companion of his son—that merely breeds contempt and self-confidence in the youth, who, feeling himself curbed by no law, comes to pursue with headstrong passion whatever takes his fancy. On the other hand he should be no formal or rigid moralist, afraid of giving his son ample proof of courteous and warm-hearted consideration, or shy of taking affectionately and even with a certain rapture to his heart the child, who is a living image of himself, than which nothing in life is sweeter to a parent. But if he must control his affection, lest the child spoiled by excessive indulgence cast away all respect and reverence for his father, he must take even more strenuous pains to avoid violent and rough severity; that crushes out love from the child's heart and brings him to the purpose and passion of hating whatever in himself he knows to be pleasing to his father.

A Man's Journey

The Seven Ages of Man

From William Shakespeare, As You Like It

All the world's a stage,
And all the men and women merely players;
They have their exits and their entrances,
And one man in his time plays many parts,
His acts being seven ages. At first, the infant,
Mewling and puking in the nurse's arms.
Then the whining schoolboy, with his satchel
And shining morning face, creeping like snail
Unwillingly to school. And then the lover,
Sighing like furnace, with a woeful ballad
Made to his mistress' eyebrow. Then a soldier,
Full of strange oaths and bearded like the pard,
Jealous in honor, sudden and quick in quarrel,
Seeking the bubble reputation
Even in the cannon's mouth. And then the justice,
In fair round belly with good capon lined,
With eyes severe and beard of formal cut,
Full of wise saws and modern instances;
And so he plays his part. The sixth age shifts
Into the lean and slippered pantaloon,
With spectacles on nose and pouch on side;
His youthful hose, well saved, a world too wide
For his shrunk shank, and his big manly voice,
Turning again toward childish treble, pipes
And whistles in his sound. Last scene of all,
That ends this strange eventful history,
Is second childishness and mere oblivion,
Sans teeth, sans eyes, sans taste, sans everything.

Odysseus Comes Home

From Homer, The Odyssey

Upon Odysseus's return to Ithaca in disguise after twenty years of wandering, his wife Penelope tricks him into revealing himself by making him jealous. Years before, he had made their bed out of a giant tree that grew right into their bedroom. She makes him jealous by leading him to think another man has rearranged his bed in his absence. Once she realizes it's really him, they embrace and he weeps at the thought of what this extraordinary woman has been through, ruling in his absence, fighting off the suitors and bringing up their son on her own. They hug for a long time—after twenty years, she doesn't want to let him go.

So she spoke to her husband, trying him out, but Odysseus spoke in anger to his virtuous-minded lady:

"What you have said, dear lady, has hurt my heart deeply. What man has put my bed in another place? But it would be difficult for even a very expert one, unless a god, coming to help in person, were easily to change its position. But there is no mortal man alive, no strong man, who lightly could move the weight elsewhere. There is one particular feature in the bed's construction. I myself, no other man, made it. There was the bole of an olive tree with long leaves growing strongly in the courtyard, and it was thick like a column. I laid down my chamber around this, and built it, until I finished it, with close-set stones. And roofed it well over, and added the compacted doors, fitting closely together. Then I cut away the foliage of the long-leaved olive, and trimmed the trunk from the roots up, planing it with a brazen adze, well and expertly, and trued it straight to a chalkline, making a bed post of it, and bored all holes with an auger. I began with this and built my bed, until it was finished, and decorated it with gold and silver and ivory. Then I lashed it with thongs of oxhide, dyed bright with purple. There is its character, as I tell you; but I do not know now, dear lady, whether my bed is still in place, or if some man has cut underneath the stump of the olive, and moved it elsewhere."

So he spoke, and her knees and the heart within her went slack as she recognized the clear proofs that Odysseus had given;

but then she burst into tears and ran straight to him, throwing her arms around the neck of Odysseus, and kissed his head, saying:

"Do not be angry with me, Odysseus, since, beyond other men, you have the most understanding. The gods granted us misery, in jealousy over the thought that we two, always together, should enjoy our youth, and then come to the threshold of old age. But now, since you have given me accurate proof describing our bed, which no other mortal man beside has ever seen, but only you and I, and there is one serving woman Aktor's daughter, whom my father gave me when I came here, who used to guard the doors for us in our well-built chamber; so you persuade my heart, though it has been very stubborn."

She spoke, and still more roused in him the passion for weeping. He wept as he held his lovely wife, whose thoughts were virtuous. And as when the land appears welcome to men who are swimming after Poseidon has smashed their strong-built ship on the open water, pounding it with the weight of wind and the heavy seas, and only a few escape the gray water landward by swimming, with a thick scurf of salt coated upon them, and gladly they set foot on the shore, escaping the evil; so welcome was her husband to her as she looked upon him, and she could not let him go from the embrace of her white arm.

Meanwhile, the bed chamber has been prepared. After their lovemaking, they sit up all night telling each other of what each has endured during their long separation. Husband and wife are the only ones who can understand each other. Did they tell everything?

Now as these two were conversing thus with each other, meanwhile the nurse and Eurynome were making the bed up with soft coverings, under the light of their flaring torches. Then when they had worked and presently had a firm bed made, the old woman went away back to bed in her own place, while Eurynome, as mistress of the chamber, guided them on their way to the bed, and her hands held the torch for them. When she had brought them to the chamber she went back. They then gladly went together to bed, and their old ritual.

At this time Telemachus and the oxherd and swineherd stopped the beat of their feet in the dance, and stopped the women, and they themselves went to bed in the shadowy palace.

When Penelope and Odysseus had enjoyed their lovemaking, they took their pleasure in talking, each one telling his story. She, shining among women, told of all she had endured in the palace, as she watched the suitors, a ravening company, who on her account were slaughtering many oxen and fat sheep, and much wine was being drawn from the wine jars. But shining Odysseus told of all the cares he inflicted on other men, and told too of all that in his misery he had toiled through. She listened to him with delight, nor did any sleep fall upon her eyes until he had told her everything.

Married or Single?

From Francis Bacon, Essays

When a man has a wife and children, Bacon tells us, he gives hostages to fortune. As a contemporary arbitrageur might put it, if you're married, you're exposed.

He that hath wife and children hath given hostages to fortune, for they are impediments to great enterprises, either of virtue or mischief. Certainly the best works, and of greatest merit for the public, have proceeded from the unmarried or childless men, which both in affection and means have married and endowed the public. Yet it were great reason that those that have children should have greatest care of future times, unto which they know they must transmit their dearest pledges. Some there are who though they lead a single life, yet their thoughts do end with themselves, and account future times impertinences. Nay, there are some other that account wife and children but as bills of charges. Nay more, there are some foolish, rich covetous, men that take pride in having no children, because they may be thought so much the richer. For perhaps they have heard some talk, *Such an one is a great rich man,* and another except to it, *Yea, but he hath a great charge of children,* as if it were an abatement to his riches. But the most ordinary cause of a single life is liberty, especially in certain self-pleasing and humorous minds, which are so sensible of every restraint, as they will go near to think their girdles and garters to be bonds and shackles.

A Son's Mixed Feelings

From John Stuart Mill, Autobiography

What would it be like if a father had complete control over his son's education? In his autobiography, the utilitarian philosopher J. S. Mill (1806–1873) recalls that his imposing father prescribed every aspect of his studies, a rigorous immersion in the classics, history, and science. The boy had no playmates and no holidays to interfere with this demanding curriculum. He was isolated from any exposure to religious faith so that he would grow up as his father's ally in "the great and decisive contest against priestly tyranny for liberty of thought." The reader senses Mill's mixed feelings about his upbringing—and especially his father's lack of tenderness toward his children.

My father, in all his teaching, demanded of me not only the utmost that I could do, but much that I could by no possibility have done. What he was himself willing to undergo for the sake of my instruction, may be judged from the fact, that I went through the whole process of preparing my Greek lessons in the same room and at the same table at which he was writing: and as those days Greek and English Lexicons were not, and I could make no more use of a Greek and Latin Lexicon than could be made without having yet begun to learn Latin, I was forced to have recourse to him for the meaning of every word which I did not know. This incessant interruption he, one of the most impatient of men, submitted to, and wrote under that interruption several volumes of his History and all else that he had to write during those years.

One of the evils most liable to attend on any sort of early proficiency, and which often fatally blights its promise, my father most anxiously guarded against. This was self-conceit. He kept me, with extreme vigilance, out of the way of hearing myself praised, or of being led to make self-flattering comparisons between myself and others. From his own intercourse with me I could derive none but a very humble opinion of myself; and the standard of comparison he always held up to me, was not what other people did, but what a man could and ought to do. He completely succeeded in preserving me from the sort of influences he so much dreaded. I was not at all aware that my attainments were anything unusual at my age. If I accidentally had my attention drawn to the fact that some other boy knew less than myself—which happened less often than might be imagined—I concluded, not that I knew much, but that he, for some reason or other, knew little, or that his knowledge was of a different kind from mine. My state of mind was not humility, but neither was it arrogance. I never thought of saying to myself, I am, or I can do, so and so. I neither estimated myself highly nor lowly: I did not estimate myself at all. If I thought anything about myself, it was that I was rather backward in my studies, since I always found myself so, in comparison with what my father expected from me. I assert this with confidence, though it was not the impression of various persons who saw me in my childhood. They, as I have since found, thought me greatly and disagreeably self-conceited; probably because I was disputatious, and did not scruple to give direct contradictions to things which I heard said. I suppose I acquired this bad habit from having been encouraged in an unusual degree to talk on matters beyond my age, and with grown persons, while I never had inculcated on me the usual respect for them. My father did not correct this ill breeding and impertinence, probably from not being aware of it, for I was always too much in awe of him to be otherwise than extremely subdued and quiet in his presence. Yet with all this I had no notion of any superiority in myself; and well was it for me that I had not.

It is evident that this, among many other of the purposes of my father's scheme of education, could not have been accomplished if he had not carefully kept me from having any great amount of intercourse with other boys. He was earnestly bent upon my escaping not only the ordinary corrupting influence which boys exercise over boys, but the contagion of vulgar modes of thought and feeling; and for this he was willing that I should pay the price of inferiority in the accomplishments which schoolboys in all countries chiefly cultivate. The deficiencies in my education were principally in the things which boys learn from being turned out to shift for themselves, and from being brought together in large numbers. From temperance and much walking, I grew up healthy and hardy, though not muscular; but I could do no feats of skill or physical strength, and knew none of the ordinary bodily exercises. It was not that play, or time for it, was refused me. Though no holidays were allowed, lest the habit of work should be broken, and a taste for idleness acquired, I had ample leisure in every day to amuse myself; but as I had no boy companions, and the animal need of physical activity was satisfied by walking, my amusements, which were mostly solitary, were in general of a quiet, if not a bookish turn, and gave little stimulus to any other kind even of mental activity than that which was already called forth by my studies. I consequently remained long, and in a less degree have always remained, inexpert in anything requiring manual dexterity; my mind, as well as my hands, did its work very lamely when it was applied, or ought to have been applied, to the practical details which, as they are the chief interest of life to the majority of men are also the things in which whatever mental capacity they have, chiefly shews itself.

It would have been wholly inconsistent with my father's ideas of duty, to allow me to acquire impressions contrary to his convictions and feelings respecting religion: and he impressed upon me from the first, that the manner in which the world came into existence was a subject on which nothing was known: that the question "Who made me?" cannot be answered, because we have no experience or authentic information from which to answer it; and that any answer only throws the difficulty a step further back, since the question immediately presents itself, Who made God? He, at the same time, took care that I should be acquainted with what had been thought by mankind on these impenetrable problems. I have mentioned at how early an age he made me a reader of ecclesiastical history; and he taught me to take the strongest interest in the Reformation, as the great and decisive contest against priestly tyranny for liberty of thought. I am thus one of the very few examples, in this country, of one who has, not thrown off religious belief, but never had it: I grew up in a negative state with no regard to it. I looked upon the modern exactly as I did upon the ancient religion, as something which in no way concerned me.

He thought human life a poor thing at best, after the freshness of youth and of unsatisfied curiosity had gone by. This was a topic on which he did not often speak, especially, it may be supposed, in the presence of young persons: but when he did it, it was with an air of settled and profound conviction. He would sometimes say, that if life were made what it might be, by good government and good education, it would be worth having: but he never spoke with anything like enthusiasm even of that possibility. He never varied in rating intellectual enjoyments above all others, even in value as pleasures, independently of their ulterior benefits. The pleasures of the benevolent affections he placed high in the scale; and used to say, that he had never known a happy old man, except those who were able to live over again in the pleasures of the young. For passionate emotions of all sorts, and for everything which had been said or written in exaltation of them, he professed the greatest contempt. He regarded them as a form of madness. "The intense" was with him a bye-word of scornful disapprobation. He regarded as an aberration of the moral standard of modern times, compared with that of the ancients, the great stress laid upon feeling. Feelings, as such, he considered to be no proper subjects of praise or blame. Right and wrong, good and bad, he regarded as qualities solely of conduct.

It will be admitted, that a man of the opinions, and the character, above described, was likely to leave a strong moral impression on any mind principally formed by him, and that his moral teaching was not likely to err on the side of laxity or indulgence. The element which was chiefly deficient in his moral relation to his children was that of tenderness. I do not believe that this deficiency lay in his own nature. I believe him to have had much more feeling than he habitually shewed, and much greater capacities of feeling than were ever developed. He resembled most Englishmen in being ashamed of the signs of feeling, and, by the absence of demonstration, starving the feelings themselves. If we consider further that he was in the trying position of sole teacher, and add to this that his temper was constitutionally irritable, it is impossible not to feel true pity for a father who did, and strove to do so much for his children, who would have so valued their affection, yet who must have been constantly feeling that fear of him was drying it up at its source. This was no longer the case, later in life and with his younger children. They loved him tenderly: and if I cannot say so much of myself, I was always loyally devoted to him. As regards my own education, I hesitate to pronounce whether I was more a loser or gainer by his severity.

Hektor and Andromache
on the Walls of Troy

From Homer, The Iliad

In contrast with the Greek hero Achilles, the Trojan prince Hektor is as much concerned with family life as with glory. From the beginning of history, men have been torn between their love for their families and their duty to the common good. In this touching scene, Andromache begs her husband to avoid the battle and not leave his child an orphan and her a widow. But he has no choice—he must fight for his country. Standing on the walls of Troy, they enjoy a moment of laughter when their baby son cries in fright at the sight of his father's plumed helmet. In the midst of war and despite a foreboding of tragedy, they retain their vibrant integrity as a family.

Hektor smiled in silence as he looked on his son, but she, Andromache, stood close beside him, letting her tears fall, and clung to his hand and called him by name and spoke to him:

"Dearest, your own great strength will be your death, and you have no pity on your little son, nor on me, ill-starred, who soon must be your widow; for presently the Achaians, gathering together, will set upon you and kill you; and for me it would be far better to sink into the earth when I have lost you, for there is no other consolation for me after you have gone to your destiny—only grief; since I have no father, no honored mother. Hektor, thus you are father to me, and my honored mother, you are my brother, and you it is who are my young husband. Please take pity upon me then, stay here on the rampart, that you may not leave your child an orphan, your wife a widow, but draw your people up by the fig tree, there where the city is openest to attack, and where the wall may be mounted."

Then tall Hektor of the shining helm answered her: "All these things are in my mind also, lady; yet I would feel deep shame before the Trojans, and the Trojan women with trailing garments, if like a coward I were to shrink aside from the fighting; and the spirit will not let me, since I have learned to be valiant and to fight always among the foremost ranks of the Trojans, winning for my own self great glory, and for my father. For I know this thing well in my heart, and my mind knows it: there will come a day when sacred Ilion shall perish, and Priam, and the people of Priam of the strong ash spear. But it is not so much the pain to come of the Trojans that troubles me, not even of Priam the king nor Hekabe, not the thought of my brothers who in their numbers and valor shall drop in the dust under the hands of men who hate them, as troubles me the thought of you, when some bronze-armored Achaian leads you off, taking away your day of liberty, in tears; and in Argos you must work at the loom of another, and carry water from the spring Messeis or Hypereia, all unwilling, but strong will be the necessity upon you; and someday seeing you shedding tears a man will say of you;

'This is the wife of Hektor, who was ever the bravest fighter of the Trojans, breakers of horses, in the days when they fought about Ilion.'

"So will one speak of you; and for you it will be yet a fresh grief, to be widowed of such a man who could fight on the day of your slavery. But may I be dead and the piled earth hide me under before I hear you crying and know by this that they drag you captive."

So speaking glorious Hektor held out his arms to his baby, who shrank back to his fair-girdled nurse's bosom screaming, and frightened at the aspect of his own father, terrified as he saw the bronze and the crest with its horse-hair, nodding dreadfully, as he thought, from the peak of the helmet. Then his beloved father laughed out, and his honored mother, and at once glorious Hektor lifted from his head the helmet and laid it in all its shining upon the ground. Then taking up his dear son he tossed him about in his arms, and kissed him, and lifted his voice in prayer to Zeus and the other immortals: "Zeus, and you other immortals, grant that this boy, who is my son, may be as I am, preeminent among the Trojans, great in strength, as am I and rule strongly over Ilion; and some day let them say of him: 'He is better by far than his father,' as he comes in from the fighting; and let him kill his enemy and bring home the blooded spoils, and delight the heart of his mother."

The Joys of Parents Are Secret

From Francis Bacon, Essays

From Francis Bacon's essay, Of Parents and Children.

The joys of parents are secret; and so are their griefs and fears. They cannot utter the one, nor they will not utter the other. Children sweeten labors, but they make misfortunes more bitter. They increase the cares of life, but they mitigate the remembrance of death. The perpetuity by generation is common to beasts, but memory, merit, and noble works are proper to men. And surely a man shall see the noblest works and foundations have proceeded from childless men, which have sought to express the images of their minds, where those of their bodies have failed. So the care of posterity is most in them that have no posterity.

Advice to a Young Man on Marrying Early

From Benjamin Franklin, Essays Humorous, Moral and Literary

Scientist, moralist, and diplomat, Benjamin Franklin (1706-1780) was an early authority on virtuous living for colonial America.

Dear Jack,

You desire, you say, my impartial thoughts on the subject of an early marriage, by way of answer to the numberless objections that have been made by numerous persons to your own. You may remember, when you consulted me on the occasion, that I thought youth on both sides to be no objection. Indeed, from the marriages that have fallen under my observation, I am rather inclined to think, that early ones stand the best chance of happiness. The temper and habits of the young are not yet become so stiff and uncomplying, as when more advanced in life; they form more easily to each other, and hence, many occasions of disgust are removed. And if youth has less of that prudence which is necessary to manage a family, yet the parents and elder friends of young married persons are generally at hand to afford their advice, which amply supplies that defect; and, by early marriage, youth is sooner formed to regular and useful life; and possibly some of those accidents or connections, that might have injured the constitution, or reputation, or both, are thereby happily prevented. Particular circumstances of particular persons may possibly sometimes make it prudent to delay entering into that state: but, in general, when nature has rendered our bodies fit for it, the presumption is in nature's favor, that she has not judged amiss in making us desire it. Late marriages are often attended, too, with this further inconvenience, that there is not the same chance that the parents should live to see their offspring educated. "Late children," says the Spanish proverb, "are early orphans." A melancholy reflection to those whose case it may be. With us in America, marriages are generally in the morning of life; our children are therefore educated and settled in the world by noon; and thus, our business being done, we have an afternoon and evening of cheerful leisure to ourselves, such as our friend at present enjoys. By these early marriages we are blessed with more children; and from the mode among us, founded by nature, of every mother suckling and nursing her own child, more of them are raised. Thence the swift progress of population among us, unparalleled in Europe. In fine, I am glad you are married, and congratulate you most cordially upon it. You are now in the way of becoming a useful citizen; and you have escaped the unnatural state of celibacy for life—the fate of many here, who never intended it, but who having too long postponed the change of their conditions, find, at length, that it is too late to think of it, and so live all their lives in a situation that greatly lessens a man's value. An odd volume of a set of books bears not the value of its proportion to the set; what think you of the odd half of a pair of scissors; it can't well cut any thing; it may possibly serve to scrape a trencher.

Pray make my compliments and best wishes acceptable to your bride. I am old and heavy, or should ere this have presented them in person. I shall make but small use of the old man's privilege, that of giving advice to younger friends. Treat your wife always with respect; it will procure respect to you, not only from her, but from all that observe it. Never use a slighting expression to her, even in jest; for slights in jest, after frequent bandyings, are apt to end in angry earnest. Be studious in your profession and you will be learned. Be industrious and frugal, and you will be rich. Be sober and temperate, and you will be healthy. Be in general virtuous, and you will be happy. At least, you will, by such conduct, stand the best chance for such consequences. I pray God to bless you both! being ever your affectionate friend,

B. Franklin

My Wife Is My Best Friend

From John Stuart Mill, Autobiography

Mill's moving tribute to his wife and "most valuable friend" Harriet Parker suggests that he found in marriage an emotional wholeness and an intellectual openness denied to him in childhood—and a partner and mentor for every sphere of his life. His marriage to this "eminently meditative and poetic" woman made him a deeper man, one whose life work was not a solitary labor but "the fusion of two minds."

It was at the period of my mental progress which I have now reached that I formed the friendship which has been the honor and chief blessing of my existence, as well as the source of a great part of all that I have attempted to do, or hope to effect hereafter, for human improvement. My first introduction to the lady who, after a friendship of twenty years, consented to become my wife, was in 1830, when I was in my twenty-fifth and she in her twenty-third year. With her husband's family it was the renewal of an old acquaintanceship. His grandfather lived in the next house to my father's in Newington Green, and I had sometimes when a boy been invited to play in the old gentleman's garden. He was a fine specimen of the old Scotch puritan; stern, severe, and powerful, but very kind to children, on whom such men make a lasting impression. Although it was years after my introduction to Mrs. Taylor before my acquaintance with her became at all intimate or confidential, I very soon felt her to be the most admirable person I had ever known. It is not to be supposed that she was, or that anyone, at the age at which I first saw her, could be, all that she afterward became. Least of all could this be true of her, with whom self-improvement, progress in the highest and in all senses, was a law of nature; a necessity equally from the ardor with which she sought it, and from the spontaneous tendency of faculties which could not receive an impression or an experience without making it the source or the occasion of an accession of wisdom. Up to the time when I first saw her, her rich and powerful nature had chiefly unfolded itself according to the received type of feminine genius.

To her outer circle she was a beauty and a wit, with an air of natural distinction, felt by all who approached her: to the inner, a woman of deep and strong feeling, of penetrating and intuitive intelligence, and of an eminently meditative and poetic nature. Married at a very early age, to a most upright, brave, and honorable man, of liberal opinions and good education, but without the intellectual or artistic tastes which would have made him a companion for her—though a steady and affectionate friend, for whom she had true esteem and the strongest affection through life, and whom she most deeply lamented when dead; shut out by the social disabilities of women from any adequate exercise of her highest faculties in action on the world without; her life was one of inward meditation, varied by familiar intercourse with a small circle of friends, of whom one only (long since deceased) was a person of genius, or of capacities of feeling or intellect kindred with her own, but all had more or less of alliance with her in sentiments and opinions. Into this circle I had the good fortune to be admitted, and I soon perceived that she possessed, in combination, the qualities which in all other persons whom I had known I had been only too happy to find singly. In her, complete emancipation from every kind of superstition (including that which attributes a pretended perfection to the order of nature and the universe), and an earnest protest against many things which are still part of the established constitution of society, resulted not from the hard intellect but from strength of noble and elevated feeling, and coexisted with a highly reverential nature. In general spiritual characteristics, as well as in temperament and organization, I have often compared her, as she was at this time, to Shelley: but in thought and intellect, Shelley, so far as his powers were developed in his short life, was but a child compared with what she ultimately became. Alike in the highest regions of speculation and in the smallest practical concerns of daily life, her mind was the same perfect instrument, piercing to the very heart and marrow of the matter; always seizing the essential idea or principle. The same exactness and rapidity of operation, pervading as it did her sensitive as well as her mental faculties, would with her gifts of feeling and imagination have fitted her to be a consummate artist, as her fiery and tender soul and her vigorous eloquence would certainly have made her a great orator, and her profound knowledge of human nature and discernment and sagacity in practical life, would in the times when such a *carriere* was open to women, have made her eminent among the rulers of

mankind. Her intellectual gifts did but minister to a moral character at once the noblest and the best balanced which I have ever met
with in life. Her unselfishness was not that of a taught system of
duties, but of a heart which thoroughly identified itself with the
feeling of others, and often went to excess in consideration for
them, by imaginatively investing their feelings with the intensity of
its own. The passion of justice might have been thought to be her
strongest feeling, but for her boundless generosity, and a loving-
ness every ready to pour itself forth upon any or all human beings
who were capable of giving the smallest feeling in return. The rest
of her moral characteristics were such as naturally accompany
these qualities of mind and heart: the most genuine modesty combined with the loftiest pride; a simplicity and sincerity which were
absolute, toward all who were fit to receive them; the utmost scorn
of whatever was mean and cowardly, and a burning indignation at
everything brutal or tyrannical, faithless or dishonorable in conduct and character; while making the broadest distinction between
mala in se and mere *mala prohibita*—between acts giving evidence of
intrinsic badness in feeling and character, and those which are only
violations of conventions either good or bad, violations which
whether in themselves right or wrong, are capable of being committed by persons in every other respect loveable or admirable.

To be admitted into any degree of mental intercourse with a
being of these qualities, could not but have a most beneficial influence on my development; though the effect was only gradual, and
many years elapsed before her mental progress and mine went forward in the complete companionship they at last attained. The
benefit I received was far greater than any which I could hope to
give; though to her, who had at first reached her opinions by the
moral intuition of a character of strong feeling, there was doubtless
help as well as encouragement to be derived from one who had
arrived at many of the same results by study and reasoning; and in
the rapidity of her intellectual growth, her mental activity, which
converted everything into knowledge, doubtless drew from me, as
it did from other sources, many of its materials. What I owe, even
intellectually, to her, is, in its detail, almost infinite; of its general
character, a few words will give some, though a very imperfect,
idea. With those who, like all the best and wisest of mankind, are
dissatisfied with human life as it is, and whose feelings are wholly
identified with its radical amendment, there are two main regions
of thought. One is the region of ultimate aims; the constituent ele-

ments of the highest realizable ideal of human life. The other is that of the immediately useful and practically attainable. In both these departments I have acquired more from her teaching, than from all other sources taken together. And, to say truth, it is in these two extremes principally, that real certainty lies. My own strength lay wholly in the uncertain and slippery intermediate region, that of theory, or moral and political science: respecting the conclusions of which, in any of the forms in which I have received or originated them, whether as political economy, analytic psychology, logic, philosophy of history, or anything else, it is not the least of my intellectual obligations to her that I have derived from her a wise skepticism, which, while it has not hindered me from following out the honest exercise of my thinking faculties to whatever conclusions might result from it, has put me on my guard against holding or announcing those conclusions with a degree of confidence which the nature of such speculations does not warrant, and has kept my mind not only open to admit it, but prompt to welcome and eager to seek, even the questions on which I have most meditated, any prospect of clearer perceptions and better evidence. I have often received praise, which in my own right I only partially deserve, for the greater practicality which is supposed to be found in my writings, compared with those of most thinkers who have been equally addicted to large generalizations. The writings in which this quality had been observed, were not the work of one mind, but of the fusion of two, one of them as preeminently practical in its judgments and perceptions of things present, as it was high and bold in its anticipations for a remote futurity.

At His Brother's Grave

From Robert G. Ingersoll, Select Orations

Robert G. Ingersoll was a nationally known lecturer, humanist critic of Biblical revelation, and a staunch Illinois Republican.

My friends: I am going to do that which the dead oft promised he would do for me.

The loved and loving brother, husband, father, friend, died where manhood's morning almost touches noon, and while the shadows still were falling toward the west.

He had not passed on life's highway the stone that marks the highest point, but, being weary for a moment, lay down by the wayside, and using his burden for a pillow, fell into that dreamless sleep that kisses down his eyelids still. While yet in love with life and raptured with the world, he passed to silence and pathetic dust.

Yet, after all, it may be best, just in the happiest, sunniest hour of all the voyage, while eager winds are kissing every sail, to dash against the unseen rock, and in an instant hear the billows roar above a sunken ship. For, whether in midsea or 'mong the breakers of the farther shore, a wreck at last must mark the end of each and all. And every life, no matter if its every hour is rich with love and every moment jeweled with a joy, will at its close become a tragedy as sad and deep and dark as can be woven of the warp and woof of mystery and death.

This brave and tender man in every storm of life was oak and rock, but in the sunshine he was vine and flower. He was the friend of all heroic souls. He climbed the heights and left all superstitions far below, while on his forehead fell the golden dawning of the grander day.

He loved the beautiful, and was with color, form, and music touched to tears. He sided with the weak, and with a willing hand gave alms; with loyal heart and with purest hands he faithfully discharged all public trusts.

He was a worshiper of liberty, a friend of the oppressed. A thousand times I have heard him quote these words: "For justice all place a temple, and all seasons, summer." He believed that happiness was the only good, reason the only torch, justice the only worship, humanity the only religion, and love the only priest. He added to the sum of human joy; and were every one to whom he did some loving service to bring a blossom to his grave, he would sleep tonight beneath a wilderness of flowers.

Life is a narrow vale between the cold and barren peaks of two eternities. We strive in vain to look beyond the heights. We cry aloud, and the only answer is the echo of our wailing cry. From the voiceless lips of the unreplying dead there comes no word; but in the night of death, hope sees a star, and listening love can hear the rustle of a wing.

He who sleeps here, when dying, mistaking the approach of death for the return of health, whispered with his last breath, "I am better now." Let us believe, in spite of doubts and dogmas, and tears and fears, that these dear words are true of all the countless dead.

And now to you who have been chosen, from among the many men he loved, to do the last sad office for the dead, we give his sacred dust. Speech cannot contain our love. There was, there is, no greater, stronger, manlier man.

Mother o' Mine

Rudyard Kipling

If I were hanged on the highest hill,
Mother o' mine, O mother o' mine!
I know whose love would follow me still,
Mother o' mine, O mother' o' mine!
If I were drowned in the deepest sea,
Mother o' mine, O mother o' mine!
I know whose tears would come down to me,
Mother o' mine, O mother o' mine!
If I were damned of body and soul,
I know whose prayers would make me whole,
Mother o' mine, O mother o 'mine!

Youth Versus Age

Francis Bacon, Essays

Young men are bold, impetuous, and drawn to extremes, Bacon tells us. Older men are cautious, garrulous, and tend to carp. What age gains in understanding, it loses in willpower.

Young men are fitter to invent than to judge, fitter for execution than for counsel, and fitter for new projects than for settled business. For the experience of age, in things that fall within the compass of it, directeth them, but in new things abuseth them. The errors of young men are the ruin of business, but the errors of aged men amount but to this, that more might have been done, or sooner. Young men in the conduct and manage of actions embrace more than they can hold; stir more than they can quiet; fly to the end, without consideration of the means and degrees; pursue some few principles which they have chanced upon absurdly; [are careless in their innovations], which draws unknown inconveniences; use extreme remedies at first; and that which doubleth all errors, will not acknowledge or retract them, like an unready horse that will neither stop nor turn. Men of age object too much, consult too long, adventure too little, repent too soon, and seldom drive business home to the full period, but content themselves with a mediocrity of success.

Why Should Not Old Men Be Mad?

William Butler Yeats

Why should not old men be mad?
Some have known a likely lad
That had a sound fly-fisher's wrist
Turn to a drunken journalist;
A girl that knew all Dante once
Live to bear children to a dunce;
A Helen of social welfare dream
Climb on a wagonette to scream.
Some think it a matter of course that chance
Should starve good men and bad advance,
That if their neighbors figured plain,
As though upon a lighted screen,
No single story would they find
Of an unbroken happy mind,

A finish worthy of the start.
Young men know nothing of this sort,
Observant old men know it well;
And when they know what old books tell,
And that no better can be had,
Know why an old man should be mad.

5

THE
STATESMAN

For the ancient Greeks and Romans, manliness could not be understood apart from a full-time devotion to the duties of public life and the cultivation of the civic virtues. As Aristotle had it in his famous axiom from the *Politics*, "Man is by nature a political animal." In our times, this statement might at first strike us as strange: We have professional politicians, after all, who are elected to concern themselves with public affairs on a full-time basis, while the rest of us devote our efforts to trying to be a good man in other areas of life besides politics—by being a good husband, father, or friend, good at one's job or vocation, or by contributing to the community through myriad other channels.

Yet when the ancients identified manliness with the civic virtues, they were not thinking of politics in the narrow way we sometimes do today. For them, politics was more than just a realm for brokering private interests. The civic association was not just a contract among individuals to protect its members from crime or foreign invasion and enable them to get on with their private lives in peace. For the ancients, the city or *polis* was an all-encompassing association. To be a citizen was a source not only of security and freedom from unjust treatment, but of aesthetic and cultural satisfaction through the community's shared traditions, and even of religious fulfillment through its common faith. By serving the common good, according to the ancients, we exercise our moral and intellectual virtues in a way that would not be possible in private life alone. By deliberating together with our fellow citizens on the great issues of war and peace, justice and injustice, nobility and baseness, we give our natures room to flower and blossom. Family life is crucially important to a republic of virtuous men because it provides children with their first habituation to good behavior, preparing them for their future lives as citizens. But, in the end, a man's public life might be said to possess an even higher dignity and importance than his private life as a husband and father. The cardinal virtues of justice, moderation, courage, liberality, and wisdom can only be expressed at their fullest through our lives as citizens.

The readings in this section, then, are about man as statesman. The Greek word for statesman, *politikos,* meant "citizen" in
the fullest sense—not someone who sits passively by while the great
affairs of state unfold, but one who takes an active part in deciding
their course, whether jointly with his peers or by taking a role at the
helm of affairs. Of course, there is always the danger that a man
convinced of his ability to lead will become overbearing and intolerant of dissenting opinions, or jealous of the talents of others;
what starts out as statesmanship can degenerate into tyranny. For
manly pride and honor have both good and bad potential. At its
highest levels it can involve an energetic commitment to justice at
home and, when necessary, the defense of one's country from
external threats. And yet unchecked pride can lead to overweening
arrogance, ambition and dreams of imperialism, and at worst to a
base desire to overthrow the common good and rule as tyrant,
indulging one's own self-serving desires at the expense of others.
Many of the readings in this section explore this problem: how can
masculine ambition be channeled away from tyrannical selfishness
and redirected toward honorable citizenship?

For these reasons, statesmanship has always been closely connected with moral and intellectual education. According to Plato's
Republic, in a just and well-ordered society, the soul of the individual citizen will mirror the virtues of the community as a whole, and
the community in turn will enable the individual citizen to exercise
his potential for excellence. Both within the individual soul and
the structure of the community at large, there must be a hierarchy
in which reason governs the passions. To achieve this harmony
within the individual soul and between the citizen and the community he serves, government must take the lead in providing a civic
education.

Young men need an education that will instill in their characters a sense of order, of harmony and justice that seems to mirror
the order of the cosmos itself. If a man's soul participates in this
pattern in the heavens, he will be steady, sober, gracious, and self-
restrained—a true gentleman. The aim of Platonic education is to
harness manly ambition and turn it away from extravagance and
profligacy toward civic virtue and the life of the mind. In his dialogues we encounter perplexed young men who want to be good,
but who are tempted by a life of pleasure or domination, and troubled by the lack of a clear moral direction from their parents,
teachers, or other authorities. Everyone tells them to be good, but

to do everything necessary to get ahead in the world and be successful! Socrates, by contrast, characterized the life of the soul as an ascent from bodily pleasures to the higher pleasures of the mind, pleasures that include the love of family and further ennoble family life by directing it toward the even higher purposes of the common good.

Readers of this section will find many variations on this fundamental classical ideal of citizenship, which identifies true manliness with the sobriety, thoughtfulness, and steadfastness required by civic affairs and a respect for learning. It is captured well by Cicero's portrait of Scipio Africanus the Younger, the great Roman general and statesman. Scipio perfectly embodies the classical hierarchy of active and contemplative virtues. To be a man, his example shows, one must demonstrate civic virtue, including military prowess, in the service of one's country and thereby reap the deserved reward of public honor. But worthy as the civic virtues and public honor are, the life of learning, art, and culture is even worthier. The intellectual virtues should govern the civic virtues so that both may flourish. Political and military prowess that might otherwise make a man too harsh and proud will be tempered by their subordination to the nobler virtues of learning and culture. A true man is strong, but in a quiet way. He is modest, generous and affable, not a boaster or a bully. This ideal of statesmanship as a balance between active and contemplative virtues endures throughout all the ages of the West, down to the American Founding Fathers and great men of the present century like Churchill.

On reflection, then, the classical ideal of statesmanship is not quite so alien to us as it might first appear. For much of that ideal of citizenship and governing is familiar to us through the influence of its modern admirers, Thomas Jefferson, Alexis de Tocqueville, and Theodore Roosevelt among them. Its influence is still with us and shapes us deeply, even if we might have lost our immediate day-to-day connection with this heritage. For even in our most pessimistic mood about the careerism or posturing of modern politicians—or over the failure of some of our own leaders to demonstrate the maturity and honesty that we might rightly expect—we can still feel inspired to recall the classical ideal. It's not all that distant, the image of strong yet just, forceful yet reflective leadership. As Jefferson tells us in a reading appearing later in this anthology, a free people must be liberally educated in the same moral and intellectual virtues praised by the ancients if they are not to lose their freedom to a demagogue. As long as free peoples and self-governing republics exist, men must aspire to rise above being mere politicians to being statesmen. For, as Dwight D. Eisenhower once wrote, "Only our individual faith in freedom can keep us free."

THE KINGLY MAN

Two Kings Clashing:
Achilles and Agamemnon

From Homer, The Iliad

Anger is necessary in a warrior, but when mixed with jealousy and wounded honor it can lead to a dangerous instability. When the Greek king of kings, Agamemnon, deprives the Greeks' greatest fighter, Achilles, of his war prize, the young warrior withdraws from the army. Achilles, a king in his own right, believes he is a better man than his lawful commander in chief, and is ready to sacrifice his own side's safety and success against the Trojans to avenge his wounded pride. It's an age-old conflict of youth versus age, and natural merit versus authority. For his part, Agamemnon has long resented Achilles's resistance to his supreme authority, as their heated argument makes plain. The ultimate consequence of Achilles's desertion of the Greeks is that the Trojans come close to defeating them, while Achilles's best friend Patroclus dies in his place. Thus Homer demonstrates that overreaching anger and pride are due for a fall. Achilles wanted the Greeks to suffer so they would realize how much they needed him. He got his wish, but at an awful price.

    Sing, goddess, the anger of Paleus's son Achilleus and its devastation, which put pains thousandfold upon the Achaians, hurled in their multitudes to the house of Hades strong souls of heroes, but gave their bodies to be the delicate feasting of dogs, of all birds, and the will of Zeus was accomplished since that time when first there stood in division of conflict Atreus's son, the lord of men and brilliant Achilleus.

Then in answer again spoke brilliant swift-footed Achilleus:

"Son of Atreus, most lordly, greediest for gain of all men, how shall the great-hearted Achaians give you a prize now? There is no great store of things lying about I know of. But what we took from the cities by storm has been distributed; it is unbecoming for the people to call back things once given. No, for the present give the girl back to the god; we Achaians thrice and four times over will repay you, if ever Zeus gives into our hands the strong-walled citadel of Troy to be plundered."

Then in answer again spoke powerful Agamemnon:

"Not that way, good fighter though you be, godlike Achilleus, strive to cheat, for you will not deceive, you will not persuade me. What do you want? To keep your own prize and have me sit here lacking one? Are you ordering me to give this girl back? Either the great-hearted Achaians shall give me a new prize chosen according to my desire to atone for the girl lost, or else if they will not give me one I myself shall take her, your own prize, or that of Aias, or that of Odysseus."

Then looking darkly at him Achilleus of the swift feet spoke:

"O wrapped in shamelessness, with your mind forever on profit, how shall any one of the Achaians readily obey you either to go on a journey or to fight men strongly in battle? I for my part did not come here for the sake of the Trojan spearmen to fight against them, since to me they have done nothing. Never yet have they driven away my cattle or my horses, never in Phthia where the soil is rich and men grow great did they spoil my harvest, since indeed there is much that lies between us, the shadowy mountains and the echoing sea; but for your sake, o great shamelessness, we followed, to do you a favor, you with the dog's eyes, to win your honor and Menelaos's from the Trojans. You forget all this or else you care nothing. And now my prize you threaten in person to strip from me, for whom I labored much, the gift of the sons of the Achaians. Never, when the Achaians sack some well-founded citadel of the Trojans, do I have a prize that is equal to your prize. Always the greater part of the painful fighting is the work of my hands; but when the time comes to distribute the booty yours is far the greater reward, and I with some small thing yet dear to me go back to my ships when I am weary with fighting. Now I am returning to Phthia, since it is much better to go home again with my curved ships, and I am minded no longer to stay here dishonored and pile up your wealth and your luxury."

Then answered him in turn the lord of men Agamemnon:

"Run away by all means if your heart drives you. I will not

entreat you to stay here for my sake. There are others with me who will do me honor, and above all Zeus of the counsels. To me you are the most hateful of all the kings whom the gods love."

"Forever quarreling is dear to your heart, and wars and battles; and if you are very strong indeed, that is a god's gift. Go home then with your own ships and your own companions, be king over the Myrmidons. I care nothing about you. I take no account of your anger. But here is my threat to you. Even as Phoibos Apollo is taking away my Chryseis, I shall convey her back in my own ship, with my own followers; but I shall take the fair-cheeked Briseis, your prize, I myself going to your shelter, that you may learn well how much greater I am than you, and another man may shrink back from likening himself to me and contending against me."

David and Goliath

From 1 Samuel (16–20)

The great biblical account of how a young man's valor serves his king, but also threatens his power.

The Philistines collected their forces for war and massed at Socoh in Judah; they camped between Socoh and Azekah at Ephes-dammim. Saul and the Israelites also massed, and camped in the Vale of Elah. They drew up their lines facing the Philistines, the Philistines occupying a position on one hill and the Israelites on another, with a valley between them. A champion came out from the Philistine camp, a man named Goliath, from Gath; he was over nine feet in height. He had a bronze helmet on his head, and he wore plate-armor of bronze, weighing five thousand shekels. On his legs were bronze greaves, and one of his weapons was a dagger of bronze. The shaft of his spear was like a weaver's beam, and its head, which was of iron, weighed six hundred shekels; and his shield-bearer marched ahead of him. The champion stood and shouted to the ranks of Israel, "Why do you come out to do battle, you slaves of Saul? I am the Philistine champion; choose your man to meet me. If he can kill me in fair fight, we will become your slaves; but if I prove too strong for him and kill him, you shall be our slaves and serve us. Here and now I defy the ranks of Israel. Give me a man," said the Philistine, "and we will fight it out." When Saul and the Israelites heard what the Philistine said, they were shaken and dismayed.

David was the son of an Ephrathite called Jesse, who had eight sons. By Saul's time he had become a feeble old man, and his three eldest sons had followed Saul to the war. The eldest was called Eliab, the next Abinadab, and the third Shammah; David was the youngest. The three eldest followed Saul, while David used to go to Saul's camp and back to Bethlehem to mind his father's flocks.

Morning and evening for forty days the Philistine came forward and took up his position. Then one day Jesse said to his son David, "Take your brothers an ephah of this parched grain and these ten loaves of bread, and run with them to the camp. These ten cream-cheeses are for you to take to the commanding officer. See if your brothers are well and bring back some token from them." Saul and the brothers and all the Israelites were in the Vale of Elah, fighting the Philistines. Early next morning David left someone in charge of the sheep, set out on his errand and went as Jesse had told him. He reached the lines just as the army was going out to take up position and was raising the war-cry. The Israelites and the Philistines drew up their ranks opposite each other. David left his things in charge of the quartermaster, ran to the line and went up to his brothers to greet them. While he was talking to them the Philistine champion, Goliath, came out from the Philistine ranks and issued his challenge in the same words as before; and David heard him. When the Israelites saw the man they ran from him in fear. "Look at this man who comes out day after day to defy Israel," they said. "The king is to give a rich reward to the man who kills him; he will give him his daughter in marriage too and will exempt his family from service due in Israel." Then David turned to his neighbors and said, "What is to be done for the man who kills this Philistine, and wipes out our disgrace? And who is he, an uncircumcised Philistine to defy the army of the living God?" The people told him how the matter stood and what was to be done for the man who killed him. His elder brother Eliab overheard David talking with the men and grew angry. "What are you doing here?" he asked. "And who have you left to look after those sheep in the wilderness? I know you, you impudent young rascal; you have only come to see the fighting." David answered, "What have I done now? I only asked a question." And he turned away from him to someone else and repeated his question, but everybody gave him the same answer.

What David had said was overheard and reported to Saul, who sent for him. David said to him, "Do not lose heart, sir. I will go and fight this Philistine." Saul answered, "You cannot go and fight with this Philistine; you are only a lad, and he has been a fighting man all his life." David said to Saul, "Sir, I am my father's shepherd; when a lion or a bear comes and carries off a sheep from the flock, I attack it and rescue the victim from its jaws. Then if it turns on me, I seize it by the beard and batter it to death. Lions I have killed and bears, and this uncircumcised Philistine will fare no better than they; he has defied the army of the living God. The Lord who saved me from the lion and the bear will save me from this Philistine." "Go then," said Saul; "and the Lord will be with you." He put his own tunic on David, placed a bronze helmet on his head and gave him a coat of mail to wear; he then fastened his sword on David over his tunic. But David hesitated, because he had not tried them, and said to Saul, "I cannot go with these, because I have not tried them." So he took them off. Then he picked up his stick, chose five smooth stones from the brook and put them in a shepherd's bag which served as his pouch. He walked out to meet the Philistine with his sling in his hand.

The Philistine came toward David, with his shield-bearer marching ahead; and he looked David up and down and had nothing but contempt for this handsome lad with his ruddy cheeks and bright eyes. He said to David, "Am I a dog that you come out against me with sticks?" And he swore at him in the name of his god. "Come on," he said, "and I will give your flesh to the birds and the beasts." David answered, "You have come against me with sword and spear and dagger, but I have come against you in the name of the Lord of Hosts, the God of the army of Israel which you have defied. The Lord will put you into my power this day; I will kill you and cut your head off and leave your carcass and the carcasses of the Philistines to the birds and the wild beasts; all the world shall know that there is a God in Israel. All those who are gathered here shall see that the Lord saves neither by sword nor spear; the battle is the Lord's, and he will put you all into our power."

When the Philistine began moving toward him again, David ran quickly to engage him. He put his hand into his bag, took out a stone, slung it, and struck the Philistine on the forehead. The stone sank into his forehead, and he fell flat on his face on the ground. So David proved the victor with his sling and stone; he struck Goliath down and gave him a mortal wound, though he had no sword. Then he ran to the Philistine and stood over him, and grasping his sword, he drew it out of the scabbard, dispatched him and cut off his head. The Philistines, when they saw that their hero was dead, turned and ran. The men of Israel and Judah at once raised the war-cry and hotly pursued them all the way to Gath and even to the gates of Ekron. The road that runs to Shaarim, Gath, and Ekron was strewn with their dead. On their return from the pursuit of the Philistines, the Israelites plundered their camp. David took Goliath's head and carried it to Jerusalem, leaving his weapons in his tent.

Next day an evil spirit from God seized upon Saul; he fell into a frenzy in the house, and David played the harp to him as he had before. Saul had his spear in his hand, and he hurled it at David, meaning to pin him to the wall; but twice David swerved aside. After this Saul was afraid of David, because he saw that the Lord had forsaken him and was with David. He therefore removed David from his household and appointed him to the command of a thousand men. David led his men into action, and succeeded in everything that he undertook, because the Lord was with him. When Saul saw how successful he was, he was more afraid of him than ever; all Israel and Judah loved him because he took the field at their head.

Saul spoke to Jonathan his son and all his household about killing David. But Jonathan was devoted to David and told him that his father Saul was looking for an opportunity to kill him. "Be on your guard tomorrow morning," he said; "conceal yourself, and remain in hiding. Then I will come out and join my father in the open country where you are and speak to him about you, and if I discover anything I will tell you." Jonathan spoke up for David to his father Saul and said to him, "Sir, do not wrong your servant David; he has not wronged you; his conduct toward you has been beyond reproach. Did he not take his life in his hands when he killed the Philistine, and the Lord won great victory for Israel? You saw it, you shared in the rejoicing; why should you wrong an innocent man and put David to death without cause?"

The Kingdom of the Lion

Aesop

The beasts of the field and forest had a Lion as their king. He was neither wrathful, cruel, nor tyrannical, but just and gentle as a king should be. He made during his reign a royal proclamation for a general assembly of all the birds and beasts, and drew up conditions for an universal league, in which the Wolf and the Lamb, the Panther and the Kid, the Tiger and the Stag, the Dog and the Hare, should live together in perfect peace and amity. The Hare said, "Oh, how I have longed to see this day, in which the weak shall take their place with impunity by the side of the strong."

The Good Prince and
the Evil Prince

From Desiderius Erasmus,
The Education of a Christian Prince

Good and bad models for the moral education of a prince.

Let the teacher paint a sort of celestial creature, more like to a divine being than a mortal: complete in all the virtues; born for the common good; yea, sent by the God above to help the affairs of mortals by looking out and caring for everyone and everything; to whom no concern is of longer standing or more dear than the state; who has more than a paternal spirit toward everyone; who holds the life of each individual dearer than his own; who works and strives night and day for just one end—to be the best he can for everyone; with whom rewards are ready for all good men and pardon for the wicked, if only they will reform—for so much does he want to be of real help to his people, without thought of recompense, that if necessary he would not hesitate to look out for their welfare at great risk to himself; who considers his wealth to lie in the advantages of his country; who is ever on the watch so that everyone else may sleep deeply; who grants no leisure to himself so that he may spend his life in the peace of his country; who worries himself with continual cares so that his subjects may have peace and quiet. Upon the moral qualities of this one man alone depends the felicity of the state. Let the tutor point this out as the picture of a true prince!

Now let him bring out the opposite side by showing a frightful, loathsome beast, formed of a dragon, wolf, lion, viper, bear, and like creatures; with six hundred eyes all over it, teeth everywhere, fearful from all angles, and with hooked claws; with never satiated hunger, fattened on human vitals, and reeking with human blood; never sleeping, but always threatening the fortunes and lives of all men; dangerous to everyone, especially to the good; a sort of fatal scourge to the whole world, on which everyone who has the interests of the state at heart pours forth execration and hatred; which cannot be borne because of its monstrousness and yet cannot be overthrown without great disaster to the city because its maliciousness is hedged about with armed forces and wealth. This is the picture of a tyrant—unless there is something more odious which can be depicted. Monsters of this sort were Claudius and Caligula. The myths in the poets also showed Busyris, Pentheus, and Midas, whose names are now objects of hate to all the human race, to be of the same type.

Theseus, the Minotaur and Other Adventures

Thomas Bulfinch, Bulfinch's Mythology

Theseus was the son of Aegeus, king of Athens, and of Aethra, daughter of the king of Troezen. He was brought up at Troezen, and when arrived at manhood was to proceed to Athens and present himself to his father. Aegeus, on parting from Aethra, before the birth of his son, placed his sword and shoes under a large stone and directed her to send his son to him when he became strong enough to roll away the stone and take them from under it. When she thought the time had come, his mother led Theseus to the stone, and he removed it with ease and took the sword and shoes. As the roads were infested with robbers, his grandfather pressed him earnestly to take the shorter and safer way to his father's country—by sea; but the youth, feeling in himself the spirit and the soul of a hero, and eager to signalize himself like Hercules, with whose fame all Greece then rang, by destroying the evildoers and monsters that oppressed the country, determined on the more perilous and adventurous journey by land.

His first day's journey brought him to Epidaurus, where dwelt a man named Periphetes, a son of Vulcan. This ferocious savage always went armed with a club of iron, and all travelers stood in terror of his violence. When he saw Theseus approach he assailed him, but speedily fell beneath the blows of the young hero, who took possession of his club and bore it ever afterward as a memorial of his first victory.

Several similar contests with the petty tyrants and marauders of the country followed, in all of which Theseus was victorious. One of these evildoers was called Procrustes, or the Stretcher. He had an iron bedstead, on which he used to tie all travelers who fell into his hands. If they were shorter than the bed, he stretched their limbs to make them fit it; if they were longer than the bed, he lopped off a portion. Theseus served him as he had served others.

Having overcome all the perils of the road, Theseus at length reached Athens, where new dangers awaited him. Medea, the sorceress, who had fled from Corinth after her separation from Jason, had become the wife of Aegeus, the father of Theseus. Knowing by her arts who he was, and fearing the loss of her influence with her husband if Theseus should be acknowledged as his son, she filled the mind of Aegeus with suspicions of the young stranger, and induced him to present him a cup of poison; but at the moment when Theseus stepped forward to take it, the sight of the sword which he wore discovered to his father who he was, and prevented the fatal draught. Medea, detected in her arts, fled once more from deserved punishment, and arrived in Asia, where the country afterward called Media, received its name from her. Theseus was acknowledged by his father, and declared his successor.

The Athenians were at that time in deep affliction, on account of the tribute which they were forced to pay to Minos, king of Crete. This tribute consisted of seven youths and seven maidens, who were sent every year to be devoured by the Minotaur, a monster with a bull's body and a human head. It was exceedingly strong and fierce, and was kept in a labyrinth constructed by Daedalus, so artfully contrived that whoever was enclosed in it could by no means find his way out unassisted. Here the Minotaur roamed, and was fed with human victims.

Theseus resolved to deliver his countrymen from this calamity, or to die in the attempt. Accordingly, when the time of sending off the tribute came, and the youths and maidens were, according to custom, drawn by lot to be sent, he offered himself as one of the victims, in spite of the entreaties of his father. The ship departed under black sails, as usual, which Theseus promised his father to change for white, in case of his returning victorious. When they arrived in Crete, the youths and maidens were exhibited before Minos; and Ariadne, the daughter of the king, being present, became deeply enamored of Theseus, by whom her love was readily returned. She furnished him with a sword, with which to encounter the Minotaur, and with a spool of thread by which he might find his way out of the labyrinth. He was successful, slew the Minotaur, escaped from the labyrinth, and taking Ariadne as the companion of his way, with his rescued companions sailed for Athens. On their way they stopped at the island of Naxos, where Theseus abandoned Ariadne, leaving her asleep. His excuse for this ungrateful treatment of his benefactress was that Minerva appeared to him in a dream and commanded him to do so.

On approaching the coast of Attica, Theseus forgot the signal appointed by his father, and neglected to raise the white sails, and the old king, thinking his son had perished, put an end to his own life. Theseus thus became king of Athens.

Henry the Fifth Rallies His Troops Before the Walls of Harfleur

From William Shakespeare, Henry V

Once more unto the breach, dear friends, once more;
Or close the wall up with our English dead!
In peace, there's nothing so becomes a man,
As modest stillness, and humility;
But when the blast of war blows in our ears,
Then imitate the action of the tiger;
Stiffen the sinews, summon up the blood,
Disguise fair nature with hard-favored rage:
Then lend the eye a terrible aspect;
Let it pry through the portage of the head,
Like the brass cannon; let the brow o'erwhelm it,
As fearfully, as doth a gallèd rock
O'erhang and jutty his confounded base,
Swilled with the wild and wasteful ocean.
Now set the teeth, and stretch the nostril wide;
Hold hard the breath, and bend up every spirit
To his full height! On, on, you noblest English,
Whose blood is fet from fathers of war-proof!
Fathers, that like so many Alexanders,
Have, in these parts, from morn till even fought,
And sheathed their swords for lack of argument,
Dishonor not your mothers; now attest,
That those, whom you called fathers, did beget you!
Be copy now to men of grosser blood,
And teach them how to war! And you, good yeomen,
Whose limbs were made in England, show us here
The mettle of your pasture; let us swear
That you are worth your breeding: which I doubt not;
For there is none of you so mean and base,
That hath not noble lustre in your eyes.
I see you stand like greyhounds in the slips,

Straining upon the start. The game's afoot;
Follow your spirit: and, upon this charge,
Cry—God for Harry! England! And Saint George!

Napoleon, Man of the World

From Ralph Waldo Emerson, Representative Men

Emerson (1803–1882) was a celebrated essayist, poet, and speaker, and the main exponent of New England Transcendentalism.

In describing the two parties into which modern society divides itself—the democrat and the conservative—I said, Bonaparte represents the democrat, or the party of men of business, against the stationary or the conservative party. I omitted then to say, what is material to the statement, namely that these two parties differ only as young and old. The democrat is a young conservative; the conservative is an old democrat. The aristocrat is the democrat ripe and gone to seed; because both parties stand on the one ground of the supreme value of property, which one endeavors to get, and the other to keep. Bonaparte may be said to represent the whole history of this party, its youth and its age; yes, and with poetic justice its fate, in his own. The counter-revolution, the counter-party, still waits for its organ and representative, in a lover and a man of truly public and universal aims.

Here was an experiment, under the most favorable conditions, of the powers of intellect without conscience. Never was such a leader so endowed and so weaponed; never leader found such aids and followers. And what was the result of this vast talent and power, of these immense armies, burned cities, squandered treasures, immolated millions of men, of this demoralized Europe? It came to no result. All passed away like the smoke of his artillery, and left no trace. He left France smaller, poorer, feebler, than he found it; and the whole contest for freedom was to be begun again. The attempt was in principle suicidal. France served him with life and limb and estate, as long as it could identify its interest with him; but when men saw that after victory was another war; after the destruction of armies, new conscriptions; and they who had toiled so desperately were never nearer to the reward—they could not spend what they had earned, nor repose on their down-beds, nor strut in their chateaux—they deserted him. Men found that his absorbing egotism was deadly to all other men. It resembled the torpedo, which inflicts a succession of shocks on anyone who takes hold of it, producing spasms which contract the muscles of the hand, so that the man cannot open his fingers; and the animal inflicts new and more violent shocks, until he paralyzes and kills his victim. So this exorbitant egotist narrowed, impoverished and absorbed the power and existence of those who served him; and the universal cry of France and of Europe in 1814 was, "Enough of him;" "*Assez de Bonaparte.*"

It was not Bonaparte's fault. He did all that in him lay to live and thrive without moral principle. It was the nature of things, the eternal law of man and of the world which baulked and ruined him; and the result, in a million experiments, will be the same. Every experiment, by multitudes or by individuals, that has a sensual and selfish aim, will fail. The pacific Fourier will be as inefficient as the pernicious Napoleon. As long as our civilization is essentially one of property, of fences, of exclusiveness, it will be mocked by delusions. Our riches will leave us sick; there will be bitterness in our laughter, and our wine will burn our mouth. Only that good profits which we can taste with all doors open, and which serves all men.

Alfred the Great,
a Model King and Man

From John Richard Green, A Short History
of the English People

A portrait of the ideal ruler, balancing valor and humanity.

Alfred was the noblest as he was the most complete embodiment of all that is great, all that is lovable, in the English temper. He combined as no other man has ever combined its practical energy, its patient and enduring force, its profound sense of duty, the reserve and self-control that steady in it a wide outlook and a restless daring, its temperance and fairness, its frank geniality, its sensitiveness to action, its poetic tenderness, its deep and passionate religion. Religion, indeed, was the groundwork of Alfred's character. His temper was instinct with piety. Everywhere throughout his writings that remain to us the name of God, the thought of God, stir him to outbursts of ecstatic adoration.

But he was no mere saint. He felt none of that scorn of the world about him which drove the nobler souls of his day to monastery or hermitage. Vexed as he was by sickness and constant pain, his temper took no touch of asceticism. His rare geniality, a peculiar elasticity and mobility of nature, gave color and charm to his life. A sunny frankness and openness of spirit breathe in the pleasant chat of his books, and what he was in his books he showed himself in this daily converse. Alfred was in truth an artist, and both the lights and shadows of his life were those of the artistic temperament. His love of books, his love of strangers, his questionings of travelers and scholars, betray an imaginative restlessness that longs to break out of the narrow world of experience which hemmed him in. At one time he jots down news of a voyage to the unknown seas of the north. At another he listens to tidings which his envoys bring back from the churches of Malabar.

And side by side with this restless outlook of the artistic nature he showed its tenderness and susceptibility, its vivid apprehension of unseen danger, its craving for affection, its sensitiveness to wrong. It was with himself rather than with his reader that he communed as thoughts of the foe without, of ingratitude and opposition within, broke the calm pages of Gregory or Boethius.

"Desirest thou power?" he asks. "But thou shalt never obtain it without sorrows—sorrows from strange folk, and yet keener sorrows from thine own kindred." "Hardship and sorrow!" he breaks out again; "not a king but would wish to be without these if he could. But I know that he cannot!"

The loneliness which breathes in words like these has often begotten in great rulers a cynical contempt of men and the judgments of men. But cynicism found no echo in the large and sympathetic temper of Alfred. He not only longed for the love of his subjects, but for the remembrance of generations to come. Nor did his inner gloom or anxiety check for an instant his vivid and versatile activity. To the scholars he gathered round him he seemed the very type of a scholar, snatching every hour he could find to read or listen to books read to him. The singers of his court found in him a brother singer, gathering the old songs of his people to teach them to his children, breaking his renderings from the Latin with simple verse, solacing himself in hours of depression with the music of the Psalms.

He passed from court and study to plan buildings and instruct craftsmen in gold work, to teach even falconers and dogkeepers their business. But all this versatility and ingenuity was controlled by a cool good sense. Alfred was a thorough man of business. He was careful of detail, laborious, methodical. He carried in his bosom a little handbook in which he noted things as they struck him—now a bit of family genealogy, now a prayer, now such a story as that of Ealdhelm playing minstrel on the bridge. Each hour of the day had its appointed task; there was the same order in the division of his revenue and in the division of the court.

Wide, however, and various as was the King's temper, its range was less wonderful than its harmony. Of the narrowness, of the want of proportion, of the predominance of one quality over another which go commonly with an intensity of moral purpose Alfred showed not a trace. Scholar and soldier, artist and man of business, poet and saint, his character kept that perfect balance which charms us in no other Englishman save Shakespeare. But full and harmonious as his temper was, it was the temper of a king. Every power was bent to the work of rule. His practical energy found scope for itself in the material and administrative restoration of the wasted land.

His intellectual activity breathed fresh life into education and literature. His capacity for inspiring trust and affection drew the hearts of Englishmen to a common center, and began the upbuilding of a new England. And all was guided, controlled, ennobled by a single aim. "So long as I have lived," said the King as life closed about him, "I have striven to live worthily." Little by little men came to know what such a life of worthiness meant. Little by little they came to recognize in Alfred a ruler of higher and nobler stamp than the world had seen. Never had it seen a king who lived solely for the good of his people. Never had it seen a ruler who set aside every personal aim to devote himself solely to the welfare of those whom he ruled. It was this grand self-mastery that gave him his power over the men about him.

Tyrants Will Always
Be with Us

Aesop

A Wolf meeting with a Lamb astray from the fold, resolved not to lay violent hands on him, but to find some plea, which should justify to the Lamb himself his right to eat him. He thus addressed him: "Sirrah, last year you grossly insulted me." "Indeed," bleated the Lamb in a mournful tone of voice, "I was not then born." Then said the Wolf, "You feed in my pasture." "No, good sir," replied the Lamb, "I have not yet tasted grass." Again said the Wolf, "You drink of my well." "No," exclaimed the Lamb, "I never yet drank water, for as yet my mother's milk is both food and drink to me." On which the Wolf seized him, and ate him up, saying, "Well! I won't remain supperless, even though you refute every one of my imputations."

The tyrant will always find a pretext for his tyranny.

The Outstandingly
Virtuous Prince

From Niccolo Machiavelli, The Prince

In his classic meditation on princely power (1513), the Renaissance philosopher explores a disturbing question: Are there any moral limits on what a ruler must do to make his people secure and prosperous?

Many have imagined republics and principalities which have never been seen or known to exist in reality; for how we live is so far removed from how we ought to live, that he who abandons what is done for what ought to be done, will rather learn to bring about his own ruin than his preservation. A man who wishes to make a profession of goodness in everything must necessarily come to grief among so many who are not good. Therefore it is necessary for a prince, who wishes to maintain himself, to learn how not to be good, and to use his knowledge and not use it, according to the necessity of the case.

Let no one marvel if in speaking of new dominions both as to prince and state, I bring forward very exalted instances, for men walk almost always in the paths trodden by others, proceeding in their actions by imitation. Not being always able to follow others exactly, nor attain to the excellence of those he imitates, a prudent man should always follow in the path trodden by great men and imitate those who are most excellent, so that if he does not attain to their greatness, at any rate he will get some tinge of it. He will do as prudent archers, who when the place they wish to hit is too far off, knowing how far their bow will carry, aim at a spot much higher than the one they wish to hit, not in order to reach this height with their arrow, but by help of this high aim to hit the spot they wish to.

I say then that in new dominions, where there is a new prince, it is more or less easy to hold them according to the greater or lesser ability of him who acquires them. And as the fact of a private individual becoming a prince presupposes either great ability or good fortune, it would appear that either of these things would in part mitigate many difficulties. Nevertheless those who have been less beholden to good fortune have maintained themselves best. The matter is also facilitated by the prince being obliged to reside personally in his territory, having no others. But to come to those who have become princes through their own merits and not by fortune, I regard as the greatest, Moses, Cyrus, Romulus, Theseus, and their like. And although one should not speak of Moses, he having merely carried out what was ordered him by God, still he deserves admiration, if only for that grace which made him worthy to speak with God. But regarding Cyrus and others who have acquired or founded kingdoms, they will all be found worthy of admiration; and if their particular actions and methods are examined they will not appear very different from those of Moses, although he had so great a Master. And in examining their life and deeds it will be seen that they owed nothing to fortune but the opportunity which gave them matter to be shaped into what form they thought fit; and without that opportunity their powers would have been wasted, and without their powers the opportunity would have come in vain.

It was thus necessary that Moses should find the people of

Israel slaves in Egypt and oppressed by the Egyptians, so that they were disposed to follow him in order to escape from their servitude. It was necessary that Romulus should be unable to remain in Alba, and should have been exposed at his birth, in order that he might become King of Rome and founder of that nation. It was necessary that Cyrus should find the Persians discontented with the empire of the Medes, and the Medes weak and effeminate through long peace. Theseus could not have shown his abilities if he had not found the Athenians dispersed. These opportunities, therefore, gave these men their chance, and their own great qualities enabled them to profit by them, so as to ennoble their country and augment its fortunes.

Those who by the exercise of abilities such as these become princes, obtain their dominions with difficulty but retain them easily, and the difficulties which they have in acquiring their dominions arise in part from the new rules and regulations that they have to introduce in order to establish their position securely. It must be considered that there is nothing more difficult to carry out, nor more doubtful of success, nor more dangerous to handle, than to initiate a new order of things. For the reformer has enemies in all those who profit by the old order, and only lukewarm defenders in all those who would profit by the new order, this lukewarmness arising partly from fear of their adversaries, who have the laws in their favor; and partly from the incredulity of mankind, who do not truly believe in anything new until they have had actual experience of it. Thus it arises that on every opportunity for attacking the reformer, his opponents do so with the zeal of partisans, the others only defend him half-heartedly, so that between them he runs great danger. It is necessary, however, in order to investigate thoroughly this question, to examine whether these innovators are independent, or whether they depend upon others, that is to say, whether in order to carry out their designs they have to entreat or are able to compel. In the first case they invariably succeed ill, and accomplish nothing; but when they can depend on their own strength and are able to use force, they rarely fail. Thus it comes about that all armed prophets have conquered and unarmed ones failed; for besides what has been already said, the character of peoples varies, and it is easy to persuade them of a thing, but difficult to keep them in that persuasion. And so it is necessary to order things so that when they no longer believe, they can be made to believe by force. Moses, Cyrus, Theseus, and Romulus would not have been able to keep their constitutions observed for so long had they been disarmed, as happened in our own time with Fra Girolamo Savonarola, who failed entirely in his new rules when the multitude began to disbelieve in him, and he had no means of holding fast those who had believed nor of compelling the unbelievers to believe. Therefore such men as these have great difficulty in making their way, and all their dangers are met on the road and must be overcome by their own abilities; but when once they have overcome them and have begun to be held in veneration, and have suppressed those who envied them, they remain powerful and secure, honored and happy.

The Patriot King

From Henry St. John, Viscount Bolingbroke,
The Idea of a Patriot King

It matters whether a ruler is noble or base. But the best kings are not necessarily men! From the 1749 treatise on virtuous government.

Machiavel is an author who should have great authority with the persons likely to oppose me. He proposes to princes the amplification of their power, the extent of their dominion, and the subjection of their people, as the sole objects of their policy. He devises and recommends all means that tend to these purposes, without the consideration of any duty owing to God or man, or any regard to the morality or immorality of actions. Yet even he declares the affectation of virtue to be useful to princes: he is so far on my side in the present question. The only difference between us is, I would have the virtue real: he requires no more than the appearance of it.

Kings who have weak understandings, bad hearts, and strong prejudices, and all these, as it often happens, inflamed by their passions, and rendered incurable by their self-conceit and presumption; such kings are apt to imagine, that the king and the people in free governments are rival powers, who stand in competition with one another, who have different interests, and must of course have different views: that the rights and privileges of the people are so many spoils taken from the right and prerogative of the crown; and that the rules and laws, made for the exercise and security of the former, are so many diminutions of their dignity, and restrains on their power.

A Patriot King will see all this in a far different and much truer light. The constitution will be considered by him as one law, consisting of two tables, containing the rule of his government, and the measure of his subjects' obedience; or as one system, composed of different parts and powers, but all duly proportioned to one another, and conspiring by their harmony to the perfection of the whole. He will make one, and but one, distinction between his rights, and those of his people: he will look on his to be a trust, and theirs a property. He will discern, that he can have a right to no more than is trusted to him by the constitution: and that his people, who had an original right to the whole by the law of nature, can have the sole indefeasible right to any part; and really have such a right to that part which they have reserved to themselves. In fine, the constitution will be reverenced by him as the law of God and of man; the force of which binds the king as much as the meanest subject, and the reason of which binds him much more.

Wisdom is neither left-handed, nor crooked: but the heads of some men contain little, and the hearts of others employ it wrong. To use my lord Bacon's own comparison, the cunning man knows how to pack the cards, the wise man how to play the game better: but it would be of no use to the first to pack the cards, if his knowledge stopped here, and he had no skill in the game; nor to the second to play the game better, if he did not know how to pack the cards, that he might unpack them by new shuffling. Inferior wisdom or cunning may get the better of folly: but superior wisdom will get the better of cunning. Wisdom and cunning have often the same objects; but a wise man will have more and greater in his view. The least will not fill his soul, nor ever become the principal there; but will be pursued in subservience, in subordination at least, to the other. Wisdom and cunning may employ sometimes the same means too: but the wise man stoops to these means, and the other cannot rise above them.

The true image of a free people, governed by a Patriot King, is that of a patriarchal family, where the head and all the members are united by one common interest, and animated by common spirit: and where, if any are perverse enough to have another, they will be soon borne down by the superiority of those who have the same; and, far from making a division, they will but confirm the union of the little state. That to approach as near as possible to these ideas of perfect government, and social happiness under it, is desirable in every state, no man will be absurd enough to deny. The sole question is, therefore, how near to them it is possible to attain? For, if this attempt be not absolutely impracticable, all the views of a Patriot King will be directed to make it succeed. Instead of abetting the divisions of his people, he will endeavor to unite them, and to be himself the center of their union: instead of putting himself at the head of his people in order to govern, or more properly to subdue, all parties. Now, to arrive at this desirable union, and to maintain it, will be found more difficult in some cases than in others, but absolutely impossible in none, to a wise and good prince.

Our Elizabeth was queen in a limited monarchy, and reigned over a people at all times more easily led than driven; and at that time capable of being attached to their prince and their country, by a more generous principle than any of those which prevail in our days, by affection. There was a strong prerogative then in being, and the crown was in possession of greater legal power. Popularity was, however, then, as it is now, and as it must be always in mixed government, the sole true foundation of that sufficient authority and influence, which other constitutions give the prince gratis, and independently of the people, but which a king of this nation must acquire. The wise queen saw it, and she saw too, how much popularity depends on those appearances, that depend on the decorum, the decency, the grace, and the propriety of behavior of which we are speaking. A warm concern for the interest and honor of the nation, a tenderness for their people, and a confidence in their affections, were appearances that ran through her whole public conduct, and gave life and color to it. She did great things, and she knew how to set them off according to their full value, by her manner of doing them. In her private behavior she shewed great affability, she descended even to familiarity; but her familiarity was such as could not be imputed to her weakness, and was, therefore, most justly ascribed to her goodness. Though a woman, she hid all that was womanish about her: and if a few equivocal marks of coquetry appeared on some occasions, they passed like flashes of lightning, vanished as soon as they were discerned, and imprinted no blot on her character. She had private friendships, she had favorites: but she never suffered her friends to forget she was their queen; and when her favorites did, she made them feel that she was so.

To Be a King

Queen Elizabeth I to the House of Commons,
November 30, 1601

Mr. Speaker, we perceive your coming is to present thanks unto us. Know I accept them with no less joy than your loves can have desire to offer such a present, and do more esteem it than any treasure, or riches; for those we know how to prize, but loyalty, love, and thanks, I account them invaluable, and though God hath raised me high, yet this I account the glory of my crown, that I have reigned with your loves. This makes that I do not so much rejoice that God hath made me to be a queen, as to be a queen over so thankful a people, and to be the means under God to conserve you in safety, and preserve you from danger, yea to be the instrument to deliver you from dishonor, from shame, and from infamy, to keep you from out of servitude, and from slavery under our enemies, and cruel tyranny and vile oppression intended against us; for the better withstanding whereof, we take very acceptable their intended helps, and chiefly in that it manifesteth your loves and largeness of hearts to your sovereign. Of myself I must say this, I never was any greedy scraping grasper, nor a strict fast-holding prince, nor yet a waster, my heart was never set upon any worldly goods, but only for my subjects' good. What you do bestow on me I will not hoard up, but receive it to bestow on you again; yea mine own properties I account yours to be expended for your good, and your eyes shall see the bestowing of it for your welfare.

Mr. Speaker, I would wish you and the rest to stand up, for I fear I shall yet trouble you with longer speech.

Mr. Speaker, you give me thanks, but I am more to thank you, and I charge you thank them of the Lower House from me; for had I not received knowledge from you, I might a' fallen into the lapse of an error, only for want of true information.

Since I was Queen, yet did I never put my pen to any grant but upon pretext and semblance made me, that it was for the good and avail of my subjects generally, though a private profit to some of my ancient servants, who have deserved well; but that my grants shall be made grievances to my people, and oppressions, to be privileged under color of our patents, our princely dignity shall not suffer it.

When I heard it, I could give no rest unto my thoughts until I had reformed it, and those varlets, lewd persons, abusers of my bounty, shall know I will not suffer it. And, Mr. Speaker, tell the House from me, I take it exceeding grateful, that the knowledge of these things are come unto me from them. And though amongst them the principal members are such as are not touched in private, and therefore need not speak from any feeling of the grief, yet we have heard that other gentlemen also of the House, who stand as free, have spoken as freely in it; which gives us to know, that no respect or interests have moved them other than the minds they bear to suffer no diminution of our honor and our subjects love unto us. The zeal of which affection tending to ease my people, and knit their hearts unto us, I embrace with a princely care far above all earthly treasures. I esteem my people's love, more than which I desire not to merit: and God, that gave me here to sit, and placed me over you, knows, that I never respected myself, but as your good was conserved in me; yet what dangers, what practices, and what perils I have passed, some if not all of you know, but none of these things do move me, or ever made me fear, but it's God that hath delivered me.

And in my governing this land, I have ever set the last judgment day before mine eyes, and so to rule as I shall be judged and answer before a higher Judge, to whose judgment seat I do appeal: in that never thought was cherished in my heart that tended not to my people's good.

And if my princely bounty have been abused; and my grants turned the hurt of my people contrary to my will and meaning, or if any in authority under me have neglected, or converted what I have committed unto them, I hope God will not lay their culps to my charge.

To be a king, and wear a crown, is a thing more glorious to them that see it than it's pleasant to them that bear it: for myself, I never was so much enticed with the glorious name of a king, or the royal authority of a queen, as delighted that God hath made me his instrument to maintain his truth and glory, and to defend this kingdom from dishonor, damage, tyranny, and oppression. But should I ascribe any of these things to myself or my sexly weakness, I were not worthy to live, and of all most unworthy of the mercies I have received at God's hands, but to God only and wholly all is given and ascribed.

The cares and troubles of a crown I cannot more fitly resemble than to the drugs of a learned physician, perfumed with some aromatical savor, or to bitter pills gilded over, by which they are made more acceptable or less offensive, which indeed are bitter and unpleasant to take; and for my own part, were it not for conscience sake to discharge the duty that God hath lay'd upon me, and to maintain his glory, and keep you in safety, in mine own disposition I should be willing to resign the place I hold to any other, and glad to be freed of the glory with the labors, for it is not my desire to live nor to reign, longer than my life and reign shall be for your good. And though you have had and may have many mightier and wiser princes sitting in this seat, yet you never had nor shall have any that will love you better.

Thus, Mr. Speaker, I commend me to your loyal loves, and yours to my best care and your further councils, and I pray you, Mr. Controuler and Mr. Secretary, and you of my council, that before these gentlemen depart into their countries, you bring them all to kiss my hand.

Who Should Pilot the Ship of State?

From Plato, The Republic

In the famous allegory for good government from The Republic, *Socrates tells Adeimantus why the state needs a "pilot."*

Conceive now such a person as this to be the pilot of a fleet or a single ship, one who surpasses all in the ship both in bulk and strength, but is somewhat deaf, and short-sighted as well, and whose skill in nautical affairs is much of the same kind; and also that the sailors are all quarreling among each other about the pilotage, each thinking he ought to be pilot, though he never learned the art, and cannot show who was his master, nor at what time he got his learning; that besides this, they all say that the art itself cannot be taught, and are ready to cut in pieces anyone who says that it can. Imagine further, that they are constantly crowding round the pilot himself, begging, and forming all schemes to induce him to commit the helm into their hands, and that sometimes even, when they do not so well succeed in persuading him as others may, they either kill these others, or throw them overboard, and after having, by mandragora or wine or something else, rendered the noble pilot incapable, they manage the ship by aid of the crew, and sail on, thus drinking and feasting, as may be expected of such people; and besides this, if any one be clever at assisting them in getting the management into their own hands, and either by persuasion or force, setting aside the pilot, they praise such an one, calling him sailor and pilot, and versed in navigation, but despise as useless everyone not of this character—not in the least considering that the true pilot must necessarily study the year, the seasons, the heavens, and stars, and winds, and everything belonging to his art, if he would be a real commander of a ship; but at the same time as respects the art and practice of governing men, whether some be willing or not, they think it impossible for a man to attain it in connection with the art of navigation. Whilst affairs are thus situated as regards ships, do you not think that the true pilot will be called by the sailors on board of ships thus regulated, a mere stargazer, trifler, and of no use to them whatever? Undoubtedly, said Adeimantus. I think then, said I, that you do not want this comparison explained, in order to see that it represents how people feel in states toward true philosophers, but that you quite understand what I mean. Perfectly, said he. First of all then, as regards this—namely, a person's wondering the philosophers are not honored in states—you must acquaint him with our comparison, and try to persuade him, that it would be much more wonderful if they were honored. I will so, replied he. And further, that it is quite true, as you were just observing, that the best of those who study philosophy are useless to the bulk of mankind: but nevertheless, for all this, they intend to lay the blame not on the philosophers, but on such as make no use of them, for it is not natural that the pilot should beg of the sailors to allow him to govern them, nor that the wise should hold attendance at the gates of the rich: and whoever wittily said this was mistaken; for this indeed is the natural method, that whoever is sick, whether rich or poor, must necessarily go to the gates of the physician, and whoever wants to be governed must wait on a person able to govern; for it is not natural that a really worthy governor should beg of the governed to subject themselves to his government. You will not be far wrong, however, in comparing our present political governors to those sailors we now mentioned, and those whom they call insignificant and star-gazers to those who are truly pilots. Quite right, said he.

The Midas Touch

From Thomas Bulfinch, Bulfinch's Mythology

What can happen when a king's wishes are too greedy.

Bacchus, on a certain occasion, found his old schoolmaster and foster-father, Silenus, missing. The old man had been drinking, and in that state wandered away, and was found by some peasants, who carried him to their king, Midas. Midas recognized him, and treated him hospitably, entertaining him for ten days and nights with an unceasing round of jollity. On the eleventh day he brought Silenus back, and restored him in safety to his pupil. Whereupon Bacchus offered Midas his choice of a reward, whatever he might wish. He asked that whatever he might touch should be turned into *gold.* Bacchus consented, though sorry that he had not made a better choice. Midas went his way, rejoicing in his new-acquired power, which he hastened to put to the test. He could scarce believe his eyes when he found a twig of an oak, which he plucked from the branch, become gold in his hand. He took up a stone; it changed to gold. He touched a sod; it did the same. He took an apple from the tree; you would have thought he had robbed the garden of the Hesperides. His joy knew no bounds, and as soon as he got home, he ordered the servants to set a splendid repast on the table. Then he found to his dismay that whether he touched bread, it hardened in his hand; or put a morsel to his lip, it defied his teeth. He took a glass of wine, but it flowed down his throat like melted gold.

In consternation at the unprecedented affliction, he strove to divest himself of his power; he hated the gift he had lately coveted, but all in vain; starvation seemed to await him. He raised his arms all shining with gold, in prayer to Bacchus, begging to be delivered from his glittering destruction. Bacchus, merciful deity, heard and consented. "Go," said he, "to the River Pactolus, trace the stream to its fountain-head, there plunge your head and body in, and wash away your fault and its punishment." He did so, and scarce had he touched the waters before the gold-creating power passed into them, and the river sands became changed into gold, as they remain to this day.

The Career of Charlemagne

From Francois P. G. Guizot,
History of France from the Earliest Times
to the Year 1848

"An able warrior, an energetic legislator, a hero of poetry." From Guizot's celebrated history of France published in 1869.

The original and dominant characteristic of the hero of this reign, that which won for him and keeps for him after more than ten centuries, the name of great, is the striking variety of his ambition, his faculties, and his deeds. Charlemagne aspired to and attained to every sort of greatness—military greatness, political greatness, and intellectual greatness; he was an able warrior, an energetic legislator, a hero of poetry. And he united, he displayed all these merits in a time of general and monotonous barbarism when, save in the church, the minds of men were dull and barred. Those men, few in number, who made themselves a name at that epoch, rallied round Charlemagne and were developed under his patronage. To know him well and appreciate him justly, he must be examined under those various grand aspects, abroad and at home, in his wars and in his government.

We have here, it will be seen, no ordinary legislator and no ordinary laws: we see the work, with infinite variations and in disconnected form, of a prodigiously energetic and watchful master, who had to think and provide for everything, who had to be everywhere the moving and the regulating spirit. This universal and untiring energy is the grand characteristic of Charlemagne's government, and was, perhaps, what made his superiority most incontestable and his power most efficient.

The energy of Charlemagne as a warrior and a politician having thus been exhibited, it remains to say a few words about his intellectual energy. For that is by no means the least original or least grand feature of his character and his influence.

Modern times and civilized society have more than once seen despotic sovereigns filled with distrust toward scholars of exalted intellect, especially such as cultivated the moral and political sciences, and little inclined to admit them to their favor or to public office. There is no knowing whether, in our days, with our freedom of thought and of the press, Charlemagne would have been a stranger to this feeling of antipathy; but what is certain is that in his day, in the midst of a barbaric society, there was no inducement to it, and that, by nature, he was not disposed to it. His power was not in any respect questioned; distinguished intellects were very rare; Charlemagne had too much need of their services to fear their criticisms, and they, on their part, were more anxious to second his efforts than to show, toward him, anything like exaction or independence. He gave rein, therefore, without any embarrassment or misgiving, to his spontaneous inclination toward them, their studies, their labors, and their influence. He drew them into the management of affairs.

It was without effort and by natural sympathy that Charlemagne had inspired them with such sentiments; for he, too, really loved sciences, literature, and such studies as were then possible, and he cultivated them on his own account and for his own pleasure, as a sort of conquest.

We Few, We Happy Few, We Band of Brothers

From William Shakespeare, Henry V

Westmoreland:
O that we now had here
But one ten thousand of those men in England
That do no work to-day!

King:
What's he that wishes so?
My cousin Westmoreland? No, my fair cousin.
If we are marked to die, we are enow
To do our country loss; and if to live,
The fewer men, the greater share of honor.
God's will! I pray thee wish not one man more.
By Jove, I am not covetous for gold.
Nor care I who doth feed upon my cost;
It yearns me not if men my garments wear;
Such outward things dwell not in my desires:
But if it be a sin to covet honor,
I am the most offending soul alive.
No, faith, my coz, wish not a man from England.
God's peace! I would not lose so great an honor
As one man more methinks would share from me
For the best hope I have. O, do not wish one more!
Rather proclaim it, Westmoreland, through my host,
That he which hath no stomach to this fight,
Let him depart; his passport shall be made,
And crowns for convoy put into his purse.
We would not die in that man's company
That fears his fellowship to die with us.
This day is called the Feast of Crispian.
He that outlives this day, and comes safe home,
Will stand a-tiptoe when this day is named
And rouse him at the name of Crispian.
He that shall see this day, and live old age,
Will yearly on the vigil feast his neighbors
[And say, "These wounds I had on Crispin's day."]
Old men forget; yet all shall be forgot,
But he'll remember, with advantages,
What feats he did that day. Then shall our names,
Familiar in his mouth as household words—
Harry the King, Bedford and Exeter,
Warwick and Talbot, Salisbury and Gloucester—
Be in their flowing cups freshly rememb'red.
This story shall the good man teach his son;
And Crispin Crispian shall ne'er go by,
From this day to the ending of the world,
But we in it shall be remembered—
We few, we happy few, we band of brothers;

For he to-day that sheds his blood with me
Shall be my brother. Be he ne'er so vile,
This day shall gentle his condition;
And gentlemen in England now abed
Shall think themselves accursed they were not here,
And hold their manhoods cheap whiles any speaks
That fought with us upon Saint Crispin's day.

MANLY LEADERS
AND CITIZENS

The Man of Character

From Charles de Gaulle,
The Edge of the Sword

By common agreement one of the greatest statesmen of the twentieth century, Charles de Gaulle organized French resistance to the Nazi occupation of World War II from abroad, eventually returning in triumph to his liberated country and serving as its president. The Edge of the Sword *offers reflections on statesmanship remarkable for their subtlety, eloquence, and realism.*

When faced with the challenge of events, the man of character has recourse to himself. His instinctive response is to leave his mark on action, to take responsibility for it, to make it *his own business.* Far from seeking shelter behind his professional superiors, taking refuge in textbooks, or making the regulations bear the responsibility for any decision he may make, he sets his shoulders, takes a firm stand, and looks the problem straight in the face. It is not that he wishes to turn a blind eye to orders, or to sweep aside advice, but only that he is passionately anxious to exert his own will, to make up his own mind. It is not that he is unaware of the risks involved, or careless of consequences, but that he takes their measure honestly, and frankly accepts them. Better still, he embraces action with the pride of a master; for if he takes a hand in it, it will become his, and he is ready to enjoy success on condition that it is really *his own*, and that he derives no profit from it. He is equally prepared to bear the weight of failure, though not without a bitter sense of dissatisfaction. In short, a fighter who finds within himself all the zest and support he needs, a gambler more intent on success than profits, a man who pays his debts with his own money lends nobility to action. Without him there is but the dreary task of the slave; thanks to him, it becomes the divine sport of the hero.

This does not mean that he carries out his purpose unaided. Others share in it who are not without the merit of self-sacrifice and obedience, and give of their best when carrying out his orders. Some there are who even contribute to his planning—technicians or advisers. But it is character that supplies the essential element, the creative touch, the divine spark; in other words, the basic fact of initiative. Just as talent gives to a work of art a special stamp of understanding and expression, character imparts its own dynamic quality to the elements of action, and gives it personality which, when all is said, makes it live and move, just as the talent of the artist breathes life into matter.

The power to vivify an undertaking implies an energy sufficient to shoulder the burden of its consequences. The man of character finds an especial attractiveness in difficulty, since it is only by coming to grips with difficulty that he can realize his potentialities. Whether or not he proves himself the stronger is a matter between it and him. He is a jealous lover and will share with no one the prizes or the pains that may be his as a result of trying to overcome obstacles. Whatever the cost to himself, he looks for no higher reward than the harsh pleasure of knowing himself to be the man responsible.

This passion for self-reliance is obviously accompanied by some roughness in method. The man of character incorporates in his own person the severity inherent in his effort. This is felt by his subordinates, and at times they groan under it. In any event, a leader of this quality is inevitably aloof, for there can be no authority without prestige, nor prestige unless he keeps his distance. Those under his command mutter in whispers about his arrogance and the demands he makes. But once action starts, criticism disappears. The man of character then draws to himself the hopes and the wills of everyone as the magnet draws iron. When the crisis comes, it is him they follow, it is he who carries the burden on his own shoulders, even though they collapse under it. On the other hand, the knowledge that the lesser men have confidence in him exalts the man of character. The confidence of those under him gives him a sense of obligation. It strengthens his determination but also increases his benevolence, for he is a born protector. If success attends upon his efforts he distributes its advantages with a generous hand. If he meets with failure, he will not let the blame fall on anybody but himself. The security he offers is repaid by the esteem of his men.

In his relationship with his superiors he is generally at a disadvantage. He is too sure of himself, too conscious of his strength to let his conduct be influenced by a mere wish to please. The fact that he finds his powers of decision within himself, and not imposed upon him by an order, often disinclines him to adopt an attitude of passive obedience. All he asks is that he shall be given a task to do, and then be left alone to do it. He wants to be the captain of his own ship, and this many senior officers find intolerable since, temperamentally incapable of taking a wide view, they concentrate on details and draw their mental sustenance from formalities. And so it comes about that the authorities dread any officer who has the gift of making decisions and cares nothing for routine and soothing words. "Arrogant and undisciplined" is what the mediocrities say of him, treating the thoroughbred with a tender mouth as they would a donkey which refuses to move, not realizing that asperity is, more often than not, the reverse side of a strong character, that you can only lean on something that offers resistance, and that resolute and inconvenient men are to be preferred to easy-going natures without initiative.

But when the position becomes serious, when the nation is in urgent need of leaders with initiative who can be relied upon, and are willing to take risks, then matters are seen in a very different light, and credit goes to whom credit is due. A sort of a ground swell brings the man of character to the surface. His advice is listened to, his abilities are praised, and his true worth becomes apparent. To him is entrusted, as a matter of course, the difficult task, the direction of the main effort, the decisive mission. Everything he suggests is given serious consideration; all his demands are met. He, for his part, does not take advantage of this change in his fortunes, but shows a generous temperament and responds wholeheartedly when he is called upon. Scarcely, even, does he taste the sweet savor of revenge, for his every faculty is brought to bear upon the action he must take.

This rallying to character when danger threatens is the outward manifestation of an instinctive urge, for all men at heart realize the supreme value of self-reliance, and know that without it there can be no action of value. In the last resort, we must, to quote Cicero, "judge all conduct in the light of the best examples available," for nothing great has ever been achieved without that passion and that confidence which is to be found only in the man of character. Alexander would never have conquered Asia, Galileo would never have demonstrated the movement of the earth, Columbus would never have discovered America, nor Richelieu have restored the authority of the crown, had they not believed in themselves and taken full control of the task in hand. Boileau would never have established the laws of classic taste, Napoleon would never have founded an empire, Lesseps would never have pierced the isthmus of Suez, Bismarck would never have achieved German unity, nor Clemenceau have saved his country, had they hearkened to the counsels of short-sighted prudence or the promptings of fainthearted modesty. We can go further and say that those who have done great deeds have often had to take the risk of ignoring the merely routine aspects of discipline. Examples are plentiful: Pelissier at Sebastopol stuffing the Emperor's threatening dispatches into his pocket unopened and reading them only after the action was over; Lanrezac saving his army after Charleroi by breaking off the battle, contrary to orders; Lyautey keeping the whole of Morocco in 1914, in the teeth of instructions issued at a higher level. After the Battle of Jutland and the English failure to take the opportunity offered them of destroying the German fleet, Admiral Fisher, then First Sea Lord, exclaimed in a fury after reading Jellicoe's dispatch: "He has all Nelson's qualities but one: he doesn't know how to disobey!"

It goes without saying that the successes achieved by great men have always depended on their possessing many different faculties. Character alone, if unsupported by other qualities, results only in rashness and obstinacy. On the other hand, purely intellectual gifts, even of the highest order, are not sufficient. History is filled with examples of men who, though they were gifted beyond the ordinary, saw their labors brought to nothing because they were lacking in character. Whether serving, or betraying, their masters in the most expert fashion, they were entirely uncreative. Notable they may have been, but famous never.

The Model Citizen

From Plutarch, Lives of the Noble Greeks
and Romans

In many ways, Marcus Brutus is Plutarch's ideal combination of active and contemplative virtues. Student of philosophy, defender of the Roman republic against ambitious usurpers like Julius Caesar, he was blessed with an extraordinary wife with whom he shared his secrets and labors. Even his enemies on the Caesarean side, such as Mark Antony, admired his nobility of character and the sincerity of his convictions. Plutarch (46–127 A.D.) wrote numerous biographies of Greek and Roman heroes and statesmen.

Marcus Brutus was descended from Junius Brutus, whose brass statue was erected by the ancient Romans in the capitol among the images of their kings. His statue has a drawn sword in its hand, in remembrance of his courage and resolution in expelling the Tarquins and destroying the monarchy. But this ancestor of Brutus had a severe and inflexible nature, like steel of too hard a temper, for his character had never been softened by study and thought. As a result, he let himself be so carried away by his rage and hatred against the tyrants that he executed even his own sons for conspiring with them. But the Brutus whose life is our present subject combined a good character with the improvements of learning and the study of philosophy. Despite a naturally grave and gentle disposition, he applied himself to business and public affairs, forging in himself a temperament that seems to have been perfectly suited for virtue. So much so, that even those who were his greatest enemies, because of his conspiracy against Caesar, said that if there had been any honorable or generous part in that whole affair, they attributed it entirely to Brutus, and attributed whatever was barbarous and cruel to Cassius, who was Brutus's relative and close friend, but not his equal in honesty and pureness of purpose.

Cato the philosopher was the brother of Brutus' mother, Servilia. Of all the Romans, this was the man his nephew most admired. Brutus strove to imitate his example, and later married his daughter, Porcia. Of all the Greek philosophers, and Brutus had heard and studied them all, the ones he admired most were the Platonists.

When Rome split into two factions, with Pompey and Caesar taking up arms against one another, and the whole empire was thrown into confusion, it was commonly thought that Brutus would take Caesar's side, since Brutus' father had been put to death by Pompey. But Brutus thought it was his duty to prefer the public interest to his own private feelings, and judging that Pompey had the better cause, sided with him. He did this even though, previously, he had refused to so much as greet or take any notice of Pompey, if he happened to meet him, for he thought it would be disgraceful to have the least conversation with his father's murderer. But now, looking upon Pompey as the general of his country, he placed himself under his command.

Well aware of the dangers they would encounter, Brutus felt that the safety of those Romans who were most honored for their virtue, birth, or courage depended upon him. Therefore, he strove, as much as possible, when in public, to hide his uneasiness, and control his thoughts; but at home, and especially at night, he was not the same man. Sometimes, against his will, his worries would make him start out of his sleep. At other times he was so absorbed in reflection and consideration of his difficulties, that his wife who lay with him, could not help but notice that he was unusually troubled, and agitated by some dangerous and perplexing matter

Porcia, as I said above, was the daughter of Cato. She was very young when she married her cousin Brutus, after the death of her first husband. Porcia, who was addicted to philosophy, loved her husband greatly, and was full of understanding and courage. She resolved, therefore, not to inquire into Brutus's secrets before she had made this trial of herself. She turned all her attendants out of her chamber, and taking a little knife, of the sort they use to cut nails with, she gave herself a deep gash in the thigh. She lost a great deal of blood. This was followed by violent pains and a shivering fever, caused by the wound. At the height of her suffering, when Brutus was extremely anxious and afflicted for her, she said to him: "I, Brutus, being the daughter of Cato, was not given to you in marriage to share only in your bed and board, like a concubine, but to share as well in all your good and all your evil fortunes. For your part, as regards your care of me, I find no reason to complain. But what evidence of my love, what satisfaction can you receive from me, if I may not share with you your hidden griefs, nor be admitted to your counsels when they require secrecy and trust? I know very well that women seem to have too weak a nature to be trusted with secrets; but surely, Brutus, a virtuous birth and education, and the company of good and honorable men, help form our characters; and I can boast that I am the daughter of Cato and the wife of Brutus. I put even more confidence in this now that I have tried myself, and find that I can withstand pain." Then she showed him her wound, and told him the trial she had made of her constancy. He was astonished, and lifting up his hands to heaven begged the gods to help him be worthy of such a wife. Then he comforted his wife.

It is reported that Caesar, when he first heard Brutus speak in public, said to his friends, "I do not know what this young man wants, but whatever he wants, he wants it vehemently." Many heard Antony himself say that Brutus was the only man who conspired against Caesar out of a sense of the glory and apparent justice of the action, but that all the rest rose up against him from private envy and malice. Moreover, it is plain from his own writings, that Brutus relied not so much upon his forces, as upon his own virtue. For he wrote in a letter to Atticus, shortly before he was to engage the enemy, that his affairs were in the best state of fortune that he could wish; that either he should prevail, and restore liberty to the people of Rome, or die which would put himself out of the reach of slavery. He wrote that while other things were certain and beyond the reach of chance, one thing was still in doubt, whether they should live or die free men. He adds further, that Mark Antony had received a just punishment for his folly, for, when he had the opportunity to have been numbered with Brutus and Cassius and Cato, he chose instead to join the likes of Octavius. He predicts that, though they would not both be defeated, they would soon fight one another. And in this he seems to have been no ill prophet.

The Mice in Council

Aesop

The need for leadership, the danger of apathy.

The Mice summoned a council to decide how they might best devise means for obtaining notice of the approach of their great enemy the Cat. Among the many plans devised, the one that found most favor was the proposal to tie a bell to the neck of the Cat, that the Mice being warned by the sound of the tinkling might run away and hide themselves in their holes at his approach. But when the Mice further debated who among them should thus "bell the Cat," there was no one found to do it.

Everything That Entitles
a Man to Praise

From Cicero,
On the Commonwealth

Cicero's On the Commonwealth *beautifully expresses the classical ideal of the manly citizen. To be a man is not only to be vigorous in service of the common good, but refined, gracious, and learned, familiar with the sublime beauties of art, music, and philosophy.*

Let us count those who treat the philosophy of life as great men—as indeed they are—let us count them as scholars and teachers of truth and excellence. But at the same time let us admit the existence of an art—whether discovered by statesmen who have faced the vicissitudes of public life or studied even by your philosophers in scholarly retirement—an art which comprises the theory of politics and the government of peoples and which, in truth, is by no means to be despised. This art, when added to great natural abilities, produces, as it has often done in the past, a type of character extraordinary and divine. And when men have felt, as did the participants in this dialogue, that, to the powers of mind received from nature and developed by experience in public affairs, they should add also scholarly interests and a richer acquaintance with life, such men must be universally conceded to be superior to all others. What, indeed, can be more glorious than the union of practical experience in great affairs with an intelligent enthusiasm for the liberal arts? Can anything be imagined more perfect than the distinction of a Publius Scipio, a Gaius Laelius, or a Lucius Philus, men who, in order not to neglect anything which might bring the highest glory to illustrious men, united the rules of conduct which they learned at home and inherited from their ancestors even with a foreign philosophy derived from Socrates? Hence I hold that a man who has been able and willing to combine these two interests, and has disciplined himself both in the ways of his ancestors and in liberal culture, has attained everything that entitles a man to praise.

The Need for Good Laws

From Aristotle,
The Nicomachaean Ethics

Unfortunately, not everyone longs to be a good citizen. In addition to beautiful words about virtue, the constraint of law and even punishment is always required to prod some men along the right path.

Before virtue can be acquired, affections congenial to it must be implanted; the love of beauty and excellence, the hatred of baseness and deformity; which preparatory discipline cannot take place, except in those states which are governed by good laws; for a life of soberness and self-command is irksome to the multitude, and peculiarly unpleasing to the headstrong impetuosity of youthful passions, which must, therefore, be bridled by the authority of law; that what is painful by nature may become pleasant through custom. The superintending aid of discipline ought not to be confined to children, but must extend to adolescence and manhood; the greater proportion of human kind remaining through life rather slaves to necessity, than subjects of reason; and more susceptible of the fear of punishment, than sensible to the charms of moral excellence. Legislators, therefore, it is said, ought to employ admonitions and chastisements, as well as punishments that are final; admonitions, for those whose character and morals render them open to conviction; chastisements, for those whose immoderate and beastly passion for selfish pleasures must be subdued and corrected by coarse bodily pains (the pains inflicted on them standing as nearly as possible in direct opposition to the pleasures which they unlawfully pursued); and total extermination, or perpetual banishment, for the extreme evils of incurable profligacy and incorrigible villainy. Since, then, the condition of the greater proportion of mankind is such that to be kept within the bounds of propriety and virtue they require not only the benefits of early instruction, but the watchfulness of perpetual discipline through life, good laws become essentially necessary for upholding this discipline by their coercive authority. The influence of fathers over their children is too feeble for that purpose; or indeed the influence of any individuals not invested with public authority. Law has a compulsive and necessary force, since it is acknowledged as the commanding voice of prudence and reason; and its power is not invidious, like that of men, who are apt to offend us when they oppose, even most justly, our favorite propensities.

Liberty Is Order,
Liberty Is Strength

From Charles James Fox,
Select Orations

As a Member of Parliament, Fox (1749–1806) was an ardent champion of liberty and the rights of man.

Liberty is order. Liberty is strength. Look round the world, and admire, as you must, the instructive spectacle. You will see that liberty not only is power and order, but that it is power and order predominant and invincible, and that it derides all other sources of strength. And shall the preposterous imagination be fostered, that men bred in liberty—the first of human kind who asserted the glorious distinction of forming for themselves their social compact—can be condemned to silence upon their rights? Is it to be conceived that men who have enjoyed, for such a length of days, the light and happiness of freedom, can be restrained, and shut up again in the gloom of ignorance and degradation? As well, sir, might you try, by a miserable dam, to shut up the flowing of a rapid river! The rolling and impetuous tide would burst through every impediment that man might throw in its way; and the only consequence of the impotent attempt would be, that, having collected new force by its temporary suspension, enforcing itself through new channels, it would spread devastation and ruin on every side. The progress of liberty is like the progress of the stream. Kept within its bounds, it is sure to fertilize the country through which it runs; but no power can arrest it in its passage; and short-sighted, as well as wicked, must be the heart of the projector that would strive to divert its course.

Comparing the Statesman
and the Soldier

From Charles de Gaulle, The Edge of the Sword

It is the task of political leaders to dominate opinion: that of the monarch, of the council, of the people, since it is from these that they draw their authority. They have no value, and can do nothing, except in the name of the sovereign power. But their abilities matter less than their skill in pleasing, and promises are more effective than arguments. The statesman, therefore, must concentrate all his efforts on captivating men's minds. He must know when to dissemble, when to be frank. He must pose as the servant of the public in order to become its master. He must outbid his rivals in self-confidence, and only after a thousand intrigues and solemn undertakings will he find himself entrusted with full power. Even when he has it in his grasp, he can never be completely open in his dealings, for he must still be concerned to please, to know how to convince prince or parliament, how to gratify popular passions and soothe the anxieties of vested interests. His authority, no matter how unquestioned, is precarious. Public opinion, that inconstant mistress, follows his lead with a capricious step, ready to stop dead should he race too far ahead, to take giant strides when he thinks it advisable to move with caution. Ungrateful, it rates at a low price the efforts he has made, and, even at the moment of success, is only too ready to listen to his opponents. But, if he makes a mistake, the pack is at his heels; if he shows signs of weakness it hurls itself upon him. What does the statesman's empire amount to? A court cabal, an intrigue in the Council, a shift of opinion in the Assembly can snatch it from him in a moment. Toppled from his pedestal he finds nothing but injustice awaiting him. Great or small, historic figure or colorless politician, he comes and goes between power and powerlessness, between prestige and public ingratitude. The whole of his life and the sum total of his work are marked by instability, restlessness, and storm, and so are very different from those of the soldier. The soldier's profession is that of arms, but the power they give him has to be strictly organized. From the moment that he embarks upon it he becomes a slave of a body of regulations, and so remains all through his active life. The army is generous but jealous. It guides his steps, supports him in his moments of weakness, develops such gifts as he may have. But it also keeps a tight hold on him, overriding his doubts and holding his enthusiasm in check. As a man he suffers much from its demands, for he must renounce his personal liberty, his chances of making money, and, sometimes, sacrifice his life, and what greater offering could there be? But at this high cost it opens the door for him to the empire of armed might. That is why, though he often grumbles at his slavery, he clings to it; nay, more, he loves it, and glories in the price he has to pay. "It is my honor!" he says.

In the company of his fellows he rises to a position of power, but by degrees, for the hierarchy of which he is a member is strict and uncompromising. For the soldier there is always yet some higher rank to attain, some recognition to be gained. On the other hand, such authority as he may wield is absolute. Supported by discipline and strengthened by tradition, it makes use of everything in the way of credit and prestige which the military order gives to him who holds command. Under the iron rod and the shield of the "regulations" he marches with a firm step along a road which, grueling though it may be, points straight ahead.

The statesman and the soldier bring, therefore, to a common

task very different characters, methods, and anxieties. The former reaches his goal by roundabout ways, the later by direct approach. The one is long-sighted though his vision may be clouded, sees realities as complex, and sets himself to master them by trickery and calculation. The other sees with clear eyes what there is to be seen straight in front of his nose and thinks it simple and capable of being controlled by resolution. In dealing with immediate problems, the statesman's first concern is what people will say of him; the soldier looks for counsel to principles.

Always Be Prepared for War

From Niccolo Machiavelli, The Prince

The best way for statesmen to avoid going to war is to be always ready to wage it.

The Romans in the provinces they took, always followed this policy; they established colonies, inveigled the less powerful without increasing their strength, put down the most powerful and did not allow foreign rulers to obtain influence in them. I will adduce the province of Greece as a sole example. They made friends with the Achaeans and the Aetolians, the kingdom of Macedonia was cast down, and Antiochus driven out, nor did they allow the merits of the Achaeans or the Aetolians to gain them any increase of territory, nor did the persuasions of Philip induce them to befriend him without reducing his influence, nor could the power of Antiochus make them consent to allow him to hold any state in that province.

For the Romans did in these cases what all wise princes should do, who consider not only present but also future discords and diligently guard against them; for being foreseen they can easily be remedied, but if one waits till they are at hand, the medicine is no longer in time as the malady has become incurable; it happening with this as with those hectic fevers, as doctors say, which at their beginning are easy to cure but difficult to recognize, but in course of time when they have not at first been recognized and treated, become easy to recognize and difficult to cure. Thus it happens in matters of state; for knowing afar off (which it is only given to a prudent man to do) the evils that are brewing, they are easily cured. But when, for want of such knowledge, they are allowed to grow so that everyone can recognize them, there is no longer any remedy to be found. Therefore, the Romans, observing disorders while yet remote, were always able to find a remedy, and never allowed them to increase in order to avoid a war; for they knew that war is not to be avoided, and can be deferred only to the advantage of the other side; they therefore declared war against Philip and Antiochus in Greece, so as not to have to fight them in Italy, though they might at the time have avoided either; this they did not choose to do, never caring to do that which is now every day to be heard in the mouths of our wise men, namely to enjoy the advantages of delay, but preferring to trust their own virtue and prudence; for time brings with it all things, and may produce indifferently either good or evil.

The Wolves to the Sheep: Give Peace a Chance

Aesop

"Why should there always be this internecine and implacable warfare between us?" said the Wolves to the Sheep. "Those evil-disposed Dogs have much to answer for. They always bark whenever we approach you, and attack us before we have done any harm. If you would only dismiss them from your heels, there might soon be treaties of peace and of reconciliation between us." The Sheep, poor silly creatures! were easily beguiled, and dismissed the Dogs. The Wolves destroyed the flock at their own pleasure.

What Is the Duty of a Statesman to the Voters?

From Edmund Burke, Speech to the Electors of Bristol

According to this famous statement in 1774 of the legislator's responsibility, it is important not simply to carry out passively the voters' wishes, but to deliberate on their behalf—even if a decision ends up going against their wishes.

Certainly, gentlemen, it ought to be the happiness and glory of a representative to live in the strictest union, the closest correspondence, and the most unreserved communication with his constituents. Their wishes ought to have great weight with him; their opinion, high respect; their business, unremitted attention. It is his duty to sacrifice his repose, his pleasures, his satisfactions, to theirs; and above all, ever, and in all cases, to prefer their interest to his own. But his unbiased opinion, his mature judgment, his enlightened conscience, he ought not to sacrifice to you, to any man, or to any set of men living. These he does not derive from your pleasure no, nor from the law and the constitution. They are a trust from Providence, for the abuse of which he is deeply answerable. Your representative owes you, not his industry only, but his judgment; and he betrays, instead of serving you, if he sacrifices it to your opinion.

To deliver an opinion, is the right of all men; that of constituents is a weighty and respectable opinion, which a representative ought always to rejoice to hear; and which he ought always most seriously to consider. But *authoritative* instructions, *mandates* issued, which the member is bound blindly and implicitly to obey, to vote, and to argue for, though contrary to the clearest conviction of his judgment and conscience, these are things utterly unknown to the laws of this land, and which arise from a fundamental mistake of the whole order and tenor of our constitution.

Parliament is not a *congress* of ambassadors from different and hostile interests; which interests each must maintain, as an agent and advocate, against other agents and advocates; but parliament is a *deliberative* assembly of *one* nation, with *one* interest, that of the whole; where, not local purposes, not local prejudices, ought to guide, but the general good, resulting from the general reason of the whole. You choose a member indeed; but when you have chosen him, he is not member of Bristol, but he is a member of *parliament*. If the local constituent should have an interest, or should form an hasty opinion, evidently opposite to the real good of the rest of the community, the member for that place ought to be as far, as any other, from any endeavor to give it effect. I beg pardon for saying so much on this subject. I have been unwillingly drawn into it but I shall ever use a respectful frankness of communication with you. Your faithful friend, your devoted servant, I shall be to the end of my life: a flatterer you do not wish for. On this point of instructions, however, I think it scarcely possible we ever can have any sort of difference. Perhaps I may give you too much, rather than too little, trouble.

From the first hour I was encouraged to court your favor, to this happy day of obtaining it, I have never promised you anything but humble and persevering endeavors to do my duty. The weight of that duty, I confess, makes me tremble; and whoever well considers what it is, of all things in the world, will fly from what has the least likeness to a positive and precipitate engagement. To be a good member of parliament is, let me tell you, no easy task; especially at this time, when there is so strong a disposition to run into the perilous extremes of servile compliance or wild popularity. To unite circumspection with vigor, is absolutely necessary; but it is extremely difficult. We are now members for a rich commercial *city*; this city, however, is but a part of a rich commercial *nation*, the interests of which are various, multiform, and intricate. We are members for that great nation, which however is itself but part of a great *empire*, extended by our virtue and our fortune to the farthest limits of the east and of the west. All these wide-spread interests must be considered; must be compared; must be reconciled, if possible. We are members for a *free* country; and surely we all know, that the machine of a free constitution is no simple thing; but as intricate and as delicate as it is valuable. We are members in a great and ancient *monarchy;* and we must preserve religiously the true legal rights of the sovereign, which form the key-stone that binds together the noble and well-constructed arch of our empire and our constitution. A constitution made up of balanced powers must ever be a critical thing. As such I mean to touch that part of it which comes within my reach. I know my inability, and I wish for support from every quarter.

At Last I Had the Authority.
I Slept Soundly.

From Winston S. Churchill, The Gathering Storm

Winston Spencer Churchill was Britain's Prime Minister during World War II and chief architect of the Allied defeat of the Third Reich. He was also a prodigiously talented historian, biographer, and essayist, exemplifying the balance of active and contemplative virtues that recurs throughout this anthology as the key to manliness. An early and persistent critic of Adolf Hitler, in his history of the World War II, Churchill describes the fall of the Chamberlain government after Hitler flagrantly violated the peace agreement he had concluded with Chamberlain at Munich. His warnings about the Nazis finally vindicated, Churchill recounts how he became Prime Minister.

I do not remember exactly how things happened during the morning of May 9, but the following occurred. Sir Kingsley Wood, Secretary of State for Air, was very close to the Prime Minister as a colleague and a friend. They had long worked together in complete confidence. From him I learned that Mr. Chamberlain was resolved upon the formation of a National Government and, if he could not be the head, he would give way to anyone commanding his confidence who could. Thus, by the afternoon, I became aware that I might well be called upon to take the lead. The prospect neither excited nor alarmed me. I thought it would be by far the best plan. I was content to let events unfold. In the afternoon, the Prime Minister summoned me to Downing Street, where I found Lord Halifax, and after a talk about the situation in general, we were told that Mr. Attlee and Mr. Greenwood would visit us in a few minutes for a consultation.

When they arrived, we three Ministers sat on one side of the table and the Opposition leaders on the other. Mr. Chamberlain declared the paramount need of a National Government, and sought to ascertain whether the Labour Party would serve under him. The conference of their party was in session at Bournemouth. The conversation was most polite, but it was clear that the Labour leaders would not commit themselves without consulting their people, and they hinted, not obscurely, that they thought the response would be unfavorable. They then withdrew. It was a bright, sunny afternoon, and Lord Halifax and I sat for a while on a seat in the garden of Number 10 and talked about nothing in particular. I then returned to the Admiralty and was occupied during the evening and a large part of the night in heavy business.

The morning of the tenth of May dawned, and with it came tremendous news. Boxes with telegrams poured in from the Admiralty, the War Office, and the Foreign Office. The Germans had struck their long-awaited blow. Holland and Belgium were both invaded. Their frontiers had been crossed at numerous points. The whole movement of the German Army upon the invasion of the Low Countries and of France had begun.

At about ten o'clock, Sir Kingsley Wood came to see me, having just been with the Prime Minister. He told me that Mr. Chamberlain was inclined to feel that the great battle which had broken upon us made it necessary for him to remain at his post. Kingsley Wood had told him that, on the contrary, the new crisis made it all the more necessary to have a National Government, which alone could confront it, and he added that Mr. Chamberlain had accepted this view. At eleven o'clock, I was again summoned to Downing Street by the Prime Minister. There once more I found Lord Halifax. We took our seats at the table opposite Mr. Chamberlain. He told us that he was satisfied that it was beyond his power to form a National Government. The response he had received from the Labour leaders left him in no doubt of this. The question, therefore, was whom he should advise the King to send for after his own resignation had been accepted. His demeanor was cool, unruffled, and seemingly quite detached from the personal aspect of the affair. He looked at us both across the table.

I have had many important interviews in my public life, and this was certainly the most important. Usually I talk a great deal, but on this occasion I was silent. Mr. Chamberlain evidently had in his mind the stormy scene in the House of Commons two nights before, when I had seemed to be in such heated controversy with the Labour Party. Although this had been in his support and defense, he nevertheless felt that it might be an obstacle to my obtaining their adherence at this juncture. I do not recall the actual words he used, but this was the implication. His biographer,

Mr. Feiling, states definitely that he preferred Lord Halifax. As I remained silent, a very long pause ensued. It certainly seemed longer than the two minutes which one observes in the commemorations of Armistice Day. Then at length Halifax spoke. He said that he felt that his position as a peer, out of the House of Commons, would make it very difficult for him to discharge the duties of Prime Minister in a war like this. He would be held responsible for everything, but would not have the power to guide the assembly upon whose confidence the life of every Government depended. He spoke for some minutes in this sense, and by the time he had finished, it was clear that the duty would fall upon me—had in fact fallen upon me. Then, for the first time, I spoke. I said I would have no communication with either of the Opposition Parties until I had the King's commission to form a Government. On this the momentous conversation came to an end, and we reverted to our ordinary easy and familiar manners of men who had worked for years together and whose lives in and out of office had been spent in all the friendliness of British politics. I then went back to the Admiralty, where, as may well be imagined, much awaited me.

The Dutch Ministers were in my room. Haggard and worn, with horror in their eyes, they had just flown over from Amsterdam. Their country had been attacked without the slightest pretext or warning. The avalanche of fire and steel had rolled across the frontiers, and when resistance broke out and the Dutch frontier guards fired, an overwhelming onslaught was made from the air. The whole country was in a state of wild confusion; the long-prepared defense scheme had been put into operation; the dykes were opened; the waters spread far and wide. But the Germans had already crossed the outer lines, and were now streaming across the causeway which enclosed the Zuyder Zee. Could we do anything to prevent this? Luckily, we had a flotilla not far away, and this was immediately ordered to sweep the causeway with fire, and take the heaviest toll possible of the swarming invaders. The Queen was still in Holland, but it did not seem she could remain there long.

As a consequence of these discussions, a large number of orders were dispatched by the Admiralty to all our ships in the neighborhood, and close relations were established with the Royal Dutch Navy. Even with the recent overrunning of Norway and Denmark in their minds, the Dutch Ministers seemed unable to understand how the great German nation, which, up to the night before, had professed nothing but friendship, and was bound by treaty to respect the neutrality of Holland, so strictly maintained, should suddenly have made this frightful and brutal onslaught. Upon these proceedings and other affairs, an hour or two passed. A spate of telegrams pressed in from all the frontiers affected by the forward heave of the German armies. It seemed that the old Schlieffen Plan, brought up to date with its Dutch extension, was already in full operation. In 1914, the swinging right arm of the German invasion had swept through Belgium, but had stopped short of Holland. It was well known then that had that war been delayed for three or four years, the extra army group would have been ready, and the railway terminals and communications adapted, for a movement through Holland. Now the famous movement had been launched with all these facilities and with every circumstance of surprise and treachery. But other developments lay ahead. The decisive stroke of the enemy was not to be a turning movement on the flank, but a break through the main front. This none of us or the French, who were in responsible command, foresaw. Earlier in the year I had, in a published interview, warned these neutral countries of the fate which was impending upon them and which was evident from the troop dispositions and road and rail development, as well as from the captured German plans. My words had been resented.

In the splintering crash of this vast battle, the quiet conversations we had had in Downing Street faded or fell back in one's mind. However, I remember being told that Mr. Chamberlain had gone, or was going, to see the King, and this was naturally to be expected. Presently a message arrived summoning me to the Palace at six o'clock. It only takes two minutes to drive there from the Admiralty along the Mall. Although I suppose the evening newspapers must have been full of the terrific news from the Continent, nothing had been mentioned about the Cabinet crisis. The public had not had time to take in what was happening either abroad or at home, and there was no crowd about the Palace gates.

I was taken immediately to the King. His Majesty received me most graciously and bade me sit down. He looked at me searchingly and quizzically of some moments, and then said: "I suppose you don't know why I have sent for you?" Adopting his mood, I replied: "Sir, I simply couldn't imagine why." He laughed and said: "I want to ask you to form a government." I said I would certainly do so.

The King had made no stipulation about the Government being national in character, and I felt that my commission was in no formal way dependent upon this point. But in view of what had happened, and the conditions which had led to Mr. Chamberlain's resignation, a Government of national character was obviously inherent in the situation. If I had found it impossible to come to terms with the Opposition Parties, I should not have been constitutionally debarred from trying to form the strongest Government possible of all who would stand by the country in the hour of peril, provided that such a Government could command a majority in the House of Commons. I told the King that I would immediately send for the leaders of the Labour and Liberal Parties, that I proposed to form a War Cabinet of five or six Ministers, and that I hoped to let him have at least five names before midnight. On this I took my leave and returned to the Admiralty.

Between seven and eight, at my request, Mr. Attlee called upon me. He brought with him Mr. Greenwood. I told him of the authority I had to form a Government and asked if the Labour Party would join. He said they would. I proposed that they should take rather more than a third of the places, having two seats in the War Cabinet of five, or it might be six, and I asked Mr. Attlee to let me have a list of men so that we could discuss particular offices. I mentioned Mr. Bevin, Mr. Alexander, Mr. Morrison, and Mr. Dalton as men whose services in high office were immediately required. I had, of course, known both Attlee and Greenwood for a long time in the House of Commons. During the eleven years before the outbreak of war, I had in my more or less independent position come far more often into collision with the Conservative and National Governments than with the Labour and Liberal Oppositions. We had a pleasant talk for a little while, and they went off to report by telephone to their friends and followers at Bournemouth, with whom, of course, they had been in the closest contact during the previous forty-eight hours.

I invited Mr. Chamberlain to lead the House of Commons as Lord President of the Council, and he replied by telephone that he accepted and had arranged to broadcast at nine that night, stating that he had resigned, and urging everyone to support and aid his successor. This he did in magnanimous terms. I asked Lord Halifax to join the War Cabinet while remaining Foreign Secretary. At about ten, I sent the King a list of five names, as I had promised. The appointment of the three Service Ministers was vitally urgent. I had already made up my mind who they should be. Mr. Eden should go to the War Office; Mr. Alexander should come to the Admiralty; and Sir Archibald Sinclair, leader of the Liberal Party, should take the Air Ministry. At the same time I assumed the office of Minister of Defence, without, however, attempting to define its scope and powers.

Thus, then, on the night of the tenth of May, at the outset of this mighty battle, I acquired the chief power in the State, which henceforth I wielded in ever-growing measure for five years and three months of world war, at the end of which time, all our enemies having surrendered unconditionally or being about to do so, I was immediately dismissed by the British electorate from all further conduct of their affairs.

During these last crowded days of the political crises, my pulse had not quickened at any moment. I took it all as it came. But I cannot conceal from the reader of this truthful account that as I went to bed at about three o'clock in the morning, I was conscious of a profound sense of relief. At last I had the authority to give directions over the whole scene. I felt as if I were walking with Destiny, and that all my past life had been but a preparation for this hour and for this trial. Eleven years in the political wilderness had freed me from ordinary party antagonisms. My warnings over the last six years had been so numerous, so detailed, and were now so terribly vindicated, that no one could gainsay me. I could not be reproached either for making the war or with want of preparation for it. I thought I knew a good deal about it all, and I was sure I should not fail. Therefore, although impatient for the morning, I slept soundly and had no need for cheering dreams. Facts are better than dreams.

Pericles's Funeral Oration and Thucydides's Assessment of His Statesmanship

From Thucydides, History of the Peloponnesian War

One of the greatest examples of political oratory in Western history, as recounted by the historian Thucydides. Pericles (495–429 B.C.) encourages his fellow citizens to serve their city loyally because it combines the advantages of a powerful democratic empire with a respect for learning, tolerance, and civilization.

In the course of this winter the Athenians, in accordance with the custom of their forefathers, buried at the public expense those who had first fallen in this war. Pericles was chosen to speak. Advancing from the sepulcher on to a platform, which had been raised to some height, that he might be heard over as great a part of the crowd as possible, he spoke to the following effect:

"The greater part of those who ere now have spoken in this place, have been accustomed to praise the man who introduced this oration into the law; considering it a right thing that it should be delivered over those who are buried after falling in battle. To me, however, it would have appeared sufficient, that when men had shown themselves brave by deeds, their honors also should be displayed by deeds—as you now see in the case of this burial, prepared at the public expense—and not that the virtues of many should be periled in one individual, for credit to be given him according as he expresses himself well or ill. For it is difficult to speak with propriety on a subject on which even the impression of one's truthfulness is with difficulty established. For the hearer who is acquainted [with the facts], and kindly disposed [toward those who performed them], might perhaps think them somewhat imperfectly set forth, compared with what he both wishes and knows; while he who is unacquainted with them might think that some points were even exaggerated, being led to this conclusion by envy, should he hear anything surpassing his own natural powers. For praises spoken of others are only endured so far as each one thinks that he is himself also capable of doing any of the things he hears; but that which exceeds their own capacity men at once envy and disbelieve. Since, however, our ancestors judged this to be a right custom, I too, in obedience to the law, must endeavor to meet the wishes and views of every one, as far as possible.

"I will begin then with our ancestors first: for it is just and becoming too at the same time, that on such an occasion the honor of being thus mentioned should be paid them. For always inhabiting the country without change, through a long succession of posterity, by their valor they transmitted it free to this very time. Justly then may they claim to be commended; and more justly still may our own fathers. For in addition to what they inherited, they acquired the great empire which we possess, and by painful exertions bequeathed it to us of the present day: though to most part of it have additions been made by ourselves here, who are still, generally speaking, in the vigor of life; and we have furnished our city with everything, so as to be most self-sufficient both for peace and for war. Now with regard to our military achievements, by which each possession was gained, whether in any case it were ourselves, or our fathers, that repelled with spirit hostilities brought against us by barbarian or Greek; as I do not wish to enlarge on the subject before you who are well acquainted with it, I will pass them over. But by what a mode of life we attained to our power, and by what form of government and owing to what habits it became so great, I will explain these points first, and then proceed to the eulogy of these men; as I consider that on the present occasion they will not be inappropriately mentioned, and that it is profitable for the whole assembly, both citizens and strangers, to listen to them.

"For we enjoy a form of government which does not copy the laws of our neighbors; but we are ourselves rather a pattern to others than imitators of them. In name, from its not being administered for the benefit of the few, but of the many, it is called a democracy; but with regard to its laws, all enjoy equality, as concerns their private differences; while with regard to public rank, according as each man has reputation for anything, he is preferred for public honors, not so much from consideration of party, as of merit; nor, again, on the ground of poverty, while he is able to do the state any good service, is he prevented by the obscurity of his position. We are liberal then in our public administration; and with regard to mutual jealousy of our daily pursuits, we are not angry with our neighbor, if he does anything to please himself; nor wear on our countenance offensive looks, which though harmless, are yet unpleasant. While, however, in private matters we live together agreeably, in public matters, under the influence of fear, we most carefully abstain from transgression, through our obedience to those who are from time to time in office, and to the laws; especially such of them as are enacted for the benefit of the injured, and such as, though unwritten, bring acknowledged disgrace [on those who break them].

"Moreover, we have provided for our spirits the most numerous recreations from labors, by celebrating games and sacrifices through the whole year, and by maintaining elegant private establishments, of which the daily gratification drives away sadness. Owing to the greatness too of our city, every thing from every land is imported into it; and it is our lot to reap with no more peculiar enjoyment the good things which are produced here, than those of the rest of the world likewise.

"In the studies of war also we differ from our enemies in the following respects. We throw our city open to all, and never, by the expulsion of strangers, exclude anyone from either learning or observing things, by seeing which unconcealed any of our enemies might gain an advantage; for we trust not so much to preparations and stratagems, as to our own valor for daring deeds. Again, as to our modes of education *they* aim at the acquisition of a manly character, by laborious training from their very youth; while *we*, though living at our ease, no less boldly advance to meet equal dangers. As a proof of this, the Lacedaemonians never march against our country singly, but with all [their confederates] together: while we, generally speaking, have no difficulty in conquering in battle upon hostile ground those who are standing up in defense of their own. And no enemy ever yet encountered our whole united force, through our attending at the same time to our navy, and sending our troops by land on so many different services: but wherever they have engaged with any part of it, if they conquer only some of us, they boast that we were all routed by them; and if they are conquered, they say it was by all that they were beaten. And yet if with careless ease rather than with laborious practice, and with a courage which is the result not so much of laws as of natural disposition, we are willing to face danger, we have the advantage of not suffering beforehand from coming troubles, and of proving ourselves, when we are involved in them, no less bold than those who are always toiling; so that our country is worthy of admiration in these respects, and in others besides.

"For we study taste with economy, and philosophy without effeminacy; and employ wealth rather for opportunity of action than for boastfulness of talking; while poverty is nothing disgraceful for a man to confess, but not to escape it by exertion is more disgraceful. Again, the same men can attend at the same time to domestic as well as to public affairs; and others, who are engaged with business, can still form a sufficient judgment on political questions. For we are the only people that consider the man who takes no part in these things, not as unofficious, but as useless; and we ourselves judge rightly of measures, at any rate, if we do not originate them; while we do not regard words as any hindrance to deeds, but rather [consider it a hindrance] not to have been previously instructed by word, before undertaking in deed what we have to do. For we have this characteristic also in a remarkable degree, that we are at the same time most daring and most calculating in what we take in hand; whereas to other men it is ignorance that brings daring, while calculation brings fear. Those, however, would deservedly be deemed most courageous, who know most fully what is terrible and what is pleasant, and yet do not on this account shrink from dangers. As regards beneficence also we differ from the generality of men; for we make friends, not by receiving, but by conferring kindness. Now he who has conferred the favor is the firmer friend, in order that he may keep alive the obligation by good will toward the man on whom he has conferred it; whereas he who owes it in return feels less keenly, knowing that it is not as a favor, but as a debt, that he will repay the kindness. Nay, we are the only men who fearlessly benefit anyone, not so much from calculations of expediency, as with the confidence of liberality.

"In short, I say that both the whole city is a school for Greece, and that, in my opinion, the same individual would amongst us prove himself qualified for the most varied kinds of action, and with the most graceful versatility. And that this is not mere vaunting language for the occasion, so much as actual truth, the very power of the state, which we have won by such habits, affords a proof. For it is the only country at the present time that, when brought to the test, proves superior to its fame; and the only one that neither gives to the enemy who has attacked us any cause for indignation at being worsted by such opponents, nor to him who is subject to us room for finding fault, as not being ruled by men who are worthy of empire. But we shall be admired both by present and future generations as having exhibited our power with great proofs, and by no means without evidence; and as having no further need, either of Homer to praise us, or anyone else who might charm for the moment by his verses, while the truth of the facts would mar the idea formed of them; but as having compelled every sea and land to become accessible to our daring, and everywhere established everlasting records, whether of evil or of good. It was for such a country then that these men, nobly resolving not to have it taken from them, fell fighting; and every one of their survivors may well be willing to suffer in its behalf.

"For this reason, indeed, it is that I have enlarged on the characteristics of the state; both to prove that the struggle is not for the same object in our case as in that of men who have none of these advantages in an equal degree; and at the same time clearly to establish by proofs [the truth of] the eulogy of those men over whom I am now speaking. And now the chief points of it have been mentioned; for with regard to the things for which I have commended the city, it was the virtues of these men, and such as these, that adorned her with them; and few of the Greeks are there whose fame, like these men's, would appear but the just counterpoise of their deeds. Again, the closing scene of these men appears to me to supply an illustration of human worth, whether as affording us the first information respecting it, or its final confirmation. For even in the case of men who have been in other respects of an inferior character, it is but fair for them to hold forth as a screen their military courage in their country's behalf; for, having wiped out their evil by their good, they did more service collectively, than harm by their individual offenses. But of these men there was none that either was made a coward by his wealth, from preferring the continued enjoyment of it; or shrank from danger through a hope suggested by poverty, namely, that he might yet escape it, and grow rich; but conceiving that vengeance on their foes was more to be desired than these objects, and at the same time regarding this as the most glorious of hazards, they wished by risking it to be avenged on their enemies, and so to aim at procuring those advantages; committing to hope the uncertainty of success, but resolving to trust to action, with regard to what was visible to themselves; and in that action, being minded rather to resist and die, than by surrendering to escape, they fled from the shame of [a discreditable] report, while they endured the brunt of the battle with their bodies; and after the shortest crisis, when at the very height of their fortune, were taken away from their glory rather than their fear.

"Such did these men prove themselves, as became the character of their country. For you that remain, you must pray that you may have a more successful resolution, but must determine not to have one less bold against your enemies; not in word alone considering the benefit [of such a spirit], (on which one might descant to you at great length—though you know it yourselves quite as well—telling you how many advantages are contained in repelling your foes;) but rather day by day beholding the power of the city as it appears in fact, and growing enamored of it, and reflecting, when you think it great, that it was by being bold, and knowing their duty, and being alive to shame in action, that men acquired these things; and because, if they ever failed in their attempt at any thing, they did not on that account think it right to deprive their country also of their valor, but conferred upon her a most glorious joint-offering. For while collectively they gave her their lives, individually they received that renown which never grows old, and the most distinguished tomb they could have; not so much that in which they are laid, as that in which their glory is left behind them, to be everlastingly recorded on every occasion for doing so, either by word or deed, that may from time to time present itself. For of illustrious men the whole earth is the sepulcher; and not only does the inscription upon columns in their own land point it out, but in that also which is not their own there dwells with everyone an unwritten memorial of the heart, rather than of a material monument. Vieing then with these men in your turn, and deeming happiness to consist in freedom, and freedom in valor, do not think lightly of the hazards of war. For it is not the unfortunate, [and those] who have no hope of any good, that would with most reason be unsparing of their lives; but those who, while they live, still incur the risk of a change to the opposite condition, and to whom the difference would be the greatest, should they meet with any reverse. For more grievous, to a man of high spirit at least, is the misery which accompanies cowardice, than the unfelt death which comes upon him at once, in the time of this strength and of his hope for the common welfare.

"Wherefore to the parents of the dead—as many of them as are here among you—I will not offer condolence, so much as consolation. For they know that they have been brought up subject to manifold misfortunes; but that happy is *their* lot who have gained the most glorious—death, as these have—sorrow, as you have; and to whom life has been so exactly measured, that they were both happy in it, and died in [that happiness]. Difficult, indeed, I know it is to persuade you of this, with regard to those of whom you will often be reminded by the good fortune of others, in which you yourselves also once rejoiced; and sorrow is felt, not for the blessings of which one is bereft without full experience of them, but of that which one loses after becoming accustomed to it. But you must bear up in the hope of other children, those of you whose age yet allows you to have them. For to yourselves individually those who are subsequently born will be a reason for your forgetting those who are no more; and to the state it will be beneficial in two ways, by its not being depopulated, and by the enjoyment of security; for it is not possible that those should offer any fair and just advice, who do not incur equal risk with their neighbors by having children at stake. Those of you, however, who are past that age, must consider that the longer period of your life during which you have been prosperous is so much gain, and that what remains will be but a short one; and you must cheer yourselves with the fair fame of these [your lost ones]. For the love of honor is the only feeling that never grows old; and in the helplessness of age it is not the acquisition of gain, as some assert, that gives greatest pleasure, but the enjoyment of honor.

"For those of you, on the other hand, who are sons or brothers of the dead, great, I see, will be the struggle of competition. For every one is accustomed to praise the man who is no more; and scarcely, though even for an excess of worth, would you be esteemed, I do not say equal to them, but only slightly inferior. For the living are exposed to envy in their rivalry; but those who are in no one's way are honored with a goodwill free from all opposition. If, again, I must say anything on the subject of woman's excellence also, with reference to those of you who will now be in widowhood, I will express it all in a brief exhortation. Great will be your glory in not falling short of the natural character that belongs to you; and great is hers, who is least talked of amongst the men, either for good or evil.

"I have now expressed *in word,* as the law required, what I had to say befitting the occasion; and, *in deed* those who are here interred, have already received part of their honors; while, for the remaining part, the state will bring up their sons at the public expense, from this time to their manhood; thus offering both to these and to their posterity a beneficial reward for such contests; for where the greatest prizes for virtue are given, there also the most virtuous men are found amongst the citizens. And now, having finished your lamentations for your several relatives, depart."

Thucydides's assessment of Pericles:

For as long as Pericles was at the head of the state in time of peace, he governed it with moderation, and kept it in safety, and it was at its height of greatness in his time: and when the war broke out, he appears to have foreknown its power in this respect also. He survived its commencement two years and six months; and when he was dead, his foresight with regard to its course was appreciated to a still greater degree. For he said that if they kept quiet, and attended to their navy, and did not gain additional dominion during the war, nor expose the city to hazard, they would have the advantage in the struggle. But they did the very contrary of all this, and in other things which seemed to have nothing to do with the war, through their private ambition and private gain, they adopted evil measures both toward themselves and their allies; which, if successful, conduced to the honor and benefit of individuals; but if they failed, proved detrimental to the state with regard to the war. And the reason was, that he, being powerful by means of his high

rank and talents, and manifestly proof against bribery, controlled
the multitude with an independent spirit, and was not led by them
so much as he himself led them; for he did not say anything to
humor them, for the acquisition of power by improper means; but
was able on the strength of his character to contradict them even at
the risk of their displeasure. Whenever, for instance, he perceived
them unseasonably and insolently confident, by his language he
would dash them down to alarm; and, on the other hand, when
they were unreasonably alarmed, he would raise them again to confidence. And so, though in name it was a democracy, in fact it was a
government administered by the first man. Whereas those who
came after, being more on a level with each other, and each grasping to become first, had recourse to devoting [not only their
speeches, but] even their *measures,* to the humors of the people. In
consequence of this, many other blunders were committed.

The Wolves to the Sheep Dogs: Give Peace a Chance

Aesop

The Wolves thus addressed the Sheep-dogs: "Why should you,
who are like us in so many things, not be entirely of one mind with
us, and live with us as brothers should? We differ from you in one
point only. We live in freedom, but you bow down to, and slave for,
men; who, in return for your services, flog you with whips, and put
collars on your necks. They make you also guard their sheep, and
while they eat the mutton throw only the bones to you. If you will
be persuaded by us, you will give us the sheep, and we will enjoy
them in common, till we all are surfeited." The Dogs listened favor-
ably to these proposals, and, entering the den of the Wolves, they
were set upon and torn to pieces.

6

THE NOBLE MAN

"LET A MAN NOBLY LIVE OR NOBLY DIE," WROTE THE TRAGIC POET Sophocles in the fifth century B.C. But what is nobility? It is an elusive concept, although many writers, artists, and thinkers have tried, in varying and often sublimely beautiful ways, to express it or give it form. "Virtue is the only true nobility," one eighteenth-century essayist advised, and should never be confused with mere conventional social status. Nobility is not a function of birth or inherited privilege, but of character and ability. "There is a natural aristocracy among men," Thomas Jefferson wrote. "The grounds of this are virtue and talents." The Victorians raised their contemplation of nobility to a high art: Alfred, Lord Tennyson wrote that it is "better not to be at all than not be noble," while the Romantic poet William Wordsworth contended that "there is one great society alone on earth, the noble Living and the noble Dead."

Nobility is often praised in war and combat, especially when the situation is dangerous or perhaps even hopeless. "What's brave, what's noble," Shakespeare has Cleopatra say after Mark Antony kills himself and she prepares to take her own life. "Let's do it after the high Roman fashion, and make death proud to take us." An ability to bear up with dignity and fortitude under the blows of fortune, whether delivered in the guise of war, natural disaster, disease, or betrayal, is one of the keys to a noble character. But nobility is just as often ascribed to qualities of mind, to large and inspiring thoughts, to subtle, capacious, and bold-minded insights into life and human nature. "What is poetry?" asks the Victorian art historian and critic John Ruskin. "The suggestion, by the imagination, of noble grounds for noble emotions." Sir Arthur Conan Doyle once observed that "of all ruins, that of a noble mind is the most deplorable."

Nobility is often associated, as well, with a virtuous character. Indeed, for some writers, nobility is the basis for all the moral virtues. Solon, the great law giver of ancient Athens, advises us to "put trust in nobility of character" rather than in the swearing of oaths. According to Cicero, "The nobler a man, the harder it is for

him to suspect inferiority in others." As with gentlemanliness, true
nobility has less to do with class origins than character: In the
words of an old English proverb, "The more noble, the more humble." A noble man will not allow himself or others to be treated like
slaves. Indeed, as Edmund Burke remarks, a truly noble nature
prefers the respect of free citizens to domination over those who
are debased: "He is noble who has priority among free men, not he
who has a sort of wild liberty among slaves." And, of course, nobility is associated with a disdain for shameful, cowardly, deceitful, or
manipulative acts—habits unworthy of a manly and honorable
character. According to many traditional authorities, it is sometimes better to be prepared for death than to go on living in a
degraded or humiliating condition—especially if the price of stay-
ing alive is to commit some act of betrayal or treachery against
another. For the most part, unfortunately, argues the Roman
philosopher Seneca, "Men do not care how nobly they live, but
only how long, although it is within the reach of every man to live
nobly, but within no man's power to live long." Since we all have to
die eventually, why not concentrate on living with dignity and
decency for whatever time is allotted to us?

The readings in this section concentrate on several important
dimensions of what it means to be a noble man—valor, integrity,
and honor. Valor in war is not a topic much in fashion today. It is
sometimes implied that even to discuss the possibility that certain
admirable human qualities might arise in situations of combat is
somehow indecent, if not a promotion of war-mongering and violence. But, as readers will discover in this section, few thoughtful
observers of combat have ever praised it unequivocally, or been
blind to the corrupting influence that the savagery of war can have
on a young man's heart and soul. Indeed, what makes these stories
and reflections about military valor so compelling is their sensitivity
to war's power either to ennoble or to debase the human character,
sometimes in the same man. In the end, however, there is something enduringly inspiring about the idea of being willing to die for
one's country, or for a just cause, whether it be Thermopylae, the
Battle of the Bulge, or struggling to abolish slavery and discrimination. It is worth recalling that the larger meaning of valor is sometimes described as moral courage. Sometimes the bravest men are
not those who are courageous in battle, but those who are steadfast
in the defense of goodness, in aiding the oppressed and helpless,
or—perhaps the hardest battle of all—triumphing over their own
worst impulses.

The ancient Greek word for "noble" was also used to mean "beautiful" or "fine," especially when applied to the soul and its virtues, and this inner beauty of character, feeling, and temper is surely what we are sensing when a man's conduct strikes us as noble. Nobility is an ideal that comprises nearly everything that is most admirable in a man. It includes the virtues of honor, justice, compassion, generosity, and honesty. But to these other virtues, nobility adds something more: a level of extraordinary, even sublime self-sacrifice and steadfastness in the face of peril or oppression, rising at times to almost superhuman heights. A man can be just by refraining from hurting others, obeying the law, and fulfilling his everyday responsibilities as a citizen, friend, or spouse—but nobility is rare. The noble man possesses what the Romans called *integritas*. Integrity is, as the word suggests, an integration of the virtues within a temperament of fortitude, compassion, and patience, and an ability to *remain oneself,* however severely tested by battle, persecution, sickness, bereavement, disappointment, and the other challenges to which man must constantly rise.

THE MAN OF VALOR

The Virtues of the Soldier

From Charles de Gaulle, The Edge of the Sword

Can we imagine life without force? No, de Gaulle argues, not only because human nature cannot change, but because ambition and passion are as necessary to noble projects as to base ones. The "virtues of the soldier are an integral part of man's inheritance." A great commander combines intelligence with instinct. War brings out men's basest instincts, but also their finest virtues. While war often serves greed and tyranny, it can also defend the oppressed and spread the ideals of civilization and religion.

Hope though we may, what reason have we for thinking that passion and self-interest, the root cause of armed conflict in men and in nations, will cease to operate; that anyone will willingly surrender what he has or not try to get what he wants; in short, that human nature will ever become something other than it is? Is it really likely that the present balance of power will remain unchanged so long as the small want to become great, the strong to . dominate the weak, the old to live on? How are frontiers to be stabilized, how is power to be controlled if evolution continues along the same lines as hitherto? Even supposing that nations should agree, for a time, to conduct their mutual relations in accordance with a sovereign code, how effective could such a code be even if enforced? "Laws unsupported by force soon fall into contempt," said Cardinal de Retz. International agreements will be of little value unless there are troops to prevent their infringement. In whatever direction the world may move, it will never be able to do without the final arbitrament of arms.

Is it possible to conceive of life without force? Only if children cease to be born, only if minds are sterilized, feelings frozen, men's needs anaesthetized, only if the world is reduced to immobility, can it be banished. Otherwise, in some form or another, it will remain indispensable, for, without it, thought would have no driving power, action no strength. It is the prerequisite of movement and the midwife of progress. Whether as the bulwark of authority, the defender of thrones, the motive power of revolution, we owe to it, turn and turn about, both order and liberty. Force has watched over civilization in the cradle; force has ruled empires, and dug the grave of decadence; force gives laws to the peoples and controls their destinies.

It is true to say that the fighting spirit, the art of war, the virtues of the soldier are an integral part of man's inheritance. They have been part and parcel of history in all its phases, the medium through which it has expressed itself. How can we understand Greece without Salamis, Rome without the legions, Christianity without the sword, Islam without the scimitar, our own Revolution without Valmy, the League of Nations without the victory of France? The self-sacrifice of individuals for the sake of the community, suffering made glorious—those two things which are the basic elements of the profession of arms—respond to both our moral and aesthetic concepts. The noblest teachings of philosophy and religion have found no higher ideals.

Should, then, those who control the accumulated strength of

France fall into discouragement, the result would be not only peril for the country but a complete rupture of civilization. Into what mad or irresponsible hands might force not fall if its control were relinquished by a wise and highly trained directorate? The time has come for a military elite once more to become conscious of the preeminent role it has to play, and to concentrate anew upon its one and only duty, which is to prepare itself for war. It must lift its head again and fix its eyes upon the heights. Only if the philosophy proper to the soldier is restored will an edge be given to the sword. In that philosophy he will find nobility of outlook, pride in his vocation, and a chance to influence the world outside himself. In it, till the day of glory dawns, he will find the sole reward worth considering.

Great war leaders have always been aware of the importance of instinct. Was not what Alexander called his "hope," Caesar his "luck," and Napoleon his "star" simply the fact that they knew they had a particular gift of making contact with realities sufficiently closely to dominate them? For those who are greatly gifted, this faculty often shines through their personalities. There may be nothing in itself exceptional about what they say or their way of saying it, but other men in their presence have the impression of a natural force destined to master events. Flaubert expresses this feeling when he describes the still adolescent Hannibal as already clothed "in the undefinable splendor of those who are destined for great enterprises."

However, while no work or action can be conceived without the promptings of instinct, these promptings are not sufficient to give the conception a precise form. The very fact that they are "gifts of nature" means that they are simple, crude, and sometimes confused. Now, a leader commands a unit, that is to say a system of complex forces with its own properties and disciplines, which can develop its power only by following a certain pattern. It is here that the intelligence comes into its own. Taking possession of the raw material of instinct, it elaborates it, gives it a specific shape, and makes of it a clearly defined and coherent whole. This done, a due application of method, by establishing the different values of this whole in their order of importance, and by apportioning to its various parts the execution of the plan in time and in space, by linking the different operations, and the phases of those operations, in such a way that they shall be carried out concurrently, will put into the hands of the commander an effective and well-tempered tool. It is essential that some such method, whether good or bad, be employed if the action is not to result in confusion. A bad method is better than no method at all.

If a commander is to grasp the essentials and reject the inessentials; if he is to split his general operation into a number of complementary actions in such a way that all shall combine to achieve the purpose common to every one of them, he must be able to see the situation as a whole, attribute to each object its relative importance, grasp the connections between each factor in the situation, and recognize its limits. All this implies a gift of synthesis which, in itself, demands a high degree of intellectual capacity. The general who has to free the essentials of his problem from the confused mass of their attendant details resembles the user of a stereoscope who has to concentrate his eyes upon the image before he can see it in relief. That is why great men of action have always been of the meditative type. They have, without exception, possessed to a very high degree the faculty of withdrawing into themselves. As Napoleon said: "The military leader must be capable of giving intense, extended, and indefatigable consideration to a single group of objects."

War stirs in men's hearts the mud of their worst instincts. It puts a premium on violence, nourishes hatred, and gives free rein to cupidity. It crushes the weak, exalts the unworthy, bolsters tyranny. Because of its blind fury many of the noblest schemes have come to nothing and the most generous instincts have more than once been checked. Time and time again it has destroyed all ordered living, devastated hope, and put the prophets to death. But, though Lucifer has used it for his purposes, so, sometimes, has the Archangel. With what virtues has it not enriched the moral capital of mankind! Because of it, courage, devotion, and nobility have scaled the peaks. It has conferred greatness of spirit on the poor, brought pardon to the guilty, revealed the possibilities of self-sacrifice to the commonplace, restored honor to the rogue, and given dignity to the slave. It has carried ideas in the baggage wagons of its armies, and reforms in the knapsacks of its soldiers. It has blazed a trail for religion and spread across the world influences which have brought renewal to mankind, consoled it, and made it better. Had not innumerable soldiers shed their blood there would have been no Hellenism, no Roman civilization, no Christianity, no Rights of Man, and no modern developments.

Not One Step Back
Unless Ordered!
The Battle of Stalingrad

From M. S. Shumilov, Colonel-General,
Hero of the Soviet Union
Two Hundred Days of Fire

The Battle of Stalingrad took a ghastly toll in lives, but it was the beginning
of the end for the German invasion of Russia in World War II.

Supported by artillery and mortars, the enemy deployed over one infantry company against a dozen marines. Potapov was wounded, but he stayed on the battlefield to direct the fire. With every new attack the Marines' strength dwindled. Only two were left to repulse the fourth attack. When the German fire subsided, the wounded Potapov crawled up unnoticed to an enemy machine-gun nest and pelted it with grenades. Here again he was hit by a German bullet. After eight hours of bitter fighting, during which 70 Germans were killed, two Marines withdrew to the Don carrying their wounded fellows on their shoulders. These men could be counted on.

Fierce fighting in the steppeland persisted day and night. The army's men were acutely aware of the danger, and stubbornly defended every inch of ground. The extent of their gallantry can be judged from enemy casualties. Between July 21 and August 1, 1942, the Nazis lost over 16,000 killed and wounded. The enemy had been bled white, but this did not mean he was abandoning his intentions. On the contrary, his advance became all the more frenzied.

Dusk had fallen. Battalion commander wrote the following note on a strip of paper: "Six attacks have been repulsed. Several dozen enemy and officers have been killed. There are two of us left. I am keeping up the fire. Muratov." The man who delivered this dispatch described the details of the fighting to regimental commander. The valiant captain had died in an uneven fight without retiring one step from his line.

"Not a step back unless ordered." This stern formula became

organically engrained in the flesh and blood of the men and their commanders and inspired discipline of the highest quality which reached the heights of utter selflessness and, as can be seen from the example of Battalion Commander Muratov, self-sacrifice. "Stand and conquer!" was the iron law of discipline on the battle-field.

Years have passed but that day is still fresh in my mind. We left our observation post knowing that the bulk of the army's forces were clear of the enemy and that any day now they would dig their heels into the city's inner fortified perimeter and confront the enemy in an organized manner. We owed this to the heroic 126th Division whose feat to this day remains unknown in its details. Thousands of heroes must be resurrected from obscurity, and this is the duty of the survivors of that unparalleled battle on August 29, 1942.

The Stalingrads, as we dubbed the veterans of the battle, were the pride and joy of the Guards units. "Where a Stalingrad stands, the enemy shall not pass!" "Where the Stalingrad strikes, the enemy shall not hold his ground." We had good ground for coining these rules of battle.

The soldier-liberator realized that sacred and just battles are fought not for the sake of glory but for the sake of life on earth. Stalingrad had risen out of the ash and shone in our souls like a beacon leading on and on to victory itself.

The Meaning of Courage

From John Fitzgerald Kennedy,
Profiles in Courage

Decorated war hero and future President John Fitzgerald Kennedy sums up the importance of courage for democratic leadership in this book from 1956.

This has been a book about courage and politics. Politics furnished the situations, courage provided the theme. Courage, the universal virtue, is comprehended by us all—but these portraits of courage do not dispel the mysteries of politics.

Motivation, as any psychiatrist will tell us, is always difficult to assess. It is particularly difficult to trace in the murky sea of politics. Those who abandoned their state and section for the national interest—men like Daniel Webster and Sam Houston, whose ambitions for higher office could not be hidden—laid themselves open to the charge that they sought only to satisfy their ambition for the Presidency. Those who broke with their party to fight for broader principles—men like John Quincy Adams and Edmund Ross—faced the accusation that they accepted office under one banner and yet deserted it in a moment of crisis for another.

But in the particular events set forth in the preceding chapter, I am persuaded after long study of the record that the national interest, rather than a private or political gain, furnished the basic motivation for the actions of those whose deeds are therein described. This does not mean that many of them did not seek, though rarely with success, to wring advantage out of the difficult course they had adopted. For as politicians—and it is surely no disparagement to term all of them politicians—they were clearly justified in doing so.

Of course, the acts of courage described in this book would be more inspiring and would shine more with the traditional luster of hero-worship if we assumed that each man forgot wholly about himself in his dedication to higher principles. But it may be that President John Adams, surely as disinterested as well as wise a public servant as we ever had, came much nearer to the truth when he wrote in his *Defense of the Constitutions of the United States*: "It is not true, in fact, that any people ever existed who love the public better than themselves."

If this be true, what then caused the statesmen mentioned in the preceding pages to act as they did? It was not because they "loved the public better than themselves." On the contrary it was precisely because they did *love themselves*—because each one's need to maintain his own respect for himself was more important to him than his popularity with others—because his desire to win or maintain a reputation for integrity and courage was stronger than his desire to maintain his office—because his conscience, his personal standard of ethics, his integrity or morality, call it what you will—was stronger than the pressure of public disapproval—because his faith that *his* course was the best one, and would ultimately be vindicated, outweighed his fear of public reprisal.

Although the public good was the indirect beneficiary of his sacrifice, it was not that vague and general concept, but one or a combination of these pressures of self-love that pushed him along the course of action that resulted in the slings and arrows previously described. It is when the politician loves neither the public good nor himself, or when his love for himself is limited and is satisfied by the trappings of office, that the public interest is badly served. And it is when his regard for himself is so high that his own self-respect demands he follow the path of courage and conscience that all benefit. It is then that his belief in the rightness of his own course enables him to say with John C. Calhoun: "I never know what South Carolina thinks of a measure. I never consult her. I act to the best of my judgment and according to my conscience. If she approves, well and good. If she does not and wishes anyone to take my place, I am ready to vacate. We are even."

This is not to say that courageous politicians and the principles for which they speak out are always right.

But is it necessary to decide this question in order to admire their courage? Must men conscientiously risk their careers only for principles which hindsight declares to be correct, in order for posterity to honor them for their valor? I think not. Surely in the United States of America, where brother once fought against brother, we did not judge a man's bravery under fire by examining the banner under which he fought.

To be courageous, these stories make clear, requires no exceptional qualifications, no magic formula, no special combination of time, place and circumstance. It is an opportunity that sooner or later is presented to us all. Politics merely furnishes one arena which imposes special tests of courage. In whatever arena of life one may meet the challenge of courage, whatever may be the sacrifices he faces if he follows his conscience—the loss of his friends, his fortune, his contentment, even the esteem of his fellow men—each man must decide for himself the course he will follow. The stories of past courage can define that ingredient—they can teach, they can offer hope, they can provide inspiration. But they cannot supply courage itself. For this each man must look into his own soul.

A Young Man's First Battle

From Leo Tolstoy, War and Peace

Tolstoy's novel unforgettably portrays the attractions and drawbacks of, on the one hand, a life devoted to martial valor and patriotic service, and, on the other, the more retiring inner life of a family man, husband, and father. In this scene, young Nicholas Rostof experiences the confusion, terror, and joy of his first battle.

The squadron in which Rostof served had barely time to mount their horses, before they found themselves face to face with the enemy. Again, as at the bridge over the Enns, there was no one between the squadron and the line of the enemy, and between them lay that terrible gap of the unknown and the dreadful, like the line that divides the living from the dead. All the men felt conscious of that line, and were occupied by the question whether they should pass beyond it or not, and how they should cross it.

The colonel came galloping along the front; and angrily replied to the questions of his officers, and like a man who in despair insists on his own way, thundered out some command. No one said anything definite, but something had given the squadron an idea that there was to be a charge. The command to fall in was given, then sabres were drawn with a clash. But as yet no one stirred. The army of the left wing and the infantry and the hussars felt that their leaders did not know what to do, and the indecision of the commanders communicated itself to the soldiers.

"If they would only hurry, hurry," thought Rostof, feeling that at last the time was at hand for participating in the intoxication of a charge of which he had heard so much from his comrades, the hussars.

"Forward, with God, children," rang out Denisof's voice, "at a trot!"

In the front rank, the haunches of the horses began to rise and fall. Grachik began to pull on the reins, and dashed ahead. At the right, Rostof could see the forward ranks of his hussars, but farther in front there was a dark streak, which he could not make out distinctly but supposed to be the enemy. Reports were heard, but in the distance.

"Charge!" rang the command, and Rostof felt how his Grachik broke into a gallop and seemed to strain every nerve. He realized that his division was dashing forward and it became more and more exciting to him. He noticed a solitary tree just abreast of him. At first this tree had been in front of him, in the very centre of that line which seemed so terrible. But now he had passed beyond it and there was not only nothing terrible about it, but it seemed ever more and more jolly and lively.

"Oh! how I will slash at them!" thought Rostof, as he grasped the handle of his sabre. "Hurrah-ah-ah-ah!" rang the cheers in the distance. "Now let us be at them if ever," thought Rostof, striking the spurs into Grachik, and overtaking the others, he urged him to the top of his speed. The enemy were already in sight before him. Suddenly, something like an enormous lash cracked all along the squadron. Rostof raised his sabre, in readiness to strike, but just at that instant Nikitenko, a hussar galloping in front of him, swerved aside from him, and Rostof felt, as in a dream, that he was being carried with unnatural swiftness forward, and yet was not moving from the spot. A hussar whom he recognized as Bondarchuk was galloping behind him and looked at him gravely. Bondarchuk's horse shied and he dashed by him.

"What does it mean? Am I not moving? Have I fallen? Am I dead?" these questions Rostof asked and answered in a breath. He was alone in the middle of the field. In place of the galloping horses and backs of the hussars, he saw all around him the solid earth and stubble. Warm blood was under him. "No, I am wounded and my horse is killed."

Grachik raised himself on his fore legs, but fell back, pinning down his rider's foot. From the horse's head a stream of blood was flowing. The horse struggled but could not rise. Rostof tried to get to his feet, but likewise fell back. His sabre-tasche had caught on the saddle. Where our men were, where the French were, he could not tell. There was no one around him.

Freeing his leg, he got up.

"Where, in which direction, is now that line which so clearly separated the two armies?" he asked himself, and could find no answer. "Has something bad happened to me? Is this the way things take place, and what must be done in such circumstances?" he asked himself again, as he got to his feet; and at this time he began to feel as though something extra were hanging to his benumbed left arm. His wrist seemed to belong to another person. He looked at his hand, but could find no trace of blood on it. "There now, here are our fellows," he exclaimed mentally, with joy, perceiving a few running toward him. "They will help me."

In front of these men ran one in a foreign-looking shako and in a blue capote. He was dark and sunburnt, and had a hooked nose. Two or three others were running at his heels.

One of them said something in a language that was strange and un-Russian. Surrounded by a similar set of men, in the same sort of shakos, stood a Russian hussar. His hands were held; just behind him, they were holding his horse.

"Is our man really taken prisoner? Yes! And will they take me too? Who are these men?" Rostof kept asking himself, not crediting his own eyes. "Can they be the French?"

He gazed at the on-coming strangers, and in spite of the fact that only a second before he had been dashing forward solely for the purpose of overtaking and hacking down these same Frenchmen, their proximity now seemed to him so terrible that he could not trust his own eyes!

"Who are they? Why are they running? Are they running at me? And why? Is it to kill me? *Me*, whom every one loves so?"

He recollected how he was beloved by his mother, his family, his friends, and the purpose of his enemies to kill him seemed incredible.

He Had Dreamed of Battles All His Life

From Stephen Crane,
The Red Badge of Courage

The classic American story of a young man coming of age on the battlefield, first published in 1895. In these opening pages the protagonist, Henry Fleming, thinks back to his initial enlistment in the Union Army. He remembers his mother's advice, his early enthusiasm about the war, and the flattering attentions of civilians as his regiment marched south to face the Confeder-

ates. He also remembers when the question that frames the book first came to him: When confronted with real battle, will I run?

The youth was in a little trance of astonishment. So they were at last going to fight. On the morrow, perhaps, there would be a battle, and he would be in it. For a time he was obliged to labor to make himself believe. He could not accept with assurance an omen that he was about to mingle in one of these great affairs of the earth.

He had, of course, dreamed of battles all his life—of vague and bloody conflicts that had thrilled him with their sweep and fire. In visions he had seen himself in many struggles. He had imagined peoples secure in the shadow of his eagle-eyed prowess. But awake he had regarded battles as crimson blotches on the pages of the past. He had put them as things of the bygone with his thought-images of heavy crowns and high castles. There was a portion of the world's history which he had regarded as the time of wars, but it, he thought, had been long gone over the horizon and had disappeared forever.

From his home his youthful eyes had looked upon the war in his own country with distrust. It must be some sort of a play affair. He had long despaired of witnessing a Greek-like struggle. Such would be no more, he had said. Men were better, or more timid. Secular and religious education had effaced the throat-grappling instinct, or else firm finance held in check the passions.

He had burned several times to enlist. Tales of great movements shook the land. They might not be distinctly Homeric, but there seemed to be much glory in them. He had read of marches, sieges, conflicts, and he had longed to see it all. His busy mind had drawn for him large pictures extravagant in color, lurid, with breathless deeds.

But his mother had discouraged him. She had affected to look with some contempt upon the quality of his war ardor and patriotism. She could calmly seat herself and with no apparent difficulty give him many hundreds of reasons why he was of vastly more importance on the farm than on the field of battle. She had had certain ways of expression that told him that her statements on the subject came from a deep conviction. Moreover, on her side, was his belief that her ethical motive in the argument was impregnable.

At last, however, he had made firm rebellion against this yellow light thrown upon the color of his ambitions. The newspapers, the gossip of the village, his own picturings, had aroused him to an uncheckable degree. They were in truth fighting finely down there. Almost every day the newspapers printed accounts of a decisive victory.

One night, as he lay in bed, the winds had carried to him the clangoring of the church bell as some enthusiast jerked the rope frantically to tell the twisted news of a great battle. This voice of the people rejoicing in the night had made him shiver in a prolonged ecstasy of excitement. Later, he had gone down to his mother's room and had spoken thus: "Ma, I'm going to enlist."

"Henry, don't you be a fool," his mother had replied. She had then covered her face with the quilt. There was an end to the matter for that night.

Nevertheless, the next morning he had gone to a town that was near his mother's farm and had enlisted in a company that was forming there. When he had returned home his mother was milking the brindle cow. Four others stood waiting. "Ma, I've enlisted," he had said to her diffidently. There was a short silence. "The Lord's will be done, Henry," she had finally replied, and had then continued to milk the brindle cow.

When he had stood in the doorway with his soldier's clothes on his back, and with the light of excitement and expectancy in his eyes almost defeating the glow of regret for the home bonds, he had seen two tears leaving their trails on his mother's scarred cheeks.

Still, she had disappointed him by saying nothing whatever about returning with his shield or on it. He had privately primed himself for a beautiful scene. He had prepared certain sentences which he thought could be used with touching effect. But her words destroyed his plans. She had doggedly peeled potatoes and addressed him as follows: "You watch out, Henry, an' take good care of yerself. Don't go a thinkin' you can lick the hull rebel army at the start, because yeh can't. Yer jest one little feller amongst a hull lot of others, and yeh've got to keep quiet an' do what they tell yeh. I know how are you, Henry.

"I've knet yeh eight pair of socks, Henry, and I've put in all yer best shirts, because I want my boy to be jest as warm and com'able as anybody in the army. Whenever they get holes, in 'em, I want yeh to send 'em rightaway back to me, so's I kin dern 'em.

"An' allus be careful an' choose yer comp'ny. There's lots of bad men in the army, Henry. The army makes 'em wild, and they like nothing better than the job of leading off a young feller like you, as ain't never been away from home much and has allus had a mother, an' a-learning 'em to drink and swear. Keep clear of them folks, Henry. I don't want yeh to ever do anything, Henry, that yeh would be 'shamed to let me know about. Jest think as if I was a watchin' yeh. If yeh keep that in yer mind allus, I guess yeh'll come out about right.

"Yeh must allus remember yer father, too, child, an' remember he never drunk a drop of licker in his life, and seldom swore a cross oath.

"I don't know what else to tell yeh, Henry, excepting that yeh must never do no shirking, child, on my account. If so be a time comes when yeh have to be kilt or do a mean thing, why, Henry, don't think of anything 'cept what's right, because there's many a woman has to bear up 'ginst sech things these times, and the Lord'll take keer of us all.

"Don't forgit about the socks and the shirts, child; and I've put a cup of blackberry jam with yer bundle, because I know yeh like it above all things. Good-by, Henry. Watch out, and be a good boy."

He had, of course, been impatient under the ordeal of this speech. It had not been quite what he expected, and he had borne it with an air of irritation. He departed feeling vague relief.

Still, when he had looked back from the gate, he had seen his mother kneeling among the potato parings. Her brown face, upraised, was stained with tears, and her spare form was quivering. He bowed his head and went on, feeling suddenly ashamed of his purposes.

From his home he had gone to the seminary to bid adieu to many schoolmates. They had thronged about him with wonder and admiration. He had felt the gulf now between them and had swelled with calm pride. He and some of his fellows who had donned blue were quite overwhelmed with privileges for all of one afternoon, and it had been a very delicious thing. They had strutted.

A certain light-haired girl had made vivacious fun at his martial spirit, but there was another and darker girl whom he had gazed at steadfastly, and he thought she grew demure and sad at sight of his blue and brass. As he had walked down the path between the rows of oaks, he had turned his head and detected her at a window watching his departure. As he perceived her, she immediately began to stare up through the high tree branches at the sky. He had seen a good deal of flurry and haste in her movement as she changed her attitude. He often thought of it.

On the way to Washington his spirit had soared. The regiment was fed and caressed at station after station until the youth had believed that he must be a hero. There was a lavish expenditure of bread and cold meats, coffee, and pickles and cheese. As he basked in the smiles of the girls and was patted and complimented by the old men, he had felt growing within him the strength to do mighty deeds of arms.

After complicated journeyings with many pauses, there had come months of monotonous life in a camp. He had had the belief that real war was a series of death struggles with small time in between for sleep and meals; but since his regiment had come to the field the army had done little but sit still and try to keep warm.

He was brought then gradually back to this old ideas. Greek-like struggles would be no more. Men were better, or more timid. Secular and religious education had effaced the throat-grappling instinct, or else firm finance held in check the passions.

He had grown to regard himself merely as a part of a vast blue demonstration. His province was to look out, as far as he could, for his personal comfort. For recreation he could twiddle his thumbs and speculate on the thoughts which must agitate the minds of the generals. Also, he was drilled and drilled and reviewed, and drilled and drilled and reviewed.

The only foes he had seen were some pickets along the river bank. They were a sun-tanned, philosophical lot, who sometimes shot reflectively at the blue pickets. When reproached for this afterward, they usually expressed sorrow, and swore by their gods that the guns had exploded without their permission. The youth, on guard duty one night, conversed across the stream with one of them. He was a slightly ragged man, who spat skillfully between his shoes and possessed a great fund of bland and infantile assurance. The youth liked him personally.

"Yank," the other had informed him, "yer a right dum good feller." This sentiment, floating to him upon the still air, had made him temporarily regret war.

Various veterans had told him tales. Some talked of gray, bewhiskered hordes who were advancing with relentless curses and chewing tobacco with unspeakable valor; tremendous bodies of fierce soldiery who were sweeping along like the Huns. Others spoke of tattered and eternally hungry men who fired despondent powders. "They'll charge through hell's fire an' brimstone t' git a holt on a haversack, an' sech stomachs ain't a-lastin' long," he was told. From the stories, the youth imagined the red, live bones, sticking out through slits in the faded uniforms.

Still, he could not put a whole faith in veterans' tales, for recruits were their prey. They talked much of smoke, fire, and blood, but he could not tell how much might be lies. They persisently yelled, "Fresh fish!" at him, and were in no wise to be trusted.

However, he perceived now that it did not greatly matter what kind of soldiers he was going to fight, so long as they fought, which fact no one disputed. There was a more serious problem. He lay in his bunk pondering upon it. He tried to mathematically prove to himself that he would not run from a battle.

Previously he had never felt obliged to wrestle too seriously with this question. In his life he had taken certain things for granted, never challenging his belief in ultimate success, and bothering little about means and roads. But here he was confronted with a thing of moment. It had suddenly appeared to him that perhaps in a battle he might run. He was forced to admit that as far as war was concerned he knew nothing of himself.

A sufficient time before he would have allowed the problem to kick its heels at the outer portals of his mind, but now he felt compelled to give serious attention to it.

A little panic-fear grew in his mind. As his imagination went forward to a fight, he saw hideous possibilities. He contemplated the lurking menaces of the future, and failed in an effort to see himself standing stoutly in the midst of them. He recalled his visions of broken-bladed glory, but in the shadow of the impending tumult he suspected them to be impossible pictures.

He sprang from the bunk and began to pace nervously to and fro. "Good Lord, what's th' matter with me?" he said aloud.

He felt that in this crisis his laws of life were useless. Whatever he had learned of himself was here of no avail. He was an unknown quantity. He saw that he would again be obliged to experiment as he had in early youth. He must accumulate information of himself, and meanwhile he resolved to remain close upon his guard lest those qualities of which he knew nothing should everlastingly disgrace him. "Good Lord!" he repeated in dismay.

In this section Henry Fleming faces the enemy after faltering at first, and in this encounter becomes a "war-devil." He had earlier fled, but now Henry stands his ground and, in Crane's words, "he had slept and, awakening, found himself a knight."

This advance of the enemy had seemed to the youth like a ruthless hunting. He began to fume with rage and exasperation. He beat his foot upon the ground, and scowled with hate at the swirling smoke that was approaching like a phantom flood. There was a maddening quality in this seeming resolution of the foe to give him no rest, to give him no time to sit down and think. Yesterday he had fought and had fled rapidly. There had been many adventures. For to-day he felt that he had earned opportunities for contemplative repose. He could have enjoyed portraying to uninitiated listeners various scenes at which he had been a witness or ably discussing the processes of war with other proved men. Too it was important that he should have time for physical recuperation. He was sore and stiff from his experiences. He had received his fill of all exertions, and he wished to rest.

But those other men seemed never to grow weary; they were fighting with their old speed. He had a wild hate for the relentless foe. Yesterday, when he had imagined the universe to be against him, he had hated it, little gods and big gods; to-day he hated the army of the foe with the same great hatred. He was not going to be badgered of his life, like a kitten chased by boys, he said. It was not well to drive men into final corners; at those moments they could all develop teeth and claws.

He leaned and spoke into his friend's ear. He menaced the woods with a gesture. "If they keep on chasing us, by Gawd, they'd better watch out. Can't stand *too* much."

The friend twisted his head and made a calm reply. "If they keep on a-chasin' us they'll drive us all inteh th' river."

The youth cried out savagely at this statement. He crouched behind a little tree, with his eyes burning hatefully and his teeth set in a curlike snarl. The awkward bandage was still about his head, and upon it, over his wound, there was a spot of dry blood. His hair was wondrously tousled, and some straggling, moving locks hung over the cloth of the bandage down toward his forehead. His jacket and shirt were open at the throat, and exposed his young bronzed neck. There could be seen spasmodic gulpings at his throat.

His fingers twined nervously about his rifle. He wished that it was an engine of annihilating power. He felt that he and his companions were being taunted and derided from sincere convictions that they were poor and puny. His knowledge of his inability to take vengeance for it made his rage into a dark and stormy specter, that possessed him and made him dream of abominable cruelties. The tormentors were flies sucking insolently at his blood, and he thought that he would have given his life for a revenge of seeing their faces in pitiful plights.

The winds of battle had swept all about the regiment, until the one rifle, instantly followed by others, flashed in its front. A moment later the regiment roared forth its sudden and valiant retort. A dense wall of smoke settled slowly down. It was furiously slit and slashed by the knifelike fire from the rifles.

To the youth the fighters resembled animals tossed for a death struggle into a dark pit. There was a sensation that he and his fellows, at bay, were pushing back, always pushing fierce onslaughts of creatures who were slippery. Their beams of crimson seemed to get no purchase upon the bodies of their foes; the latter seemed to evade them with ease, and come through, between, around, and about with unopposed skill.

When, in a dream, it occurred to the youth that his rifle was a impotent stick, he lost sense of everything but his hate, his desire to smash into the pulp the glittering smile of victory which he could feel upon the faces of his enemies.

The blue smoke-swallowed line curled and writhed like a snake stepped upon. It swung its ends to and fro in an agony of fear and rage.

The youth was not conscious that he was erect upon his feet. He did not know the direction of the ground. Indeed, once he even lost the habit of balance and fell heavily. He was up again immediately. One thought went through the chaos of his brain at the time. He wondered if he had fallen because he had been shot. But the suspicion flew away at once. He did not think more of it.

He had taken up a first position behind the little tree, with a direct determination to hold it against the world. He had not deemed it possible that his army could that day succeed, and from this he felt the ability to fight harder. But the throng had surged in all ways, until he lost directions and locations, save that he knew where lay the enemy.

The flames bit him, and the hot smoke broiled his skin. His rifle barrel grew so hot that ordinarily he could not have borne it upon his palms; but he kept on stuffing cartridges into it, and pounding them with his clanking, bending ramrod. If he aimed at some changing form through the smoke, he pulled his trigger with a fierce grunt, as if he were dealing a blow of the fist with all his strength.

When the enemy seemed falling back before him and his fellows, he went instantly forward, like a dog, who, seeing his foes lagging, turns and insists upon being pursued. And when he was compelled to retire again, he did it slowly, sullenly, taking steps of wrathful despair.

Once he, in his intent hate, was almost alone, and was firing, when all those near him had ceased. He was so engrossed in his occupation that he was not aware of a lull.

He was recalled by a hoarse laugh and a sentence that came to his ears in a voice of contempt and amazement. "Yeah infernal fool, don't yeh know enough t' quit when there ain't anything t' shoot at? Good Gawd!"

He turned then and, pausing with his rifle thrown half into position, looked at the blue line of his comrades. During this moment of leisure they seemed all to be engaged in staring with astonishment at him. They had become spectators. Turning to the front again he saw, under the lifted smoke, a deserted ground.

He looked bewildered for a moment. Then there appeared upon the glazed vacancy of his eyes a diamond point of intelligence. "Oh," he said, comprehending.

He returned to his comrades and threw himself upon the ground. He sprawled like a man who had been thrashed. His flesh seemed strangely on fire, and the sounds of the battle continued in his ears. He groped blindly for his canteen.

The lieutenant was crowing. He seemed drunk with fighting. He called out to the youth: "By heavens, if I had ten thousand wild cats like you I could tear th' stomach outa this war in less'n a week!" He puffed out his chest with large dignity as he said it.

Some of the men muttered and looked at the youth in awe-struck ways. It was plain that as he had gone on loading and firing and cursing without the proper intermission, they had found time to regard him. And they looked upon him as a war devil.

The friend came staggering to him. There was some fright and dismay in his voice. "Are yeh all right, Fleming? Do yeh feel all right? There ain't nothin' th' matter with yeh, Henry, is there?"

"No," said the youth with difficulty. His throat seemed full of knobs and burrs.

These incidents made the youth ponder. It was revealed to him that he had been a barbarian, a beast. He had fought like a pagan who defends his religion. Regarding it, he saw that it was fine, wild, and, in some ways, easy. He had been a tremendous figure, no doubt. By this struggle he had overcome obstacles which he had admitted to be mountains. They had fallen like paper peaks, and he was now what he called a hero. And he had not been aware of the process. He had slept and, awakening, found himself a knight.

On Courage

From Aristotle,
The Nicomachean Ethics

The same evils which terrify one person are not formidable to another; though there are some of such an irresistible nature, as to shake the firmest minds, and to inspire fear into all possessed of understanding. But those objects of terror which surpass not the strength of human nature, differing from each other in magnitude, as well as do the grounds of confidence, courage will discriminate between real and apparent dangers; and make us meet the former, as brave men ought, unshaken and dauntless, subjecting the instinctive emotions of fear to the dictates of reason and of honour. For we betray our weakness, not only when we fear things really not formidable, but when we are affected in an undue degree, or at an improper time, by objects of real danger. A brave man avoids such errors; and, estimating things by their real worth, prefers the grace and beauty of habitual fortitude to the delusive security of deformed cowardice. Yet he is not less careful to avoid that excess of intrepidity, which, being rarely met with, is like many other vices, without a name; though nothing but madness, or a most stupid insensibility, can make any man preserve, amidst earthquakes and inundations, that unshaken composure, which has been ascribed to the Celts. An overweening estimate of the causes of confidence, and a consequent excess of courage, is called audacity; a boastful species of bravery, and the mere ape of true manhood. What the brave man *is*, the rash and audacious man wishes to *appear;* he courts and provokes unnecessary dangers, but fails in the hour of trial; and is, for the most part, a blustering bully, who, under a semblance of pretended courage, conceals no inconsiderable portion of cowardice. But the complete and genuine coward easily betrays himself, by fearing either things not formidable, or things formidable, in an undue degree; and his failing is the more manifest, because it is accompanied with plain indications of pain; he lives in continual alarm, and is therefore spiritless and dejected; whereas courage warms our breasts, and animates our hopes. Such then is the character of true courage, as opposed to audacity on one hand, and cowardice on the other. It holds the middle place between those vicious extremes; it is calm and sedate; and though it never provokes danger, is always ready to meet even death in an honorable cause.

The Coward

From Theophrastus,
The Characters

Now, cowardice would seem to be a failure of spirit caused by fear. On shipboard the coward is the sort of man who mistakes a rocky headland for a pirate brig, and who asks if there are unbelievers aboard when a big wave hits the side. Or he will show up suddenly alongside the helmsman, trying to find out what the weather means or if they are halfway yet; and he explains to the nearest listener that his fright was caused by a dream. Since he expects the worst, he strips off his coat and hands it to a servant—or he pleads, "Get me safe to shore!"

Suppose, again, that he is on active duty. As the infantry advances into battle, he shouts for his friends from home to come over by him. He wants them to stop for a look round before they go farther, it's a job he says, to tell which is the enemy. And as soon as he starts hearing the shouts and seeing men drop, he explains to those on either side of him that all the excitement made him forget to take his sword. So back he runs to the tent, then he sends his orderly out on reconnaissance, hides the sword under a pillow, and takes his time pretending to hunt for it. Also, in case he looks out and sees a wounded man he knows being brought in, he runs to help carry him and tells him, "Keep your spirits up!" He will nurse the man, clean out his wound, sit by him to keep the flies off: anything to avoid going back and facing the enemy. What's more, when the call to battle stations sounds he stays right where he is. "Oh, go to hell with that damned bugling all the the time" is his response. "Won't you ever let the poor fellow get some sleep?" And with blood from the other man's wound all over him, he explains to troops coming back from the front, "Managed to save at least one of my boys, anyway," just as if he had risked his own neck. He makes the men from his part of town come in to see the patient, too, and he keeps on explaining to everybody, "Brought him here myself—carried him the whole way."

"Oh, to Die, to Die for Him!"

From Leo Tolstoy,
War and Peace

The Czar reviews his troops. Young Rostof is brought to a peak of martial and patriotic ecstasy as he imagines dying in battle for the splendid and kindly emperor.

Early in the morning, the soldiers, elegantly spruced and attired, began to move, falling into line in front of the fortress. Here thousands of legs and bayonets moved along with streaming banners, and at the command of their officers, halted or wheeled, or formed into detachments, passing by other similar bodies of infantry, in other uniforms.

There, with measured hoof beats and jingling of trappings came the cavalry gayly dressed in blue, red, and green embroidered uniforms with gayly-dressed musicians ahead, riding coal-black, chestnut, and gray horses.

Rostof standing in the front rank of Kutuzof's army, which the emperor first approached, shared the feeling experienced by every man in that army, a feeling of self-forgetfulness, a proud consciousness of invincibility and of passionate attachment to him on whose account all this solemn parade was prepared. He felt that only a single word from this man was needed for this mighty mass, including himself as an insignificant grain of sand, to dash through fire and water, to commit crime, to face death or perform the mightiest deeds of heroism, and therefore he could not help trembling, could not help his heart melting within him at the sight of this approaching Word.

"Hurrah! Hurrah! Hurrah!" was roared on all sides, and one regiment after another welcomed the sovereigns with the music of the general march, then renewed huzzas, the general march and huzzas on huzzas, which growing louder and louder, mingled in one overpowering deafening tumult.

Until the sovereign came quite close, every regiment in its silence and rigidity seemed like a lifeless body, but as soon as the sovereign came abreast of it, the regiment woke to life and broke out into acclamations which mingled with the roar extending down the whole line past which the sovereign rode. Amid the tremendous deafening tumult of these thousands of voices, through the midst of the armies, standing in their squares as motionless as though they had been carved out of granite, moved easily, carelessly, but symmetrically, and above all with freedom and grace, the hundreds of riders constituting the suites, and in front of all—two men, the emperors! Upon them, and upon them alone, were concentrated the suppressed but eager attention of all that mass of warriors.

The handsome young Emperor Alexander in his Horseguards' uniform and three-cornered hat worn point forward, with his pleasant face and clear but not loud voice, was the cynosure of all eyes.

Rostof stood not far from the buglers, and his keen glance recognized the emperor while he was still far off, and followed him as he drew near. When the Sovereign had approached to a distance of twenty paces, and Nikolai could clearly distinguish every feature of his handsome and radiant young face, he experienced a sense of affection and enthusiasm such as he had never before felt. Everything, every feature, every motion seemed to him bewitching in his sovereign.

Pausing in front of the Pavlograd regiment, the monarch said something in French to the Emperor of Austria and smiled.

Seeing this smile, Rostof himself involuntarily smiled also, and felt a still more powerful impulse of love toward his sovereign. He felt a burning desire to display this love in some way. He knew that this was impossible, and he felt like weeping.

The sovereign summoned the regimental commander and said a few words to him.

"My God! what would happen to me, if the sovereign were to address me!" thought Rostof. "I should die of happiness!"

The emperor also addressed the officers,—

"Gentlemen," said he, and Rostof listened as to a voice from heaven. How happy he would have been now if he only could die for his Tsar! "I thank you all from my heart! You have won the standards of St. George, prove yourselves worthy of them!"

"Oh, to die, to die for him!" thought Rostof.

After the sovereign had ridden past almost all the regiments, the troops began to move in front of him in the "ceremonial march," and Rostof, on his Bedouin, which he had recently bought from Denisof, rode at the end of his squadron, that is, alone, and in a most conspicuous position before his sovereign.

Just before he came up to where the emperor was, Rostof, who was an admirable horseman, plunged the spurs in Bedouin's flanks, and urged him into that mad, frenzied gallop which Bedouin always took when he was excited. Pressing his foaming mouth back to his breast, arching his tail, and seeming to fly through the air, and spurning the earth, gracefully tossing and interweaving his legs, Bedouin, also conscious the emperor's eyes were fastened on him, dashed gallantly by.

Rostof himself, keeping his feet back, and sitting straight in his saddle, feeling himself one with his horse, rode by his sovereign with disturbed but beatific face; "a very devil," as Denisof expressed it.

"Bravo!" exclaimed the emperor.

"My God! how happy I should be if he would only bid me to dash instantly into the fire!" thought Rostof.

When the review was ended, the officers who had just come from Russia and those of Kutuzof's division, began to gather in groups and talk about the rewards of the campaign, about the Austrians and their uniforms, about their line of battle, about Bonaparte, and what a desperate position he had got himself into now, especially if Essen's corps should join them, and Prussia should take their side.

But more than all else in each of these circles, the conversation was about the Emperor Alexander, and every word that he had spoken was repeated, and everything that he had done was praised, and all were enthusiastic over him.

All had but one single expectation: under the personal direction of the sovereign, to go with all speed against the enemy. Under the command of the emperor himself, it would be an impossibility not to win the victory over any one in the world: so thought Rostof and the majority of the officers.

After this review, all were more assured of victory than they would have been after the winning of two battles.

The Good War

From Studs Terkel,
The Good War

American World War II veterans recall their experiences in the European and Pacific campaigns.

ROBERT RASMUS

I've lived about thirty-eight years after the war and about twenty years before. For me it's B.W. and A.W.—before the war and after the war. I suspect there are lots of people like me. In business, there'll be times when I say, This really worries the heck out of me, but it's really minor compared to having to do a river crossing under fire. (Laughs.)

I get this strange feeling of living through a world drama. In September of '39 when the Germans invaded Poland, I was fourteen years old. I remember my mother saying, "Bob, you'll be in it." I was hoping she'd be right. At that age, you look forward to the glamour and have no idea of the horrors.

Sure enough, I was not only in the army but in the infantry. Step by logistic step, our division was in combat. You're finally down to one squad, out ahead of the whole thing. You're the point man. What am I doing out here—in this world-cataclysmic drama—out in front of the whole thing? (Laughs.)

You saw those things in the movies, you saw the newsreels. But you were of an age when your country wasn't even in the war. It seemed unreal. All of a sudden, there you were right in the thick of it and people were dying and you were scared out of your wits that you'd have your head blown off. (Laughs.)

I was acutely aware, being a rifleman, the odds were high that I would be killed. At one level, animal fear. I didn't like that at all. On the other hand, I had this great sense of adventure. My gosh, going across the ocean, seeing the armies, the excitement of it. I was there.

You have to understand the culture of our company. Most of

our privates were college types. They had been dumped en masse into these infantry divisions. The cadre of noncommissioned officers were old-timers. They were mostly uneducated country types, many of them from the South. There was a rather healthy mutual contempt between the noncoms and the privates. This sergeant was the most hated man. One of the nineteen-year-olds, during maneuvers, was at the point of tears in his hatred of this man who was so unreasonable and so miserable. He'd say, "If we ever get into combat, I'm gonna kill 'im. First thing I'll do." Who's the first one killed? This sergeant. I'm sure it was enemy fire. I would bet my life on it. I'm sure the guys who said they would kill him were horrified that their wish came true.

I'm sure our company was typical. We had x percent of self-inflicted wounds. There's no question that a guy would blow his toe off to get out of combat. People would get lost. These combat situations are so confused that it's very easy to go in the other direction. Say you get lost, get sick, get hurt. By the time you get back to your outfit, a couple of days have gone by.

We remember examples of Caspar Milquetoast: ordinary people showing incredible heroism. But you have to accept the fact that in a cross section of people—in civilian life, too—you've got cowards and quitters. Our radio man shot up his radio: he thought we were going to be captured. Panic. I became a bazooka man because our bazooka man threw his weapon away and I picked it up. He ran off.

Our captain said, "Pick up the bodies. We don't leave our dead to the enemy." We're now cut off and have to join the rest of our battalion. We had to improvise stretchers. I took off my field jacket and turned the arms inside out. We poked rifles through the arms and fashioned a stretcher. We got the sergeant on ours and, jeez half his head was blown off and the brains were coming out on my hands and on my uniform. Here's the mama's boy, Sunday school, and now I'm really in it.

I remember lying in that slit trench that night. It was a nightmare. I'd now seen what dead people look like, the color out of their face. I think each person in my squad went through this dream of mine. Daylight came and we moved out into another town. This is twenty-four hours of experience.

Those who really went through combat, the Normandy landings, the heavy stuff, might laugh at this little action we'd been in, but for me . . . We were passing people who were taking over from us, another company. We had one day of this. Our uniforms were now dirty and bloody and our faces looked like we'd been in there for weeks. Now *we* had the feeling: you poor innocents.

We weren't able to bring those bodies back with us. The mortar fire became too much. The next morning, our squad was assigned to go far back and recover the bodies. It was sunshine and quiet. We were passing the Germans we killed. Looking at the individual German dead, each took on a personality. These were no longer an abstraction. These were no longer the Germans of the brutish faces and the helmets we saw in the newsreels. They were exactly our age. These were boys like us.

Looking back on the war, in spite of the really bad times, it was certainly the most exciting experience of my life. As a character in *Terry and the Pirates* once put it so eloquently, "We shot the last act in the first reel." As I see it, at that young age, we hit the climax. Everything after that is anticlimactic.

E. B. (Sledgehammer) Sledge

There was nothing macho about the war at all. We were a bunch of scared kids who had to do a job. People tell me I don't act like an ex-Marine. How is an ex-Marine supposed to act? They have some Hollywood stereotype in mind. No, I don't look like John Wayne. We were in it to get it over with, so we could go back home and do what we wanted to do with our lives.

I was nineteen, a replacement in June of 1944. Eighty percent of the division in the Guadalcanal campaign was less than twenty-one years of age. We were much younger than the general army units.

To me, there were two different wars. There was the war of the guy on the front lines. You don't come off until you are wounded or killed. Or, if lucky, relieved. Then there was the support personnel. In the Pacific, for every rifleman on the front lines there were nineteen people in the back. Their view of the war was different than mine. The man up front puts his life on the line day after day after day to the point of utter hopelessness.

The only thing that kept you going was your faith in your buddies. It was just a case of friendship. I never heard of self-inflicted wounds out there. Fellows from other services said they saw this in Europe. Oh, there were plenty of times when I wished I had a million-dollar wound. (Laughs softly.) Like maybe shootin' a toe off. What was worse than death was the indignation of your buddies. You couldn't let 'em down. It was stronger than flag and country.

With the Japanese, the battle was all night long. Infiltratin' the lines, slippin' up and throwin' in grenades. Or runnin' in with a bayonet or saber. They were active all night. Your buddy would try to get a little catnap and you'd stay on watch. Then you'd switch off. It went on, day in and day out. A matter of simple survival. The only way you could get it over with was to kill them off before they killed you. The war I knew was totally savage.

The Japanese fought by a code they thought was right: *bushido.* The code of the warrior: no surrender. You don't really comprehend it until you get out there and fight people who are faced with an absolutely hopeless situation and will not give up. If you tried to help one of the Japanese, he'd usually detonate a grenade and kill himself as well as you. To be captured was a disgrace. To us, it was impossible, too, because we knew what happened in Bataan.

PETER BEZICH

People in America do not know what war is. I do, and anybody that was in the service. The Russians know. The Polish know. The Jewish know. But the American people have no idea what all-out war is. We never tasted it. I hope we never do.

My brother, he was the all-American kid, Jack Armstrong. He's being elevated in the military. He's a career man. They're checking out his background and all that bull, the FBI. They came to my dad, to his job, and they said somethin' about Russia and all that. This is just after the war, right? And they said, "What're you? Communists or somethin'? You know Russia's our enemy." The curtain and all that stuff. My dad says, "Hey, weren't they fightin' with us?" The government was sayin' they're our allies, and all of a sudden they turn it around and the Russians are no good.

They wanted to know about my brother. Did he have any leanings to the left? Did he do this? Did he do that? I said, "You couldn't find a more all-American kid than my brother." He was in the Battle of the Bulge, yeah.

Now we come to my two sons and Vietnam. I get mad about that patriotism. If your house is on fire, I'll help you put out the fire. If you argue with your wife, I'm not gonna get in between. It's like we had our revolution here. When they talk about reds and redniks, we did our fighting here. The American Revolution. Look what the French did there. We got sucked in by the French.

My war's over, right? Then they come up with Vietnam. My one son was gettin' outa school and he went to Vietnam for a year and a half. The other son refused to be drafted. It wasn't on religious principles, because we're not church people. He said killing was against his principles. Steve didn't burn no draft cards. He said, "I'll go to Vietnam and build hospitals." He was in construction, with me. They even interviewed the guys at work. Steve was the nicest kid you could know. He's a do-gooder. He donates one day a week to Shedd Aquarium for no pay. He's an all-American kid. It's a shame. It has ruined his life.

What he did took more guts than what I did. These big heroes grab him, put 'im in county jail. The kid never had a ticket in his life. It's like takin' a flower and cuttin' it and just throwin' it in a corner.

In Flanders Fields

Lieutenant-Colonel John McRae, M.D.

In Flanders fields the poppies blow
Between the crosses, row on row,
That mark our place; and in the sky
The larks, still bravely singing, fly
Scarce heard amid the guns below.

We are the Dead. Short days ago
We lived, felt dawn, saw sunset glow,
Loved and were loved, and now we lie,
In Flanders fields.

Take up our quarrel with the foe:
To you from failing hands we throw
The torch; be yours to hold it high.
If ye break faith with us who die
We shall not sleep, though poppies grow
In Flanders fields.

THE MAN OF INTEGRITY
AND HONOR

The Great-Souled Man

From Aristotle, The Nicomachean Ethics

Can a man be proud without being arrogant and overbearing? In modern times, we tend to think not. But the ancients believed that a justified pride in one's accomplishments was an important part of manly self-respect. Moreover, it could be the basis for good behavior toward others. For Aristotle, a man who possesses "greatness of soul" will not stoop to treat others unjustly or unkindly because it would reveal his need for others as objects of exploitation. He is generous and decent toward others precisely because he doesn't need anything from them. In the Ethics, *Aristotle tells us that pride is the crown of all the moral virtues, including courage, self-control and generosity. The proud man is the source of his own self-esteem, amply confirmed by the honor he receives from his fellow citizens.*

Magnanimity, or greatness of soul, as the name imports, is conversant about great things; what these are let us first consider; contemplating not the quality itself, but the person actuated by it, which will bring us to precisely the same conclusions. A magnanimous man is he, whose character being of great worth, is estimated by himself at its full value. He who forms a grossly false estimate of himself is a fool; and none of the virtues are consistent with folly: while the man who, conscious of his defects, appreciates his small merits by a fair and just standard, may be praised for his good sense and modesty, but cannot pass for magnanimous; which epithet always implies dignity and excellence; this beauty of the mind requiring, like that of the body, elevation and magnitude; for persons of a diminutive stature are not called beautiful, but neat and elegant. A mean-spirited man underrates his own merits; and the vainglorious boaster arrogates to himself merits, of which he is by no means possessed; but the more solid merit he possesses, his vainglory is the less; whereas mean-spiritedness is the greater in proportion to the excellence of the worth which is so improperly appreciated by its possessor; for how contemptible would he be, even to himself, were his real character of little or no value! The magnanimous man estimates himself at the highest rate, yet no higher than he ought; and conscious of his inward worth, thinks himself entitled to whatever is held most precious; to what the most exalted of men claim as the highest of all rewards and to what all men confer on the gods as their acknowledged due; in a word, to honor, the greatest and most invaluable of external goods.

True magnanimity then is a thing most difficult, since it implies the perfection of moral rectitude. It delights, moderately, in great honors bestowed by the deserving, as meeting with its due, or less: for with perfect virtue no honor can be fully commensurate. It accepts, however, such honors, because nothing better can be bestowed; but of vulgar honors, or from vulgar men, it is altogether disdainful; and is as insensible to their reproach, as careless of their applause. Wealth, power, good or bad fortune, it will meet and sustain with the same dignified composure, neither elated with prosperity nor dejected by adversity; for to a magnanimous man those things are desirable chiefly as the signs of honor; and, if he bears honor itself with moderation, much more must he thus bear those things which are only its signs, and desired merely on its account, since to him who thinks not too highly of honor, nothing besides can possibly appear great.

A man of magnanimity neither courts dangers, nor willingly encounters them on slight occasions. But when a worthy occasion requires it, he is unsparing of his life, thinking that to live is not, under all conditions, desirable. Magnanimity condemns trivial honors; and disdains, even in great things, to act a secondary role. It is slow in action, and averse to exertion, except when great honor may be obtained, or great actions are to be performed: not busied about many things, but confined to those which are great and splendid. A magnanimous man is as open in his hatred as in his friendship; for concealment is the part of fear; he regards truth more than opinion, and shows himself manifestly in his words and actions, declaring his mind with full freedom; which indicates both his own love of truth and his contempt for the opinions of others: but this openness of character is liable to one exception, for he is much given to *irony*, dissembling his merits before the vulgar, who are unworthy to appreciate them. He can show undue complaisance for no one's humors, except those of his friends; for flattery is a low and servile vice. He is not prone to admire, for he deems nothing great. He is not mindful of injuries, which his magnanimity teaches him to despise. He is no man's panegyrist or slanderer; he talks not of himself, nor does he blame others; not speaking ill even of his enemies, except when their insolence excites his indignation. As to things of small import, or even daily use, he is no petitioner or complainer: for that would show too much concern about them. His possessions are distinguished for their beauty and elegance rather than for their fruitfulness and utility; because the former qualities are more nearly allied to that independence and all-sufficiency to which he aspires. The gait of a magnanimous man is slow; his tone of voice grave, his pronunciation firm. Haste and rapidity betoken too much solicitude. *He* therefore is seldom in haste who deems few things worthy of his pursuit; nor is he often eager who thinks few things of importance: quickness and sharpness of voice proceed from earnestness and eagerness. Such then are the characteristics of magnanimity.

A Counterfeit Man

From William Shakespeare, As You Like It

Rosalind: Were it not better,
Because that I am more than common tall,
That I did suit me all points like a man?
A gallant curtle-axe upon my thigh,
A boar-spear in my hand; and, in my heart
Lie there what hidden woman's fear there will,
We'll have a swashing and a martial outside,
As many other mannish cowards have
That do outface it with their semblances.

Moral Courage

From Charles Dickens,
A Tale of Two Cities

Not all bravery is on the battlefield. In one of Dickens's best-known novels, Sidney Carton exchanges his life for another falsely convicted.

They said of him, about the city that night, that it was the peacefullest man's face ever beheld there. Many added that he looked sublime and prophetic.

One of the most remarkable sufferers by the same axe—a woman—had asked at the foot of the same scaffold, not long before, to be allowed to write down the thoughts that were inspiring her. If he had given an utterance to his, and they were prophetic, they would have been these:

"I see Barsad, and Cly, Defarge, the Vengeance, the Juryman, the Judge, long ranks of the new oppressors who have risen on the destruction of the old, perishing by this retributive instrument, before it shall cease out of its present use. I see a beautiful city and a brilliant people rising from this abyss, and, in their struggles to be truly free, in their triumphs and defeats, through long years to come, I see the evil of this time and of the previous time of which this is the natural birth, gradually making expiation for itself and wearing out.

"I see the lives for which I lay down my life, peaceful, useful, prosperous and happy, in that England which I shall see no more. I see Her with a child upon her bosom, who bears my name. I see her father, aged and bent, but otherwise restored, and faithful to all men in his healing office, and at peace. I see the good old man, so long their friend, in ten years' time enriching them with all he has, and passing tranquillity to his reward.

"I see that I hold a sanctuary in their hearts, and in the hearts of their descendants, generations hence. I see her, an old woman, weeping for me on the anniversary of this day. I see her and her husband, their course done, lying side by side in their last earthly bed, and I know that each was not more honored and held sacred in the other's soul, than I was in the souls of both.

"I see that child who lay upon her bosom and who bore my name, a man winning his way up in that path of life which once was mine. I see him winning it so well, that my name is made illustrious there by the light of his. I see the blots I threw upon it, faded away. I see him, foremost of just judges and honored men, bringing a boy of my name, with a forehead that I know and golden hair, to this place—then fair to look upon, with not a trace of this day's disfigurement—and I hear him tell the child my story, with a tender and a faltering voice.

"It is a far, far better thing that I do, than I have ever done; it is a far, far better rest that I go to than I have ever known."

Conquer Fortune
with Patience

From Leon Battista Alberti,
On the Duties and Education of Children

If a young man cultivates the virtues of courage, intelligence, and modesty, he will triumph over adversity by mastering his own inner impulses.

Be brave and courageous, for adversity is the proving ground of virtue. Is there any man who can gain as much praise and fame for his brave spirit, firm will, great intellect, zeal, and skill in favorable and peaceful circumstances, as he can in difficult times and adversity? So conquer Fortune, with patience. Overcome men's iniquity by persevering in virtue. Adapt yourselves to the times and to necessity with wisdom and prudence. Conform to the usages and customs of men of modesty, good breeding, and discretion. Above all, strive with all your intelligence, skill, zeal, and deeds first to be virtuous, then to appear so. Let nothing be dearer to you, do not desire anything before virtue. You shall first determine that wisdom and knowledge are to be preferred to everything else, and then you will see that the favors of Fortune are of little value. Only honor and fame will have first place in your desires, and you will never prefer wealth to praise. To gain honor and esteem, you will never think of avoiding any undertaking, no matter how arduous and strenuous, and you will persevere in it. You will be satisfied to expect from your labors nothing more than gratitude and renown. Do not doubt, however, that the virtuous will enjoy the fruits of their labors sooner or later.

The Generous Majesty of His Nature: Lawrence of Arabia

From Winston S. Churchill,
Great Contemporaries

Despite great changes in the ideals of manliness over the centuries, until roughly World War II, there is an impressive consistency in the way in which the higher kind of manliness is understood and extolled by European and American writers. Consider this brief, eloquent essay on T. E. Lawrence, "Lawrence of Arabia," by Winston Churchill. In form and content, Churchill's praise of Lawrence could almost have been written by Aristotle or Cicero, so closely and naturally does it adhere to the tradition of masculine refinement and honor that reaches back to antiquity. Lawrence, according to Churchill, embodied that same hierarchy of active and contemplative virtues we find stretching through the European tradition back to the ancients. He was a great general, statesman, and leader. But, even more admirable from Churchill's viewpoint, he was an outstanding scholar and author. Admirable as the life of active virtue may be, we are told once again, the life of the mind is even more to be admired. "An epic, a prodigy, a tale of torment, and in the heart of it—a Man."

I did not meet Lawrence till after the war was over. It was the spring of 1919, when the Peace-makers, or at any rate the Treaty-makers, were gathered in Paris and all England was in the ferment of the aftermath. So great had been the pressure in the War, so vast its scale, so dominating the great battles in France, that I had only been dimly conscious of the part played in Allenby's campaigns by the Arab revolt in the desert. But now someone said to me: "You ought to meet this wonderful young man. His exploits are an epic." So Lawrence came to luncheon. Usually at this time in London or Paris he wore his Arab dress in order to identify himself with the interests of the Emir Feisal and with the Arabian claims then under harsh debate. On this occasion, however, he wore plain clothes, and looked at first sight like one of the many clean-cut young officers who had gained high rank and distinction in the struggle.

I did not see Lawrence again for some weeks. It was, if my memory serves me right, in Paris. He wore his Arab robes, and the full magnificence of his countenance revealed itself. The gravity of his demeanor, the precision of his opinions; the range and quality of his conversation; all seemed enhanced to a remarkable degree by the splendid Arab head-dress and garb. From amid the flowing draperies his noble features, his perfectly chiseled lips and flashing eyes loaded with fire and comprehension shone forth. He looked what he was, one of Nature's greatest princes. We got on much better this time, and I began to form that impression of his strength and quality which since has never left me. Whether he wore the prosaic clothes of English daily life or afterward in the uniform of an Air Force mechanic, I always saw him henceforward as he appears in Augustus John's brilliant pencil sketch.

I began to hear much more about him from friends who had fought under his command, and indeed there was endless talk about him in every circle, military, diplomatic and academic. It appeared that he was a savant as well as a soldier: an archaeologist as well as a man of action: a brilliant scholar as well as an Arab partisan.

An important post was offered to Lawrence, and to the surprise of most people, though not altogether to mine, he accepted at once.

Lawrence's term as a Civil Servant was a unique phase in his life. Everyone was astonished by his calm and tactful demeanor. His patience and readiness to work with others amazed those who knew him best. Tremendous confabulations must have taken place among these experts, and tension at times must have been extreme. But so far as I was concerned, I received always united advice from two or three of the very best men it has ever been my fortune to work with. It would not be just to assign the whole credit for the great success which the new policy secured to Lawrence alone. The wonder was that he was able to sink his personality, to bend his imperious will and pool his knowledge in the common stock. Here is one of the proofs of the greatness of his character and the versatility of his genius. He saw the hope of redeeming in a large measure the promises he had made to the Arab chiefs and of reestablishing a tolerable measure of peace in those wide regions. In that cause he was capable of becoming—I hazard the word—a humdrum official. The effort was not in vain. His purposes prevailed.

The next episode was the writing, the printing, the binding and the publication of his book, *Seven Pillars of Wisdom*. This is perhaps the point at which to deal with this treasure of English literature. As a narrative of war and adventure, as a portrayal of all that the Arabs mean to the world, it is unsurpassed. It ranks with the greatest books ever written in the English language. If Lawrence had never done anything except write this book as a mere work of the imagination his fame would last—to quote Macaulay's hackneyed phrase—"as long as the English language is spoken in any quarter of the globe." *The Pilgrim's Progress, Robinson Crusoe, Gulliver's Travels* are dear to British homes. Here is a tale originally their equal in interest and charm. But it is fact, not fiction. The author was also the commander. Caesar's *Commentaries* deal with larger numbers, but in Lawrence's story nothing that has ever happened in the sphere of war and empire is lacking. When most of the vast literature of the Great War has been sifted and superseded by the epitomes, commentaries and histories of future generations, when the complicated and infinitely costly operations of its ponderous armies are the concern only of the military student, when our struggles are viewed in a fading perspective and a truer proportion, Lawrence's tale of the revolt in the desert will gleam with immortal fire.

We read of grim camel-rides through sun-scorched, blasted lands, where the extreme desolation of nature appalls the traveler. With a motor-car or airplane we may now inspect these forbidding solitudes, their endless sands, the hot savage wind-whipped rocks, the mountain gorges of a red-hot moon. Through these with infinite privation men on camels with shattering toil carried dynamite to destroy railway bridges and win the war, and, as we then hoped, free the world.

Here we see Lawrence the soldier. Not only the soldier but the statesman: rousing the fierce peoples of the desert, penetrating the mysteries of their thought, leading them to the selected points of action and as often as not firing the mine himself. Detailed accounts are given of ferocious battles with thousands of men and little quarter fought under his command on these lava landscapes of hell. There are no mass-effects. All is intense, individual, sentient—and yet cast in conditions which seemed to forbid human existence. Through all, one mind, one soul, one willpower. An epic, a prodigy, a tale of torment, and in the heart of it—a Man.

The impression of the personality of Lawrence remains living and vivid upon the minds of his friends, and the sense of his loss is in no way dimmed among his countrymen. All feel the poorer that he has gone from us. In these days dangers and difficulties gather upon Britain and her Empire, and we are also conscious of a lack of outstanding figures with which to overcome them. Here was a man in whom there existed not only an immense capacity for service, but that touch of genius which everyone recognizes and no one can define. Alike in his great period of adventure and command or in these later years of self-suppression and self-imposed eclipse, he always reigned over those with whom he came in contact. They felt themselves in the presence of an extraordinary being. They felt that his latent reserves of force and willpower were beyond measurement. If he roused himself to action, who should say what crisis he could not surmount or quell? If things were going very badly, how glad one would be to see him come round the corner.

Part of the secret of this stimulating ascendancy lay of course in his disdain for most of the prizes, the pleasures and comforts of life. The world naturally looks with some awe upon a man who appears unconcernedly indifferent to home, money, comfort, rank, or even power and fame. The world feels, not without a certain apprehension, that here is someone outside its jurisdiction; someone before whom its allurements may be spread in vain; someone strangely enfranchised, untamed, untrammeled by convention, moving independently of the ordinary currents of human action; a being readily capable of violent revolt or supreme sacrifice, a man solitary, austere to whom existence is no more than a duty, yet a duty to be faithfully discharged. He was indeed a dweller upon the mountain tops where the air is cold, crisp and rarefied, and where the view on clear days commands all the Kingdoms of the world and the glory of them.

Lawrence was one of those beings whose pace of life was faster and more intense than the ordinary. Just as an airplane only flies by its speed and pressure against the air, so he flew best and easiest in the hurricane. He was not in complete harmony with the normal. The fury of the Great War raised the pitch of life to the Lawrence standard. The multitudes were swept forward till their pace was the same as his. In this heroic period he found himself in perfect relation both to men and events.

Lawrence has a full measure of the versatility of genius. He held one of those master keys which unlock the doors of many kinds of treasure-houses. He was a savant as well as a soldier. He was an archaeologist as well as a man of action. He was an accomplished scholar as well as an Arab partisan. He was a mechanic as well as a philosopher. His background of somber experience and reflection only seemed to set forth more brightly the charm and gaiety of his companionship, and the generous majesty of his nature.

Toussaint L'Ouverture: Soldier, Statesman, Martyr

From Wendell Phillips, Select Orations

A tribute to the leader of the Haitian independence movement, Toussaint L'Ouverture (1743–1803), by the American abolitionist crusader Wendell Phillips (1811–1844).

If I stood here to tell you the story of Napoleon, I should take it from the lips of Frenchmen, who find no language rich enough to paint the great captain of the nineteenth century. Were I to tell you the story of Washington, I should take it from your hearts—you, who think no marble white enough on which to carve the name of the Father of his country. But I am to tell you the story of a negro who has left hardly one written line. You remember Macaulay says, comparing Cromwell with Napoleon, that Cromwell showed the greater military genius, if we consider that he never saw an army until he was forty; while Napoleon was educated from a boy in the best military schools in Europe. Cromwell manufactured his own army; Napoleon at the age of twenty-seven was placed at the head of the best Europe ever saw. They were both successful; but, says Macaulay, with such disadvantages, the Englishmen showed the greater genius. Whether you allow the inference or not, you will at least grant that it is a fair mode of measurement. Apply it to this negro. Cromwell never saw an army till he was forty; this man never saw a soldier till he was fifty. Cromwell manufactured his own army—out of what? Englishmen—the best blood in Europe. Out of the middle class of Englishmen—the best blood of the island. And with it he conquered what? Englishmen—their equals. This man manufactured his army out of what? Out of what you call the despicable race of negroes, debased, demoralized by two hundred years of slavery, one hundred thousand of them imported into the island within four years, unable to speak a dialect intelligible even to each other. Yet out of this mixed, and as you say, despicable mass he forged a thunderbolt and hurled it at what? At the proudest blood in Europe, the Spaniard, and sent him home conquered; at the most warlike blood in Europe, the French, and put them under his feet, at the pluckiest blood in Europe, the English, and they skulked home to Jamaica.

I would call him Napoleon, but Napoleon made his way to empire over broken oaths and through a sea of blood. This man never broke his word. I would call him Cromwell, but Cromwell was only a soldier, and the state he founded went down with him into his grave. I would call him Washington, but the great Virginian held slaves. This man risked his empire rather than permit the slave-trade in the humblest village of his dominions.

You think me a fanatic, for you read history, not with your eyes but with your prejudices. But fifty years hence, when Truth gets a hearing, the Muse of history will put Phocion for the Greek, Brutus for the Roman, Hampden for England, Fayette for France, choose Washington as the bright consummate flower of our earlier civilization, then, dipping her pen in the sunlight, will write in the clear blue, above them all, the name of the soldier, the statesman, the martyr, Toussaint L'Ouverture.

If

Rudyard Kipling

If you can keep your head when all about you
Are losing theirs and blaming it on you;
If you can trust yourself when all men doubt you,
But make allowance for their doubting too;
If you can wait and not be tired by waiting,
Or, being lied about, don't deal in lies,
Or, being hated, don't give way to hating,
And yet don't look too good, nor talk too wise;

If you can dream—and not make dreams your master;
If you can think—and not make thoughts your aim;

If you can meet with triumph and disaster
And treat those two imposters just the same;
If you can bear to hear the truth you've spoken
Twisted by knaves to make a trap for fools,
Or watch the things you gave your life to broken,
And stoop and build 'em up with wornout tools;

If you can make one heap of all your winnings
And risk it on one turn of pitch-and-toss,
And lose, and start again at your beginnings
And never breathe a word about your loss;
If you can force your heart and nerve and sinew
To serve your turn long after they are gone,
And so hold on when there is nothing in you
Except the Will which says to them: "Hold on";

If you can talk with crowds and keep your virtue,
Or walk with kings—nor lose the common touch;
If neither foes nor loving friends can hurt you;
If all men count with you, but none too much;
If you can fill the unforgiving minute
With sixty seconds' worth of distance run—
Yours is the Earth and everything that's in it,
And—which is more—you'll be a Man my son!

The Happy Warrior

William Wordsworth

Who is the happy Warrior? Who is he
That every man in arms should wish to be?
—It is the generous Spirit, who, when brought
Among the tasks of real life, hath wrought
Upon the plan that pleased his boyish thought:
Whose high endeavors are an inward light
That makes the path before him always bright:
Who, with a natural instinct to discern

What knowledge can perform, is diligent to learn;
Abides by this resolve, and stops not there,
But makes his moral being his prime care;
Who, doomed to go in company with Pain,
And Fear, and Bloodshed, miserable train!
Turns his necessity to glorious gain;
In face of these doth exercise a power
Which is our human nature's highest dower;
Controls them and subdues, transmutes, bereaves
Of their bad influence, and their good receives:
By objects, which might force the soul to abate
Her feeling, rendered more compassionate;
Is placable—because occasions rise
So often that demand such sacrifice;
More skillful in self-knowledge, even more pure,
As tempted more; more able to endure,
As more exposed to suffering and distress;
Thence also, more alive to tenderness.
—'Tis he whose law is reason; who depends
Upon that law as on the best of friends;
Whence, in a state where men are tempted still
To evil for a guard against worse ill,
And what in quality or act is best
Doth seldom on a right foundation rest,
He labors good on good to fix, and owes
To virtue every triumph that he knows:
—Who, if he rise to station of command,
Rises by open means; and there will stand
On honorable terms, or else retire
And in himself possess his own desire;
Who comprehends his trust, and to the same
Keeps faithful with a singleness of aim;
And therefore does not stoop, nor lie in wait
For wealth, or honors, or for worldly state;
Whom they must follow; on whose head must fall,
Like showers of manna, if they come at all:
Whose powers shed round him in the common strife,
Or mild concerns of ordinary life,
A constant influence, a peculiar grace;
But who, if he be called upon to face
Some awful moment to which Heaven has joined
Great issues, good or bad for human kind,

Is happy as a Lover; and attired
With sudden brightness, like a Man inspired;
And, through the heat of conflict, keeps the law
In calmness made, and sees what he foresaw;
Or if an unexpected call succeed,
Come when it will, is equal to the need:
—He who, though thus endued as with a sense
And faculty for storm and turbulence,
Is yet a Soul whose master-bias leans
To homefelt pleasures and to gentle scenes;
Sweet images! which, wheresoe'er he be,
Are at his heart; and such fidelity
It is his darling passion to approve;
More brave for this, that he hath much to love:—
'Tis, finally, the Man who lifted high,
Conspicuous object in a Nation's eye,
Or left unthought-of in obscurity,—
Who, with a toward or untoward lot,
Prosperous or adverse, to his wish or not—
Plays, in the many games of life, that one
Where what the most doth value must be won:
Whom neither shape of danger can dismay
Nor thought of tender happiness betray;
Who, not content that former worth stand fast,
Looks forward, persevering to the last,
From well to better, daily self-surpast:
Who, whether praise of him must walk the earth
Forever, and to noble deeds give birth,
Or he must fall, to sleep without his fame,
And leave a dead unprofitable name—
Finds comfort in himself and his cause;
And, while the mortal mist is gathering, draws
His breath in confidence of Heaven's applause:
This is the happy Warrior; this is He
That every Man in arms should wish to be.

The Value of Adversity
to a Great Man

From Seneca, On Providence

Lucius Annaeus Seneca (5 B.C.–65 A.D.) was a Roman author of philosophical and literary works.

Success comes to the common man, and even to the commonplace ability; but to triumph over the calamities and terrors of mortal life is the part of a great man only. Truly, to be always happy and to pass through life without a mental pang is to be ignorant of one half of nature. You are a great man; but how do I know it if Fortune gives you no opportunity of showing your worth?

True worth is eager for danger and thinks rather of its goal than of what it may have to suffer, since even what it will have to suffer is a part of its glory. Warriors glory in their wounds and rejoice to display the blood spilled with luckier fortune. Those who return from the battle unhurt may have fought as well, but the man who returns with a wound wins the greater regard. God, I say, is showing favor to those whom he desires to achieve the highest possible virtue whenever he gives them the means of doing a courageous and brave deed, and to this end they must encounter some difficulty in life. You learn to know a pilot in a storm, a soldier in the battle-line. How can I know with what spirit you will face poverty, if you wallow in wealth? How can I know with what firmness you will face disgrace, ill fame, and public hatred, if you attain to old age amidst rounds of applause—if a popularity attends you that is irresistible, and flows to you from a certain leaning of men's minds? How do I know with what equanimity you would bear the loss of children, if you see around you all that you have fathered? I have heard you offering consolation to others. If you had been offering it to yourself, if you had been telling yourself not to grieve, then I might have seen your true character. Do not, I beg of you, shrink in fear from those things which the immortal gods apply like spurs, as it were, to our souls. Disaster is Virtue's opportunity. Justly may those be termed unhappy who are dulled by an excess of good fortune, who rest, as it were, in dead calm upon a quiet sea;

whatever happens will come to them as a change. Cruel fortune bears hardest upon the inexperienced; to the tender neck the yoke is heavy. The raw recruit turns pale at the thought of a wound, but the veteran looks undaunted upon his own gore, knowing that blood has often been the price of his victory. In like manner God hardens, reviews, and disciplines those whom he approves, whom he loves.

No proof of virtue is ever mild. If we are lashed and torn by Fortune, let us bear it; it is not cruelty but a struggle, and the oftener we engage in it, the stronger we shall be. The staunchest member of the body is the one that is kept in constant use. We should offer ourselves to Fortune in order that, struggling with her, we may be hardened by her. Gradually she will make us a match for herself.

Triumphing over Adversity

From Frederick Douglass,
Narrative of the Life of Frederick Douglass

Despite the horrors of his life as a slave in the American South, Frederick Douglass (1818–1895) educates himself. Resisting an oppressive overseer gives the young man a sense of manhood and a resolve to be free.

I lived in Master Hugh's family about seven years. During this time, I succeeded in learning to read and write. In accomplishing this, I was compelled to resort to various stratagems. I had no regular teacher. My mistress, who had kindly commenced to instruct me, had, in compliance with the advice and direction of her husband, not only ceased to instruct, but had set her face against my being instructed by anyone else. It is due, however, to my mistress to say of her, that she did not adopt this course of treatment immediately. She at first lacked the depravity indispensable to shutting me up in mental darkness. It was at least necessary for her to have some training in the exercise of irresponsible power, to make her equal to the task of treating me as though I were a brute.

My mistress was, as I have said, a kind and tender-hearted woman; and in the simplicity of her soul she commenced, when I first went to live with her, to treat me as she supposed one human being ought to treat another. In entering upon the duties of a slave-

holder, she did not seem to perceive that I sustained to her the relation of a mere chattel, and that for her to treat me as a human
being was not only wrong, but dangerously so. Slavery proved as
injurious to her as it did to me. When I went there, she was a pious,
warm, and tender-hearted woman. There was no sorrow or suffering for which she had not a tear. She had bread for the hungry,
clothes for the naked, and comfort for every mourner that came
within her reach. Slavery soon proved its ability to divest her of
these heavenly qualities. Under its influence, the tender heart
became stone, and the lamblike disposition gave way to one of
tigerlike fierceness. The first step in her downward course was in
her ceasing to instruct me. She now commenced to practice her
husband's precepts. She finally became even more violent in her
opposition than her husband himself. She was not satisfied with
simply doing as well as he had commanded; she seemed anxious to
do better. Nothing seemed to make her more angry than to see me
with a newspaper. She seemed to think that here lay the danger. I
have had her rush at me with a face made all up of fury, and snatch
from me a newspaper, in a manner that fully revealed her apprehension. She was an apt woman; and a little experience soon
demonstrated, to her satisfaction, that education and slavery were
incompatible with each other.

From this time I was most narrowly watched. If I was in a separate room any considerable length of time, I was sure to be suspected of having a book, and was at once called to give an account
of myself. All this, however, was too late. The first step had been
taken. Mistress, in teaching me the alphabet, had given me the
inch, and no precaution could prevent me from taking the *ell.*

The plan which I adopted, and the one by which I was most
successful, was that of making friends of all the little white boys
whom I met in the street. As many of these as I could, I converted
into teachers. With their kindly aid, obtained at different times and
in different places, I finally succeeded in learning to read.

Master Thomas ridiculed the idea that there was any danger of
Mr. Covey's killing me, and said that he knew Mr. Covey; that he was
a good man, and that he could not think of taking me from him;
that should he do so, he would lose the whole year's wages; that I
belonged to Mr. Covey for one year, and that I must go back to him,
come what might; and that I must not trouble him with any more
stories, or that he would himself *get hold of me,* which meant that he

would whip me. I remained all night, and, according to his orders,
I started off to Covey's about nine o'clock; and just as I was getting
over the fence that divided Mrs. Kemp's fields from ours, out ran
Covey with his cowskin, to give me another whipping. Before he
could reach me, I succeeded in getting to the cornfield; and as the
corn was very high, it afforded me the means of hiding. He seemed
very angry, and searched for me a long time. My behavior was altogether unaccountable. He finally gave up the chase, thinking, I
suppose, that I must come home for something to eat; he would
give himself no further trouble in looking for me. I spent that day
mostly in the woods, having the alternative before me—to go home
and be whipped to death, or stay in the woods and be starved to
death. That night, I fell in with Sandy Jenkins, a slave with whom I
was somewhat acquainted. Sandy had a free wife who lived about
four miles from Mr. Covey's; and it being Saturday, he was on his
way to see her. I told him my circumstances, and he very kindly
invited me to go home with him. I went home with him, and talked
this whole matter over, and got his advice as to what course it was
best for me to pursue. I found Sandy an old advisor. He told me,
with solemnity, I must go back to Covey; but that before I went, I
must go with him into another part of the woods, where there was a
certain *root*, which if I would take some of it with me, carrying it
always on my right side, would render it impossible for Mr. Covey, or
any other white man, to whip me. He said he had carried it for
years, and since he had done so, he had never received a blow, and
never expected to while he carried it. I at first rejected the idea,
that the simple carrying of a root in my pocket would have any such
effect as he had said, and was not disposed to take it; but Sandy
impressed the necessity with much earnestness, telling me it could
do no harm, if it did no good. To please him, I at length took the
root, and, according to his direction, carried it upon my right side.
This was Sunday morning. I immediately started for home; and
upon entering the yard gate, out came Mr. Covey on his way to
meeting. He spoke to me very kindly, bade me drive the pigs from
a lot near by, and passed on toward the church. Now, this singular
conduct of Mr. Covey really made me begin to think that there was
something in the *root* which Sandy had given me; and had it been
on any other day than Sunday, I could have attributed the conduct
to no other cause than the influence of that root; and as it was, I
was half inclined to think the *root* to be something more than I at
first had taken it to be. All went well till Monday morning. On this
morning, the virtue of the *root* was fully tested. Long before day-

light, I was called to go and rub, curry, and feed the horses. I obeyed, and was glad to obey. But whilst thus engaged, whilst in the act of throwing down some blades from the loft, Mr. Covey entered the stable with a long rope; and just as I was half out of the loft, he caught hold of my legs, and was about tying me. As soon as I found what he was up to, I gave a sudden spring, and as I did so, he holding to my legs, I was brought sprawling on the stable floor. Mr. Covey seemed now to think he had me, and could do what he pleased; but at this moment—from whence came the spirit I don't know—I resolved to fight; and, suiting my action to the resolution, I seized Covey hard by the throat; and as I did so, I rose. He held on to me, and I to him. My resistance was so entirely unexpected, that Covey seemed taken all aback. He trembled like a leaf. This gave me assurance, and I held him uneasy, causing the blood to run where I touched him with the ends of my fingers. Mr. Covey soon called out to Hughes for help. Hughes came, and while Covey held me, attempted to tie my right hand. While he was in the act of doing so, I watched my chance, and gave him a heavy kick close under the ribs. This kick fairly sickened Hughes, so that he left me in the hands of Mr. Covey. This kick had the effect of not only weakening Hughes, but Covey also. When he saw Hughes bending over with pain, his courage quailed. He asked me if I meant to persist in my resistance. I told him I did, come what might, that he had used me like a brute for six months, and that I was determined to be used so no longer. With that, he strove to drag me to a stick that was lying just out of the stable door. He meant to knock me down. But just as he was leaning over to get the stick, I seized him with both hands by his collar, and brought him by a sudden snatch to the ground. By this time, Bill came. Covey called upon him for assistance. Bill wanted to know what he could do. Covey said, "Take hold of him, take hold of him!" Bill said his master hired him out to work, and not to help to whip me; so he left Covey and myself to fight our own battle out. We were at it for nearly two hours. Covey at length let me go, puffing and blowing at a great rate, saying that if I had not resisted, he would not have whipped me half so much. The truth was, that he had not whipped me at all. I considered him as getting entirely the worst end of the bargain; for he had drawn no blood from me, but I had from him. The whole six months afterwards, that I spent with Mr. Covey, he never laid the weight of his finger upon me in anger. He would occasionally say, he didn't want to get hold of me again. "No," thought I, "you need not; for you will come off worse than you did before."

This battle with Mr. Covey was the turning-point in my career as a slave. It rekindled the few expiring embers of freedom, and revived within me a sense of my own manhood. It recalled the departed self-confidence, and inspired me again with a determination to be free. The gratification afforded by the triumph was a full compensation for whatever else might follow, even death itself. He only can understand the deep satisfaction which I experienced, who has himself repelled by force the bloody arm of slavery. I felt as I never felt before. It was a glorious resurrection, from the tomb of slavery, to the heaven of freedom. My long-crushed spirit rose, cowardice departed, bold defiance took its place; and I now resolved that, however long I might remain a slave in form, the day had passed forever when I could be a slave in fact. I did not hesitate to let it be known of me, that the white man who expected to succeed in whipping must also succeed in killing me.

What Is a Man?

From William Shakespeare,
Hamlet

Can too much thinking undermine a man's resolve?

How all occasions do inform against me
And spur my dull revenge. What is a man,
If his chief good and market of his time
Be but to sleep and feed? A beast, no more.
Sure he that made us with such large discourse,
Looking before and after, gave us not
That capability and godlike reason
To fust in us unused. Now, whether it be
Bestial oblivion, or some craven scruple
Of thinking too precisely on th' event—
A thought which, quartered, hath but one part wisdom
And ever three parts coward—I do not know
Why yet I live to say, "This thing's to do,"
Sith I have cause, and will, and strength, and means
To do't. Examples gross as earth exhort me.

Witness this army of such mass and charge,
Led by a delicate and tender prince,
Whose spirit, with divine ambition puffed,
Makes mouths at the invisible event,
Exposing what is mortal and unsure
To all that fortune, death, and danger dare,
Even for an eggshell. Rightly to be great
Is not to stir without great argument,
But greatly to find quarrel in a straw
When honor's at the stake. How stand I then,
That have a father killed, a mother stained,
Excitements of my reason and my blood,
And let all sleep, while to my shame I see
The imminent death of twenty thousand men
That for a fantasy and trick of fame
Go to their graves like beds, fight for a plot
Whereon the numbers cannot try the cause,
Which is not tomb enough and continent
To hide the slain? O, from this time forth,
My thoughts be bloody, or be nothing worth!

There Was a Time When Our Forefathers Owned This Great Island

Red Jacket,
On the Religion of the White Man and the Red

A leader defends the nobility and integrity of his people. In 1805, the Native American leader Red Jacket spoke to a council of the Six Nations after a Christian missionary had proposed that he work among them.

Friend and Brother: It was the will of the Great Spirit that we should meet together this day. He orders all things; and has given us a fine day for our council. He has taken his garment from before the sun, and caused it to shine with brightness upon us. Our eyes are opened that we see clearly, our ears are unstopped that we have been able to hear distinctly the words you have spoken. For all these favors we thank the Great Spirit, and Him only.

Brother, listen to what we say. There was a time when our forefathers owned this great island. Their seats extended from the rising to the setting sun. The Great Spirit had made it for the use of Indians. He had created the buffalo, the deer, and other animals for food. He had made the bear and the beaver. Their skins served us for clothing. He had scattered them over the country and taught us how to take them. He had caused the earth to produce corn for bread. All this He had done for His red children because He loved them. If we had some disputes about our hunting-ground, they were generally settled without the shedding of much blood.

But an evil day came upon us. Your forefathers crossed the great water and landed on this island. Their numbers were small. They found friends and not enemies. They told us they had fled from their own country for fear of wicked men and had come here to enjoy their religion. They asked for a small seat. We took pity on them, granted their request, and they sat down among us. We gave them corn and meat; they gave us poison in return.

The white people, brother, had now found our country. Tidings were carried back, and more came among us. Yet we did not fear them. We took them to be friends. They called us brothers. We believed them and gave them a larger seat. At length their numbers had greatly increased. They wanted more land; they wanted our country. Our eyes were opened, and our minds became uneasy. Wars took place. Indians were hired to fight against Indians, and many of our people were destroyed. They also brought strong liquor among us. It was strong and powerful, and has slain thousands.

Brother, our seats were once large and yours were small. You have now become a great people, and we have scarcely a place left to spread our blankets. You have got our country, but are not satisfied; you want to force your religion upon us.

Brother, you say there is but one way to worship and serve the Great Spirit. If there is but one religion, why do you white people differ so much about it? Why not all agree, as you can all read the book?

Brother, we do not understand these things: we are told that your religion was given to your forefathers, and has been handed down from father to son. We also have a religion which was given to *our* forefathers, and has been handed down to us: it teaches us *to be thankful for all favors received, to love each other, and to be united: we never quarrel about religion.*

Brother, we do not want to destroy your religion, or take it from you. We only want to enjoy our own.

My Forefathers Were Warriors

Tecumseh to Governor Harrison, 1810

The great Shawnee chief Tecumseh (1768–1813) tried to organize a tribal confederacy to check the relentless westward advance of the white settlers.

It is true I am a Shawnee. My forefathers were warriors. Their son is a warrior. From them I take only my existence; from my tribe I take nothing. I am the maker of my own fortune; and oh! that I could make that of my red people, and of my country, as great as the conceptions of my mind, when I think of the Spirit that rules the universe. I would not then come to Governor Harrison to ask him to tear the treaty and to obliterate the landmark; but I would say to him, "Sir, you have liberty to return to your own country."

The being within, communing with past ages, tells me that once, nor until lately there was no white man on this continent; that it then all belonged to red men, children of the same parents, placed on it by the Great Spirit that made them, to keep it, to traverse it, to enjoy its productions, and to fill it with the same race, once a happy race, since made miserable by the white people, who are never contented but always encroaching. The way, and the only way, to check and to stop this evil, is for all the red men to unite in claiming a common and equal right in the land, as it was at first, and should be yet; for it never was divided, but belongs to all for the use of each. For no part has a right to sell, even to each other, much less to strangers—those who want all, and will not do with less.

The white people have no right to take the land from the Indians, because they had it first; it is theirs. They may sell, but all must join. Any sale not made by all is not valid. The late sale is bad. It was made by a part only. Part do not know how to sell. It requires all to make a bargain for all. All red men have equal rights to the unoccupied land. The right of occupancy is as good in one place as in another. There cannot be two occupations in the same place. The first excludes all others. It is not so in hunting or traveling; for there the same ground will serve many, as they may follow each other all day; but the camp is stationary, and that is occupancy. It belongs to the first who sits down on his blanket or skins which he has thrown upon the ground; and till he leaves it, no other has a right.

The Hero Deepened

From Homer, The Iliad

Achilles kills Hektor and is still so furious that he refuses to return the fallen Trojan's body for a decent burial. Instead, he violates Hektor's body by dragging it around the walls of Troy behind his chariot. Achilles's mother warns him that the gods are angry at his disrespect for such a worthy adversary. The gods admire manly pride, but demand that worthy men honor one another even in enmity; Achilles is exercising a vengeance proper only to the gods themselves.

In his weakness Hektor of the shining helm spoke to him:
"I entreat you, by your wife, by your knees, by your parents, do not let the dogs feed on me by the ships of the Achaians, but take yourself the bronze and gold that are there in abundance, those gifts that my father and the lady my mother will give you, and give my body to be taken home again, so that the Trojans and the wives of the Trojans may give me in death my rite of burning."
But looking darkly at him swift-footed Achilleus answered:
"No more entreating of me, you dog, by knees or parents, I wish only that my spirit and fury would drive me to hack your meat away and eat it raw for the things that you have done to me. So there is no one who can hold the dogs off from your head, not if they bring here and set before me ten times and twenty times the ransom, and promise more in addition, not if Priam son of Dardanos should offer to weigh out your bulk in gold; not even so shall the lady your mother who herself bore you lay you on the death-

bed and mourn you: no, but the dogs and the birds will have you all for their feasting."

Then dying, Hektor of the shining helmet spoke to him:

"I know you well as I look upon you, I know that I could not persuade you, since indeed in your breast is a heart of iron. Be careful now; for I might be made into the gods' curse upon you, on that day when Paris and Phoibos Apollo destroy you in the Skaian gates, for all your valor."

He spoke, and as he spoke the end of death closed in upon him, and the soul fluttering free of the limbs went down into Death's house mourning her destiny, leaving youth and manhood behind her. Now though he was a dead man brilliant Achilleus spoke to him:

"Die: and I will take my own death at whatever time Zeus and the rest of the immortals choose to accomplish."

His honored mother came close to him and sat down beside him, and stroked him with her hand and called him by name and spoke to him:

"My child, how long will you go on eating your heart out in sorrow and lamentation, and remember neither your food nor going to bed? It is a good thing even to lie with a woman in love. For you will not be with me for long, but already death and power-ful destiny stand closely above you. But listen hard to me, for I come from Zeus with a message. He says that the gods frown upon you, that beyond all other immortals he himself is angered that in your heart's madness you hold Hektor beside the curved ships and did not redeem him. Come, then, give him up and accept ransom for the body."

Priam, the King of Troy, comes to the Greek camp to beg for his son's body to be returned. As the old man clings like a supplicant to the young man's knees, Achilles's heart melts as he thinks of his own father far away. Hektor gets his burial rites. At the end of the poem, Achilles is deepened and humanized by his ability to enter into the suffering of someone besides himself. Mourning tran-scends the divisions of war, and Achilles is a full man at last.

Tall Priam came in unseen by the other men and stood close beside him and caught the knees of Achilleus in his arms, and kissed the hands that were dangerous and manslaughtering and had killed so many of his sons. As when dense disaster closes on one who has murdered a man in his own land, and he comes to the country of others, to a man of substance, and wonder seizes on those who behold him, so Achilleus wondered as he looked on Priam, a godlike man, and the rest of them wondered also, and looked at each other. But now Priam spoke to him in the words of a suppliant:

"Achilleus like the gods, remember your father, one who is of years like mine, and on the door-sill of sorrowful old age. And they who dwell nearby encompass him and afflict him, nor is there any to defend him against the wrath, the destruction. Yet surely he, when he hears of you and that you are still living, is gladdened within his heart and all his days he is hopeful that he will see his beloved son come home from the Troad. But for me, my destiny was evil. I have the noblest of sons in Troy, but I say not one of them is left to me. Fifty were my sons, when the sons of the Achaians came here. Nineteen were born to me from the womb of a single mother, and other women bore the rest in my palace; and of these violent Ares broke the strength in the knees of most of them, but one was left me who guarded my city and people, that one you killed a few days since he fought in defense of his country. Hektor; for whose sake I come now to the ships of the Achaians to win him back from you, and I bring you gifts beyond number. Honor then the gods, Achilleus, and take pity upon me remembering your father, yet I am still more pitiful; I have gone through what no other mortal on earth has gone through; I put my lips to the hands of the man who has killed my children."

So he spoke, and stirred in the other a passion of grieving for his own father. He took the old man's hand and pushed him gently away, and the two remembered, as Priam sat huddled at the feet of Achilleus and wept close for manslaughtering Hektor and Achilleus wept now for his own father, now again for Patroklos. The sound of their mourning moved in the house. Then when great Achilleus had taken full satisfaction in sorrow and the passion for it had gone from his mind and body, thereafter he rose from his chair, and took the old man by the hand, and set him on his feet again, in pity for the gray head and the gray beard, and spoke to him and addressed him in winged words:

"Ah, unlucky, surely you have had much evil to endure in your spirit. How could you dare to come alone to the ships of the Achaians and before my eyes, when I am one who has killed in such numbers such brave sons of yours? The heart in you is iron. But bear up, nor mourn endlessly in your heart, for there is not anything to be gained from grief for your son; you will never bring him back; sooner you must go through yet another sorrow."

In answer to him again spoke the aged Priam the godlike:

"Do not, beloved of Zeus, make me sit on a chair while Hektor lies yet forlorn among the shelters; rather with all speed give him back, so my eyes may behold him, and accept the ransom we bring you, which is great. You may have joy of it, and go back to the land of your own fathers, since once you have permitted me to go on living myself and continue to look on the sunlight."

Then looking darkly at him spoke swift-footed Achilleus:

"No longer stir me up, old sir. I myself am minded to give Hektor back to you."

The Ascent

From Aleksandr Solzhenitsyn,
The Gulag Archipelago

Marcus Aurelius believed that if a man's soul is free, he is free in the highest sense whether he is an emperor or a slave. Sometimes men experience tyranny of such an overwhelmingly terrifying and degrading kind that their very souls are transmuted. Though at first they may be passive victims, their torment and suffering gradually purify them of their earthly attachments and vanity, liberating the soul from the body and from ambitions for worldly prestige and power. Losing everything most people could not live without, such men achieve an extraordinary spiritual strength that their oppressors cannot touch. In one of our century's most moving affirmations of the power of the human spirit to survive the worst humiliations and pain inflicted by tyranny, Aleksandr Solzhenitsyn reflects on how his long years of imprisonment in the Gulag miraculously improved him and made him a better man.

And the years go by . . .

Not in swift staccato, as they joke in camp—"winter-summer, winter-summer"—but a long drawn-out autumn, an endless winter, an unwilling spring, and only a summer that is short. In the Archipelago . . . summer is short.

Even one mere year, whew, how long it lasts! Even in one year how much time is left for you to think! For 330 days you stomp out to line-up in a drizzling, slushy rain, and in a piercing blizzard, and in a biting and subzero cold. For 330 days you work away at hateful, alien work with your mind unoccupied. For 330 evenings you squinch up, wet, chilled, in the end-of-work line-up, waiting for the convoy to assemble from the distant watchtowers. And then there is the march out. And the march back. And bending down over 730 bowls of gruel, over 730 portions of grits. Yes, and waking up and going to sleep on your multiple bunk. And neither radio nor books to distract you. There are none, and thank God.

And that is only one year. And there are ten. There are twenty-five . . .

And then, too, when you are lying in the hospital with dystrophy—that, too, is a good time—*to think.*

Think! Draw some conclusions from misfortune.

And all that endless time, after all, the prisoners' brains and souls are not inactive?! In the mass and from a distance they seem like swarming lice, but they are the crown of creation, right? After all, once upon a time a weak little spark of God was breathed into them too—is it not true? So what has become of it now?

For centuries it was considered that a criminal was given a *sentence* for precisely this purpose, to think about his crime for the whole period of his sentence, be conscience-stricken, repent, and gradually reform.

But the Gulag Archipelago knows no pangs of conscience! Out of one hundred natives—five are thieves, and their transgressions are no reproach in their own eyes, but a mark of valor. They dream of carrying out such feats in the future even more brazenly and cleverly. They have nothing to repent. Another five . . . *stole* on a big scale, but not from people; in our times, the only place where one can steal on a big scale is from the state, which itself squanders the people's money without pity or sense—so what was there for such types to repent of? Maybe that they had not stolen more and divvied up—and thus remained free? And, so far as another 85 percent of the natives were concerned—they had never committed any crimes whatever. What were they supposed to repent of? That they had thought what they thought? (Nonetheless, they managed to pound and muddle some of them to such an extent that they did repent—of being so depraved . . . Let us remember the desperation of Nina Peregud because she was unworthy of Zoya Kosmodemyanskaya.) Or that a man had surrendered and become a POW in a hopeless situation? Or that he had taken employment under the Germans instead of dying of starvation? (Nonetheless, they managed so to confuse what was permitted and what was forbidden that there were some such who were tormented greatly: I would have done better to die than to have earned that bread.) Or that while working for nothing in the collective-farm fields, he had taken a mite to feed his children? Or that he had taken something from a factory for the same reason?

No, not only do you not repent, but your clean conscience, like a clear mountain lake, shines in your eyes. (And your eyes, purified by suffering, infallibly perceive the least haze in other eyes; for example, they infallibly pick out stool pigeons. And the Cheka-GB is not aware of this capacity of ours to see with the eyes of truth—it is our "secret weapon" against that institution. And State Security slips up here with us.)

It was in this nearly unanimous consciousness of our innocence that the main distinction arose between us and the hard labor prisoners of Dostoyevsky, the hard-labor prisoners of P. Yakubovich. There they were conscious of being doomed renegades, whereas we were confidently aware that they could haul in any free person at all in just the same way they had hauled us in; that barbed wire was only a nominal dividing line between us. In earlier times there had been among the majority . . . the unconditional consciousness of personal guilt, and among us . . . the consciousness of disaster on a mammoth scale.

Just not to perish from the disaster! It had to be survived.

Wasn't this the root cause of the astounding rarity of camp suicides? Yes, rarity, although every ex-prisoner could in all probability recall a case of suicide. But he could recall even more escapes. There were certainly more escapes than suicides! (Admirers of socialist realism can praise me: I am pursuing an optimistic line.) And there were far more self-inflicted injuries, too, than there were suicides! But this, too, is an act indicating love of life—a straightforward calculation of sacrificing a portion to save the whole. I even imagine that, statistically speaking, there were fewer suicides per thousand of the population in camp than in freedom. I have no way of verifying this, of course.

But Skripnikova recalls how a man thirty years old hanged himself in 1931 in the women's toilet in Medvezhyegorsk—and hanged himself on the very day he was to be released! So maybe it was out of a feeling of disgust for the *freedom* of that time? (Two years earlier his wife had abandoned him, but he had not hanged himself then.) Well, the designer Voronov hanged himself in the club of the main camp center of Burepolom. The Communist Party official Aramovich, a second-termer, hanged himself in 1947 in the garret of the machinery-repair factory in Knyazh-Pogost. In Kraslag during the war years Lithuanians who had been reduced to a state of total despair—mainly because nothing in their former lives had prepared them for our cruelties—marched on infantrymen so as to get themselves shot down. In 1949, in the interrogation cell in Vladimir-Volynsk, a young fellow stunned by his interrogation tried to hang himself, but Boronyuk pulled him down in time. At the Kaluga Gates a former Latvian officer who was hospitalized in the camp infirmary began to creep stealthily up some stairs—they led to the incomplete, empty upper stories. The "zechka" nurse saw him and went in pursuit. She caught up with him on the open balcony of the sixth floor. She caught him by the bathrobe, but the suicide slipped off the robe and stepped off into nothingness dressed in his underwear—and flashed past like a white streak of lightning in plain sight of busy Bolshaya Kaluzhskaya Street on a sunny summer day. When Emmi, a German Communist, learned about her husband's death, she left the barracks in subzero weather undressed so as to catch cold. The Englishman Kelly, in the Vladimir Special Purpose Prison, very skillfully cut his veins with the door wide open and the jailer right there on the threshold.

I repeat: There are many others who can recount similar cases—but nonetheless, out of tens of millions who have served time, their total number will be small. Even among these examples, it is clear that a much greater proportion of suicides is accounted for by foreigners, Westerners; for them the transition to the Archipelago . . . was a more shattering blow than for us, so they put an end to it. And suicides were frequent among the loyalists too (but not among the hard-heads). And one can understand why—after all, their heads must have got thoroughly mixed up and filled with incessant buzzing. How could they stand it? (Zosia Zaleska, a Polish noblewoman who had devoted her entire life to the "cause of Communsim" by serving in the Soviet intelligence service, tried to commit suicide three times during her interrogation: she tried to hang herself—they pulled her down; she cut her veins—but they stopped her; she jumped onto the window sill on the seventh floor—but the drowsy interrogator managed to grab hold of her by her dress. They saved her life three times—so they could shoot her.)

But what if one has nothing to repent of—what then, what then does the prisoner think about all the time? "Poverty and prison . . . give wisdom." They do. But—where is it to be directed?

Here is how it was with many others, not just with me. Our initial, first prison sky consisted of black swirling storm clouds and black pillars of volcanic eruptions—this was the heaven of Pompeii, the heaven of the Day of Judgment, because it was not just anyone who had been arrested, but I—the center of this world.

Our last prison sky was infinitely high, infinitely clear, even paler than sky-blue.

We all (except religious believers) began from one point: we tried to tear our hair from our head, but our hair had been clipped close! . . . How could we? How could we not have seen those who informed against us?! How could we not have seen our enemies? (And how we hated them! How could we avenge ourselves on them?) And what recklessness! What blindness! How many errors! How can they be corrected? They must be corrected all the more swiftly! We must write . . . We must speak out . . . We must communicate . . .

But—there is nothing that we can do. And nothing is going to save us! At the appropriate time we will sign Form 200. At the appropriate time the tribunal will read us our sentence in our presence, or we will learn it in absentia from the OSO.

Then there begins the period of transit prisons. Interspersed with our thoughts about the future camp, we now love to recall our past: How many unused opportunities there were! How many flowers we left uncrumpled! . . . When will we now make up for it? If I only manage to survive—oh, how differently, how wisely, I am going to live! The day of our future *release*? It shines like a rising sun!

And the conclusion is: Survive to reach it! Survive! At any price!

This is simply a turn of phrase, a sort of habit of speech: "at any price."

But then the words swell up with their full meaning, and an awesome vow takes shape: to survive *at any price*.

And as soon as you have renounced that aim of "surviving at any price," and gone where the calm and simple people go—then imprisonment begins to transform your former character in an astonishing way. To transform it in a direction most unexpected to you.

And it would seem that in this situation feelings of malice, the disturbance of being oppressed, aimless hate, irritability, and nervousness ought to multiply. But you yourself do not notice how, with the impalpable flow of time, slavery nurtures in you the shoots of contradictory feelings.

Once upon a time you were sharply intolerant. You were constantly in a rush. And you were constantly short of time. And now you have time with interest. You are surfeited with it, with its months and its years, behind you and ahead of you—and a beneficial calming fluid pours through your blood vessels—patience.

You are ascending . . .

Formerly you never forgave anyone. You judged people without mercy. And you praised people with equal lack of moderation. And now an understanding mildness has become the basis of your uncategorical judgments. You have come to realize your own weakness—and you can therefore understand the weakness of others. And be astonished at another's strength. And wish to possess it yourself.

The stones rustle beneath our feet. We are ascending . . .

With the years, armor-plated restraint covers your heart and all your skin. You do not hasten to question and you do not hasten to answer. Your tongue has lost its flexible capacity for easy oscillation. Your eyes do not flash with gladness over good tidings nor do they darken with grief.

For you still have to verify whether that's how it is going to be. And you also have to work out—what is gladness and what is grief.

And now the rule of your life is this: Do not rejoice when you have found, do not weep when you have lost.

Your soul, which formerly was dry, now ripens from suffering. And even if you haven't come to love your neighbors in the Christian sense, you are at least learning to love those close to you.

Those close to you in spirit who surround you in slavery. And how many of us come to realize: It is particularly in slavery that for the first time we have learned to recognize genuine friendship!

And also those close to you in blood, who surrounded you in your former life, who loved you—while you played the tyrant over them . . .

Here is a rewarding and inexhaustible direction for your thoughts: Reconsider all your previous life. Remember everything you did that was bad and shameful and take thought—can't you possibly correct it now?

Yes, you have been imprisoned for nothing. You have nothing to repent of before the state and its laws.

But . . . before your own conscience? But . . . in relation to other individuals?

Looking back, I saw that for my whole conscious life I had not understood either myself or my strivings. What had seemed for so long to be beneficial now turned out in actuality to be fatal, and I had been striving to go in the opposite direction to that which was truly necessary to me. But just as the waves of the sea knock the inexperienced swimmer off his feet and keep tossing him back onto the shore, so also was I painfully tossed back on dry land by the blows of misfortune. And it was only because of this that I was able to travel the path which I had always really wanted to travel.

It was granted me to carry from my prison years on my bent back, which nearly broke beneath its load, this essential experience: *how* a human being becomes evil and *how* good. In the intoxication of youthful successes I had felt myself to be infallible, and I was therefore cruel. In the surfeit of power I was a murderer, and an oppressor. In my most evil moments I was convinced that I was doing good, and I was well supplied with systematic arguments. And it was only when I lay there on rotting prison straw that I sensed within myself the first stirrings of good. Gradually it was disclosed to me that the line separating good and evil passes not through states, nor between classes, nor between political parties either—but right through every human heart—and through all human hearts. This line shifts. Inside us, it oscillates with the years. And even within hearts, overwhelmed by evil, one small bridgehead of good is retained. And even in the best of all hearts, there remains . . . an unuprooted small corner of evil.

Since then I have come to understand the truth of all the religions of the world: They struggle with the *evil inside a human being* (inside every human being). It is impossible to expel evil from the world in its entirety, but it is possible to constrict it within each person.

And since that time I have come to understand the falsehood of all the revolutions in history: They destroy only *those carriers* of evil contemporary with them (and also fail, out of haste, to discriminate the carriers of good as well). And they then take to themselves as their heritage the actual evil itself, magnified still more.

The Nuremberg Trials have to be regarded as one of the special achievements of the twentieth century: they killed the very idea of evil, though they killed very few of the people who had been infected with it. (Of course, Stalin deserves no credit here. He would have preferred to explain less and shoot more.) And if by the twenty-first century humanity has not yet blown itself up and has not suffocated itself—perhaps it is this direction that will triumph?

Yes, and if it does not triumph—then all humanity's history will have turned out to be an empty exercise in marking time, without the tiniest mite of meaning! Whither and to what end will we otherwise be moving? To beat the enemy over the head with a club—even cavemen knew that.

"Know thyself!" There is nothing that so aids and assists the awakening of omniscience within us as insistent thoughts about one's own transgressions, errors, mistakes. After the difficult cycles of such ponderings over many years, whenever I mentioned the heartlessness of our highest-ranking bureaucrats, the cruelty of our executioners, I remember myself in my captain's shoulder boards and the forward march of my battery through East Prussia, enshrouded in fire, and I say: "So were *we* any better?"

When people express vexation, in my presence, over the West's tendency to crumble, its political short-sightedness, its divisiveness, its confusion—I recall too: "Were we, before passing through Archipelago, more steadfast? Firmer in our thoughts?"

And that is why I turn back to the years of my imprisonment and say, sometimes to the astonishment of those about me: *"Bless you, prison!"*

Lev Tolstoi was right when he *dreamed* of being in prison. At a certain moment that giant began to dry up. He actually needed prison as a drought needs a shower of rain!

All the writers who wrote about prison but who did not themselves serve time there considered it their duty to express sympathy for prisoners and to curse prison I . . . have served enough time there. I nourished my soul there, and I say without hesitation:

"Bless you, prison, for having been in my life!"

(And from beyond the grave come replies: It is very well for you to say that—when you came out of it alive!)

7

THE AMERICAN MAN

Manhood in America has been a complicated matter, from its earliest days forward. European traditions about the meaning of manliness, including relationships between husbands and wives and fathers and children, migrated to the New World along with the settlers—and yet many early Americans left Europe precisely because they found those older feudal and theocratic patterns of authority oppressive. From the beginning, Americans have prized individual freedom. For the early colonists, this meant above all freedom of conscience to worship as they saw fit. As the new American people grew and put down deeper roots in the soil of the continent, this belief in individual liberty was extended to business, political debate and personal life.

The American founding was thus a kind of experiment in encouraging individual freedom to flourish without impediment or competition from earlier European models of virtue and the common good. But it would be misleading to say that American individualism had no connection at all with those earlier traditions of manliness, fatherhood, and statesmanship. The influence of John Locke and Adam Smith on the principles of the American founding is widely noted, and neither of those philosophers endorsed unbridled selfishness or spontaneous impulse. On the contrary, they argued that an education in moral character was necessary if individual liberty was not to degenerate into licence and anarchy.

Adam Smith is best known for his formulation of the "hidden hand" argument in favor of capitalist free enterprise, on the grounds that markets generally correct their own errors and distribute the rewards of hard work to the meritorious. But Smith based this endorsement of the work ethic on the education of what he called "the inner man" in the moral and intellectual virtues that prevent us from becoming totally absorbed in moneymaking. For Smith firmly believed that men will not treat each other honestly in their business dealings unless those commercial relationships are guided by a wider moral training based on reason and sympathy.

Locke, whose portrait Jefferson hung in a prominent place at Monticello, is perhaps best known for his defense of the individual's right to acquire property. But Locke never maintained that property rights were the basis for all other rights. According to Locke, the first law of nature is the individual's right to freedom from tyranny and other forms of criminal violence and oppression. The practice of this fundamental natural right includes the right to acquire property, worship, move about, and engage in public debate. The right to property is only one among a number of liberties that flow from and demonstrate our more fundamental right to freedom from tyranny.

Locke and his American disciples did not view liberal democracy as a product of the free enterprise economic system. On the contrary, it is liberal democracy that creates and sustains a market economy, and justifies it only to the extent that it facilitates the freedom and dignity of every member of society. Accordingly, like Adam Smith, Locke was also keenly interested in educating young men in the virtues of character, compassion and tolerance necessary for exercising one's rights responsibly. His advice in favor of more flexible and open-minded approaches to child-rearing would become a kind of ideal for American education:

"The business of education . . . is not, as I think, to make [students] perfect in any one of the sciences, but so to open and dispose their minds as may best make them capable of any, when they shall come to apply themselves to it. If men are for a long time accustomed only to one sort or method of thoughts, their minds grow stiff in it, and do not readily turn to another. It is therefore to give them this freedom, that I think they should be made to look into all sorts of knowledge, and exercise their understandings in so wide a variety and stock of knowledge." Free your mind, in other words, and success will follow.

By the time the young French aristocrat Alexis de Tocqueville toured America in the 1830s, eager to acquaint Europeans with this strange, boisterous new society, Americans bore the stamp of this Enlightenment philosophy of individualism on their national character. As Tocqueville remarked, Americans were from the start natural Cartesians—followers of the French rationalist Rene Descartes—even though most may never have read the philosopher's work. Descartes had argued that individuals should take nothing on faith, but subject every belief and observation to their own autonomous powers of reasoning. Doubt everything! was his motto, and although Americans had little taste for philosophy, Tocqueville observed, they practiced this skepticism every day. To this day, indeed, Americans are self-reliant and deeply suspicious of any kind of inherited collective authority. Historically, they have resisted outdated European notions of duty to family, clan, class, and church. Believing democracy and equality to be the only legitimate principles of government, they show no trace of the European deference to aristocracy, and little patience for European traditions of reserve, delicacy, or decorum.

Tocqueville believed there was a clear-cut and unavoidable choice between the American and European ways of life. Both had their merits and shortcomings, but they could not be combined. As the readings in this section suggest, however, there may have been more overlap in the long run than the French aristocrat thought possible. Whether one examines the American brand of heroism in statesmanship and battle, or the evolution of the American character in personal life and family affairs, some themes are uniquely American while others have roots in the older traditions of classical antiquity, feudal Europe and the Renaissance. Age-old aspects of the manly virtues—valor, statesmanship, chivalry and family life—were subjected to unprecedented new challenges as Americans extended their creed of democratic individualism across the mysterious and sometimes dangerous continent. What evolved was a uniquely American hybrid of these ancient aspirations to virtuous manhood.

THE AMERICAN HERO

Freedom in All Just Pursuits

From Thomas Jefferson,
Notes on the State of Virginia

American democracy and civilization brought new complexities to the meaning of manliness. In some ways, Americans drew upon the older classical ideals to provide a model for democratic virtue. In his Notes on the State of Virginia, *Jefferson says the greatest happiness comes from the freedom that a liberal education bestows to develop our highest capacities for just pursuits. Echoing the classical ideal stretching back to Plato and Aristotle, Jefferson maintains that an educated citizenry is essential to good government. True manliness is impossible without learning. Through the study of ancient history and the Greek and Roman classics, young Americans will learn about the high points of moral and intellectual excellence from the past.*

Their memories may be stored with the most useful facts from Grecian, Roman, European and American history. The first elements of morality too may be instilled into their minds such as, when further developed as their judgments advance in strength, may teach them how to work out their own greatest happiness, by showing them that it does not depend on the condition of life in which chance has placed them, but is always the result of a good conscience, good health, occupation, and freedom in all just pursuits. The learning of Greek and Latin, I am told, is going into disuse in Europe. I know not what their manners and occupations may call for; but it would be very ill-judged in us to follow their example in this instance. There is a certain period of life, say from eight to fifteen or sixteen years of age, when the mind like the body is not yet firm enough for laborious and close operations. If applied to such, it falls an early victim to premature exertion; exhibiting, indeed, at first, in these young and tender subjects, the flattering appearance of their being men while they are yet children, but ending in reducing them to be children when they should be men. The memory is then most susceptible and tenacious of impressions; and the learning of languages being chiefly a work of memory, it seems precisely fitted to the powers of this period, which is long enough too for acquiring the most useful languages, ancient and modern. As soon as they are of sufficient age, it is supposed they will be sent on from the grammar schools to the university. By that part of our plan which prescribes the selection of the youths of genius from among the classes of the poor, we hope to avail the State of those talents which nature has sewn as liberally among the poor as the rich, but which perish without use, if not sought for and cultivated. But of the views of this law none is more important, none more legitimate, than that of rendering the people the safe, as they are the ultimate, guardians of their own liberty. History, by apprising them of the past, will enable them to judge of the future; it will avail them of the experience of other times and other nations; it will qualify them as judges of the actions and designs of men; it will enable them to know ambition under every disguise it may assume; and knowing it, to defeat its views. In every government on earth is some trace of human weakness, some germ of corruption and degeneracy, which cunning will discover, and wickedness insensibly open, cultivate and improve. Every government degenerates when trusted to the rulers of the people alone. The people themselves therefore are its only safe depositories. And to render even them safe, their minds must be improved to a certain degree.

The Call to Arms

Patrick Henry, Select Orations

The immortal summons to revolution delivered in 1775 by the brilliant orator and statesman (1736–1799).

The question before the House is one of awful moment to this country. For my own part, I consider it as nothing less than a question of freedom or slavery; and in proportion to the magnitude of the subject ought to be the freedom of the debate. It is only in this way that we can hope to arrive at truth, and fulfill the great responsibility which we hold to God and our country. Should I keep back my opinions at such a time, through fear of giving offense, I should consider myself as guilty of treason toward my country, and of an act of disloyalty toward the Majesty of Heaven, which I revere above all earthly kings.

Mr. President, it is natural to man to indulge in the illusions of hope. We are apt to shut our eyes against a painful truth, and listen to the song of that siren, till she transforms us into beasts. Is this the part of wise men, engaged in a great and arduous struggle for liberty? Are we disposed to be of the number of those, who, having eyes, see not, and having ears, hear not, the things which so nearly concern their temporal salvation? For my part, whatever anguish of spirit it may cost, I am willing to know the worst, and to provide for it.

There is no longer any room for hope. If we wish to be free— if we mean to preserve inviolate those inestimable privileges for which we have been so long contending—if we mean not basely to abandon the noble struggle in which we have been so long engaged, and which we have pledged ourselves never to abandon, until the glorious object of our contest shall be obtained—we must fight! I repeat it, sir, we must fight! An appeal to arms and to the God of Hosts is all that is left us!

They tell us, sir, that we are weak—unable to cope with so formidable an adversary. But when shall we be stronger? Will it be the next week, or the next year? Will it be when we are totally disarmed, and when a British guard shall be stationed in every house? Shall we gather strength by irresolution and inaction? Shall we acquire the means of effectual resistance by lying supinely on our backs and hugging the delusive phantom of hope, until our enemies shall have bound us hand and foot?

Sir, we are not weak if we make a proper use of those means which the God of nature has placed in our power. Three millions of people armed in the holy cause of liberty, and in such a country as that which we possess, are invincible by any force which our enemy can send against us. Besides, sir, we shall not fight our battles alone. There is a just God who presides over the destinies of nations, and who will raise up friends to fight our battles for us. The battle, sir, is not to the strong alone; it is to the vigilant, the active, the brave. Besides, sir, we have no election. If we were base enough to desire it, it is now too late to retire from the contest. There is no retreat but in submission and slavery! Our chains are forged! Their clanking may be heard on the plains of Boston! The war is inevitable—and let it come! I repeat it, sir, let it come!

It is in vain, sir, to extenuate the matter. Gentlemen may cry, Peace, Peace—but there is no peace. The war is actually begun! The next gale that sweeps from the north will bring to our ears the clash of resounding arms! Our brethren are already in the field! Why stand we here idle? What is it that gentlemen wish? What would they have? Is life so dear, or peace so sweet, as to be purchased at the price of chains and slavery? Forbid it, Almighty God! I know not what course others may take; but as for me, give me liberty or give me death!

It Is Natural to Believe in Great Men

From Ralph Waldo Emerson,
Representative Men

It is natural to believe in great men. If the companions of our childhood should turn out to be heroes, and their condition regal it would not surprise us. All mythology opens with demigods, and the circumstance is high and poetic; that is, their genius is paramount. In the legends of the Gautama, the first men ate the earth and found it deliciously sweet.

Nature seems to exist for the excellent. The world is upheld by the veracity of good men: they make the earth wholesome. They who lived with them found life glad and nutritious. Life is sweet and tolerable only in our belief in such society; and, actually or ideally, we manage to live with superiors. We call our children and our lands by their names. Their names are wrought into the verbs of language, their works and effigies are in our houses, and every circumstance of the day recalls an anecdote of them.

The search after the great man is the dream of youth and the most serious occupation of manhood. We travel into foreign parts to find his works—if possible, to get a glimpse of him.

Our religion is the love and cherishing of these patrons. The gods of fable are the shining moments of great men. We run all our vessels into one mold. Our colossal theologies of Judaism, Christianism, Buddhism, Mahometism, are the necessary and structural action of the human mind. The student of history is like a man going into a warehouse to buy cloths or carpets. He fancies he has a new article. If he goes to the factory, he shall find that his new stuff still repeats the scrolls and rosettes which are found on the interior walls of the pyramids of Thebes. Our theism is the purification of the human mind. Man can paint, or make, or think, nothing but man. He believes that the great material elements had their origin from his thought. And our philosophy finds one essence collected or distributed.

If now we proceed to inquire into the kinds of service we

derive from others, let us be warned of the danger of modern studies, and begin low enough. We must not contend against love, or
deny the substantial existence of other people. I know not what
would happen to us. We have social strengths. Our affection toward
others creates a sort of vantage or purchase which nothing will supply. I can do that by another which I cannot do alone. I can say to
you what I cannot first say to myself. Other men are lenses through
which we read our own minds. Each man seeks those of different
quality from his own, and such as are good of their kind; that is, he
seeks other men, and the *otherest*. The stronger the nature, the
more it is reactive. Let us have the quality pure. A little genius let us
leave alone.

The Glory of Our Fathers

From Josiah Quincy,
July 4th Oration on the American Revolution

When we speak of the glory of our fathers, we mean not that
vulgar renown to be attained by physical strength, nor yet that
higher fame to be acquired by intellectual power. Both often exist
without lofty thought, or pure intent, or generous purpose. The
glory which we celebrate was strictly of a moral and religious character; righteous as to its ends; just as to its means. The American
Revolution had its origin neither in ambition, nor avarice, nor
envy, nor in any gross passion; but in the nature and relation of
things, and in the thence resulting necessity of separation from the
parent state. Its progress was limited by that necessity. During the
struggle, our fathers displayed great strength and great moderation
of purpose. In difficult times, they conducted with wisdom; in
doubtful times, with firmness; in perilous, with courage; under
oppressive trials, erect; amid great temptations, unseduced; in the
dark hour of danger, fearless; in the bright hour of prosperity,
faithful.

It was not the instant feeling and pressure of the arm of despotism that roused them to resist, but the *principle* on which that arm
was extended. They could have paid the *stamp-tax*, and the *tea-tax*,

and other impositions of the British government, had they been increased a thousandfold. But *payment* acknowledged the *right;* and they spurned the consequences of that acknowledgment. In spite of those acts they could have lived, and happily; and bought, and sold, and got gain, and been at ease. But they would have held those blessings, on the tenure of dependence on a foreign and distant power; at the mercy of a king, or his minions; or of councils, in which they had no voice, and where their interests could not be represented, and were little likely to be heard. They saw that their prosperity in such case would be precarious, their possessions uncertain, their ease inglorious.

But, above all, they realized that these burdens, though light to them, would, to the coming age, to us, their posterity, be heavy, and probably insupportable.

Democracy and the Great Man

From Alexis de Tocqueville,
Democracy in America

Based on a nine-month visit to the United States during 1831 and 1832, a young French nobleman, Alexis de Tocqueville, produced Democracy in America, *regarded ever since as the single most powerful and prescient diagnosis of democratic civilization in the New World. Here, Tocqueville wonders whether there is a place for great men in the democratic interpretation of history.*

Historians who write in aristocratic ages generally attribute everything that happens to the will and character of particular men, and they will unhesitatingly suppose slight accidents to be the cause of the greatest revolutions. With great sagacity they trace the smallest causes and often leave the greatest unnoticed.

Historians who live in democratic ages show contrary tendencies.

Most of them attribute hardly any influence over the destinies of mankind to individuals, or over the fate of a people to the citizens.

Thus historians who live in democratic times do not only refuse to admit that some citizens may influence the destiny of a people, but also take away from the peoples themselves the faculty of modifying their own lot and make them depend either on an inflexible providence or on a kind of blind fatality. According to them each nation is inexorably bound by its position, origin, antecedents, and nature to a fixed destiny which no efforts can change. Generation is firmly bound to generation, and so going back from age to age, from necessity to necessity, they reach the origin of the world, forging a tight, enormous chain which girds and binds the human race.

Not content to show how events have occurred, they pride themselves on proving that they could not have happened differently. They see a nation which has reached a certain point in its history, and they assert that it was bound to have followed the path that led it there. That is easier than demonstrating how it might have taken a better road.

In reading historians of aristocratic ages, those of antiquity in particular, it would seem that in order to be master of his fate and to govern his fellows a man need only be master of himself. Perusing the histories written nowadays, one would suppose that man had no power, neither over himself nor over his surroundings. Classical historians taught how to command; those of our own time teach next to nothing but how to obey. In their writings the author often figures large, but humanity is always tiny.

If this doctrine of fatality, so attractive to those who write history in democratic periods, passes from authors to readers, infects the whole mass of the community, and takes possession of the public mind, it will soon paralyze the activities of modern society and bring Christians down to the level of Turks.

I would add that such a doctrine is particularly dangerous at the present moment. Our contemporaries are all too much inclined to doubts about free will, since each of them feels himself confined on every side by his own weakness. But they will freely admit the strength and independence of men united in a body social. It is important not to let this idea grow dim, for we need to raise men's souls, not to complete their prostration.

The Sword of Washington!
The Staff of Franklin!

From John Quincy Adams,
Select Orations

Adams, who became President of the United States in 1825, pays tribute to two of the founding fathers.

The *Sword of Washington!* The *Staff of Franklin!* O, sir, what associations are linked in adamant with these names! Washington, whose sword was never drawn but in the cause of his country, and never sheathed when wielded in his country's cause! Franklin, the philosopher of the thunderbolt, the printing-press, and the ploughshare! What names are these in the scanty dialogue of the benefactors of human kind! *Washington* and *Franklin!* What *other* two men whose lives belong to the eighteenth century of Christendom have left a deeper impression of themselves upon the age in which they lived, and upon all after time?

Washington, the warrior and the legislator! In war, contending, by the wager of the battle, for the independence of his country, and for the freedom of the human race—ever manifesting, amid its horrors, by precept and by example, his reverence for the laws of peace, and for the tenderest sympathies of humanity; —in peace, soothing the ferocious spirit of discord, among his own countrymen, into harmony and union, and giving to that very sword, now presented to his county, a charm more potent than that attributed, in ancient times, to the lyre of Orpheus.

Franklin! The mechanic of his own fortune; teaching, in early youth, under the shackles of indigence, the way to wealth, and, in the shade of obscurity, the path to greatness; in the maturity of manhood, disarming the thunder of its terrors, the lightning of its fatal blast; and wresting from the tyrant's hand the still more afflictive scepter of oppression: while descending into the vale of years, traversing the Atlantic Ocean, braving, in the dead of winter, the battle and the breeze, bearing in his hand the Charter of Independence, which he had contributed to form, and tendering, from the self-created nation to the mightiest monarchs of Europe, the olive-branch of peace, the mercurial wand of commerce, and the amulet of protection and safety to the man of peace, on the pathless ocean, from the inexorable cruelty and merciless rapacity of war.

And, finally, in the last stage of life, with fourscore winters upon his head, under the torture of an incurable disease, returning to his native land, closing his days as the chief magistrate of his adopted commonwealth, after contributing by his counsels, under the Presidency of Washington, and recording his name, under the sanction of devout prayer, invoked by him to God, to that Constitution under the authority of which we are here assembled, as the representatives of the North American people, to receive, in their name and for them, these venerable relics of the wise, the valiant, and the good founders of our great confederated republic—these sacred symbols of our golden age. May they be deposited among the archives of our Government! And may every American who shall hereafter behold them, ejaculate a mingled offering of praise to that Supreme Ruler of the Universe, by whose tender mercies our Union had been hitherto preserved, through all the vicissitudes and revolutions of this turbulent world; and of prayer for the continuance of these blessings, by the dispensations of Providence, to our beloved country, from age to age, till time shall be no more!

Illustrious Man!

From Charles James Fox,
Select Orations

The English politician pays tribute to the foreign policy of George Washington.

How infinitely superior must appear the spirit and principles of General Washington in his late address to Congress compared with the policy of modern European courts! Illustrious man! Deriving honor less from the splendor of his situation than for the dignity of his mind.

It must, indeed, create astonishment, that, placed in circumstances so critical, and filling a station so conspicuous, the character of Washington should never once have been called in question—that he should, in no one instance, have been accused either of improper insolence, or of mean submission, in his transactions with foreign nations. It has been reserved for him to run the race of glory without experiencing the smallest interruption to the brilliancy of his career. The breath of censure has not dared to impeach the purity of his conduct, nor the eye of envy to raise its malignant glance to the elevation of his virtues. Such has been the transcendent merit and the unparalleled fate of this illustrious man!

Happy Americans! While the whirlwind flies over one quarter of the globe, and spreads everywhere desolation, you remain protected from its baneful effects by your own virtues, and the wisdom of your government.

Separated from Europe by an immense ocean, you feel not the effect of those prejudices and passions which convert the boasted seats of civilization into scenes of horror and bloodshed. You profit by the folly and madness of the contending nations, and afford, in your more congenial clime, an asylum to those blessings and virtues which they wantonly contemn or wickedly exclude from their bosom! Cultivating the arts of peace, under the influence of freedom, you advance, by rapid strides, to opulence and distinction.

Such Men Cannot Die

From Edward Everett, Select Orations

A tribute to two American heroes from the eminent orator and statesman, Edward Everett (1794–1865).

No, fellow-citizens, we dismiss not Adams and Jefferson to the chambers of forgetfulness and death. What we admired, and prized, and venerated in them, can *never* die, nor, dying, be forgotten. I had almost said that they are now beginning to live—to live that life of unimpaired influence, of unclouded fame, of unmingled happiness, for which their talents and services were destined. They were of the select few, the least portion of whose life dwells in their physical existence; whose hearts have watched while their senses slept; whose souls have grown up into a higher being; whose pleasure is to be useful; whose wealth is an unblemished reputation; who respire the breath of honorable fame; who have deliberately and consciously put what is called life to hazard, that they may live in the hearts of those who come after. Such men do not, *can* not die.

To be cold, and motionless, and breathless, to feel not and speak not: this is not the end of existence to the men who have breathed their spirits into the institutions of their country, who have stamped their characters on the pillars of the age, who have poured their hearts' blood into the channels of the public prosperity. Tell me, ye who tread the sods of yon sacred height, is Warren dead? Can you not still see him, not pale and prostrate, the blood of his gallant heart pouring out of his ghastly wound, but moving resplendent over the field of honor, with the rose of heaven upon his cheek, and the fire of liberty in his eye?

Tell me, ye who make your pious pilgrimage to the shades of Vernon, is Washington indeed shut up in that cold and narrow house? That which made these men, and men like these, cannot die. The hand that traced the charter of independence is, indeed, motionless, the eloquent lips that sustained it are hushed; but the lofty spirits that conceived, resolved, matured, maintained it, and which alone, to such men, "make it life to live," *these* cannot expire:

"These shall resist the empire of decay,
When time is o'er, and worlds have passed away:
Cold in the dust the perished heart may lie,
But that which warmed it once, can never die."

Manly Honor in Democracy and Aristocracy

From Alexis de Tocqueville, Democracy in America

The feudal aristocracy was born of war and for war; it won its power by force of arms and maintained it thereby. So nothing was more important to it than military courage. It was therefore natural to glorify courage above all other virtues. Every manifestation thereof, even at the expense of common sense and humanity, was therefore approved and often even ordained by the manners of the time. The fantastic notions of individuals could affect only the details of such a system.

That a man should regard a tap on the cheek as an unbearable insult and feel bound to kill the man who struck him thus in single combat is an arbitrary rule; but that a noble should not tranquilly suffer an insult, and was dishonored if he let himself be struck without fighting—that was a result of the basic principles and needs of a military aristocracy.

Among opinions current among Americans one still finds some scattered notions detached from the old European aristocratic conception of honor, but they have no deep roots or strong influence. It is like a religion whose temples are allowed to remain but in which one no longer believes.

Amid these half-effaced notions of an exotic honor some new opinions have made their appearance, and these constitute what one might call the contemporary American conception of honor.

I have shown how the Americans are continually driven into trade and industry. The origin, social conditions, political institutions, and even the very land they live in irresistibly impel them in this direction. Hence they now form an almost exclusively industrial and trading community placed in the midst of a huge new country whose exploitation is their principal interest. That is the characteristic trait which now distinguishes the Americans most particularly from all other nations.

But all those turbulent virtues which sometimes bring glory but more often trouble to society will rank lower in the public opinion of this same people. One could disregard them without forfeiting the esteem of one's fellow citizens, and perhaps by acquiring them one might run a risk of losing it.

American and European medieval conceptions of honor agree on one point: both rank courage first of virtues and count it the greatest moral necessity for a man. But the two conceptions envisage courage in a different light.

In the United States martial valor is little esteemed; the type of courage best known and best appreciated is that which makes a man brave the fury of the ocean to reach port more quickly, and face without complaint the privations of life in the wilds and that solitude which is harder to bear than any privations, the courage which makes a man almost insensible to the loss of a fortune laboriously acquired and prompts him instantly to fresh exertions to gain another. It is chiefly courage of this sort which is needed to maintain the American community and make it prosper, and it is held by them in particular esteem and honor. To betray a lack of it brings certain shame.

In America I have sometimes met rich young men temperamentally opposed to any uncomfortable effort and yet forced to enter a profession. Their characters and their wealth would have allowed them to stay idle, but public opinion imperiously forbade that and had to be obeyed. But among European nations where an aristocracy is still struggling against the current that carries it away, I have often met men whose needs and inclinations constantly goaded them to action, who yet remained idle so as not to lose the esteem of their equals, and who found boredom and discomfort easier to face than work.

"Towering Genius Disdains a Beaten Path."

From Abraham Lincoln,
Address to the Young Men's Lyceum
in Springfield, Illinois (1838)

Can a democracy find room for "an Alexander, a Caesar or a Napoleon? Never!" A surprising viewpoint from the future president, twenty-two years before his inauguration.

As a subject of the remarks of the evening, *the perpetuation of our political institutions,* is selected.

In the great journal of things happening under the sun, we, the American People, find our account running, under date of the nineteenth century of the Christian era. We find ourselves in the peaceful possession, of the fairest portion of the earth, as regards extent of territory, fertility of soil, and salubrity of climate. We find ourselves under the government of a system of political institutions, conducing more essentially to the ends of civil and religious liberty, than any of which the history of former times tells us. We, when mounting the stage of existence, found ourselves the legal inheritors of these fundamental blessings. We toiled not in the acquirement or establishment of them—they are a legacy bequeathed us, by a *once* hardy, brave, and patriotic, but *now* lamented and departed race of ancestors. Theirs was the task (and nobly they performed it) to possess themselves, and through themselves, us, of this goodly land; and to uprear upon its hills and its valleys, a political edifice of liberty and equal rights; 'tis ours only, to transmit these, the former, unprofaned by the foot of an invader; the latter, undecayed by the lapse of time, and untorn by [usurpation—to the latest generation that fate shall permit the world to know. This task of gratitude to our fathers, justice to] ourselves, duty to posterity, and love for our species in general, all imperatively require us faithfully to perform.

How, then, shall we perform it? At what point shall we expect the approach of danger? By what means shall we fortify against it? Shall we expect some transatlantic military giant, to step the Ocean, and crush us at a blow? Never! All the armies of Europe, Asia and Africa combined, with all the treasure of the earth (our own excepted) in their military chest; with a Buonaparte for a commander, could not by force, take a drink from the Ohio, or make a track on the Blue Ridge, in a trial of a thousand years.

At what point then is the approach of danger to be expected? I answer, if it ever reach us, it must spring up amongst us. It cannot come from abroad. If destruction be our lot, we must ourselves be its author and finisher. As a nation of freemen, we must live through all time, or die by suicide.

I hope I am over wary; but if I am not, there is, even now, something of ill-omen amongst us. I mean the increasing disregard for the law which pervades the country; the growing disposition to substitute the wild and furious passions, in lieu of the sober judgment of Courts; and the worse than savage mobs, for the executive ministers of justice. This disposition is awfully fearful in any community; and that it now exists in ours, though grating to our feelings to admit, it would be a violation of truth, and an insult to our intelligence, to deny. Accounts of outrages committed by mobs, form the everyday news of the times. They have pervaded the country, from New England to Louisiana; —they are neither peculiar to the eternal snows of the former, nor the burning suns of the latter; —they are not the creature of climate—neither are they confined to the slaveholding, or the non-slaveholding States. Alike, they spring up among the pleasure hunting masters of Southern slaves, and the order loving citizens of the land of steady habits. Whatever, then, their cause may be, it is common to the whole country.

I know the American People are *much* attached to their Government; —I know they would suffer *much* for its sake; —I know they would endure evils long and patiently, before they would ever think of exchanging it for another. Yet, notwithstanding all this, if the laws be continually despised and disregarded, if their rights to be secure in their persons and property, are held by no better tenure than the caprice of a mob, the alienation of their affections from the Government is the natural consequence; and to that, sooner or later, it must come.

Here then, is one point at which danger may be expected.

The question recurs "how shall we fortify against it?" The answer is simple. Let every American, every lover of liberty, every well wisher to his posterity, swear by the blood of the Revolution, never to violate in the least particular, the laws of the country; and never to tolerate their violation by others. As the patriots of seventy-six did to the support of the Constitution and Laws, let every American pledge his life, his property, and his sacred honor; —let every man remember that to violate the law, is to trample on the blood of his father, and to tear the [charter?] of his own, and his children's liberty. Let reverence for the laws, be breathed by every American mother, to the lisping babe, that prattles on her lap—let it be taught in schools, in seminaries, and in colleges; —let it be written in Primmers, spelling books, and in Almanacs; —let it be preached from the pulpit, proclaimed in legislative halls, and enforced in courts of justice. And, in short, let it become the *political religion* of the nation; and let the old and the young, the rich and the poor, the grave and the gay, of all sexes and tongues, and colors and conditions, sacrifice unceasingly upon its altars.

But, it may be asked, why suppose danger to our political institutions? Have we not preserved them for more than fifty years? And why may we not for fifty times as long?

The experiment is successful; and thousands have won their deathless names in making it so. But the game is caught; and I believe it is true, that with the catching, end the pleasures of the chase. This field of glory is harvested, and the crop is already appropriated. But new reapers will arise, and *they*, too, will seek a field. It is to deny, what the history of the world tells us is true, to suppose that men of ambition and talents will not continue to spring up against us. And, when they do, they will as naturally seek the gratification of their ruling passion, as others have so done before them. The question then, is, can that gratification be found in supporting and maintaining an edifice that has been erected by others? Most certainly it cannot. Many great and good men sufficiently qualified of any task they should undertake, may ever be found, whose ambition would aspire to nothing beyond a seat in Congress, a gubernatorial or a presidential chair; *but such belong not to the family of the lion, or the tribe of the eagle,* [.] What! Think you these places would satisfy an Alexander, a Caesar, or a Napoleon? Never! Towering genius disdains a beaten path. It seeks regions hitherto unexplored. It sees *no distinction* in adding story to story, upon the monuments of fame, erected to the memory of others. It *denies* that it is glory enough to serve under any chief. It *scorns* to tread in the footsteps of *any* predecessor, however illustrious. It thirsts and burns for distinction; and, if possible, it will have it, whether at the expense of emancipating slaves, or enslaving freemen. Is it unreasonable then to expect, that some man possessed of the loftiest genius, coupled with ambition sufficient to push it to its utmost stretch, will at some time, spring up among us? And when such a one does, it will require the people to be united with each other, attached to the government and laws, and generally intelligent, to successfully frustrate his designs.

Distinction will be his paramount object; and although he would as willingly, perhaps more so, acquire it by doing good as harm; yet, that opportunity being past, and nothing left to be done in the way of building up, he would set boldly to the task of pulling down.

Here, then, is a probable case, highly dangerous, and such a one as could not have well existed heretofore.

Another reason which *once was;* but which, to the same extent, is *now no more,* has done much in maintaining our institutions thus far. I mean the powerful influence which the interesting scenes of the revolution had upon the *passions* of the people as distinguished from their judgment. By this influence, the jealousy, envy, and avarice, incident to our nature, and so common to a state of peace, prosperity, and conscious strength, were, for the time, in a great measure smothered and rendered inactive while the deep rooted principles of *hate,* and the powerful motive of *revenge,* instead of being turned against each other, were directed exclusively against the British nation. And thus, from the force of circumstances, the bases principles of our nature, were either made to lie dormant, or to become the active agents in the advancement of the noblest of cause[s?]—that of establishing and maintaining civil and religious liberty.

But this state of feeling *must fade, is fading, has faded,* with the circumstances that produced it.

I do not mean to say, that the scenes of the revolution *are now* or *ever will be* entirely forgotten; but that like everything else, they must fade upon the memory of the world, and grow more and more dim by the lapse of time. In history, we hope, they will be read of, and recounted, so long as the Bible shall be read; —but even granting that they will, their influence *cannot be* so universally known, nor so vividly felt, as they were by the generation just gone to rest. At the close of that struggle, nearly every adult male had been a participator in some of its scenes. The consequence was, that of those scenes, in the form of a husband, a father, a son or a brother, a *living history was* to be found in every family—a history bearing the indubitable testimonies of its own authenticity, in the limbs mangled, in the scars of wounds received, in the midst of the very scenes related—a history, too, that could be read and understood alike by all, the wise and the ignorant, the learned and the unlearned. But *those* histories are gone. They *can* be read no more forever. They *were* a fortress of strength; but, what invading foe-men could *never do,* the silent artillery of our time *has done;* the leveling of its walls. They are gone. They *were* a forest of giant oaks; but the all-restless hurricane has swept over them, and left only, here and there, a lonely trunk, despoiled of its verdure, shorn of its foliage; unshading and unshaded, to murmur in a few more gentle breezes, and to combat with its mutilated limbs, a few more ruder storms, then to sink, and be no more.

They *were* the pillars of the temple of liberty; and now, that they have crumbled away, that temple must fall, unless we, their descendants, supply their places with other pillars, hewn from the solid quarry of sober reason. Passion has helped us; but can do so no more. It will in future be our enemy. Reason, cold, calculating, unimpassioned reason, must furnish all the materials for our future support and defence. Let those [materials] be moulded into *general intelligence,* [*sound*] *morality* and, in particular, *a reverence for the constitution and laws;* and, that we improved to the last; that we remained free to the last; that we revered his name to the last; [tha]t, during his long sleep, we permitted no hostile foot to pass over or desecrate [his] resting place; shall be that which to le[arn the last] trump shall awaken our Wash[ington.

Upon these] let the proud fabric of freedom r[est, as the] rock of its basis; and as truly as has been said of the only greater institution, "*the gates of hell shall not prevail against it.*"

Why There Are So Many Men of Ambition in the United States but So Few Lofty Ambitions

From Alexis de Tocqueville,
Democracy in America

The first thing that strikes one in the United States is the innumerable crowd of those striving to escape from their original social condition; and the second is the rarity, in a land where all are actively ambitious, of any lofty ambition. Every American is eaten up with longing to rise, but hardly any of them seem to entertain very great hopes or to aim very high. All are constantly bent on gaining property, reputation, and power, but few conceive such things on a grand scale.

It is also important to remember that those who destroy an aristocracy once lived under its laws; they have seen its splendors and have unconsciously imbibed the feelings and ideas which it conceived. At the moment, therefore, of the dissolution of an aristocracy, its spirit still hovers over the masses, and its instincts are preserved long after it has been conquered.

Thus ambitions are on the grand scale while the democratic revolution lasts; that will no longer be true some considerable time after it has finished.

Men do not in one day forget the memory of extraordinary events which they have witnessed; and the passions roused by revolution by no means vanish at its close. A sense of instability is perpetuated amid order. The hope of easy success lives on after the strange turns of fortune which gave it birth. Longings on a vast scale remain, though the means to satisfy them become daily less. The taste for huge fortunes persists, though such fortunes in fact become rare, and on all sides there are those who eat out their hearts in secret, consumed by inordinate and frustrated ambition.

But little by little the last traces of the battle are wiped out and the relics of aristocracy finally vanish. The great events which accompanied its fall are forgotten. Peace follows war, and order again prevails in a new world. Longings once more become proportionate to the available means. Wants, ideas, and feelings again learn their limits. Men find their level, and democratic society is finally firmly established.

When we come to take stock of a democratic people which has reached this enduring and normal state, it appears very different from the scene we have been contemplating. And we easily come to the conclusion that although high ambitions swell while conditions are in process of equalization, that characteristic is lost when equality is a fact.

When great fortunes have been divided up and education has spread, no one is absolutely deprived of either education or property. When both the privileges and the disqualifications of class have been abolished and men have shattered the bonds which once held them immobile, the idea of progress comes naturally into each man's mind; the desire to rise swells in every heart at once, and all men want to quit their former social position. Ambition becomes a universal feeling.

But equality, though it gives every citizen some resources, prevents any from enjoying resources of great extent, and for this reason desires must of necessity be confined within fairly narrow limits. Hence in democracies ambition is both eager and constant, but in general it does not look very high. For the most part life is spent in eagerly coveting small prizes within reach.

It is not so much the small scale of their wealth as the constant and strenuous efforts requisite to increase it which chiefly diverts men in democracies from high ambitions. They strain their faculties to the utmost to achieve paltry results, and this quickly and inevitably limits their range of vision and circumscribes their powers. They could well be much poorer and yet be more magnanimous.

The few opulent citizens of a democracy constitute no exception to this rule. A man who raises himself gradually to wealth and power contracts in the course of this patient ascent habits of prudence and restraint which he cannot afterward shake off. A mind cannot be gradually enlarged, like a house.

Much the same applies to the sons of such a man. They may, it is true, have been born into a high position, but their parents were humble. They have grown up among feelings and ideas from which it is difficult later to escape. One may suppose that they inherit their father's instincts together with his property.

On the other hand, one may find some poor offshoot of a

powerful aristocracy whose ambition is vast, for the opinions traditional to his race and the whole spirit of his caste for some time yet buoy him up above his actual fortune.

Another impediment making it far from easy for men of democratic ages to launch on great ambitions is the length of time that must elapse before they are in a position to undertake any such matter. "It is a great advantage," says Pascal, "to be a man of quality, for it brings one man forward at eighteen or twenty, whereas another must wait till he is fifty, which is a clear gain of thirty years." Ambitious men in democracies generally have to do without those thirty years. Equality, while it allows any man to reach any height, prevents his doing so fast.

In a democratic society, as elsewhere, there are only a few great fortunes to be made. As the careers leading thereto are open without discrimination to every citizen, each man's progress is bound to be slow. When all candidates seem more or less alike and it is difficult to make any choice between them without violating the principle of equality which is the supreme law of democratic societies, the first idea which comes to mind is to make them all go forward at the same rate and submit to the same tests.

Therefore, as men become more alike and the principle of equality has quietly penetrated deep into the institutions and manners of the country, the rules of advancement become more inflexible and advancement itself slower. It becomes ever more difficult to reach a position of some importance quickly.

From hatred of privilege and embarrassment in choosing, all men, whatever their capacities, are finally forced through the same sieve, and all without discrimination are made to pass a host of petty preliminary tests, wasting their youth and suffocating their imagination. So they come to despair of ever fully enjoying the good things proffered, and when at last they reach a position in which they could do something out of the ordinary, the taste for it has left them.

In China, where equality has for a very long time been carried to great lengths, no man graduates from one public office to another without passing an examination. He has to face this test at every stage of his career, and the idea is now so deeply rooted in the manners of the people that I remember reading a Chinese novel in which the hero, after many ups and downs, succeeds at last in touching his mistress's heart by passing an examination well. Lofty ambition can hardly breathe in such an atmosphere.

What has been said about politics applies to everything else.

Equality produces the same results everywhere. Even where no law regulates and holds back advancement, competition has this effect.

Hence great and rapid promotion is rare in a well-established democracy. Such events are exceptions to the general rule. Their very singularity makes men forget how seldom they occur.

The inhabitants of democracies do in the end get a glimpse of all these truths. They do at length appreciate that while the law opens an unlimited field before them, and while all can make some easy progress there, no one can flatter himself that his advance is swift. They see a multitude of little intermediate obstacles, all of which have to be negotiated slowly, between them and the great object of their ultimate desires. The very anticipation of this prospect tires ambition and discourages it. They therefore discard such distant and doubtful hopes, preferring to seek delights less lofty but easier to reach. No law limits their horizon, but they do so for themselves.

I have said that high ambitions were rarer in democratic ages than under aristocracies. I must add that when, despite all natural obstacles, they do appear, they wear another face.

I think that ambitious men in democracies are less concerned than those in any other lands for the interests and judgment of posterity. The actual moment completely occupies and absorbs them. They carry through great undertakings quickly in preference to erecting long-lasting monuments. They are much more in love with success than with glory. What they especially ask from men is obedience. What they most desire is power. Their manners almost always lag behind the rise in their social position. As a result, very vulgar tastes often go with their enjoyment of extraordinary prosperity, and it would seem that their only object in rising to supreme power was to gratify trivial and coarse appetites more easily.

I confess that I believe democratic society to have much less to fear from boldness than from paltriness of aim. What frightens me most is the danger that, amid all the constant trivial preoccupations of private life, ambition may lose both its force and its greatness, that human passions may grow gentler and at the same time baser, with the result that the progress of the body social may become daily quieter and less aspiring.

I therefore think that the leaders of the new societies would do wrong if they tried to send the citizens to sleep in a state of happiness too uniform and peaceful, but that they should sometimes give them difficult and dangerous problems to face, to rouse ambition and give it a field of action.

Moralists are constantly complaining that the pet vice of our age is pride.

There is a sense in which that is true; everyone thinks himself better than his neighbor and dislikes obeying a superior. But there is another sense in which it is very far from the truth, for the same man who is unable to put up with either subordination or equality has nonetheless so poor an opinion of himself that he thinks he is born for nothing but the enjoyment of vulgar pleasures. Of his own free will he limits himself to paltry desires and dares not face any lofty enterprise; indeed, he can scarcely imagine such a possibility.

Thus, far from thinking that we should council humility to our contemporaries, I wish men would try to give them a higher idea of themselves and of humanity; humility is far from healthy for them; what they most lack, in my view, is pride. I would gladly surrender several of our petty virtues for that one vice.

His Life Now Is Grafted Upon the Infinite

From Henry Ward Beecher,
Select Orations

A tribute to Lincoln in 1865 from the influential Congregational minister, abolitionist, and orator.

There is no historic figure more noble than that of Moses the Jewish lawgiver. There is scarcely another event in history more touching than his death. He had borne the great burdens of state for forty years, shaped the Jews to a nation, filled out their civil and religious polity, administered their laws, guided their steps, or dwelt with them in all their journeyings in the wilderness; had mourned in their punishment, kept step with their march, and led them in wars, until the end of their labors drew nigh. The last stage was reached. Jordan only lay between them and the promised land. Then came the word of the Lord unto him, "Thou mayest not go over. Get thee up into the mountain, look upon it, and die."

From that silent summit, the hoary leader gazed to the north, to the south, to the west, with hungry eyes. The dim outlines rose up. The hazy recesses spoke of quiet valleys between the hills. With eager longing, with sad resignation, he looked upon the promised land. It was now to him a forbidden land. It was a moment's anguish. He forgot all his personal wants, and drank in the vision of his people's home. His work was done. There lay God's promise fulfilled.

Again a great leader of the people has passed through toil, sorrow, battle, and war, and come near to the promised land of peace, into which he might not pass over. Who shall recount our martyr's sufferings for this people? Since the November of 1860, his horizon has been black with storms. By day and by night he trod a way of danger and darkness. On his shoulders rested a government dearer to him than his own life. At its integrity millions of men were striking at home. Upon this government foreign eyes lowered. It stood like a lone island in a sea full of storms; and every tide and wave seemed eager to devour it. Upon thousands of hearts great sorrows and anxieties have rested, but not on one such, and in such measure, as upon that simple, truthful, noble soul, our faithful and sainted Lincoln. He wrestled ceaselessly, through four black and dreadful purgatorial years, wherein God was cleansing the sin of his people as by fire.

At last the watcher beheld the gray dawn for the country. The mountains began to give forth their forms from out the darkness; and the East came rushing toward us with arms full of joy for all our sorrows. Then it was for him to be glad exceedingly, that had sorrowed immeasurably. Peace could bring to no other heart such joy, such rest, such honor, such trust, such gratitude. But he looked upon it as Moses looked upon the promised land. Then the wail of a nation proclaimed that he had gone from among us. Not thine the sorrow, but ours, sainted soul.

And now the martyr is moving in triumphal march, mightier than when alive. The nation rises up at every stage of his coming. Cities and states are his pall-bearers, and the cannon beats the hours with solemn progression. Dead, dead, dead, he yet speaketh! Is Washington dead? Is Hampden dead? Is David dead? Is any man that ever was fit to live dead? Disenthralled of flesh, and risen in the unobstructed sphere where passion never comes, he begins his illimitable work. His life now is grafted upon the infinite, and will be fruitful as no earthly life can be. Pass on, thou that hast overcome! Your sorrows, oh people, are his peace! Your bells, and bands, and muffled drums, sound triumph in his ear. Wail and weep here; God makes it echo joy and triumph there. Pass on!

Four years ago, oh Illinois, we took from your midst an untried man, and from among the people. We return him to you a mighty conqueror. Not thine anymore, but the nation's; not ours, but the world's. Give him place, oh ye prairies! In the midst of this great continent his dust shall rest, a sacred treasure to myriads who shall pilgrim to that shrine to kindle anew their zeal and patriotism. Ye winds that move over the mighty places of the West, chant requiem! Ye people, behold a martyr whose blood, as so many articulate words, pleads for fidelity, for law, for liberty!

I Have a Dream

Martin Luther King Jr.

Delivered before the Lincoln Memorial on August 28, 1963, this is the best-known speech of the illustrious and heroic civil rights leader. In keeping with his deeply held theological convictions, Dr. King believed that a man's inner spiritual strength to do good came through renouncing violence, and that no Americans could be free so long as any Americans were oppressed.

I am happy to join with you today in what will go down in history as the greatest demonstration for freedom in the history of our nation.

Fivescore years ago, a great American, in whose symbolic shadow we stand today, signed the Emancipation Proclamation. This momentous decree came as a great beacon light of hope to millions of Negro slaves who had been seared in the flames of withering injustice. It came as a joyous daybreak to end the long night of their captivity.

But one hundred years later, the Negro still is not free; one hundred years later, the life of the Negro is still sadly crippled by the manacles of segregation and the chains of discrimination; one hundred years later, the Negro lives on a lonely island of poverty in the midst of a vast ocean of material prosperity; one hundred years later, the Negro is still languished in the corners of American society and finds himself in exile in his own land.

So we've come here today to dramatize a shameful condition. In a sense we've come to our nation's capital to cash a check. When the architects of our republic wrote the magnificent words of the Constitution and the Declaration of Independence, they were signing a promissory note to which every American was to fall heir. This note was the promise that all men, yes, black men as well as white men, would be guaranteed the unalienable rights to life, liberty, and the pursuit of happiness.

It is obvious today that America has defaulted on this promissory note in so far as her citizens of color are concerned. Instead of honoring this sacred obligation, America has given the Negro people a bad check; a check which has come back marked "insufficient funds." We refuse to believe that there are insufficient funds in the great vaults of opportunity of this nation. And so we've come to cash this check, a check that will give us upon demand the riches of freedom and security of justice.

We have also come to this hallowed spot to remind America of the fierce urgency of now. This is no time to engage in the luxury of cooling off or to take the tranquilizing drug of gradualism. Now is the time to make real the promises of democracy; now is the time to rise from the dark and desolate valley of segregation to the sunlit path of racial justice; now is the time to lift our nation from the quicksands of racial injustice to the solid rock of brotherhood; now is the time to make justice a reality for all God's children. It would be fatal for the nation to overlook the urgency of the moment. This sweltering summer of the Negro's legitimate discontent will not pass until there is an invigorating autumn of freedom and equality.

Nineteen sixty-three is not an end, but a beginning. And those who hope that the Negro needed to blow off steam and will now be content, will have a rude awakening if the nation returns to business as usual.

There will be neither rest nor tranquillity in America until the Negro is granted his citizenship rights. There whirlwinds of revolt will continue to shake the foundations of our nation until the bright day of justice emerges.

But there is something that I must say to my people who stand on the warm threshold which leads into the palace of justice. In the process of gaining our rightful place we must not be guilty of wrongful deeds.

Let us not seek to satisfy our thirst for freedom by drinking from the cup of bitterness and hatred. We must forever conduct our struggle on the high plane of dignity and discipline. We must not allow our creative protest to degenerate into physical violence.

Again and again we must rise to the majestic heights of meeting physical force with soul force.

The marvelous new militancy which has engulfed the Negro community must not lead us to a distrust of all white people, for many of our white brothers, as evidenced by their presence here today, have come to realize that their destiny is tied up with our destiny and they have come to realize that their freedom is inextricably bound to our freedom. This offensive we share, mounted to storm the battlements of injustice, must be carried forth by a biracial army. We cannot walk alone.

And as we walk, we must make the pledge that we shall always march ahead. We cannot turn back. There are those who are asking the devotees of civil rights, "When will you be satisfied?" We can never be satisfied as long as the Negro is the victim of the unspeakable horrors of police brutality.

We can never be satisfied as long as our bodies, heavy with fatigue of travel, cannot gain lodging in the motels of the highways and the hotels of the cities. We cannot be satisfied as long as the Negro's basic mobility is from a smaller ghetto to a larger one.

We can never be satisfied as long as our children are stripped of their selfhood and robbed of their dignity by signs saying "for whites only." We cannot be satisfied as long as a Negro in Mississippi cannot vote and a Negro in New York believes he has nothing for which to vote. No, we are not satisfied, and we will not be satisfied until justice rolls down like waters and righteousness like a mighty stream.

I am not unmindful that some of you have come here out of excessive trials and tribulations. Some of you have come fresh from narrow jail cells. Some of you have come from areas where your quest for freedom left you battered by the storms of persecution and staggered by the winds of police brutality. You have been the veterans of creative suffering. Continue to work with the faith that unearned suffering is redemptive.

Go back to Mississippi; go back to Alabama; go back to South Carolina; go back to Georgia; go back to Louisiana; go back to the slums and ghettos of the northern cities, knowing that somehow this situation can, and will be changed. Let us not wallow in the valley of despair.

So I say to you, my friends, that even though we must face the difficulties of today and tomorrow, I still have a dream. It is a dream deeply rooted in the American dream that one day this nation will rise up and live out the true meaning of its creed—we hold these truths to be self-evident, that all men are created equal.

I have a dream that one day on the red hills of Georgia, sons of former slaves and sons of former slave-owners will be able to sit down together at the table of brotherhood.

I have a dream that one day, even the state of Mississippi, a state sweltering with the heat of injustice, sweltering with the heat of oppression, will be transformed into an oasis of freedom and justice.

I have a dream my four little children will one day live in a nation where they will not be judged by the color of their skin but by the content of their character. I have a dream today!

I have a dream that one day, down in Alabama, with its vicious racists, with its governor having his lips dripping with the words of interposition and nullification, that one day, right there in Alabama, little black boys and black girls will be able to join hands with little white boys and white girls as sisters and brothers. I have a dream today!

I have a dream that one day every valley shall be exalted, every hill and mountain shall be made low, the rough places shall be made plain, and the crooked places shall be made straight and the glory of the Lord will be revealed and all flesh shall see it together.

This is our hope. This is the faith that I go back to the South with.

With this faith we will be able to hew out of the mountain of despair a stone of hope. With this faith we will be able to transform the jangling discords of our nation into a beautiful symphony of brotherhood.

With this faith we will be able to work together, to pray together, to struggle together, to go to jail together, to stand up for freedom together, knowing that we will be free one day. This will be the day when all of God's children will be able to sing with new meaning— "my country 'tis of thee; sweet land of liberty; of thee I sing; land where my fathers died, land of the pilgrim's pride; from every mountain side, let freedom ring"—and if America is to be a great nation, this must become true.

So let freedom ring from the prodigious hilltops of New Hampshire.

Let freedom ring from the mighty mountains of New York.

Let freedom ring from the heightening Alleghenies of Pennsylvania.

Let freedom ring from the snow-capped Rockies of Colorado.

Let freedom ring from the curvaceous slopes of California.

But not only that.

Let freedom ring from Stone Mountain of Georgia.

Let freedom ring from Lookout Mountain of Tennessee.

Let freedom ring from every hill and molehill of Mississippi, from every mountainside, let freedom ring.

And when we allow freedom to ring, when we let it ring from every village and hamlet, from every state and city, we will be able to speed up that day when all of God's children—black men and white men, Jews and Gentiles, Catholics and Protestants—will be able to join hands and to sing in the words of the old Negro spiritual, "Free at last, free at last; thank God Almighty, we are free at last."

A Man Among Men

From Theodore Roosevelt,
The Americanism of Theodore Roosevelt

An address by TR on service and citizenship at the Harvard Union in 1907.

Unless democracy is based on the principle of service by everybody who claims the enjoyment of any right, it is not true democracy at all. The man who refuses to render, or is ashamed to render, the necessary service is not fit to live in a democracy. And the man who demands from another a service which he himself would esteem it dishonorable or unbecoming to render is to that extent not a true democrat. No man has a right to demand a service which he does not regard as honorable to render; nor has he a right to demand it unless he pays for it in some way, *the payment to include respect of the man who renders it.* Democracy must mean mutuality of service rendered, and of respect for the service rendered.

The educated man who seeks to console himself for his own lack of the robust qualities necessary to bring success in American politics by moaning over the degeneracy of the times instead of trying to better them, by railing at the men who do the actual work of political life instead of trying himself to do the work, is a poor creature, and, so far as his feeble powers avail, is a damage and not a help to the country.

You may come far short of this disagreeable standard and still be a rather useless member of society. Your education, your cultivation, will not help you if you make the mistake of thinking that it is a substitute for instead of an addition to those qualities which in the struggle of life bring success to the ordinary man without your advantages. Your college training confers no privilege upon you save as tested by the use you make of it. It puts upon you the obligation to show yourselves better able to do certain things than your fellows who have not had your advantages. If it has served merely to make you believe that you are to be excused from contact with the actual world of men and events, then it will prove a curse and not a blessing. If on the other hand you treat your education as a weapon the more in your hands, a weapon to fit you to do better in the hard struggle of effort, and not as excusing you in any way from taking part in practical fashion in that struggle, then it will be a benefit to you.

Let each of you college men remember in after life that in the fundamentals he is very much like his fellows who have not been to college, and that if he is to achieve results, instead of confining himself exclusively to disparagement of other men who have achieved them, he must manage to come to some kind of working agreement with these fellows of his. There are times, of course, when it may be the highest duty of a citizen to stand alone, or practically alone. But if this is a man's normal attitude—if normally he is unable to work in combination with a considerable body of his fellows—it is safe to set him down as unfit for useful service in a democracy. In popular government results worth having can only be achieved by men who combine worthy ideals with practical good sense; who are resolute to accomplish good purposes, but who can accommodate themselves to the give and take necessary where work has to be done, by combination. Moreover, remember that normally the prime object of political life should be to achieve results and not merely to issue manifestoes—save, of course, where the issuance of such manifestoes helps to achieve the results. It is a very bad thing to be morally callous, for moral callousness is disease. But inflammation of the conscience may be just as unhealthy so far as the public is concerned; and if a man's conscience is always telling him to do something foolish he will do well to mistrust its workings. The religious man who is most useful is not he whose sole care is to save his own soul, but the man whose religion bids him strive to advance decency and clean living and to make the world a better place for his fellows to live in; and all this is just as true of the ordinary citizen in the performance of the ordinary duties of political life. . . .

In short, you college men, be doers rather than critics of the deeds that others do. Stand stoutly for your ideals; but keep in mind that they can only be realized, even partially, by practical methods of achievement. Remember always that this Republic of ours is a very real democracy, and that you can only win success by showing that you have the right stuff in you. The college man, the men of intellect and training, should take the lead in every fight for civic and social righteousness. He can take that lead only if in a spirit of thoroughgoing democracy he takes his place among his fellows, not standing aloof from them, but mixing with them, so that he may know, may feel, may sympathize with their hopes, their ambitions, their principles—and even their prejudices—as an American among Americans, as a man among men.

Were We Truly Men?

John Fitzgerald Kennedy

What defines a man? In his 1952 inaugural speech as a Senator-elect from Massachusetts, John F. Kennedy gave an eloquent answer.

For of those to whom much is given, much is required. And when at some future date the high court of history sits in judgment on each of us, recording whether in our brief span of service we fulfilled our responsibilities to the state, our success or failure, in whatever office we hold, will be measured by the answers to four questions:

First, were we truly men of courage, with the courage to stand up to one's enemies, and the courage to stand up, when necessary, to one's associates, the courage to resist public pressure as well as private greed?

Second, were we truly men of judgment, with perceptive judgment of the future as well as the past, of our own mistakes as well as the mistakes of others, with enough wisdom to know what we did not know, and enough candor to admit it?

Third, were we truly men of integrity, men who never ran out on either the principles in which we believed or the people who believed in us, men whom neither financial gain nor political ambition could ever divert from the fulfillment of our sacred trust?

Finally, were we truly men of dedication, with an honor mortgaged to no single individual or group, and compromised by no private obligation or aim, but devoted solely to serving the public good and the national interest?

Courage, judgment, integrity, dedication—these are the historic qualities of the Bay Colony and the Bay State, the qualities which this state has consistently sent to Beacon Hill here in Boston and to Capitol Hill back in Washington. And these are the qualities which, with God's help, this son of Massachusetts hopes will characterize our government's conduct in the four stormy years that lie ahead. Humbly I ask His help in this undertaking; but aware that on earth His will is worked by men, I ask for your help and your prayers as I embark on this new and solemn journey.

MANHOOD IN AMERICA

The Democratic Dad

From Alexis de Tocqueville,
Democracy in America

Although in some ways American civilization drew upon and developed European ideals of manliness from the ancient, medieval and Renaissance eras, life in the new world was so different from anything in the European heritage that new experiences of manliness and fatherhood were bound to emerge. Alexis de Tocqueville, in Democracy in America, *registers a European aristocrat's impression of how the meaning of family life has changed in America because of democratic equality. There are no Catos in Ohio. The old paterfamilias of Roman fame—the father who rules like a benevolent but absolute king over his family—cannot survive transplanting to the new world. As Tocqueville sees it, democracy weakens the father's authority over his children, but increases the open display of affection between them. Your*

children don't think you're a king. But you can shoot hoops with them or
have a pillow fight. This would not have gone down well in ancient Rome.

In America the family, if one takes the word in its Roman and aristocratic sense, no longer exists. One only finds scattered traces thereof in the first years following the birth of children. The father then does, without opposition, exercise the domestic dictatorship which his sons' weakness makes necessary and which is justified by both their weakness and his unquestionable superiority.

But as soon as the young American begins to approach man's estate, the reins of filial obedience are daily slackened. Master of his thoughts, he soon becomes responsible for his own behavior. In America there is in truth no adolescence. At the close of boyhood he is a man and begins to trace out his own path.

It would be wrong to suppose that this results from some sort of domestic struggle, in which, by some kind of moral violence, the son had won the freedom which his father refused. The same habits and principles which lead the former to grasp at independence dispose the latter to consider its enjoyment as an incontestable right.

So in the former one sees none of those hateful, disorderly passions which disturb men long after they have shaken off an established yoke. The latter feels none of those bitter, angry regrets which usually accompany fallen power. The father has long anticipated the moment when his authority must come to an end, and when that time does come near, he abdicates without fuss. The son has known in advance exactly when he will be his own master and wins his liberty without haste or effort, as a possession which is his due and which no one seeks to snatch from him.

In countries organized on the basis of an aristocratic hierarchy, authority never addresses the whole of the governed directly. Men are linked one to the other and confine themselves to controlling those next on the chain. The rest follows. This applies to the family as well as to all associations with a leader. In aristocracies society is, in truth, only concerned with the father. It only controls the sons through the father; it rules him, and he rules them. Hence the father has not only his natural right. He is given a political right to command. He is the author and support of the family; he is also its magistrate.

In democracies, where the long arm of the government reaches each particular man among the crowd separately to bend him to obedience to the common laws, there is no need for such an intermediary. In the eyes of the law the father is only a citizen older and richer than his sons.

When conditions generally are very unequal and this inequality is permanent, the conception of superiority works on the imagination of men. Even if the law gave no parental prerogatives, custom and public opinion would supply them. But when men are little different from one another and such differences are not permanent, the general conception of superiority becomes weaker and less defined. It would be useless for a legislator to put the man who obeys in a position of great inferiority compared to him who gives the orders; mores bring these two men close to one another and daily put them more on a level.

So, then, if I do not see any particular privileges accorded to the head of a family in the legislation of an aristocratic people, I can nonetheless rest assured that his power is much respected there and of wider extent than in a democracy, for I know that, whatever the laws may be, the superior will always seem higher and the inferior lower in aristocracies than in democracies.

When men are more concerned with memories of what has been than with what is, and when they are much more anxious to know what their ancestors thought than to think for themselves, the father is the natural and necessary link between the past and the present, the link where these two chains meet and join. In aristocracies, therefore, the father is not only the political head of the family but also the instrument of tradition, the interpreter of custom, and the arbiter of mores. He is heard with deference, he is addressed always with respect, and the affection felt for him is ever mingled with fear.

When the state of society turns to democracy and men adopt the general principle that it is good and right to judge everything for oneself, taking former beliefs as providing information but not rules, paternal opinions come to have less power over the sons, just as his legal power is less too.

A perusal of the family correspondence surviving from aristocratic ages is enough to illustrate the difference between the two social states in this respect. The style is always correct, ceremonious, rigid, and cold, so that natural warmth of heart can hardly be felt through the words.

But among democratic nations every word a son addresses to his father has a tang of freedom, familiarity, and tenderness all at once, which gives an immediate impression of the new relationship prevailing in the family.

I think that I may be able to sum up in one phrase the whole sense of this chapter and of several others that preceded it. Democracy loosens social ties, but it tightens natural ones. At the same time as it separates citizens, it brings kindred closer together.

An American Father: Robert E. Lee

From Captain Robert E. Lee,
Recollections and Letters of General Robert E. Lee

The two representative men of the North and South, Lincoln and Lee, present a fascinating study in contrasts. Lincoln, who dedicated his public life to a just cause, was a troubled husband and a distracted father, pursuing his duties to his family against an undertow of melancholy. Lee, who in his public life defended the Confederacy, and therefore the evil of slavery, was by contrast a model gentleman, father, and leader of youth in his private and post-war life. Idolized by his children, he was firm and set high standards for them, and they dreaded his bad opinion. And yet he was also a warm and loving father who rough-housed with them and took an interest in everything that concerned their happiness, including their love lives. He took pleasure in his duty to his family, softening his demanding standards with gentleness and wry humor. Famed as a warrior, Lee nevertheless took a keen interest in the family household, including its economy and aesthetic comforts—not only because his disabled wife needed his help, but because Lee liked living graciously and didn't think it was beneath a man to enjoy beautiful and orderly surroundings. Perhaps most impressively, his fatherly care extended from his own children to the young men at Washington College, where he ended his life as a much loved president. Despite his extraordinary feats on the battlefield, Lee always prized liberal education and learning above martial fame and tried to instill the same conviction in his students. This memoir was written by his son, Captain Robert E. Lee.

The first vivid recollection I have of my father is his arrival at Arlington, after his return from the Mexican War.

From that early time I began to be impressed with my father's character, as compared with other men. Every member of the household respected, revered and loved him as a matter of course, but it began to dawn on me that every one else with whom I was thrown held him high in their regard. At forty-five years of age he was active, strong, and as handsome as he had ever been. I never remember his being ill. I presume he was indisposed at times; but no impressions of that kind remain. He was always bright and gay with us little folk, romping, playing, and joking with us. With the older children, he was just as companionable, and I have seen him join my elder brothers and their friends when they would try their powers at a high jump put up in our yard. The two younger children he petted a great deal, and our greatest treat was to get into his bed in the morning and lie close to him, listening while he talked to us in his bright, entertaining way. This custom we kept up with until I was ten years and over. Although he was so joyous and familiar with us, he was very firm on all proper occasions, never indulged us in anything that was not good for us, and exacted the most implicit obedience. I always knew that it was impossible to disobey my father. I felt it in me, I never thought why, but was perfectly sure when he gave an order that it had to be obeyed. My mother I could sometimes circumvent, and at times took liberties with her orders, construing them to suit myself; but exact obedience to every mandate of my father was a part of my life and being at that time. He was very fond of having his hands tickled, and, what was still more curious, it pleased and delighted him to take off his slippers and place his feet in our laps in order to have them tickled. Often, as little things, after romping all day, the enforced sitting would be too much for us, and our drowsiness would soon show itself in continued nods. Then, to arouse us, he had a way of stirring us up with his foot—laughing heartily at and with us. He would often tell us the most delightful stories, and then there was no nodding. Sometimes, however, our interest in his wonderful tales became so engrossing that we would forget to do our duty—when he would declare, "No tickling, no story!" When we were a little older, our elder sister told us one winter the ever-delightful "Lady of the Lake." Of course, she told it in prose and arranged it to suit our mental capacity. Our father was generally in his corner by the fire, most probably with a foot in either the lap of myself or youngest sister—the tickling going on briskly—and would come in at different points of the tale and repeat line after line of the poem—much to our disapproval—but to his great enjoyment.

My father was the most punctual man I ever knew. He was

always ready for family prayers, for meals, and met every engagement, social or business, at the moment. He expected all of us to be the same, and taught us the use and necessity of forming such habits for the convenience of all concerned. I never knew him late for Sunday service at the Post Chapel. He used to appear some minutes before the rest of us, in uniform, jokingly rallying my mother for being late, and for forgetting something at the last moment. When he could wait no longer for her, he would say that he was off and would march along to church by himself, or with any of the children who were ready. There he sat very straight—well up the middle aisle—and, as I remember, always became very sleepy, and sometimes even took a little nap during the sermon. At that time, this drowsiness of my father's was something awful to me, inexplicable. I know it was very hard for me to keep awake, and frequently I did not; but why he, who to my mind could do everything that was right, without any effort, should sometimes be overcome, I could not understand, and did not try to do so.

It was against the rules that the cadets should go beyond certain limits without permission. Of course they did go sometimes, and when caught were given quite a number of "demerits." My father was riding out one afternoon with me, and, while rounding a turn in the mountain road with a deep woody ravine on one side, we came suddenly upon three cadets far beyond the limits. They immediately leaped over a low wall on the side of the road and disappeared from our view. We rode on for a minute in silence; then my father said: "Did you know those young men? But no; if you did, don't say so. I wish boys would do what is right, it would be so much easier for all parties!"

Lee writes to his wife:

"You do not know how much I have missed you and the children, my dear Mary. To be alone in a crowd is very solitary. In the woods, I feel sympathy with the trees and birds, in whose company I take delight, but experience no pleasure in a strange crowd. I hope you are all well and will continue so, and, therefore, must again urge you to be very prudent and careful of those dear children. If I could only get a squeeze at that little fellow, turning up his sweet mouth to 'keese baba!' You must not let him run wild in my absence, and will have to exercise firm authority over all of them. This will not require severity or even strictness, but constant attention and an unwavering course. Mildness and forbearance will strengthen their affection for you, while it will maintain your control over them."

In a letter to one of his sons he writes as follows:

"I cannot go to bed, my dear son, without writing you a few lines, to thank you for your letter, which gave me great pleasure. . . . You and Custis must take great care of your kind mother and dear sisters when your father is dead. To do that you must learn to be good. Be true, kind and generous, and pray earnestly to God to enable you to keep His Commandments 'and walk in the same ways all the days of your life.' I hope to come on soon to see that little baby you have got to show me. You must give her a kiss for me, and one to all the children, to your mother, and grandmother."

My father had had nearly four years' experience in charge of the young men at West Point. The conditions at that place, to be sure, were very different from those at the one to which he was now going, but the work in the main was the same—to train, improve and elevate. I think he was influenced, in making up his mind to accept this position, by the great need of education in his State and in the South, and by the opportunity that he saw at Washington College for starting almost from the beginning, and for helping, by his experience and example, the youth of his country to become good and useful citizens.

In addition to his duties as a college president, my father had to make all the arrangements for his new home.

My mother was an invalid and absent, and as my sisters were with her, everything down to the minutest detail was done by my father's directions and under his superintendence. He had always been noted for his care and attention to little things, and that trait, apparent in him when a mere lad, practiced all through his busy and eventful life, stood him in good stead now. The difficulties to be overcome were made greater by the scarcity and inaccessibility of supplies and workmen and the smallness of his means. In addition, he conducted a large correspondence, always answering every letter. To every member of his family he wrote continually, and was interested in all our pursuits, advising and helping us as no one else could have done.

My father was much interested in all the arrangements of the house, even to the least thing. He would laugh merrily over the difficulties that appalled the rest of us. Our servants were few and unskilled, but his patience and self-control never failed. He often teased my sisters about their experiments in cookery and household arts, encouraging them to renewed efforts after lamentable failures. When they succeeded in a dish for the table, or completed any garment with their own hands, he was lavish with his praise. He would say:

"You are all very helpless; I don't know what you will do when I am gone," and "If you want to be missed by your friends—be useful."

He at once set to work to improve all around him, laid out a vegetable garden, planted roses and shrubs, set out fruit and yard trees, made new walks and repaired the stables, so that in a short time we were quite comfortable and very happy. He at last had a home of his own, with his wife and daughters around him, and though it was not the little farm in the quiet country for which he had so longed, it was very near to it, and it gave rest to himself and those he loved most dearly.

His duties as president of Washington College were far from light. His time was fully occupied, and his new position did not relieve him from responsibility, care and anxiety. He took pains to become acquainted with each student personally, to be really his guide and friend. Their success gratified and pleased him, and their failures, in any degree, pained and grieved him. He felt that he was responsible for their well-doing and progress, and he worked very hard to make them good students and useful men.

The grounds and buildings of the college soon began to show his care, attention, and good taste. In all his life, wherever he happened to be, he immediately set to work to better his surroundings.

The professors and students of the two institutions of learning were constant visitors, especially in the evenings, when young men came to see the girls. If his daughters had guests, my father usually sat with my mother in the dining-room adjoining the drawing-room. When the clock struck ten he would rise and close the shutters carefully and slowly, and, if that hint was not taken, he would simply say "Good night, young gentlemen." The effect was immediate and lasting, and his wishes in that matter, finally becoming generally known, were always respected. Captain W., who had very soon found out the General's views as to the time of leaving, was told on one occasion that General Lee had praised him very much.

"Do you know why?" said the Captain. "It is because I have

never been caught in the parlor at ten o'clock. I came very near it last night, but got out into the porch before the General shut the first blind. That's the reason he called me a 'fine young man.'"

"A Natural Made Gentleman"

From William H. Herndon,
Letters and Papers

Sometimes a man's virtues are tested by an unhappy marriage and shine through in spite of it. Lincoln's marriage was bleak, but his remorse over his inability to love his wife as she would have liked seemed to intensify his resolve to fulfill his duties to the family conscientiously. Lincoln's gentleness and love of justice persevered through the sadness of his marital life and a life-long streak of melancholy. He is a great exemplar of Aristotle's maxim that virtue begins as habit and ends up as one's true disposition. As his memoirist Herndon concludes, despite his humble origins, Lincoln was a "natural made gentleman."

Mr. Lincoln was the best man, the kindest, tenderest, noblest, loveliest, *since Christ.* He was better and purer than Washington; and in mind he stands incomparable, grandly looming up. He is now the great central figure of American History. God bless Abraham Lincoln!

Again—did you know that Mr. Lincoln was "*as crazy as a loon*" *in this city in 1841;* that he did not sit, did not attend to the Legislature, but in part, if any (special session of 1841); that he was then deranged? Did you know that he was forcibly arrested by his special friends here at that time; that they had to remove all razors, knives, pistols, etc., from his room and presence, that he might not commit suicide? Did you know that his crazy bout was partly caused by *that old original love* coming in conflict with *new relations about to be assumed?* His fidelity *was sublime.* Did you know that all Lincoln's struggles, difficulties, etc., between himself and wife were partly, if not wholly, caused by Mrs. L's cognition that Lincoln did not love her, and *did love another?* Lincoln told his wife that he did not love her, did so before he was married to her; she was cognizant of the fact that Lincoln loved another. Did you know that the *Hell* through which Lincoln passed was caused by these things? Mrs. Lincoln's knowledge that Lincoln did not love her and did love another caused much trouble between them. I say, Lincoln told her *he did not love her.* The world does not know her, Mrs. L.'s sufferings, her trials, and the causes of things. Sympathize with her. I shall never rob Mrs. Lincoln of her justice—justice due her. Poor woman! She will yet have her rewards.

Mrs. Lincoln will scold me, poor woman, without knowing I am her friend, determined to put her right before the world for all time. She too had borne her cross, and she shall have justice if I live. Would that I could but talk to you one hour. Mr. and Mrs. Lincoln's marriage was an unfortunate one, and I say to you that what I know and shall tell only ennobles both—that is to say, it will show that Mrs. L. has had cause to suffer, and be almost crazed, while Lincoln self-sacrificed himself rather than to be charged with dishonor. Such a man the world never saw—and never will see again. God bless him—so pure, so tender, so good, so honorable, so noble, so lovely, the very noblest and loveliest man since this orb began to spin. Mr. Lincoln was shoved through her furnace, but, poor woman, she rebelled! Lincoln suffered as it were by crucifixion for forty-five or fifty years; and that process caused his glory, and yet the world doesn't, it seems, want to know it. You have perceived that I am not a very orthodox Christian and yet I believe that Lincoln was God's chosen one.

You wish to know more about Lincoln's domestic life. The history of it is a sad, sad one, I assure you. Many and many a time I have known Lincoln to come down to our office, say at 7 a.m., sometimes bringing with him his then young son Bob. Our office was on the west side of the public square and upstairs. The door that entered our office was, the up half, of glass, with a curtain on the inside made of calico. When we did not wish anyone to see inside, we let down the curtain on the inside. Well, I say, many and many a time have I known Lincoln to come down to our office, sometimes Bob with him, with a small lot of cheese, crackers, and "bologna" sausages under his arm; he would not speak to me, for he was full of sadness, melancholy, and I suppose of the devil; he would draw out the sofa, sit down upon it, open his breakfast, and divide between Bob and himself. I would as a matter of course know that Lincoln was driven from home, by a club, knife, or tongue, and so I would let down the curtain on the inside, go out, and lock the door behind me, taking the key out and with me. I would stay away, say an hour, and then I would go into the office on one pretense or another, and if Lincoln did not then speak, I did as before, go away, etc. In the course of another hour I would go back, and if Lincoln spoke, I knew it was all over, i.e., his fit of sadness, etc. Probably he would say something or I would, and then he would say: "Billy, that puts me in mind of a story," he would tell it, walk up and down the room, laughing the while, and now the dark clouds would pass off his withered and wrinkled face and the God-blessed sunshine of happiness would light up *those* organs o'er which the emotions of that good soul played their gentle dance and chase. Friend, I can see all this now acting before me and am sad.

In the winter of 1857 the Supreme Court was in session and Lincoln had an important suit to argue. He came in the clerk's office, the law library room too; his nose was plastered up, fixed up with court plaster. Now for the facts. Lincoln had on the day before become somewhat abstracted, thoughtful, and let the fire in Mr. and Mrs. Lincoln's sitting room nearly die out. Mrs. Lincoln came to the door of the sitting room from the kitchen and said: "Mr. Lincoln, put some wood on the fire." Lincoln did not hear her and neglected the repair of the fire. Mrs. Lincoln came to the sitting room again and said, "Mr. Lincoln, mend up the fire," it having got low down. Lincoln did not hear Mrs. Lincoln; she came in again and picked up a stick of wood and said: "Mr. Lincoln, I have told you now there three times to mend the fire and you have pretended that you did not hear me. I'll make you hear me this time," and she blazed away at Lincoln with a stick of stovewood and hit him on the nose and thus banged it up. Someone in the courtroom asked Lincoln what was the matter; he made an evasive reply in part to the question. Lincoln's girl stated this, if others did not know it. From what I know of the facts, it is more probable that it is true than untrue. I believe it; it went around among the members of the bar as true. Many such quarrels did take place between Lincoln and his wife. Lincoln's domestic life was a home hell on this globe.

Mr. Lincoln was a kind of fatalist in some aspects of his philosophy, and skeptical in his religion. He was a sad man, a terribly gloomy one—a man of sorrow, if not of agony. This, his state, may have arisen from a defective physical organization, or it may have arisen from some fatalistic idea, that he was to die a sudden and a terrible death. Some unknown power seemed to buzz about his consciousness, his being, his mind, that whispered in his ear: "Look out for danger ahead!" This peculiarity in Mr. Lincoln I had noticed for years, and it is no secret in this city. He has said to me more than once: "Billy, I feel as if I shall meet with some terrible end." He did not know what would strike him, nor when, nor where, nor how hard; he was a blind intellectual Samson, struggling and fighting in the dark against the fates. I say on my own personal observation that he felt this for years. Often and often I have resolved to make or get him to reveal the causes of his misery, but I had not the courage nor the impertinence to do it.

When you are in some imminent danger or suppose you are, when you are suffering terribly, do you not call on some power to come to your assistance and give you relief? I do, and all men do. Mr. Lincoln was in great danger, or thought he was, and did as you and I have done; he sincerely invoked and fiercely interrogated all intelligences to give him a true solution of his state—the mysteries and his destiny. He had great, too great, confidence in the common judgment of an uneducated people. He believed that the common people had truths that philosophers never dreamed of; and often appealed to that common judgment of the common people over the shoulders of scientists. I am not saying that he did right. I am only stating what I know to be facts, to be truths.

To sum up, let us say that here is a very sensitive, diffident, unobtrusive, natural-made gentleman; his mind was strong and deep, sincere and honest, patient and enduring, with a good heart filled with the love of mercy and with a conscience that loved justice, having no vices, only negative defects with many positive virtues; he is strong, self-reliant, honest, full of practical sagacities, manly, noble; he stands high in the foremost [ranks] of man in all ages, their equal, if not their superior, one of the very best types of free institutions and this Christian civilization; and if I were to deliver a eulogy freed from all rhetoric of extravagant eulogy, I say here was a man in his general life [who?] thought strongly, willed firmly, and acted nobly, and in whose life and death the world is lifted to a higher plane of existence.

Men and Women in America

From Alexis de Tocqueville,
Democracy in America

Among aristocratic peoples birth and fortune often make a man and a woman such different creatures that they would never be able to unite with one another. Their passions draw them together, but social conditions and the thoughts that spring from them prevent them from uniting in a permanent and open way. The necessary result of that is a great number of ephemeral and clandestine connections. Nature secretly gets her own back for the restraint imposed by laws.

Things do not happen in the same way when equality of conditions has swept down all the real or imaginary barriers separating man and woman. No girl then feels that she cannot become the wife of the man who likes her best, and that makes irregular morals before marriage very difficult. For however credulous passion may make us, there is hardly a way of persuading a girl that you love her when you are perfectly free to marry her but will not do so.

The same cause is at work, though in a more indirect way, after marriage.

Nothing does more to make illegitimate love seem legitimate in the eyes both of those who experience it and of the watching crowd than forced marriages or ones entered into by chance.

In a country where the woman can always choose freely and where education has taught her to choose well, public opinion is inexorable against her faults.

The severity of the Americans is in part due to this cause. They regard marriage as a contract which is often burdensome but every condition of which the parties are strictly bound to fulfill, because they knew them all beforehand and were at liberty not to bind themselves to anything at all.

The same cause which renders fidelity more obligatory also renders it easier.

The object of marriage in aristocratic lands is more to unite property than persons, so it can happen sometimes that the husband is chosen while at school and the wife at the breast. It is not surprising that the conjugal tie which unites the fortunes of the married couple leaves their hearts to rove at large. That is the natural result of the spirit of the contract.

But when each chooses his companion for himself without any external interference or even prompting, it is usually nothing but similar tastes and thoughts that bring a man and a woman together, and these similarities hold and keep them by each other's side.

I would say that while democratic peoples allow women the right to choose their husbands freely, they have been careful to educate their understanding beforehand and to give their wills the strength necessary for such a choice; but the girls who in an aristocracy secretly escape from paternal authority to throw themselves into the arms of a man whom they have had neither time nor capacity to judge lack all these guarantees. One should not be surprised that they make ill use of their free choice the first time they avail themselves of it, nor that they make such cruel mistakes when, without receiving a democratic education, they wish, in marriage, to follow democratic customs.

Men Who Greatly Dared

From Theodore Roosevelt,
The Americanism of Theodore Roosevelt

There was scant room for the coward and the weakling in the ranks of the adventurous frontiersmen—the pioneer settlers who first broke up the wild prairie soil, who first hewed their way into the primeval forest, who guided their white-topped wagons across the endless leagues of Indian-haunted desolation, and explored every remote mountain-chain in the restless quest for metal wealth. Behind them came the men who completed the work they had roughly begun: who drove the great railroad system over plain and desert and mountain pass; who stocked the teeming ranches, and under irrigation saw the bright green of the alfalfa and the yellow of the golden stubble supplant the gray of the sagebrush desert; who have built great populous cities—cities in which every art and science of civilization are carried to the highest point—on tracts which, when the nineteenth century had passed its meridian, were still known only to the grim trappers and hunters and the red lords of the wilderness with whom they waged eternal war.

Such is the record of which we are so proud. It is a record of men who greatly dared and greatly did; a record of wanderings wider and more dangerous than those of the Vikings; a record of endless feats of arms, of victory after victory in the ceaseless strife waged against wild man and wild nature. The winning of the West was the great epic feat in the history of our race.

We have then a right to meet today in a spirit of just pride in the past. But when we pay homage to the hardy, grim, resolute men who, with incredible toil and risk, laid deep the foundations of the civilization that we inherit, let us steadily remember that the only homage that counts is the homage of deeds—not merely of words. It is well to gather here to show that we remember what has been done in the past by the Western pioneers of our people, and that we glory in the greatness for which they prepared the way. But lip-loyalty by itself avails very little, whether it is expressed concerning a nation or an ideal. It would be a sad and evil thing for this country if ever the day came when we considered the great deeds of our forefathers as an excuse for our resting slothfully satisfied with what has been already done. On the contrary, they should be an inspiration and appeal, summoning us to show that we too have courage and strength; that we too are ready to dare greatly if the need arises; and, above all, that we are firmly bent upon that steady performance of everyday duty which, in the long run, is of such incredible worth in the formation of national character.

It is character that counts in a nation as in a man. It is a good thing to have a keen, fine intellectual development in a nation, to produce orators, artists, successful business men; but it is an infinitely greater thing to have those solid qualities which we group together under the name of character—sobriety, steadfastness, the sense of obligation toward one's neighbor and one's God, hard common sense, and, combined with it, the lift of generous enthusiasm toward whatever is right. These are the qualities which go to make up true national greatness.

The worst development that we could see in civic life in this country would be a division of citizens into two camps, one camp containing nice, well-behaved, well-meaning little men, with receding chins and small feet, men who mean well and who if they are insulted feel shocked and want to go home; and the other camp containing robust and efficient creatures who do not mean well at all. I wish to see our side—the side of decency—include men who have not the slightest fear of the people on the other side. I wish to see the decent man in any relation of life, including politics, when hustled by the man who is not decent, able so to hold his own that the other gentleman shall feel no desire to hustle him again. My plea is for the virtue that shall be strong and that shall also have a good time.

Young Husbands

From Albert J. Beveridge,
The Young Man and the World

Albert J. Beveridge's The Young Man and the World *(1906) was a collection of essays that had originally appeared in* The Saturday Evening Post. *His book reflects a taste for popular moralizing and uplift widespread at the turn of the century. It's a characteristic exhortation to Victorian virtue in an American context.*

Your father made the old home. Prove yourself worthy of him by making the new home. He built the roof-tree which sheltered you. Build you a roof-tree that may in its turn shelter others. What abnormal egotism the attitude of him who says, "This planet, and all the uncounted centuries of the past, were made for *me* and nobody else, and I will live accordingly. I will go it alone."

"I wish John had not married so young," said a woman of wealth, fashion, and brilliant talents in speaking of her son.

"Why, how old was he?" asked her friend. "Twenty-five,"said she; "he ought to have waited ten years longer." "I think not," was the response of the world-wise man with whom she was conversing. "If he got a good wife he was in great luck that he did not wait longer."

"No," persisted the mother, "he ought to have taken more time 'to look around.' These early marriages interfere with a young man's career."

This fragment of a real conversation, which is typical of numberless others like it, reveals the false and shallow philosophy which, if it becomes our code of national living, will make the lives of our young people abnormal and our twentieth-century civilization artificial and neurotic. Even now too many people are thinking about a "career." Mothers are talking about "careers" for their sons. Young men are dreaming of their "careers."

It is assumed that a young man can "carve out his career" if his attention is not distracted and his powers are not diminished by a wife and children whom he must feed, clothe, and consider. The icy selfishness of this hypothesis of life ought to be enough to reject it without argument. Who is any man, that he should have a "career"? And what does a "career" amount to, anyway?

I am assuming that you are man enough to be a man—not a mere machine of selfishness on the one hand, or an anemic imitation of masculinity on the other hand. I am assuming that you think—and, what is more important, feel—that Nature knows what she is about; that "God is not mocked"; and that therefore you propose to live in harmony with universal law.

Therefore, I am assuming that you have established, or will establish, the new home in place of the old home. I am assuming that you will do this before there is a gray hair in your head or a wrinkle under your eye.

Of course nobody means that young men should hurl themselves into matrimony. The fact that it is advisable for you to learn to swim does not mean that you should jump into the first stream you come to, with your clothes and shoes on. Undoubtedly you ought first to get "settled"; that is, you ought to prepare for what you are going to do in life and begin the doing of it. Don't take this step while you are in college. If you mean to be a lawyer, you ought to get your legal education and open your office; if a business man, you should "get started"; if an artisan, you should acquire your trade, etc. But it is inadvisable to wait longer.

It is not necessary for you to "build up a practice" in the profession, or make a lot of money in business, or secure unusual wages as a skilled laborer. Begin at the beginning, and live your lives together, share your hardships together, and let your fortune, good or ill, be of your joint making.

Of course you will spend all of your extra time at home. That is what home is for. Live in your home; do not merely eat and sleep there. It is not a boarding-house, remember that. Books are there, and music and a human sympathy and a marvelous care for you, under whose influence alone the soul of a young man grows into real grandeur, power, and beauty. And be sure that you let each day have its play-hour.

Speaking of politics, I have always thought men, young and

old, ought to consult their wives and families about how they cast their ballot. What right has any man to vote as he individually thinks best? He is the head of the family, after all. This Republic is not made up of individuals; it is made up of families. Its unit is not the boarding-house, but the home.

Of course, being an American and a gentleman, you will have the American gentleman's conception of all womanhood, and his adoring reverence for the one woman who has blessed him with her life's companionship. You will cherish her, therefore, in that way which none but the American gentleman quite understands. You will be gentle with her, and watchful of her health and happiness.

You will be ever brave and kind, wise and strong, deserving that respect which she is so anxious to accord you; earning that devotion which by the very nature of her being she must bestow on you; winning that admiration which it is the crowning pride of her life to yield to you; and, finally, receiving that care which only her hands can give, and a life-long joy which, increasing with the years, is fullest and most perfect when both your heads are white and your mutual steps no longer wander from the threshold of that "new home" which you built in the beginning of your lives, and which is now the "old home" to your children, who beneath its roof "rise up and call you blessed."

Moral Force Gives a Man Both Fearlessness and Tranquillity

From Ralph Waldo Emerson,
Sermons

It is quite important to observe that more is required of you than to say and do what is agreed on all hands to be right. I have said, every man is an original mind. It follows, that there is some peculiar merit which it is yours to seek and find. You must work after your own fashion, and not after that of anybody else. You must be virtuous and wise in your own way, as much as you must speak in your own tone, and not mimic other people's. The first resolute efforts at a virtuous life, are often embarrassed by vain attempts to cooperate in those good works which are most in vogue. There are, perhaps, many benevolent projects—certain plans of instruction, or of charity, or of public reform, which interest the community, but which fail to affect you. Let them alone. If you have given them a fair examination, and doubt their efficacy, or are satisfied that you have not power to forward them, do not praise them because they are popular and because other people think they ought to have your support. Do not use a stronger expression in commending the best cause than your own feeling will justify. Do not put at risk the integrity of your own character, and neutralize the force of your own talents by giving a half support to any thing which, however good it may be, is not good for you—is not the place appointed for you. There is something—be assured, there is something—which does seem to you good and wise. Praise that; aid that; give yourself to that; and not the less because you find yourself in the minority, no, nor even if you should find yourself alone.

It is wonderful the amount of moral force which strict consistency of character—the habit of regarding not only what is true in words, but what is true for himself, a fit object for his advocacy—bestows upon the words of a single-minded person. You feel that it is not he who speaks, so much as truth and reason which speak through him.

One more mark of the man we describe is his fearlessness and habitual tranquillity. God rewards those who obey him with peace. The person who implicitly follows the leading of his own mind casts off from himself the responsibility of his words and actions and throws that responsibility upon God. Whilst a man rests upon the simple perception of the rectitude of his action, he has nothing to do with consequences. He is above them. He has nothing to do with the effect of his example. God will take care of his example. He is following God's finger and cannot go astray. Whilst I walk according to my conscience, I know I shall never be ashamed. When I have adhered to it, I know my conduct is capable of explanation though I may have wholly forgotten the circumstances.

I have enumerated some of the traits of this desirable character. I wish it was in my power to show the striking contrast to the tameness and slavishness of our ordinary habits that is presented by a life thus springing ever fresh from an active mind; to show the grace and the power of a man not hampered by little fears nor mean ambition but walking in the world with the free step of Adam in the Garden, which was all his own by the highest right; a man who when known is found to unite every endearing sportive grace to a sublime self-subsistency.

I see fragments of this character everywhere; they make the sweetness and virtue of society, but the individual in high or in humble life who holds this purpose steadily before him—how rarely is he found.

Finally, in answer to any, if such there be, who shall say, "This quality of genuineness or truth of character is good, but is there not something better?" I will add the remark that the conviction must be produced in our minds that this *truth of character is identical with a religious life;* that they are one and the same thing; that this voice of your own mind is the voice of God, that the reason why you are bound to reverence it is because it is the direct revelation of your Maker's will, not written in books many ages since nor attested by distant miracles but writ in the flesh and blood, in the faculties and emotions of your constitution.

Family Life and the Average Man's Duty

From Theodore Roosevelt, The Americanism of Theodore Roosevelt

The Nation is in a bad way if there is no real home, if the family is not of the right kind; if the man is not a good husband and father, if he is brutal or cowardly or selfish, if the woman has lost her sense of duty, if she is sunk in vapid self-indulgence or has let her nature be twisted so that she prefers sterile pseudo-intellectuality to that great and beautiful development of character which comes only to those whose lives know the fullness of duty done, or effort made and self-sacrifice undergone.

In the last analysis the welfare of the State depends absolutely upon whether or not the average family, the average man and woman and their children, represent the kind of citizenship fit for the foundation of a great nation; and if we fail to appreciate this we fail to appreciate the root morality upon which all healthy civilization is based.

There are certain old truths which will be true as long as this world endures, and which no amount of progress can alter. One of these is the truth that the primary duty of the husband is to be the homemaker, the breadwinner for his wife and children, and that the primary duty of the woman is to be the helpmeet, the housewife, and mother. The woman should have ample educational advantages; but save in exceptional cases the man must be, and she need not be, and generally ought not to be, trained for a lifelong career as the family breadwinner.

Of course there is now and then a man who in some given crises plays the hero although on other occasions he plays the brute—there are such cases; but it is a mighty unsafe thing to proceed upon the assumption that because a man is ordinarily a brute he will therefore be a hero in a crisis. Disregarding the exceptions, and speaking normally, no man can be of any service to the State, no man can amount to anything from the standpoint of usefulness to the community at large, unless first and foremost he is a decent man in the close relations of life. No community can afford to think for one moment that great public service, that great material achievement, that ability shown in no matter how many different directions, will atone for the lack of a sound family life.

Multiplication of divorces means that there is something rotten in the community, that there is some principle of evil at work which must be counteracted and overcome or widespread disaster will follow. In the same way, if the man preaches and practices a different code of morality for himself than that which he demands that his wife shall practice, then no profession on his part of devotion to civic ideals will in the least avail to alter the fact that he is fundamentally a bad citizen. I do not believe in weakness. I believe in a man's being a man; and for that very reason I abhor the creature who uses the expression that "a man must be a man" in order to excuse his being a vile and vicious man.

The Whistle

From Benjamin Franklin,
Essays Humorous, Moral and Literary

Franklin wrote this story for his nephew.

When I was a child, at seven years old, my friends on a holiday, filled my pockets with coppers. I went directly to a shop where they sold toys for children; and, being charmed with the sound of a *whistle,* that I met by the way in the hands of another boy, I voluntarily offered him all my money for one. I then came home, and when whistling all over the house, much pleased with my *whistle,* but disturbing all the family. My brothers and sisters and cousins, understanding the bargain I had made, told me I had given four times as much for it as it was worth. This put me in mind what good things I might have bought with the rest of the money; and they laughed at me so much for my folly that I cried with vexation; and the reflection gave me more chagrin than the *whistle* gave me pleasure.

This, however, was afterward of use to me, the impression continuing on my mind; so that often, when I was tempted to buy some unnecessary thing, I said to myself, *Don't give too much for the whistle;* and so I saved my money.

As I grew up, came into the world, and observed the actions of men, I thought I met with many, very many, who *gave too much for the whistle.*

When I saw any one too ambitious of court favor, sacrificing his time in attendance on levees, his repose, his liberty, his virtue, and perhaps his friends, to attain it, I have said to myself, *This man gave too much for his whistle.*

When I saw another fond of popularity, constantly employing himself in political bustles, neglecting his own affairs, and ruining them by that neglect; *He pays indeed,* says I, *too much for this whistle.*

If I knew a miser, who gave up every kind of comfortable living, all the pleasure of doing good to others, all the esteem of his fellow-citizens, and the joys of benevolent friendship, for the sake of accumulating wealth; *Poor man,* says I, *you do indeed pay too much for your whistle.*

When I meet a man of pleasure, sacrificing every laudable improvement of the mind, or of his fortune, to mere corporeal sensations; *Mistaken man*, says I, *you are providing pain for yourself instead of pleasure: you give too much for your whistle.*

If I see one fond of fine clothes, fine furniture, fine equipages, all above his fortune, for which he contracts debts, and ends his career in prison; *Alas*, says I, *he has paid dear, very dear, for his whistle.*

When I see a beautiful, sweet-tempered girl, married to an ill-natured brute of a husband; *What a pity it is,* says I, *that she has paid so much for a whistle.*

In short, I conceived that great part of the miseries of mankind were brought upon them by the false estimates they had made of the value of things, and by their giving too much for their *whistles.*

The College Man

From Albert J. Beveridge,
The Young Man and the World

Watch out for tobacco, alcohol, and those Eastern colleges.

You can succeed—I repeat it—college or no college; all you have to do in the latter case is to put on a little more steam. And remember that some of the world's sages of the practical have closed their life's wisdom with the deliberate opinion that a college education is a waste of time, and an over-refinement of body and of mind.

Still, with all this in mind, my advice is this: Go to college. Go to the best possible college for *you.* Patiently hold on through the sternest discipline you can stand, until the course is completed. It will not be fatal to your success if you do not go; but you will be better prepared to meet the world if you do go. I do not mean that your mind will be stored with much more knowledge that will be useful to you if you go through college than if you do not go through college.

Probably the man who keeps at work at the business he is going to follow through life, during the years when other men are studying in college, acquires more information that will be "useful" to him in his practical career. But the college man who has not thrown away his college life comes from the training of his alma mater with a mind as highly disciplined as are the wrist and eye of the skilled swordsman.

Nobody contends that a college adds an ounce of brain power. But if college opportunities are not wasted, such mind as the student does have is developed up to the highest possible point of efficiency. The college man who has not scorned his work will understand any given situation a great deal quicker than his brother who, with equal ability, has not had the training of the university.

The spirit with which you enter college is just as important as going to college at all. It is more important. For if a man has the spirit that will get for him all that a college education has to give, it will also make him triumph in a contest with the world, even if he does not get his college education. It will only be a little harder for him, that is all.

But if a man has not that mingled will and wish for a college education flaming through his young veins that makes him capable of any sacrifice to get through college, I do not see what good a college education will do him—no, nor any other kind of an education. The quicker such a man is compelled to make his own living without help from any source, the better for him.

This one word of definite helpfulness on this subject: Do not choose any particular college because you want to be known as a Yale man, a Harvard man, a Princeton man, or any other kind of man. Remember that the world cares less than the snap of its fingers what particular *college* man you are.

What the world cares about is that you should *be* a man—a real *man*.

Nobody cares what college you went to. Nobody cares whether you went to college at all.

But everybody cares whether you are a real force among men; and everybody cares more and more as it becomes clearer and clearer that you are not only a force, but a trained, disciplined force. That is why you ought to go to college—to be a trained, disciplined force. But how and where you got your power—the world of men and women is far too interested in itself to be interested in that.

When you do finally go to college, take care of yourself like a man. I am told that there are men in college who have valets to attend them, their rooms, and their clothes. Think of that!

While I am on this subject I might as well say another thing:

Do not think that you have got to smoke in order to be or look like a college man. A pipe in the mouth of a youth does not make him look like a college man, or any other kind of man. It merely makes him look absurd, that is all. And if there is ever a time on earth when you do not need the stimulus of tobacco, it is while you are in college.

Tobacco is a wonderful vegetable. It is, I believe, the only substance in the world which at the same time is a stimulant and a narcotic, a heart excitant and a nerve sedative. Very well. You are too young yet to need a heart stimulant, too young to need anything to quiet your nerves.

If at your tender age your nerves are so inflamed that they must be soothed, and if at the very sunrise of your life your heart is so feeble that it must be forced with any stimulant, you had better quit college. College is no place for you if you are such a decadent; yes, and you will find the world a good deal harder place than college.

Cut out tobacco, therefore. For a young fellow in college it is a ridiculous affectation—nothing more. Why? Because you do not need tobacco; that is why. At least you do not need it yet. The time may come when you will find tobacco helpful, but it will not be until you have been a long while out of college. As to whether tobacco is good for a man at any stage of life the doctors disagree, and "where doctors disagree, who shall decide?"

Ruskin says that no really immortal work has been done in the world since tobacco was introduced; but we know that this is not true. I would not be understood as having a prejudice for or against the weed. Whether a full-grown man shall use it or not is something for himself to decide. Personally I liked it so well that I made up my mind a long time ago to give it up altogether.

But there is absolutely no excuse for a man young enough to still be in college to use it at all. And it does not look right. For a boy to use tobacco has something contemptible about it. I will not argue whether this is justified or not. That is the way most people feel about it. Whether their feeling is a prejudice or not, there is no use of your needlessly offending their prejudice and this is to be taken into account. For you want to succeed, do you not? Very well. You cannot mount a ladder of air; you must rise on the solid stepping-stones of the people's deserved regard.

And, of course, you will not disgrace yourself by drinking. There is absolutely nothing in it. If you have your fling at it you will learn how surely Intoxication's apples of gold turn to the bitterest ashes in eating. But when you do find how fruitless of everything but regrets dissipation is, be honest with yourself and quit it. Be honest with the mother who is at home praying for you, and quit it. But this is weak advice. Be honest with that mother who is at home praying for you, and *never begin it*. That's the thing—*never begin it!*

In a word, be a man; and you will be very little of a man, very little indeed, if you have got to resort to tobacco and liquor to add to your blood and conduct that touch of devilishness which you may think is a necessary part of manliness. Indeed, between fifteen and thirty years of age your veins will be quite full enough of the untamed and desperate. I do not object in the least to this wild mustang period in a man's life.

Is a fellow to have no fun? you will say. Of course, have all the fun you want; the more the better. But if you need stimulants and tobacco to key you up to the capacity for fun, you are a solemn person indeed.

One thing I must warn you against, and warn you supremely: the critical habit of mind which somehow or other a college education does seem to produce. This is especially true of the great universities of our East.

A Man Must Be a Nonconformist

From Ralph Waldo Emerson, Sermons

There is a time in every man's education when he arrives at the conviction that envy is ignorance; that imitation is suicide; that he must take himself for better or worse as his portion; that though the wide universe is full of good, no kernel of nourishing corn can come to him but through his toil bestowed on that plot of ground which is given to him to till. The power which resides in him is new in nature, and none but he knows what that is which he can do, nor does he know until he has tried. Not for nothing one face, one character, one fact, makes much impression on him, and another none. It is not without preestablished harmony, this sculpture in the memory. The eye was placed where one ray should fall, that it might testify of that particular ray. Bravely let him speak the utmost syllable of his confession. We but half express ourselves, and are ashamed of that divine idea which each of us represents. It may be safely trusted as proportionate and of good issues, so it be faithfully imparted, but God will not have his work made manifest by cowards. It needs a divine man to exhibit anything divine. A man is relieved and gay when he has put his heart into his work and done his best; but what he has said or done otherwise shall give him no peace. It is a deliverance which does not deliver. In the attempt his genius deserts him; no muse befriends; no invention, no hope.

Trust thyself: every heart vibrates to that iron string. Accept the place that divine providence has found for you, the society of your contemporaries, the connexion of events. Great men have always done so, and confided themselves childlike to the genius of their age, betraying their perception that the Eternal was stirring at their heart, working through their hands, predominating in all their being. And we are now men, and must accept in the highest mind the same transcendent destiny; and not inched in a corner, not cowards fleeing before a revolution, but redeemers and benefactors, pious aspirants to be noble clay under the Almighty effort let us advance on Chaos and the Dark.

What pretty oracles nature yields us on this text in the face and behavior of children, babes, and even brutes. That divided and rebel mind, that distrust of a sentiment because our arithmetic has computed the strength and means opposed to our purpose, these have not. Their mind being whole, their eye is as yet unconquered, and when we look in their faces, we are disconcerted. Infancy conforms to nobody: all conform to it; so that one babe commonly makes four or five out of the adults who prattle and play to it. So God has armed youth and puberty and manhood no less with its own piquancy and charm, and made it enviable and gracious and its claims not to be put by, if it will stand by itself. Do not think the youth has no force, because he cannot speak to you and me. Hark! In the next room who spoke so clear and emphatic? It seems he knows how to speak to his contemporaries. Good Heaven! It is he! It is that very lump of bashfulness and phlegm which for weeks has done nothing but eat when you were by, and now rolls out these words like bell-strokes. It seems he knows how to speak to his contemporaries. Bashful or bold then, he will know how to make us seniors very unnecessary.

The nonchalance of boys who are sure of a dinner, and would disdain as much as a lord to do or say aught to conciliate one, is the healthy attitude of human nature. How is a boy the master of society;

independent, irresponsible, looking out from his corner on such people and facts as pass by, he tries and sentences them on their merits, in the swift, summary way of boys, as good, bad, interesting, silly, eloquent, troublesome. He cumbers himself never about consequences, about interest; he gives an independent, genuine verdict. You must court him; he does not court you. But the man is as it were clapped into jail by his consciousness. As soon as he has once acted or spoken with eclat he is a committed person, watched by the sympathy or the hatred of hundreds, whose affections must now enter into his account. There is no Lethe for this. Ah, that he could pass again into his neutral, godlike independence! Who can thus lose all pledge and, having observed, observe again from the same unaffected, unbiased, unbribable, unaffrighted innocence, must always be formidable, must always engage the poet's and the man's regards. Of such an immortal youth the force would be felt. He would utter opinions on all passing affairs, which being seen to be not private but necessary, would sink like darts into the ear of men and put them in fear.

These are the voices which we hear in solitude, but they grow faint and inaudible as we enter into the world. Society everywhere is in conspiracy against the manhood of every one of its members. Society is a joint-stock company, in which the members agree, for the better securing of his bread to each shareholder, to surrender the liberty and culture of the eater. The virtue in most request is conformity. Self-reliance is its aversion. It loves not realities and creators, but names and customs.

Whoso would be a man, must be a nonconformist.

A foolish consistency is the hobgoblin of little minds, adored by little statesmen and philosophers and divines. With consistency a great soul has simply nothing to do. He may as well concern himself with his shadow on the wall. Out upon your guarded lips! Sew them up with packthread, do. Else if you would be a man speak what you think today in words as hard as cannon balls, and tomorrow speak what tomorrow thinks in hard words again, though it contradict every thing you said today. Ah, then, exclaim the aged ladies, you shall be sure to be misunderstood! Misunderstood! It is a right fool's word. Is it so bad then to be misunderstood? Pythagoras was misunderstood, and Socrates, and Jesus, and Luther, and Copernicus, and Galileo, and Newton, and every pure and wise spirit that ever took flesh. To be great is to be misunderstood.

No Man Is Happy If
He Does Not Work

From Theodore Roosevelt,
The Americanism of Theodore Roosevelt

I wish to preach, not the doctrine of ignoble ease, but the doctrine of the strenuous life, the life of toil and effort, of labor and strife; to preach that highest form of success which comes, not to the man who desires mere easy peace, but to the man who does not shrink from danger, from hardship, or from bitter toil, and who out of these wins the splendid ultimate triumph.

A life of slothful ease, a life of that peace which springs merely from lack either of desire or of power to strive after great things, is as little worthy of a nation as of an individual. I ask only that what every self-respecting American demands from himself and from his sons shall be demanded of the American Nation as a whole. Who among you would teach your boys that ease, that peace, is to be the first consideration in their eyes—to be the ultimate goal after which they strive? You men of Chicago have made this city great, you men of Illinois have done your share, and more than your share, in making America great, because you neither preach nor practice such a doctrine. You work yourselves, and you bring up your sons to work. If you are rich and are worth your salt, you will teach your sons that though they may have leisure, it is not to be spent in idleness; for wisely used leisure merely means that those who possess it, being free from the necessity of working for their livelihood, are all the more bound to carry on some kind of non-remunerative work in science, in letters, in art, in exploration, in historical research—work of the type we most need in this country, the successful carrying out of which reflects most honor upon the Nation. We do not admire the man of timid peace. We admire the man who embodies victorious effort; the man who never wrongs his neighbor, who is prompt to help a friend, but who has those virile qualities necessary to win in the stern strife of actual life. It is hard to fail, but it is worse never to have tried to succeed.

In the last analysis a healthy state can exist only when the men and women who make it up lead clean, vigorous, healthy lives; when the children are so trained that they shall endeavor, not to shirk difficulties, but to overcome them; not to seek ease, but to know how to wrest triumph from toil and risk. The man must be glad to do a man's work, to dare and endure and to labor; to keep himself, and to keep those dependent upon him.

As it is with the individual, so it is with the nation. It is a base untruth to say that happy is the nation that has no history. Thrice happy is the nation that has a glorious history. Far better it is to dare mighty things, to win glorious triumphs, even though checkered by failure, than to take rank with those poor spirits who neither enjoy much nor suffer much, because they live in the gray twilight that knows not victory nor defeat. If in 1861 the men who loved the Union had believed that peace was the end of all things, and war and strife the worst of all things, and had acted up to their belief, we would have saved hundreds of thousands of lives, we would have saved hundreds of millions of dollars. Moreover, besides saving all the blood and treasure we then lavished, we would have prevented the heartbreak of many women, the dissolution of many homes, and we would have spared the country those months of gloom and shame when it seemed as if our armies marched only to defeat. We could have avoided all this suffering simply by shrinking from strife. And if we had thus avoided it, we would have shown that we were weaklings, and that we were unfit to stand among the great nations of the earth. Thank God for the iron in the blood of our fathers, the men who upheld the wisdom of Lincoln, and bore sword or rifle in the armies of Grant!

I preach to you, then, my countrymen, that our country calls not for the life of ease but for the life of strenuous endeavor. The twentieth century looms before us big with the fate of many nations. If we stand idly by, if we seek merely swollen, slothful ease and ignoble peace, if we shrink from the hard contests where men must win at hazard of their lives and at the risk of all they hold dear, then the bolder and stronger peoples will pass us by, and will win for themselves the domination of the world. Let us therefore boldly face the life of strife, resolute to do our duty well and manfully; resolute to uphold righteousness by deed and by word; resolute to be both honest and brave, to serve high ideals, yet to use practical methods. Above all, let us shrink from no strife, moral or physical, within or without the nation, provided we are certain that the strife is justified, for it is only through strife, through hard and dangerous endeavor, that we shall ultimately win the goal of true national greatness.

Your work is hard. Do you suppose I mention that because I pity you? No; not a bit. I don't pity any man who does hard work worth doing. I admire him. I pity the creature who doesn't work, at whichever end of the social scale he may regard himself as being. The law of worthy work well done is the law of successful American life.

Work and love, using each in its broadest sense—work, the quality which makes a man ashamed not to be able to pull his own weight, not to be able to do for himself as well as for others without being beholden to any one for what he is doing. No man is happy if he does not work. Of all miserable creatures the idler, in whatever rank of society, is in the long run the most miserable. If a man is utterly selfish, if utterly disregardful of the rights of others, if he has no ideals, if he works simply for the sake of ministering to his own base passions, if he works simply to gratify himself, small is his good in the community. I think even then he is probably better off than if he is an idler, but he is of no real use unless together with the quality which enables him to work he has the quality which enables him to love his fellows, to work with them and for them for the common good of all.

8

THE INVISIBLE MAN

As WE ENTER THE NEW MILLENNIUM, THE MEANING OF MANLIness is increasingly unclear and fragmented. The Rolling Stones' paean to alienation, "Shattered," might serve as an anthem for our disaffection with traditional ideals. Up until at least World War II, a more or less continuous tradition from Plato to Theodore Roosevelt had codified a subtle, complex, and yet common vision of manhood. In the last few generations, by contrast, the meaning of manliness seems to have exploded into a million shards of shrapnel. What follows is a sampling of those fragments, from a statement by rebel icon James Dean to a sketch of teenage Goth culture, as conveyed by fiction, lyrics, poetry, and journalism.

Some of these fragments are bleak indeed. They speak of homelessness both physical and spiritual, of aimlessness and despair; of young men who have forgotten what it is to feel, or who cannot put those feelings into words because no one has taught them the vocabulary of love and honor. Hence, while they have strong passions, and strong loves, those passions often remain mute, baffled, and stifling because they can find no release and relief in the expression of honest and delicate sentiments.

But the panorama isn't all bleak. Contemporary man may be an invisible man, but you can still see his shadow as he walks those lonely streets. As often as these fragments are depressing and nihilistic, just as often they are full of naive wonder, generous feeling, a longing for heroism and adventure, and a burning desire to be decent toward others and be treated decently in return. Through the shadows there are occasional flares of brilliance, honest and authentic intimations of what men have lost, and of what it still could mean to be a good man, husband, parent, and citizen. No one who knows many young people today is likely to capitulate entirely to despair. Young men still want heroes, and they still want to be heroes. They still want to fall in love and prove themselves worthy of their beloved's affection. The young man who may be invisible today will soon reemerge into the sunlight.

REBELLION AND DESPAIR

The End of Something

From Ernest Hemingway,
In Our Time

The twentieth century brought a new kind of brutality to both love and war. Heroism and chivalry seemed outmoded in both spheres. Ernest Hemingway's characters embody this shift from the traditional vocabulary of romance to baffled inarticulateness: "Love isn't fun anymore."

We were in a garden at Mons. Young Buckley came in with his patrol from across the river. The first German I saw climbed up over the garden wall. We waited till he got one leg over and then potted him. He had so much equipment on and looked awfully surprised and fell down into the garden. Then three more came over further down the wall. We shot them. They all came just like that.

In the old days Hortans Bay was a lumbering town. No one who lived in it was out of sound of the big saws in the mill by the lake. Then one year there were no more logs to make lumber. The lumber schooners came into the bay and were loaded with the cut of the mill that stood stacked in the yard. All the piles of lumber were carried away. The big mill building had all its machinery that was removable taken out and hoisted on board one of the schooners by the men who had worked on the mill. The schooner moved out of the bay toward the open lake carrying the two great saws, the traveling carriage that hurled the logs against the revolving, circular saws and all the rollers, wheels, belts and iron piled on a hull-deep load of lumber. Its open hold covered with canvas and lashed tight, the sails of the schooner filled and it moved out into the open lake, carrying with it everything that had made the mill a mill and Hortons Bay a town.

The one-story bunk houses, the eating-house, the company

store, the mill offices, and the big mill itself stood deserted in the acres of sawdust that covered the swampy meadow by the shore of the bay.

Ten years later there was nothing of the mill left except the broken white limestone of its foundations showing through the swampy second growth as Nick and Marjorie rowed along the shore. They were trolling along the edge of the channel-bank where the bottom dropped off suddenly from sandy shallows to twelve feet of dark water. They were trolling on their way to the point to set night lines for rainbow trout.

"There's our old ruin, Nick," Marjorie said.

Nick, rowing, looked at the white stone in the green trees.

"There it is," he said.

"Can you remember when it was a mill?" Marjorie asked.

"I can just remember," Nick said.

"It seems more like a castle," Marjorie said

Nick said nothing. They rowed on out of sight of the mill, following the shore line. Then Nick cut across the bay.

"They aren't striking," he said.

"No," Marjorie said. She was intent on the rod all the time they trolled, even when she talked. She loved to fish. She loved to fish with Nick.

Close beside the boat a big trout broke the surface of the water. Nick pulled hard on one oar so the boat would turn and the bait spinning far behind would pass where the trout was feeding. As the trout's back came up out of the water the minnows jumped wildly. They sprinkled the surface like a handful of shot thrown into the water. Another trout broke water, feeding on the other side of the boat.

"They're feeding," Marjorie said.

"But they won't strike," Nick said.

He rowed the boat around to troll past both the feeding fish, then headed it for the point. Marjorie did not reel in until the boat touched the shore. They pulled the boat up the beach and Nick lifted out a pail of live perch. The perch swam in the water in the pail. Nick caught three of them with his hands and cut their heads off and skinned them while Marjorie chased with her hands in the bucket, finally caught a perch, cut its head off and skinned it. Nick looked at her fish.

"You don't want to take the ventral fin out," he said. "It'll be all right for bait but it's better with the ventral fin in."

He hooked each of the skinned perch through the tail. There were two hooks attached to a leader on each rod. Then Marjorie rowed the boat out over the channel-bank, holding the line in her teeth, and looking toward Nick, who stood on the shore holding the rod and letting the line run out from the reel.

"That's about right," he called.

"Should I let it drop?" Marjorie called back, holding the line in her hand.

"Sure. Let it go." Marjorie dropped the line overboard and watched the baits go down through the water.

She came in with the boat and ran the second line out the same way. Each time Nick set a heavy slab of driftwood across the butt of the rod to hold it solid and propped it up at an angle with a small slab. He reeled in the slack line so the line ran taut out to where the bait rested on the sandy floor of the channel and set the click on the reel. When a trout, feeding on the bottom, took the bait it would run with it, taking line out of the reel in a rush and making the reel sing with the click on.

Marjorie rowed up the point a little so she would not disturb the line. She pulled hard on the oars and the boat went way up the beach. Little waves came in with it. Marjorie stepped out of the boat and Nick pulled the boat high up the beach.

"What's the matter, Nick?" Marjorie asked.

"I don't know," Nick said, getting wood for a fire.

They made a fire with driftwood. Marjorie went to the boat and brought a blanket. The evening breeze blew the smoke toward the point, so Marjorie spread the blanket out between the fire and the lake.

Marjorie sat on the blanket with her back to the fire and waited for Nick. He came over and sat down beside her on the blanket. In back of them was the close second-growth timber of the point and in front was the bay with the mouth of Hortons Creek. It was not quite dark. The fire-light went as far as the water. They could both see the two steel rods at an angle over the dark water. The fire glinted on the reels.

Marjorie unpacked the basket of supper.

"I don't feel like eating," said Nick.

"Come on and eat, Nick."

"All right."

They ate without talking, and watched the two rods and the fire-light in the water.

"There's going to be a moon tonight," said Nick. He looked across the bay to the hills that were beginning to sharpen against the sky. Beyond the hills he knew the moon was coming up.

"I know it," Marjorie said happily.

"You know everything," Nick said.

"Oh, Nick, please, cut it out! Please, please, don't be that way!"

"I can't help it," Nick said. "You do. You know everything. That's the trouble. You know you do."

Marjorie did not say anything.

"I've taught you everything. You know you do. What don't you know, anyway?"

"Oh, shut up," Marjorie said. "There comes the moon."

They sat on the blanket without touching each other and watched the moon rise.

"You don't have to talk silly," Marjorie said. "What's really the matter?"

"I don't know."

"Of course you know."

"No I don't."

"Go on and say it."

Nick looked on at the moon, coming up over the hills.

"It isn't fun anymore."

He was afraid to look at Marjorie. Then he looked at her. She sat there with her back toward him. He looked at her back. "It isn't fun anymore. Not any of it."

She didn't say anything. He went on. "I feel as though everything was gone to hell inside of me. I don't know, Marge. I don't know what to say."

He looked on at her back.

"Isn't love any fun?" Marjorie said.

"No," Nick said. Marjorie stood up. Nick sat there, his head in his hands.

"I'm going to take the boat," Marjorie called to him. "You can walk back around the point."

"All right," Nick said. "I'll push the boat off for you."

"You don't need to," she said. She was afloat in the boat on the water with the moonlight on it. Nick went back and lay down with his face in the blanket in the fire. He could hear Marjorie rowing on the water.

He lay there for a long time. He lay there while he heard Bill come into the clearing walking around through the woods. He felt Bill coming up to the fire. Bill didn't touch him, either.

"Did she go all right?" Bill said.

"Yes," Nick said, lying, his face on the blanket.

"Have a scene?"

"No, there wasn't any scene."

"How do you feel?"

"Oh, go away, Bill! Go away for a while."

Bill selected a sandwich from the lunch basket and walked over to have a look at the rods.

Oh Damn Them All,
Thought the Adolescent

From John Cheever,
Bullet Park *(1966)*

John Cheever chronicled the spiritual emptiness behind the affluence of suburbia in the 1950s and '60s. For an adolescent, the suburbs are a plush prison of frustration and artificiality.

The lights of Powder Hill twinkled, its chimneys smoked and a pink plush toilet-seat cover flew from a clothesline. Seen at an improbable distance by some zealous adolescent, ranging over the golf links, the piece of plush would seem to be the imprimatur, the guerdon, the accolade and banner of Powder Hill behind which marched, in tight English shoes, the legions of wife-swapping, Jew-baiting, booze-fighting spiritual bankrupts. Oh damn them all, thought the adolescent. Damn the bright lights by which no one reads, damn the continuous music which no one hears, damn the grand pianos that no one can play, damn the white houses mortgaged up to their rain gutters, damn them for plundering the ocean for fish to feed the mink whose skins they wear and damn their shelves on which there rests a single book—a copy of the telephone directory, bound in pink brocade. Damn their hypocrisy, damn their cant, damn their credit cards, damn their discounting the wilderness of the human spirit, damn their immaculateness, damn their lechery and damn them above all for having leached from life that strength, malodorousness, color and zeal that give it meaning. Howl, howl, howl.

"Most Young Men Do Not Stand Like Ramrods or Talk Like Demosthenes."

James Dean's defense of
Rebel Without a Cause *(1955)*

At the age of twenty-four, James Dean was an avatar of moody confusion and yearning to an entire generation of young men.

Since I'm only 24 years old, I guess I have as good an insight into this rising generation as any other young man my age. And I've discovered that most young men do not stand like ramrods or talk like Demosthenes. Therefore, when I do play a youth, such as in Warner Bros. *Rebel Without a Cause,* I try to imitate life. The picture deals with the problems of modern youth. It is the romanticized conception of the juvenile that causes much of our trouble with misguided youth nowadays. I think the one thing this picture shows that's new is the psychological disproportion of the kids' demands on the parents. Parents are often at fault, but the kids have some work to do, too. But you can't show some far-off idyllic conception of behavior if you want the kids to come and see the picture. You've got to show what it's really like, and try to reach them on their own grounds. You know, a lot of times an older boy, one of the fellows the young ones idolize, can go back to the high school kids and tell them, "Look what happened to me! Why be a punk and get in trouble with the law? Why do these senseless things just for a thrill?" I hope *Rebel Without a Cause* will do something like that. I hope it will remind them that other people have feelings. Perhaps they will say, "What do we need all that for?" If a picture is psychologically motivated, if there is truth in the relationship in it, then I think that picture will do good. I firmly believe *Rebel Without a Cause* is such a picture.

What Then Shall We Choose?
Weight or Lightness?

From Milan Kundera,
The Unbearable Lightness of Being

If every second of our lives recurs an infinite number of times, we are nailed to eternity as Jesus Christ was nailed to the cross. It is a terrifying prospect. In the world of eternal return the weight of unbearable responsibility lies heavy on every move we make. That is why Nietzsche called the idea of eternal return the heaviest of burdens (*das schwertze Gewicht*).

If eternal return is the heaviest of burdens, then our lives can stand out against it in all their splendid lightness.

But if heaviness of burdens crushes us, we sink beneath it, it pins us to the ground. But in the love poetry of every age, the woman longs to be weighed down by the man's body. The heaviest of burdens is therefore simultaneously an image of our life's most intense fulfillment. The heavier the burden, the closer our lives come to the earth, the more real and truthful they become.

Conversely, the absolute absence of a burden causes man to be lighter than air, to soar into the heights, take leave of the earth and his earthly being, and become only half real, his movements as free as they are insignificant.

What then shall we choose? Weight or lightness?

Video Games Get Very Very Ugly: Masochism, Mutilation, Prostitution

Charles Mandel,
The Globe and Mail *[Toronto] (1998)*

What role if any do video games play in the disturbing spate of violent acts recently committed by young males? This essay provides a disturbing look at what your son may actually be doing at his computer.

Duke Nukem runs forward, grabs the shotgun and pumps a round into the chamber. "Groovy," intones the video-game hero in his gravelly voice, just before he starts blasting alien scum into a gory pulp.

Sound violent? Not to some video-game developers, apparently. Major U.S. software companies are about to make such infamous "splatter" games as Duke Nukem and Doom seem like child's play as they prepare to release a new wave of titles this fall that enable players to manipulate photorealistic images of humans into acts of torture, mutilation and even—if you can believe it—prostitution.

Interplay Productions proudly promotes its Wild 9 as the first-ever action game that encourages players to torture enemies. Shiny Entertainment, a subsidiary of Interplay, is completing work on Messiah, a game in which a cherub tries to cleanse the world of corruption. "Ever seen a body with 10,000 volts run through it?" the game's advertising slogan teases. "Want to?"

Not to be outdone, Virgin Interactive is set to release Thrill Kill, a series of gladiator-style battles between demented characters that bite and tear at each other in a torture-chamber setting.

And Max Payne, a vigilante-style game (whose hero is not-so-subtly named after the "maximum pain" he likes to inflict on his victims), is coming soon from 3D Realms and Remedy Entertainment. The game recently inspired editors of *PC Gamer Magazine* to exclaim: "While Duke Nukem raised a few eyebrows with his testosterone-charged quips, alienbashing violence and girl-happy lifestyle, Max Payne's vendetta-fueled exploits and shocking amount of violence are likely to have the senators squealing."

Other pain-packing titles due out in the next year include Deathtrap Dungeon and Dungeon Keeper II (which, according to Computer Gaming World Magazine, "offers improved graphics, more creatures and better ways to torture").

What is also striking about such games is that they are being released by large, well-established companies. Interplay, for example, is one of the largest U.S.–based entertainment-software publishers, with sales in the past six months of $81 million. And Virgin Interactive is the software arm of Richard Branson's multibillion-dollar British media conglomerate.

But then, the stakes are high. Since video-gaming giant GT Interactive Software acquired Duke Nukem from creator Formgen in 1996, the company has sold more than four million copies globally. Those sales have helped solidify GT Interactive's position as the second largest entertainment-software publisher in the United States, after Electronic Arts, with annual revenue of $531 million. In total, the U.S. gaming market was worth $1.3 billion in 1997, according to market-research firm PC Data. Globally, the figure is $17 billion.

While game developers say the violence is aimed purely at adults, others point out there are few safeguards to prevent the software from falling into the hands of children. Stephen Kline, a professor of communications at Simon Fraser University in Burnaby, British Columbia, who has taught courses on video-gaming culture, recently released a study that concludes parents tend to pay no attention to what their kids play. And, according to Kline's survey of 650 youth, video games—whether computer-based CD-ROM's or Nintendo, Sony or Sega console games—help shape children's outlook on the world.

"Heavy gamers show different kinds of judgments than light gamers," Kline said in an interview. "Female gamers especially—and there are some—show the classic desensitization effect. They rate things like blood and guts, rape and sexual aggression as less offensive, as less violent, than the light and moderate gamers."

Kline's study states that roughly one in four children is addicted to gaming (specifically, 24 percent play between seven and 30 hours a week).

That's not all. In this new world of gaming, where there's violence there often is sex. Fallout 2, a soon-to-be released game set in a postnuclear holocaust era, features the chance to "fall in love, get married and pimp your spouse for a little extra chump change. Hey, it's a dark and dangerous world." Prostitution also features prominently in the aforementioned Messiah, whose characters include several scantily clad hookers.

Mayhem Milestones

While not all of the following games made a killing at the cash register, they rank as classic carnage moments. Chris Charla, editor of the gaming magazine *Next Generation,* walked us through some psycho highlights of the past 22 years:

Death Race 2000: This arcade-style game from 1976 was the first of the very violent titles. A forerunner to today's graphically vivid Carmageddon, the object is to run over people who on contact would turn into little white crosses.

Splatterhouse: A sort of cross between the Halloween movie series and the *Texas Chainsaw Massacre.* You are a man in a hockey mask armed with a chainsaw running through a house killing monsters.

Mortal Kombat: Released in the late eighties, it was among the first to explore the martial-arts theme. The key action is to rip your opponent's heart out.

Wolfenstein 3D: In 1992, graphics technology had progressed to the point where the player could move through three-dimensional space and thus get close, personal and very gory. The revolutionary Wolfenstein 3D fired the opening salvo in the 3D revolution.

Night Trap: With its full-motion video sequence of a woman in a scanty night dress being pursued by monsters, this game caused U.S. senators in 1993 to raise a hue and cry and call for a rating system.

Carmaggedon: The British Board of Film and Video Classification refused a rating certificate to Carmaggedon in 1997, when the British press were still fussing over the recent release of David Cronenberg's controversial film *Crash.*

Postal: A 1997 game consisting of an armed man shooting unarmed bystanders in settings such as fast-food restaurants. It nearly triggered a U.S. postal strike in protest.

Sin: Shooting took on a new level of realism in this 1997 release. A shot in the arm, for example, causes the victim to collapse in a way that is different from, say, a blow to the head.

On the horizon: Thrill Kill, a viciously violent fight game, promises to be among the more shocking titles this fall.

Television's Virus of Violence and the Jonesboro Schoolyard Shootings

Lieutenant-Colonel Dave Grossman,
The Virginian-Pilot *[Hampton Roads, VA] (1998)*

In this hard-hitting essay, a retired infantry officer and expert on the psychology of violence lays the blame for Jonesboro and other shooting sprees by young males squarely at the doorstep of the television networks. There is a direct link, Colonel Grossman argues, between television's glamorization of violence and alienated boys' search for recognition through violent acts.

Folks here noticed something interesting about the network television crews that swarmed in like the second of some series of biblical plagues two months ago. What we noticed about the TV folks was this: They have blood on their hands, and they know it, yet they dare not admit it.

The U.S. television networks will stick their lenses anywhere and courageously expose anything. Like flies crawling on open wounds, they find nothing too private or too shameful for their probing—except themselves, and their share of guilt in the terrible crime that happened here.

That crime, as the world now knows, was the March 24 schoolyard shooting deaths of four schoolgirls and a teacher. Ten others were wounded and two boys, 11 and 13, are in jail, charged with the murders.

And it happened in Jonesboro, my home. Before retiring here, I spent almost a quarter of a century as an army infantry officer and a psychologist, learning how to enable people to kill. Believe me, we are very good at it. And just as the army enables killing, we are doing the same thing to our kids—but without the military's safeguards.

The TV networks are responsible for traumatizing and brutalizing our children as they watch violent acts—a thousand a month, according to the latest research financed by the cable industry itself—at a young, vulnerable age when they cannot tell the difference between reality and fantasy. Children really only know what they have been taught, and we have taught them, ever so cleverly, to laugh and cheer at violence. In Jonesboro, we saw an indication of just how good a job we have done.

I spent the first three days after the shooting at Westside Middle School, counseling teachers, students and parents. One high-school teacher told me about the reaction she got when she informed her students that someone was shooting at their little brothers, sisters and cousins in the middle school.

"They laughed," she told me in amazement. "They laughed."

We have raised a generation of barbarians who have learned to associate violence with pleasure, like the Romans who cheered and snacked as the Christians were slaughtered in the Colosseum.

A TV commentator told me not long after the shootings, "Well, we only have one real violent show on our network, *NYPD Blue*. I'll admit that it's bad, but it's only one night a week."

I wondered how she would feel if someone said, "Well, I only beat my wife in front of the kids one night a week." The effect is the same. According to *USA Weekend*, *NYPD Blue* star Kim Delaney was shocked to discover that underage viewers watch her show, which is rated TV–14 for gruesome crimes, raw language and explicit sex. "You're not supposed to know who I am!" she told a group of young children who recognized her.

The copycat aspect of the Jonesboro murders is another twist to juvenile crime that the TV networks would rather not talk about.

Research in the 1970s demonstrated the effect of "cluster suicides," in which the local TV reporting of teen suicides was directly responsible for causing numerous copycat suicides of young, impressionable teenagers. Somewhere in every population there are potentially suicidal kids who will say to themselves, "Well, I'll show all those people who have been mean to me. I know how to get my picture on TV, too."

Today, TV stations generally do not "do" suicides. But when pictures of teenage *killers* appear on TV, the effect is the same: Somewhere there is a potentially violent little boy who says to himself, "Well, I'll show all those people who have been mean to me. I know how to get my picture on TV, too."

And thus we get clusters of copycat murders that work their way across the United States like a virus spread by the six o'clock news. In the latest outbreak, in Springfield, Oregon, on Thursday, a 15-year-old high-school student who'd been suspended a day earlier for bringing a gun to school returned with his .22-caliber rifle and two handguns and opened fire in a packed cafeteria. When the rampage was over, two students were dead and 22 injured. The bodies of his parents were found later at his home.

The lineage of the Jonesboro shootings can first be picked up less than six months before, at Pearl, Mississippi. A 16-year-old boy was accused of killing his mother and then going to his school and shooting nine students, two of whom—one his ex-girlfriend—died.

Two months later, it spread to Paducah, Kentucky, where a 14-year-old boy was arrested for killing three students and wounding five others.

A very important step occurred in Stamps, Arkansas, 15 days after Pearl and just a little over 90 days before Jonesboro. A 14-year-old boy, angry at his schoolmates, hid in the woods and fired at children as they came out of school. Sound familiar? Only two children were injured in this crime, so most of the world didn't hear about it. But it got great regional TV coverage, and two little boys across the state in Jonesboro couldn't have helped but hear about it.

This is not to say that TV violence is the only reason for these terrible murders. The easy availability of guns, the prevalence of family breakdown, the violence kids absorb from Hollywood movies and video games—all of these are topics that the TV industry would much rather tell us about. But while they focus on the mote in the eye of their neighbors, we are obliged to point out the huge, bleeding splinter in their electronic eye.

The data linking TV violence and violent crime is more scientifically sound than that linking tobacco and cancer. More than 200 studies have identified a clear cause-and-effect relationship. Thus, we are probably very close to a time when the TV networks will be treated like the tobacco industry and brought to their knees by lawsuits.

The American Medical Association, the American Academy of Pediatrics and the American Psychiatric Association, as well as their equivalents in other nations, have made definitive, unequivocal statements about the link between violence in the media and violent crime. The APA, in its 1992 report "Big World, Small Screen," said flatly that the "scientific debate is over." With few exceptions, every nation that has fed violent images to its children as entertainment is paying the same tragic price.

You may ask: But what about the responsibility of parents to "just turn it off"? Every single one of the parents of the 15 shooting victims in Jonesboro could have protected their children from TV violence in this way, and it wouldn't have done a bit of good, because, somewhere, there were two little boys whose parents didn't "just turn it off."

On the night of the shootings, clergy and counselors were working in small groups in the hospital waiting room, comforting relatives and friends of the shooting victims. Then they noticed one woman who had been sitting silently, alone.

A counselor went up to the woman and discovered that she was the mother of one of the girls who had been killed. She had no friends, no husband, no family with her as she sat in the hospital, stunned by her loss. "I just came to find out how to get my little girl's body back," she said. But the body had been taken to Little Rock, 160 kilometers away, for an autopsy. In her dazed state of mind, her very next concern was, "I just don't know how we're going to pay for the funeral. I don't know how we can afford it."

That little girl was truly all she had in all the world. Come to Jonesboro, my friend, hunt up this mother, and tell her how she should "just turn it off."

Every parent desperately needs to be warned of the impact of TV on children, just as we would warn parents of a rampant carcinogen. But our key means of public education in America is the national TV networks—using the public airwaves we have licensed to them. And they are stonewalling.

The hard-hitting investigative reporters of shows such as *60 Minutes* have always been our heroes. They are the ones we counted on to swoop down like Superman and rescue us from corporate oppressors. But now it is the networks that are the irresponsible, heartless corporate killers who put profits ahead of lives. Our heroes are nothing more than hypocrites.

In the days after the Jonesboro shootings, I was interviewed for Canadian national TV, the BBC, and many U.S. and international radio stations and newspapers. But the U.S. television networks simply would not touch this aspect of the story. Never, in my experience as a historian and a psychologist, have I seen any institution in America so clearly abusing their publicly licensed authority and power to cover up their guilt.

Time after time, idealistic young network producers contacted me, fascinated by the irony that an expert in the field of violence and aggression was living right here in Jonesboro and was at the school almost from the beginning. But unlike the stories in all the other media, these network items always died a sudden, silent death when the powers-that-be said, "Yeah, we need this story like we need a hole in the head."

Many times since the shooting, I have been asked, "Why weren't you on TV talking about the stuff in your book?"—meaning *On Killing: The Psychological Cost of Learning to Kill in War and Society* (Little Brown, 1996). And every time my answer had to be, "The TV networks are burying this story. They know they are guilty and they want to delay the inevitable retribution as long as they can."

I accuse. I accuse the U.S. TV networks of inciting the violent deaths of thousands of innocent Americans across many decades, and I accuse them of abusing the public airwaves in a conspiracy to cover up their guilt.

I've been there, and I am angry. I've seen the horror and the blood and the death of the innocents, and I personally have heard some of the world's foremost experts lay the blame squarely on the doorstep of TV. And I personally have seen the networks kill this story.

I'm mad as hell at the hypocrisy of the U.S. TV networks. And, in the name of the people of Jonesboro, Arkansas, and in the name of all innocent lives sacrificed on this altar of glass, I hereby publicly challenge the networks to honestly discuss and examine their guilt.

NBC, ABC, CBS, Fox and all you others, turn the cameras on yourselves and see: You have the blood of innocents on your hands.

Why the U.S. Won't Go to War

Michael Kelly,
The Times *of London (1997)*

The rise of nihilistic violence at home (Jonesboro, Littleton, and a string of less-well-publicized incidents) is ironically paralleled by a strong aversion for military combat abroad. The U.S. is willing to use massive force (Iraq, Kosovo), but apparently only if its ground troops are spared direct contact with the enemy. Thus, as Michael Kelly observes, Americans are spared the painful lesson known to other peoples: that there are things worth fighting and dying for.

In the summer and autumn of 1995, as the war in Bosnia was winding down, I spent a couple of months in Bihac, a small, handsome mountain city in the northwest corner of the country then entering its last days under Serbian siege. Bihac was defended by the Bosnian Army's V Corps, which had built itself up from a few platoons of local volunteers armed with Kalashnikovs and hunting rifles into a great, if unconventional, fighting force. For more than two years the V Corps held off a vastly better-armed encircling force, and the war they fought was more like 1917 than 1995.

The soldiers at the front lived for months at a time in slit trenches and scant bunkers of sandbags and tree branches, dug in along wooded ridges and hills. They had, for most of the war, so little ammunition that it was common for troops to go into battle with 20 rounds apiece. They fought in short, furious, bursts, emerging from their holes in the mud to charge the enemy line in shooting, stabbing, shrieking onslaughts that usually ended with everyone on one side or the other wounded or dead.

These soldiers were mostly young and mostly untrained, but they had become greatly familiar with war and familiarity had bred its usual contempt. While they still feared death, they no longer respected it. This had some unhappy consequences. There was a lot of mental depression in Bihac. But the devaluation of life had also served its great purpose. It had freed the people from their normal inhibitions about killing and being killed, and this in turn had kept them from being killed. Accepting death, it turned out, was indispensable to defeating death.

This is a troubling idea to contemplate as the United States worries, again, about what to do about Baghdad. Saddam Hussein's ability to agitate America rests on his understanding that America has developed a phobia of military death. While the Americans have become weirdly numb to the horror of death in the civilian sphere (on the streets, in the movies), they have evolved what amounts to a zero tolerance policy for death on the battlefield, and not just American death, any death. In Bosnia, America watched the Serbs conduct a genocidal campaign, and did nothing of practical import for three years, because they didn't want to be—responsible for anyone being killed—not even the perpetrators of genocide.

The Gulf conflict was, per capita, probably the most death-free war ever waged. In all the war, there was only one scene of really troubling mass slaughter, the savaging by air and by tank of the Iraqi forces fleeing home from their rout in Kuwait. And this scene ended the war.

Looking at the burned, exploded bodies a few days after the attack, it seemed obvious to me that the war must instantly end; there could be no justification for continuing unilateral slaughter. This seemed obvious to a lot of other people too, some of them professional military men and some of them advisers to the President. So the war ended, abruptly and disastrously, with Saddam Hussein in power and protected by the well-paid, heavily armed Republican Guard, which American forces could have destroyed in a few days then.

It seems obvious to me now that what seemed obvious to me then was the usual result of a little knowledge intruding suddenly on total ignorance. I had never seen the results of war, and the results horrified me out of my wits. In this, I was of course typical of my generation of reporters. The result is, in matters military, a press corps that is forever suffering a collective case of the vapors. At the least exposure to the most unremarkable facts of military life—soldiers can be brutes and pigs, generals can be stupid, bullets can be fatal—we are forever shocked, forever reaching for the sal volatile.

The media's generational horror at war's truths reflects the larger society's views, and this larger society includes the military itself. Not since Vietnam has America faced a serious war, involving a serious level of death (and Vietnam's 58,000 American coffins were a fraction of the butcher's bills paid in the great wars), and that conflict ended a quarter of a century ago. We are a nation in which there are fewer and fewer people, and they are older and older people, who accept what every 12-year-old in Bihac knows: that there are things worth dying for, and killing for.

So, Americans will let Saddam Hussein stall them until he has hidden what weapons of mass deaths he needs to hide, and then he will let the UN inspectors back in, and the Americans will live with that. Or they will inflict some suffering on Iraq, and kill some people, but not too many, because the people—the American people, that is—will not be able to stand the pictures. And the Americans can live with that too. But one of these days, somebody—the North Koreans come to mind—is going to start a real war. And then we will find out what we can really live with.

Gender Traits Tie
T.V. Execs in Knots

Brian Lowry,
Los Angeles Times *(1998)*

Some may deny that men and women are different, but in the business world, understanding those differences is connected to big profits. For instance, men and women watch television in very different ways; the viewing habits of men are harder to pin down because they have shorter attention spans. Women are loyal to their shows, prefer dramas, and pay attention to the story line. Men prefer action scenes, military hardware, sports, and incessant channel surfing. What a surprise!

When the CBS series *JAG* is screened for test audiences, producers have noticed that while the more emotional scenes resonate with women, it's the military drama's "hardware" that causes the dials to rise among men.

"When you come to an action scene, the women will drop off, and the men will peak incredibly," says executive producer Donald P. Bellisario. The consistency of that dynamic underscores how men and women watch television differently, as well as changes in a wired-for-cable world that contribute to such a rift, prompting many couples to adjourn to separate rooms to watch TV on their own.

The major networks find attracting men especially difficult, which helps explain a dizzying series of sports TV deals as programmers seek showcases to reel in that audience at least temporarily. The frenzy peaked in January, when Disney (through ABC and ESPN), CBS and Fox agreed to pay a mind-boggling $17.6 billion for broadcast rights to National Football League games.

Beyond being drawn to different genres, research indicates that men are generally less willing to commit time to an ongoing TV series and more apt to flip around during commercial breaks.

"Men have fewer appointment shows," says Kelly Kahl, CBS' vice president of scheduling, adding that with the exception of sports events—such as the recent National Collegiate Athletic Association basketball championship—"our ability to get men in front of the set is minimal."

The gender disparity begins with simple math: Women out-number men and generally watch more television. According to estimates by Nielsen Media Research, the average woman 18 and older—a population estimated at 100.6 million in the United States—tunes in 4½ hours daily, about 40 minutes more than aver-age for the country's 92.3 million adult males.

"It's much easier to reach women any place on television. There's more of us and we spend more time watching," says Jean Pool, executive vice president of North American media-buying services at J. Walter Thompson. "It's just a fact and always has been that men are harder to reach on television than women."

The data become more significant when coupled with an anecdotal observation that hasn't eluded women or stand-up comics—namely, men are more likely to channel-surf, flipping idly from station to station.

"(A woman) will watch a two-hour movie, and the guy will watch 15 things during the same time," says Tim Brooks, senior vice president of research at USA Networks.

A *Los Angeles Times* poll conducted in September concluded that four out of 10 men said they always or frequently change chan-nels when a commercial comes on, compared to 28 percent of women; by contrast, 7 percent of men said they never flip around during a program, as opposed to 17 percent of women.

"Men are masters of the remote control, and they will surf more easily than women do. That's clearly a challenge," says Artie Bulgrin, vice president of research and sales development at cable sports network ESPN. "Sports, out of all the TV genres, is certainly the most vulnerable to switching."

In descending order, men polled by the *Times* cited network news, network sports, cable sports, movies, comedies and cable news as the programming they watched most. Women also led their list with network news but followed with comedies, dramas, soap operas and movies.

Women were more than twice as likely to mention dramas among their favorite forms of programming, while four times as many men chose sports. Based on a breakdown of prime-time net-works series, the current television season's No. 1 show among men, *Monday Night Football*, doesn't crack the Top 20 with women.

Other programs exclusive to the men's roster include Fox's Sunday lineup of *The X-Files, King of the Hill* and *The Simpsons*, as well as NBC's *Law & Order*. Shows unique to women were *Diagnosis Murder, Cosby, Mad About You, Promised Land* and *Everybody Loves Raymond*.

"In the broader strokes, women tend to be more story-oriented, men more action- and comedy-oriented," Smith says.

Many popular programs cross gender lines, especially *Seinfeld*, which is second on both lists. Other shows preferred by both men and women include *Friends, Touched by an Angel, 60 Minutes, Home Improvement, Frasier* and *The Drew Carey Show*.

In shows common to both, however, the percentage of the female population that tunes in is invariably higher.

"Choice" is the operative word in television. Based on Nielsen data, roughly three-quarters of all households have two or more TV sets and, with increasing frequency, men, women and children scatter to watch the programs they want separately.

Cable, of course, has exacerbated the problem of getting families to watch together, by providing channels catering to a wide variety of highly specific interests.

Women appear to be more willing to watch programs that traditionally appeal to men than the other way around, including those that contain violence.

Networks have experienced some success tinkering with shows that possess a stronger male following in order to make them more attractive to women. NBC's *Law & Order* replaced two members of the originally all-male cast with women, for example, in a conscious effort to make the long-running show more accessible to them.

One of the casualties gradually inflicted by such advances as multiple televisions and VCRs is family viewing, and the days when everyone crowded around one TV together to watch *Bonanza* or *The Cosby Show*. With digital technology that promises to expand the number of channels further, the day may be coming, in fact, where Bruce Springsteen won't sing about "57 channels and nothing on" but rather a channel with something on—viewed alone—for every one of us.

Marginal Men

From Barbara Ehrenreich,
Essays, Thought and Style *(1996)*

Two vicious murders of teenage girls on Long Island are the occasion for
Barbara Ehrenreich's reflections on the sources of violence in young males.
When a young man's pride has no honorable outlet (like a decent job), it will
degenerate into violence and "the politics of gesture."

Crime seems to change character when it crosses a bridge or a
tunnel. In the city, crime is taken as emblematic of the vast injus-
tices of class and race. In the suburbs, though, it's intimate and psychological—resistant to generalization, a mystery of the individual
soul. Recall the roar of commentary that followed the murderous
assault on a twenty-eight-year-old woman jogging in Central Park.
Every detail of the assailants' lives was sifted for sociological significance: Were they poor? How poor? Students or dropouts? From
families with two parents or one? And so on, until the awful singularity of the event was lost behind the impersonal grid of Class,
Race, and Sex.

Now take the Midtown Tunnel east to the Long Island
Expressway, out past the clutter of Queens to deepest suburbia,
where almost every neighborhood is "good" and "social pathology"
is something you learn about in school. Weeks before the East
Harlem youths attacked a jogger, Long Islanders were shaken by
two murders which were, if anything, even more inexplicably
vicious than the assault in Central Park. In early March, the body of
thirteen-year-old Kelly Tinyes was found in the basement of a house
just down the block from her own. She had been stabbed, strangled, and hit with a blunt instrument before being mutilated with a
bayonet. A few weeks later, fourteen-year-old Jessica Manners was
discovered along the side of a road in East Setauket, strangled to
death, apparently with her own bra, and raped.

Suspects have been apprehended. Their high-school friends,
parents, and relatives have been interviewed. Their homes and cars
have been searched; their photos published. We know who they

hung out with and what they did in their spare time. But on the scale of large social meanings, these crimes don't rate. No one is demanding that we understand—or condemn—the white communities that nourished the killers. No one is debating the roots of violence in the land of malls and tract homes. Only in the city, apparently, is crime construed as something "socioeconomic." Out here it's merely "sick."

But East Setauket is not really all that far from East Harlem. If something is festering in the ghetto, something very similar is gnawing away at Levittown and East Meadow. A "way of life," as the cliché goes, is coming to an end, and in its place a mean streak is opening up and swallowing everything in its path. Economists talk about "deindustrialization" and "class polarization." I think of it as the problem of *marginal men:* they are black and white, Catholic and Pentecostal, rap fans and admirers of technopop. What they have in common is that they are going nowhere—nowhere legal, that is.

Consider the suspects in the Long Island murders. Twenty-one-year-old Robert Golub, in whose basement Kelly Tinyes was killed, is described in *Newsday* as an "unemployed bodybuilder." When his high-school friends went off to college, he stayed behind in his parents' home in Valley Stream. For a while, he drove a truck for a cosmetics firm, but he lost that job, in part because of his driving record: his license has been suspended twelve times since 1985. At the time of the murder, he had been out of work for several months, constructing a life around his weight-lifting routine and his dream of becoming an entrepreneur.

Christopher Loliscio, the suspect in the Manners case, is nineteen, and, like Golub, lives with his parents. He had been in trouble before, and is charged with third-degree assault and "menacing" in an altercation that took place on the campus of the State University at Stony Brook last December. Loliscio does not attend college himself. He is employed as a landscaper.

The suburbs are full of young white men like Golub and Loliscio. If they had been born twenty years earlier, they might have found steady work in decent-paying union jobs, married early, joined the volunteer fire department, and devoted their leisure to lawn maintenance. But the good blue-collar jobs are getting sparser, thanks to "deindustrialization"—which takes the form, in Long Island, of cutbacks in the defense and aerospace industries. Much of what's left is likely to be marginal, low-paid work. Nationwide, the earnings of young white men dropped 18 percent between 1973 and 1986, according to the Census Bureau, and the earnings of male high-school dropouts plunged 42 percent.

Landscaping, for example—a glamorous term for raking and mowing—pays four to five dollars an hour; truck driving for a small firm is in the same range: not enough to pay for a house, a college education, or even a mid-size wedding reception at the VFW hall.

And even those modest perquisites of life in the subyuppie class have become, in some sense, "not enough." On Long Island, the culture that once sustained men in blue-collar occupations is crumbling as more affluent settlers move in, filling the vacant lots with their new, schooner-shaped, $750,000 homes. In my town, for example, the last five years saw the bowling alley close and the blue-collar bar turn into a pricey dining spot. Even the volunteer fire department is having trouble recruiting. The prestigious thing to join is a $500-a-year racquetball club; there's just not much respect anymore for putting out fires.

So the marginal man lives between two worlds—one that he aspires to and one that is dying, and neither of which he can afford. Take "Rick," the twenty-two-year-old son of family friends. His father is a machinist in an aerospace plant which hasn't been hiring anyone above the floor-sweeping level for years now. Not that Rick has ever shown any interest in his father's trade. For one thing, he takes too much pride in his appearance to put on the dark green company-supplied work clothes his father has worn for the past twenty years. Rick has his kind of uniform: pleated slacks, high-tops, Italian knit cardigans, and a $300 leather jacket, accessorized with a gold chain and earring stud.

To his parents, Rick is a hard-working boy for whom things just don't seem to work out. For almost a year after high school, he worked behind a counter at Crazy Eddie's, where the pay is low but at least you can listen to rock and roll all day. Now he has a gig doing valet parking at a country club. The tips are good and he loves racing around the lot in the Porsches and Lamborghinis of the stockbroker class. But the linchpin of his economic strategy is living at home, with his parents and sisters, in the same room he's occupied since third grade. Rick is a long way from being able to afford even a cramped, three-bedroom house like his family home; and, given the choice, he'd rather have a new Camaro anyway.

If this were the seventies, Rick might have taken up marijuana, the Grateful Dead, and vague visions of a better world. But like so many of his contemporaries in the eighties, Rick has no problem with "the system," which, in his mind, embraces every conceivable hustle, legal or illegal. Two years ago, he made a tidy bundle dealing coke in a local dance club, bought a $20,000 car, and smashed it up. Now he spends his evenings as a bouncer in an illegal gambling joint—his parents still think he's out "dancing"—and is proud of the handgun he's got stowed in his glove compartment.

Someday Rick will use that gun, and I'll probably be the first to say—like Robert Golub's friends—"but he isn't the kind of person who would hurt *anyone.*" Except that even now I can sense the danger in him. He's smart enough to know he's only a cut-rate copy of the upscale young men in GQ ads and MTV commercials. Viewed from Wall Street or Southampton, he's a peon, a member of the invisible underclass that parks cars, waits on tables, and is satisfied with a five-dollar tip and a remark about the weather.

He's also proud. And there's nowhere for him to put that pride except into the politics of gesture; the macho stance, the seventy-five-mile-per-hour takeoff down the expressway, and eventually maybe, the drawn gun. Jobs are the liberal solution; conservatives would throw in "traditional values." But what the marginal men— from Valley Stream to Bedford-Stuyvesant—need most of all is *respect.* If they can't find that in work, or in a working-class lifestyle that is no longer honored, they'll extract it from someone weaker— a girlfriend, a random jogger, a neighbor, perhaps just any girl. They'll find a victim.

THE CONFUSIONS OF LOVE

The Dangerous Game of Dating

Jonathan Foreman,
The Women's Quarterly

What constitutes a "date"? An English observer of American women is puzzled by its many meanings.

People back in my homeland of England often ask me if American women are as sexually aggressive as they have heard. British males who don't really know this country are convinced that American women are all fierce, perpetually complaining feminists who throw themselves at men with startling force and frequency. "Is it true they just come up to you in bars and ask you to sleep with them?" one fellow asked.

The truthful answer is, "Uh, not usually." American women are no more likely to be sexually hyperactive than their British counterparts; in fact, British women are a far better bet if you meet them at a bar. (Surveys have shown that the Brits are the most promiscuous people in Western Europe—far more so than the French.)

Despite this society's openness about sex, American women often have remarkably frustrating sex lives. This is not because American women are in any way prudish. On the contrary. It is mainly because the rules of "dating" wreak such havoc on relations between the sexes.

I have lived in this country for a decade, my father was American, I spent all my school vacations in California, and I still don't really understand what Americans mean by "dating." It is hard to believe, I know, but we simply don't have "dating" in England. This is not as strange as it sounds. We still have sex lives; we still marry and have children. Indeed, we have successfully done all these things for centuries. So far as I know, "dating" scarcely exists outside the United States.

For example, I once heard one of my American female colleagues say, "I'm dating three guys right now, nothing serious." I was stunned. Could she really be sleeping with three men simultaneously? A lawyer friend explained she was not sleeping with them, she was merely "dating" them—in other words, going out to dinner with them. I asked this friend if that meant that any time a man has dinner with a woman they are on a date. Not at all, she explained. For a dinner to be a date, there has to be romantic intent.

At this point, I thought I understood dating. It was a kind of reconnaissance made in a restaurant before two people embarked on a relationship; no carnal activity was involved except eating.

But there are many times when the context is less clear. If I meet an unmarried woman and she tells me she has been dating someone for three weeks, or three years, what does that mean? Is she single? (As a European, I would be happy to treat all women as potential lovers—I was brought up to look at a woman's eyes, not her ring finger—but as I live here I prefer to avoid misunderstandings.)

There are a host of ancillary questions, all of which depend on correct interpretation of this mysterious concept. How do I know if a lunch, dinner, or drink with a woman constitutes a "date"? Many American women feel they should not sleep with you, or in extreme cases, even kiss you, until the second or third "date." Yet some women don't count a dinner date if she has invited the man out, or if neither person has used the actual phrase, "It's a date."

More quaintly, others require the man to pay for the woman if the occasion is to count as a "date." (Presumably such women see dating as a transaction that is partly financial: Each of the three dates is an installment paid in advance. The man's return takes the form of what lawyers call consortium: a combination of company, domestic work, and sexual favors.)

What I want to know is how many dates have to take place before you can say you are "dating" someone? Why should "dating" someone imply exclusivity? And can you sleep with a woman without "dating" her?

This last goes to the root of what is wrong with the idea of "dating." For the foreigner, the whole weird system with its vagueness and simultaneous rigidity speaks to a linguistic shortage. Americans simply don't have enough words to describe all the variations of sexual relationships. And they are uncomfortable in relationships that are not easily defined by phrases like "engaged to," "one-night stand," or "going out with." This is especially true of American women who are well known to enjoy long, late-night conversations during which they and their consorts endeavor to define and describe their "relationship."

The confused notion of the "date" stems in large part from its origins in a 1950s suburban mating ritual. The original date was essentially a way of formalizing fraternization in an era when arranged marriages were old-fashioned, chaperones were impractical, and automobiles let teenagers escape parental discipline.

In an era when people married young, you were only supposed to date someone if the relationship had a chance of "going somewhere." A date was presumed to be the first step on the road to marriage. Hence, parental disapproval if their child dated somebody from the wrong race or class.

We never developed the dating system in England because we couldn't afford cars in the 1950s, or suburbs for that matter. And English cars, for all their elegance, were either too small and uncomfortable for sex, or driven only by the chauffeur. So we developed a system so fluid and practical it is barely a system at all.

I really came to understand it as a student at Cambridge in the early 1980s. First, everyone drank a great deal (but not beer) and flirted all the time. I would have dinner (or lunch, tea, or drinks) with female friends. Sometimes we would sleep together afterward. With some girls this became a regular event. With other girls you would sleep with them only once, but continue to see them as friends.

With still others, the friendship would always be platonic. It was only when you started to have sex with someone regularly that the nomenclature of your relationship became important. And the questions were: Was this an affair, should you try to keep it secret, or would you start "going out"? It was simple, and great fun.

And it continued when we all moved to London and started jobs, except that about a quarter of the people I knew married within three years of graduation. Three years later another quarter were hitched. After a decade, three quarters if not more of my contemporaries have tied the knot, proving that the English model makes for both happy single people and coupling off at a reasonably young age. It is New York, and not London, that is prowled by thousands of anxious thirty-something men and women, all nervously watching their mirrors for signs of decreasing value.

The dating system may have worked well in 1950s suburbia, but it doesn't work in big cities today. Politically correct puritanism is one reason. Human mating rituals conducted without benefit of drinking, smoking, and dancing are either joylessly crude or excessively calculated. Without flirtation, they become very dreary indeed. And these days flirting is a dying art. Badly executed flirtation can cost you your career and may land you in court.

Also, in the golden age of the 1950s people who "dated" usually knew each other from their high school or by parental introduction. Questions of suitability were thus settled long before the actual "date," the main point of which seems to have been to test sexual chemistry. Today, "dating" frequently involves asking someone very boring, bureaucratic questions about their career, their family, and interests.

Blind dates are the worst of all, essentially a job interview with your sexual self-esteem at stake. And they can wreck your relationships with the people who set you up. Not only might your date reject you, but when you see her you instantly know what league your friends think you are in.

The answer, of course, is not to "date." Ask people out to dinner. Go out for coffee in the afternoon. Don't only ask people who are suitable, and don't think of it as "step one" in some kind of scientific experiment. Your oldest and best friend could be the one for you, or your boss. That is what romance is all about: spontaneity, adventure—all things incompatible with "dating."

Collecting Broken Glass

From Nino Ricci, In a Glass House

Ricci's trilogy of novels follows Vittorio Innocente, a boy transplanted from Italy to the New World in the 1950s, as he struggles to learn from a father rendered weak and embittered by financial burdens, cultural dislocation, and the betrayal of his wife—Vittorio's mother, who died giving birth to another man's child while en route to join her husband in Canada. Broken in spirit, Mario Innocente makes gestures toward raising his son, and yet the example he sets leaves the boy sullen and confused.

For several weeks after the planting, my father and I were alone on the farm. Gelsomina came by on Saturdays to do laundry and cook up soup and sauce for the following week; the baby remained at Tsi' Alfredo's. But though we were together more often now, my father seemed still merely a kind of element I had to move through, my body tensing against him like a single hard muscle when he was near, taking in only his animal scent and then the shape he cut like black space in a landscape.

For a week or so he had me clean out an old chicken coop in a barn. The coop was crammed with all manner of refuse, busted packing crates, hoops of thick wire, old farm implements with decayed leather harnesses; every morning a swallow would swoop out in a swift arc from a nest there when my father and I came in, slashing a quick hieroglyph in the air like a secret signal before disappearing in the branches of a mulberry tree across the lane. My father would give me a few terse instructions before he went off on his own chores; but then as soon as he'd gone everything he said became a haze. When he came back to check on me he'd see my mistakes at once.

"I told you to pile those crates against the other wall, where they'd be out of the way." And in fifteen minutes of swift, precise work he'd redo what I'd spent a whole morning on.

After the barn, he set me to work collecting broken glass in the alleys between the greenhouses. But now it was exactly the mistakes he warned me about in advance that I invariably fell into.

"Don't fill the wheelbarrow too full," he said, "or you'll spill it."

But I did pile it too full; and even feeling its weight begin to lean as I lifted its handles, already seeing in my mind how it would spill, watching the image unfurl there like a premonition, still I tried to push it forward. There was a tremendous crash when it tilted, the glass splintering through the wall of one of the greenhouses. In a moment my father was standing over me, his face flushed.

"*Per la madonna*—" It was the first time I had seen his anger so plain and uncurbed, so ice-hard. "Is it possible you can't do anything the way I tell you?"

I had steeled myself instinctively against a blow. But the blow didn't come, and afterwards, when my father bent quick and silent to pick up the glass I had spilled, he appeared chastened by his outburst as if he had been the one who had suffered some humiliation.

He left me less on my own from then on, often keeping me beside him to be his helper. He'd make comments sometimes while he worked, or curse some problem in a way that was oddly intimate and frank, as if he'd forgotten I was merely a child. But usually he was silent, the work taking him over, bringing out in him a hard-edged concentration that seemed to free me from him even though it was exactly then that I was most aware of him, the tawny muscles of his arms and neck, the patches of sweat on his clothes, his ghostly familiarity like a mirror I looked into.

At noon, he'd send me home ahead of him to put soup on the stove or set the water heating for pasta for our lunch. If we ran out of the food Gelsomina had left, he'd fry up onion and eggs, scraping the eggs onto our plates with a casual violence, a mash of grease and broken yolks and scorched whites, though I preferred them to the porcelain-smooth ones Gelsomina used to prepare. He listened to the radio while we ate, odd music at first and then a voice, the same one every day, my father turning the volume up when it came on.

"*Mbeh*," he'd say afterwards, "maybe we'll get a little more sun after all, if you can believe all the stupidities they say on that thing."

Once when we were all hoeing beans in the front field, someone came to visit us, a gray-haired man in a checked suit and dark glasses. He pulled up in the courtyard in a large blue car and came toward us smiling broadly, his hand outstretched.

"Mario," he said. "Mario, Mario, *como stai, paesano?*"

After his greeting, he and my father began to speak in what must have been English. They talked for a long time, and I had the sense from the way my father was laughing and smiling that speaking in English brought out some different person in him, one more relaxed and good-humored. But when the man had gone, my father grew canny.

"That was the guy I bought the farm from," he said. "Those Germans—*paesano* this, *paesano* that, everyone's a *paesano*. But the old bastard just wanted to make sure I don't forget to pay him."

And yet he was smiling, the old man's visit apparently having heartened him.

He took me into town with him that night to a sort of bar, a long dim room with a counter on one side and a row of rickety tables on the other. There were several men talking around one of the tables at the back, a few wearing the striped gray-and-white uniform that my father had worn when he'd worked at the factory. My father nodded in greeting toward them, but his good mood appeared to pass from him suddenly. He ordered an ice cream for me and a coffee for himself from the man behind the counter; but one of the men at the table had turned to him.

"*Dai*, Mario, let's get a game going. We need a fourth, these others here are too afraid to put a little money on the table."

My father stared into his coffee.

"Maybe they're the smart ones," he said. "Nobody gives you something for nothing."

"What are you saying, for the fifty cents we play for you couldn't even buy a whore in Detroit."

The other men laughed.

"*Sì*, fifty cents," my father said, still talking into his cup though his energy was clearly drawn toward the men now. "It took half a day to make that when I came here—"

"Oh, always the same story! *Dai*, sit down, you'll be a rich man soon, when the checks start coming in from the farm."

"The farm—at least what I made before, I could put in my pocket. Now I'm just working for the bank. And then that damned German, still worried about the four cents I owe him—"

"What does he have to do with it? Didn't he get his money from the Farm Credit?"

My father had turned to face them. With the mention of the German his good humor began to return.

"*Mbeh*, we kept a little back because of all the work that had to be done, he'd left the place to rot like that. So today he comes around, in his suit and new car, still thinking about those few pennies, though the contract says he doesn't see another cent until October—"

"*Che scostumat'*. What did you tell him?"

"Don't think he was stupid enough to say a word about the money. You know how they are, always smiling, *amico, paesano*. But the whole time he was looking around, checking to see how things were, asking about the crop, about the prices. So I smiled too. I told him if he wanted to see how the crop was, he could come back in July and I'd give him a bushel of beans."

The other men laughed.

"And he'll be back for those beans, too," one of them said.

My father stayed to play cards.

"You can be my banker," he said, pulling up a chair for me beside him.

"That means every time he wins," one of the others said, "you take five percent."

"And if he loses he gives you the farm."

They played until late, making laconic conversation at first but then becoming more and more involved in the game. At the end my father gave me some change from the money he'd won.

"What are you doing, Mario," one of the men said, "you want to spoil him? That's half a day's wages."

The Sinking of Mature Romance

Michael Medved,
The Ottawa Citizen *(1998)*

From the Duke and Duchess of Windsor to the movie Titanic, *Michael Medved laments, modern pop culture undermines the idea of love as a mature partnership by exalting florid romanticism, sexual flamboyance, and narcissism.*

In February, Sotheby's in New York staged a gala auction honoring one of the most celebrated couples of the 20th century—and inadvertently emphasized the emptiness and destructiveness of the most common contemporary concepts of romance.

This royal garage sale brought in some $23 million U.S. by selling off 40,000 possessions of the late Duke and Duchess of Windsor. The items purchased ranged from monogrammed china toothbrush cups and an elaborately painted porcelain commode to the Duchess's mink garters and a boxed slice of their 1937 wedding cake. The Windsors accumulated their tacky treasures during 35 years of marriage, most of which they spent as rulers of a "15-acre kingdom" outside of Paris following his abdication from the British throne for the sake of "the woman he loved."

This dramatic gesture, in which England's handsome young monarch (he spent only 11 months as Edward VIII) gave up his kingdom to marry a twice-divorced American commoner, captured the imagination of most of the world. A look back on Edward's decision some 60 years later, however, suggests the dangers of allowing passion and sentiment to rule our lives and the lives of our children.

Edward and his wife, the former Wallis Warfield Simpson, bore no offspring and remained painfully irrelevant—and vaguely sympathetic to Hitler—during his country's hour of maximum trial (and maximum heroism) in the Second World War. They hosted many glittering dinner parties, accumulated a great deal of fashionable jewelry, but ultimately struck most acquaintances and observers as hopelessly shallow and even pathetic.

Edward gave up a kingdom but what, precisely, had he gained? He began his affair with Mrs. Simpson while she was still living with her second husband, allowing his sexual obsession to overrule all sense of morality and duty.

Unfortunately, popular culture regularly exalts precisely this sort of decision—celebrating couples who defy convention and rationality in the name of some higher "love." This is by no means a new theme in Western civilization, but with its amplification by movies, TV and pop music it has become an especially destructive one for our children. Even cartoons for six-year-olds (*The Little Mermaid, Pocahontas*) glorify the idea of barely pubescent young people disregarding their parents' expectations and displaying deeper wisdom by following their hearts—and hormones

On a more substantive level, we all thrill to the emotions evoked by Romeo and Juliet (and by the deathless poetry Shakespeare provides for them), but as the popular recent movie version with Leonardo DiCaprio and Claire Danes forcefully reminds us, the relationship of the world's most famous romantics culminated in the double suicide of two teenagers. In the abstract, we may view their fate as noble and grand, but would any sane parents welcome the notion of their own children following the path of these two "star cross'd lovers"?

Nor should parents accept the handsome lead characters in the smash hit *Titanic* as a suitable standard for romance. This motion picture, with all its cinematic grandeur, can sweep away the resistance of even the most skeptical viewers and obscure the crucial context of its central relationship. After all, 17-year-old Rose (Kate Winslet) meets earnest but penniless Jack (Leonardo DiCaprio) on board the great ship and then less than five days later, despite the fact that she's engaged to another man, makes love to him in the backseat of a car being transported in the ship's hold. This fleeting but overwhelming experience transforms her entire life, and continues to haunt her more than 80 years later.

This florid romanticism hardly classifies as the "loveless sex" so regularly (and appropriately) condemned in recent entertainment, but in a sense it may be even more dangerous for our kids. Though conventional wisdom suggests that the irresponsible behavior of unattached males accounts for most of the destructive sexual activity among today's youth, the changed values of females have resulted in even deeper damage.

Many, if not most, boys have always sought to take advantage of available girls, pushing sexuality just as far as those girls would let them; social order has always depended on the young woman's ability (and determination) to draw a line and say no. Most of the females who now say yes, endangering their own futures and the institution of marriage itself, do not do so out of commitment to the "Playboy philosophy"; they do so for the sake of what they view as grand, timeless, life-changing passions. For these young women, notions of premarital surrender in the cause of lofty, irrational love will prove far more seductive than the allure of recreational sex.

As an alternative, responsible adults should stress a more wholesome sense of romanticism—emphasizing joyous fulfillment rather than tragic doom, offering a warming hearth rather than a consuming bonfire, bringing young people closer to their parents rather than dividing them, honoring life rather than death. Despite tortured romantic conventions that have been rattling around our culture since medieval times, common sense and lasting love are anything but incompatible; they are, in fact, indispensably connected.

Rather than accepting the ardent young lovers on board *Titanic* (or in hundreds of lesser films) as appropriate examples of romantic commitment, consider some of the older couples, with dozens of grandchildren and decades of unflagging friendship and devotion, who seem to turn up in nearly all American families. Mature love involves a productive life together, shared values, common commitment to faith and the future, rather than indulging in flamboyant but empty gestures like those perpetrated by the Duke and Duchess of Windsor. If we can teach our children that romance at its best involves embracing, rather than abdicating responsibility, then their love lives may leave behind more substantive contributions than mink garters and moldy wedding cake.

Enchanting and Repulsive:
What Is Gothic?

From Michelle Wauchope,
What Is Gothic? An Exploration of Youth Culture

The shootings at Columbine High School drew attention to the "Goth" sub-culture, since the accused were dressed in that fashion. Is Goth some dark celebration of Satanism and evil? Or is it an update of late-nineteenth-century Decadence with a few Vampiric touches added? Goth is a worldwide phenomenon, as this essay posted on the Net by a first-year Australian university student testifies. In its stylistic and erotic flamboyance, she observes, "Romanticism and beauty become juxtaposed with the shock value of punk."

The Gothic subculture has been in existence for around sixteen years, making it one of the most enduring of youth cultures. However, what Gothic really is about is rarely known outside "the scene."

This is due in part to the nonconfrontational nature of the subculture, as well as mainstream media's omission to report on things and events pertaining to the Gothic subculture.

As with any youth culture, music and fashion are major contributors to the Gothic identity and is what attracts most people to the scene. Unlike many youth cultures, Gothic also has a strong literature base.

Behind the music and fashion, is a specific fascination with the darker side of life. The people in the scene share a familiar outlook on life, as well as often having similar past histories.

While the subculture started in England, there are now people all over the world who consider themselves Gothics. In Australia there is a particularly active scene.

While the phenomena of youth cultures has often been explored, both in the media and in various cultural and psychological studies, little research has been conducted on the Gothic subculture. As a result, very little is known about what constitutes Gothic.

The Gothic subculture is one of the most misunderstood of youth cultures, often referred to as a "cult" and blamed for youth suicides. While it does celebrate horror, the darker side of life and often Gothics have a blatant disregard for organized religion, this is a matter of personal choice and not a form of "cult" or peer pressure.

There are rules and modes of behavior within the scene, however what they are is hard to define. There is frequent discussion about "what constitutes Gothic" by the Gothics themselves, but no one has come up with any concrete answers.

The Gothic movement can be linked to a single London nightclub called the Batcave, which opened in 1981. It sprang up from what remained of the punk scene and as such, many bands now synonymous with Gothic were first known as Punk. The Batcave fostered these bands as well as their audience. This first wave of Goths took the elements of punk that they liked; the spirit of rebellion, the shocking edge of fashion and music, a high pleasure principle and a penchant for all things black.

These original "Gothics" were reputedly so named by *NME* and *Sounds*. These music magazines took the term from Siouxsie Sioux (of the Banshees) who used it to describe the new direction her punk band was taking. The pop journalists used it as a pigeonhole for many bands around at the time, actually covering three separate styles of music with the label, as they were only occupied with the look of the Gothics.

The fans of these bands used elements of punk as a statement, adopting bondage and fetish wear as well as aspects of German expressionism, but along the way adopted various regalia from the Victorian era, blending the term "Gothic" with Gothic Literature. Now the two are synonymous. Romanticism and beauty became juxtaposed with the shock value of punk.

The Batcave was the crucial meeting point, the place to dress up and be seen. It encouraged the narcissistic and elitist attitude carried by most Gothics over the rest of society, but it must also be seen that this attitude is a feature of most youth cultures.

In the second wave, the connection with Gothic literature became the driving force. The original idea of fun was replaced with intelligent introspection. The Gothic subculture became a refuge for the freaks of society, the people who valued escapism and angst more than reality and anger. These new pale-faced, black-swatched, hair-sprayed night dwellers used the look to scare and repel, to avoid acceptability. It was this new breed of Gothics that elicited the most derision and they were painted as morbid and maudlin. This image set up links between suicide and "other evils" with the subculture in the minds of "normal" people.

Recently there has been another wave of ideas, this time called "Dark Wave." It has taken the separate genres of Industrial and Techno music and fused it with the dark elements of Gothic.

"Dark Wave" has also been adopted by many as an alternative label to "Gothic," avoiding the negative connotations the word has come to represent.

Literature has also received new lifeblood with many techno-culture books being popular reading, as well as the propagation of "net.goths" (Goths on the Internet). Goth debates thrive on the Internet, as it is one of the few mediums [where] such debate can flourish. In the real world, debate on Gothic is taboo. The unwritten rule is if you don't know if something is Gothic or not, then you can't be Gothic. Also there is a reluctance for Gothics to proclaim themselves as such, or to talk about the subculture, creating a paradox.

While other subcultures that emerged at the same time as Gothic, such as New Romantic and New Wave, have come and gone, the movement continues to replenish itself with fresh blood of new bands and fans.

The Gothic subculture is small in comparison to other more mainstream youth cultures, such as rave and hip-hop. The resulting lack of media coverage, coupled with the unusual dress and behavioral standards of the Gothics, has created many misconceptions about the subculture.

"Supposedly" Gothic guys are all gay because they wear makeup and nail polish. While the scene encourages androgyny and makes no distinction between gay and straight, mainstream society is not as open-minded. Consequently, male Gothics are often the targets of homophobic attacks, both verbal and physical.

Gothics are apparently all Satanists. This misconception can be attributed to the wearing and idolizing of religious and pagan symbols and imagery, as well as the rejection of organized religion. What the "normal" people fail to understand is that Satanism is also an organized religion, and thus just as likely to be rejected by the Gothic community. More importance is placed on individual strength; structured religion is looked down upon as an emotional crutch for the weak. The rejection of organized religion is usually made through disillusionment with hypocritical religious people.

The Gothic love of introspective music, penchant for dark imagery and romanticizing of death, is often blamed for teenage suicide. This is a reactionary response and a fallacy. It ignores many other important factors involved in suicides, pushing the blame on a perceived "influence" rather than the problems within the victim's life. It also ignores the fact that many people gain stability and friends from the Gothic culture, and are out to have fun rather than withdrawing into themselves.

Gothics allegedly lead a promiscuous lifestyle. Many "normals" go to Gothic nightclubs believing that "Goths are easy." Monogamy is preferred by most Goths, although other relationship types are more accepted within the subculture than elsewhere. This presumption of sexual promiscuity is based more on the body worshiping style of dress many Goths adopt. Bondage and fetish wear, while often worn for their shock value and "kinky-ness," are certainly not seen as obscene or inappropriate clothing.

Vampirism is another trait attributed to Gothics. While some may involve themselves in drinking blood, either their own or a partner's, most Gothics are merely interested in the erotic romance embodied by the vampires in Gothic literature. Within the Gothic scene, people who claim to be Vampires are treated as fools and jokes.

There are many "looks" in the Gothic subculture, but black is by far the dominant color in the Gothic wardrobe. While it is a color symbolising death and mourning as well as "evil," it also has the practical side of being easy to coordinate. Other colors make an appearance more as an accessory. These are usually jewel colors or plain white.

Fabric plays an important role in clothes. Rich fabrics—silk, satin, velvet, embroidery borrowed from Victorian or Medieval imagery—as well as P.V.C. and leather from the Punks are just as important as the color or cut of the clothes.

Gothic makeup is often similar to that of the German expressionists, with heavy eyeliner and a white pancake base. The need to be pale leads many Gothics to shun sunlight; this in turn adds fuel to the perceptions of vampirism and of general mystique.

Accessories play an important role. Boots, collars, studs and chains tend to be favorites. Lots of silver jewelry is a must, bracelets, earrings, necklaces and rings, either of a religious or pagan nature.

Although the "look" plays an important role both as a form of identification and as a personal statement, many Goths also denounce them as superficial trappings and not a true indicator of a "real" Gothic. This concept is in direct opposition to the "old Goth" way of thinking.

Gothic literature is not tied down to a particular time period. While it proliferated throughout the Victorian era, the devices and imagery used in that time period are still being used in "Modern

Gothic." Many works considered as being Gothic literature also existed long before the Romantic age.

Authors such as Edgar Allan Poe, Bram Stoker, Mary Shelley, Kafka and H. P. Lovecraft are still widely read, as are poets and philosophers such as Baudelaire, Byron, Shelley and Nietzsche.

There is no concrete rule as to behavior or philosophy. The Gothic subculture is a dynamic structure, fusing the best bits from many past cultures with current ideas. It is for this reason that Gothic is just as relevant today as it was sixteen years ago.

A few general concepts can be stated with some reasonable authority. Open-mindedness is prized above all else. Gothics consider themselves "above" normal society and pride themselves on tolerance, intelligence and understanding. Whether or not they maintain this standard is debatable. Often Gothics become disdainful and intolerant of outsiders and petty-minded as to the "standards of Gothic."

A celebration of the mind is also often encountered. Education is considered important, and even those who haven't undertaken tertiary studies are often verbose on the topic of literature. Perhaps because of this, there is less drug use than in other youth cultures. This is not to say it doesn't exist, just that the people who take them and the quantities involved tend to be less when compared with current youth cultures such as "Rave" or "Indy-kids."

Dad? I Wish I'd Known You When You Were Little

From Raymond Carver,
Bicycles, Muscles, Cigarettes *(1988)*

A quiet story of a father recalling his father for his son.

"I'm sorry," Hamilton said. "I'm sorry you had to see something like that," Hamilton said to his son.

They kept walking and when they reached their block, Hamilton took his arm away.

"What if he'd held up a knife, Dad? Or a club?"

"He wouldn't have done anything like that," Hamilton said.

"But what if he had?" his son said.

"It's hard to say what people will do when they're angry," Hamilton said.

They started up the walk to their door. His heart moved when Hamilton saw the lighted windows.

"Let me feel your muscle," his son said.

"Not now," Hamilton said. "You just go in now and have your dinner and hurry up to bed. Tell your mother I'm all right and I'm going to sit on the porch for a few minutes."

The boy rocked from one foot to the other and looked at his father, and then he dashed into the house and began calling, "Mom, Mom!"

He sat on the porch and leaned against the garage wall and stretched his legs. The sweat had dried on his forehead. He felt clammy under his clothes.

He had once seen his father—a pale, slow-talking man with slumped shoulders—in something like this. It was a bad one, and both men had been hurt. It had happened in a cafe. The other man was a farmhand. Hamilton had loved his father and could recall many things about him. But now he recalled his father's one fistfight as if it were all there was to the man.

He was still sitting on the porch when his wife came out.

"Dear God," she said and took his head in her hands. "Come in and shower and then have something to eat and tell me about it. Everything is still warm and Roger has gone to bed."

But he heard his son calling him.

"He's still awake," she said.

"I'll be down in a minute," Hamilton said. "Then maybe we should have a drink."

She shook her head. "I really don't believe this yet."

He went into the boy's room and sat down at the foot of the bed.

"It's pretty late and you're still up, so I'll say goodnight," Hamilton said.

"Goodnight," the boy said, hands behind his neck, elbows jutting.

He was in his pajamas and had a warm fresh smell about him that Hamilton breathed deeply. He patted his son through the covers.

"You take it easy from now on. Stay away from that part of the neighborhood, and don't let me ever hear of you damaging a bicycle or any other personal property. Is that clear?" Hamilton said.

The boy nodded. He took his hands from behind his neck and began picking at something on the bedspread.

"Okay, then," Hamilton said, "I'll say goodnight."

He moved to kiss his son, but the boy began talking.

"Dad, was Grandfather strong like you? When he was your age, I mean, you know, and you—"

"And I was nine years old? Is that what you mean? Yes I guess he was," Hamilton said.

"Sometimes I can hardly remember him," the boy said. "I don't want to forget him or anything, you know? You know what I mean, Dad?"

When Hamilton did not answer at once the boy went on. "When you were young, was it like it is with you and me? Did you love him more than me? Or was it just the same?" the boy said abruptly. He moved his feet under the covers and looked away. When Hamilton still did not answer, the boy said, "Did he smoke? I think I remember a pipe or something."

"He started smoking a pipe before he died, that's true," Hamilton said. "He used to smoke cigarettes a long time ago and then he'd get depressed or something or other and quit, but later he'd change brands and start again. Let me show you something," Hamilton said. "Smell the back of my hand."

The boy took the hand in his, sniffed it, and said, "I guess I don't smell anything, Dad, what is it?"

Hamilton sniffed the hand and then the fingers. "Now I can't smell anything either," he said. "It was there before, but now it's gone." Maybe it was scared out of me he thought. "I wanted to show you something. All right, it's late now. You better go to sleep," Hamilton said.

The boy rolled onto his side and watched his father walk to the door and watched him put his hand to the switch. And then the boy said, "Dad? You'll think I'm pretty crazy, but I wish I'd known you when you were little. I mean, about as old as I am right now. I don't know how to say it, but I'm lonesome about it. It's like—it's like I miss you already if I think about it now. That's pretty crazy, isn't it? Anyway, please leave the door open." Hamilton left the door open, and then he thought better of it and closed it halfway.

Born to Lose in 1962

Social Distortion,
Somewhere Between Heaven and Hell *(1992)*

I was brought in this world 1962
I didn't have much choice you see
But by the time I was eight I could tell it was too late.
I was already barking up the wrong tree.
When I was in school you thought I was a fool, in trouble breaking
    all the rules.
I was absent from class, my daddy spanked my bare ass, but I sure
    tried hard to be cool.
Born to lose was what they said,
You know I was better off dead.
Born to lose, you're just bad news,
You don't get no second chance.
It was a hot summer night in mid July,
A hangover and a black eye.
Your momma said I was a loser, a dead end cruiser, and deep
    inside
I knew that she was right. . . .

Sex and That Postmodernist Girl

From David Foster Wallace,
Brief Interviews with Hideous Men *(1998)*

If you're not confused about love in the nineties already, read this one.

K—: "What does today's woman want. That's the big one."

E—: "I agree. It's the big one all right. It's the what-do-you-call . . . "

K—: "Or put another way, what do today's women *think* they want versus what do they really deep down *want*."

E—: "Or what do they think they're supposed to want."

Q.

K—: "From a male."

E—: "From a guy."

K—: "Sexually."

E—: "In terms of the old mating dance."

K—: "Whether it sounds Neanderthal or not, I'm still going to argue it's the big one. Because now the whole question today's become such a mess."

E—: "You can say that again."

K—: "Because now the modern woman has an unprecedented amount of contradictory stuff laid on her about what it is she's supposed to want and how she's expected to conduct herself sexually."

E—: "The modern woman's a mess of contradictions that they lay on themselves that drives them nuts."

K—: "It's what makes it so difficult to know what they want. Difficult but not impossible."

E—: "Like take your classic Madonna-versus-whore contradiction. Good girl versus slut. The girl you respect and take home to meet Mom versus the girl you just fuck."

K—: "Yet let's not forget that overlaid atop this is the new feminist-slash-postfeminist expectation that women are sexual agents, too, just as men are. That it's okay to be sexual, that it's okay to whistle at a man's ass and be aggressive and go after what you want. That it's okay to fuck around. That for today's woman it's almost mandatory to fuck around."

E—: "With still, underneath, the old respectable-girl-versus-slut thing. It's okay to fuck around if you're a feminist but it's also not okay to fuck around because most guys aren't feminists and won't respect you and won't call you again if you fuck around."

K—: "Do but don't. A double bind."

E—: "A paradox. Damned either way. The media perpetuates it."

K—: "You can imagine the load of internal stress all this dumps on their psyches."

E—: "Come a long way baby, my ass."

K—: "That's why so many of them are nuts."

E—: "Out of their minds with internal stress."

K—: "It's not even really their fault."

E—: "Who wouldn't be nuts with that kind of mess of contradictions laid on them all the time in today's media culture?"

K—: "The point being that this is what makes it so difficult, when for example you're sexually interested in one, to figure out what she really wants from a male."

E—: "It's a total mess. You can go nuts trying to figure out what tack to take. She might go for it, she might not. Today's woman's a total crapshoot. It's like trying to figure out a Zen koan. Where what they want's concerned, you pretty much have to just shut your eyes and leap."

K—: "I disagree."

E—: "I meant metaphorically."

K—: "I disagree that it's impossible to deduce what it is they really want."

E—: "I don't think I said *impossible*."

K—: "Though I do agree that in today's postfeminist era it's unprecedentedly difficult and takes some serious deductive fire-power and imagination."

E—: "I mean if it were really literally *impossible* then where would we be as a species?"

K—: "And I do agree that you can't necessarily go just by what they *say* they want."

E—: "Because are they only saying it because they think they're supposed to?"

K—: "My position is that actually most of the time you *can* figure what they want, I mean almost logically deduce it, if you're willing to make the effort to understand them and to understand the impossible situation they're in."

E—: "But you can't just go by what they say, is the big thing."

K—: "There I'd have to agree. What modern feminists-slash-post-feminists will *say* they want is mutuality and respect of their individual autonomy. If sex is going to happen, they'll say, it has to be by mutual consensus and desire between two autonomous equals who are each equally responsible for their own sexuality and its expression."

E—: "That's almost word for word what I've heard them say."

K—: "And it's total horseshit."

E—: "They all sure have the empowerment-lingo down pat, that's for sure."

K—: "You can easily see what horseshit it is if you start by recognizing the impossible double bind we've already discussed."

E—: "It's not all that hard to see."

Q.

K—: "That she's expected to be both sexually liberated and autonomous and assertive, and yet at the same time she's still conscious of the old respectable-girl-versus-slut dichotomy, and know that some girls still let themselves be used sexually out of a basic lack of self-respect, and she still recoils at the idea of ever being seen as this kind of pathetic roundheel sort of woman."

E—: "Plus remember the postfeminist girl now knows that the male sexual paradigm and the female's are fundamentally different—"

K—: "*Mars and Venus.*"

E—: "Right, exactly, and she knows that as a woman she's naturally programmed to be more high-minded and long-term about sex and to be thinking more in relationships terms than just fucking terms, so if she just immediately breaks down and fucks you she's on some level still getting taken advantage of, she thinks."

K—: "This, of course, is because today's postfeminist era is also today's postmodern era, in which supposedly everybody now knows everything about what's really going on underneath all the semiotic codes and cultural conventions, and everybody supposedly knows what paradigms everybody is operating out of, and so we're all as individuals held to be far more responsible for our sexuality, since everything we do is now unprecedentedly conscious and informed."

E—: "While at the same time she's still under this incredible biological pressure to find a mate and settle down and nest and breed; for instance, go read this thing *The Rules* and try to explain its popularity any other way."

K—: "The point being that women today are now expected to be responsible both to modernity and to history."

E—: "Not to mention sheer biology."

K—: "Biology's already included in the range of what I mean by *history*."

E—: "So you're using *history* more in a Foucaultian sense."

K—: "I'm talking about history being a set of conscious intentional human responses to a whole range of forces of which biology and evolution are a part."

E—: "The point is it's an intolerable burden on women."

K—: "The real point is that in fact they're just logically incompatible, these two responsibilities."

E—: "Even if modernity *itself* is a historical phenomenon, Foucault would say."

K—: "I'm just pointing out that nobody can honor two logically incompatible sets of perceived responsibilities. This has nothing to do with history, this is pure logic."

E—: "Personally, I blame the media."

K—: "So what's the solution."

E—: "Schizophrenic media discourse exemplified by, like, for example *Cosmo*—on one hand be liberated, on the other make sure you get a husband."

K—: "The solution is to realize that today's women are in an impossible situation in terms of what their perceived sexual responsibilities are."

E—: "I can bring home the bacon mm *mm* mm *mm* fry it up in a pan mm *mm* mm *mm*."

K—: "And that, as such, they're naturally going to want what any human being faced with two irresolvably conflicting sets of responsibilities is going to want. Meaning that what they're *really* going to want is some way *out* of these responsibilities."

E—: "An escape hatch."

K—: "Psychologically speaking."

E—: "A back door."

K—: "Hence the timeless importance of: *passion*."

E—: "They want to be both responsible and passionate."

K—: "No, what they want is to experience a passion so huge, overwhelming, powerful, and irresistible that it obliterates any guilt or tension or culpability they might feel about betraying their perceived responsibilities."

E—: "In other words what they want from a guy is *passion*."

K——: "They want to be swept off their feet. Blown away. Carried off on the wings of. The logical conflict between their responsibilities can't be resolved, but their postmodern *awareness* of this conflict can be."

E——: "Escaped. Denied."

K——: "Meaning that, deep down, they want a man who's going to be so overwhelmingly passionate and powerful that they'll feel that they have no choice, that this thing is bigger than both of them, that they can forget there's even such a *thing* as postfeminist responsibilities."

E——: "Deep down, they want to be irresponsible."

K——: "I suppose in a way. I agree, though I don't think they can really be faulted for it, because I don't think it's conscious."

E——: "It dwells as a Lacanian cry in the infantile unconscious, the lingo would say."

K——: "I mean it's understandable, isn't it? The more these logically incompatible responsibilities are forced on today's females, the stronger their unconscious desire for an overwhelmingly powerful, passionate male who can render the whole double bind irrelevant by so totally overwhelming them with passion that they can allow themselves to believe they couldn't help it, that the sex wasn't a matter of conscious choice, that they can be held responsible for, that ultimately if *anyone* was responsible it was the *male.*"

E——: "Which explains why the bigger the so-called feminist, the more she'll hang on you and follow you around after you sleep with her."

K——: "I'm not sure I'd go along with that."

E——: "But it follows that the bigger the feminist, the more grateful and dependent she's going to be after you've ridden in on your white charger and relieved her of responsibility."

K——: "What I disagree with is E——'s scornful use of *so-called.* I just don't think that today's feminists are being consciously insincere in all their talk about autonomy. Just as I don't think they're strictly to blame for the terrible bind they've found themselves in. Though deep down I do have to agree that women are historically ill-equipped for taking genuine responsibility for themselves."

Q.

E——: "I don't suppose either of you saw where the Little Wranglers' room was in this place."

K——: "I don't mean that in any kind of just-another-Neanderthal-male-grad-student-putting-down-women-because-he's-too-insecure-to-countenance-their-sexual-subjectivity way. And I'd go to the wall to defend them against scorn or culpability for a situation that is clearly not their fault."

E—: "Because it's getting to be time to answer nature's page, if you know what I mean."

K—: "I mean, even looking at the evolutionary aspect, you have to agree that a certain lack of autonomy-slash-responsibility was an obvious genetic advantage as far as primitive human females went, since a weak sense of autonomy would drive a primitive female toward a primitive male to provide food and protection."

E—: "While your more autonomous, butch-type female would be out hunting on her own, actually competing with the males for food."

K—: "But the point is that it was the less self-sufficient less autonomous females who found mates and bred."

E—: "And raised offspring."

K—: "And thus perpetuated the species."

E—: "Natural selection favored the ones who found mates instead of going out hunting. I mean, how many cave paintings of female hunters do you ever see?"

K—: "Historically, we should probably note that once the quote-unquote *weak* female has mated and bred, she shows an often spectacular sense of responsibility where her offspring are concerned. It's not that females have no capacity for responsibility. That's not what I'm talking about."

E—: "They do make great moms."

K—: "What we're talking about here is single adult preprimipara females, their genetic-slash-historical capacity for autonomy, for as it were *self*-responsibility, in their dealings with males."

E—: "Evolution has bred it out of them. Look at the magazines. Look at romance novels."

K—: "What today's woman wants, in short, is a male with both the passionate sensitivity and the logical firepower to discern that all her pronouncements about autonomy are actually desperate cries in the wilderness of the double bind."

E—: "They all want it. They just can't *say* it."

K—: "Putting you, today's interested male, in the paradoxical role of almost their therapist or priest."

E—: "They want absolution."

K—: "When they say, 'I am my own person,' 'I do not need a man,' 'I am responsible for my own sexuality,' they are actually telling you precisely what they want you to make them forget."

E—: "They want to be rescued."

K——: "They want you on one level wholeheartedly to agree and respect what they're saying and on another, deeper level to recognize that it's all complete horseshit and to gallop in on your white charger and overwhelm them with passion, just as males have been doing since time immemorial."

E——: "That's why you can't take what they say at face value or it'll drive you nuts."

K——: "Basically it's all still an elaborate semiotic code, with the new postmodern semions of autonomy and responsibility replacing the old premodern semions of chivalry and courtship."

E——: "I really do have to see a man about a prancing pony."

K——: "The only way not to get lost in the code is to approach the whole issue logically. What is she really saying."

E——: "No doesn't mean yes, but it doesn't mean no, either."

K——: "I mean, the capacity for logic is what distinguished us from animals to begin with."

E——: "Which, no offense, but logic's not exactly a woman's strong suit."

K——: "Although if the whole sexual *situation* is illogical, it hardly makes sense to blame today's woman for being weak on logic or for giving off a constant barrage of paradoxical signals."

E——: "In other words, they're not responsible for not being responsible, K——'s saying."

K——: "I'm saying it's tricky and difficult but that if you use your head it's not impossible."

E——: "Because think about it: if it was really *impossible,* where would the species be?"

K——: "Life always finds a way."

Each Other

Patrick Buckley

A college application, later published in the New York Post, *expresses a teenager's vision of the importance of male role models—within the family or without.*

April 25, 1992, was a day that forever changed my life. A month earlier the friendly UPS man had delivered a box that contained some plans and many pieces of wood. The plans were for a complicated radio-controlled sailboat that I had ordered as a birthday present from a model company. I had been building model cars since I was nine but when I opened this box I was blown away. It was just wood. There were no plastic parts nicely designed to fit together or any photo instructions. The only direction given was one large blueprint.

For one or two weeks I struggled, trying to figure out where to begin. There was no one in my house who could help. My mother was certifiably *mechanically impaired* and I rarely saw my father, who lived in Florida. So on that hot April day, I decided to do something that most cynical New Yorkers would regard as a waste of time. I decided to go to the model-boat basin in Central Park in search of someone who would help to build my boat. As I trekked across the park with my mom, she told me not to be disappointed if we couldn't find anyone who could help.

"People in New York are very busy," she warned, trying to soften the blow of any potential rejection. "But maybe someone can refer us to a class or a book that will help." My mother was always very protective of me and I knew, even at that early age, how it pained her that I didn't have a father in my life. She was pessimistic, but my resolve increased as we neared the boat pond. I had been there many times just to look at the boats and to climb on the nearby bronze *Alice in Wonderland* sculpture.

As we neared the basin, my enthusiasm grew as the masts of model sailboats bobbing on the water appeared through the trees. The boats were on average four or five feet long and had six- to eight-foot-tall masts. They were very large models that inspired awe in children, including me. In front of the boathouse were a number of men walking around with radio controls. As I was a shy 11-year-old, my mom started doing most of the talking. Then I noticed an older gentleman with a small number of people around him. He didn't have a radio control, but he was answering questions and handing out sheets of information about model suppliers.

My mom and I started asking him questions. His name was Hal and he had been building models since he was 9 years old. He was now 72. A well-mannered gentleman, he'd grown up in Brooklyn, served in the Navy during WWII, and had worked as a top engineer for the Bell Laboratories. I told him about the model sailboat kit I'd received for my birthday and that I didn't know where to begin. I'm not sure what I expected him to do. Maybe, I innocently thought, he has a sheet that will explain the art of wooden model building. What happened was something I could never imagine.

"Well, if you like, I could help get you organized and maybe give you a hand with the first step," Hal said, to my surprise. We made an appointment to meet after school the next day and that "first step" turned into over three hundred hours. Three hundred hours of after-school work that included first finishing my homework and then intense, complicated, fascinating, and detailed instruction on the fine art of boat building. For hours each day, designs were drawn with precision, plans were carefully studied, and materials and tools were meticulously handled. We logged our hours, created a budget that we honored, turned our beautiful living room into a wood shop replete with sawdust, paint fumes, tools, and stains, and patiently and painstakingly crafted our boat.

Every day, rain, shine, or snow, Hal arrived on time and ready for work. For years my father, and then my stepfather, had broken many promises to me. My dad would say he'd come, and time and time again he wouldn't show up. I remember my stepfather turning to me and saying "I don't have time for this sh—!" when I came to him as a 5-year-old with my hand-drawn invitation to an important school event. Missed school plays, missed graduations, missed birthdays, missed athletic events . . . camping trips that never happened: that was what I was used to. Hal never broke a single promise to me. Not once. Even when he was sick (he'd had several heart attacks and suffered from heart disease), he would show up on time, ready to go to work.

Hal and I worked diligently for a year on that boat. At times, it was a real struggle for me to stay on course because, as an 11-year-old, my attention often wandered and the work was not always exciting. But Hal's dedication profoundly influenced me. By his own example, he taught me important lessons about how to be organized, how to set priorities, and how to be responsible. He also, through working with me on the design of the electronics for the boat, played a pivotal role in developing my passion for science.

In May 1993, we launched the *Marilu,* named after my godmother. I'm proud to say that she is the most photographed boat in the park. She has a 6-foot mast, a 4-foot cherry-red hull, and a varnished mahogany deck that you can see your reflection in. The following September, we started work on a second boat. The *Sequin,* a model tugboat from Maine, took over 500 hours to build and was complete with radio-controlled steam, a detailed interior of the captain's cabin, and double-planked hull—all built from scratch.

When I was 11, Hal explained to me that he had always wanted to give back for all the opportunities he's been given, but he'd never found a way to do it. At the time I did not fully understand what he meant. Now, as a 17-year-old, when I reflect on the experience of building boats with him, I understand that through being his student and friend, he had not only helped me but I helped him, by filling that missing part of his life.

My friendship with Hal has taught me so many great lessons about patience, loyalty, endurance, education, and commitment. It has also affirmed my optimism about life and helped me to understand that despite the heartache and losses we may have, we also have, if we look and if we believe, the most important and powerful gift of all: *each other.*

"I Don't Want to Sacrifice Myself or My Family."

Interview with Kurt Cobain by Robert Hilburn,
Los Angeles Times *(1992)*

Kurt Cobain and Courtney Love were one of those iconic couples of the adversarial culture, a grunge Antony and Cleopatra. Cobain's suicide note was an extraordinary farewell from an unhappy man full of love for his family and "the guilt and empathy I have for everyone." This interview with Cobain a few weeks after the birth of his daughter reveals the complicated man behind the icon.

"I don't want my daughter to grow up and someday be hassled by kids at school. . . . I don't want people telling her that her parents were junkies."

Kurt Cobain, the 25-year-old leader of the acclaimed and hugely successful rock group Nirvana, is sitting in the living room of his Hollywood Hills apartment, holding Frances, his and Courtney Love's 4-week-old baby.

It's Cobain's first formal interview in almost a year, and it takes time to open up.

A shy, sensitive man, he speaks easily about his daughter, but there's one thing he's uncomfortable talking about even though he knows he has to.

Nirvana is the hottest new band to come along in years, and several of the articles on the group have speculated about Cobain's alleged drug use.

He now admits that he's used drugs, including heroin, but never as much as has been rumored or reported in the rock press. He also says in a quiet, but forceful, way that he is now drug-free.

"There's nothing better than having a baby," says Cobain disarmingly.

"I've always loved children. I used to work summers at the YMCA and be in charge of like 30 preschool kids.

"I knew that when I had a child, I'd be overwhelmed and it's true. I can't tell you how much my attitude has changed since we've got Frances. Holding my baby is the best drug in the world."

Yet Cobain, whose music speaks eloquently about the anger and alienation of youth, worries that the persistent rumors are threatening to turn him into a stereotype of a wasted rock 'n' roller. He also doesn't want to be a bad role model for the group's teenage fans.

He knows some people won't believe him when he says drugs are no longer part of his life, but he still feels compelled to speak out.

"I would say I tried to set the record straight," he says, when asked how he'd respond to someone who questions his sincerity. "That's all I can do. We have a lot of young fans and I don't want to have anything to do with inciting drug use. People who promote drug use are [expletive]. I chose to do drugs. I don't feel sorry for myself at all, but have nothing good to say about them. They are a total waste of time."

While it was Cobain's songwriting skills that enabled the band to achieve mainstream success, it was his link to the underground/punk world that made him uneasy in the mainstream spotlight. Not only did the mainstream represent compromise and superficiality to him, but he also felt overwhelmed by the pressures that were thrust upon him.

"I guess I must have quit the band about 10 different times in the last year," he says, handing the baby to his wife, who has joined him in the living room.

"I'd tell my manager or the band, but most of the time I would just stand up and say to Courtney, 'OK, this is it.' But it would be over in a day or two. . . . The music is usually what brings me back.

"The biggest thing that affected me was all the insane rumors, the heroin rumors . . . all this speculation going on. I felt totally violated. I never realized that my private life would be such an issue."

Danny Goldberg, an Atlantic Records executive who remains one of the managers of the band, confirmed in a separate interview that he's seen a dramatic change in Cobain since last spring.

"Kurt is someone who had a hard time dealing with the unexpected intensity of the success," Goldberg said. "He came from a very difficult background, literally didn't have his own apartment when I first started managing him. Then, in a matter of a few months, he became an international celebrity. He got confused for a while, but seems to have bounced back. He has a healthy baby and is functioning the best I've ever seen him."

Goldberg says he thinks becoming a father has helped Cobain get a perspective on his career and life.

"I believe the day (last spring) I saw a change was when he had these ultrasound (pictures) of the baby. They are like little black-and-white Polaroid photos and you see the baby's hands and things in the womb. He put it up on his wall at home.

"I think that took him out of thinking about himself and made him start thinking about the next phase of his life, where no matter what happens, this person was going to be in his life. He came out of the 'Oh, man, I was a punk rocker and now I'm a rock star and I never wanted to be a rock star' attitude. He was so thrilled about having a baby."

Back in his apartment, Cobain takes his daughter from his wife and reflects on the future. He is looking forward to what he thought only a few months ago might be impossible: recording another album.

"We've been wanting to record a really raw album for almost a year and it looks like we are finally ready to do it," he says. "I have been prescribed some stomach medicine that has helped ease the pain and I've been going to a pain management clinic. I also meditate. We'd like to put the album out before we go on tour again early next year."

He pauses after the mention of touring. The band followed the MTV Awards with concerts in Seattle and Portland, but they were the group's only U.S. dates this year.

"We might not go on any more long tours," he says, hesitantly. "The only way we could tour is if I could find some way to keep my stomach from acting up. We could record and play shows once in a while, but to put myself in the physical strain of seven months of touring is too much for me. I would rather be healthy and alive. I don't want to sacrifice myself or my family."

9

CONCLUSION: A RETURN TO MANLINESS?

Is it too soon to speak of a return to manliness at the end of the twentieth century? In the last section of this anthology, readers can sample what might be taken as a series of distress calls from the Zeitgeist. It would take another book as long as this one to chronicle exactly how—let alone why—a nobly inspiring tradition of manliness that stretches more or less continuously from classical Athens to the lifetimes of our parents and grandparents should, in the last thirty years, have come close to perishing. Doubtless it has something to do with what I call the Myth of the '60s. People of my generation who came of age during that decade entertained the fantastic notion that human beings could invent themselves literally out of nothing, free of any inherited religious or historical traditions, motivated by a desire for the pure, uninhibited freedom to do exactly as one pleased. Like all utopian projects, it was a fantasy that few, if any, of us actually achieved (or, in our heart of hearts, even seriously wanted). But we did manage to establish it as a cultural orthodoxy, passing on to the next generation much of our disastrous presumption in believing that nothing just, good, or true had happened in human history before our time. Most of those of my generation who pioneered this ill-fated revolution had themselves received a traditional liberal education in the humanities and sciences. They battened off the very tradition they worked assiduously to undermine. It was their children who became the true children of the revolution, victims of the myth that humans can "construct" their "identities" out of nothing. The disappearance of the positive tradition of manliness through relentless simplification and caricature, to the point where it bears no resemblance to its actual teachings, is one by-product of that vast shipwreck of culture.

And yet it would be a great mistake to see in these distress calls from the Zeitgeist grounds for only despair or pessimism. In fact, as a baby boomer, I take great encouragement in many ways from the sensibilities and tastes of young people in their twenties and thirties today. Students today are often criticized by their elders for their lack of political commitment, but I find them mercifully free of the ideological fixations of my own generation. Depending on the specific issue, most of them are capable of holding views from every shade in the political spectrum, defying the old left-wing/right-wing labels. Even aesthetically, the minimalist ethos of the '90s has been vastly more appealing than the bloated hippie establishmentarianism of the seventies, with its aging, paunchy Woodstock legends and drug-dealers-turned-moguls. That pale, hollow-cheeked, emaciated kid who frightens you with his shaved head and Doc Martens might well own his own business—and be a lover of the Great Books. You needn't assume the gay men you know are necessarily left wing—they could be cultural conservatives, while liberal on other issues.

As far as the problem of manliness is concerned, the excerpts in the last section are, on balance, at least as encouraging as they are discouraging. It's easy to be dismayed by the foul language, the hardened attitude to casual loveless sex, the worship of mindless violence, the cheap attitudinizing and wish to scandalize the grown-ups. Yes, it's all there. But, as the readings in the earlier sections demonstrate, to some extent young men have always been this way at their worst—cocky, libidinous, disdainful of their elders based on nothing, prone to violence. And, let's not forget, sometimes they're right to be angry. Sometimes their parents *are* utterly contemptible, their teachers boring, their jobs mindless and exploitive.

The difference between today's young man and his predecessors is the lack of a framing tradition for guidance, an orderly, challenging and intelligent process by which a young man can grow out of that immaturity by channeling those rambunctious energies into learning and duty. But, given the languishing of that framing tradition in recent decades, what is perhaps more remarkable than the nihilism so easily observable in youth culture is how many sound and justified frustrations, and dignified if unclarified longings, still shine through to us from these contemporary fragments. Not only is the passion still instinctual, but so is the search for an intelligible and satisfying outlet. Crude and raw though they may sometimes be, the lyrics, poems, stories, music, and styles of young people in the '90s still evoke a longing for heroism, adventure, self-overcoming, spiritual testing, romantic love, family life, and service to a noble calling. In the spirit of that cautious optimism about the return of manliness, I offer some concluding observations.

I began this book by remarking that the last three decades had witnessed one of the most remarkable efforts at social engineering in human history—a state-sponsored campaign, organized throughout the education system and in all major public institutions, to eradicate the psychological and emotional differences between men and women. Two generations have been brought up as the products of this vast experiment. From the moment they enter kindergarten to their final courses in university, they are required to subscribe to a new doctrine of human relations without precedent in known experience: that there are no inherent differences in character between men and women.

This doctrine now influences everything in contemporary society from how children and young adults are schooled, to pension plans, gender quotas for hiring, the enforcement of laws relating to domestic violence, and admission to military academies. And yet, as everyone with eyes to see and ears to listen realizes, this pervasive public orthodoxy bears little resemblance to the actual world of boys and girls and men and women in which we all live, and has had virtually no long-acting effect on the behavior of either sex. Everywhere you look, you will see the pronounced differences between male and female psychology, motivation, interests, and sentiments. These differences should not, and for the most part now do not, have any bearing on the equal opportunity of women to compete on an equal basis as individuals for the earned rewards of hard work and talent. But they are, and for the most part should be respected as important dimensions of the quality of our personal lives, and how our personal lives lead us in distinct ways to responsible interactions with our friends, loved ones, and fellow citizens. The psychological and emotional differences between men and women are not barriers to their friendship and mutual respect. On the contrary, they are the only sure basis for them, because they are rooted in human nature, providing men and women with different paths to the same goals. Instead of men and women fencing themselves off from those emotional differences, we should each be learning from the other about the plenitude and richness of our shared human destiny. As Socrates tells Callicles in Plato's dialogue the *Gorgias,* until you can be sure that a single other human being has benefited from intimacy with you, you are not fit to go into a wider forum and presume to tell others their duties or how they should live.

One of the most encouraging signs about contemporary youth culture is that it is precisely here, on the margins of respectable society where the energies of young people in their teens and twenties can find release, that a sensitivity to the emotional and aesthetic differences between men and women remains and may even be increasing, and in a way that is completely compatible with the equality of women and men. One of my favorite films is Fellini's *Satyricon,* because of the way it takes you beneath the marble facade of the Roman Empire's splendid civic hypocrisy—a military autocracy tricked out as the Stoic defender of republican dignity—into the underworld of Epicurean license, a kaleidoscope of polymorphous sexuality in which senators frolic with slaves. There is a broad, if hardly precise, analogy with our world in the closing years of the twentieth century. Beneath our arid public orthodoxy about men and women—the world of the right-thinking upper middle classes with their Birkenstocks and pasta machines, where the men are sensitive and the women empowered, and both work at interchangeable jobs as lawyers, academics, and civil servants—there lies the fecund subterranean realm of youth culture, which utterly repudiates this upper realm even as it confusedly tries to profess its values. Every decade or so, one of these beautiful young gods gives up his life, like Osiris or Dionysus, so that his dismemberment might reinvigorate the festivals of the bacchantes. In the '90s, the beautiful young death couple Kurt Cobain and Courtney Love reign, as different from each other as could be: he the fallen warrior, she the punk queen of hearts tending the ashes of her fallen hero like a postmodernist Isis. Both are a touch androgynous, not because they lack male or female sexuality but because, on the contrary, they have it in abundance. Like aristocratic nonconformists of the past such as Alcibiades, they cultivate androgyny as a sign of their excess of feeling and will, and their unity of style. A real man and a real woman, equal in their differences, both exceedingly strong antinomian personalities who exude love, ambition, and longing.

The prevailing public orthodoxy forbids us to entertain the thought that men and women, while equal in their intellectual and moral capacities for a successful and fulfilling life, might be different in their temperaments, emotional rhythms and sensitivity to others, and that each sex might be, in some cases, better suited for certain kinds of activity than the other. But, given the tension between the daylight realm of orthodoxy and the subterranean realm of youth culture, it is plain that many people, especially young men and women, find the idea of a genderless society unbelievable, restrictive, and boring. Moreover, the sheer unreality of this model, its naive and arrogant expectation, perennially doomed to failure by human nature, that some kind of gender-neutral new human personality will emerge from decades of relentless social engineering and propaganda, is arguably increasing tension and hostility between men and women. Precisely because young people, in particular, are too passionate to make themselves over into junior yuppies dedicated to careers and to orderly, respectable relationships bereft of stress and adventure (which is what the orthodoxy requires of them), they try superficially to accommodate themselves to the upper realm of Birkenstocks and Laura Ashley, while banishing their less manageable impulses to the Dionysian underworld of dance clubs, raves, booze cans, body piercing, recreational drugs, and our whole plethora of aesthetic and erotic subcultures.

I know that some of my readers must be wondering by this point how a writer who worked for the first Reagan administration transition team could have taken leave of his senses so fully as to speak in anything but horrified tones of the after-hours pursuits of young people today. But I was also a student and friend for many years of Allan Bloom, and while I cannot say what he would think of my specific observations, I can say that I write from a position very much in sympathy with his own understanding of, and insight into, the longings of the young. I hasten to add that my sympathies toward this Dionysian realm are strictly qualified, and I will get to that qualification in a moment. But I am sympathetic, because this fecund underworld is the only place left where young people can express their intimations of erotic release. Erotic obsession can lead down a dark alleyway toward every imaginable depth of degradation. But it can also stir in us a longing for transcendence, through our absorption in someone or something higher and better than ourselves. No matter how jaded a young man is, no matter how much premature and bad experience he has had with drugs and exploitive sex, the simple but profound moment of dawning need will prompt in him the words men's hearts have always spoken: I love you, I admire you, I need you. When we love others for their bodily beauty, it is possible to stay there and sample only the limited and repetitive pleasures of physical lust. But most people, even in their enthrallment with the beloved's bodily beauty, glimpse through that shell a beauty of soul and spirit that draws them upward, because they need those virtues to achieve some sort of repose in their own hearts and minds. The sheen of the hair, the flush in the face, the curve of the lips—none of these is merely physical. They are embodiments of the soul's capacity for nobility, shining through the fleshly carapace like fire shining through ivory.

And yet, and yet—here is where the qualification must come.

Taken on its own terms, the Dionysian world of youth culture is ultimately just as much a distortion of human psychology, character, and satisfied longing as the daylight realm of nine-to-five productivity and middle-class feminist orthodoxy that it repudiates. Why? Because to experience the passions there, one must by and large sacrifice any sense of reason or balance. The heart may still prompt us to find those natural words of love. But it is hard for a young man to hear that inner voice in the din of the surrounding subcultures, all of which urge him to gratify his spontaneous impulses without regard for the accompanying excesses of vulgarity, coarseness, and self-absorption. Indeed, there is an insidious connection between the daylight and nighttime realms, because many of the nine-to-fivers are engaged in converting the nighttime images of the Dionysian realm into commodities for our daytime amusement. What starts as criminal lust seeps up into the pederastic flirtations of underwear ads or movies about snuff films to titillate suburban moviegoers at Cinema 1–2–3–4–5–6–7–8 off the interstate.

Socrates was initiated into the mysteries of the god Eros by a wise and majestic woman, the mysterious prophetess Diotima. As she tells him, there is a logic peculiar to love. Diotima's Ladder ranks the objects of erotic longing in a hierarchy, ascending from bodily love upward through family life, the civic virtues, and, on the highest rung, philosophical contemplation. Properly explored and articulated, our erotic attachment to another leads us in and of itself to cultivate the virtues of character—moderation, honesty, gratitude, compassion, and honor—that make us worthy of love in the eyes of the beloved. We try to be virtuous because we want to be worthy of being loved. But, in today's world, the orderly side of the human soul has been sucked into the desert of contemporary legal proceduralism and the redesigning of the human personality to rid it of precisely these same erotic longings and their potential for bringing our virtues of character to fruition. As a consequence of this artificial and agonizing split between an arid public rationality and uncontrolled private impulse, the passion experienced in the subcultures of music and entertainment rarely advance beyond the first rung of Diotima's Ladder—sheer carnal desire. Raves, dance clubs, casual drugs, piercing, being in a band, cheating, swapping, experimenting with bondage and sadomasochism—here, one can experience that side of Eros that sweeps us away in the sheer passion and excitement of love, the release from the boundaries of the body through mortification, the thrill of losing oneself in a crowd all excited by the same primal rhythms. But it can't get you any further. You never advance further up the rungs of Diotima's Ladder toward transcendence. Eros remains on the level of ecstasy (the name of this popular party drug is very revealing). But young people are hard pressed to find the quiet place where their passion for another acts as a mirror in which to see themselves through the eyes of the one they love, and so find an erotic motive to perfect their virtues. If the wisdom of the West about manliness contained in this anthology could be summed up in two words, they would be: Love perfects. It is this very idea that is at the heart of the traditions that have shaped our civilization—and that has well-nigh been lost in the changes our society has seen in the last half century. If contemporary man is to regain his sense of purpose, of nobility, of his place in the world, he cannot do better than to look to the past, and to take to heart its lessons about virtue, manliness, and—above all—love.